Y0-BVP-573

421 N.
ENter

# Communicating

Through Writing and Speaking in Business

# Communicating
## Through Writing and Speaking in Business

### C. W. Wilkinson
*Professor of English and Chairman*
*Business and Technical Communication Courses*
*University of Florida*

### Dorothy C. Wilkinson
*Assistant Professor of Business Communication*
*College of Commerce and Business Administration*
*University of Alabama*

### Gretchen N. Vik
*Professor of Business Communication*
*Information Systems Department*
*College of Business Administration*
*San Diego State University*

Ninth Edition   1986

Homewood, Illinois   60430

The previous editions of this text were published under the title
*Communicating through Letters and Reports.*

ISBN 0-256-03534-2

Library of Congress Catalog Card No. 85-81220

*Printed in the United States of America*

1 2 3 4 5 6 7 8 9 0  K  3 2 1 0 9 8 7 6

# Preface

This Ninth Edition should continue the leadership role its eight predecessors have held successively since 1955.

Through years in business and industry consulting, professional associations, and extensive reading, as well as academic experience teaching in several universities, we've collected the best thinking about business communication as it has evolved since the 50's.

We have updated, added to, and rearranged the text. Its slightly changed title reflects the evolution in ways of teaching and learning its more comprehensive coverage of business communication.

At least a fair share of the work and contents in this edition are products of its bright, well-educated, and broadly experienced new coauthor. Dr. Gretchen Vik's varied experience and hard work have been very helpful in writing this edition and will no doubt help the book remain the leader in business communication.

Our purpose is, as always, to teach the skills and strategies necessary to be an effective business communicator in both writing and speaking. Teachers familiar with the previous eight editions will find that we've retained the basic three message plans as well as the popular checklists (useful as summaries of message strategies and specific techniques the accompanying chapters explain in detail). The Concise Writer's Handbook (now Appendix C) still contains the thorough, authoritative, and helpful writing style tips and time-saving and instructional set of paper-marking symbols.

The basic changes are:

- A revised and expanded chapter on communication and semantic theory, pragmatically discussed.
- An added chapter on how the automated office will affect your work as a future manager.
- More material on intercultural business communication.
- Revised chapters on message strategies, explaining and illustrating the basic plans of various good-news, disappointing, and persuasive messages.
- Added sections on forms development and writing job descriptions.
- Revised job communication sections with new résumés and more on interviewing.

- An expanded section on oral communication, including listening.
- Ample cases in two appendixes, one of cases applying specific principles and one of case series involving various principles and strategies.

Besides adding cases and examples in both the text and the *Instructor's Manual,* we've updated and revised both volumes; but the theory and application pointers that have helped so many students in past editions are still here. With the additions and revisions, the text again includes the established past practices as well as the current material about how offices and communication will change in the future.

Students and teachers of college courses in communicating through writing and speaking will find the book easily adaptable to varying standards, student abilities, and breadths of coverage (one, two, or three courses). By attention to only the major principles and easier questions, exercises, and cases, freshmen and sophomores of average ability can use the book effectively. By attention to all the refinements and the more difficult cases, upperclassmen in our best universities and businesspeople who are taking extension courses will find it among their most challenging texts.

Preparing effective business communications is *not* an easy task. It doesn't come naturally to most people. To go beyond the usual low level of business writing and speaking, you'll need to study the principles and illustrations carefully and then make a concentrated effort to write your messages and plan your speeches. Try to go *beyond* the basic facts we give you in the cases, *beyond* the reminders in the checklists, and *up* to the clear, graceful, and concise style and diplomatic tone of the illustrations. By applying the principles we discuss, you can become a more effective communicator in business.

C. W. Wilkinson
Dorothy C. Wilkinson
Gretchen N. Vik

# Contents

# Part One

## Background for Business Communication

# Chapter Outline

# 1

# Overview of Business Communication

## Why Study Business Communication?

The main reasons you should study business communication are:

1. You are almost certain to write many business letters, memos, and reports during the rest of your life, regardless of the kind of work you do. These are the most common forms of written communication for managing business affairs, and everybody has business affairs to manage.

2. Your degree of failure or success in managing many of those affairs will depend on whether you write well or merely copy old style and format from communications in your file.

3. Through systematic study and practice you can learn to write more effectively and thus greatly increase your chances of success in handling your personal business or business affairs on a job.

4. You will often have to present your ideas and plans orally, to your department, potential clients, or the public. Studying business communication will help you become a better-organized and persuasive speaker.

5. With word processing/data processing systems within the reach of even the smallest offices and businesses, employers put even more of a premium on people who write clearly, concisely, and correctly. Electronic messages, like the ones still sent on paper, require attention to style and clear, interesting, inconspicuous writing.

In the next few years, as computerized data/word processing becomes a common part of the office, we can look forward to an increased emphasis on writing that quickly and effectively communicates the message—exactly what *Communicating through Writing and Speaking in Business* teaches.

## Other Things You Learn

In learning to communicate in business, you will also learn some principles of practical psychology that will enable you to get along better professionally and socially with other people.

When you improve your ability to write clear, concise, persuasive, and natural English (which is the desirable language in business), you gain accuracy and naturalness in phrasing anything else you have to write or speak.

Through your study of letters and memos you will get further insight into the ways of the business world: practices used in getting people to buy, handling orders, gaining and refusing credit, making collections, adjusting claims, and selecting employees.

You will learn how to save time and money on business writing. As a good business writer, you can often write one letter to settle a business transaction that would require two or three from an untrained writer. By using form letters and form paragraphs, you can cut down on costs when the form message will do the job. When, however, you have situations requiring individual letters, you will recognize them and know better than to waste money on forms.

Perhaps most important of all, you will realize that every letter and memo you write is an item in your overall public relations—and you will try to make each one win, instead of lose, friends.

## Costs to Business

The Dartnell Corporation, which assesses business costs, finds that a business letter costs about $8 to produce and mail. With the volume of business mail (about 75 billion pieces of first-class mail alone) in the United States, that's big business—and a very practical reason to make sure each piece of mail does its intended job.

Your communication skills can gain or lose you business, a job, or a promotion, because your style and tone (as well as clarity and organization) strongly affect whether your audience will see things your way.

## Advantages of Written Communication

Despite the cost of a letter, it is often the most economical way to transact business. You can't go far (not even across town, if you figure your time and traveling expense) or talk much by long distance during business hours or say much in a telex for the cost of a letter. But for that money you can put your message in a letter and send it anywhere in the country and almost anywhere in the world.

Even if you do talk to another person, you do not have a written record, as you do if you follow the almost universal business practice of making a copy of your letter. Because a letter and its answer can make a written contract, letters often replace personal calls and telephone calls even when the two parties are in the same city.

Telex, teletype, and facsimile transmission provide written records of communications and have the added advantage of being virtually immediate, though only people with access to the systems can receive messages. But their cost makes them impractical unless a company can make heavy use of them. This fact generally restricts their use to large organizations with numerous locations. Electronic messages without a printed copy have the same disadvantages as telephone calls, of course.

Still another advantage of a written communication is that both the writer and the reader can handle it at their most convenient times. Moreover, the reader usually gives it full attention without raising partially considered objections and without interruption, a decided psychological advantage.

## Emphasis in Business and Schools

When executives began to realize how much written communication cost, how important it was to the smooth operation of their firms, and how few of their employees were capable writers, many of them started training and correspondence control programs.

At General Electric, Westinghouse, Southern Pacific, Marshall Field's, the New York Life Insurance Company, and the big mail-order houses (Montgomery Ward, Spiegel's, and Sears, Roebuck), to mention only a few of the leaders, such programs have demonstrated the economy and efficiency resulting from improved correspondence. Even these firms, however, prefer to hire people who can already write rather than train people to write on company time.

Many of the executives who are aware of the importance of written communication are graduates of the few schools that have taught business writing since early in the 1900s. These business leaders are the main reason why today in the majority of respectable colleges and universities literally thousands of students are studying and practicing how to write more effectively for business. Without exception, surveys by such organizations as Delta Sigma Pi, the American Assembly of Collegiate Schools of Business, and the Association for Business Communication have confirmed the high regard of former students for the work.

## Common Misconceptions

Some people—mostly for lack of information—wonder why business communication is a university course. Somehow, they think that the course is about letter writing only, or about learning to write the trite, wordy, and nearly meaningless expressions so common at the beginnings and endings of letters untrained writers usually prepare.

On the contrary, a good course in business communication will teach you to write and speak naturally, concisely, and clearly. You'll learn to present information so that your reader/audience is most apt to see things your way; you don't manipulate your reader, but rather use an indirect approach.

Some people criticize business communication as a "practical study." It certainly is practical, for the ability to write good business messages is useful. But it is also a cultural study because its primary purposes are the development of (1) your ability to maintain pleasant relations with others and (2) your language effectiveness.

## Why the High Regard for Business Communication?

One of the reasons courses in business communication have found increasing favor with students, recruiters, executives, and college administrators is that they are blends of the cultural and the practical.

The business correspondent communicates to an individual for a definite, practical purpose—and must do so with the same exactness as other good writers and speakers. *Action* is usually the goal. Since the quality of persuasion is most important to the business communicator, knowledge of practical psychology is essential.

The successful business writer or speaker must learn tact, patience, consideration of the other person, a necessarily optimistic attitude, and the value of saying things pleasantly and positively instead of negatively. These are the reasons why you can expect more successful social and business relations with other people after a thorough, conscientious, and repeated analysis and application of the principles of good communication in this book.

Furthermore, the effective business writer or speaker must learn to be concise, interesting, and easy to follow—to hold a reader's/audience's attention. The good communicator therefore edits carefully to phrase ideas more effectively in writing than in talking.

Reader analysis, planning, and editing establish good habits of expression—habits that carry over to the spoken message; so you will learn to talk better if you learn to write better.

The use of the language—in clear, concise adaptation to one's readers/ listeners so that they can absorb the message with the least amount of effort and the greatest amount of pleasant reaction—is an art.

Successful business communication is also the result of a conscious use of principles that have evolved since the turn of the century. No one would claim that business communication is an exact and thoroughly developed science, but prominent business writers who have experimented with letters and memos for over 80 years have given us a near-scientific framework of empirical principles as a starting point. You can therefore approach business communication with considerable knowledge of what good writing principles are and when, where, and how to apply them.

## The Communication Process and Semantic Principles

### The Communication Process

One of the areas studied that can help you become a better business writer and speaker is communication theory. While theoretical discussions can go to extremes and involve many social scientific "models," basic communication is a commonsense process. The parts of this process are *symbols* (to carry the meaning), *channels* (to send the message), and a *sender* (you) and a *receiver* (your intended audience).

Whether you are writing or talking, reading or listening, you are doing one half (*sending* or *receiving*) of the two-way process of communication.

Essential to this process are *symbols*—usually words. (We are not concerned here with smoke signals, smiles, gestures, winks, and other forms of nonverbal communication—though they are all parts of the whole communication story.) When you have an idea to convey to somebody, you cannot just hand it over; you necessarily use symbols of some kind. In oral communication, these are sounds; written, they become words, figures, charts, and other marks on paper. The first step in communication, then, is to formulate your ideas into symbols.

These sounds or written symbols do not communicate, however, until they go through some *channel* (letter, memo, report, conversation, speech, press conference, etc.) from you to the receiver.

Then, to complete the communication process, the receiver has to interpret these symbols back into an idea.

This three-step process of *symbolizing, transmitting,* and *interpreting,* though simple-sounding, nevertheless involves many possibilities for breakdown.

Since communication has different physical, psychological, and verbal contexts for both sender and receiver, these areas of *context* are sources of communication breakdown. (Electronic communications can also have noises that interfere with communication.) You can therefore improve communication by taking these possibilities for interference into account when you choose your channel and transmit your message.

You can't do much about the physical context, such as people's eyesight and hearing problems, nor can you always control office space or traffic noise. You *can* control psychological context to a certain extent by timing letters to arrive on the better days of the week and by paying attention to you-attitude and the psychology of refusals.

You can see that choosing a channel and transmitting your message are not the most difficult parts of the communication process. *Symbolizing* and *interpreting* the message are the parts that will cause you the greatest problems. The reason? The symbols won't necessarily mean the same thing to you and your receiver. The study of meaning in language forms (our communication symbols, or verbal context) is called *semantics.*

## Some Basic Semantic Principles

Fundamental to communication is this general principle: *The symbols used must stand for essentially the same thing in the minds of the sender and the receiver.*

Since words are the symbols used to communicate, think of the potential problems in attaching meaning to words. For one thing, words have both a **connotative** and **denotative** meaning.

For example, the word *claim* has a denotative (or dictionary) meaning of "state to be true." But often the connotative meaning is the one the recipient thinks of first. If you write a customer and say, "You claim that you followed the instructions," that customer is likely to think that you don't believe it, because the connotation of *claim* is often "You *say* this is true, but I have my doubts." Thus to communicate best you may need to choose words that are as neutral in connotation as possible.

Another example of connotation and denotation is the way you use different adjectives to describe positive, neutral, and negative things. For example, you may describe your best friend as "slender," your same-size boss as "thin," and your rival for the public affairs job as "skinny." Keep in mind that words in many contexts convey much more than their dictionary definitions.

When the sender and the receiver attach different meanings to the same words or use different words even though they intend the same meaning, semanticists call it **bypassing,** because the messages thus sent pass but do not connect. You need to stress clarity when sending messages and to avoid jargon the receiver might not understand. Your responsibility as a receiver is to *ask questions* if you're not sure what the sender means.

*Diction* is another aspect of communicating with words—you need to choose the proper word to represent your idea. Sometimes the problem is remembering which of two easily confused words to use, as in the choice between *affect* and *effect.* Other times the problem lies in a choice between two words often misused, such as *imply* and *infer, eager* and *anxious,* or *less* and *fewer.* In these cases your receiver will probably figure out what you meant to say, but your inept wording will probably slow down the message while the receiver makes this translation. (Look in Appendix C under **Dic** for more examples of often-confused pairs of words.)

Semanticists also talk about *levels of abstraction* when they discuss how words carry meaning. High-level abstractions are the hair-trigger words like *communism, crook,* and *homosexual* that have such strong emotional meaning for people that you should avoid them. Low-level abstractions are apt to cause you more problems in business communication, though. These are the words, usually nouns, that name things in groups by ignoring small differences, such as the general word *machines,* rather than brand names or specific types.

Of course, *abstracting,* by its very nature, means focusing on some details and omitting others. In your business communications you will normally be limited by time, space, and purpose anyway. You *can't* give all the details, nor would you want to. When you give highlights, be as objective as you can. No two people will ever see or report things the same way, but you owe it to your reader or listener not to give a slanted view. You don't want to be a victim of the allness fallacy, described later in this section.

If you write a memo asking for funds to buy *machines,* your request will probably not be granted. You'll be more likely to achieve success if you justify the purchase of *microcomputers,* or even more specifically, *IBM PCs.* To communicate well, you must use words specific enough for the necessary precision.

Other aspects of word choice that you need to consider are the level of language your audience will best understand (avoid technical jargon if your receiver is a layperson or not in your technical field; don't write in a condescending tone to your subordinates) and general rules of grammar. The way you put words together, or even punctuate and spell them, can make a vast difference in communication.

To a reader who follows the English system of placing modifiers as close as possible to the things they modify, "Only three men passed the first screening" does not mean the same as "Three men passed the first screening only."

To a reader who knows anything about the punctuation of essential and nonessential clauses, "The prices which are higher than those last year for the same items are simply too high" does not mean the same as "The prices, which are higher than those last year for the same items, are simply too high."

To get the right idea, the reader has to assume that the writer didn't know how to handle participles when writing "Having hung by the heels in the 30-degree temperature overnight, we found the venison made an excellent breakfast." Remember the fundamental principle: *The symbols used must stand for essentially the same thing in the minds of the sender and the receiver.*

If you could enter the receiver's world and operate according to the same assumptions, communication would be simpler. Since you usually can't do this, as in many business situations where you know the receiver only sketchily if at all, considering the general principles of semantics can help you communicate better.

*1. Words are merely symbols for the things they represent.* Words do not have meanings themselves but only the power to evoke or represent meanings in our minds. As mentioned earlier, words are more apt to have personal connotations than common denotations. Think, for example, of specific features that come to your mind when you hear or see the word *president.* If you make a list of the features and compare it with the list of one of your classmates, you'll find many differences in the way two people view the same term.

*2. No two things are exactly alike.* To be absolutely precise, you'd need a different word or symbol for naming each item that exists. Obviously, such precision is impractical—and unnecessary for most purposes. General words, naming whole groups of things similar in one or more aspects, help you classify things. You save words by talking about somewhat similar things collectively instead of individually. As long as what you say or do with such a group applies equally well to all members of the group, you can communicate effectively.

You run into trouble, however, when you group things on the basis of a few similarities and then act as if all things in the group were identical. Such a situation exists when colleges try to treat all freshmen alike because all are first-year students, ignoring the great variety of interests and abilities in the individuals.

If you ignore differences and stress only similarities, you may unfairly *stereotype* groups of individuals. Some common personnel stereotypes in the past, for example, were that married employees were more stable, that women couldn't be assigned jobs requiring travel, and that accountants needed only technical skills rather than additional people skills and marketing skills.

As a communicator, you can help solve the problem of categorizing by using words that are specific enough for your purposes. When you intend your statement to apply equally to a number of somewhat similar things (perhaps all new customers), be efficient and use the group name. On the other hand, when significant differences exist in the group, make clear which members of the group you are talking about. "Businesspeople who do such and such things are unethical" is quite different from "Businesspeople are unethical."

When you make *analogies* comparing two things, you point to the similarities between the two things to help your receiver understand the unknown item in terms of a known item. When you talk about a team player in business, for example, you're making an analogy to sports teams and how the players interact for the good of the group.

To use analogies so they help the communication process rather than hinder it, remember that analogies are never exact (because no two things are ever exactly alike) and that an analogy never *proves* anything. A comparison may be helpful, in other words, but significant differences can exist to change the impact of generally similar background conditions. Stock market and weather forecasters often err because they fail to consider the differences in generally similar background conditions.

*3. A statement is never the whole story.* Even reporting the simplest event, you omit some details. Even if you think you cover the standard *who, where, when, why, what,* and *how,* another reporter could easily add more details and more specifics on each of them.

This idea of incompleteness concerns you as a communicator because of the dangers of ignoring it—what semanticists call the *allness* fallacy. If you consider only parts of a whole and judge the whole, you're in danger of the logical fallacy of hasty generalization and unsound conclusions. Remember the six blind men who each described an elephant so differently because each had felt a different part? If you forget that you do not have all the facts, you are in danger of closing your mind to other facts and points of view. Recognizing that you never have the whole story, on the other hand, helps keep you open-minded and tolerant.

*4. Perception involves both the perceived and the perceiver.* Since you never tell the whole story, you select those things that seem important to you. What you say, then, depends as much on you (the kind of person you really are, different from anybody else) as on what the whole story really is. Another person would filter out different things; hence neither of you can be strictly objective.

Recognizing this point can prevent disagreements by making you cautious about using *is* dogmatically. Instead of saying "My friend is honest," you'd be more realistic to say, "My friend *seems* to be honest."

You also need to avoid projecting your own characteristics and feelings onto others. You may assume that your subordinates will work overtime to get an important project done, as you would do. If you want to make *sure* they will do so, be certain to communicate this expectation clearly.

*5. Statements or actions based on whims, feelings, imaginings, preconceptions, customs, traditions, and platitudes are questionable.* Instead of accepting these subjective types of information, get all the facts you can and evaluate them as objectively as you can. This is why, as a report writer, you always answer the questions "What are the facts?" and "How do you know?" no matter what else you do in the report. You also use *think* rather than *feel* when you state your reasoned conclusions.

When considering your collected facts, you should ask, "How do you know that this information is reliable?" The disagreements among authorities in almost every field should warn you to question authoritative statements or at least to check them against your own experience. Also check the dates of your facts, since even well-established teachings of science changed after the discovery of new evidence by such researchers as Harvey, Pasteur, and Reed. More recently, discoveries in outer space have been bringing into question many of the established principles that astronomers and physicists have followed for years.

*6. Facts, inferences, and value judgments are not the same thing.* Things that you can see, feel, or hear (sense data) are considered more reliable than inferences (opinions or conclusions), as you know if you've ever heard a court trial. You can see why if you consider the nature of sense data, inferences, and value judgments. Sense data usually approach certainty; inferences vary all the way from near certainty to slight probability (usually depending mainly on how many verifiable facts form the basis for them); and value judgments are nearly always debatable.

Of course, you can't hold up every action waiting for exact facts. As a practical matter, you make and act on inferences all the time. You take calculated risks based on some data. The danger in inferences is not in acting on them but in acting on them *as if* they were completely reliable.

To avoid deluding yourself and others with whom you communicate, try to remind yourself and forewarn others of the *bases* on which your statements rest. If you are reporting a client complaint to another manager, for example, be sure to indicate that "he said this trust seemed to increase his tax exposure rather than save him money," rather than "this trust arrangement will cost him money."

*7. Some either-or, black-white classifications are legitimate, but most are not.* The question is *whether your two-part classifications are mutually exclusive.* The division of anything into two parts—either-or, black-white—is usually fallacious. Imagine dividing things into categories of blue and not blue, for example. In the real world of varying colors, this would be as hard a task as dividing employees into categories of hardworking and not hardworking. Where do you draw the line?

If you use two-valued classifications for things that cannot exist simultaneously (such as married or not married), you are being true to reality. But most things are continua, with gradations, shadings, or degrees between the extremes. For them, you need a "how-much index." Applying black-white logic to them ignores the gray.

Fortunately for you as a communicator, English contains not only somewhat similar nouns of varying degrees of specificity and strength but also a large supply of adjectives and adverbs with similar variations. Adjectives and adverbs also have three standard degrees of comparison such as *good, better, best* and *speedily, more speedily, most speedily.* In addition, you can always add specific details such as times and weights.

*8. Things change significantly with time.* Nature is a dynamic process;

so significant aspects of a present situation may not have existed in the past and may not continue in the future. Some semanticists use indexing to differentiate among the various times they refer to when mentioning people, places, or things. Indexing thus helps emphasize differences rather than similarities. (Indexing is extremely distracting in print, of course. "Jane $_{1983}$ is not Jane $_{1986}$" is a true statement, but would certainly bog a reader down.)

To recognize how important this principle is, spend some time thinking in terms of differences only. Don't think of similarities, but notice unique, individual things around you. You will quickly see that considering differences is important but that considering *all* differences *all* the time would be time-consuming and unnecessary.

If you *don't consider time* in connection with statements sent or received, you can end up with what semanticists call a frozen evaluation (as happens when your parents still treat you like a child the first time you come home from college). A good example of *considering time* is the practice of universities readmitting students after a specified length of time, after dropping them for poor scholarship or rule infractions.

The main things the study of semantics should show you are that words are very powerful and that knowledge of semantics can help make powerful writers. Using the right adjective can promote a certain attitude about a product, as advertising people know, just as using the wrong abstractions (such as beauty, which means very different things to different people) can block communication. You'll learn in Chapter 8 how sales increase more from referring to the specific good qualities of a product than from selling it in glowing generalities.

Alert receivers will ask you as a writer or speaker to prove your assertions and give them the facts. You'll communicate more fully if you differentiate among your facts, assumptions, and value judgments for the receiver.

## Nonverbal Communication

Not all communication involves spoken language, of course. Some people go so far as to say that less than half the meaning we get comes from words. Nonverbal communication can come from *how* we say things, what we wear, and all sorts of other nonverbal cues.

Without being taught the subject in school, each of us knows how to communicate nonverbally. We've learned our culture as we grew up, and nonverbal conventions are a part of that culture. You do need to be aware of the differences in nonverbal cues from one culture to another, however, as discussed in Chapter 4.

Nonverbal communication cues can be conscious or unconscious—

we choose to wear certain clothes to a job interview, for example, but may not be aware of how our posture reflects our mood. When you listen, you communicate with the speaker by your facial expressions, movements, and position whether you realize it or not.

**Kinds of Nonverbal Cues.** *Body movement* such as gestures, position, and actual movement can tell your listeners a lot about how you feel about them. (The study of the meaning of body movement is called *kinesics;* it includes all movements that show meaning, including *facial expressions* and *eye movements.*)

You also tend to judge people you meet by *physical characteristics* and the *artifacts* they wear (uniforms, pins, makeup, even perfume).

One nonverbal area with strong cultural differences is *touching.* In our culture touching is socially restricted after childhood, but many other cultures allow adults to touch one another more freely. (Again, see Chapter 4 for more information on cultural differences in international business.) Think of how you react in a crowd, trying not to touch strangers. Think of the information you get about another person when shaking hands.

*Paralanguage* describes *how* a person speaks, a nonverbal cue that also gives you much information about a person's mood, social status, education, and possibly even self-esteem.

*Proxemics* describes our use of space. Think of the different distances you stand from a person at work, your friend met in the hall, and a loved one. Most people in the U.S. culture find less than 18 inches to be uncomfortably close unless there's some romantic or family attachment, but people in other cultures use much less space than we do even when talking to strangers.

In addition to this space code, cultures have a *time code.* Consider the various amounts of lateness acceptable in your life—to class, to a formal meeting, to a dinner party. Again, other cultures have time codes different from ours.

**How Verbal and Nonverbal Cues Relate.** Verbal and nonverbal cues relate to each other in some commonsense ways:

- A nonverbal cue and a verbal one may **emphasize** or **amplify** the same information, as when we warn someone to be quiet or cautious in words and by gesture. The nonverbal may add to the verbal, as when a person says he's angry and is tense and speaks loudly and often quickly. Shrugs and other emphatic gestures also add meaning to words.

- The nonverbal and verbal cues may also **contradict** each other. We tend to trust most the nonverbal cues in a case of this type, as when someone says she has time to talk but continues to go through papers on her desk without looking at you.

- Sometimes a nonverbal cue **substitutes** for words. You may have explained your needs through gesture in a foreign country, or beckoned to a person too far away to call by name.
- Nonverbal cues also **regulate** and **control** our conversation, for it is through them that you show your speaking partner how fast to go, when to explain further, and when to stop.

You can see that what you *don't* say can help or hurt you. You might want to study semantics and nonverbal behavior in more depth using library sources and periodicals.

Knowing how the process of communication works and how semantics and nonverbal communication can help you communicate will make you a more effective communicator with all levels of receivers, from laypeople to technical experts. In addition to these outside audiences, you'll need to learn how best to handle the various levels of employees you'll meet at work.

# Office Politics/Intraoffice Communication

When you go to work, you'll have people above you, below you, and equal to you on the organization chart. You'll also have people who actually operate in a different way from what their place on the organization chart would indicate—who have more or less power than their titles would seem to give them. You need to approach these three groups (superiors, subordinates, and peers) in different ways if you want to be an effective communicator.

For example, higher-level audiences need clear, sharp presentation. They may actually need more detail than lower-level employees, though, because subordinates may already understand the technical details. Within a firm, upward and downward communication require extra attention to the audience's relationship to the writer.

## Attention to Audience

No matter what kind of message you are writing, one of the most important planning steps you go through is audience analysis. Most business communications have one main reader or group of readers and then secondary readers whose interests and needs you must also consider. One rather structured way of analyzing your audience is to use a chart like the following.

|  | Reader 1 | Reader 2 |
|---|---|---|
| 1. *Who* is my audience? (Name or job title) |  |  |
| 2. What *attitude* do I expect this person to have toward my information? |  |  |
| 3. What *attitude* do I want this person to have after I've presented the information? |  |  |
| 4. What *action* (if any) do I want this person to take as a result of my message? |  |  |
| 5. What is the *most important* thing to tell this person? |  |  |

Too often, a writer tries to cover more material than the reader wants or needs to make a decision. If an entire communication doesn't get read, your message may not get through. Tell the audience only as much as it needs to know. Question 5, on the most important thing to tell your audience, is the most critical question. *Focus* your message for greatest impact.

## Upward, Downward, and Peer Communication

Attention to audience is an attribute of good professional writing, because you communicate more efficiently when you take into account your reader's or listener's background knowledge, interest in and opinions about the topic, and action on your information or request.

*Upward communication,* for example, requires tactful recognition of the differences in position between the writer and the receiver, decisive tone, summaries of information presented, a combination of facts and recommendations, and an objective attitude.

*Upward* communications need to sound decisive and thorough, and to summarize the points presented, usually before presenting supporting facts. Obvious efforts to impress or please a supervisor or signs of a cringing attitude don't create the right impression—or get your wishes accomplished.

*Downward communication,* on the other hand, should sound diplomatic rather than overbearing, while remaining clear, complete, and persuasive to get the task done.

*Downward* communications need to sound clear and objective; too many memos to subordinates are condescending and aggressive instead. Let people know what you want them to do, and tell *why* if you want to motivate the desired action. Almost all people react better to a reasonable request than to an arbitrary order.

*Peer communication* can sometimes be more formal than other types, and can use more technical language and often more detail, because this audience knows more about the technical areas discussed.

In communicating with your peers, you finally have a chance to use the language of the job and not have to think of it pejoratively, as jargon. Peer communication lets you use technical terms common to the field, and may allow for more personal writing as well. You will, however, need solid data to persuade peers, who are often more aware of hidden agendas than outsiders can be. The trade-off to more research, however, is the lack of a need to explain basics that peers already understand.

An exception to the underexplaining principle would be the proposal, usually written for peer reviewers. Usually proposals require total explanation and a great deal of marketing writing to sell your ideas.

## Expert to Nonexpert

To communicate with laypeople and many clients, you'll need to pay special attention to language. For a project to be sold, or a development explained, the audience must be able to understand the concept. This means not much jargon, maybe some definitions, and above all a clear sense of purpose and focus.

One of the marketing skills in demand in many technical fields is the ability to focus a presentation on key selling points. Part of this focus, of course, relies on clarity and concise, specific writing.

## Managerial Image—Choosing Stationery and Letterhead

One issue you will face as a manager is how to give your reading audience a positive first impression of your firm. The first impression your reader gets is important; so even though it sounds like a small detail, you need to choose pleasing and unobtrusive stationery.

The appearance of an individualized letter or memo is like a person's appearance: Since it is not the most important thing, the less attention it attracts to itself, the better. The wording, a desirable tone reflecting goodwill, and the persuasive qualities are more influential than the looks of a letter in determining its success or failure. Just as some listeners will reject the messages of speakers who do not come up to expected standards of appearance, however, so will many readers reject a written message that calls attention to its format and thereby distracts from the content.

A personalized (individualized) letter sent by first-class mail will nearly always get a reading. Flashy designs and lavish colors may distract the reader's attention from the important feature—your message.

Direct mail/marketing (sales) letters are sometimes justifiable exceptions. Because they are frequently mass mailings (not individualized), they often must struggle to get read at all. In striving to capture attention, their writers may use computer-simulated personalization, cartoons, gadgets, bright colors, important-seeming messages on the envelopes, and other gimmicks. Except for such direct mail, however, the physical letter should serve only as a vehicle for your message. The reader should not notice it since it would distract attention from the message.

A memo, by its nature, should never need to work for a reader's attention. A neat, clean, conventional appearance is always the goal.

**Stationery.** The first thing your reader will notice if it is inappropriate is your stationery. The most common business stationery—and therefore the least noticed—is 20-pound white bond with some rag content in 8½ by 11-inch sheets. Variations acceptable under appropriate circumstances include heavier and lighter paper, different sizes, and various unobtrusive colors and shades.

Paper heavier than 20-pound is more expensive and too stiff for easy folding, and paper lighter than 20-pound is too flimsy and transparent. (If used, carbon copies are usually on very light paper because it is cheaper, takes less file space, and allows a greater number of clear carbon copies.)

The main off-standard sizes are Executive or Monarch letterheads (7½ by 10½ or 11 inches, used mainly by top executives) and half sheets (8½ by 5½ inches, used most frequently in intracompany memos or notes).

Though white is the standard, only the rainbow and your sense of appropriateness to your kind of business set the limits for color variations. Some tests have shown that colored papers sometimes produce better results in sales mailings. If you are sending out large mailings, however, you may be wise to run your own test on a small sample to see what color works best for that particular situation.

Paper with some rag content is more expensive than all-pulp paper, but it gives the advantages of pleasant feel, durability, and resistance to yellowing. With the advent of word processing and the use of white-out products to facilitate typing corrections, the erasable papers have found only a limited market in business and industry.

Whatever your choice of paper for letter and memo sheets, be sure you use the same quality and color for envelopes and second pages.

The acceptable variations in stationery allow you to reflect the personality of your business, just as you select clothes appropriate to your personality. The big points are *appropriateness* and *inconspicuousness.* In selecting paper for your letterheads, then, you should have a good reason before choosing something other than 20-pound white bond, 8½ by 11 inches. Anything else may distract the reader's attention from your message.

**Letterhead.** The main trend in letterheads for many years has been toward simplicity. Letterheads once took up a good part of the sheet with slogans, names of officers, and pictures of the firm's plant and product. Good modern letterheads usually take no more than 2 inches at the top and may occupy just a corner. They use wording, design, color, and graphic techniques to convey the necessary information and communicate a desirable image of the firm represented.

The minimum content is the name, address, and telephone number of the firm, including area and ZIP codes. Sometimes an added trademark or slogan indicates the nature of the business. Firms doing much nationwide or international business frequently give a toll-free telephone number and/or an address for cablegrams or telex.

Recent years have shown a marked movement toward the use of color in stationery. This trend has resulted partly from increased acceptance of colored paper and color printing and partly from heightened awareness of the role of letterheads as representatives of a company. Firms wishing to present a modern image are turning to carefully designed graphics, such as the imaginative use of special colors and blind embossing. Good designers, however, are careful to avoid garish combinations and tasteless designs.

**Placement on the Page.** Even with appropriate paper and a well-designed letterhead, you can still spoil the appearance (and thus distract from the message) unless you place the letter on the page properly. Two methods are in common use: the standard-line plan and the less-popular picture-frame plan.

*Standard-Line Plan.* The standard-line plan of placing a letter on the page saves time and money because typewriters set to the company's standard line (usually 6 inches—60 spaces in pica type or 72 of elite) give all letters the same side margins. The top margin is about the same as the side margins, and the bottom margin is about 1½ times as wide. By varying from the standard spacing between letter parts (more or less between the date and inside address, for example, or three spaces instead of two between paragraphs), you can adjust letters of differing lengths.

Memos almost always use the standard-line plan, in keeping with their intended saving of time and money.

*Picture-Frame Plan.* The idea of the picture-frame plan is that a rectangle drawn around the typed letter (not including a printed letterhead) should look like a picture framed in the marginal white space. You determine the width of side margins according to your letter length and make the top margin about the same. The bottom margin will take care of itself automatically. It should be about 1½ times as long (deep) as the other margins.

For short letters (100 words or less), leave about 2-inch margins at the top and sides. For long letters (over 250 words), leave at least 1-inch margins. Split the difference for middle-length letters.

Word processors make using the picture-frame plan much easier. Once a letter is in the machine's memory, an operator can quickly configure it with any desired margins. In only a minute or two the operator can print out versions with different margins to see how they look *if appearance is important enough to justify the extra time and effort.* But even with word processing, the standard-line plan is by far the more popular.

## How Your Text Approaches Business Communication

After discussing how office automation will affect the offices you will work in, your text covers the basic skills, principles, and plans you will use in preparing business messages.

Generally, all business messages—whether letter, memo, report, oral report, or telephone call—contain only three types of information. You may need to send *good news,* in which case you write or speak directly. You may have a *disappointing* or a *persuasive* message to send, in which case you write or speak indirectly. The text covers these three types of strategy in Part Two, along with the elements of effective business style.

Part Three, Psychological Planning for Effectiveness, tells you in more detail how to handle good news, disappointing messages, and persuasive messages (including selling ideas and services through requests, collections, and proposals and selling personal services through job letters and résumés).

Part Four applies the principles of good communication to speaking, listening, interviewing, and conferring. Part Five covers the special concerns of reporting for management decisions, among them adding graphics, using more headings, and giving extra attention to organization.

Both of these parts, like Part Three, use many examples to *show* as well as *tell* you about how to succeed as a business communicator.

All the cases for applying communication principles appear in two appendixes (one of chapter-related cases and one of case-series that combine communication problems arising out of an initial situation and its results). A concise writer's handbook follows the cases, to provide answers to your questions about style and usage in business.

If this sounds like a lot of material to cover in one term, it is. If your course doesn't last two terms, as it does in many schools with separate communication and report courses, your instructor will choose which topics to cover in the shortened time. Once you've mastered the basics, you can apply them in communication situations whether you've had time to work on them in class or not—but a two-term class gives you a better chance to really work on longer reports and more oral reports.

The principles of business communication that you'll learn in this book will make you better able to take advantage of opportunities to get your point across, whether to sell a product, get yourself promoted, or convince a friend to see the movie you chose.

If you pay attention to office politics and communication theory, you'll be more apt to succeed in business than people who haven't learned these principles. As you begin to reach the higher ranks of management, you'll have to present your ideas well in both writing and speaking, so that you can convince top management of their worth.

## Questions and Exercises

1. Go to the library and find a recent survey on the importance of communication skills to businesspeople. What is the rank of writing skills? What about speaking skills?

2. What parts of the communication process cause senders the most trouble? The receivers?

3. Write 5 to 10 specific features of two of the following terms as you visualize them
   —professor
   —lawyer
   —astronaut
   —doctor
   —accountant

Now compare your list with a classmate's list. What is different about your lists? Why is this so?

4. Label the following as fact, inference, or value judgment:
   —x is America's finest city.
   —Venus is called the evening star.
   —Natural vitamins are more healthful for you.
   —Television causes children to be violent.
   —Nonsmokers can get lung disease from being around smokers.
   —The surgeon general says that smoking can be hazardous to your health.
   —I bought new tires for my car last week.
   —Now I'll get better gas mileage because the tires are properly inflated for once.
   —Michelin tires are always the best.

5. In a paragraph or two, define a term common to your chosen profession by analogy to something a lay reader would know. (Example: CPA, focus group, cafeteria benefit plan, rate of return.)

6. Name three valid two-part classifications.

7. What approach would you use to tell your boss about cost overruns on your current project? How would you tell an equal-level manager that one of her employees has made a mistake in dealing with a client (you found out because he's your neighbor)? How do you give a subordinate instructions?

8. What nonverbal behavior are you most aware of?

9. What should a manager consider when choosing company stationery and letterhead? Why?

# Chapter Outline

**How Technology Has Helped the Office**
**Commonly Adopted Kinds of Office Automation**
    Word Processors
    Microcomputers
    Local Area Networks
    Telecommuting
    Electronic Mail
    Micrographics
    Teleconferencing
    Voice Recognition/Reproduction
    Artificial Intelligence
**The Downside of Office Automation**
    Productivity versus People
    Management Problems
    VDT Problems
**Evolutionary Aspects of Office Life**
    Position and Spacing of Letter Parts
    OCR Envelope Handling
    Interoffice Memorandums
    Efficient Use of Forms
    Adaptations for International Business Communication
**Questions and Exercises**

# 2

# You and the Automated Office

The offices you will go to work in may be very different from those where your parents began work, and probably among the biggest differences will be the equipment available to make your jobs easier.

As a future manager, you will need to be familiar with the possibilities of office automation so you can help your company evaluate what aspects of automation to use.

Of course, the largest companies are the ones most apt to use the newest equipment. Smaller businesses often have less need as well as less budget for innovation. A recent *Business Week* survey found, however, that even industry leaders like GE have only about 25 percent penetration of office automation equipment.

Various aspects of the automated office that you may encounter are word processors, microcomputers, local area networks (LANs), telecommuting, electronic mail, micrographics, and teleconferencing.

This chapter discusses current and future applications of the automated office, analyzes advantages and disadvantages of the new equipment, and finally offers examples of parts of office life that have remained the same—well-written letters and memos, both national and international.

## How Technology Has Helped the Office

Some advantages common to the different types of office automation technology are:

- reduction of repetitive work, whether retyping corrected reports or recalculating cost projections;
- reduction of cost, whether from labor force reduction, time savings, or mail or travel costs;
- increase in quickly available, current reports with useful graphics;

- increase in time spent on creative work rather than on daily tasks; and
- possible decrease in need for layers of management.

# Commonly Adopted Kinds of Office Automation

### Word Processors

The piece of office equipment you're probably most familiar with now is the word processor, which had joined or replaced the typewriter in 86 percent of U.S. companies by late 1984. (Usage is increasing fairly fast, as the figures were 69 percent in 1982 and 75 percent in 1983.) Because the word processor (even in its simplest form of an electronic typewriter) has some memory capability, you can without retyping save and revise letters, memos, reports, tables, or instructions.

Because corrections and revisions do not require typing over a whole page or document, clerical productivity increases with word processor use. Companies able to quantify their productivity gains find an increase of from one fourth to one half (43 percent of companies) or from one half to three fourths (25 percent of companies). Even a one-fourth increase would be significant in most offices, of course. Because revision is so comparatively easy, however, one danger is that some managers may lose productivity gains by trying to make every report absolutely flawless.

Word processing isn't, however, just a clerical tool. You'll find that you can write faster on your own by cutting out turnaround time as you revise format, appearance, writing style, and content on your own terminals without waiting for a secretary's revision. You might revise and polish your writing more because text-editing changes are so easy to make. For team-written reports, in many instances a diskette (instead of cut-and-pasted report copies) goes back and forth.

Software can also help you work more productively in other ways than proofreading for errors. It can check for consistent usage in hyphenated adjectives, the spelling of unusual names, the terms used throughout a series of manuals, matching formats, and similar cross-references. Programs such as STYLE and DICTION (Bell Laboratories) can analyze the readability of documents. (STYLE figures readability scores and indicates *be* verbs, passive verbs, number of adjectives, and sentence length. DICTION targets misused phrases and wordy passages, much as the Department of Commerce computer rejects *utilize* for *use* and other poor word choices in letters and memos.)

One of the most useful characteristics of the word processor is the availability of form paragraphs and messages in its memory that are quickly usable without retyping except to personalize. (Chapter 6 treats form paragraphs in more detail.) You just need to be sure to add the personalized inserts, unlike the fund raiser who sent a letter saying "Thank you for your generous gift of $.00, which we received on. . . ."

By using a program like GRAMMATIK (Wang Electronic Publishing), you can edit out sexist words. The program tags around 100 gender-specific words and offers alternative forms, substituting such nonsexist words as *guard* for *watchman, representative* for *spokesman,* and *attendant* for *bellboy.*

The following helpful products will go beyond checking a limited number of spellings or grammatical constructions:

- automatic and instantaneous spell checking, and
- automatic grammar checking
  missed tenses in a sentence
  awkward or uncommon phrasing
  missing quotation marks
  suggested alternatives to correct the faulty constructions.

Electronic dictation is also a future possibility for your office. As a manager, you will dictate directly to a computer that will store "voiceprints" for several thousand words and then type them out.

## Microcomputers

In the years before the microcomputer, computers had generally become more powerful, smaller, and less costly. What happened with the introduction of the microcomputer was more than just a continuation of this trend. A qualitative shift made computers truly available on a practical and individual basis.

The cost breakthrough was important because the hardware was now readily affordable; but newer, more powerful software that was easy to use also played a large part in the transformation of the office. You, as a manager, no longer have to explain your needs to someone in the data processing department or learn how to program a computer. While "user-friendliness" is still more a marketing point than a reality, in some cases computer software can enable you to use the computer directly.

In addition to word processing, using individual microcomputers gives you other valuable software tools: electronic spreadsheets, computer graphics, integrated software packages, and specific applications such as accounting software, professional time and billing programs, data bases, and even training packages in areas such as sales. Some of these applications are especially useful to managers.

An *electronic spreadsheet* allows you to change figures and project "what-if" forecasts to decide among possible future actions without doing time-consuming hand calculations.

*Integrated software packages* combine a spreadsheet and graphics with word processing and telecommunications (a phone-line hookup for direct communication with larger computers or data bases) so that you need not keep changing software to perform different tasks. After entering numbers into a table, for example, you can convert them into graph form and then insert them into a memo—all without changing disks.

Like other graphics, *computer graphics* (used on 2.5 million personal computers by 1986) get ideas across faster than narrative alone—and graphics produced by computer software save your firm the time and cost of having the art department produce charts, slides, labeled figures, and other visual aids. Originally, computer graphics seemed to be limited to pie charts and bar graphs generated from spreadsheet data, but improved technology permits newer multicolored high-resolution graphics printed on slides or transparencies. Now even small computers have extensive graphics capability, and if your company has a mainframe computer, it can produce very sophisticated graphics.

*Matrix printers* increase the sharpness of graphics, and *laser printers* make black-and-white production graphics possible. (With the latter, you can get 10 different charts in less than a minute, so the people in your organization can have charts to work from, rather than bulky printouts.) Color production graphics are more possible all the time as equipment improves, but these are still quite expensive.

An integrated software package can now integrate computer graphics with text on a screen, and a photocomposer can print them on the same page. Quality of resolution is improving in this field, and equipment prices are dropping very rapidly.

Your company will also be able to cut the cost of slides needed for presentations by using in-house computers for preparation ($8 per slide) rather than an outside service bureau ($50 per slide). A *digital film recorder* hooks to your large computer and creates very high resolution color slides, giving you security for your information as well as faster production time and cost savings.

*Lettering fonts* are also improving with the addition of decorative letter designs such as those found on Apple's Macintosh. Another helpful feature of the newest graphics packages is the *chartbook.* This shows you a selection of finished chart examples (such as Gantt and cost versus budget); all you need to do is fill in the data.

These new developments in computer graphics will probably double their use from 1 in 15 white-collar workers to 1 in 8, according to business predictions. More than six times as many dollars go to computer graphics in business now as went to them in 1981 (from $1.8 billion to $11.8 billion).

*Scheduling and time-management programs* range from electronic calendars and Rolodexes to extensive project management software, including Gantt and PERT charts. The more sophisticated programs show when portions of the project will be completed, when resources are in use on different tasks, and when potential scheduling problems might occur.

*Data base programs* help you and researchers evaluate large amounts of data quickly and can provide quick, up-to-date access to stock market quotations, airline schedules, and even shopping choices. (Chapter 14 discusses data base programs for researchers.)

## Local Area Networks

In some of your companies, personal computers and multifunction local area networks (LANs) will replace the word processor. These networks are desktop machines and workstations linked together by sophisticated cabling to central mainframes or midsize computers that exchange data with other mainframes through electronic messages, voice mail, and videoconferencing systems.

LANs are a method of coordinating computers so that your company can benefit from the use of shared resources. Usually a LAN serves a limited area such as a single building. Made up of a software package and several types of hardware, a LAN can support digitalized voice, data, and video and can link communication points within a facility.

Using LANs to integrate workstations can increase productivity on existing equipment and provide managers with greater control of resources. Two kinds of networks appear in Figures 2–1 and 2–2.

**Figure 2–1 / PC Local Area Network**

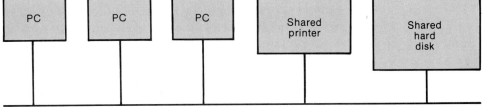

**Figure 2–2 / Multiuser Micro**

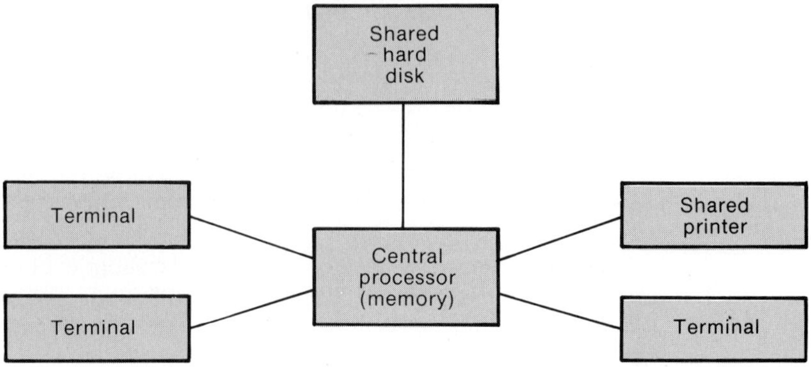

## Telecommuting

At one point, so-called cottage computing was apparently going to allow you as a manager to work at home via your (or the company's) personal computer. After all, the technology existed, with relatively inexpensive computers and modems readily available. Neither companies nor large numbers of employees, however, are willing to give up the at-the-office interaction with other workers and managers.

As a result, while some employees work at home part of the time, this part of the hoped-for electronic revolution probably won't take the place of team building and face-to-face meetings in your company. A Honeywell survey found that 56 percent of the company's workers would go to the office every day even if they had an identical computer to work on at home and that 36 percent would work at home only half of the time.

Another problem not thought of when hopes were so high for telecommuting was organized labor's negative attitude. As with the home knitting industry, labor unions claim that people working at home, linked to the office via computer, could violate minimum wage and child labor laws. With legalized home work, some predictions indicate as many as 10–15 million telecommuters by 1990, even though only 20,000–30,000 or so are working at home now. As a manager, you'll need to consider whether telecommuting can help *your* company.

In addition to saving commuting time and fuel, telecommuting gives home-workers more time with their families, scheduling flexibility, and a sense of being their own boss in responsibility for work completion. The company with home-workers increases productivity 15–20 percent and reduces overhead costs 10 percent. Telecommuting should lower turnover, which will in turn cut training costs. Unless employers exploit home-workers, as unions fear, telecommuting seems to be a way of using new technology to improve both work productivity and working conditions for employees who *want* to work at home and who *need* less interaction at work to complete their tasks successfully.

## Electronic Mail

In addition to regular mail, a business's choices of mail today include express mail, air freight (with next-day office-to-office delivery and rate reductions for volume users), and electronic mail (facsimile, telex, and voice mail).

From answering services to answering machines, people have tried to overcome the problem of not being able to reach the person with whom they want to communicate. Electronic mail (messages sent via computer) and voice mail (a voice instead of data recording) also help solve the problem by making the message available when the receiver is available to receive it.

The five technologies usually included in electronic mail systems individually or in various combinations are:

- computer-based message systems,
- facsimile systems,
- partially electronic mail,
- communicating word processors, and
- voice mail.

*Computer-based message systems* allow individual computers or terminals to communicate with one another. The communication can be direct, using such software as E-Mail (written by C. Dennis Jones specifically for the IBM PC), or through a specialized network that links users, such as the Freedom Network from Graphnet. (Both ways of communicating appear in Figures 2–3 and 2–4.)

Computer-based message systems enable a reader to answer, forward, delete, create, and edit messages. Some systems also indicate message length, urgency, and security level.

**Figure 2–3 / A Direct Communication**

Computer A ⟶ Computer B

**Figure 2–4 / A Network Communication**

User A ⟶ Network ⟶ User B
User C
User D

*Facsimile* is a remote photocopying device that transfers an exact copy of a document from one facsimile (or fax) device to another via telephone lines, satellite links, or packet-switched networks. If your company has the newest machines, they can transmit or receive messages in 20 seconds per page, with little or no operator intervention.

These machines compare very favorably with machines still used currently that transmit a page in six minutes, with operators monitoring at both ends. Assuming your company sent five pages a day via facsimile, at 50 cents a minute phone charges, the older machines cost $300 a month compared to $50 a month for the faster machine.

The advantages of speed and exact duplication of documents, signatures, drawings, and charts do need to be balanced against equipment cost and possible loss of security when you use network service.

*Partially electronic mail* consists of messages you create or transmit electronically but convert to hard copy during some phase of the delivery process. MCI, Federal Express, and other companies offer this service at relatively low cost. For this type of electronic mail, your sending company needs to buy equipment that can generate an electronic message but does not need equipment in every branch office to receive messages.

*Communicating word processors* can originate and transmit documents to similar machines, either by typing or by optical character recognition (OCR). A telex system is an example of a communicating word processor system, as is an in-house word processing system that transmits documents to other locations for editing, review, or printing.

As with other electronic mail systems, this type eliminates needless retyping of your documents.

*Voice mail* is a computer-assisted device for recording voice messages. Such a system ranges from a telephone answering machine to an integrated system tied into your PBX. The more sophisticated voice mail systems can send messages to a whole group at once and can rank-order your messages for callback. Voice mail is best for quick, personal messages rather than detailed messages with numerical data, as you don't get printed documentation of calls. It does eliminate "telephone tag," which occurs when people have to call back repeatedly and leave messages for one another.

Electronic mail systems need security precautions, just as do paper memos. As a manager, you should consider some rules requiring confirmation of sending and receiving a message, and passwords to limit access.

## Micrographics

Microfilm, microfiche, computer output micrographics (COM), and updatable microfiche are all part of micrographics, an important technology for efficient and effective information handling. Computer-aided retrieval (CAR) also allows you access to large files via a computer-based index.

Microfacsimile takes input images from microfiche or microfilm and transmits them by facsimile for output as a CRT image, on paper, or as micrographics. Coupled with CAR, this technology provides on-line remote access to typed, printed, handwritten, and drawn documents. Computer output microfilm (COM) allows your company to produce documents on microforms instead of regular computer printouts. This obviously saves a great deal of paper and filing space.

Micrographics can save both paper and filing space and time. The computer-aided forms of micrographics have the advantages of both small space and speed of access, but even the currently used micrographics forms of microfilm and microfiche can help eliminate some of the paper found in most offices.

## Teleconferencing

Teleconferencing of different types is one solution to increasing travel and time costs in multilocation companies. The possible types:

- audioconferencing (conference calling),
- videoconferencing (television with audio),
- audiographic (voices and visuals carried by regular phone lines), and
- computer conferencing (use of terminals over phone lines),

can all save travel time, costs, and stress on key personnel (managers, specialist technicians, leaders of dispersed teams). While even a simple cost-benefit analysis can track travel and salary costs, electronic meetings can also save you indirect costs of burnout (turnover, reduced performance, stress).

Teleconferencing *can* be expensive if your company needs full color, full motion, high fidelity, and a full-room setup. Lesser systems, however, are not necessarily inferior for many applications. Audioconferencing, for example, has served well for press conferences, long-distance training, information gathering, and problem solving. A national real estate firm uses teleconferencing to give information about changing interest rates and market trends and to manage training sessions among franchise staffs in 40 cities. An insurance firm director used teleconferencing to explain a new insurance policy to 30 salespeople in different branches.

By 1983, over 30 IBM locations in the United States were interconnected with audio, facsimile, and video image transmission from specially equipped conference rooms. IBM's experience was that using the videoconferencing network increased both productivity and communication. (A typical room setup appears in Figure 2–5.)

Because videoconferences must be organized well in advance, participants usually have time to come to your meeting prepared. The most successful videoconferences are among working professionals, as these

**Figure 2–5 / A Videoconferencing Room Layout**

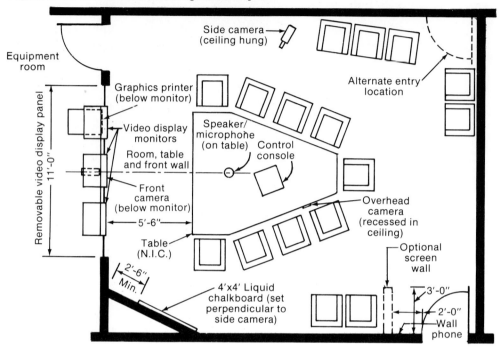

people need to be completing projects rather than flying from city to city for meetings.[1]

*Cost and Time Savings.* Even telephone conferencing can save your business a lot of money. In five months in 1981, audioconferencing saved Celanese Corporation in New York 97 business trips and $28,000 in air travel alone. Honeywell, Inc. calculates a saving of $15,000 in travel costs for each audioconference. At an extreme end, Hoffman-LaRouche, a New Jersey pharmaceutical firm, saved $200,000 by holding a national sales conference by telephone—a conference involving 1,000 people at 40 locations.

*Disadvantages.* Overuse of teleconferencing might lower morale in some fields because of decreased personal contact. Some fields, such as sales,

[1] Marilyn D. Egel and O. E. Katter, Jr., "Videoconferencing: A User Experience," in *1983 IEEE Professional Communication Society Conference Proceedings* (Atlanta, IEEE-PCS, 1983), pp. 99–101.

may be inappropriate for teleconferencing because face-to-face contact and interaction are necessary. It's possible that teleconferencing could increase *unproductive* time because easily arranged electronic meetings become too common (like some other unnecessary meetings).

Employees who consider travel a benefit may miss it. And, as with all the new office technology, once the technology is in use, management must keep a supportive and evaluative eye on the process to find profitable and unprofitable uses for it in the organization's functions.

## Voice Recognition/Reproduction

Consumer electronics experts see a new stage of the automated office revolution in machines that can listen and even talk back to you. Existing products can generate speech for telephones and personal computer prompts, alarm systems, and telephone-access data retrieval. Products that will soon be available to you will be able to recognize and store speech—a service applicable in voice typewriters, speech filing cabinets, dictation systems, and voice mail. Total speech recognition is at least a decade away from practical use, but your future possibilities seem very exciting.

Currently, the user lists words and their related commands and then places the words on a computer screen. The user points to a word and says it out loud several times (to allow for the fact that a person doesn't say a word the same way every time). At this point, the user's voice can control the speech command system. The computer matches unknown voice commands with the set of commands it knows; when the voice command and the internal set match up, the computer performs the related command.

## Artificial Intelligence

The fifth generation of computers, now under study in both the United States and Japan, will be able to make more sophisticated language judgments than those now possible. From a business communication point of view, this aspect may help you with word processing and report writing, since software will enable writers to evaluate their work instead of merely editing out objective errors. Many companies are working to develop artificial intelligence systems applications, such as drilling analyses for oil companies, greater fields of vision and mobility for robots, and financial planning and credit scoring. Some of these uses may eventually affect your work.

# The Downside of Office Automation

### Productivity versus People

Office automation has psychological effects that require attention. *Managers* see the equipment as helping employees work faster, but *workers* see it as a way to gain more control of their jobs and more intellectual challenge. This conflict between productivity and people can cause some real problems. Office automation can serve for repetitive daily tasks *and* to improve problem solving, communication, and strategy development. Most applications common so far use only the first ability—to perform daily tasks more productively.

Around 90 percent of secretaries think that office automation has had a positive effect on their work, 70 percent think automated equipment has given them more time for more challenging work, and 75 percent expect automation to open new career opportunities.

A recent Honeywell survey found that 90 percent of "knowledge workers" (managers, analysts, accountants, engineers, planners, and administrators in corporate production, development, marketing, legal, and financial departments) think that desktop computers and related technology let them make better-informed decisions and give them more time for creative work.

Office automation and increased computer use have caused the number of middle-management jobs to grow. Theoretically, new technology should reduce the number of layers of management, but this depends on the top people's policy and evaluation. Automation doesn't require workers with higher technical skills, though, as the newest equipment is designed for someone with no special skills at all and is "user-friendly."

### Management Problems

Computer workstations for managers need only a few functions; many models on the market are designed for technical specialists and are more costly and complex than necessary. Some offices, however, *need* more complex machinery, if only for future uses. The biggest problem facing you as a manager is choosing the best *system* for your needs. You may buy each piece of equipment without enough regard for how it will combine with other equipment under your control, or in other parts of the organization. You may not do a thorough enough needs assessment (both short- and long-range) to know what equipment is suitable for the problems you need solved.

Another problem you might encounter is with the video display terminals (VDTs) your staff will use.

### VDT Problems

A problem with word processing that didn't occur with typewriters is the constant need to refocus your eyes to adjust to the different distances involved:

- 14–30 inches to the screen,
- 18 inches to the keyboard, and
- 15–30 inches to reference papers.

To reduce the resulting eyestrain, your operators should place all reference papers "at the same distance as the screen and close beside it," according to experts.

Another potential problem with VDT screens is the possibility of radiation-caused illnesses or birth defects. Since controversy still exists over whether the radiation from VDTs causes birth defects, companies should consider transferring VDT workers into other jobs during pregnancy. An alternative is providing lead aprons to protect the fetus from radiation.

The problem may actually be stress- rather than radiation-related. Office automation has great potential for reducing the stress of office work, because repetitive tasks especially lend themselves to automation. If managers place too much emphasis on productivity, they may actually increase stress. Careful management of technology can increase efficiency, effectiveness, and systematization. You will need special managerial skill to balance efficiency and effectiveness against quality of working life.

## Evolutionary Aspects of Office Life

Regardless of the increases in technology for the office now and in the future, some things will remain the same. Businesses will still need well-written letters, memos, electronic messages, and reports. Sending mail electronically or meeting via satellite link instead of in person also requires more, rather than less, attention to organization, psychology, and clarity.

As a manager, you still need to be able to tell staff members if reports and shorter messages look right—both in overall format and crucial details like proofreading. A summary of conventional format follows.

### Position and Spacing of Letter Parts

**Standard Parts.** The usual business letter has six standard parts. *As a general rule, single-space within parts and double-space between parts.* But note exceptions as they come up in the following explanation. (Letter layouts appear in Figures 2–6 and 2–7.)

**Figure 2–6 / Block Form, Picture-Frame Layout,
Open Punctuation**

*RICHARD  D.  IRWIN · INC.*

1818 RIDGE ROAD · HOMEWOOD, ILLINOIS 60430          TELEPHONE: (312) 798-6000

November 12, 19--

Lightning Software Company
154 June Street
Alpena, Michigan 49707

Attention:  Manager of Office Services

This letter is in block form (no indentation), open punctuation
(nothing after the salutation or complimentary close), and picture-
frame layout.

Though picture-framing a letter takes additional time, some people
feel the resulting appearance is worth it.  With a good word
processing system, however, the task is simple.  (We used one
to prepare this letter.)

Note that all the elements of the letter begin at the left margin.
This plan is a big time-saver since the typist or word processing
operator does not need to set and use tabs and remember which
elements to tab.  This layout tends to give the letter a "modern"
look and is quite acceptable today.

Sincerely yours

RICHARD D. IRWIN, INC.

*Mrs. Jean Cauthen*

Mrs. Jean Cauthen
Manager, Office Procedures

jc/fv

PUBLISHERS OF BOOKS IN ECONOMICS AND BUSINESS

**Figure 2–7 / Page Layout Examples**

A: Block form, mixed punctuation

B: Semiblock form, open punctuation

C: No letterhead, block form, indented
paragraphs, mixed punctuation

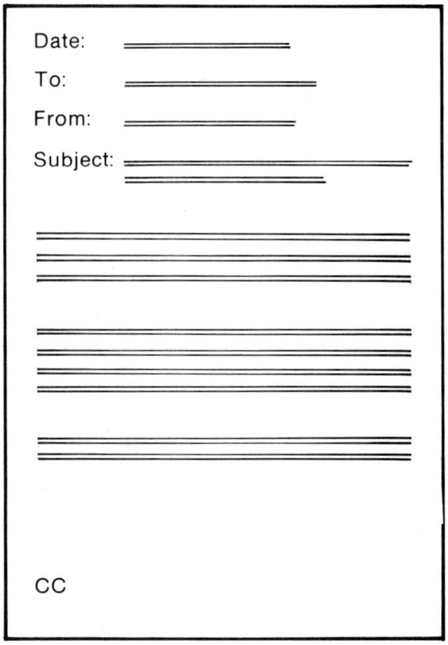

D: Memo form

The conventional *heading* or the first part of a letter on paper with no letterhead (illustrated in Figure 2–7C) usually includes the sender's address (but not name) and the date. It establishes both top and side margins because it is the first thing on the page. Such a heading is usually three lines but often more. Thus it affects the number of words you can fit into a given typewriter setting. Some writers are moving the sender's address to below the signature or title.

On printed stationery you can write the dateline as a unit with the letterhead or as a separate part. As a unit with the letterhead, the typed-in date should go for best appearance according to the design of the printed part. Usually it retains the balance by appearing directly under the center of a symmetrical letterhead; often it rounds out one that is off balance. As a separate part, it fixes the upper left corner of the letter in block style. Thus it is the *first exception* to the general rule of double-spacing between letter parts.

The *inside address* includes the title, name, and address of the person to receive the letter, including the ZIP code. The beginning of the address establishes the upper left corner of the letter if the date is a unit with a printed letterhead. Otherwise, it begins at the left margin, two to six spaces lower than the dateline. So it is the *second exception* to double spacing between letter parts. (*Warning:* Be careful to spell names right and to use proper titles. People do not like seeing their names misspelled or with the wrong title.) Standard practice calls for some form of title—professional, honorary, or courtesy.

The *salutation* or friendly greeting, the third standard part, begins at the left margin a double space below the inside address and ends with a colon (:) or no punctuation whatsoever. The wording must match the first line of the address, disregarding any attention line. If you address an individual, the salutation must fit (usually "Dear" plus title and name); if you address a firm or other group, you must choose an appropriate salutation.

Since a salutation is the first indication of the formality of a letter, you should give some thought to the implications of how you greet your reader and how you match the tone of your salutation in the complimentary close. The main forms for letters addressed to persons are (in descending order of formality, with appropriate complimentary closes):

| | |
|---|---|
| Dear (appropriate title plus surname) | Yours truly (or) Sincerely yours |
| Dear (given name) | Sincerely yours (or) Cordially yours |
| Dear (given name, nickname) | Cordially (or) Regards (or some more familiar phrasing, as long as it is in good taste) |

In line with the trend toward informal friendliness of business letters, most business writers use the person's name in the salutation when they can and match the friendly tone with some form of *sincerely* or *cordially*.

In recent years, however, new developments have made more difficult the problems of (1) addresses and salutations to women and (2) salutations to mixed-sex groups and business firms. Since the abbreviation "Ms." came into our language to solve the earlier problem of how to address a woman of unknown marital status, many women have come to dislike it. But—many other women dislike the old forms of Miss and Mrs. (even when right, according to past practice); and most rightly resent the use of "Gentlemen" for a firm or group involving even one woman.

Of course, if a woman has given you her preference (as she should— see "signature block" later), you would use it. Beyond that, here are some not completely satisfactory guidelines to choices for handling the two problems.

1. For addressing a woman when you don't know her preference of courtesy title, you can *(a)* continue the standard forms of a few years ago (Miss or Mrs. when you know and Ms. when you don't), though you may thereby antagonize some women; *(b)* (if you're on a comfortable first-name basis) use only the first name in the salutation; or *(c)* telephone her office and ask her preference.

2. For salutations to mixed-sex groups and business firms, you can use titles, such as "Dear Sales Manager." If you must write to a group, it's best to find out a name to whom you should write.

3. If a person has signed the letter sent to you "J. Smith," you can address him or her as "Dear J. Smith" even though using a first and last name in a salutation is normally awkward-sounding.

The *body* or message of the letter begins a double space below the salutation. Usually you single-space within paragraphs and double-space between, though for the standard-line layout in very short letters you may use double spacing, with triple spacing between paragraphs.

Since the body is all one part, regardless of the number of paragraphs, the standard double spacing between paragraphs is a *third exception* to the general rule of spacing. In any case the number of paragraphs affects the fit of a letter to a given typewriter setting. A letter of 250 words in seven paragraphs, for example, will take at least four more lines than a letter of the same number of words in three paragraphs. Yet you should not overlook the chance to improve readability by such means as keeping paragraphs short and itemizing points when helpful.

The *complimentary close* (worded appropriately according to the descending scale of formality illustrated earlier) goes a double space below the last line of the body. It may begin at the center of the page, in line with the beginning of a typed heading, in line with the dateline used as a separate part (Figure 2–7B), at a point to space it evenly between the center and right margin of the letter, or (in full block,

Figure 2–7A) flush at the left margin. The most common forms employ one of three key words—*cordially, sincerely,* and *truly*—each ordinarily used with *yours.* Juggling the order of the key word and *yours* or adding *very*—as *Yours truly, Yours very truly, Very truly yours*—makes little difference. The key word is the main consideration. *Sincerely* is the most common.

Proper form for the *signature block* depends on whether the letter is about your private affairs or about the business of the company where you are an employee. In writing about your own business, space four times below the complimentary close and type your name (Figure 2–7C). The typed name is important for legibility—and consideration for your reader. Then pen your signature above it.

If you're writing about company business and the company is to be legally responsible for the letter, however, the company name should appear above the signature (Figures 2–6 and 2–7A, 2–7B). That the letter is on company stationery makes no difference. So if you want to protect yourself against legal involvement, type the company name in *solid capitals* a double space below the complimentary close; then make the quadruple space for your signature before your typed name. You also give your title on the next line below the typed name or, if there is room, put a comma and your title on the same line with your name. Thus you indicate that you are an agent of the company legally authorized to transact business.

| | |
|---|---|
| Very truly yours,<br>ACME PRODUCTS, INC. | Sincerely yours,<br>LOVEJOY AND LOEB |
| *John Y. Bowen* | *Phyllis Bentley* |
| John Y. Bowen<br>Comptroller | (Miss) Phyllis Bentley,<br>Treasurer |

Because the possibility of legal involvement is usually remote, many writers prefer to omit the company name from the signature block in the hope of gaining a more personal effect through a letter from an individual instead of a company. If you feel that way, you can set up the signature block as follows:

| | |
|---|---|
| Cordially yours, | Sincerely yours, |
| *H. P. Worthington* | *Phyllis B. Hudson* |
| H. P. Worthington<br>Assistant Public<br>Relations Manager | (Mrs.) Phyllis B. Hudson<br>Treasurer |

Before you do, however, we suggest that you (1) get official agreement to bail you out of any legal involvement and (2) remember that some readers feel greater security in dealing with a company instead of an individual.

Women's signatures bring up a special problem. Note that in all the men's signatures illustrated, no title precedes the names. Without some indication, however, the person who answers a woman's letter does not know what courtesy title to give her. (For help on how to solve this problem, see our discussion of salutations.) As a matter of consideration, a woman should indicate how she wants to be addressed—the way Miss Bentley, who became Mrs. Hudson, did in the preceding examples.

**Special Parts.** Besides the six standard parts of a business letter, you will often find use for one or more of seven widely used special parts.

You can use an *attention line* in a letter addressed to a company if you want a certain individual to read it but don't know the person's name. "Attention: Purchasing Agent" or "Attention, Purchasing Agent" will do the job. In either position, flush at the left margin or centered, put it between the inside address and salutation with a double space above and below. Remember, however, *that an attention line has no effect on the salutation, which relates to the inside address instead.*

A *subject line* may save words by telling your reader quickly what the letter is about or by referring to former correspondence for necessary background. It usually appears at the left margin a double space below the salutation; but when space is at a premium, it may appear centered on the same line as the salutation. To make it stand out, either underscore it or use solid capitals. The informal "About" is increasing in use. And more and more correspondents omit the word *Subject* or its equivalent. The position and wording make clear what the subject line is.

*Initials* of the dictator and the typist often appear at the left margin a double space below the last line of the signature block. The trend is toward omitting the dictator's initials because of repetition from the signature block; but if used, they come first (usually in unspaced capitals), separated from the typist's by a colon, a diagonal, a dash, or an asterisk. A good method that saves time is to lock the shift and type CRA:MF or just write all in lowercase as cra/mf. Some writers place the typed name here and omit it from the signature block.

An *enclosure notation,* a single or a double space below the identifying initials (or in their place), is a reminder to the person putting up the mail to actually make the enclosure. Sometimes offices use an asterisk in the left margin at the line in the body referring to the enclosure. You may spell out Enclosure or abbreviate it Encl. or Enc., followed by a number indicating how many enclosures or by a colon and words indicating what the enclosures are.

*Copy* designations (carbon copy or photocopy) are useful when other persons need to know the contents of the letter. The names of people to receive copies appear after CC (or Cc or cc or just Copy to) at the left margin, a single or double space below the initials (or the enclosure notation). If you don't want the addressee to know others are receiving copies of the letter or memo, you can type Bc and the names on the copies only, to indicate "blind copies." Occasionally you may see PC (photocopy) or XC (Xerox copy).

*Postscripts* are rare in business today in the original sense of after-thoughts. Rather than reveal poor planning, the modern business writer would have the letter typed over, or in informal correspondence might add a handwritten note. (Incidentally, some research evidence suggests that such notes actually increase pulling power—probably because they give a letter or memo a more personal touch.)

The main use of postscripts now is as punch lines. Since they have the advantage of the emphatic end position, writers often plan them to emphasize an important point. The well-planned postscript that ties in with the development of the whole message and stresses an important point is effective, especially if handwritten.

When you do decide to use a postscript, it should be the last thing on the page, a double space below the last of the preceding parts. The "P.S." is optional; position and wording clearly indicate what it is.

*Second-page headings* are essential for filing and for reassembling mul-tipage letters that become separated. Since pages after the first should be on plain paper, even when the first page has a printed letterhead, for identification they should carry at least the addressee's name, the date, and the page number, typed down from the top the distance of the side margin something like one of the following:

```
Mr. C. R. Jeans        -2-        March 21, 19--
```

or

```
Mr. C. R. Jeans
March 21, 19--
Page 2
```

or (for speed and equal acceptability)

```
Mr. C. R. Jeans, March 21, 19--, page 2
```

The body of the letter continues a triple or quadruple space below this.

**Forms of Indention and Punctuation.** The illustrative letter (Figure 2–6) shows you how to use the letter parts just listed. Figure 2–7 shows other common letter forms and a basic memo form. Points you should keep in mind are:

1.  The two big trends in letter form continue to be toward simplicity and timesaving.

2.  All consistent forms are correct, but some forms call attention to themselves and characterize their users.

3.  When you go to work for a company, you should use your employer's preferred form unless and until you can persuade the company to change.

## OCR Envelope Handling

Proper form for the main address on envelopes has changed considerably in recent years. To speed up and economize on mail handling, the Postal Service has moved steadily toward machine sorting of mail—LSM (letter sorting machine) and OCR (optical character recognition) handling. How you address your letter will determine its handling—and the difference could determine whether it goes out in today's mail!

1. Traditionally, the main address—blocked the same as the inside address, and with the ZIP code—should go in the lower half of the envelope, with the beginning and ending points of the longest line equal distances from the edges.

2. For the faster OCR handling, you must follow specific requirements for the main address, as explained and illustrated in Figure 2–8 on a No. 10 envelope (4⅜ by 9½ inches).

a. Single-space, capitalize everything, omit all punctuation, use block style. No proportional spacing of characters; no italic or script; do not spell out any numbers. All address information must be in the last three lines, with the street address or box number immediately above the city–state–ZIP code (which should be the last line). If the ZIP code will not fit, it may go on the left margin immediately below the city and state.

Put a minimum of two and a maximum of five spaces between the state and the ZIP code. The full state name is preferable for OCR, but the two-letter abbreviation is acceptable. Put apartment numbers, suite numbers, and so forth on the same line as the street address if possible. For mail addressed to a foreign country, follow the same rules. Include the postal delivery zone number (if any). The name of the country must be the last item in the address.

b. Put nothing to the left, right, or below the address, which must begin at least an inch from the left edge and be more than half an inch from the bottom. Any codes should be part of the address and immediately above the addressee's name.

c. Use both the ZIP code and the full state name or two-letter state abbreviation.

d. Keep typewriter or printer type clean and ribbons fresh so as to provide clear, crisp impressions.

Enjoying the economies of window envelopes (largely through typing

**Figure 2–8 / No. 10 Envelope Addressed for OCR Handling**

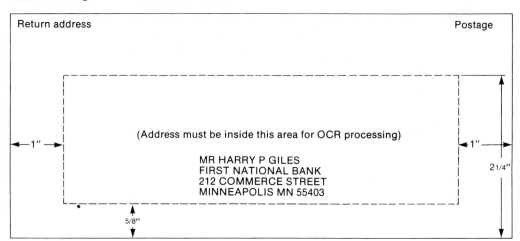

the addresses only once) requires folding the letter so that the inside address shows through the window without showing any other part. For OCR handling, window envelopes must follow additional rules (for which see your postmaster).

## Interoffice Memorandums

The business letter is still the main form of written communication *between* companies and individuals or other companies. But interoffice memorandums (commonly called memos) now replace many letters as message carriers, especially *within* companies.

Memos first came into widespread use largely to combat the high costs of producing business letters. Since the major cost of a letter or memo is the time spent in composing and dictating, however, about the only cost savings in memos today come from not using expensive letterheads, envelopes, and postage and from the easier job of typing them.

The main reasons now for using memos are:

1. The situation does not justify the expense of a letter.
2. Face-to-face communication is not possible or not desirable.
3. The information is too complex for oral communication.
4. One or both parties desire a written record.
5. The receiver asks for a written communication as a way of providing time to think about the problem or obtain additional information before responding.

For anyone in a medium or large company, memos will be the most common form of written communication with other people in the firm, especially those in other locations and including those both above and below you on the organization chart. What they know about you and how they think of you will depend on how you communicate with them—in short, on your memos.

Early in your career, especially, your only contacts with higher echelons in your organization will probably be the reports and memos you send up. Further, as you progress in your career, you will have to demonstrate your abilities as a manager—often by the memos you send down to your subordinates directing their activities. And finally, in dealing with your peers, you will find that memos are important tools in establishing and maintaining your position.

Memos vary widely in format, from simple handwritten "From the desk of . . ." notes to carefully designed forms with interleaved carbon copies and provisions for assuring an answer and proper filing. But since they usually go from one person to another in the same organization, memo messages are less formal than letters. Whether handwritten, typed, or sent via electronic mail, they share with letters the single purpose of communicating information in writing so as to effect an action.

Memos have conventional, stylized *headings* (Figures 2–7D and 2–9). The universal elements are a date line, a *To* line (addressee's name with courtesy title—and job title unless known to all who get copies, or in a very informal message), a *From* line (writer's name—and identifying position title unless known), and a *Subject* line. (Leaving plenty of room to make the subject clear and precise is a good idea. The more comprehensively you describe the subject here, the less you will have to say in the body to introduce it and identify it before you can say anything of significance.)

The *body* begins two or three lines under the *Subject* line and continues until you've said what you need to, which may take three lines or 30 pages. No salutation or complimentary close appears, though three other items may appear when needed. When the memo needs authentication, the writer signs or initials it next to the From line, or underneath the body, following personal or company preference. A typist's initials may appear at the bottom, as on a letter. If copies are to go to other people, the typist may also type a copy designation and the names of receivers.

Notice these details in the illustrative memo: Since some of its readers might not have known who R. F. Noonan was, he gave his official title. The careful phrasing of subject line indicates the contents concisely.

Because memos are usually less formal than letters in both format and language, some writers give them inadequate attention. That is a mistake, and it can be a very bad one. *Just about everything about letters in this book also applies to memos.* Whether your memos will accomplish their purpose depends on the writing style, their organization, the princi-

**Figure 2–9 / Typical Multicopy Memo**

Date:      May 21, 1985
To:        All Flight Crew Members
From:      R. F. Noonan, Chief Pilot
Subject:   <u>Wearing of Uniform</u>

   Please review your Basic Manual on the requirements
for wearing the uniform while on duty or deadheading, as
some lapses have been reported lately.

   All cockpit members are to wear the complete uniform
when beginning all flight sequences but may leave the
coat on board when the temperature is above 76° F. You
must wear epaulets and ties (with shirt collars buttoned)
whenever you leave the flight station and passengers are
on board. You must wear hats on leaving the aircraft.

   With increased competition from new airlines, it's
especially important that we project a professional and
efficient image. Check pilots will be emphasizing uniform
procedure, and I will interview every crew member who
does not comply.

ples of successful business communication discussed in the first two parts of the book, and even their appearance. Memos deserve care in preparation, just as letters do, for they are important to your company's success, and yours.

The tips here and elsewhere in this book apply to "electronic mail" as well as to the conventional kind. Whether your reader sees your message on a CRT (video) screen or on paper, the four tests of a good letter or memo still apply, as do all the techniques of clear, concise, readable writing.

In addition to sending many paper and electronic memos, one other way you'll communicate in business is through forms.

## Efficient Use of Forms

According to national surveys, 30 percent of all working hours in the average corporation go to processing forms or reports, and inefficient forms and procedures waste more than 28 percent of that time.

Some experts (according to Alfred J. Moran, Jr., "Fighting the Paper War—and Winning," *Financial Executive* 50, September 1982 pp. 52–55) say the total U.S. market for business forms in 1980 was $4.3 billion. Reducing form operations 10 percent would thus result in savings of about $430 million. Moran says (p. 52) that "if one applies a 40:1 industry-adopted ratio of clerical costs to business forms expenditures, we are describing $17.2 billion annually in potential savings through increased efficiency in purchasing, storing, filing, filling out, retaining, and destroying of business forms." For every dollar a company spends on actual business forms, it spends up to $40 using the forms.

You have probably filled out job applications that had spaces too small for the needed information or categories that didn't make sense. In applying for a loan, you may have struggled with the bank's or credit union's jargon. The federal government's many forms are notorious for complexity. The 1040EZ income tax form (though specifically written to help lower-income, lower-education-level taxpayers fill out their own forms) is not at all easy to understand. Even having your mail held at the post office is a chore until you find out that you need a "Change of Address" form to accomplish it.

Because nearly every organization uses forms (and business operations would stop if the flow of forms were shut off), you'll probably be involved with them and perhaps will have some control over their administration.

**Forms Administration.** Effective forms administration has three parts: analysis, design, and control. If you work with forms analysis, you'll have to find out what is presently being done, how the form is going to be used, how it is being used (if it is a revised form), where and when it is used, who uses it, how long it takes to complete, and how to fill it out.

And if you work with form design, you'll be involved in layout and composition. You should design computer input and output forms (and those for other types of automation) using the same techniques for non-computerized forms. One problem seems to be that when computer-system groups design forms, they tend to orient the forms to the machine rather than to the respondents. Forms used for computer input are often called "source documents." Source documents should be prepared for easy conversion to machine-processible form without sacrificing quality from the respondent's viewpoint.

If you are involved in control, you'll study all the organization's present forms and decide whether or not to stock new ones. You'll have to control inventory, to allocate costs, and to recognize and get rid of obsolete forms.

Since form design relates most to your study of business communication, we'll concentrate on that phase of forms administration.

**Forms Design—Layout and Phrasing.** The following guidelines should help you.

1. Show a form number, and have a meaningful title.
2. Allow enough space for answers. For vertical spacing, three writing lines per inch is enough space for most people's handwriting, and three lines per inch is ideal for typewritten responses. For horizontal spacing for answers up to 10 characters, allow 1 inch for every 5 characters.
3. Use upper left captions when possible.
4. Write captions that clearly define the information you want.
5. Place check boxes in front of the questions you want answered.
6. Use screens (shaded areas) and other visual aids to guide eyes.
7. Have adequate margins (generally ⅜ inch all around the form).
8. Make the form give easy-to-understand instructions.
9. Show the distribution and routing in instructions (in margin, or at the bottom, or even in red).
10. If you use codings (color, pictorial, different shapes), be sure that they are clear and effective. Remember that color coding can be tricky because 1 male in 20 has color-defective vision. Size coding and shape coding (such as squares for males and circles for females) must be logical and pretested to assure response. You can use large letters, silhouettes (of various familiar appliances, persons, or vehicles), pictorial symbols (such as for different corporation divisions), or multiple geometric shapes.
11. Have appropriate and logical sequencing and blocking of material.
12. Design headings (if you use them) to use either words or coded symbols to identify the form, contents, and sections.

13. Keep your form uncluttered.

14. Use single word or brief phrases (e.g., "Name" instead of "What is your name?").

15. Use familiar and easy-to-understand words, terms, and abbreviations.

16. Avoid ambiguities, idioms, compound questions, too technical terms.

Readability of forms depends not only on good layout and verbal content but also on the kind of paper and printing used.

**Forms Paper and Printing.** Most forms are printed on nonglossy bond paper, which is available in many grades. For single-sheet forms printed on one side use 16-pound, while on two sides use 20-pound. Multiple-part forms should have 15–16-pound for first and last parts and 11–12-pound for middle parts.

Forms can come with carbon paper or carbonless paper (produces multiple copies without carbon), and they can come as single sheets, padded sheets, or unit sets (two or more sheets held together) or books (number of units have a cover and are stapled together).

### Figure 2–10 / Postal Consumer Card

| ① RETAIN POST OFFICE COPY | ② MAIL (Under Cover) ACTION COPY UPON COMPLETION OF ACTION | ③ MAIL CUSTOMER COMMENT COPY IMMEDIATELY |
| --- | --- | --- |

☆ U.S. GOVERNMENT PRINTING OFFICE: 1980 — 308 - 536

| CUSTOMER CONTACTED YOU BY ☐ PHONE ☐ LETTER ☐ IN PERSON | DATE (Month, Day, Year) | RECORDING EMPLOYEE: | Q1 552 147 |
| --- | --- | --- | --- |

| NAME | ADDRESS (No., Street and City) | STATE | ZIP CODE | DAY PHONE (8:00 AM - 5:00 PM) |

● IS THIS ☐ SUGGESTION ☐ COMPLAINT ☐ COMPLIMENT AND OTHER

● If this is a problem with a specific mailing, please complete the following:

Please give information on the other person involved in this mailing or if complaint is a change of address problem, enter previous address

| WAS IT | WAS MAILING | DID IT INVOLVE | |
| --- | --- | --- | --- |
| LETTER | FIRST—CLASS | DELAY | WAS THE PERSON NAMED BELOW ☐ SENDER ☐ RECEIVER ☐ CHANGE OF ADDRESS |
| PACKAGE | PRIORITY | | NAME |
| NEWSPAPER/ MAGAZINE | SPECIAL DEL'Y | NON-RECEIPT | |
| | CERTIFIED | | |
| ADVERTISEMENT | REGISTERED | DAMAGE | ADDRESS |
| | INSURED | | |
| ELECTRONIC TRANS/MAILGRAM | EXPRESS MAIL | MISDELIVERY | CITY | STATE | ZIP CODE |
| | OTHER | | |

● IF NOT SPECIFIC MAIL PROBLEM, IS IT
☐ HOURS OF SERVICE ☐ SELF SERVICE POSTAL EQUIPMENT ☐ MONEY ORDER ☐ POSTAL PERSONNEL

● Please give essential facts

PS FORM 4314-P
July 1979
U.S. POSTAL SERVICE
**CONSUMER SERVICE CARD**
RESOLVED BY: ____  DATE ____
POST OFFICE COPY 1

This compact uncluttered Consumer Service Card (which has two carbons) gives clear numbered routing instructions in red and uses single words or short, understandable phrases that save space and enhance readability. The four black bullets add interest and call the reader's attention to important parts of the form. All boxes are to the left of the questions.

Print size should be a minimum of 8 point for easy reading for most people but should be increased for elderly respondents. Unembellished characters are easier to read than embellished ones with flares and segmented letters. (For more discussion on paper and printing, read William V. Nygren, *Business Forms Management,* AMACOM, New York, 1982, and John H. Burgess, *Human Factors in Forms Design,* Nelson-Hall Publishers, Chicago, 1984).

In conclusion, remember that forms will probably increase in importance and use in future offices because of the possibilities of quickly compiling and processing large amounts of data about customers, products, and work tasks. As a manager, be sure to follow the recommended techniques and remember the 40:1 ratio of usage cost to form cost. If you can save just 2.5 percent on processing/usage costs, you will save the entire cost of the form itself.

## Adaptations for International Business Communication

Though Chapter 4 treats communication for international business, the differences in letter formats and formalities seem more appropriate here. Even though you can get by with most of the U.S. practices, you can improve your relations with people of different cultures by making a few minor adaptations in the appearance and cordiality of your letters.

In other countries business stationery varies from onionskin to heavy parchmentlike paper in white or light colors—generally in 8½ by 11-inch size but often on legal-size or metric-size paper. Thus your present letterhead will serve well, though onionskin or very thin paper can reduce the cost of overseas airmail postage.

Besides the company name, type of business, and address, many international firms include their trademark, name of bank or banker, and cable, telephone, and telex numbers in their letterheads. Sometimes import and export registration numbers also appear. In the absence of a letterhead your overseas business friends will generally follow the suggestions given earlier for the format of personal letters—and you can do the same.

Many U.S. businesses operate internationally, through branch offices, the export and import of goods, or foreign investments. Since much of the world has accepted English as the language of business (a recent *Journal of Business Communication* survey showed that 95–99 percent of the correspondence of such businesses to other countries was in English[2]), the main concern of business writers is clarity, not translation. The areas given special attention are personal titles, a different dateline

---

[2] Retha H. Kilpatrick, "International Business Communication Practices," *Journal of Business Communication,* 21 (Fall 1984), pp. 33–44.

style, and different closings. Block or modified block styles are the most common ones used. Other findings:

- more foreign companies use U.S. dateline format (month, day, year) than vice versa;
- Dear (Title/Surname) is the most popular salutation for both U.S. and foreign companies, but more foreign correspondents use their equivalents of "Dear Sir";
- "Sincerely" and "Sincerely yours" are by far the most popular closings both here and abroad.

In keeping with their more formal style and stronger expressions of cordiality, your international business friends use most of the special parts we do except for postscripts and enclosure notations. A frequent enclosure notation is a request for confidentiality—in Spanish *Confidencial,* in French *Confidentiel,* in Italian *Riservata* (or, for strictly confidential, *Riservatissima*), in German *Vertraulich.*

International firms usually address the reader by name (if known) or by a job title (Dear Vice President) or a general (though usually sexist) salutation: Gentlemen, Dear Sir(s), and so on. You can fairly safely follow your usual practice for salutations; but be a little more formal, preferably by selecting an expression from the receiver's language.

The French are *Monsieur (Sir), Madame (Madam),* or *Mademoiselle (Miss),* and (to a company) *Messieurs (Gentlemen),* but never *Cher Monsieur (Dear Sir)* or *Chère Madame* unless you are personally acquainted with the reader.

In Italy *Egregio Signore (Distinguished Gentleman)* precedes the name for a gentleman and *Gentile Signora (Genteel Lady)* for a lady (or sometimes only *Signore* or *Signora*). Spanish writers use *Muy señor mio (My Dear Sir)* or *Muy señor nuestro (Our Dear Sir).*

For obvious reasons, we can't illustrate salutations of each country, but these examples give you a little taste and show you the wide variation.

You can safely use American-style complimentary closes by making them a little more formal (unless you know the reader). To an older person or superior the French prefer *Veuillez agréer (Pleasant wishes), Monsieur (Madame, Mademoiselle);* but you will also see added phrases like *l'expression de mes (nos) sentiments distingués* or *sentiments dévoués (the expression of my, or our, special/devoted feelings).* In Italy writers use *cordiali saluti (cordial greetings)* for a friendly letter.

Multilingual word processing is now a possibility—words are encoded in the computer's memory in varied languages, typed on the keyboard in the original language, and rendered in the new language. The complexity of translating from a left-to-right language such as English into a right-to-left or ideographic language is obviously enormous. Automatic translation from "one language to another is a far more distant goal."[3] Computer translation or even dual language documents obviously have great implications for companies doing international business.

## Questions and Exercises

1. Name and discuss the impact of the office automation tools you have encountered in your career so far.

2. What are the advantages and disadvantages of word processing in an office?

3. What are other common uses of microcomputers in an office besides word processing? Which ones do you expect to use most?

4. What is telecommuting? Do you expect your employees to use it?

5. Have you received any electronic mail yet? To what uses could you put an electronic mail system in your future office?

6. How does teleconferencing save money for a business?

7. What advantages besides cost does teleconferencing have? What disadvantages?

8. What products have you encountered so far that have voice commands?

9. Discuss potential problems of office automation.

10. In the list of standard parts of a letter, which (if any) have you never seen in use? Do you think that it (or they) should not have been listed?

11. In the list of special parts of a letter, which (if any) have you never seen in use? Do you think it (or they) should not have been listed?

12. Which format appeals to you most for electronic mail messages? Why?

13. Describe the main differences between U.S. and international business letter style.

---

[3] Joseph D. Becker, "Multilingual Word Processing," *Scientific American,* July 1984, p. 107.

# Part Two
## Basic Skills and Principles

# Chapter Outline

**How to Make Your Writing Clear**
Plan for Unity, Coherence, Progress, and Proper Emphasis
Make It Easy and Interesting to Read
Use Accurate Wording, Punctuation, Grammar, and Sentence Structure
**How to Express Things Interestingly**
Depend Mainly on Content
Put the Emphasis where It Belongs
State Ideas Concisely but Adequately
Be Vivid; Avoid Indefiniteness
Be Natural; Avoid Triteness and Pomposity
Vary Sentence Pattern, Type, and Length
**How to Keep Your Style Inconspicuous**
Choose the Right Level of Usage
Follow the Conventions
**How to Handle Two New Language Problems**
Avoid Sexist Language
Adapt Language in International Business
**Exercises**

# 3

## Using an Effective Style

As you prepare your business message (written or oral), keep asking yourself: *Is it in a clear, interesting, and inconspicuous style?*

- If it is foggy instead of clear, you'll only confuse and annoy instead of communicating. You may therefore get no response—or one you don't want.
- If it is dull instead of interesting, you'll be ignored (and waste your time).
- And if your style calls attention to itself because of something unexpected, inappropriate, or incorrect, it will distract attention from what you're saying and cause doubt that your facts and reasoning are any more reliable than your language.[1]

### How to Make Your Writing Clear

Conciseness helps clarity as well as interest because your reader avoids the job of separating the important from the unessential, and vividness helps by giving a sharp picture. But other more important aids to clearness are

- Planning for unity, coherence, progress, and proper emphasis.
- Making your writing easy and interesting to read.
- Using accurate wording, punctuation, grammar, and sentence structure.

---

[1] The principles in this chapter are mostly in terms of writing, but they also apply to speaking—except as modified in Chapter 11. This efficient arrangement thus covers the language skills for both written and oral business communication without wordy and annoying repetition of "writing and speaking," "writer or speaker," and "reader or listener."

## Plan for Unity, Coherence, Progress, and Proper Emphasis

You can't plan anything more than a simple message by just thinking as you write. So think your message through before you start to write or dictate. If you are answering a letter or memo, underscore points in it to be covered.

Clear writing is usually the product of a three-step process that stresses organization and coherence.

1. Planning requires specific answers to four questions:

a. *What effect do I want to produce?* Decide specifically what you want to happen. Good organization should result in a oneness by showing how every part relates to the general theme.

b. *Who is the reader?* Until you make a clear estimate of what your reader is like, you cannot apply the principles of adaptation (in Chapter 5).

c. *What facts and ideas must I present to produce the desired effect on this kind of reader?*

d. *What is the best order of presenting the items listed?*

You can organize well only by answering specifically all four of the preliminary-planning questions. In preparing a nonroutine message, you usually need to spend about 40 percent of your total preparation time on preliminary planning.

2. The second step is continuous, fast writing. You follow your preliminary plan and *keep going.* Write the entire piece without stopping. Only that way will you be efficient (using only about 20 percent of the time) and get the natural coherence that comes from following a chain of thought straight through.

3. In the third step (using about 40 percent of your time), you revise for tone (Chapter 4) and conciseness, coherence, and correctness. You may also need to reorganize a bit by shifting words, sentences, or whole paragraphs into better position. But usually the main work on organization through revision will be a few changes in wording for better coherence (see **Coh** 3 in Appendix C).

Although you should not leave out any necessary bridges between parts, the fewer you can use and still make the sequence of thought clear, the better. Try especially to avoid overformal and slowing references like *the latter, the above-mentioned,* and *namely.*

## Make It Easy and Interesting to Read

Your responsibility as a writer is to present ideas interestingly enough to get a reading and clearly enough for your reader to understand with the least possible effort. As the difficulty of understanding an idea increases, people are more inclined to lose interest and skip it. Anytime your reader has to back up and reread or has to slow down to understand, you may arouse disgust and be ignored or misunderstood. For example:

> In promulgating your esoteric cogitations or articulating your philosophical or psychological observations, circumspectly eliminate platitudinous ponderosity. Studiously manipulate your communications to manifest clarified conciseness, compact comprehensibleness, coalescent consistency, and a concatenated cogency with intelligibility and vivacity but without rodomontade or thrasonical bombast. Sedulously eschew polysyllabic profundity, pompous prolixity, psittaceous vacuity, and vapid verbosity.

*Considering your Gunning Fog Index*[2] is a good move toward clear writing. By doing so, you can quickly learn how to adapt your writing to the abilities of your readers. You'll also see that the factors that lead to a favorable index are the things this book teaches, especially in this chapter.

Figuring the Gunning Fog Index is a simple, three-step process.

1. Find the average sentence length (ASL) by
   a. Taking several representative 100-word samples, counting anything with space around it as a word—including figures.
   b. Counting the sentences involved in the samples, stopping in each sample with the sentence ending nearest the 100-word point.
   c. Dividing the total word count by the sentence count. The result is the first factor in the formula—the average sentence length.
2. Find the PHW (percentage of hard words—three or more syllables) in the total sample—not including capitalized words (proper names), combinations of easy words (like *afternoon, businesslike, bookkeeper*), figures, or verb forms made into three syllables by *-ed* or *-es* endings *(dribbled, enriches).*
3. Add number 1 above (the average sentence length) and number 2 (the percentage of hard words), and multiply the sum by 0.4. For example, suppose you have ASL 19 and PHW $14 = 33 \times 0.4 = 13$ (Fog Index and grade level). Then the material is properly adapted to college freshmen but too difficult for people with less reading ability. If the figures had been $24 + 16 \times 0.4 = 16$, a reader would need college-senior reading ability.

*Using words your reader understands* is important in making your writing easy to read. You will usually be wise to choose the more commonly known of two words. People with little education will understand you better, and educated readers will appreciate your making their job easy. Small words can say all the things you want to say. If you have 50

---

[2] In Robert Gunning, *The Technique of Clear Writing,* McGraw-Hill, New York, 1952—revised in 1968 and 1973.

percent more syllables than words, your writing requires more reader effort than it should.

For an example that illustrates what it advises about clear writing, we quote Arthur Kudner, a man well known for his way with words. "Big, long words name little things. All big things have little names, such as life and death, peace and war, or dawn, day, night, hope, love, home. Learn to use little words in a big way; they say what you mean. When you don't know what you mean, use BIG words. . . . That often fools little people."

*Keeping your sentences reasonably short and direct* will also help make your writing easy to read and hence clear. An average of 17–20 words is a healthy one for readability.

If the average length is not too much above 20, smooth sequence of thought and directness are more important than the word count. To avoid involved, indirect sentences, look at the punctuation. If you have to punctuate a sentence heavily, you will be wise to rephrase it more directly or break it into two or three sentences.

*Using short, well-organized paragraphs* will also help clarity and readability. The usual pattern is a topic sentence followed by supporting or developing details. But if one sentence says all you need to on the topic, start the next topic—in another paragraph.

Frequently a single-sentence paragraph is highly desirable to give an idea the emphasis you want!

Especially in letters, long paragraphs are uninviting and hard to read. First and last paragraphs of more than four lines and others of more than eight are likely candidates for breaking up.

*Making frequent personal references* (names of people and pronouns referring to them) also helps make your writing interesting and readable. Since you and your reader are the two persons most directly involved in the actions, desires, and benefits you write and talk about in business, most of your pronouns will be "you"—or "you" understood—and "I" or (when clear) "we." (If you're ever tempted to use *we* without clear meaning, however, remember what Mark Twain once said: "The only people entitled to use the indefinite *we* are kings, editors, and people with tapeworms.")

*Itemizing key points and tabulating significant figures* can also help make your whole letter, memo, or paragraph clear and easy to read. For instance, if your topic sentence mentions three big advantages in using XYZ equipment, the three will stand out more clearly and emphatically if you number them and list them on separate lines.

## Use Accurate Wording, Punctuation, Grammar, and Sentence Structure

Conventions, not rules, establish proper usage of words, punctuation, and grammar. The important thing is to use words with the exact meaning the reader attaches to them. To that purpose **D** in Appendix C gives a list of frequently misused words.

Remember, too, that words and sentences sometimes change meanings according to what precedes and succeeds them. For instance, a would-be secretary brought laughs when the last two sentences in an ad for a job read "No bad habits. Willing to learn." (For proper word relations, guard particularly against the errors discussed in **Mod** 1 and 2 in Appendix C).

The difficulties of accurate expression stem partly from the way words pick up related meanings (connotations, in addition to their denotations or dictionary meanings). Consider the difference between *cheap* and *inexpensive* or between *house* and *home.* And note that *hope, trust,* and *if* can suggest doubt. "You claim" or "you say" even suggests doubt of the reader's truthfulness.

The words you use should quickly give not only the general idea but the precise idea. If you say *soon* or *later,* your reader doesn't know just when you mean. If you say *checks, notes, stocks, etc.,* nobody can tell whether you mean to include bonds. (Etc. is clear only in such statements as "I am particularly interested in the odd-numbered questions, 1, 3, 5, etc." But it then becomes unnecessary, as it usually does when it is clear.)

A large vocabulary enables you to choose the precise word to give the exact idea. But if you don't use judgment to stay within the reader's vocabulary, you will sometimes use words that leave the reader in the dark or slow up the pace. For example, you may be inclined to write *actuarially;* but most readers will get the meaning more quickly if you write *statistically.*

Punctuation marks, like words, mean only what a reader takes them to mean. They can help by breaking your sentences into thought groups if you follow the conventions (**P1–P14** in Appendix C). But if you use a system of your own and your reader interprets according to the standard system, you mislead just as if you used words in unfamiliar ways. For instance, if you put up a sign to mean

No Parking: Reserved for Our Customers

you will certainly mislead people if you write:

No Parking Reserved for Our Customers

Like faulty wording, faulty punctuation not only confuses but distracts the reader's mind from the key idea. You've surely seen the laughable highway sign "Slow Men Working."

Fortunately, the system of English punctuation is well established (by conventions, not by rules), and most readers know at least the main parts of the conventions. Unfortunately, many people who know how to *read* most punctuation marks do not know the conventions well enough to use the marks precisely *in writing*. If you have any doubts about troublesome areas of punctuation, see the symbol **P** in Appendix C for explanation and illustration.

So-called errors in grammar and sentence structure also mislead readers. They also slow up reading and produce indefiniteness, disrespect, and distrust. The statement "You should not plant strawberries where tomatoes have grown for several years" will mislead readers if you mean "Wait several years before planting strawberries where tomatoes have grown." And the dangling participle in "Smelling of liquor, the officer arrested the reckless driver" (**Mod** 1) did lead to a police officer's being questioned about drinking on duty.

Faulty grammar can confuse too—though often only temporarily. Most readers will understand despite wrong verb forms like "He come to my house at 10 P.M.," the wrong choice between *lie* and *lay,* and shifts in number like "The Acme Company is located in Chicago. They manufacture. . . ." Those same understanding readers will, however, notice the bad English, become amused and/or sympathetic, and lose respect for and confidence in the obviously ignorant or careless writer. All these reactions are *distractions from the message* because the style calls attention to itself—becomes conspicuous.

# How to Express Things Interestingly

## Depend Mainly on Content

In writing for business and industry, you should depend mainly on content, not style, to arouse and hold your reader's interest. Usually you have an inquiry or other indication that your reader is interested in your general subject.

If bare facts have insufficient appeal to get attention, you can make them both interesting and persuasive if you *show how those facts point to benefits for the reader* (you-attitude; **YA** in Appendix C). In writing about a product, for example, merely giving the physical facts may be dull. But if you interpret the facts as providing reader benefits (psychological description; **PD** in Appendix C), the content is more interesting: "Made of aluminum, the Gizmo is light and rust-free—you don't need to paint." And if you write so that the reader imagines successfully using the product and enjoying its benefits (dramatized copy; **DC** in Appendix C), the content is even more interesting.

A good message can become dull, however, if poorly presented. Wordiness, indefiniteness, triteness, pompousness, monotony, and difficult reading are the most common offenders. By replacing these with their opposites, you will speed up and clear up your message—and make it interesting.

## Put the Emphasis where It Belongs (*Emp* and *Sub* in Appendix C)

Since content is the greatest means of gaining interest, the big ideas of your message deserve the major emphasis.

Though you may use minor mechanical means of controlling emphasis (underscoring, capitalizing, itemizing, using two colors)—and sometimes secondary means such as repetition, explanation (versus mere implication for reducing emphasis), and direct statements that the topic is important or of little consequence—your four primary means are (1) position, (2) space, (3) phrasing, and (4) structure.

The most significant ideas need to appear in the emphatic beginning and ending *positions* of the letter or memo, of your paragraphs—even of your sentences, oral or written.

In addition, you write more about points you want to stress. If you write 10 lines about the efficiency of a piece of equipment and 2 lines about its convenience, by *space* you emphasize efficiency more than convenience.

As a third major means of emphasis, you should select concrete, specific words and *phrasing* to etch welcome or important ideas in your reader's mind. When an idea is unwelcome or insignificant, choose general words that merely identify, not stress. *General:* "The typewriter needs several new parts and. . . ." *Specific:* "Your versatile IBM Memory Typewriter will. . . ."

Because an independent clause carries more emphasis than a dependent one, you can also stress or subordinate ideas through your choice of *sentence structure.* An important idea calls for statement in one independent clause (a simple sentence). Sometimes, however, you have two equally important and closely related ideas; so you should put the two independent clauses together in a compound sentence. If you have two related ideas of *different* importance, a complex sentence of one independent and one dependent clause divides the emphasis properly. You may have noticed, for example, that the minor mechanical means of stressing ideas appear parenthetically in a dependent clause. The four primary means, however, are itemized; then each gets a separate paragraph of discussion—and emphasis by independent-clause statement and by means of space.

In messages carrying ideas that the reader will welcome, then, use those ideas to begin and end the messages. They usually should begin and end paragraphs. They should take up most of the space. Their phrasing should be specific. And they should enjoy the benefits of independent-clause construction. Conversely, you should embed unwelcome or unimportant ideas in a middle paragraph, cover them just enough to establish their meaning, and strip them of the emphasis of concrete, specific words.

Controlling emphasis is a technique you can put into immediate successful use—in the next message you prepare. You should work first on emphasis by position, since that technique is effective and easy to use. At first you will have to think about getting important ideas at the beginnings and ends of your letters, memos, and even paragraphs; but you will be surprised how quickly this procedure becomes almost automatic . . . and how it will improve your effectiveness.

The letter and memo examples in this book use the principles for appropriate emphasis and its opposite—subordination. Two special points, however, deserve your attention right here:

1. You may be inclined to write something the reader already knows. If it serves no purpose, think and omit it. But if you need to say it as a basis for something else you want to say, put it subordinately. That is, do not put it in an independent clause: not "Winter will soon be here . . ." but "Since winter will soon be here, . . . ."

2. When you need to refer to an enclosure or other part of your message (say a graph), word your reference to emphasize what to do with it or get from it. Don't emphasize that it is enclosed: not "Enclosed is (or worse, "Please find") . . ." but something like "You'll find further details of construction and users' satisfaction in the enclosed pamphlet."

Here's a test of whether you're on the right track: To *de*-emphasize a word like *enclosed,* be sure you use it as an adjective before the thing enclosed (the pamphlet) and not as the verb of the sentence. (See **Emp** 2 in Appendix C.)

## State Ideas Concisely but Adequately (*Conc* and *Dev* in Appendix C)

Every word you can spare without reducing effectiveness is wasteful if it remains. But if you leave out necessary information and vivid details to achieve brevity, you fail to develop enough interesting ideas to hold or persuade your reader. You therefore face the dilemma of length.

A first step in the solution of that dilemma is a clear *distinction between brevity and conciseness.* Brevity is mere shortness. Sacrificing completeness because of a mistaken notion about the importance of brevity is a common mistake. A message lacking information necessary to interest and persuasion is wasteful; it produces no result.

What people really want—what you want—is conciseness (making every word contribute to your purpose). Conciseness comes, not from omitting details that contribute to clearness, persuasiveness, or interest, but from saying all you should say in as few words as possible.

Experience and long practice may teach you to compose complete and concise messages. While gaining that experience, however, you will do well to follow four guidelines.

1. Avoid expressing ideas that don't deserve to be put into words. Cut out everything that has no bearing on your topic and your purpose.

2. Don't waste words saying what the reader already knows. For example:

| Poor | Improved |
|---|---|
| Three days ago you asked us to investigate the problem of discomfort among your office workers. [Assumes that the reader has a short memory.] We have made our study. [Obviously, since you're reporting results.] Too low humidity is apparently the main cause of your trouble. Your building is steam-heated. [Doesn't the reader know?] Therefore our solution is to . . . . | Too low humidity is apparently the main cause of your workers' discomfort. Since your building is steam-heated, your solution is to . . . . |

To show the reasoning behind your suggestion, you do need to mention the steam heat; but the subordinating *since* implies "Of course you and I know this, but it has to go in for completeness of logic."

3. As a general principle, in answering a recent letter or memo, don't waste words to say "I have your letter of . . ." or to tell what it says. Instead of

You asked us to let you know when the new model of the Clarion micro transcriber came on the market. It is obtainable now.

you can say the same thing with

The new Clarion micro transcriber is now available.

That clearly implies that you got the letter and the idea of "You asked us to let you know."

Of course, if the inquiry is not recent, or if somebody other than the original inquirer may handle your answer, you may need to refer to the communication you are answering. Even then a subject line will save words and allow the first sentence to say something important.

| **Rather than this** | **You might better write** |
| --- | --- |
| On February 20 you inquired about our experience with Mr. James H. Johnson. We are glad to tell you about his work for us. | Mr. James H. Johnson, about whom you inquired on February 20, was a steady conscientious bookkeeper here for 18 months. |
| Johnson was a steady, conscientious worker during the 18 months he kept books for us. | |

Similarly, in most refusals you can save words and your reader's feelings by eliminating the negative statement of what you won't do and concentrating on what you will do. You thus imply the negative idea and gain not only conciseness but interest and acceptability. For illustrations, see "Positive Statement" late in Chapter 5.

4. If your first draft contains any wasteful expressions, revision should eliminate them as well as *deadwood phrases* (those which contribute nothing).

Consider the following incomplete list of offenders, in which a line blocks out the deadwood or the concise statement follows in parentheses:

~~free~~ gifts

~~old~~ adage

long ~~period of~~ time

is ~~at this time~~

at ~~a price of~~ $50

~~important~~ essentials

enclosed ~~herewith~~

remember ~~the fact~~ that

held a meeting (met)

main problem is ~~a matter of~~ cost

we shipped your ~~order for a~~ ⅜-inch drill

~~in the opinion of~~ Mr. Johnson (thinks)

~~falsely~~ padded expense accounts

during ~~the course of~~ the evening

~~engaged in~~ making a survey

~~the color of~~ the X is blue

until ~~such time as~~ you can

in regard to (about, regarding)

in the development of (developing)

in this day and age (today, now)

the soldering process proved ~~to be of an~~ unsatisfactory ~~nature~~

the general consensus of opinion among most students is that (most students think that)

~~the trouble with~~ the light was

that is the situation ~~at this time~~ (now)

the Rock-a-File is quite different ~~in character~~

made the announcement that (announced)

for the purpose of providing (to provide)

at an early date (soon) [if you have to be indefinite]

decide at a meeting ~~which will be held~~ Monday

eliminate needless words ~~that may be present~~

~~there is~~ only one point ~~that~~ is clear, ~~and that is~~

the price was higher than I expected ~~it to be~~

the workers ~~are in a position to~~ (can) accept or reject

~~that it was~~ too dim

in ~~the state of~~ Texas

neat ~~in appearance~~

at ~~the hour of~~ 4:00

eight ~~in number~~

circular ~~in shape~~

throughout the ~~entire~~ week

~~at a~~ later ~~date~~

during ~~the year of~~ 1986

costs ~~the sum of~~ $10

came ~~at a time~~ when

at all times (always)

in the event that (if)

put in an appearance (came)

during the time that (while)

these facts ~~serve to~~ give an idea

if ~~it is~~ possible, let me have

~~according to~~ Mr. Johnson (says)

arrived at the conclusion (concluded)

Often you can avoid such clutter by changing a clause to one word:

- all the people who are interested in (interested people)
- buying new machines that are expensive (buying expensive new machines)
- using processes that are outmoded (using outmoded processes)
- saving work that does not need to be done (saving unnecessary work)

The worst form of clutter, however, combines wasted words with clichés:

| Poor | Better |
|---|---|
| If we are not mistaken | We believe |
| In accordance with your request | As requested |
| We would therefore ask that you kindly investigate | Please investigate |
| We now have a letter from our Sparta office advising that | Our Sparta office writes that |
| A check in the amount of | A check for |
| We wish you would furnish us with | Please send us |
| We are not in a position to | We cannot |
| Let us hear from you in regard to | Write us about |
| Your early attention to this matter will be greatly appreciated | Please act promptly on this |
| They bring out the point that | They point out that |
| Will you please arrange to send | Please send |

| | |
|---|---|
| We should like to ask whether you have received our shipment of | Have you received our shipment of |
| Upon consulting our records, we find that your order reached us on | Your order arrived on |

## Be Vivid; Avoid Indefiniteness

Even good content concisely stated can be uninteresting, however, if you give only an inactive or fuzzy picture. You therefore need to use one or more of five techniques to be vivid:

1. Most things happen because people make them happen. The interesting, natural, and clear way to discuss those happenings, therefore, is to talk about those *people in action.* That is why you should make people the subject or object of most sentences.

Since each reader is most interested in personally related things, interest in your message will depend on how you put that person into the picture as the main actor. "You can save 30 minutes at dinnertime with a Pronto pressure cooker" is more vivid than "A Pronto pressure cooker saves 30 minutes at dinnertime." (For psychological reasons, if a point is a criticism and hence unpleasant, however, make your actor a third person or your message impersonal, rather than accuse. See **Accus** in Appendix C.)

2. Consistent use of people as subjects will help produce *active rather than passive voice.* The passive "30 minutes at dinnertime can be saved" lacks vividness because it omits the all-important *who.* Besides, passive constructions are usually longer, weaker, and fuzzier than active ones **(Pas).** Excessive use of "to be" verbs *(be, is, am, are, was, were, been, being)* usually produces flat wording, partly because it leads to a passive style. If the basic verb in more than half your sentences derives from *to be,* your style will seem flat.

"There are" and "It is" beginnings **(Exp**letives) delay the real idea of the sentence and frequently produce the unemphatic passive voice. The sentence "There are 1 million people in Cincinnati" is not so vivid as "One million people live in Cincinnati." "It was felt that . . ." becomes more vivid when rephrased as "We felt. . . ." (See **Exp** in Appendix C.)

You can eliminate most passives and expletives if you will *think* — that is, conscientiously try to use action verbs. People live, run, eat, buy—in short, act. They do not just exist, as indicated by *is, was, were, have been.* The price of stock *creeps up, rises, jumps, zooms*—or *plummets.* For vividness (and for economy), make verbs do a big share of the work. The more action you can pack into your verbs, the more specific and concrete you can make your sentences.

When you use active verbs and cut out passives and expletives, through your show of self-confidence you gain another desirable style quality— *force.* You appear more confident by standing up and being counted, by taking responsibility for what you say—instead of dodging, hedging, or hiding behind language evasions. A coward will hide behind passives, expletives, and little toothpulling qualifiers:

> It is believed that you might do well to. . . . (Who believes? Not sure, huh?—"might"? Hedging your bets?)

> A mistake has been made in your accounts that. . . . (Who made it? Hiding behind a passive, huh?—like a scared kid hiding behind mother's skirt.)

Other little qualifiers, like *might,* that rob sentences of their strength are *often-frequently-sometimes, most-some, may-perhaps-maybe-probably.* Before using any of them, ask yourself, "Do I need the word to avoid the risk of exaggeration, or am I too timid or cowardly?" Conversely, you do not want to come across as an overconfident, unreliable, cocksure, arrogant exaggerator by too ready use of categoricals like *the only way, always-never, everywhere-nowhere, everybody-nobody,* and *best-worst*—especially in intercultural communication. (Most other peoples resent the "grains of salt" they have to learn to take with some Americans' exaggerations.)

3. When you *use concrete rather than abstract language,* you give sharper mental pictures. When you say *superiority, efficiency,* and *durability* in telling about a product, your words are abstract; they give only hazy ideas. To make the picture sharp and lively, give the evidence back of the abstraction. If you think your product is of highest quality, you must have reasons for thinking so. To establish the idea of superiority in cloth, for instance: Thread count? Number of washings before fraying? Tensile strength? Resistance to shrinkage and fading?

In job applications you need to put across the ideas of your sociability, initiative, and dependability. But just claiming that you have those abstract qualities will make you look more conceited than competent. You can both avoid the conceit and present concrete, convincing evidence, however, by citing leadership in specific activities and offices held in organizations, ideas and plans you originated, attendance records, and completed projects. Thus you give active, vivid evidence of these qualities and convince your reader.

4. You further eliminate haziness and dullness when you *use specific rather than general words.* An investment, for instance, may be a stock (common or preferred), a bond, or a piece of real estate. The closer you can come to picturing the special type of thing named, the more specific and hence the more vivid your message is. When you are inclined to say *contact,* for example, do you mean write, go see, telephone? You present a sharper picture if you name the specific action.

5. Even when you are specific and concrete, unless you *give enough details to make the picture clear,* you will fail to be vivid. Specifications for a house may call for painting it, for example; but unless they tell the kind of paint, how many coats, and what colors, the painter does not know what to do. You need to flesh out skeletons to bring them to life, even if this sacrifices some brevity.

Comparisons can also help you explain the unknown or variable in vivid terms of the known. *Slowly* becomes sharper if you say "about as fast as you normally walk." "A saving of 2 percent when paid within 10 days" becomes more vivid if you add "$3.30, or a free box of Lane's choice chocolates, on your present invoice of $165."

## Be Natural; Avoid Triteness and Pomposity (*Nat* in Appendix C)

All kinds of trite expressions and jargon dull interest. We even call them "bromides" ("flat, commonplace statements," Webster says) because bromides are sleep-inducing medicines.

Unfortunately too many people in business learn all they know about business writing from the bad letters and memos they receive and thus continue an outmoded, inappropriate, and unnatural style. Like parrots, they use expressions unthinkingly. One person meeting another on the street would not say, "I am glad to say that we have received your letter of March 14, and in response we wish to state that. . . ." A good business writer would not write it either, but more likely, "Those tonnage figures for April were just what I needed," or "Your suggestions about the committee memberships helped a lot in my decision. Thanks." The first is slow, vague, roundabout, and stilted; the others are clear, direct, and natural.

Pompous language (puffed-up, roundabout, and big-wordy) is as dull and confusing as the use of bromides. Why many people write "We will ascertain the facts and advise accordingly" when in conversation they would say "We'll find out and let you know" is a mystery. A Washington blackout order during wartime originally read: "Obscure the fenestration with opaque coverings or terminate the illumination." A high official who wanted the message understood revised it to read: "Pull down the shades or turn out the lights."

Stuffed-shirt writers use a phrase or clause when a well-chosen verb would express the idea better. For example: "Smith raises the objection that . . ." instead of "Smith objects that (or objects to). . . ." One writer stretched a simple "Thank you" to "I wish to assure you that it has been a genuine pleasure to have been the recipient of your gracious generosity."

Good writers avoid bromides and pompous wording to make their messages natural. Common advice is "Write as you talk." Don't, however, take that advice literally. The informal style appropriate in business is more precise and concise than conversation. What the advisers mean is that you should not stiffen up, use big words and trite expressions, or get involved in complicated and formal sentences when you write. Rather, let the words flow out naturally and informally with the general tone and rhythm of the language people (rather than "stuffed shirts") actually use.

| Write (or talk) like this | Not like this |
|---|---|
| Many people | A substantial segment of the population |
| Know well | Are fully cognizant of |
| Object | Interpose an objection |
| Wait | Hold in abeyance |
| Carry out the policy | Effectuate (or implement) the policy |
| As you requested | Pursuant to your request |
| Before, after | Prior to, subsequent to |
| Get the facts | Ascertain (secure) the data |
| Find it hard to | Encounter difficulty in |
| Big difference | Marked discrepancy |
| Begin (or start) | Initiate (or institute) |
| Complete (or finish) | Consummate |
| In the first place | In the initial instance |
| Haste makes waste | Precipitation entails negation of economy |
| Make unnecessary | Obviate the necessity of |
| Think of | Conceptualize |
| Here is | Enclosed please find |
| Now | At this point in time |
| About | With regard to |
| Because | Due to the fact that |
| Soon | At an early date |
| Consider | Take under consideration |

## Vary Sentence Pattern, Type, and Length

Unvaried sentence pattern, type, length, or rhythm causes many a mind to wander. Though much necessary variety will come naturally from phrasing things well, revision can enliven your style by removing a dull sameness.

The normal English sentence pattern is subject-verb-complement. Most of your sentences should follow that sequence; but if all of them do, they produce monotony. Particularly noticeable are series of sentences beginning the same way, especially with "I" or "We." (One critical lecturer stressed the point by laughing at such "we-we" letters.) The following list suggests possible variations of sentence beginnings:

*With a subject:*

A simple way to key returns is to use different return envelopes with the several letters being tested.

*With a clause:*

Because human beings are unpredictable, you cannot rivet the sales process to a formula.

*With a phrase:*

For this reason, you should test to find which letter pulls best before making a large mailing.

*With a verb:*

Should you find that all pull about the same, you have the usual dilemma!

*With correlative conjunctions:*

Not only the lack of appealing ideas but also the stodgy writing causes many business messages to fail in their purposes.

*With an adverb:*

Ordinarily, students like courses in business communication.

*With a verbal:*

Allowing plenty of time, the student started the report early in the semester.

*With an infinitive:*

To be a successful business letter writer, a student must be able to lose selfishness in contemplation of the reader's problem.

*With adjectives:*

Congenial and cooperative, Dorothy worked many nights until midnight when we faced a deadline.

Proper emphasis of ideas is the main reason for varying sentence type, but the variation also avoids monotony and retains interest. Choosing sentence structure in terms of needed emphasis (as explained earlier) will nearly always result in enough variety to prevent monotony.

Sameness of sentence length (and to some extent, paragraph length) can become as monotonous as unvarying sentence pattern and type. Together they produce an interest-killing rhythm characteristic of a childish style. For that reason, business communicators need to learn an easily understandable style without limiting themselves to a child's monotonous short-word vocabulary and unvaried short, simple sentences.

# How to Keep Your Style Inconspicuous

A reader's starting point of interest is what you say, not how you say it. In a well-ordered sentence a reader will receive no jolt. Your style, therefore, becomes noticeable and distracting only if you do something unexpected with it. Simplicity and naturalness are good guides on the right road.

If you make your style too flowery, formal, or stiff for the situation, or if you make it too flippant and familiar, it will distract from your message and arouse doubts about your sense of appropriateness. (An obvious striving for such style is a sign of immaturity.)

If you violate any of the conventions of word choice, spelling, punctuation, sentence structure, or grammar, your unconventional practice will both distract the reader and raise doubts about your general knowledge and ability. For instance, if you cause the reader to say, "Why, that writer can't even spell," the *even* strongly implies "So of course I can't depend on such a person to know anything else either."

The two main ways a writer may do something unexpected with style and thus draw undue attention to it are

1. Choosing the wrong level of usage for the situation.
2. Violating any of the more common conventions of word choice, spelling, punctuation, grammar, or sentence structure.

Either of them will distract the reader and weaken the impact of the important thing—your message.

## Choose the Right Level of Usage

The appropriate level of language, like proper dress, is a highly variable thing. What is effective in one situation may not be suitable in another, just as a tuxedo is out of place for a day at the office or a wiener roast, blue jeans for a formal party, or a bathing suit for church.

The first step in choosing the right level of usage is to think about the situation in the light of five communication factors (sometimes called the communication formula):

1. A writer (or speaker) who has
2. A particular message to communicate through
3. A medium (letter, memo, report, interview, speech) to
4. A definite readership (or audience) for
5. A definite purpose (in business, a *practical* purpose—not entertainment).

If any of the factors change, the situation shifts so that a formerly good sentence may become bad, or vice versa. Still, many thoughtless writers almost ignore the last two factors—readership and purpose. Only in view of all of them can you classify the situation and choose the appropriate level of usage.

Having classified the communication situation, you can take the second step by considering the nature of the different levels of usage. Some linguists/philologists have distinguished as many as seven levels, but a more functional modern classification names three: informal, formal, and illiterate.

*Informal English* is the most useful for most functional speaking and writing. In it the emphasis is more on being functional than on being elegant. Its general tone is that of the natural speech of educated people in their usual business and social affairs. That—rather than a literal interpretation of the words—is the meaning of the often-heard advice that you should write as you talk.

But informal English is a broad category. When it approaches the formal, it does not allow slang, shoptalk, contractions, or omission of relative pronouns and other connecting words. (Almost any paragraph in this book illustrates this dignified-informal level.) Some misguided writers insist on the highly questionable requirement of impersonal style (no pronouns referring to writer or reader) for reports and research papers at this dignified-informal level of usage.

Near the deep end of the informal level of usage is what we call "familiar-informal." Its whole attention is on content and to heck with style. It's OK if you're writing to somebody you know pretty well or if the two of you have lots in common. As in this paragraph, it uses contractions, a light touch, and rather simple sentence structure and words.

*Formal English* is characterized by precision and elegance of diction, sentence structure, and grammar. Like the person dressed in formal clothes, it often appears stiff and unnatural. It admits of no contractions, ellipses, or indignities of any kind. Its words are frequently somewhat rare and long, with histories traceable back to the first word families of Old French or Latin. It is often fraught with abstruse literary and historical allusions, perhaps to impress the reader with the writer's erudition. Rather than concerning itself with facilitating the reader's comprehension, it employs lengthy and labyrinthine sentences and paragraphs more fanciful than functional, more rhythmical than reasoned, more literary than literate, more artificial than accurate, and more absurd than acceptable.

Abused formal English has no reason for being. Even in its best sense, formal English is nearly always unsuitable for business writing. It calls attention to itself as inappropriate in all but the most formal occasions.

*The illiterate level of usage* is the third one of them three we dun named. It ain't got no bizness in bizness. Ya see, folks who reads letters spects you ta right right. If'n ya writes wrong, . . . . (Again the paragraph illustrates—not for use or scorn but to give sympathy and to encourage the writer to do better.)

An easy way to choose the appropriate level of usage for a situation is to ask yourself which type of dress would be most suitable if you were going to see your reader and talk your message. If the answer is formal dress, choose formal English or dignified-informal. If the answer is an everyday business suit, use the broad middle ground of informal English. If the answer is sport clothes, use familiar-informal.

## Follow the Conventions

You have already seen how following the conventions of wording, punctuation, sentence structure, and grammar affects clarity. But violations of those and other conventions have an even more important bearing on keeping your style inconspicuous. If you go contrary to the conventions (something your reader doesn't expect of an educated writer), you distract attention from your message *and* lose the reader's respect and confidence.

Even in the following first paragraph of a letter from a hotel manager to an association president, you know what the writer means, despite poor sentence structure; but you are distracted and you can't hold much respect for the manager or the hotel.

```
Your recent convention over with and successful,
we are wondering if since then you have decided on
the next year's meeting city, and you jotting down
on the margin of this letter the city and dates
selected, this will be indeed appreciated.
```

From this, don't you get the impression that the sloppy language probably means the hotel might not be a very well run, clean place to stay?

*Spelling* is probably the most exactly established convention in the English language. Though the dictionary spells a few words two ways, it lists most of them in only one way. Because of this definiteness, most readers (even relatively uneducated ones) will notice your errors and look down on you for them. So unless you are willing to appear uneducated, you had better learn English spelling. (You will find some helpful guidelines under **Sp** in Appendix C.)

Poor *word choice* that is close enough to meet the basic requirement of clarity is usually not so noticeable as misspelling, but it may be distracting and even degrading. Among the thousands of possible bad choices, the pairs listed under **Diction** in Appendix C give the most trouble. If you are unsure of any of the distinctions, look up the words; any educated reader will notice if you confuse them.

Variations from *standard punctuation* may lead to misunderstanding, but more frequently they distract and retard the reader. If you have trouble with punctuation, study the material under **P** in Appendix C.

*Grammar and sentence structure* are so closely related that you should consider them together. They have a definite bearing on clarity (as previously explained), but they have more significance in terms of making your style inconspicuous. Most of the troubles come from

- A writer's having heard uneducated people speak unconventionally, particularly family and fellow workers. (Solution: Observe the skills of effective writers and speakers, study writing, practice.)
- Simple carelessness. (Solution: Proofread and revise.)
- Trying to use big words and complicated sentence structures before mastering them. (Solution: Remember that they are unnecessary to dignity or effectiveness; write simply, at least until you can use more involved structures precisely and clearly.)
- Following some misguiding "rules of English." (Solution: Learn what the true conventions are according to language scholars, ignore misguiding "rules" and unjustifiable restrictions on the language, and give your attention to the more important aspects of good style—clarity, interest, inconspicuousness.)

Here is a realistic interpretation of some points that language scholars make in contradiction to statements of some less well informed people:

- A split infinitive is undesirable only if it is awkward or unclear.
- *And, but,* and *so* are good sentence beginnings if they deserve the emphasis they get there. The same applies to *however* and other transitional words, but some people object only to *and, but,* and *so.*
- Prepositions are perfectly good at the ends of sentences if you want them to have the emphasis they would get there.
- One-sentence paragraphs are perfectly good. The ban on them is nonsense. Often a one-sentence paragraph, especially the first or last in a letter, is just what you need.
- Passive voice is usually undesirable because it is weak, wordy, and awkward; but it still exists in the language because it is useful in some situations (to avoid direct accusations, for example). To ban it completely is high-handed.
- What some people still call colloquial expressions and slang are important and useful parts of the language; when the situation calls for the informal level of usage, they can improve language effectiveness.

Appendix C covers some common violations of the conventions and gives suggestions for avoiding criticism.

## How to Handle Two New Language Problems

Two language problems that have long existed are now demanding serious consideration: (1) sexist communications and (2) writing in international business. Both are important exceptions to the generally good advice to "follow the conventions" of the English language.

### Avoid Sexist Language

For efficiency in language (and no doubt partly as a reflection of the attitude of male dominance), English has never developed universal- or dual-sex personal pronouns. Conventionally, English-speaking people have blithely used the male forms *(he, his, him)* when the sex of the person referred to was unknown or the intention was to include either or both sexes. Recent improvements in the attitude toward women are therefore running into a language problem.

Largely through the efforts of organized women's groups, most reputable speakers, writers, and publishers are learning and practicing ways to circumvent the sexist convention and make the language give women fair recognition.

Though we can't explain all the how-to's in this book (which is largely about something else), here's a list of the main ways:

- Shift to the plural, where pronouns are the same form for both sexes.
- Phrase (or rephrase) errant sentences to avoid the need for third-person singular pronouns. *The* can often replace them.
- Identify the individual involved; then refer back with the appropriate pronoun. (By this means you'll also enhance your style through specificness and gain human interest by picturing a person in action.) Remember, however, that some of both females and males are of high station in life and some of low; so keep a balance. Otherwise, you will show sexism by stereotyping one sex regularly in high-station activities and the other in low.
- Use gender-free terms (suitable in some cases) and other means to avoid the word or syllable *man* in many expressions also involving women: *sales representative* (or, in a store, *salesclerk*) instead of *salesman; police officer* instead of *policeman; mail carrier* instead of *mailman* or *postman.* The names of job categories are nearly all gender free: professor, secretary, manager, lawyer, plumber, doctor, teacher, minister, accountant, farmer, banker, retailer . . . . *Person* may serve the purpose in some places, such as *chairperson* and *salesperson.* (But beware of using laughable constructions such as *personager* and *unpersonned.* )

You can even more easily desex such female terms as *hostess, waitress, actress,* and *drum majorette* by simply omitting or changing the female-designating ending. In their basic forms, these words all include both sexes. Many similar words do too—but check an up-to-date dictionary to be sure. You can also (at the expense of a few words) change the phrasing to the *person serving/waiting on; performing* or the *performer; leading the band.* But

- Try to avoid doubling as a solution (*she or he, she/he,* or the reverse).
- Ignore (or try to educate) those people who object to the word or syllable *man* where they think it means (but does not) only a male person: *man* or *mankind* (in the original and still first-listed meaning of "all humans," as in "Man does not live by bread alone"); and in such words as *manual, manufacture,* and *manipulate.*
- See Chapter 2 for suggestions on the special problem of courtesy titles in addresses and salutations.

As you see, the main solutions to the sexist-language problem lie in (1) being fair-minded and alert to it and (2) adapting the language we have.

## Adapt Language in International Business

Since you will probably be involved somewhat in the fast-growing field of international business (as you'll see in Chapter 4), you can be thankful for your knowledge of English. It is the most widely understood and used language in the field.

Still, you will need help—some of which this book gives. Though the authors (collectively) have traveled in 29 foreign countries and understand four foreign languages, the best help this book can give you involves no instruction on any of them.

Rather, it gives you

- suggestions for *adapting* your English for better foreign understanding,
- other readily available means of avoiding or solving the language problems, and
- insights into major cultural and sociological differences that (if ignored) are more troublesome than language problems. You'll find them mainly in the next chapter, with occasional specific references throughout the book.

\*    \*    \*    \*    \*

*(All the cases for all the chapters are in Appendixes A and B. You should, therefore, read the first five chapters quickly but thoroughly so that you can put all the basic principles to use even in your first letter or memo.*

*Since you will remember the principles of good style better if you practice them, however, you may profit by working through at least some of the following exercises.)*

## Exercises

A.  Without looking at the following 10 words (printed upside down), get somebody to pronounce them for you to spell (in writing). Then check them against the spelling tips (under **Sp** in Appendix C) to understand why the spelling of each is as it is.

twenty-five, chargeable, deceived, traveling, disastrous, coping, alleys, don-keys, (All) ladies' references.

B.  Rewrite more vividly and specifically.

1.  X City [a big city you know well] has many advantages as a convention site.

2.  Watches are now available in great variety.

C.  Rewrite in modern language.

1.  We beg to advise that there is a balance due of $23 in the above-captioned account in your name.

2.  Your order of recent date for a catalog will be sent under separate cover.

3.  In reference to your request for an instruction booklet, please find same attached hereto.

4.  Enclosed herewith is a draft in the amount of twenty-three dollars ($23).

5.  We trust you will send check in full payment at your earliest convenience.

D.  As an exercise in properly handling passives, study the subject (look it up in the Index and under **Pas** in Appendix C); then rewrite the following passage from a company's management report, changing all passive sentences to active and all active ones to passive.

A report was drawn up and reviewed when a change was needed. Rearrangements were made. Even the largest division was rearranged so that each employee was given knowledge of all the tasks involved. Throughout the four-year program, a running account of the costs and savings in each department was kept by the company to determine net gains. Workers found their work to be more challenging and much more interesting after the change.

E. Rewrite the following "sentences" (or be prepared to discuss as your teacher directs). Some of them have more than one thing wrong. You may also benefit from finding (in Appendix C) the appropriate symbol(s) for criticism of each and reading the discussion of the symbol(s).

1. They came on mopeds wearing shorts and wide straw hats.

2. The executives decided that the simplest solution was for each to have their own garage key.

3. Remember that as the dictator you are responsible for errors, not the typist.

4. This afternoon there will be a meeting in the south and north ends of the Church. Children will be baptised at both ends.

5. The parole board decided that Jones was mentally ill after listening to three psychiatrists.

6. I would like to take this opportunity to thank you for letting me attend the court reporter session last week in San Antonio.

7. It is my personal opinion that the responsibility of the department lays with human resource development and it should take action upon this matter.

8. Please be advised that effective June 1, 19—, checks written for our International Buildings Company Health Protection Plan will be processed by the Associated Group Services, Inc. of Y City, State.

9. The Ladies of the Church have cast off clothes of every kind and they may be seen in the church basement on Friday afternoon.

10. The Lincoln City's shelter home provides sanctuary for victims of domestic violence and their children.

# Chapter Outline

**Tone**
Acceptable Balance of Personalities
Courtesy
Sincerity
Gratitude
**Service Attitude**
Resale Material
Sales Promotion Material
Special Goodwill Messages
**Adaptations to Intercultural Business**
Why Study Cross-Cultural Business?
Self-Analysis as the Start
Self-Preparation for Cross-Cultural Business
Group Behavioral Attributes
Varied Work Motivations
Trust
Family Affiliation
Fatalism
Religion
Language
Etiquette and Morals
Dangers of Polycentrism and Ethnocentrism
Equacentrism
**Questions and Exercises**

# 4
# Promoting Goodwill, Domestic and Intercultural

Most writing in business, industry, or government requires attention to tone—whether you're answering questions, providing quick information, persuading, refusing, or calling attention to some need or some condition that should be changed. Wherever you are on the executive ladder, you need to be careful about the tone of your message.

Whether you write to the CEO or a new clerk, you want to select words that will best convey your meaning without sounding either too weak and childlike or too condescending and parental.

The key is to sound like an adult and concentrate on issues and problems—with a little bit of psychological "stroking." Such phrases as "I know how you must have felt," "You're right," "We're glad to tell you . . . ," and "We appreciate your patience . . ." stroke your reader and help establish a friendly tone.

No business firm or individual intentionally drives away customers or friends by creating ill will or by seeming indifferent. For lack of conscious effort and know-how to build goodwill, however, many people in business do drive others away.

Proper *tone* and *service attitude* are the methods of winning and retaining friendliness and confidence—that is, goodwill (or disposition to return to you because you treat people well). Good business communication can help produce that positive disposition by developing a friendly, confident feeling through proper tone and service attitude.

## Tone

No doubt you have heard someone complain, "It isn't *what* he said—it's the *way* he said it!" Inflections and modulations of voice, facial expressions, hand gestures—all affect the tone of a spoken remark. The point applies in writing too. If you want your writing to build good relationships, you *will make a conscious effort to control the tone.*

Basic to a desirable tone is a balance of personalities (writer's and reader's) acceptable to both. Without an attitude of mutual respect, you will have difficulty achieving the other qualities necessary for good tone—courtesy, sincerity, and proper gratitude.

## Acceptable Balance of Personalities

As a good business writer, you will need to subordinate your own wishes, reactions, and opinions. You can, however, overdo the suggestion "Make it *big you* and little me." Anything you say that looks too steeply up to or down on the reader will throw the relationship off balance.

*Undue humility* usually backfires. No reader expects a writer to be so humble as in the following.

```
I'm sorry to ask a busy person like you to take
valuable time to help me, but without your help I
do not know how to proceed. Since you are a world
authority on . . . , and I know nothing about
it. . . .
```

*Flattery* also causes readers to question the sincerity of some writers, especially obvious flattery in an attempt to get the reader to do something.

```
As you know, I highly respect your professional
opinion. Your invaluable advice has helped our
company improve.

Your eminent position in commercial aviation, Mr.
Pogue, is the subject of much admiration.
```

Instead of gaining favor, the writer loses face and the reader's faith.

Passing deserved compliments or giving credit where credit is due, however, is something else—the good manners of anybody except a boor. So when you want to indicate your sincere awareness of the reader's position or accomplishment, make the compliment subordinately.

| Obvious flattery | Better |
|---|---|
| You are receiving this questionnaire because you are an authority on heat treating. | As an authority in heat treating, how do you think the passage of HR-724 will affect waste disposal? |

Now the compliment gets such a light touch that it may give a faint glow of satisfaction, and consideration of the question precludes unfavorable reaction.

As you see, handling a compliment subtly is frequently a question of inserting a complimentary phrase in a statement intended primarily to accomplish something else:

> After successful experience in the field, would
> you say that any single area of preparation is
> more important than others for effective public
> relations work?
>
> How, in your opinion, will passage of HR-724
> affect waste disposal?

More frequent than undue humility and flattery, however, is a writer's implication of too much self-respect and too little for the reader. Lack of respect usually reflects itself in (1) condescension ("talking down" to the other person), (2) preachiness (*didacticism* is another word for it), and (3) bragging.

*Condescension* implies that the writer feels superior to the reader and shows little respect. No one wants to be considered a nobody and talked down to as was done in this memo from a senior-level manager to a junior manager:

> We agreed not to continue funding your project.
> Stop all further efforts, and prepare a thorough
> report on what benefits have been realized to date
> on this project, if any.

**Revised, better**

> The valuable amount of time and effort you put
> into trying to make the Americana project viable
> is widely recognized. We all hoped that the
> project would prove successful.
>
> Since matters have turned out differently, we
> will have to discontinue the project in three
> months. In that time, please prepare a thorough
> report on what benefits we have realized to date.

Another business executive, though attempting to be bighearted, insulted a reader with "The machine is probably not defective, but a firm of our standing can afford to take it back and give you a new one." In the same category are "I am surprised that you would question the adjustment procedure of a firm like Blank's" and "You are apparently unaware of the long history of satisfactory customer relations at Blank's." Even "We shall allow you to" has condescending connotations not present in "We shall be glad to" or "Certainly you may."

A particular danger lies in writing to children, who are not lacking in respect for their own ways of looking at things. When the secretary of a boys' club requested that a department store manager contribute some boxing gloves to the club, the manager answered: "When you grow up to have the heavy business responsibilities I have, and you're asked for contributions by all kinds of charitable organizations, you'll understand why I cannot make a donation to your club."

A condescending attitude even crops up in job applications in statements like "You may call me at 743–4601." The implication is that the writer is permitting the reader a privilege, when just the opposite is true.

Repeated use of such phrases as "we think," "we believe," and "we suggest" often appears to be condescension. Such a sense of superiority is almost certain to erect a barrier of incompatibility or cause a sputter like "Well, Bigshot, I can think for myself!"

*Preachiness* (didacticism), an extension of condescension, is undesirable because, when you tell your reader what ought to be done, you imply reader ignorance or incapability and thus suggest your superiority.

A flat and obvious statement (see **Obv** in Appendix C) is frequently irritating because it implies stupidity, even though the writer's intention is good.

```
Selecting the best available personnel for the
various operations is one of the most important
things you do. Therefore you should. . . .
```

Even corporation executives, sales writers, and job applicants are sometimes flat, obvious, and preachy:

| Flat and preachy | Better |
|---|---|
| As I told you, you ought to know we have to increase all prices 7 percent. If you haven't notified our customers already—do so at once! | Remember, Jim, to notify our customers about the price increase of 7 percent. This price increase compares favorably with the varying national indicators of inflation and cost of living. |
| The business cycle is changing from a seller's market to a buyer's market. You are going to need a strong force of good salespeople. | Now that business is shifting from a seller's market to a buyer's market, you're probably thinking about the strong force of good salespeople you'll need to meet competition. |

```
Do you want Ferguson's        Good service at the
to keep growing and keep      right prices is not the
getting better? Of            only reason Ferguson's
course you do! That's         has grown as it has over
why you should employ         the last five years. The
only those who want to        team of Ferguson men and
move steadily forward         women has been equally
and push Ferguson's on        responsible.
to even greater heights.
```

As you see, careful phrasing can eliminate most of the irritation due to preachiness—and the psychological browbeating in the third example (**BB** in Appendix C). Often the key is to subordinate information that is obvious or known to the reader but must, for a reason, be included. Put it in the middle of a paragraph, preferably in a phrase or dependent clause.

*Bragging* is another undesirable extension of the writer's ego. Conscious use of superlative wording ("newest," "latest and greatest," "outstandingly superior," "final word") is a flagrant and obvious way to make your reader react unfavorably—and not believe you. Even experienced writers sometimes annoy readers with undesirable—and almost always unsupported—references to size of company, efficiency of operations, or quality of product, like:

```
We could never have become so big, successful,
and prestigious if we had not always . . . .
```

```
Even in a firm as large and as well run as Bowen
and Bowen, such incidents are bound to happen
occasionally.
```

```
You are unfortunately a victim of routine made
necessary by the vastness of an institution so
well operated as the White Sands Hotel.
```

A desirable balance of personalities between reader and writer (eliminating undue humility, flattery, condescension, preachiness, and bragging) will help improve the tone of your writing; but it will not assure courtesy, the second element in desirable tone.

## Courtesy

Being courteous is being considerate of the other person's feelings by exercising patience and tact. But often one's immediate, emotional, or unthinking reaction is an impatient or tactless expression. For that reason, one famous lecturer regularly suggests the use of a "soaking drawer"— a special drawer in the desk to put nasty-toned letters and memos overnight, for revision the next day.

The idea is good. Courtesy often requires a cool, conscious effort to be understanding and forgiving, to anticipate another's likely reaction, and to avoid offense. Sleeping on a nasty message can provide the better conditions. Besides that, correspondents need to keep in mind the major causes of discourtesy and to respect a French proverb that says, "To speak kindly does not hurt the tongue."

*Anger* is almost certain to cause loss of both friendliness toward you and confidence in you. Most people have a good deal of self-respect and confidence in the wisdom of their decisions. An attack on them produces a wave of anger and self-defense. Such sentences as the following are almost sure to produce that result:

```
I'm writing in vigorous rejection of your letter
so smugly announcing price increases of 7 percent.
I'm disgusted with your escalating price pattern
and certainly intend to tell all my professional
contacts in the Chicago, Milwaukee, and New York
areas how AYC conducts business.

What's going on in the office at your place?

We certainly have no intention of letting you get
away with that!
```

Crude slang or profanity, especially if in a display of heightened feeling, is likely to be interpreted as anger, whether or not it is intended as such. Don't use either. (And don't try to be coy and cute with quotation marks for questionable slang—or dashes in words that are obviously profanity.)

Petulance (peevishness or fretfulness) is simply anger in a modified degree. Here is how a junior-level corporation officer wrote another junior-level officer: "When do you expect to finish that report? You've had feedback from our committee for more than three weeks. That ought to be long enough to do a simple report." A calm request that the work be finished as soon as possible because of the need for the report would probably bring just as quick action, and it would leave the reader in a better mood to do a good job.

Both anger and petulance are the result of impatience and unwillingness to accept the responsibilities of successful human relations.

*Accusations,* on the other hand, are usually the result of insensitivity to how another person will react to a remark. You cannot cultivate tact (skill in dealing with others without giving offense) without a deep and almost constant concern for the feelings of others. The sensitive, thoughtful person knows that people do not like to be reminded of their carelessness or ignorance—and that they will react unfavorably to the person who insists upon reminding them.

The other person may not always be right; but if you are going to keep the greatest friendliness (goodwill), you will remember not to call attention to errors if you can avoid doing so—or, when necessary, to do it with the least likely offense (in impersonal style or by implication).

| **Accusing** | **Revised, better** |
|---|---|
| Much as we dislike doing so, we shall have to delay your purchase order number B¢33084, dated June 26. | Since we want you to be entirely satisfied with the wire you ordered June 26 (your purchase order B-33084), please tell us whether you want shielded or unshielded insulation? |
| You neglected to specify which insulation you want on the wire. | |
| Kindly check our specifications, and this time specify whether you want shielded or unshielded wire. | Shielded insulation is a little more expensive, but it meets all regulations--including the new FAA RMS-625/4. |
| We have enclosed an envelope for your convenience. | Just check the appropriate box on the enclosed reply card and sign as authorization. As soon as we receive it, your wire will be on its way. |

The contrast between the two versions of that letter points to an important principle in business communications: *When you have sincere compliments to give, personalize them for full effect; on the contrary, when you are inclined to point the accusing finger, shift to impersonal, passive, or other unaccusing phraseology.*

*Unflattering implications* are usually the result of tactlessness combined with suspicion or distrust.

The adjustment correspondent who says, "We are investigating shipment of the goods *you claim* you did not receive," need not be surprised to receive a sharp reply. Similarly, "We *are surprised* to receive your report" and "We *cannot understand* why you have had trouble with the Kold-Hold when other people like it so well" establish by implication semiaccusing doubts of the other person's reasonableness, honesty, or intelligence.

And the sales writer who begins a message by implying doubts about a reader's alertness can expect few returns from the letter:

Alert hardware dealers everywhere are stocking No-Flame, the fire-resistant. . . . Are you prepared to meet the demands of your home-building customers?

In similar vein the phrases "Do you realize . . .?" and "Surely you are . . ." immediately suggest doubts that the reader or listener measures up on either score. Such lack of tact is usually unintentional. Most people, however, do not question whether it is intentional; the result is ill will.

*Sarcasm,* on the other hand, is generally deliberate. And it is extremely dangerous in business correspondence. The smile that accompanies friendly sarcastic banter cannot find its way onto paper; unfriendly sarcasm is sheer malice. It is the direct opposite of the attitude necessary for a tone of goodwill because it shows a lack of respect for the other person and a deliberate attempt to belittle. The sales manager sending the following memo to a group of employees who have fallen short of their quotas would build no goodwill:

```
Congratulations on your magnificent showing!
We're only $50,000 short this week. How do you do
it?
```

The United Way leader who included the following in a public report could hardly expect future cooperation from the people indicated:

```
The ABC employees, with an assigned goal of $800,
magnificently responded with $452. Such generosity
should not go unmentioned.
```

*Curtness,* born of impatience and a false sense of what constitutes desirable business brevity, reflects indifference and thus seems discourteous. A poor letter like the following, reflecting such lack of interest, destroys much of the favorable impression made by even a good booklet.

```
We have your request for our booklet and are
enclosing same. Thanking you for your interest, we
are. . . .
```

This writer might very well have converted a casual inquiry into a sale by taking the time to show interest in serving with a letter like the following, with its good service attitude, positive and specific resale material, and action ending (all discussed later):

```
Here is your copy of Siesta's booklet Color at
Mealtime.
When you read it, you'll understand why we say
that in Siesta you can now have handsome
dinnerware that is sturdy enough for everyday use,
yet surprisingly inexpensive.
No photography, however, can do justice to the
delicacy of some Siesta shades or to the
brilliance of others.
```

```
Your friendly local dealer will be glad to show
you a selection of Siesta. Unless the stock is
complete, the dealer will be glad to order
additional colors for your examination.

See your dealer soon and start enjoying Siesta's
color at mealtime.

You can find Siesta in Omaha at (address of
dealer).
```

This letter adapts easily as a form letter with only the last sentence and the inside address and salutation individually processed.

*Stereotyped language* is another mark of discourtesy because it suggests indifference. Writers of messages like the following jargonistic disgrace can expect little feeling of friendliness from their readers:

```
We have your letter of the 19th and in reply wish
to state that the interest on your mortgage is now
$361.66.

We trust this is the information you desired, and
if there is any other way we can oblige, please do
not hesitate to call upon us.
```

Since stereotyped language is primarily a question of style, see **Nat** in Appendix C for fuller discussion and more examples.

*Untidy physical appearance* is another factor affecting the apparent courtesy of letters and memos. Avoid sleazy paper, poor placement, strike-overs, messy erasures, dim or clogged type, poorly matched type and processed material, and penciled signatures.

In putting your best foot forward through courtesy, however, you must be careful. Overdone attempts to be courteous may seem insincere and thus destroy the third element in desirable tone.

## Sincerity

When a reader or listener feels the first flashes of doubt, with an unexpressed reaction of "Well, I'll take that with a grain of salt," confidence in the writer or speaker wanes—because of apparent insincerity.

Sincere cordiality is entirely free of hypocrisy. It is unwillingness to exaggerate. Inappropriate cordiality (usually unbelievable and sometimes distasteful) is commonly the result of effusiveness, exaggeration, or undue familiarity. (Flattery and undue humility often sound insincere, but they relate more closely to the balance of personalities discussed in a preceding section.)

*Effusiveness* means gushiness. It is excessive politeness, which often is insincere and always *sounds* insincere. "Overdone" means the same thing. You can sound effusive simply because you've used too many and/or too strong adjectives and adverbs:

```
Your excellent choice of being a stockholder in
our fine company we consider a distinct compliment
to the superb management and quality of our
product.

We are extremely happy to place your name on our
list of highly valued customers who have open
accounts with us, and we sincerely want you to
know that we have hundreds of most loyal employees
all very eager and anxious to serve you.
```

The plain fact is that in a business relationship such highly charged personal reactions do not exist—and businesspeople know it. Phrases like "do all we can" and simply "happy" or "pleased" are appropriate because they are believable. In avoiding effusiveness, you'll do well to watch especially overused words like *very, indeed, genuinely, extremely, really,* and *truly*—which begin to gush in a very short time.

*Exaggeration* is stronger, and therefore even more destructive of sincerity. The person who wrote, "Work is a pleasure when you use these precision-made tools," appears to be overstating the case to a carpenter-reader, as does the personnel director who said, "Tellco, the amazing company with revolutionary ideas, just hired a sensational sales representative with a great personality."

Superlatives and other forms of strong wording are among the most frequent reasons why so many letters sound insincere. The trite "more than glad" is nearly always an insincere attempt to exaggerate a simple "glad." And "more than happy," if translated literally, could mean only slaphappy. The classic illustration is the misguided "What could be finer than. . . ?"

Exaggerated wording is nearly always challenging. Few things are actually *amazing, sensational, revolutionary, ideal, best, finest,* or *perfect.* Simple, accurate, specific statements of quality and value not only avoid the impression of insincerity; they are often more forceful than the general superlatives.

*Undue familiarity* also causes people to lose favor. Sometimes it crops out merely because the writer or speaker is uncouth. The reader or hearer may feel sympathy for the person who does not know how to act with people—but will probably not have the disposition to return for more uncouthness.

Undue familiarity usually results from (1) calling the reader by name too frequently or writing or speaking in too informal language to a stranger and (2) making references to subjects that are too personal for business discussions. For an obvious purpose, the writer or speaker pretends a closeness of friendship that does not exist. Like other forms of pretense, this brings resentment. In the following letter giving information about fashions for stout women, the jocularity falls flat and insults.

```
WELCOME, Mrs. McKinney, to the WORLD OF FASHION
FOR STOUT WOMEN! Now you can order direct from us
and not worry about endless shopping in
Springfield. Just sit down in your big chair and
flip through our colorful order catalog--noting
the casual as well as dressy outfits that appeal
to you.
By calling 800-986-3646, you can order from our
friendly employees as many outfits as you want. Or
you can fill out the enclosed order blank--
whichever is easy for you in your busy McKinney
household.
Since you'll be entertaining in your lovely home
on Claymount Circle, you'll certainly want to look
at the hostess gowns pictured on page 98. And for
working among your flowers, notice the casual
clothes on page 13. Notice how reasonable our
prices are--just right to fit the McKinney budget.
Yet, the variety of styles, fabrics, and sizes
gives you a wide selection. Clothes in woven
poplin, cotton, polyester knit, even silk come in
solids, prints, stripes, and pinstripes (to make
you look slimmer).
So, Mrs. McKinney, forget that diet you thought
you'd go on last Monday (after a weekend of
partying). Just order from us and enjoy the WORLD
OF FASHION FOR STOUT WOMEN.
```

Using the reader's name four times in such a short space suggests fawning with the help of the computer. References to "entertaining in your lovely home" and "after a weekend of partying" could offend or misfire.

## Gratitude

In business communication as in social relations, proper handling of deserved gratitude is a significant point in the tone of relationships. When people extend favors, they expect to receive some recognition; and everybody except the self-centered, boorish, or inept gives it. Probably because of early training, most of us have little trouble showing gratitude properly in face-to-face relations; but in business writing the what, when, and how seem to be problems for many.

Suggestions for ways of improving:

1. When the reader has already done you a favor—
   a. Don't begin with "Thank you . . ." unless that is your most important or most likely acceptable point. Instead, go ahead with your message and
      (1) Let the overall pleasant spirit show your good feeling without wasting words saying "Thanks . . ." explicitly, or
      (2) Tuck the expression in a subordinate position and word it to give due (not overdue) emphasis.
   b. If you feel that you must begin with gratitude, be sincere (don't gush or exaggerate) and word your expression to relate naturally to what follows— perhaps as a "buffer" (explained in the next chapter).

| Original | Revised |
|---|---|
| Thank you for your brochure on <u>Dietary Guidelines to Lower Cancer Risk</u>. | Your important brochure on <u>Dietary Guidelines to Lower Cancer Risk</u> will help everyone--so many thanks. |
| Thank you for becoming a charter member of X County Children's Museum. | You and many other concerned parents and friends are helping the X County Children's Museum to become a reality. Thanks! |

2. When you want to show gratitude for future favors (asked for or hoped for),
   a. Don't express it in the present tense ("I appreciate") or in unqualified future indicative mood ("I will appreciate . . ."). Either way presumes that the reader will do as you ask, and you have no right to be so presumptuous.
   b. Either
      (1) Qualify the future indicative with an "iffy" or questioning request ("I shall appreciate it if you will . . ." or "Will you please . . . ?), or
      (2) Use the future conditional ("I would appreciate your . . .").

| Original | Revised |
|---|---|
| I will appreciate your phoning me for an appointment. | I would appreciate your phoning me for an appointment. |
| I appreciate your phoning me for an appointment. | Will you please phone me . . . for an appointment. |

See the Index for further help on handling gratitude in special situations.

## Service Attitude

In addition to using a desirable tone as a means of maintaining good relationships, wise business communicators show that their concern extends beyond making a profit or other purely selfish interests. They're like the very successful business executive who said that the difference between the average person and the exceptional person usually lies in three words—"and then some." The top people, he said, "did what was expected of them—and then some. They met their obligations and responsibilities—and then some. They were good friends to their friends—and then some. . . ."

A business organization obviously must make profits if it is to exist; both reader and writer accept that premise—but you don't need to talk about it. Instead, let your messages remind others of your thoughtfulness and genuine desire to be of service—to meet your obligations, and then some—through:

1. Resale material on the goods, services, and/or the house.
2. Sales promotional material on other goods (and/or services in some cases).
3. Special-occasion messages.

### Resale Material

Often you need to assure a customer of the wisdom of an earlier choice of goods and services—or of the house (business firm) chosen to do business with—and thus stress satisfaction. In *keeping the goods sold,* resale material helps keep unfilled orders on the books, fosters repeat orders, and forestalls complaints. It is an effective device in meeting competition.

As applied in business to goods and services, resale means favorable talk about something the customer has already "bought"—that is, by purchase, practice, or approval, although it may not yet be delivered. Most buyers would feel better about the stock they bought upon reading the following resale in the company's annual report:

```
New marketing campaigns, new products, and
significant improvements in production and
processing efficiencies led to record sales and
profits for American Home Foods in 198-.
```

One of the most prestigious restaurants in Austin, Texas, helps promote its fine dinners by sticking this little sign into the skin of each baked potato served:

```
For goodness' sake Don't skin me! I've been
rubbed, tubbed, and scrubbed. I'm clean as a
```

```
whistle . . . and a lot tastier. You may eat me
skin and all--for I'm an Idaho Potato--baked and
served the XXX way.
```

Such material is *most effective when it is relatively short and when it is specific.* Tell a customer buying a shirt, for instance, that

```
It will launder rapidly and easily because of the
no-iron finish.
```

or

```
The seams are double-lockstitched for long life.
Made from long-staple California cotton, your
Pallcraft shirt will give you the wear you expect
from a shirt of this quality.
```

But don't try to tell *all* these points in a resale passage. And for your own greatest effectiveness, don't try to get by with a lame generality like "Pallcraft shirts are a good buy."

Used most frequently in acknowledgments, resale material on the goods may also appear in certain credit, collection, and adjustment messages, as you'll see later.

*Resale material on the house* consists of pointing out customer-oriented policies, procedures, guarantees, and special services, sometimes called "the little extras" (the "and then somes") that a good firm (the "house") provides its customers—retail, wholesale, or industrial. Resale is especially helpful in the beginning of a business relationship. But any time you add a new service, improve an old one, or expand a line is an appropriate occasion to tell customers about the firm's continued attempt to give satisfaction. The following excerpt from a message to a dealer is typical:

```
Along with your shipment of Lane candies are some
display cards and window stickers which you'll
find valuable aids in bringing these delicious
candies to the attention of your customers. Our
Advertising Department will regularly furnish you
with seasonal displays and will be glad to help
you on any special display problem in connection
with the sale of Lane's.
```

Retail stores often invite customers to fashion shows and special sales, or they send colorful brochures with handy order blanks and toll-free order numbers. Salesclerks often call customers to tell them about special purchases. The following letter went to past customers only:

Next Wednesday . . .

November 16, you can trim your 198- Christmas expenses substantially.

Come to Starberg Bonus Day, when we reduce every item in the store by 20 percent for one day only. And as you shop, enjoy refreshments that will be served until 9:00 P.M.

Included are brand names like Rolex and others that are never sale-priced, plus our entire collection of newly arrived Christmas merchandise.

Please join us.

Resale passages are the writer's (or speaker's) attempts to confirm or increase the buyer's faith in goods, services, or the firm in which committed interest already exists. Sales promotion material (on new and different goods or services) seeks to promote interest in *something else* the firm can supply.

## Sales Promotion Material

For a number of reasons, sales promotion material about related products is desirable in annual reports and in some acknowledgment, credit, collection, and even adjustment messages. The most obvious business reason is that regardless of what you try to market, you must constantly seek to sell more of it to more customers all the time. In terms of communication, however, *the most significant reason is the concrete demonstration that the firm desires to be of further service*. A third function of sales promotion material is that it can end a message naturally and easily, with emphasis on further service. The following example illustrates the point:

We shipped your carpenter's tools, as itemized on the enclosed invoice, UPS delivery this morning. They should reach you by October 15. Thank you for your check, which covers all charges.

*Resale*

The Crossman level with aluminum frame is stronger and weighs less than wooden ones, and it will remain bright and true. The tempered steel used in the Flex-Line tape is permanently oiled; so you can be sure it will easily and rapidly unwind and rewind every time you use it.

*Sales promotion*

> When you receive the fall and winter catalog we're sending separately, turn to page 126 and read the description of the Bradford 6½-inch electric handsaw. To enjoy the savings in time and energy this efficient piece of equipment offers, use the handy order blank at the back of the catalog.

You'll need to observe three precautions in the use of sales promotion material:

1. Above all, it should reflect the *desire to be of service* rather than the desire to sell more goods. It is low-pressure sales effort, comparable to the way a salesclerk, after selling a woman a pair of shoes, may casually pick up a matching or complementary purse and say, "Perhaps you'd like to examine this purse, which goes with your shoes so well." If another sale results, that's good. But if not, it's still good: most customers are pleased because of the demonstrated interest in their welfare or happiness.

If, however, the insatiable sales appetite of "I want to sell you more" shows through selfish, greedy terminology, you neither promote sales nor please the customer, retail or mercantile. When emphasis is on *order* instead of *service*, Greedy Gus overtones are almost inevitable:

| **Greedy Gus Original** | **Service-minded Revision** |
|---|---|
| We also sell attractive summer purses, nylon hosiery, and costume jewelry to complete your excellent line of goods. We are sending you our catalog. And we hope to fill many more orders for you. | The summer purses and costume jewelry shown on pages 29 to 32 of the accompanying catalog have also sold well for many of our other customers--and we think would for you. |

2. *Appropriateness* is also a factor. When a woman buys a suit, a natural item to call to her attention is a blouse. A man buying a suit may be interested in matching or blending shirts, ties, or shoes. But to tell a purchaser of heavy-duty truck tires about the good buy you now have in refrigerators or the buyer of a washing machine about your special on tires would be questionable most of the time. Almost always, *sales promotion material should be on items related to those under consideration.*

3. Before using sales promotion material, consider also *the kind of message* you are writing. A message requiring further action on the reader's part needs final emphasis on that action, not on sales material.

Both resale and sales promotion material help sell more merchandise, but they are even more effective as goodwill builders because they imply positively and emphatically the general statement "We are eager to serve you well."

### Special Goodwill Messages

To demonstrate continuing interest in the customer and the desire to serve, special goodwill letters also subtly use sales promotion material and resale material on the goods and the house. Many businesspeople refer to them as the "letters you don't have to write—but should." Since the customer does not expect them, since they usually bring something pleasant, and since your reader knows you do not have to write them, they are doubly welcome and thus builders of goodwill.

Because they are of great variety in function and occasion, and because you can write them with greater understanding and skill after studying some other kinds of business messages, however, the full treatment of them appears in Chapter 6. Suffice it to say here that your study of special goodwill messages will reinforce the central theme of the preceding chapters: consideration for the other person.

## Adaptations to Intercultural Business

Successful business relations with other peoples of the world also depend heavily on their goodwill, which similarly depends on proper tone and service attitude. Some adaptation of American ways are necessary, however, because of differing social, religious, and business attitudes and activities.

Though this brief overview cannot hope to give you the whole anthropological, sociological, and political pictures of the varied cultures of the world, it can (and does) give you the basic principles with some specifics, suggest a broadminded and tolerant viewpoint, alert you to some potholes to avoid, and refer you to some major current sources of further information if needed.

### Why Study Cross-Cultural Business?

Approximately one of every eight U.S. jobs is currently dependent (directly or indirectly) on the nation's stake in world trade. At current growth rates U.S. international trade will have grown to almost $4 trillion by the year 2000 (30 percent of an annual GNP of $13 trillion). Nearly one of every three U.S. jobs will owe its existence (at least partly) to international commerce.

Very likely you will be involved in this global business and will realize that you need to know some of the differences from domestic business so that you can predict, adapt, and/or control relationships and operations. Obviously, you can't know all the differences; but you can know certain norms of religious, demographic, and behavioral attributes that may alter the methods of conducting business with other countries.

One of the basic problems in communication between people of different cultures, races, economic backgrounds, and even sexes is that when people don't have much in common or know much about each other, they tend to be cautious and sometimes subconsciously hostile. Whether you are directly or indirectly involved with peoples of other cultures, therefore, you will do a better job if you are aware of the many differences and the reasons for the differences.

The more you perceive yourself to be like another person (even though that person be from a far distant land), the more you can persuade and the more you can be persuaded. The more you feel you are different from another person, the harder it will be to see eye to eye.

## Self-Analysis as the Start

Before you accept an overseas position, you should analyze yourself to see if your personality has the traits that personnel practitioners say are desirable for a successful sojourner overseas:

1. Initiative, because sometimes no one else will be there to suggest what to try next.
2. Positive attitudes toward people who may differ markedly in race, creed, color, values, personal habits, and customs, to help produce cooperation instead of conflict.
3. High motivation, to fight frustrations.
4. Skills in communication (oral, written, and nonverbal).
5. Flexibility both to accept and to try new ways to prevent blockages.
6. Ability to deal with temporary setbacks (stress) and to adapt, to preclude frustration, conflict, anxiety, and feelings of alienation.
7. Physical fitness and mental alertness, in yourself and all members of your party, for the inevitable occasions calling for quick decisions and actions (sometimes with heavy loads).
8. Curiosity, perseverance, sense of humor, and patience, for occasions when everything seems to fall apart.

Ironically, the very qualities that make a person successful in the United States—being aggressive and efficient, driving a hard bargain—may guarantee failure in some areas abroad, where such behavior often breaks local customs.

### Self-Preparation for Cross-Cultural Business

Before starting a job that takes you away from home, find out as much as you can about the culture. If possible, visit the country where you'll be stationed and get acquainted with the people. Learn at least a little of the language. Your foreign colleagues will be most pleased if you can speak their language—even if you speak haltingly and with some mistakes. Language courses—and even records, tapes, and tutors—can help. Some companies offer language training as part of cross-cultural training courses. Encourage your family or other companions to study language, for they too will have to mix and mingle with their counterparts overseas.

The language problem may not be so great as you expect, however. Many businesspeople in Asia and the Pacific Islands have been studying and using English for at least 25 years. Earlier editions of your textbook have made it the leading text in Japan and the Pacific Islands (as in the United States) since 1962 (when Professor Stephen G. Long—on leave from the University of Florida—started teaching in the Orient and the Pacific Islands).

Concurrently, the members of JBEA (Japanese Business English Association) started the now-widespread teaching of business communication in English at many Japanese universities. So today the main college-level language is English.

Collectively, therefore, certain differences in courtesies and customs may be as significant problems as the language differences in dealing with Asian and Pacific Islands people:

- First names are out (even socially).
- The Japanese bow instead of shaking hands (and even loathe touching).
- The Asian people go even further than this book suggests in applying bad-news strategy—in both oral and written messages. (You may have to chat over tea before you get the essence of a negative message.)
- And if a Japanese burps in the middle of a meal, it means only that the food is relaxing and enjoyable.

Some multinational firms are offering cross-cultural training courses at company headquarters for their employees who will work abroad. The best programs are custom-designed to meet a client's specific needs in a certain country. Videotaped role-play exercises often are the core of the training programs. Programs may include classes on native history, politics, religion, business customs, social etiquette, along with audiovisual presentations and readings. Discussions with foreign nationals and recently returned expatriates are usually part of the package. (See "Foreign Handbook," *Savvy,* 5:71–84, April 1984.)

Another kind of cross-cultural training course that is open to the business public trains managers to negotiate in any culture. Trainees learn to identify five styles and 12 kinds of behavior that effective negotiators use.

A number of business schools have courses on international business for undergraduates and graduates. Even if your school does not have such courses, you can take enough foreign languages, political science, sociology, and math to prepare yourself for work overseas.

The Experiment in International Living, a private, nonprofit organization, has been a leader in international educational exchange since 1932. For more information, write the U.S. Headquarters, Kiplin Road, Brattleboro, VT 05301.

To find out where the current jobs are, you might read the monthly publication *International Employment Hotline* (P.O. Box 6170, McLean, VA 22106). Each job is listed with its job title under the name of the country, with requirements and the name of the employer to contact. If there is a language requirement, it is mentioned. You respond promptly to a listing with a cover letter and résumé. You should handwrite your cover letter if the employer is in Europe, because Europeans often use graphologists to screen applicants and handwriting samples are often required. And unlike U.S. employers, many employers in Europe and the Middle East want to see your recent photo.

Perhaps your campus has a chapter of AIESEC ("eye-sek"), a French acronym for the International Association of Economics and Management Students (Association Internationale des Étudiants en Sciences Économiques et Commerciales). The purpose of AIESEC (founded in 1948) is to identify a select group of students with outstanding leadership potential and train them to become effective future international managers and leaders. AIESEC accomplishes its purpose through the international exchange program and the management of local committee operations.

Each year over 3,000 students and graduates, from more than 400 universities and colleges in 59 countries, get traineeships in companies worldwide. AIESEC-U.S. (14 W. 23rd Street, New York, NY 10010) places over 300 foreign members annually in U.S. companies and an equal number of American members abroad.

Whether you have AIESEC or not, you can talk with people who have spent time in the country where you'll live. Visit banks and companies that are involved in international trade, and talk with the people who are on the global scene. Perhaps you can talk with some freight forwarders, telex operators, a vice consul or trade commissioner, diplomats, interpreters, international bankers, or winners of the E award (U.S. presidential award to outstanding companies that do business with foreign countries).

Study the kinds of business documents that you'll be reading and writing. Other countries use letter and other document formats and styles different from ours. A quick study of the following letterhead tells you that the firm is incorporated (an indication of substance), as well as its mailing address, cable, telex, telephone, and logo. Don't worry if you can't read the first line.

# 艾吉企業股份有限公司
# AGIS ENTERPRISE CO., LTD.

Mailing address:      or      Mailing address:

P.O. Box 698                   P.O. Box 46-225 Taipei, Taiwan
Taichung, Taiwan              CABLE: "AGIS" Taipei, Taiwan
R.O.C.                        TELEPHONE
TEL: (042) 514858             (02) 5618529, (02) 5622491
                              TELEX: 24661 LONTING Taipei

The accepted dateline reads the year, month, and day (and time sometimes). To eliminate confusion, write out the name of the month (1986 May 11 10:30 A.M.). For example, a German and a U.S. business executive could get very confused if the month were not written out, since the German would write 11.5 and the American 5/11 for May 11.

Much business is done through telex and the freight forwarders. An example of a telex message:

```
RCA MAR 14 0833

ST DOCKS MBL

68234 NUJAME EM

ATTN: MR.GERRY P. ROBINSON

      GEN.SALES MANAGER


AM KEEN TO OFFER SERVICES TO PROMOTE TRADE THRU MOBILE PORT

AMONGST ARAB IMPORTERS, ALSO CAN PUT AS LIAISON MY FULL OFFICE

FACILITIES AT YR DISPOSAL.

PLS TLX ADVISE IF FEEL INTERESTED.

RGDS

JAMEEL H RAFFAT

SHARJAH (UAE)

68234 NUJAME EM

REPLY TO THIS TELEX VIA RCA
```

For more examples of forms and advice on how to sell products or services to customers in other countries, write the U.S. Department of Commerce, Washington, DC 20402, and ask for a copy of its "How to Build an Export Business."

If you make an oral presentation abroad, you'll have the same kind of visual aids to help you as you have in the United States. (Most overseas business representatives like visual aids.) A presentation in the host country's language will help make your project successful. An understanding of your host's culture adds interest and compatibility.

Before you make a presentation or write a letter, memo, or report, do your research. A starting place might be with the behavior attributes. Every society has its norms of behavior (attitudes, values, and beliefs) that make the societal culture.

## Group Behavioral Attributes

All countries' populations can be subdivided into groups, and individuals have memberships in more than one group (often determined at birth because of sex, family, age, caste, race, or national origin). The type of membership often reflects the degree of access to economic resources, social relations, prestige, and power.

**Women in the Work Force.** From a business standpoint, group membership may determine who is available for a certain job. The sheltering of women in Saudi Arabia, for example, shows up in education figures and work-force figures (ratio of males to females in elementary school is 2.8 to 1 and in universities, 10 to 1). Even in countries where women constitute a large portion of the working population, vast differences appear in the types of jobs considered "male" or "female." In the Sudan, for example, 74 percent of the manufacturing employees are women, while the figure is just 5 percent in next-door Egypt. In Switzerland women hold 48 percent of administrative and managerial positions as compared to just 14 percent in Canada. In Rumania 25 percent of the engineering students are women, compared to only 2 percent in Argentina.

In Japan women must contend with traditions and customs that require a great deal of patience and flexibility. Though often paid well in positions of responsibility, American businesswomen may be asked to wear the uniforms of Japanese female clerical workers or to pour tea. The rules of the workplace and the rules of protocol are very different. Americans who haven't been to Japan often think that because Japanese women seem to be oppressed, then American women will be oppressed in the same way. But Western women experience little sexual discrimination. Westerners remain foreigners whether they marry a Japanese, master the subtleties of the language, live in Japanese housing, or show a decade of loyalty to a Japanese firm. The only way to win complete acceptance is to be born Japanese.

**Age and Job Capability.** Some countries loosely correlate age and wisdom. The result is that advancement depends largely on seniority, with upper-level managers commonly over 70. In the United States retirement at 60 or 65 was mandatory in many companies until recently, and relative youthfulness is an advantage for moving ahead.

In Japan, conversely, young U.S. company representatives are often not quite accepted at first. For example, one under-30 woman sent to open a commercial real estate office in Tokyo reported that Japanese companies could hardly believe the company would send someone that young to start an office.

**Class Structure and Jobs.** Class structure among groups can affect an individual's preparation for a given job. In countries with poor public education systems, wealthy and elite groups send their children to private schools, whereas children from groups with average to low incomes can afford only inferior schools. Class structure within groups can be rigid. Firestone found, for example, that Liberians could work on plantations only by permission from their tribal chiefs (who required a Firestone payoff for their approval).

Although it is dangerous to look on any group of people and class them in stereotypes, one theory (as G. Cameron Hurst III discusses in the *Universities Field Staff International Reports*) is that the Japanese are strongly group-oriented and place supreme value on consensus and loyalty. The resulting image, whose key elements you now find in much English-language literature on Japan, is:

1. Japanese feelings generally radiate to and from the group.
2. Human relations within Japanese groups are harmonious.
3. Feelings of unity and loyalty within groups develop along vertical lines.
4. Because Japanese groups are structured vertically, mobilizing the members to accomplish group goals is relatively easy.
5. Because of the high degree of cultural, linguistic, and social homogeneity of society, the Japanese have a strong sense of belonging to a single society.
6. Japanese society (culturally and socially) is closed to foreigners.
7. Within Japanese social groups, informal relationships are relatively important.

One element not generally mentioned except by Japanese friends is that Japanese take pride in their work because they do not want to bring shame to their group—especially their family.

## Varied Work Motivations

The reasons for working and the relative importance of work among human activities depend largely on the interrelationship of the cultural and economic environment of the country where a person lives. The differences in motivation can help explain management styles, product demand, and levels of economic development.

**The Protestant Work Ethic.** Predominantly Protestant countries (as Max Weber, a German sociologist, observed) are the most economically developed because they view work as a means of salvation. People with this Protestant ethic prefer to transform productivity gains into additional output rather than additional leisure. In the United States, where incomes allow for more leisure than in any other country in the world, the general public is contemptuous of the millionaire who contributes nothing to society and of the capable person who lazily lives on government handouts. In contrast, the people of India generally consider living a simple life with minimum material achievements a desirable end in itself.

The USSR tried to shift from a six- to five-day workweek and found it had problems of alcoholism and other delinquent behavior because the people did not know what to do with the newfound leisure time.

One study, trying to determine why some parts of Latin America developed a higher economic level and desire for material achievement than others, attributed differences within Colombia to the fact that some Spanish settlers did their own work rather than using slave or near-slave labor. The Spanish settlers in Antioquia developed a work ethic, and today their descendants are the important industrial leaders of Colombia.

**TAT Groupings.** Some national differences in economic development depend on the individual's desire to achieve. Thematic apperception tests (TATs) may measure these differences. Individuals look at pictures and tell stories based on them. If an individual describes family and friends, the concern is primarily for affiliation; if an individual speculates about who is boss, the main interest is power; and if an individual emphasizes ways of doing things better, a need for achievement *(n ach)* is predominant.

Three other attributes distinguish the high-need achiever: (1) liking situations that involve personal responsibility for finding solutions to problems, (2) setting moderate achievement goals for taking calculated risks, and (3) wanting concrete feedback on performance.

One study (among managers in the United States, northern and southern Italy, Turkey, and Poland) found that the U.S. and Polish managers had substantially higher *n ach* scores, whereas the Italians and Turks had a higher affiliation need. The study helps explain situations in which

U.S. and local managers in Italy and Turkey react differently. In the job of purchasing, for example, a manager with a high affiliation need may be much more concerned with developing an amiable and continuing relationship with suppliers than with reducing costs and speeding delivery.

In contrast, another study used questionnaires to compare U.S., Japanese, and Korean managers on the importance to them of organizational goals. On all the eight goals except the last (productivity, growth, efficiency, profit maximization, stability, industry leadership, employee welfare, and social welfare), the nationalities showed significant differences in response.[1] Could these differences have arisen because of each country's value system and patterns of child rearing?

**Maslow's Needs Hierarchy.** Maslow's motivation theory is that the hierarchy of human needs goes thus: physiological, then safety, social status, self-esteem, and self-actualization. The idea is that a person tries to fulfill the lower-order (physiological and safety) needs before going on to the higher ones; and once a need is fulfilled, it is no longer a motivator.

Clearly Maslow's hierarchy does not fit all societies equally well. In each society certain occupations carry a greater reward perception than others. That perception may stem from economic, social, or prestige factors. In one study, U.S. students placed physicians in the highest rank (possibly because of high financial rewards), while the Japanese put college professors on top (probably because of the importance the Japanese attach to education and "clean" occupations).

Because educated people in Latin America are reluctant to dirty their hands or associate directly with operative workers, there's a problem in getting lower-level managers. In Latin America the people think that there is a leisure class, a class that works with its mind, and a class that works with its hands. Another problem in Latin American and some other countries is the degree of importance attached to business as a profession. In many countries people with the educational qualifications to work in business prefer to work at government positions.

Another difference centers on the desire to work for a business versus the desire to run one's own business. For example, people in Belgium and France seem to prefer to go into business for themselves. The number of retail establishments in either of those countries compared on a per capita basis with the U.S. figures shows the difference. United States businesses in Mexico also find it hard to keep good local managers because such managers want to work for themselves after gaining experience.

---

[1] H. J. Kornadt, L. H. Eckensberger, and W. B. Emminghaus, "Cross-Cultural Research on Motivation and Its Contribution to a General Theory of Motivation," in *Handbook of Cross-Cultural Psychology,* vol. 3, ed. Harry C. Triandis and Walter Lonner, Allyn & Bacon, Boston, 1980, p. 239.

Likewise, African workers typically join the urban labor force only temporarily, after which they prefer to return to their old agricultural endeavors, even though these endeavors usually give them less income.

Jobs with low prestige usually go to people whose skills are in low demand. Teenagers in the United States often begin work as baby-sitters, grocery baggers, and newspaper carriers but grow out of menial jobs through age and education. In less developed countries, however, such jobs are not transient and are filled with adults who have little chance of moving on to better (higher-reward) positions.

As you see, how people are motivated to work is a powerful behavior attribute; but also affecting a working situation is the degree of trust that one person has in another person.

## Trust

The greater the trust, the more people have the ability and eagerness to establish rapport with others. Where trust is high, managers and subordinates participate and avoid authoritative decision making.

Generally U.S. citizens have high trust and get right to the point in a business discussion. Note how fast people in the United States are to accept new products (for they have a strong belief that the other party is not developing something simply to cheat them). On the other hand, most other people want more cues as to whether they can trust others in a business relationship. They will spend a great amount of time in preliminary discussion before getting down to business.

In Greece, for example, nearly all transactions among individuals are with cash rather than check. So in Greece and other countries with similar environments, it is difficult to raise funds through the sale of company shares because people want to place their funds in visible assets that they can control themselves.

## Family Affiliation

In the United States a family usually involves a man, a woman, and minor children, but in some parts of the world you may find in the same household several generations of the same family (vertically extended or horizontally extended—aunts, uncles, cousins).

Such large vertical or horizontal families living together have an effect on business. Rewards from an individual's work may be less effective since they may be divided among more people. Geographic mobility reduces because a move would require several people to find new jobs. Purchasing decisions can be more complicated because of the interrelated roles of family members. Even where the extended family does not live together, it may reduce mobility so that family members may remain near relatives. These people may take care of their security and social needs within the family rather than at the workplace.

## Fatalism

If workers believe strongly in self-determination, they may be more willing to work hard to achieve goals and to blame and reward themselves and others for performance. A belief in fatalism may be a barrier to the acceptance of such a basic cause-effect relationship. Religious differences also play a role here. Conservative Christian, Buddhist, Hindu, and Moslem societies tend to view occurrences as "the will of God." In this type of social climate it is hard to persuade personnel to plan ahead. Even getting workers to cooperate in accident or damage prevention could be difficult. Even managers in fairly developed societies have national differences.

Some cultures equate forecasting and planning with prophesying, which is contrary to their religious teachings. To them God—and God alone—determines the future. Such a philosophy can get in the way of forecasting and planning business procedure.

## Religion

Religion affects people's views of life, death, the hereafter, superstitions—even their dress, holidays, and work attitudes. Where it is highly unified and pervasive, therefore, religion can be the heart of a country's whole culture.

The Hindus and Buddhists are less attached to worldly goods than the Judeo-Christians. Buddhism, Confucianism, Taoism, and Hinduism dominate the Oriental cultures.

Religion expresses the philosophy of a people about many important facets of life—such as the role of women. Some societies enshrine women; others treat them as equals; and others treat them as chattels.

Not only the treatment of women but also that of elders and children varies from one culture to another. The hierarchy in other cultures as well as the patrilineal (descent through the male line of the family) plays a part in business throughout the world.

Where Americans regard change as an improvement, Chinese revere tradition (though this is changing); Latin Americans are fatalistic. Once you understand the differences in a religion, you will better understand the culture that stems from that religion. And the better you understand the culture, the better you can communicate. So you see, it is most important that you study the religion of your host country as well as the language.

## Language

**Written and Spoken.** Linguistic experts have determined that very primitive societies have complex languages that reflect the environment in which people live. Because of varied environments, translating directly from one language to another is hard. In Spanish, for example, no single word means everyone who works in a business organization. The word *empleados* refers to white-collar workers, and the word *obreros* refers to laborers. The differentiation reflects the substantial class difference attributed to each group.

Differences exist within the same language. The terms *corn, maize,* and *graduate studies* in the United Kingdom translate to *wheat, corn,* and *undergraduate studies,* respectively, in American English. The terms *public schools* and *private schools* have opposite meanings in Britain's English and American English. To an English person a lift is an elevator, a dustbin a garbage can, a bonnet the hood of a car. . . .

United States firms generally use the abbreviation Inc. for incorporated; but in Canada and the United Kingdom it is Ltd., while in Germany and Austria A G is correct. France, Italy, Spain, Portugal, and Latin America use S. A.; Sweden uses A. B.; and Japan, K. K.

American advertisers sometimes lose sight of the fact that advertising copy intended for the United States may be quite ineffective abroad even if properly translated. Expressions that are highly idiomatic or narrowly American in meaning can be hazardous. Another pitfall is the translation of advertising copy containing words that have multiple meanings and definitions or that lack direct equivalents in various foreign languages. An advertising headline that depends on a play on words peculiar to American English will not be understood sensibly in other tongues, sometimes including Britain's English.

To avoid the hazards of cross-cultural advertising (twisted messages to foreign cultures), you or your corporation should do appropriate cultural research prior to introducing a new product abroad or launching an advertising campaign in a foreign language.

Advertisers get into trouble when they rely on their own sets of cultural ideas and fail to perceive that different cultures may view a specific product, together with its advertising, quite differently. For example, a famous American designer advertised to the Latin American market a perfume that had fresh camellia scent. The fragrance did not move from the shelves of stores in Latin America because camellias are the flowers used for funerals in most of Latin America.

Cross-cultural advertisers have to evaluate—for compatibility with cultural norms—the products they introduce into a culture. For example, a toothpaste claiming to give users white teeth was especially inappropriate in many areas of Southeast Asia where betel-nut chewing is a habit among the well-to-do and the resulting black teeth are a sign of high social status.

Though certain concepts—such as the avoidance of physical pain and the sanctity of the family—are fairly universal across cultures, others (like the connotations of white teeth) quite proper in one culture may be totally unthinkable elsewhere. People in the United Kingdom, for example, often drink hot milk-based beverages just before going to bed (for supposed sleep-inducing qualities). In Thailand, however, people often drink these same hot drinks outside the home and generally on the way to work for their supposed invigorating properties. To advertise such drinks similarly in the two countries would be laughable folly.

Will there always be a problem of communication even with new advanced technologies? Among the extraordinary possibilities now on the drawing board are automatic translation devices that, in minutes, deliver an English text to a distant point in another language. Although these machines can translate, will they solve the problems we've discussed?

The world has approximately 3,000 languages, though estimates run as high as 10,000 with the inclusion of dialects—India alone counting 15 languages and 200 dialects. Can such a machine take the English idiom "You deserve a break today" and say it in Spanish so that Hispanics understand? To convey the same message, McDonalds's Hispanic agency rewrote the song to say: "You deserve to enjoy your own moment." If Tony the Tiger were to say, "They're great!" in Spanish, the phrase could be construed to mean, "They're large!"

Not all communication is through a formal language, however—much of it is through a silent language.

**Silent Language.** People communicate through the colors they wear, the distance surrounding them, gestures, dress, prestige clues, time, and even manners, morals, and etiquette.

Certain *colors* convey meanings to us based on experience within our own cultures. The United States and most Western countries have historically associated black with death, for example, while white in parts of the Far East and purple in Latin America have the same connotation. Colors of products and their ads must relate to the buyer's frame of reference.

The *distance* people keep between them during conversation is a learned process that differs in varied cultures. Americans prefer about 76 centimeters (30 inches) for face-to-face impersonal conversation, while Arabs want a distance of half that. Latin Americans and Vietnamese want to be closer when talking than do Americans. Polynesian men embrace and rub each other's backs. Some Europeans kiss the sides of the face. Americans seem to prefer to be individually cased in an imaginary bubble that protects them and keeps them from breathing down the other person's neck.

The human body is capable of over 270,000 different *gestures*, and the meanings of quite similar ones vary with where you are. Snapping the fingers of both hands and slipping an open palm over a closed fist are vulgar gestures (thus meanings) to the French. They also consider a firm and pumping handshake uncultured. When dealing with Arabs, don't cross your legs so that the sole of your foot points toward someone— it is impolite. Don't turn your back on an Iranian—that, too, is impolite.

Head shaking in some cultures has nothing to do with saying yes or no. Turks signal "No" by moving the head backward while rolling the eyes upward. In parts of India, rolling the head slowly from side to side means something like "Yes, go on; I'm listening."

The type of climate and kind of culture influence the way people dress. The type of *dress* can give the wrong silent message, however, as when some top managers from America dressed in plaid suits and white buck shoes lost a big deal with some Japanese businesspeople who said they didn't trust these Americans because of the kind of dress they wore.

*Clues* concerning a person's relative position may be difficult for people of different cultures to understand. A U.S. businessperson may underestimate the importance of a foreign counterpart who has no large private office with thick carpeting and large desk. Likewise, the foreigner may do the same if the U.S. counterparts open their own garage doors and mix their own drinks. In the United States our habits of social informality are more subtle (or gross, depending on the value position); so our desires for prestige are satisfied not by how people behave toward us but by how much they knowingly or secretly envy us. In the United States there's much reliance on objects as prestige clues.

*Time* is another confusing area. For a business appointment in the United States at 3 P.M., one usually plans to arrive a bit early; for a dinner at someone's home, one arrives on time or a few minutes late; but for a cocktail party, one may arrive a bit later. In a foreign country the accepted punctuality may change drastically. A person from the United States making a business call in Latin America, for instance, may consider it discourteous that the Latin American does not invite the visitor into the office at the appointed time. The Latin American and his wife may find it equally discourteous if the U.S. businessperson arrives at their home at the invited time for dinner. Americans generally view time as money, a resource to be saved or wasted; Latin Americans regard time in relation to other priorities. Mexicans, like other Latin Americans and the Japanese, begin interviews, meetings, and letters with an exchange of personal greetings before business discussions.

Africans view time as flexible and not rigid or segmented. People may arrive several hours late. The term *African time* means the same as the term *hora Peruana* in Spanish. In contrast, Germans are precise about time.

## Etiquette and Morals

Customs that one culture accepts may not be accepted in another. Eating habits differ, from eating with hands to eating with silverware to eating with chopsticks. The way of holding the silverware even varies between Americans and Europeans.

If a U.S. businessperson in the Far East does not take a small gift to the Far Eastern counterpart, that official may not only consider it a breach of etiquette but may also feel that the businessperson places little emphasis on the meeting and has little interest in it. On visiting most homes in Japan or Europe, you take gifts. If you decide to take flowers, avoid red roses in Germany and white chrysanthemums in France, Belgium, and Japan because they are the kinds of flowers used at funerals. Also avoid taking perfume or cologne to the Japanese because they do not like such products.

Conversely, typical Western products such as blue jeans or sunglasses will please the people—especially the Chinese. But do not expect to be invited into private homes—such an invitation is not the custom. And don't expect to offer or receive a 30-minute business lunch with a European, who would prefer visiting and doing business over a two-hour lunch in a quiet restaurant.

"In the Middle East . . . hosts are insulted if guests bring food or drink to their homes because it implies that they are not good hosts. . . . In many parts of Latin America, cutlery or handkerchiefs should not be given because these gifts imply a cutting off of a relationship or the likelihood of a tearful event. And giving a clock to someone in China is not a good idea, either. The Chinese word for clock sounds the same as their word for funeral," according to David A. Ricks, *Big Business Blunders: Mistakes in Multinational Marketing,* Dow Jones-Irwin, Homewood, Ill. 1983, p. 10.

Ricks goes on to say that even the manner of presenting a gift is important. In most parts of Asia private giving is best—to avoid embarrassment; but in the Middle East public presentation is best to reduce any impression of bribery.

In some places it is common practice to give payments to government officials for their services. The "going rate" is rather easily determined and is usually graduated on the basis of ability to pay. In countries that do not have means of collecting income taxes and do not pay their civil servants well, such payments are a fairly efficient means of taxation (though to foreign firms and their home-country constituents they look like bribes).

Far Eastern countries, where even holding hands in public is not acceptable, changed a Western ad showing a male and female in close contact and banned U.S. movies because of violent scenes. Taiwan does not permit U.S. films that depict male actors with long hair. Latin America cuts from U.S. films scenes showing bare breasts. Even Helsinki banned Donald Duck comic books because of complaints about Donald's "racy lifestyle" and morals. The Finns did not like seeing his bare bottom and his relationship with Daisy.

Many countries seek to protect children from exploitation. For example, candy companies must show a toothbrush in their ads in the Netherlands. In the United Kingdom an ad agency would violate the rules if it used someone like Captain Kangaroo or Mister Rogers in a commercial before 9 P.M. France forbids children from endorsing products on TV. Because Austria does not allow companies to use children in commercials, some advertisers have resorted to hiring dwarfs and showing animated drawings of children instead. Parker Brothers (producer of children's games), plays it safe and shows just the hands of children playing with games or turning the pages of books.

Some countries don't allow analgesic ads at all, and some won't allow companies to mention whether doctors recommend the product. Cigarette companies, also, are having a tough time keeping their brand names and images before the public. In Britain, which outlaws the Marlboro cowboy, Philip Morris Inc. couldn't even show a chuck wagon and a lit campfire in its ads because that would indicate that the cowboy was lurking nearby.

Besides recognizing international differences in etiquette and morals, silent language, spoken and written language, religions, trust, family affiliations, fatalism, and varied work motivations, you should examine the attitude of your corporation toward foreign operations. Is your firm guilty of polycentrism or ethnocentrism?

## Dangers of Polycentrism and Ethnocentrism

If you and your company become overwhelmed by the differences (real and imaginary, large and small), you are guilty of polycentrism. If a company is overly polycentric in its view, it stands the risk of being so overly cautious that it shies away from certain areas or from transferring home-country practices or resources that may work well abroad. An international firm must usually perform some functions differently from the local firms against which it competes.

More likely, however, you or your company can become too imbued with the idea that what worked at home should work abroad. If so, you are guilty of ethnocentrism. One form of this comes from forgetting that there are differences, because you have become so accustomed to certain cause-effect relationships in your home country. A belief in ethnocentrism can make for many pitfalls—so many in fact that whole books are now available on international corporation blunders.

Another form involves recognizing differences but assuming that the introduction of the needed changes is easily achieved. Between the extremes of polycentrism and ethnocentrism are desirable hybrid business practices that are not exactly patterned after either the international company's home operations or those of the typical host-country firm. For lack of a better word, we'll call this Equacentrism.

## Equacentrism

A firm may not only change things abroad but may also alter its own product and activities to fit the foreign environment. In this way it may learn things useful in its own home operations. Foreign operations give companies opportunities of experimenting with adaptations to local environments, experiments that may later be applied to the United States or to a small segment of its society.

Coca-Cola learned years ago that it had to adapt its drink formula to the taste of the country where it distributed. R. J. Reynolds Tobacco has set up a joint venture with China and will produce a Sino-American cigarette that will satisfy Chinese smokers (and the packages will not have to carry any warning about the dangers of smoking). Reynolds and Chinese officials are exploring a possible future deal involving Kentucky Fried Chicken—again to please Chinese eaters.

Adapting to taste is one thing. When changes do not interfere with deep-seated customs, then accommodation is much more likely. When Sears, Roebuck opened its first retail store in Spain, one of the main problems was with suppliers. Sears used the same practices as it used in the United States. Among the many changes that Sears tried to introduce at the start were payments by check, firm delivery dates, standard sizes, no manufacturer's labels, and large orders. Suppliers balked or did things their old way and claimed forgetfulness.

A Spanish textile factory opened in Guatemala and tried to install training methods, work hours, and many other production "improvements" that were commonplace in more developed areas. People refused to work to the point that soldiers were called in to protect the factory from the community.

The management retracted and gave in on those things that were most important to the workers. These included a four-hour period between shifts so that male workers could attend to agricultural duties and so that female workers could do home chores and nurse their infants. To make up the time, the laborers were willing to work Saturday afternoons in order to compensate for lost production during the breaks.

One way of avoiding undue problems if possible changes are to be introduced is to promote participation. If managers can discuss the possibility of change, then they may learn how strong the resistance is, how to stimulate the recognition of a need for improvement, and how to dampen fears of adverse consequences among workers who otherwise might feel they have no say in their own destinies.

Another way to avoid undue problems is reward sharing. A worker may not see any benefit in making a change, and until the worker does, there's little incentive to shift to new work practices. For example, a U.S. corporation manufacturing electrical appliances in Mexico moved workers easily from radio to black-and-white television production. When the time came to work on color television, however, defects increased. Investigations showed that workers were eager to turn out a high-quality black-and-white set because they or their friends might be consumers. The prices of the color set, though, were so far beyond their reach that they had no incentive to be careful in their production. The U.S. firm therefore developed a bonus system for quality, with rewards in monetary compensation or prestige.

By finding the local channels of influence, an international firm may locate opinion leaders to help speed up the acceptance of change. In Ghana government health workers frequently ask permission and seek the help of village witch doctors before inoculating people or spraying huts to fight malaria. In this way they achieve the desired result without destroying the important social structure. One U.S. firm operating in Mexico sent low-level workers rather than supervisors to the parent plant in the United States. These workers returned as heroes among their peers and were believed and emulated when they demonstrated new work habits.

It would be an extreme of ethnocentrism to believe that all knowledge emanates from one's home country. In the case of U.S. firms, more are realizing that in many activities the United States lags behind. Their foreign operations, therefore, give them opportunities to experiment with adaptations to local environments.

With the right planning, studying, and working, perhaps you can be a part of a foreign operation and have such interesting and well-paid opportunities of adapting to local environments.

For further study of international business you might like to look into the programs at the American Graduate School of International Management, Glendale, Arizona (called Thunderbird School); Baruch College, New York; Brigham Young University, Provo, Utah; George Washington University, Washington, D.C.; Lauder Institute of the Wharton School of Business, Philadelphia; Pace University, New York; MIBS (Master of International Business Study), University of South Carolina, Columbia.

## Questions and Exercises

1. Make up an example of stroking for an imaginary someone who is under your direction on the job and has written an excellent report for you.

2. Name three of the five common errors that can prevent an acceptable balance of personalities.

3. Why is stereotyped language a mark of discourtesy?

4. Besides quality, selection, convenience (closeness), and price, on what other bases do you choose the places where you buy food, clothing, shelter (unless your own home); meals out, snacks and drinks, entertainment; transportation vehicles (and service on them)?

5. Be ready (on request) to cite a specific instance of some businessperson's *(a)* not keeping a proper balance of personalities with you, *(b)* lack of courtesy, *(c)* lack of sincerity, *(d)* lack of proper gratitude, *(e)* lack of service attitude.

6. Conversely (to 5), cite an instance of good *(a)* balance, *(b)* courtesy, *(c)* sincerity, *(d)* gratitude, *(e)* service attitude.

7. *(a)* What are the two best ways to convey necessary faultfinding (accusing) to another person in a letter or memo? *(b)* Which would you use, and how would you use it, if you were finding fault with a person (1) under you in a job? (2) over you in a job?

8. How could you improve your personality in order to be more acceptable for an overseas assignment?

9. How do you think you would measure on a thematic apperception test (TAT)?

10. After visiting an office of a CEO or the president of your university, describe the prestige clues you noticed.

11. What values in your culture do you consider superior to those of another culture?

12. What values in your culture do you consider inferior to those of another culture?

13. When you think of an English, Japanese, and Arabian business executive, what pictures come to your mind? What are the main differences?

14. In Germany the line "Kellogg makes cornflakes the best they've ever been" would be disapproved because of rules against making competitive claims. Can you think of any other U.S. advertisement that would be disapproved for the same reason?

*Improve the tone in each of the following:*

1. We were disappointed to learn that you are not taking advantage of our offer of a week's free advertising space. This was a favor we offered at no benefit to us.

2. Due to an error in processing your order, it will be billed twice to your account. A credit has been issued, and we hope you have not been inconvenienced.

3. You must comply with our request. We shall have to institute legal action against you if you don't remit the full amount of your liability by March 1.

4. We regret to inform you that the merchandise you ordered is not available. Because of this, we have been forced to cancel your order.

5. You are mistaken in your assumption that we will pay this bill!

6. We note in your letter of May 29 that you claim not to have received your order. We will look into this and, if necessary, send a second shipment without delay.

# Chapter Outline

# 5

# Considering Persuasion Principles

In business you're nearly always trying to sell something—whether it's an idea, a product, or a service. Your business communications, therefore (unless just reporting information), try to produce an action or a reaction that may soon lead to an action.

If you are going to be successful in that mission, you'll want to make conscious use of five principles that have proved helpful in getting the desired response:

1. Planned presentation in the light of your objective.
2. You-viewpoint interpretation.
3. Adaptation—even personalization when possible.
4. Positive statement.
5. Success consciousness.

## Planned Presentation

You can make your job of beginning a letter, memo, report, or talk simple if you will classify it according to one of the following three probable reactions of your reader(s) or listener(s).

1. Will they welcome it? That is, does it say things they will be glad to hear or at least not unhappy to hear? Does it take action they have requested? Does it request action they are prepared to take?
2. Will the basic message displease them? Does it contain bad news?
3. Or does it request action they are probably not already willing to take—and therefore require persuasion?

### Good-News or Neutral Messages

When you are doing what the other person wants you to do, *the first sentence should contain the big idea*—whether your message goes to

**Figure 5–1 / Good-News and Neutral Messages**

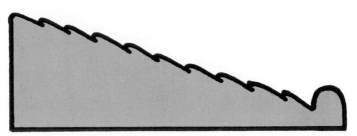

somebody of equal, lower, or higher rank. Then you follow up with necessary details in order of relative importance or natural sequence. Frequently messages of this kind (including oral ones) end with a short punch line recalling the benefits of the good news in the beginning, as suggested by Figure 5–1.

Letters, memos, and talks that merely seek or transmit business information follow the same basic order. Among them are inquiries and replies about job or credit applicants and facts about an organization, its personnel, or its products. All of these are neutral situations (neither very pleasing nor displeasing), readily taken for granted.

> Aloha and Congratulations, Jim!
>
> You have earned a week's trip to the leadership conference at the Royal Hawaiian in Honolulu, Oahu, February 7–14. You won this glorious vacation because you were in the top 2 percent in sales last year. General Selectric pays for all your and your wife's expenses, including flights on United.
>
> All winners meet for a hospitality hour at the Hilton Airport Motel, 4–7 P.M., Los Angeles, February 7. As you'll see on the enclosed itinerary, in Hawaii you'll have plenty of time for sight-seeing, swimming, playing tennis or golf, dancing, eating, and shopping. One day we'll island-hop to Maui, Kauai, and the big island, Hawaii.
>
> So that I can make your reservations, please let me know your plans by January 15.

A note of caution is in order here, however: In good-news messages to people whose native language is not English (particularly Latin and Oriental people), *the desirable directness must not rule out their conventional beginning expressions of courtesy, politeness, and cordiality.*

### Disappointing Messages

Bad-news messages—those that say no or "yes, but . . ."—should not be direct, especially if they go up the status ladder. If you have to tell someone that you can't give the booklet requested, that you can't fill an order as specified, that you can't extend credit, that you can't offer the requested job, or that you can't make the adjustment desired, you have a situation that is goodwill-killing—if you blurt out the disappointing information immediately.

Assuming that you are a fair-minded person who has good reasons when you refuse anything, you can do better. In most cases you can show that some of your reasons are beneficial to the other person—as when a mother refuses her child something for the child's good. The following psychology of refusing therefore depends on your having good reasons, as does any satisfactory refusal.

If you start pleasantly and give justifying reasons *before* a refusal, your logical reasons fall on a logical mind. Your good reasons can therefore convince the other (logical) person that you *are* justified—and to accept your refusal without irritation because you show the justice of it. This psychology directs you to a rather specific strategy for all refusals.

To soften the effect, you try to catch favorable interest in your opening remarks with *something from the situation on which both of you can agree—but carefully NOT misleading on the major point.* Effective business communicators use this kind of pleasant beginning (commonly called a "buffer") for two reasons: (1) to suggest that they are reasonable persons who can see two sides of the question and (2) to set the stage for a review of the facts. A good buffer will therefore be

- Pleasant, usually agreeing with something the other person has said.
- Relevant, thus quickly showing the subject.
- Equivocal, avoiding any implication that the main answer is yes or no.
- Transitional, carefully worded for a natural movement into the explanation.

This word of caution about buffers is due, however: In being pleasant and agreeable, be careful about the third point and do *not* say something that later seems contradictory. A buffer inconsistent with later statements loses more than its effectiveness.

After you establish compatibility, you analyze the circumstances sympathetically and understandingly, giving the reasons why you can't do what the other person wants you to do. *Only after you have tactfully prepared the way with these justifying reasons do you want to reveal or even imply the disappointing news.*

You further attempt to soften the blow by such subordinating means as embedding the refusal, giving it minimum space or time, and making a positive statement when you have to state it. But better, you can usually

**Figure 5–2 / Disappointing Messages**

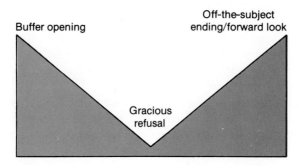

make the refusal clear by implication. Certainly you do not want to stress it—and if you are communicating with an Asian, you go even further with these subordinating devices to convey a negative message gently.

Graphically, your procedure looks like the line in Figure 5–2. The following positive refusal illustrates the strategy:

Your comments, Professor McGinnis, on the effectiveness of the "More Business" series are helpful to us at Read's who worked on these practical guides for users of direct marketing.

When we first planned the booklets for our customers, we had in mind a checklist for a business using direct marketing extensively rather than a thoroughgoing treatment suitable for a textbook. Accordingly, we set our quota for noncommercial users at a low figure--partly because we did not expect many requests.

Since the series has proved so popular with our customers, we have been distributing our limited copies only to commercial users, although we are glad to make available what we can to educational institutions.

Perhaps you can use the extra copy--sent to you this morning--as a circulating library for your students. Two or three days' use should be ample for most of them, and they're perfectly welcome to quote anything they care to.

Will you give us the benefit of your suggestions for making the series more extensive and helpful after you have had an opportunity to test its teachability?

## Persuasive Messages

For even the third basic kind of situation, starting need not be difficult. Just figure out something you can offer that the reader or listener wants, needs, or at least is interested in. Preferably it will be a promised or implied benefit, thus catching attentive interest from the start. You then develop your message in concrete pictures of the benefits available for complying with your suggestion. After enough evidence for conviction, you are in a psychological position to ask for the action you want. Figure 5–3 illustrates the plan.

**Figure 5–3 / Persuasive Messages**

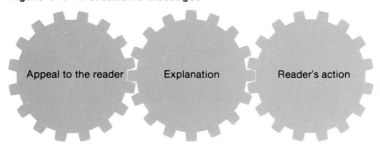

Appeal to the reader    Explanation    Reader's action

Prospecting (cold turkey) sales and application letters, executive memos calling for improved operations, persuasive requests, and some collections follow this strategy, as in the following persuasive request for a confidential manual:

How often have you received--even from well-educated people--letters that are not worth your attention?

As a public relations director and an employer, you are of course interested in this problem. And I, as a teacher of business communication, am too. Here at Harwood we're turning out several hundred students each year who are better trained in writing effective letters and memos than the usual college graduate. We'd like to be sure, however, that we're up-to-date in giving them what business wants.

Quite likely, you know, some of these students will someday be writing for companies like yours. Wouldn't they be better prepared if we stressed the ideas that you have emphasized in your recent

correspondence manual? Both the students and
business firms would benefit from your letting us
have a copy for our teaching files. Of course,
we'd handle the material with whatever confidence
you specify, and we'd be most grateful for this
practical teaching aid.

But the ones especially benefiting from your
sending a copy would be the students and business
firms like GE. Will you send us a copy today?

The planned steps in all persuasion are here. You get attentive interest
quickly by promising or mentioning a prospective benefit, give explanation
backing up that promised benefit, forestall or minimize any objections
you can foresee, and confidently ask for the action you want.

## You-Viewpoint

The you-viewpoint or you-attitude is a state of mind: bringing out and
emphasizing the benefits to the other person resulting from your suggestion or decision and subordinating or eliminating (but not denying) your
own.

Of course, it isn't pure unselfishness. When you try to sell something,
obviously you are trying to make some money; but you don't need to
put that idea into words. When you attempt to collect, obviously you
want the money; you don't need to put that idea into words. When
you apply for a job, obviously you either want or need work to earn
some money; you don't need to put that idea into words. When you
try to step up the corporation ladder or change company policy, you
don't need to put those ideas into words. Both parties involved *assume*
all these ideas. Putting them into words merely sounds selfish, wastes
words, and helps your cause not one bit.

Nor is the you-attitude a question merely of politeness, courtesy, or
good manners. The business reason for you-viewpoint presentation is
that it gets results. *When you show that you are aware of and are doing
something about another person's needs or problems, your suggestion will
get a favorable reaction.* In other words, you can get the action you
want if—and only if—you show benefits worth the cost and trouble.

So in persuasive messages (asking for action the other person is not
already motivated to take) you show by central theme and wording that
you are thinking of what you can offer in return for the action you
request at the end.

The you-viewpoint requires imagination, certainly. The old story of
how the village half-wit found the mule is apt ("Why, I just thought,
'If I was a mule, where would I go?'"). The ability to visualize someone

else's desires, circumstances, and probable reactions and write or speak in those terms is the answer. It requires that you be able to play many roles. Whether you communicate to managers, doctors, or merchants, you try to see things through *their* eyes.

You are more likely to communicate in terms of another person if you use *you* and *your* more often than the first-person pronouns *I, me, mine, we, us, our.* But if you apply that test alone, the sentence "We want your check" has more you-viewpoint than "We want our check," when obviously neither has any. The you-attitude sentence might well read, "To keep your account in the preferred-customer class, please send your check for $142.63 today." What is significant is that the *you*-viewpoint is there.

| We-Viewpoint | You-Viewpoint |
|---|---|
| We have a dividend reinvestment plan. We can defer the payment of federal income taxes on dividends that are reinvested in new shares of our common stock. | As a stockholder, you can defer federal income taxes on your dividends reinvested in new shares of common stock. |
| We have spent six years making Janus diskettes fast-selling. | Back of your Janus diskettes are six years of successful testing and improvement. Because we verify every sector on every disk, you will virtually never get a "Bad sector on A:DOS" error. |

Making your reader or listener the subject or object of most sentences will help you keep you-viewpoint interpretation too. As you've already seen in the discussion of writing interestingly (in Chapter 3), psychological description and dramatized copy are *effective because they keep the reader involved and show that you have the you-viewpoint.* The only way to get it in the first place, however, is to subordinate your own reactions to those you estimate are the other person's and to show that attitude clearly by your wording.

An example of well-intentioned writing that is fundamentally bad (because writer-dominated) is the conventional thank-you beginning: "We are glad to have . . . ." It emphasizes the personal reaction of the writer rather than something the reader is interested in knowing. The same is true of the common, and weak, speech openings "I'm glad to be here . . ." and Thank you for . . . ."

If you agree with a request or can fill an order, an opening like the following has more you-viewpoint because it is something your reader wants to know:

```
Your suggestion of getting the general manager's
help on our planning is in effect. I've made the
arrangements.

Your . . . should arrive (prepaid UPS) by Friday,
June 7.
```

If you can't do as suggested, a favorable comment is a good example of you-viewpoint:

```
Having our chief accountant in on our planning
session would indeed be a good idea if she were
not already committed to an out-of-town assignment
at the time.
```

When somebody has done you a favor and your main message is appreciation, some form of thank-you may be one of the best beginnings you could use. In other situations, in place of the conventional "Dear Mr. Miller," the salutation "Thank you, Mr. Miller!" has directness and enthusiasm that are heartwarming. The first paragraph may then concentrate on a more significant point:

```
Those articles about palletization that you
suggested contain some of the best information
I've been able to uncover.
```

But doesn't the statement of the significance you attach to your reader's contribution adequately establish your appreciation, without wasting words with "Thank you"?

That question does not imply that an expression of gratitude is improper (see "Gratitude" in Chapter 4), but it should be a reminder that (1) you usually have something more important to put in the emphatic beginning position and (2) besides, you can accomplish the same thank-you function with some statement that will place more emphasis on your reader—where it should be!

## Adaptation

The preceding remarks concerning planned presentation and you-viewpoint apply whether you're writing a memorandum, making a speech, or sending a special or form letter. The closer you can come to making your reader or listener nod in agreement and think "That's what I want to hear," the greater your possibilities for a favorable reception.

When you can make the other person also think "That sure fits me," you have an additional advantage. Successful adaptation gives the feeling that you had the one person specifically in mind.

Even in addressing a large number of people, you will usually have identifiable common characteristics (of geography, age, educational level, vocation, or income status, for example). By thinking about them, you can adapt your persuasion points, language, and style and make references to circumstances and events recognized as fitting each member of the group.

## Adapting Talking Points

In adapting talking points (or theme), you simply *seek out and emphasize those reasons you believe will be most influential in causing the particular receivers to take the action or have the reaction you want.* Specifically, you would try to sell a word processor to a secretary on the basis of ease of operation, to an office manager on the basis of ease of maintenance and durability, but to a purchasing agent on the basis of long-range cost. A car may appeal to one person on the basis of economy, power, or dependability of operation; to another the appeals of appearance, status, and comfort may be stronger.

Accordingly, you adapt your talking points for increased persuasiveness. This is a fairly simple procedure when you are dealing with one person, and it is entirely possible in a group if you study the characteristics common to all the people involved.

## Adapting Language and Style

You adapt language and style, in general, in the light of the other person's (or persons') age, educational level, and vocation (which influence social and economic position). As years, education, professional and social prestige, and financial status increase, you are safer in using longer sentences, uncommon words, and more formal language (but remember the discussion of readability in Chapter 3).

Sometimes you will want to use the specialized terms of vocational classes such as doctors, lawyers, accountants, and insurance people. Although some of these terms are too specialized for a general audience, to specialists they convey the impression that you understand their special problems. The application of this suggestion means that when you write or talk to doctors, references to patients, laboratories, diagnoses, and the like help; to a person in insurance, prospects, premiums, and expirations are likely referents. Accountants (especially those in the IRS) feel at home with your use of such terms as gross income, deductions, exemptions, interest, dividends, capital gains, and especially Form 1040!

### Referring to Common Experiences

Better adaptation than language and style, however, are references to common experiences. A reference to vocation, to a geographic factor, to some home and family status—in fact, to any activity or reaction you can be reasonably sure your readers or listeners have experienced—rings the bell of recognition and makes them feel that very definitely you are talking to them and about their conditions.

In a letter to managers, for instance, the following reference would almost universally bring positive recognition:

```
When the computer breaks down and the maintenance
crew is preoccupied . . . .
```

To stockbrokers:

```
Predictions for a market gain of . . . .
```

To nurses working in a hospital:

```
When your last rounds are made and the
patients . . . .
```

To students:

```
You rush to class and the class has . . . (been
dismissed, moved).
```

Any of the preceding phrases could go into a form or an individualized message. The more specifically you can phrase these references to make them pinpoint one person, however, the more effective your adaptation will be.

### Personalizing

The starting purpose of specific adaptation is, of course, to further the impression that you have prepared the message for the individual. To heighten the feeling of friendliness, business communicators sometimes use names or other individualizing references in a few of the sentences. At about the middle, much as you use a friend's name in conversation, or near the end, in the same way you frequently use a person's name in ending a conversation, such references as the following help give the impression that your message is for one person rather than a group:

```
Your Dallas commercial designers and interior
planners will be glad to call on you and answer
any questions, Mr. Weiler.
```

Lest you overvalue the effectiveness of this name-calling, however, remember these shortcomings and dangers:

1. It is a somewhat mechanical process and probably the least effective means of adapting.

2. In typing names on forms, you may do more harm than good unless you match type perfectly. Of course, a word processor can do the job neatly.

3. And, as you saw under "Undue Familiarity" in Chapter 4, using a person's name too frequently (as is done in many computerized letters) may do more harm than good by seeming unctuous and fawning.

You can also increase the feeling of friendliness in letters by the wording of your salutation and complimentary close (as explained in Chapter 2). Of far greater significance, however, are adaptation of talking points and lifelike references to the reader's activities—in other words, dramatized copy, as explained in Chapter 3 and illustrated in this chapter.

The following letter answers the lady's questions in a sound sales presentation and enhances the persuasiveness of the message with special references (such as the references to the attendant and the power failure mentioned in her inquiry) that could apply to no one but the reader:

Dear Mrs. Jackson:

The Stair-Traveler you saw in the June Home and Yard will certainly make daily living easier for you and your attendant. You can make as many trips upstairs and downstairs as you care to every day and still follow your doctor's advice.

Simply sit down on the bench (the size of a dressing-table stool) and press the button. Gently and smoothly your Stair-Traveler takes you upstairs just a little faster than ordinary walking. Should the electricity fail in Greenbriar while you're using your Stair-Traveler, automatic brakes bring it to a gentle stop until the current comes on. Then you just press the button to start it again.

Folded back against the wall when not in use, the Stair-Traveler's simple, straight lines of mahogany will blend in well with your antiques. Your Stair-Traveler will be right at home on your front straight stairway, Mrs. Jackson. It will be more convenient for you there, and the installation is simple and economical. Notice the folded Stair-Traveler on page 3 of the enclosed booklet; it looks somewhat like a console table.

To explain how simple and economical installing your Stair-Traveler can be, Mr. J. B. Nickle, our Springfield representative, will be glad to call at a time convenient for you. Just use the enclosed postcard to let him know when that will be.

Such specialized references do increase costs when they mean writing an individual message rather than using a form. Even in form paragraphs and entire form letters, however, you can make some adaptation to the reader's situation.

You can find out a great deal about your reader through a telemarketing service or buying/renting a mailing list that has names of people with common characteristics of vocation, location, age, sex, finances, and buying and living habits. You can also get valuable information from reports, memos, and letters you receive; sales representatives' reports; and credit records (including credit reports). You won't make your message do all it could do if you don't use these characteristics to adapt it according to talking points and endow it with the marginal pulling power of known references to familiar events, activities, places, or persons.

## Positive Statement

Your letters, memos, and oral communications have greater prospects for success if you focus on positive ideas too—because people respond more favorably to a positive prospect than to a negative one.

Saying the cheerful, positive thing that people want to hear rather than the unpleasant or unhappy, negative thing is really just an extension of you-viewpoint. It comes from staying optimistic yourself and presenting a positive picture—at least subordinating any negative idea. Translated into business communication procedures, *it is stressing what something is rather than what it is not, emphasizing what the firm or product can and will do rather than what it cannot do, leading with action rather than apology or explanation, and avoiding words that convey basically unpleasant ideas.*

Test after test of both advertising copy and letter copy has demonstrated the wisdom of positive statement. That is why years ago successful copywriters warned against the denied negative and today's effective writer or speaker will make the following positive statements rather than their negative counterparts:

| Negative | Positive |
|---|---|
| I have no experience other than being an accounting intern for Filbey and Filbey one summer. | Working as an accounting intern for Filbey and Filbey one summer taught me . . . . |

| Negative | Positive |
|---|---|
| We are sorry that we do not have the annual report ready. | After checking with the Production Department, we can assure you that our annual report will be mailable February 26. |
| We cannot ship in lots of less than 12. | To keep down packaging costs and to help customers save on shipping costs, we ship in lots of 12 or more. |

A special form of negativism is the challenging question that invites a negative answer. Although it contains no negative wording, "What could be finer than money in your checking account?" will elicit, among other answers, "Stocks, bonds, real estate!" Such questions—along with the apparently harmless "Why not try a Blank product?"—get people out of step with you and, because they invite a negative response, are deterrents to the success of your suggestion.

Keeping your messages positive also means deliberately excluding negative words. You can't be "sorry" about something without recalling the initial unhappy experience. You can't say "unfortunately" without restating some gloomy aspect of a situation. Nor can you mention "delay," "broken," "damages," "unable to," "cannot," "inconvenience," "difficulty," "disappointment," and other negatives without making people react against you rather than with you. Even a "however," after you've been talking pleasant things, will surely give a kind of sinking feeling.

*The effective way is through accentuating the positive, eliminating the negative where possible, and otherwise subordinating it* (see **Emp** and **Neg** in Appendix C).

## Success Consciousness

Success consciousness is the favorable, positive attitude that your reader or listener will do what you ask or accept the decision you present. To reflect this attitude, guard against any phrasing that suggests that you may fail.

Success consciousness is your own conviction that your explanation is adequate, your suggestion legitimate and valuable, and your decision the result of adequate evidence and logical, businesslike reasoning. Thus assured yourself, you are not likely to suggest that you are unsure of your ground. The sales writer who says

```
If you'd like to take advantage of this
timesaving piece of equipment,. . . .
```

would be better off not to remind the reader of the option to reject the proposal. Simply omitting the phrase *if you'd like* establishes a tone of greater confidence. The one word *if* is the most frequent destroyer of success consciousness.

Likewise, when tempted to say

```
Why not try a simple order?
```

you should remember that the suggestion is stronger with the elimination of *why not*, which not only suggests that you are not sure but invites reasons for not doing what you want.

*Hope* and its synonym *trust* are second only to *if* as destroyers of success consciousness. In proposing an adjustment, the sentence

```
We hope you'll approve of our decision.
```

gains success consciousness (and thus better response) when reworded:

```
With this extension of your contract for our
professional personnel-screening services, you can
continue to select only high-quality employees in
these critical times.
```

By assumption (implication)—by definitely omitting the doubtful-sounding expression—the seller seems to say, "Of course, you and I realize that this is what you want."

In refusals something like the following sentence sometimes appears in an otherwise well-written message:

```
We trust you will understand our position.
```

Usually, however, it appears in a poor one. And it is most frequently the result of inadequate explanation. If so, revise your explanation so that it is convincing—and substitute some positive, confident statement for the weak-kneed expression.

Even in simple replies the problem arises with such a sentence as

```
We hope this is the information you wanted.
```

The implications of doubt disappear quickly and easily with

```
We're glad to send you this information.
```

This principle of success consciousness applies in all types of business writing and speaking, but it is most significant in sales situations—and especially in the action ending.

A word of caution against high-pressure presumptuousness is in order here, however. To omit a reference to an alternative is one thing; to imply that no alternative exists is quite another! The job applicant who so boldly and confidently asks

```
When may I come in to see you?
```

gives the impression that the prospective employer has no alternative but to set up an interview. Such presumptuousness may irritate—at a critical time. Rephrased in a manner like the following, a request for an interview would strike most people favorably:

```
Will you name a convenient time when I may come
in and tell you more about why I believe I am the
aggressive sales representative you're looking
for?
```

The proper degree of success consciousness requires careful wording, particularly at the end. Basically, you need to consider what your purpose is.

Sometimes you want someone to take no overt action on the topic—as in most negative messages and some good-news messages. In that case, you may end with a pleasant comment or further support for something said earlier (thanks or resale, for example), with an off-the-subject comment (usually a pleasant look to the future, perhaps sales promotion material), or with something else pleasant. Certainly you want to avoid suggesting inadequacy of treatment and such jargon as "Please do not hesitate . . ." or "Feel free to. . . ." And in negative messages guard particularly against referring to the trouble you've supposedly cleared up.

At other times you are asking for action that is simple, easy, and likely—as in most good-news messages (no strong reader resistance). Here a subtle reference to that action is most appropriate:

```
I shall appreciate your answers to . . . .
You are cordially invited to . . . .
When you send in your check for the $27.50 now
due, please . . . .
```

In persuasive letters, memos, proposals, and talks your push for action—to overcome resistance—must continue to the end. Here particularly, such words as *if, trust,* and *hope* show a lack of success consciousness that is self-defeating.

As you see, each situation requires a quite different ending. You will do well, therefore, to keep in mind the principle of success consciousness as you study the discussions, illustrations, and checklists for different business messages throughout this book.

One important general point deserves your attention here, however: Even though the earlier part of the message may have indicated a desired action, you need to *refer to, suggest, ask for, or push for that action at the end.*

# Exercises

1. From your own experience, tell an instance where you or somebody else applied or ignored the principles of planned presentation in
   a. A good-news message.
   b. A bad-news message.
   c. A situation calling for persuasion.

2. From your own experience, tell an instance in which you or somebody else used or ignored the you-attitude; then tell how it might have been (for better or worse).

3. From your own experience, provide an example of effective or ineffective adaptation; then tell how it might have been (for better or worse).

4. From the many points you would like to get across to varied people, cite one in positive-statement form (and provide a less positive statement for comparison).

5. Give an instance of a politician's (preferably presidential) use of success consciousness—whether effective or ineffective and whether justified or patently pretended.

6. Give any evidence or reasoning (not speculation) you can that any of the principles in this chapter might not work equally well in some other culture.

*Rewrite for you-attitude, positive aspect, and goodwill:*

7. You cannot have an IRA unless you pay $2,000.

8. No more than 18 people should sign up for our management seminar.

9. I regret to inform you that beginning October 1, 198-, our premium for hospitalization insurance has increased.

10. You did not return your proxy material. Unfortunately, we do not have the authority to vote your shares on one or more of the matters to be acted upon at the meeting.

11. You failed to send us the check for $210 you owe us. Won't you drop it in the mail today?

## Applications of Part Two Principles

A. From a current magazine, book, or newspaper, find a passage (or passages) using sexist language in at least five sentences. Rephrase the sentences to eliminate the sexism, and submit your work in a form that shows clearly the original and the revision.

B. For the second paragraph under the section "Make It Easy and Interesting to Read" (early in Chapter 3):

1. Figure the Fog Index.
2. Rewrite it as best you can.
3. Figure the Fog Index on your rewrite.

C. Which is better, and why?

1. a. I am enclosing a letter from Marvin E. Grimm of Bohn Manufacturing Company, telling why he recommended Pace's Gilsonite asphalt.
   b. The enclosed letter from Marvin E. Grimm shows why he recommends Pace's Gilsonite asphalt.
2. a. We also checked with the Better Business Bureau and got nothing but reassurance when we were told that there had been no complaints of any kind regarding Pace's Gilsonite asphalt.
   b. The Better Business Bureau assures us that Pace does the job smoothly and efficiently.
3. a. For the reasons listed on the attached sheet, the cost runs to $5,000, or about 2½ times as much as your proposal.
   b. I regret to inform you that the cost runs 2½ times as much as your proposal.
4. a. You have been kind, helpful, and considerate in letting us come to a decision. Call us anytime.
   b. We want to thank you for your help, time, patience in our deliberations. Feel free to call me anytime.

D. As a practice exercise, set up one of the following messages in acceptable format, content, and wording as your instructor directs:

1. *Letterhead:* Visacharge, P.O. Box 21245, Greensboro, NC 27420. *Inside address:* S. C. Suderburg, 464 Sheffield Drive, Winston-Salem, NC 27104. *Signature block:* Sincerely yours, James E. Holmes III, Bank Card Department. *Subject:* Account No.: 4560 0302 0230 8952.

*Body:* The cost of maintaining inactive Visacharge accounts has over the years become prohibitive. For this reason, we can no longer continue to issue replacement cards on accounts that have been inactive for extended periods. Since you have not chosen to make regular use of your account, we unfortunately have no alternative but to cancel it and ask that all cards in your possession be destroyed. We regret that this is necessary and trust that you will not be inconvenienced. We would welcome any inquiries that you may wish to make. If we can be of any assistance to you, call us toll free.

2. *Letterhead:* City Bank, 8976 Cornwall Avenue, Cape Girardeau, MO 63710. Use current date. *Inside address:* Mrs. C. M. Worm, Rt. 2, Box 534-F, Evergreen, MO 64890. *Signature block:* Sincerely, H. M. Granger, Loan Officer.

*Body:* We can't give you the $3,000 loan you asked for because you have less-than-satisfactory credit record. We don't like to loan money to elementary school teachers for they don't make a good salary and they often don't work in the summer. Also divorced people have more financial problems than the marrieds.

3. *Letterhead:* The Patrician Group, 402 Park Avenue, New York, NY 10022. Use current date. *Inside address:* Mr. Jeffrey Simon, 32 River Oaks, Williston, VT 04598. *Signature block:* Cordially, Marian D. Ryan, President.

*Body:* We know that you are a relatively wealthy man, Mr. Simon, and that you are proud of your country. We want your donation so that we can help the poor and starving children in Africa.

We are a reputable organization, so send $100, $200, $500, $1,000. If you don't give, your conscience will bother you. Remember those pictures on TV and in the magazines of the pot-bellied hungry children who didn't ask to be brought into this world.

4. *Letterhead:* Widget Machines, 987 West Second Street, Dayton, OH 45498. Use current date. *Inside address:* Provident Mutual Insurance Company, Canyon Office Complex, Little Rock, AR 72204. *Signature block:* Yours very truly, Sydney Hampton, Director of Sales. Attention line: Attention General Agent.

*Body:* You can tell your secretary that she won't make errors using Widget word processors. When one of your top salesmen dictates his sales report over the phone, all she has to do is convert his dictation to the word processor. And even if she can't spell (as many secretaries can't), Widget does the spelling for her.

Because I know you are a busy General Agent, I'm not going to keep using this Widget to tell you about what a fine product it is, but am enclosing a descriptive folder that tells all. If you are interested in seeing how our product can save you money and time, I'll have our salesman in your area make a call on you. To get him to come around, fill out the enclosed self-addressed stamped card.

5. *Company name:* Continental. Use current date. Memo to: James T. Moore, Research and Development. From Richard Welch, Director of Marketing. No subject line.

*Body:* I wish to congratulate you on your recent promotion and increase in pay. But I'm sorry that others like Jim Borden who has been with the company 25 years got passed over. Guess you have some in or know-how that pleases the CEO.

# Part Three

## Psychological Planning for Effectiveness

# Chapter Outline

**Direct Inquiries**
**Favorable Replies**
   Replies without Sales Possibilities
   Replies with Sales Possibilities
**Short Transmittal Messages**
**Form Enclosures, Letters, and Documents**
   Enclosures
   Form Letters, Memos, and Paragraphs
   Short Note Replies
**Orders**
**Standard Acknowledgments**
**Credit Approvals**
   Establishing the Basis for Credit
   Explanation of Terms
   Stimulating Sales
   Making the Customer Feel Welcome and Appreciated
**Simple Claims and Adjustment Approvals**
   Direct Claims
   Adjustment Approvals
**Special Goodwill Messages**
   Giving Deserved Praise
   Expressing Appreciation
   Sending Seasonal Greetings
   Conveying Sympathy
   Extending Welcomes and Invitations
   Anticipating Resistance
   Improving Services
**Questions and Exercises**

# 6

# Good-News and Goodwill Messages

Though businesspeople use the telephone for many of the simpler kinds of neutral and good-news messages discussed in this chapter, they are also using more and more letters and memos. For efficiency in handling varied situations as a manager, employee, or individual conducting your own business affairs, therefore, you need the skills and techniques to write the messages well.

As you learned in Chapter 5, messages that please the receiver should be direct. The emphasis should be on speed, specificness, completeness, and conciseness. Inquiries, favorable replies, credit approvals, adjustment approvals, and special goodwill letters are typical direct-style messages.

Most of the communications you're likely to prepare in doing business internationally (Chapter 4) will also be direct exchanges of information. Often they will be by telex or short covering letters supplemented by standardized forms for establishing credit, quoting prices and terms or conditions, and invoicing shipments.

## Direct Inquiries

Any firm that wants to stay in business welcomes inquiries about products, services, operations, and personnel. The possibility of making a sale will motivate a reply concerning the firm's products. An inquiry about routine operations will get a reply out of simple business friendship. Requests for information about job and credit applicants get ready answers because giving such information is established business courtesy and is reciprocating.

In a direct inquiry, therefore, your problem is making clear exactly what you want, so that the willing responder can give you the necessary information as quickly and easily as possible. Resolve this problem by beginning directly and being specific and concise, as in this interoffice memo:

> What day in October will you schedule the annual
> R&D Plans Board meeting? I want to be sure both my
> department heads will be free to attend.
>
> Will we meet in the main conference room at
> headquarters as we did last year?

Out-of-the-ordinary questions involving special conditions require detailed answers for satisfaction. Because they also require explanation before the reader can get a clear picture, they are better set out in expository paragraph form, as in the following:

> Where will the World Business Communication
> Convention meet this year, and when? I believe
> Professor Arvind M. Velankar of Pune, India, said
> that the meeting would be in Tokyo in November.
>
> Since I'll be spending all of November in Japan,
> I could easily be a part of the meeting and even
> present a paper on some of the problems we face in
> cross-cultural communication.
>
> I presented such a paper at the American
> Marketing Association last April in New York.
>
> With all the cutbacks for travel, I'll not have
> much spending allowance. What will be the costs
> for the registration fee and a hotel room for one
> person?

Similarly, personnel and credit inquiries (though less frequently written than they used to be) should begin with the key question and follow with necessary explanations and specific questions.

*Credit inquiries* from one business house to another are as direct, concise, and specific as those about products—and are usually forms.

When special circumstances arise that the form does not cover, however, you'll need to write a special letter. Like any direct request, it should get right down to business with the key question, followed by any needed explanation and specifics.

> Have your credit experiences with X been
> satisfactory? . . .
>
> We'd especially like to have your explanation of
> why he did not list your firm when he applied for
> credit with us . . . .

When you ask your readers to give information about people, as in inquiries about job and credit applicants, both of you face a special problem—*compliance with the libel and other laws.* You have a duty to help protect your information source. Of course, truth is the most important protection, but truth alone is not complete protection in some states and under all circumstances.

You can help by making the reply what lawyers call a *privileged* communication. You show that you have an interest to protect, and you promise to keep the information confidential.[1] As a matter of courtesy, but with no legal significance, you also say that the inquiry was authorized (if true), and you express appreciation and offer to return the favor.

You can increase your chances of getting an answer, or a faster answer, if you can justifiably ask for it by a certain date. (People are inclined to put things off—especially if the benefit is not obvious and immediate.) Therefore, you should consider justifying and end-dating:

> Because Mr. Bowers wants our decision by the end
> of the month, we would especially appreciate your
> answer by the 25th.

Getting credit information on potential overseas buyers may be a little more difficult, but you have various sources that will help you.

1. Banks and other companies (references).
2. The *World Traders Data Reports* (U.S. Department of Commerce).
3. Dun & Bradstreet's International Division reports.
4. The Export-Import Bank of the United States.
5. The Foreign Credit Interchange Bureau (bulletins on foreign markets and economic conditions, credit interchange reports, worldwide collections service, and consultation services).

The most important considerations about direct inquiries are to get started in a hurry, to be as specific in your questions as you can, and to explain enough (but only enough) for your reader to answer well and easily. The accompanying Direct Inquiry Checklist will help, although it is not an outline, a prescription, a coverall, or a cure-all.

None of the checklists in this book are. And they are especially not outlines. If you try to use the appropriate checklist as an outline, you will simply not be able to come up with a good message to handle the particular situation. Instead, use the checklists for their intended purposes. First, draft your message. Then (though not all points apply to every case), use the checklist to make sure you have covered everything and said everything appropriately. (Your teacher probably will.)

---

[1] You go ahead and promise confidentiality despite the fact that you can't keep the information confidential under certain conditions. The Fair Credit Reporting Act empowers the subject of such a report to see what was said to whom and by whom if the information bears on a turndown for credit, insurance, or employment.

## Direct Inquiry Checklist

1. Get this message under way quickly.
   a. Maybe use a subject line showing the nature of the inquiry.
   b. Make your question(s) specific and direct: "What would be your reaction if Mr. Bowers . . . ?"

2. Be careful about the form and wording of the questions.
   a. Don't hint; ask directly: "What does the . . . ?"
   b. Word questions to get what you want—not just yes or no when you need an explanation. Avoid questions phrased to suggest a certain answer, too broad questions (". . . any information you have"), and double-barreled questions (". . . whether . . . and, if so, . . . ?").
   c. For a series of questions, explain and itemize (tabulate).

3. Ask the minimum number of questions in the best order.

4. Express gratitude cordially in first person, future tense—not "Thank you in advance." If appropriate, offer to reciprocate.

5. Leave your reader clear as to what you want, and stimulate action (maybe justify and ask for an answer by a certain date).

6. In inquiries about people, establish the privileged aspects.
   a. Show an interest to protect; promise confidential treatment.
   b. If the inquiry is authorized, say so (for courtesy, not legal reasons).

## Favorable Replies

Any company or person desiring the goodwill of others replies to all reasonable inquiries—and does so promptly. If a delay is necessary, some explanation should go quickly, indicating the reason and approximately when to expect a complete answer.

> Your request for information about robotization is one for Mr. J. S. McConnough, our industrial engineering specialist, who will be in Denver for another 10 days.
>
> Shortly after he returns to the office, he will write you.

Because some inquiries ask only for assistance, whereas others readily indicate a potential customer (and a quite different reply), this discussion properly divides into (1) replies to inquiries without apparent sales possibilities (including reports dealing with personnel and credit applicants) and (2) replies to inquiries with sales possibilities (often called invited sales).

## Replies without Sales Possibilities

When someone asks you something, you properly say either yes or no—in a direct (favorable) or indirect reply. An undecided, noncommittal response like "Well, I'll think it over" is a refusal and needs to be handled accordingly (Chapter 7).

In favorable replies without sales possibilities, particular points to watch are the direct beginning, completeness of coverage, and (when appropriate) resale.

**Direct Beginning.** The fundamental principle in all favorable replies is to say yes immediately and thus gain increased goodwill, as well as save time and words.

The direct beginning can even establish many ideas by implication, thus shortening your message:

> We are glad to send you these last three annual reports of National Reaper, Inc. and to add your name to our mailing list to receive future copies as they come out, around March 1 each year.

The direct beginning also establishes a cheerful, ungrudging tone and eliminates pompousness. Observe the difference between the following slow, grudging, jargonistic original and the revision:

| Indirect, Wordy, Grudging | Direct, Compact, Cheerful |
|---|---|
| We have your request for our <u>HOW</u> book. | Here is your copy of the <u>HOW</u> book. |
| It was prepared primarily for material-handling engineers, and so we were not prepared for the numerous requests we have received from schools. We are sending you one, however, and hope you find it helpful. If there is any other way we can be of assistance, please do not hesitate to call on us. | We prepared it after extensive research by our material-handling engineers with the help of consultants and plant workers who specialize in material-handling methods. No doubt you'll find it useful. |

Note that the revised version not only begins directly but makes comments on the book showing that it is something special. In such situations, where you send helpful information, you have every reason to enhance

## Favorable Reply Checklist

1. Quickly show that you are doing as asked, maybe in a subject line.
2. Completeness, specificness, and correctness are essential.
   a. Answer every question—direct or implied.
   b. Evaluate when evaluation will be helpful. But do more than editorialize with "fine," "splendid," "excellent." Give specifics.
3. Watch your tone.
   a. Don't do anything grudgingly or parade your generosity.
   b. In a personnel report: *report*, don't recommend; beware of superlatives.
4. Watch space, word choice, and position to avoid overemphasis; but don't ignore shortcomings and mislead.
5. Give information about a person only when asked because of an interest to protect; then require confidentiality.
6. When sending something tangible, add a few enhancing words.
7. End graciously and confidently.
   a. An expression of willingness nullifies any possible curt impression.
   b. Don't suggest inadequacy: "I hope" or "If this is not . . . ."

its desirability (and hence your goodwill). Also note that the direct beginning makes unnecessary any reference to the inquiry and saves space.

**Completeness of Coverage.** Obviously, you need to take up every question in an inquiry—to avoid extra correspondence or reader disgust. At times, of course, you can't answer—because you don't know, or because you can't reveal the information. In either case, simply tell your reader so, but don't ignore the question.

In most cases in which you give information about a credit applicant, all you'll need to do is look at your customer's record and fill in the blanks provided on the inquiry. But when some atypical factor presents itself (or when the inquiring firm does not provide blanks), you'll need to write a special message.

In addition to the standard information, you may need to incorporate explanations of the effects of local conditions on the size and timing of purchases or on paying habits. And of course any unusual question requires special attention. Since it is usually the reason for the special letter, it often merits the beginning position.

Completeness of coverage does not, however, mean recommendation. Note that the personnel report does not recommend the applicant—as it should not—and hence that such letters should not be called "letters of recommendation."

But in replying about people, completeness *does* require *covering the legal aspects.* You could get into trouble by sending damaging information without meeting the obligations of doing so. Conversely, if you play it straight, you need have no fear.

Legally and morally you are on safe ground only if your report meets the requirements of a *privileged* communication. First, *don't volunteer information about job or credit applicants;* send it *only if requested by somebody with an interest to protect,* and subordinately make that clear. Beyond that, you owe the inquirer, the person reported on, and the state *the truth as you see it (including your evaluations and opinions), good faith to avoid misleading or malice, and reasonable care to be right about facts.*

The accompanying Favorable Reply Checklist summarizes the most important points to keep in mind as you write replies complying with a request that has no sales possibilities. It applies equally to overseas personnel reports but not credit reports.

A bigger difference in strategy that does serve well in both domestic and overseas replies, however, is one for **situations with favorable sales prospects.** The basic plan shifts to match the significant change in THE PSYCHOLOGY OF THE SITUATION.

## Replies with Sales Possibilities

Failure to answer the preceding kinds of inquiries will mark you as uncooperative and probably lose you lots of goodwill; but failure to answer inquiries with direct sales possibilities is business suicide.

When someone inquires about your goods or services, clearly an unsatisfied need or desire exists and the inquiry implies that you might satisfy it. You have an interested, potential customer—a prospect.

Since you don't have to get attention (because you already have it), your only problems are to start favorably, answer all questions, subordinate unfavorable information, handle price positively, and stimulate action.

**Getting Started Positively.** The thing the reader most wants to know is the information requested—as specifically as you can give it (not your expressions of pleasure or gratitude). But you will want to check the importance and nature of the questions before framing your reply. The most important one you can answer favorably should be your start:

```
In making the Rover bicycle you saw advertised in
U.S. Youth, we use lightweight, high-grade steel
of the same quality used in motorbikes.
```

Such positiveness stimulates enthusiasm and increases the desire to read further.

**Answering All Questions.** In some instances you cannot give all the requested information. For example, the letter about the Stair-Traveler (Chapter 5) could not give cost details because installation varies according to the placement of the machine in a particular home. The visit of the representative would have to clear up that point. But *if you cannot supply an answer, do not ignore the question.* Indicate that you are supplying the information some other way or that you are getting it.

Most of the time you can give all the requested information, even though it runs to considerable length. The following reply has you-viewpoint and positiveness, and it answers all the questions (which you can easily list as you read the answers).

The reconditioned Lektrasweep you asked about has a 6-inch upholstery brush, a 6-inch lampshade brush, a 12-inch prober, a plastic blower attachment, and a 12-inch rug brush.

These are the same attachments that come with vacuum cleaners costing $40 to $80 more. Were we to include a 1-hp motor (necessary only for spraying attachments), the price would have to be considerably higher. Since most users want their Lektrasweeps for cleaning purposes only, we eliminate the spray attachments and give you a good low-cost cleaner operating efficiently on a 1/2-hp motor.

I believe we have the machine you'll find convenient for your cleaning. The quiet operation of the motor, allowing you to carry on a normal conversation, is especially desirable in small living quarters. Another convenience is the 20-foot cord, which enables you to clean an entire room from one wall plug.

The Lektrasweep guarantee protects you for a full two years. If any parts fail because of defective materials or workmanship, specially trained service personnel at the central plant will put your Lektrasweep in service again and return it to you within a week. If the machine shows evidence of proper care, we absorb the charges for servicing and new parts and return your Lektrasweep, charges prepaid.

Next time you're in Madison, come in and let us demonstrate a Lektrasweep. After a thorough test of its effectiveness, you'll see why we are so confident of the Lektrasweep.

> To get your Lektrasweep before you can come to
> Madison, use the enclosed order blank and reply
> envelope to send us your payment and instructions.
> You can be enjoying easy Lektrasweeping the day
> after we hear from you.

This was a particularly difficult reply because so many of the questions had to be answered with limitations, reservations, or an implied no.

To get full value out of the reply about Lektrasweeps, you need to look a second time. It effectively illustrates two aspects of you-viewpoint especially important in all sales writing:

1. *Psychological description.* Except in the first paragraph about the Lektrasweep, every time the letter gives a physical fact about the product, it tells and emphasizes a resultant benefit. As you look again, see how many more pieces of psychological description you can find like the italicized part of ". . . 20-foot cord, *which enables you to clean an entire room from one wall plug.*"

2. *Dramatized copy,* the most effective kind of sales writing, gets the reader to imagine actually using and enjoying the benefits of the product.

For further help on answering all questions, see the second group of form enclosures later in this chapter.

**Subordinating Unfavorable Information.** Only a very poor sales writer would have started the Lektrasweep reply with

> No, the Lektrasweep does not have a 1-hp motor.

or even with

> The Lektrasweep is equipped with a 1/2-hp motor.

The letter wisely begins and ends with positive ideas and positively establishes the negative answers of "No, the Lektrasweep does not have a 1-hp motor; no, we do not repair in the home; and no, we do not offer a free trial."

**Handling Price.** When you have a genuine bargain that the reader will recognize as such, the price may be the best lead you can choose.

Most of the time, however, you are trying to sell on the bases of quality and benefits received at an established price. And most of the time you are writing to someone who wishes the price were less! For these reasons, in most cases good sales writers attempt to minimize the effect of price by one or more of several methods:

- Introducing price after presenting most of the sales points.
- Stating price in terms of a unit ("$1.67 a wrench" rather than "$20 a dozen").

- Identifying the daily, monthly, or even yearly cost based on an estimated life of the product ("10 cents a night" for a good mattress sounds much easier to pay than "$365").
- Suggesting a series of payments rather than the total (an alumnus is more likely to contribute "$10 a month for the next year" than to contribute "$120 next year").
- Comparing the price with the cost of some product or activity that the reader accepts readily. ("For the price of six cigarettes a day your child can have better schools" was the punch line of an ad promoting a school-bond drive.)
- Associating the price with a reminder of the benefits to be gained.

You can always apply the first and last of the suggestions. You may want to use the others as indicated by the following varying factors:

- In general, the higher the income bracket of your readers, the less the desirability for applying the techniques.
- The higher the price and the less familiar your readers are with your product or service, the greater the desirability for minimizing price. Minimizing price has more effect on consumers than on dealers or business or industrial customers.

Sometimes you can shift the burden of price discussion to an enclosure or a sales representative. But *when you are trying to close a sale, you must identify what it is going to cost and help your reader justify the expenditure.*

**Securing Action.** Having convinced your reader that your product or service is worth the price, you want to get action before a change of mind, before any of the other things that could happen do happen.

A word of caution here, however: The bromidic, high-pressure, general expressions like "Act today!" "Do it now!" "Don't delay!" are more likely to produce reactions ranging from indifference to disgust than the favorable reaction you seek.

Instead, in all persuasive messages, your good action ending:

- Makes clear the specific action you want your reader to take.
- Clears up any question about how to take the action.
- Makes the action easy (and makes it sound as easy as possible).
- Supplies a stimulus to action, preferably immediate action.

On finishing your letter, your reader should know exactly what you want done. The psychological urge is stronger if you *name the explicit action* rather than resort to the vague "Let us hear from you soon" or any of its equivalents.

Facilitating devices—order blanks, order cards, and postcards or envelopes already addressed and requiring no postage—remove some of the

## Invited Sales Checklist

1. Quickly give a direct, favorable answer to a key question.

2. Arrange points for coherence and favorable information at the beginning and end of paragraphs as well as the whole. Embed touchy points.

3. Answer every question, specifically (and as positively as possible).

4. Use psychological description (you-viewpoint) and dramatization.
   a. Put the product to work for the reader, and give a visual image of benefits.
   b. Use words sparingly on insignificant physical description.

5. If you use an enclosure for details, economy, and pictures, don't mention it too early; but emphasize what to do with it or get from it, not that it's enclosed.

6. Adaptation is easy here; the inquiry gives you cues. Maybe use the name once and/or make a reference to hometown, firm, or organization—or (better) a commonplace action or event characteristic of the reader's job, community, area, or economic status.

7. Try to cushion the shock of price when you have to state it, minimizing it and making it and the payment method clear.

8. In a full-fledged four-point action ending (what to do, how, aids to easy action, stimulus to promptness), confidently ask the reader to act.

work in taking action. References to them—*preferably directing the reader to use them*—make the action easy, and more likely.

Moreover, careful wording can increase your chances. "Write us your choice" suggests more work than "Check your choice of colors on the enclosed card." "Jot down," "just check," "simply initial" are examples of wording that suggests ease and rapidity and reduces your reader's reluctance.

The final suggestion for a good action ending—that of supplying a stimulus to action—is a matter of motivation (a reader benefit)! Talk of limited supply, price rises after a certain date, introductory offers for a limited time, premiums, and the like is all very well *provided it is true* and *provided it is specific,* so that the reader is likely to accept it. But in the final analysis your reader buys for what the product contributes to life; and you always have that to offer. So when you ask for money, *mention again what benefits will result.*

Such a stimulus comes appropriately as the ending idea. This placement emphasizes the service attitude—rather than the greed stressed if you end with dollars-and-cents talk or the mechanics of ordering.

Desirably, the stimulus is short—often only a phrase, at most a short sentence, restating the theme. The Stair-Traveler letter, for example, could have ended effectively with

```
Mr. J. B. Nickle, our Kansas City representative,
will be glad to call at a time convenient for you.
Fill out and mail the enclosed postcard, and he
will come to your home and explain how simply and
economically your Stair-Traveler can make your
daily living more pleasurable.
```

For another example, reread the ending about the Lektrasweep.

Invited sales are persuasive presentations. You should therefore apply all the fitting points discussed in Chapter 5. The accompanying Invited Sales Checklist summarizes the most significant points.

## Short Transmittal Messages

A frequent kind of written communication is the short (in-house or external) covering letter or memo sending information, ideas, or material. Though these notes are not always favorable replies, they usually are welcome. (Illustrated on the next page.)

Whether such a message sends requested information, a perceptive interpretation of known or new facts, or a new-idea suggestion, for young people early in their careers it is a primary (and maybe the only) means of contact with upper management. Such writing therefore deserves care.

*Tone* is the starting point in that care—especially in self-initiated interpretations and suggestions. (No executive likes to have an underling imply the executive's stupidity for not having seen the new idea.)

Early use of identifying dates, file numbers, and other references is helpful. The real significance (and feather in your cap), however, is in *reliable information, wise interpretation of data, and helpful suggestions or questions* on the use of the information. A reputation for diplomatically providing such facts and ideas (requested or volunteered) is a good ladder to promotions and salary increases in almost any organization.

## Form Enclosures, Letters, and Documents

Invited sales messages (and various other kinds) do take time and therefore money. Unless a firm has practically unlimited money and trained personnel, it will have to use form messages some of the time for speed and economy in handling them. (To that purpose a section of Chapter 2 discusses the preparation and use of forms.)

```
X MOTOR DIVISION              INNER-ORGANIZATION
NATIONAL CORPORATION               MESSAGE

TO:       Mr. A. J. High   Location  Charlotte Zone
FROM:     M. J. Whistle    Location: Charlotte Zone
SUBJECT:  X COLLEGE OF      Date      May 1, 198-
          PROFESSIONAL
          SELLING
```

As you know, George Hightower, Sales Manager of LaPointe X, and I attended the Basic Selling Course of the X College here in Charlotte. I hope that the observations we made will be beneficial to future sessions.

1. Time allotted was too short for the material. Careful evaluation of forms and examples can solve this problem.
2. Instruction was excellent. Both instructors were well prepared and knowledgeable of the subject matter. They kept the attention of the group and led class participation well.
3. Homework assignments were excellent; all attendants performed well during role-play situations.
4. Planners should select class participants more carefully to obtain quality candidates for the classes rather than just to fill available spaces.

Should you have any questions, please call.


Copy to: Mr. M. R. Bornsen

Form enclosures and letters can decrease the cost of correspondence by cutting the time needed for dictation, transcription, handling, and filing—despite the best of office equipment. The big problem is to determine when you can save enough in costs to justify the loss in effectiveness. Before you can decide, however, you need to know the potentials of forms.

## Enclosures

Three classes of *form enclosures* deserve your attention:

1. Forms that are the basic reason for the mailing.
2. Forms that give supplementary information.
3. Forms that aid the reader in responding.

Since items in the *first group* are the key things in the envelopes (checks, requested pamphlets, brochures, and the like), they deserve to come to the reader's attention immediately. In some cases they may properly be the only thing necessary. In most situations, however, you should *make something of them* by saying something about them—even if for no reason but goodwill.

You've already seen earlier in this chapter the reasons and approaches for comment when transmitting requested booklets. Similarly, simple and typical covering letters (often forms themselves) beginning something like the following could hardly help making their readers feel better.

        This check will tell you more clearly than words
        that when we guarantee satisfaction with Acme
        products or your money back, we mean it.

        Here is your current quarterly dividend check
        (our 200th without interruption, raised to 50
        cents a share this time), and our thanks for your
        continued confidence in Rushman.

        The enclosed check paying for your services as
        consultant carries with it our thanks for the good
        advice you gave us.

Unlike the first group of form enclosures, the enclosures in the *second group* are *not* the basic reason for writing but are *helpful to give additional details* and thus avoid cluttering and lengthening the main message. Most frequently useful in sales letters as brochures and detailed price lists, they also help in job application letters (as résumés) and in answers to various inquiries about products (as installation, operating, and repair guides).

As supplements, these informative enclosures do not deserve mention until late in the message—usually the next-to-last paragraph, *after* the key points and *near enough to the end* that the reader will finish before turning to the enclosure (perhaps never to return). As with the first group, the important thing to say about these enclosures is *not* their mere existence—*not* "We have enclosed . . . ," and certainly *not* "Enclosed please find . . ." (the reader has probably already found)—but what the reader should get from them.

```
As you'll see from the enclosed brochure. . . .
```

```
The illustrations and explanations on pages 3 and
4 of the enclosed installation guide will answer,
better than I can, your questions about wiring the
two thermostats in combination.
```

The *third useful group* of form enclosures (reader aids in replying) naturally deserve mention only in the ending—where you ask for action. Order blanks and reply or return cards and envelopes (usually stamped and addressed—but *not* properly called "self-addressed," unless you insist on being trite, jargonistic, illogical, and wordy) can often help you get an answer when the reader might not go to the trouble necessary without them. As in referring to other form enclosures, the point to stress is *not* the idea that they are enclosed but the suggestion that the reader use them.

If you'll use the word *enclosed* as an adjective instead of a verb, you'll probably put the emphasis where it belongs in referring to all three classes of form enclosures, like this:

```
By filling out and mailing the enclosed reply
card promptly, you . . . .
```

```
Sending in your order today on the enclosed form
will bring you . . . .
```

### Form Letters, Memos, and Paragraphs

Although most readers like the implied extra consideration of the individual letter, few businesspeople will object to a form letter *because* it is a form but only if it seems to give them less attention than they desire. New customers and those writing you about important affairs are most likely to feel that way. Anybody, however, will rightly object to a sloppy form or a form message that does not contain the necessary information. And many people will object to a form that tries to masquerade as an individualized message but fails. The undisguised form, however, can successfully carry its message in many situations.

```
As I'm writing this letter,
The Richmond U.S. Government Money Market Trust
Is paying your fellow members xx.x% net annualized
yield.
If you really want to hold your own against
inflation, compare that with what your checking
and savings accounts are giving you.
The Trust has three beneficial features:
    1.  Your money is available simply by writing a
        check (minimum of $500).
    2.  You pay no sales charge when you put your
        money in or when you take it out.
    3.  The Trust will invest your money exclusively
        in securities that the U.S. government issues
        or guarantees--the safest security
        investments.
You can invest with as little as $500; but the
larger your investment, the greater your return.
The sooner you act, the sooner your dollars will
be doing more for you.
You have the prospectus giving you important
details about the Trust. Complete the application
and write your check for this powerful new way of
fighting inflation. Use the enclosed postage-paid
envelope.
```

Even the signature of this letter is printed. Thus a reply that would cost several dollars if individually handled runs to no more than 50 cents. And the firm gains extra goodwill by answering promptly.

You can print *strict form* messages by the thousands at low cost. And you can adapt them in talking points and references even to a large mailing list. They can answer an inquiry (or order), express gratitude, convey some evidence of service attitude, and look forward to future business relations, as in the following postcard acknowledgment:

```
We will give your recent order our immediate
careful attention and follow your shipping
instructions exactly.
You may be sure we appreciate this opportunity to
serve you and shall be happy to do so when you
again order computer supplies.
```

But completely printed letters have limitations. Personalizing is impossible. And if you print the body and then insert individual inside addresses and salutations, you will have greatly increased costs and likely discrepancies between the two types. Unless you sell only one product or have a different form for each product, you can't include resale talk on the goods, although you can for the firm.

*Fill-ins* enable you to be more specific than you can be in a strict form. For example, the strict form above could read like this as a fill-in (the filled-in parts are in parentheses):

```
Today we shipped you (400 MRP118520SD 20-pocket
Microfiche Reference Panels @ $3.14, 6 TPZ11854BL
blue 4" capacity Trapezoid Ring Binders @ $26.35)
as ordered on (purchase order no.) via (UPS).

Thank you for your order and for giving us this
opportunity to prove that MagiComp is your fastest
and most complete source for all your computer
supplies and accessories.
```

Sophisticated equipment can type out the entire form, picking up the fill-ins from data about the order already on record. Such word processing equipment can also personalize letters and memos, change paragraphs to relate to different products or orders, and in general, keep your forms from looking like impersonal communication.

International business communication, for example, makes much use of forms. The usual method of assuring payment when exporting is to get a letter of credit (issued by a bank at the importer's request). Your international banker will check out the foreign bank. A U.S. bank can confirm a letter of credit and thus guarantee payment.

The preceding comments can apply to form paragraphs as well as to whole letters or memos. The procedure is to write an excellent paragraph covering each frequently recurring point in the firm's correspondence. Usually half a dozen ending paragraphs and a dozen beginnings will cover most situations. Other paragraphs will be about the various products, procedures, and policies of the company. Each company correspondent and each typist then gets a book of the coded paragraphs recorded for use in word processing equipment.

A dictator could code a letter simply 13, 27, 16, 42. That would mean a four-paragraph letter made up of those standard paragraphs in that order. If no ready-made paragraph covers what should be in the second paragraph, dictation would be "13, special, 16, 42," followed by the wording for the special second paragraph. If the same point comes up frequently enough, the firm should prepare a good paragraph for it and put it into the correspondent's book.

Because such paragraphs get frequent use, they should get careful preparation so they are better than most people would write quickly under the pressure of dictation. Obviously, the same advantage applies to an entire form message.

Even if you spend 10 hours on one message, when you send it to a thousand people, dictation time and transcription time are only a fraction of the time individual messages would require. Thus forms cut correspondence costs, reduce the burdensome human aspects of the ever-increasing correspondence problems of management, and expedite replies to people who want information quickly.

Certain *dangers* exist, however. *The greatest is the tendency to use a form when it simply does not apply.* When a person asks if Sure-Clip T nuts can withstand temperatures up to 2,400° F, answering that "Sure-Clip T nuts are specially finished to resist corrosion and be compatible with a wide range of ferrous and nonferrous metals" is nice but doesn't answer the question.

One good solution, if a form does not answer one of the specific questions, is to add a postscript. If you cannot answer all questions by adding a little to an existing form, you need to write an individual message.

Another danger is in broadcasting that the message is a form with such references as

```
To all our customers:
Whether you live in Maine or California . . . .
```

In a letter or memo the personal touch pays off. The wording of even a form letter, then, should *give each reader the feeling that it fits.* And remember that in every test ever made, the form letter that makes no pretense of being anything else results in more returns than the imperfectly disguised form, whether the slipup is due to poor mechanics or inept wording.

The suggestions made about forms in this chapter can help with *any repetitive writing situation.* So except for occasional incidental references pointing out the ease or wisdom of form treatment in a particular situation, the remainder of this book deals with individualized, personalized messages because:

1. You can learn more about communication principles and their application that way.

2. As a result of such specific study and practice, you will write much better forms when you need to.

3. In most circumstances calling for a letter or memo, an individualized copy will do a more effective job for you than a form.

## Short Note Replies

In an effort to expedite many day-to-day answers to inquiries (and reduce correspondence costs), many executives turn to the short note reply

(SNR). One leading copying-machine manufacturer explains this way in its advertising:

1. Just jot a personal note on the margin of the letter you received—no wasted time in dictation.
2. Insert the letter and a sheet of copy paper into a copying machine.
3. In just four seconds you have the letter ready to mail back to the sender—plus the copy for your files.

Certainly most readers will appreciate the thoughtfully fast answer. The practice seems to be gaining favor—rightly so.

## Orders

Buying and selling by mail and telephone has long involved much more than just the big mail-order houses. It includes mail sales through large department stores; national marketing of seasonal and regional produce like fruit, game, syrup, and candy; farmers' orders for various supplies, machinery, and replacement parts; office equipment and supplies from manufacturers and distributors; and even industrial tools and materials.

Since most catalogs include well-designed order blanks and addressed envelopes, you'll rarely need to write a letter to order something, but when you do:

1. *Begin directly and specifically,* as in "Please send me . . . ."
2. *Describe the goods adequately* (quantity; catalog item number and page number; name of product and appropriate details—size, model, color, grade or quality; unit price; and total price).

In ordering replacement parts for machines, be sure to give the name and model number of the machine and the name and number of the part. If you have no parts list, the number may be on the part.

3. *Write a single-spaced paragraph for each item.*
4. *Make clear how you expect to pay.*
5. *Tell where to ship the goods,* and when and how if it matters to you.

The following typical order illustrates the five points:

```
Please send me the following items listed in your
current spring and summer catalog:

1  60  C 6587L  Glass casting rod, Model
                162, extra-light action,
                5 ft. 8 in. . . . . . . . . . . . $18.95
```

```
1  60  CP 6302  Pflueger Summit reel,
                  Model 1993L . . . . . . . . . . . .    33.75
2  60  C 6846   Cortland "Cam-o-flage" nylon
                  casting line, 10-lb. test,
                  100-yd. lengths @ $4.30 . . . .     8.60
       Total  . . . . . . . . . . . . . . . . . . . . .  $61.30
```

The enclosed check for $69.63 covers the price, sales tax, and parcel post charges.

As I plan to go fishing a week from next Saturday (June 26), I will want the equipment by that time.

Because of their advantages, phone orders are increasing, particularly in credit sales. Although a phone service may cost a company as much as $1.75 per order, it has subtle advantages. Phone orders are nearly always on credit, and credit orders usually are larger than cash orders (an average 35 percent larger). The customer calls when in a buying mood and therefore might buy more if the handler of the call suggests appealing merchandise. Credit card customers are also least likely to return merchandise.

The one disadvantage to phone customers is that the 30-day fulfillment law does not protect them. The law—that a company must either fill orders within 30 days or inform customers of their refund options—applies to cash orders only.

Telephone order service is expensive, however, because of the cost of operators, equipment, and a WATS line. If business is limited to the Christmas season, it may not pay to keep a full-time operator staff.

Because in-house operators generally can answer customers' questions, supply inventory information (what's in or out of stock), and talk about allied merchandise, they are better than answering bureaus—for both the buyer and the seller.

(The related topic, telemarketing, appears in Chapter 8.)

## Standard Acknowledgments

A buyer (retail, mercantile, or industrial) expects to get ordered products quickly and to be appreciated. So acknowledgments should be an effective means of increasing goodwill and promoting business. To give less is to make a customer for somebody else, as a U.S. Department of Commerce survey found: "Seeming indifference is responsible for at least 67 percent of lost customers." Thus no reason justifies not acknowledging orders promptly and appreciatively.

To that purpose most large firms now have automated devices to handle these situations. Whether keyed in, scanned in optically (as at the grocery checkout), or beamed in, the code is the language that becomes the computer input. There the orders usually go through a dry run (an edit run) that checks for errors. The computer then processes the orders and prepares shipping labels.

The company now also has a mailing list of customers for use or sale. As annual Christmas-sales promotions, some companies, such as Figi's, send their Christmas-present customers a list of what they ordered the preceding year and for whom.

Regardless of increasing automation, however, some person (like you) has to determine the wording of the acknowledgments to promote goodwill and further sales. To reduce costs, most large-volume sellers-by-mail use forms to acknowledge all but unusual orders. By arranging for fill-ins (underscored here), you can even personalize the message, as in this one from a large department store:

```
As you requested, we have sent the pocket
calculator to Mrs. M. W. Colby.


Thank you for calling on us. We try to make our
service convenient. Order from us again when we
can serve you.
```

When a large or unusual order comes in, however—or even a small first order from a new customer—the opportunity to make a lasting relationship is too great to leave to anything but a well-written, personalized complete acknowledgment.

Clearly a *standard acknowledgment* of an order you can fill immediately is a good-news letter. The beginning should tell immediately the *when* and *how* of shipment, preferably timed and worded to indicate that it's on the way, and identify what it includes, the charges, and (here or later) the financial arrangements if necessary.

To a new customer a hearty welcome, resale, and a forward look are even more important than to an old customer; and service attitude and appreciation are important to every customer.

The middle section of a standard acknowledgment is the place for financial details, resale talk of more than phrase length, and explicit evidence of your service attitude. For instance, in acknowledging dealers' orders, you might talk about having your sales representative set up window and counter displays, offer free envelope stuffers (small promotional pamphlets about your products for the dealer to send to customers), or describe your radio, TV, and magazine ads that call customers' attention to your products and help the dealer sell more.

Encouragement to future ordering (just preceded by any appropriate sales promotion material) is almost invariably the best ending for the standard acknowledgment. The accompanying Standard Acknowledgment Checklist outlines the previous points.

Here's an example of how the parts go together for an effective personalized acknowledgment covering all points specifically:

> You should receive your eight cases of Tuff Paper towels in time for Friday afternoon shoppers; we sent them by prepaid express this morning.
>
> The $3.27 voucher attached to this letter is your change after we deducted $76.80 charges and $4.93 express from your $85 check.
>
> You'll find these Tuff Paper towels have a fast turnover, Mr. Ford, because homemakers like the way they soak up grease, dust off spots, and save cloth towels from many dirty jobs. And you'll like their attractive small packaging that takes up a minimum of display and shelf space. Your markup figures out at exactly 29 percent.
>
> For more information about Tuff Paper dishrags and window washers, colorful shelf paper your customers will like for their pantries, and other paper products every household needs, look in the enclosed booklet. Notice that each article carries the usual Tuff Paper margin of profit!
>
> Perhaps you'd like to take advantage of our regular terms of 2/10, n/60 on future orders. If so, we'll be glad to consider your credit application when you fill in and return the enclosed form.

The trouble with this kind of acknowledgment is that it is costly. In many cases, however, a form can serve as an acknowledgment (especially for small orders from established customers). Certainly a form like this could handle the Tuff Paper situation or a repeat of it.

> You should receive the Tuff Paper products you ordered in just a few days; they are already on the way.
>
> You'll find that Tuff Paper products have a fast turnover; homemakers like them for many messy household cleaning jobs.
>
> You will like their attractive packaging (taking little display space) and the sizable markup!
>
> Read the enclosed booklet about Tuff Paper dishrags, window washers, colorful shelf paper, and other paper products every household needs.

Use the handy order blank and business reply
envelope when you need additional Tuff Papers your
customers will be asking for.

## Standard Acknowledgment Checklist

1. Emphasize the good news (sending the goods—not an order) in the first sentence, preferably also indicating method, arrival time, and use.
   a. Clearly identify the order by one or more of date, number, content.
   b. Clear up any uncertainty about payment details.
2. Resale and appreciation are important parts of acknowledgments.
3. Service attitude and sales promotion material are especially important to new customers.
   a. For a consumer: delivery schedules, free installation, maybe credit possibilities (invite application without promising approval).
   b. For an industrial customer: full stock, quick shipment, custom or special capabilities, maybe credit.
   c. For a dealer: sales and service representatives, manuals, displays, and advertising aids and programs (mats, envelope stuffers, etc.).
4. Encourage future orders.

## Credit Approvals

In naming what they commonly call the four C's of credit—the bases for evaluating individual as well as corporate credit applicants, domestic or international—credit specialists name character first, followed by capacity, capital, and conditions.

*Character* is honesty. In credit, it is meeting obligations as one promises to do.

*Capacity* is the ability to earn the means for payment.

*Capital* is the already available money behind the debtor. It may be in cash or other forms.

*Conditions* (plural) has two parts. One is general business trends. The other is special or local conditions or the trends of the debtor's business.

Because these four C's—especially the first two—are reflections of "personal" qualities of an individual or business, credit communications are open to dangerous negative possibilities. When you question honesty, earning ability, or judgment, you are treading on potentially dangerous ground. With tact, patience, and a positive attitude, however, communications about credit can be goodwill builders.

One of the fundamental concepts that will help you write successfully about credit is this: The credit privilege has to be *earned.* For that reason, you should not talk about *granting* credit. More appropriate terminology is *approval* or *extension* of credit.

On the basis of one or more of the four C's, an individual or firm merits credit. For many, character is the primary reason. Anticipating those who may be unable or unwilling to pay is one of the primary functions of the credit manager. But approving only gilt-edged applications will seriously curtail sales. Accordingly, a credit manager must be sales-minded, and well informed about the firm's goods, to help build customer confidence and increase sales.

Since marginal risks are often vital for profitable operations, evaluating and encouraging borderline cases must get careful attention. When the information you receive about an applicant is favorable, you will of course approve the application and set up the account. Because of the sheer weight of numbers, most retail credit approvals are form messages like the following:

THE J. P. BOWEN COMPANY

Is pleased to open a charge
account for you and welcome you to
our family of regular patrons

Such a notification sent promptly is certainly better than nothing. Yet it falls far short of what a good credit message can do to strengthen the credit relationship, promote goodwill, forestall collection problems, and stimulate sales—especially for mercantile and industrial credit.

## Establishing the Basis for Credit

In credit approvals you may take advantage of the simple, obvious psychology of praise or approval. If you place a customer on the credit list because of a prompt-pay rating, you should say so. The reference should not be lengthy; in fact, the best way is to subordinate it in the extension of credit or the explanation of terms. Thus it reminds the customer that credit is an earned privilege that requires care, thought, and effort to maintain. Thus established, it may serve as an effective collection appeal if payment becomes slow.

## Explanation of Terms

Unless a firm wants to encourage delayed payments, the initial extension of credit should make unmistakably clear how you expect payments. *How far to go with the explanation depends on the reader's credit knowledge and reputation.* To those you think know and respect credit practices, you would tell only what the terms are. (Explaining that 2/10, n/30 means a deduction of 2 percent if paid in 10 days or pay the whole in 30 days would insult such a reader.) To a reader who is new to credit business or barely passes your credit evaluation, however, you had better make the terms not only clear and emphatic but concrete (i.e., show the prompt-pay benefits as savings).

Few credit approvals to consumers identify a limit (although one may go on the office record), whereas most business credit arrangements and consumer bank credit cards like Visa and MasterCard include limits as parts of the explanation of terms. To prevent the limit from appearing to be a penalty, with consequent negative reactions, a good writer phrases it in positive language:

> Under our regular terms of 2/10, n/60, your No-Flame will cost you only $1,176 if you send your check by May 2; the full $1,200 is due on June 21. At any one time you may carry as much as $2,500 worth of No-Flame or other Bronson products on account.

To stop with the approval, the basis, and the terms would be foolish, however; a good credit writer can also help to further sales—through the goodwill elements of resale material on goods, resale on the house, or sales promotion material on allied goods. All should focus on repeat sales.

## Stimulating Sales

In credit approvals, sales-building passages should definitely be low pressure. The writer of the following, you will note, is careful to tie in a service-to-you reference to all sales-building passages and thus make the customer feel welcome rather than pounced upon:

> Your company's fine record of promptly paying invoices, confirmed by the references you supplied, certainly qualifies you for an open account with Rutherford Chemicals.
>
> Now your company is only a telephone call away from one of the country's largest stocks of laboratory chemicals, and we promise "same day" shipment for almost every order.
>
> We will invoice your purchases and date the invoices two days after the date of shipment. Terms are 2/10, net 45, up to $4,000, and we are sure you will want to take advantage of the discount for prompt payment.
>
> Since we regularly stock every item in our catalog, you will experience almost invariably prompt shipment from Rutherford. In fact, over the past two years we have achieved a 98.5 percent of

"same day" shipments, a point of pride among our
people.

## Credit Approval Checklist

1. The direct opening should approve credit quickly.
   a. When you are shipping goods, saying so quickly also implies credit approval.
   b. An early touch of resale is desirable, but move fast to the credit explanation.
   c. By invoice or tabulation, take care of legal details: item prices, freight charges.
2. Clear up the credit agreement/relation.
   a. For restraint, explain how the customer earned credit.
   b. For people who might not understand or respect credit terms, explain by
      (1) Applying the terms to a purchase (present or future).
      (2) Concretizing the discount figures (maybe a free item, a month's phone bill . . .).
      (3) Bringing in prompt-pay education (implying your confidence).
   c. To reduce its negative tone, give credit-limit talk a you-viewpoint introduction and positive statement (maybe label it temporary).
3. For a resale or sales promotional ending:
   a. Reassure about the reader's choice.
   b. Mention your services and selling aids concretely.
   c. Consider selling some seasonal or allied goods.
   d. Point to future orders.

### Making the Customer Feel Welcome and Appreciated

Credit-approval writers nearly all seem to know that making new credit customers feel welcome and appreciated helps promote frequent and continued use of the account (increasing sales and profits). Indeed, they so often begin by welcoming the customer to "our growing number of satisfied customers" that the writing is not only bad but stereotyped. *The customer is more interested in finding out the decision on the application. So that decision should get the emphatic beginning position.*

If you approve the credit (implied by sending the goods immediately when the application accompanies an order), establish the basis, explain the terms positively, and then follow with resale and sales promotion material, your reader will not doubt whether you appreciate business.

The relevant checklist summarizes the major suggestions, although, as always, you should apply them with discretion. They don't all apply in all cases.

# Simple Claims and
# Adjustment Approvals

Claims offer you the opportunity to get adjustments on unsatisfactory goods and services. If you are a seller and therefore receive claims, welcome them! They offer you an opportunity to discover and correct defects in your goods and services, but your adjustment letters are excellent opportunities for you to build or destroy goodwill.

Any claim and adjustment situation necessarily involves negatives. One of the major jobs in writing either claim or adjustment messages, therefore, is to keep negatives from making the situation worse. What you have learned about goodwill, resale, and handling negative material is especially important in adjustments.

In three kinds of situations you may have reason to write a persuasive claim: (1) you've tried a simple (direct) one and been turned down; (2) you know you're dealing with a tightfisted firm; or (3) the claim is unusual, or the facts leave at least some doubt about the justice of the claim. Such persuasive claims appear in Chapter 9.

Here the discussion is about direct claims—situations where you have facts clearly justifying the claim and you are supposedly dealing with a fair person or firm.

### Direct Claims

You will probably write good direct claims if you remember these five often-forgotten points (which serve as a checklist for direct claims):

1. *If you think you have a just claim, go ahead.* Progressive firms like claims because they suggest ways of improvement. Many firms even advertise this request: "If you like our products, tell others; if you don't, tell us." Often firms encourage claims by "double-your-money-back" guarantees and the like.

2. *Keep your shirt on! When things go wrong, the firm surely did not intend to mistreat you. Almost certainly the person handling your claim had nothing to do with the dissatisfaction. So restrain your anger or sarcasm!*

Most manufacturers know that ZD (zero-defect) production is an ideal rarely achieved even by the best quality controls. So nearly always they expect to replace or repair defective merchandise. This is more efficient than to insist on perfection in manufacturing—and consequently higher prices. The consumer who gets defective merchandise and takes the attitude that the seller tried to cheat, then, is usually wrong.

Furthermore, in most cases all that's necessary to get satisfaction is to make a simple claim and calmly give the justifying facts.

```
Your last shipment to us (our order No. A-1753,
your invoice No. 45602, dated May 6, 1986) was
incorrect. Instead of the socket-head set screws
with cups we ordered, you sent screws with flat
points. We were able to hold this shipment of
screws intact, having opened only one box.

Will you please rush us 5,000 5-40 × 1/4-inch
socket-head set screws, black finish, with cup
points. Our plant manager says we have enough of
the proper screws on hand to last us through June
12; so we must have the replacement screws by
then.

How shall we ship the screws with flat points
back to you? Do you want to cancel your invoice
No. 45602 or let it cover the replacement order?
We want to take your 2 percent cash discount.
```

To be nasty to the almost certainly innocent person who handles your claim is to be unfair and unreasonable, even foolish. Instead of creating a favorable mood that will help you get satisfaction, you turn this possible ally against you if you write in a nasty mood.

3. *Give the facts—calmly, specifically, thoroughly.* Usually a firm will grant an adjustment merely on the strength of a customer's adequate explanation of what is wrong and suggestions for a fair settlement. So unless you have good reason to believe otherwise, assume that the firm will be cooperative. Little or no persuasion seems necessary; hence you use no appeal beyond a possible brief reference to the guarantee, reputation for fair dealing, and the like.

This kind of direct claim may start with the requested action, or it may start with the history of the case. Beginning with the history of the case is a little less antagonizing and a little more persuasive.

The middle part is a carefully planned, complete, and specific explanation of the facts. A test of the adequacy of the explanation is to ask whether it is all you would want to know if you had to decide on the claim—and whether it is convincing. Hence you may need to use other evidence to back up your word. The ending, then, is a request for action. It should be as specific as the conditions will permit.

4. *When you know just what is wrong and what is necessary to set things right, you should make a definite claim; otherwise, explain and ask for an inspection.*

Sometimes you can be sure that the only fair adjustment is a refund of your money or a complete replacement of the product. On other occasions you can see that replacement of a part will correct the trouble.

You therefore ask definitely for what is necessary to make things right, as in the preceding claim.

Sometimes, however, the product just isn't right, but you don't know exactly what is wrong. Your claim then should be an explanation of how the product is failing to satisfy you and a request for the necessary action. You can make your own estimate and request that action, call in third parties to estimate (as on automobile insurance claims), or ask the firm to investigate and take the indicated action.

5. *Sometimes a touch of humor can relieve the pressure in small claims.* Several dangers confront you, however, if you decide to be humorous:

1. A failing attempt to be funny is worse than no attempt.
2. Humor may make you write a longer letter than necessary.
3. Humor making the reader the butt will nearly always arouse resentment.
4. Humor that verges on the vulgar or sacrilegious may offend.

## Adjustment Approvals

**Adjustment Policies.** Invariably a claim represents loss of time and money—and maybe goodwill and confidence in the goods or in the firm. The adjustment writer's key job is to minimize those losses by satisfying customers as far as possible at a reasonable cost to the company.

Some companies try to dodge the basic problem by almost literally adopting the policy that the customer is always right. They figure that the few unfair claims cost less in adjustment losses than the liberal policy pays in goodwill.

Other firms take the opposite view and make all sales final. Usually they depend on low prices rather than goodwill to attract a type of customer to whom price is the strongest possible appeal.

The great majority take the middle ground between those two extremes: *Treat each claim on its merits, and lean a bit toward giving the customer the benefit of the doubt for the sake of unquestioned fairness and the resulting goodwill.*

Generally a customer will not leave a firm or product after only one disappointment if the firm applies this honest and reasonable policy with finesse. Carrying out the recommended policy therefore requires

1. Careful analysis and classification of each claim according to the cause of dissatisfaction and consequently what adjustment is fair.
2. Retaining a reasonable attitude even with (sometimes) angry claimants.
3. Skill in the use of the tools and techniques of adjustment.

**Analysis and Classification of Adjustments.** If the evidence in a claim (and from inspection when deemed necessary) shows clearly that the company or the product was at fault, you may replace the article free with a perfect one, repair it free, or take it back and refund the money.

The last is the least desirable for both buyer and seller. The purchaser bought the article to get the service it would render. If you take it back, you give the purchaser a problem—to make other arrangements or do without that service. If you replace or repair it, you give the service, regain goodwill, and make a satisfied customer who will perhaps buy from you again and pass on the good word about you and your products to other prospects.

If the dissatisfaction is clearly the buyer's fault, you will ordinarily refuse the claim. In rare cases you may decide that a compromise or even a full-reparation adjustment will be wise because of the amount of goodwill you regain at small cost. The weakness in this decision is that it implies your acceptance of responsibility and increases your difficulty in regaining confidence in your goods and service. (See Chapter 7 for more detail.)

Whatever your action when the buyer is at fault, your major job is justifying your decision and (usually) educating the customer. By educating the buyer in the proper use and care of the product, you may establish the responsibility by implication, avoid irritating the claimant, and prevent future trouble.

When you decide to approve the adjustment, you will write a favorable reply, as discussed earlier. In answering claims, you have a legal and ethical obligation to be fair.

**Attitude of the Adjuster.** If a firm's adjuster thinks most claims are dishonest or from chronic gripers, this attitude will show and eventually reduce the number of claims—and probably the firm's sales too. People won't continue to trade where they are considered dishonest or unreasonable—as most are not. (In an extensive survey, out of 5 million customers only 2,712 tried to take advantage of one firm in five years.)

Claims are an invaluable clue to weaknesses in a company's products, methods, services, or personnel. If you start with the attitude that a claimant may be misinformed but is honest and reasonable, you will be right most of the time; and you will do much better. You will use claims as pointers to improve your firm's goods and operations, and your adjustment letters will thank customers for their help. (Even claims where the buyer seems completely at fault may point to a need for better instructions to users.) But more important, you create a pleasant climate in which people will buy more freely because they know they can get reasonable adjustments if anything goes wrong.

In addition to this sound attitude, you need a thick skin to be an adjuster. Many claimants are not calm. As a wise adjuster, therefore, you will ignore personal taunts. Remember the old saying, "You can't win an argument with a customer; even when you win you lose." So defend your firm, your products, and yourself insofar as you can by explanations; otherwise, accept the claims made. Thus you can create a climate of goodwill and good business.

**Adjustment Tools and Techniques.**
*Using Resale.* Since the adjustment writer's main job is to regain goodwill and confidence, you will find resale a highly useful tool. Indeed, the main job of an adjuster is essentially the same as the purpose of resale— to recover or strengthen goodwill and confidence in the integrity and efficiency of a firm and/or the quality of its goods. Naturally, then, resale is the main tool for doing that job.

*Making Positive Explanations.* Effective resale is impossible, however, unless you avoid the following special pitfalls that frequently trap the untrained adjuster:

1. Inadequate or inept explanation that leaves the customer thinking slipshod methods of manufacturing or marketing caused the trouble. (Explain how careful you really are—the high frequency of satisfaction.)
2. Dwelling on the reader's dissatisfaction or likelihood of being a lost customer.
3. Passing the buck by attributing the difficulty to a new clerk or an act of God.
4. Trying to hide in the bigness of your firm. About the only way you can use bigness as an acceptable explanation is to sell it in terms of customer benefits along with its weaknesses.
5. Stressing your openhandedness. The customer does not want to be considered a beggar.
6. Suggesting future trouble. You only put undesirable ideas into the customer's head if you say, "If you have any more difficulty, let us know," or even, "I don't believe you'll have any more difficulty." In fact, a big problem in adjustments is how to subordinate the inherent negatives in them.

*Handling Inherent Negatives.* As an adjustment writer, you need to be a master of the techniques for dealing with negatives. You'll do well to remember the definition of *negative* as anything unpleasant to the reader. Moreover, you should remember that *a good business communicator avoids negative material when possible and otherwise subordinates it.* You'll find that you can usually avoid most of the goodwill killers like the following, which creep into the work of untrained adjusters:

| you claim | policy | damaged | delay |
|---|---|---|---|
| you say | amazed | broken | inconvenience |
| you state | fault | defective | regret |
| you (plus any accusing verb) | surprised | unable | sorry |

Prune out such negative wording (and implications). Substitute positive phrasing.

## Adjustment Approval Checklist

1. Begin pleasantly—with the adjustment. Open with the full reparation—a statement of your action.
2. Explain fully, honestly, and reassuringly any favorable facts.
   a. Establish the reason for the mishap.
   b. Give evidence of normally high-quality goods and service, or explain changes you are making.
3. Ask for any necessary cooperation from the customer.
4. Close pleasantly with a forward look.

**Adjustment-Approval Messages.** Since an adjustment approval is good news, answer the big question as fast as you can, without any grudging tone or emphasis on the dissatisfaction.

Approving the adjustment gives you a basis for resale talk on the house. Use it as evidence that you stand behind guarantees and treat the customer right, or something similar.

Somewhere, but not necessarily right after the good news and its interpretations, express appreciation for the claimant's report (it helps the firm keep goods and services up to par). This "thank-you" does several important things quickly:

1. It shows that you are fair-minded, not distrusting or bitter.
2. It is basically resale (you are interested in retaining/improving your standards for goods and services).
3. It makes the customer feel good because a claim seems welcome and appears to get careful consideration.

Of course, if you are taking any steps to prevent recurrence of such claims, you should explain them (to rebuild confidence) and give the customer as much credit as the facts allow: "On the basis of helpful suggestions like yours, we have decided . . . ."

Your explanation of the situation will be important. If you explain specifically how your firm tries to see that everything goes well, most people will accept this as due precaution and will understand that mistakes do occasionally creep in, despite reasonable care—ZD production is an unattainable ideal.

If you have statistics to show how effective your system is, they may be effective in rebuilding the customer's confidence and goodwill. Be careful, though, not to present such data in a way that seems to say the reader must be odd to have trouble when nearly all your other customers don't.

End looking forward, not backward. A light touch of resale can provide you with a sincere, success-conscious look to future business. The following letter sends the check in the first sentence, then gives a clear explanation and strong resale (in answer to the claim near the end of Chapter 9):

> Here's your check as a refund on the XXX suit you purchased, for we support our salespeople in whatever they promise a customer.
>
> The person who told you that we would have no sale on XXX suits was, however, sincere. The XXX manufacturers have never before offered their suits at reduced prices, but one week before our summer clothing sale this year they notified us that they were permitting a reduction for the first time.
>
> We thank you for calling our attention to this situation, and we are glad to enclose our check for $21.87.
>
> When you again need clothing, see our salespeople. You can rely on what they tell you, with full confidence that we will back them up.

Sometimes you will need the customer's help on details such as filling out blanks for recovery of damages from a transportation company or returning defective articles. Cover such points in the one letter and make the reader's action as easy as possible:

> To simplify getting the insurance due from the Postal Service on the first shipment, we are sending a form completely filled out except for your signature. Will you please sign it and use the reply envelope to mail it back?

## Special Goodwill Messages

In the preceding chapters you have seen that all business communications should retain and try to increase the other person's favorable attitude toward you, even when you're working primarily on something else.

Certain situations, however, call for messages that have no immediate purpose other than cementing friendly relations. Although such special goodwill messages may not ask for any immediate action, indirectly they pave the way for smooth personal relationships within businesses, for continued business from old customers, and for new business from prospects.

Because people know you do not have to express them, these unexpected special goodwill messages are particularly effective in overcoming the impression of indifference—indifference within a firm, to business given, to the general public welfare, and to serving new customers. Since many of our non-American business friends (particularly the Orientals and Latins) look upon business relations as more personal than we do, goodwill messages are particularly important in business relations with them—to avoid appearing indifferent.

Many goodwill messages used to go out as separate individualized mailings. Because of the high cost of mailing individual letters, however, goodwill messages today often go out by phone or on printed forms (with invoices and bills or in annual reports, newspapers, and magazines).

Regardless of form, the messages serve such a significant purpose that they are numerous—and someone has to compose them. This section will help you phrase them and use them properly.

In theory, goodwill messages sell only friendship. Some do no more than that—ostensibly. But we should admit to ourselves that a letter on a firm's letterhead, signed by a representative of the firm, is promotional, regardless of its personal nature. The cultivation of business is inherent in the circumstance itself. Though no business writer need be reluctant to establish the virtues of a firm's services and goods and to place them at the disposal of the reader, blatant promotion under the guise of a goodwill message will probably bring resentment. *The main thing to guard against is appearing to be offering only friendship in the first part and then shifting to an obvious, immediate sales pitch.*

Some of these "unnecessary" special goodwill messages are so personal that to use an obvious form would be insulting, to include sales or even resale talk would be ludicrous, and to write very much would probably result in gushiness. Notes giving deserved praise or extending sympathy certainly fall into this category. Those expressing appreciation, extending seasonal greetings, issuing invitations, accompanying favors (or services), or offering helpful information also do if they are strictly for purposes of goodwill; but most of these are forms including sales-building talk and thus are promotional.

### Giving Deserved Praise

Although letters and notes praising people do not have to contain the word *congratulations,* you are recognizing a significant event or accomplishment in the life of your reader: a job promotion, election to an office, receiving an honor, winning a contest, graduation, marriage, birth of a child, or completion of a new plant, office, project, or report.

```
When I saw that you had been named plant manager
of Tri-States, I was delighted!
```

It's a well-earned recognition.
And it couldn't happen to a more deserving
person!

Any good effects of the foregoing passages would disappear if the writer
followed with such an idea as "Now that you're earning more, surely
you'd like to consider more insurance" or ". . . buy more clothes."

Thank you for doing so much to make our first
annual management meeting a success. Your
willingness to participate indicates exactly what
kind of professional you are.

I thought your talk on our booming international
business went very well, and I have heard several
comments from individuals indicating that your
presentation has been of considerable value (and
use) to them.

We share your pride and happiness in the
completion of the new Henderson plant.
It is a criterion of business, as well as civic,
accomplishment.
Good wishes from all of us.

A note like the following from any manager would certainly engender
good feeling (and probably stimulate the reader to do even better work):

Your analysis of production difficulties at the
Saginaw plant was one of the clearest, most easily
read reports I've ever been privileged to study.
We're carrying out some of your recommendations
immediately.
Several of us look forward to discussing the
report with you when you return to the home
office. In the meantime, thanks for a job well
done.

Many people in both their business and their private lives have discovered
the gratifying responses of associates, customers, and personal friends
to the receipt of a newspaper or magazine clipping of interest to the
reader. A simple greeting (it may be no more than "Good morning")
and a line or two like "This clipping made me think of you" or "I
thought you might be interested in this clipping" are enough, followed
by a note like:

> Let me add my commendation to those you've
> undoubtedly already received as a result of the
> enclosed clipping.

## Expressing Appreciation

You have observed that most congratulatory messages also involve an element of thanks. Likewise, most thank-you letters contain some commendatory passages. It's really just a question of where you want your emphasis to go.

Strictly goodwill thank-you messages—in response to a favor extended, for work on a project (member of a fund-raising team, for example), or for a contribution—often have their origins in civic, educational, and religious surroundings rather than in business.

This thank-you pleased the volunteer who helped open a theater for arts at a school:

> You and our other volunteers planned and handled
> the opening of Jefferson Center with care and
> skill. All of the events associated with the
> theater's debut will be recalled as peak
> experiences for the community.
>
> As a committed volunteer, you have helped the
> School of Arts achieve a level of community
> involvement and appreciation never before
> realized. Over 3,000 people have toured Jefferson
> Center in the two weeks following the Gala
> Opening.

> For the 32,000 youths of Athens . . .
> Thanks a million!
> Your generous gift to the new "Y" building is
> another evidence of your concern for the boys and
> girls of our city and county.
>
> We appreciate your cooperation in this project.
> As citizens and parents, we'll all be happy about
> our "Y" for years to come.

*Any* time is a good time to express appreciation to good customers for handling accounts satisfactorily. Even the notation on a current bill, "One of the pleasures of being in business is serving a good customer like you," has a heartening effect.

> Thank you for using your newly opened account.
> Surely you found it a quick, convenient way to
> shop at Tilford's.

```
To make sure our merchandise and service are just
the way you want them, we'll always welcome any
comments you may have about improvements you would
like us to make.
We want to continue to serve you well, and we
pledge our efforts to keep your trust.
```

Because of the rush of business, such messages too often go out only around holiday and special-event times. By arriving unexpectedly and without apparent reason at some other time, something like the following note is probably a more effective pleasant reminder of the firm's appreciation:

```
Believe us--
--we appreciate your continued business.
And to hold your friendship and patronage, we
certainly intend to continue giving you the sort
of service and honest values you deserve. See us
again when we can serve.
```

```
Your check this morning in prompt payment of your
last purchase made me think, "I wish all our
accounts were handled so efficiently."
It's a real pleasure to service an account like
yours, and we thank you sincerely for your
cooperation.
```

When a firm expresses appreciation to an individual, it expects no reply. And when an individual takes the time to pay a business firm a compliment or express appreciation for good service, no answer is *required*. But you establish yourself as courteous and polite if you do reply.

When a company receives suggestions for improved service, some of which will be outright complaints requiring adjustments, an acknowledgment *is* required, particularly if it has invited the suggestion.

```
You are quite right, Mr. Von Bergen. The exhaust
on your new Servaire portable air compressor
should point away from the air intake, not toward
it.
That is how we originally designed the
compressor. But apparently we did not make clear
to our dealer how to install the pipe when
assembling the unit for sale to you. We're glad
you were able to reinstall it correctly.
```

As a result of your experience, we are altering
the exhaust flange mounting to make it impossible
to install the exhaust improperly. Thank you for
telling us about the problem.

### Sending Seasonal Greetings

A modified form of thank-you is the season greeting (also used by firms
in the Orient). By far the most common times are around Christmas
and New Year.

Business firms, too, pause at this season to
count their blessings.

Good friends and customers like you are one of
our greatest blessings.

So we want to tell you how much we appreciate
your business at the same time we send heartiest
wishes for A VERY MERRY CHRISTMAS AND A HAPPY,
SUCCESSFUL NEW YEAR!

### Conveying Sympathy

Unlike seasonal greetings, congratulatory and thank-you messages are
practically always individualized. Expressions of sympathy—the most
personal of special goodwill messages—must be.

Admittedly, condolences are among the most difficult special goodwill
messages to write because of the melancholy circumstances (which you
can reduce by avoiding specifics). But certainly everyone appreciates
them.

Sorry, Sam--

--to hear that you're in the hospital again.

But with rest and good care you'll be back at
work soon.

I've always valued you as a friend and
appreciated you as a business associate; so for
two reasons I hope all goes well with you.


We were genuinely distressed to learn of the
death of Mrs. Guin, your partner and our good
friend for many years.

We respected her as a good business associate who
insisted on high standards in serving the public
and was always just, fair, and cooperative in her
relations with us. We admired the good judgment,

> vision, and integrity she showed as a business
> leader in your community.
>
> To you who saw these and other fine qualities in
> greater detail and frequency than we were
> privileged to, we offer our sympathy.

Such a letter will necessarily have an emotional impact. But that effect can be less if you will refrain from quoting Scripture or poetry. And sepulchral overtones will not be so powerful if you accept death as the inevitability it is and use the word itself rather than euphemisms like "passed away," "passed to his reward," and "departed." Emphasize the good characteristics and the outstanding contributions of the dead individual rather than the sorrow and anguish of the survivor. Accept the thought that good, worthwhile people continue to exert their influence in the hearts and minds of those who knew them.

Adversity also strikes in other forms—fires, floods, accidents and lawsuits, labor unrest, and work stoppage. When it does, the victim(s) will appreciate a message that says, "We're your friends; we understand the significance of this to you; we hope everything will work out well."

## Extending Welcomes and Invitations

One of the most popular forms of goodwill message greets newcomers to a community and offers to be of assistance, particularly during the orientation period. Almost always it is an invitation to come in and get acquainted; it also emphasizes the services of the inviting firm.

A bank or other firm with commercial/profit aspirations would have to be subtle, however, to have its welcome accepted at face value—and not use a hard-selling "come and do business with us."

Someone connected with credit, for example, could easily maintain a list of newcomers to the community and mail a welcoming form (which does not promise credit but only invites the application).

The invitation to a special event extended in the following letter would probably be read with interest. It builds goodwill because it expresses a desire to render service; no sales promotion (except that inherent in the action itself) distracts:

> How are you going to be up-to-date with all the
> new income tax regulations by April 15?
>
> If you've not read all the fine print, then join
> Chris Lawrence, a broker with Murial Launch
> Investments, from 7-9 for three Monday nights
> starting February 1 in the Seminar Room of the
> City Library. Chris has handouts, gives solid
> advice, listens to your problems. You come to the
> seminar as Murial Launch's guest.

```
Just indicate on the addressed-stamped card that
you'll be at the free seminar February 1.
```

The following to a new shareholder is typical of what many corporations do to cement goodwill.

```
On behalf of the Board of Directors and employees
of Pushman, I welcome you as a Pushman
stockholder.
Through your shares in Pushman, you participate
in ownership of one of America's leading
corporations . . . one with a bright and promising
future.
Your company has operations in virtually every
part of the world, activities that reach into a
broad range of products and services that help
make human life better.
As your company progresses, you will receive
regular reports. I've enclosed your company's
latest annual report to give you an in-depth view
of our achievements and status last year.
Again, welcome to Pushman. We look forward to
sharing with you.
```

## Anticipating Resistance

In the interest of forestalling complaints and minimizing dissatisfaction, many business executives give advance notice when they foresee something like an interruption of service, a curtailment of service, or a necessary price increase. In almost all instances these notices (often only postcards) must be obvious forms. They need to stress service—improved service, if possible; at least, maintaining superior service or quality of goods—as an antidote to the inherently negative material that the message has to establish.

This message from a power company is typical (dates and times varied according to areas and so were stamped in). Notice, again, the effective psychology of good news first (justifying the bad), bad news embedded in the middle, and a pleasant ending.

```
To provide better service for you and our other
customers in your area, we have installed new
equipment, which we plan to place in service
April 15, 19--
between 1 and 2 P.M.
```

> To safeguard the workers who do this work, we
> shall have to shut off power during this time.
> Service will resume as promptly as possible. We
> appreciate your cooperation in making this
> improved service possible.

A notification of a coming price increase is even more unwelcome. But with specific details justifying the increase, it may be successful in retaining the goodwill of some otherwise lost customers. The following notice went to all customers, riding free with their monthly bills:

> It's been a tough year, hasn't it? Wages have
> gone up, costs of materials and supplies have gone
> up, utility bills have gone up, insurance has gone
> up, transportation costs have gone up.
>
> Of course, this isn't news to you. Everybody's in
> the same boat. Including us.
>
> Our highly trained operators need more money, our
> costs for machines and supplies are rising,
> electricity is more expensive . . . everything is
> more expensive.
>
> To continue to give you the same prompt,
> efficient service we have in the past, and to add
> new technological advances as they become
> available, we have to increase our charges. The
> rates on the attached rate sheet will go into
> effect July 1.
>
> Thus we can and do continue to guarantee, as
> always, the same high-quality service you expect.

Such a notice as the preceding can be even more convincing (and hence effective) if you can give the specifics of your cost increases for the past few months or years.

## Improving Services

To find out how to improve their services, hospital administrators (like other administrators) often use a goodwill message along with a special request asking the recipient to complete a questionnaire. It can sometimes ride free with the bill. Whether it brings helpful suggestions, complaints, unreasonable ideas, or no response, it will build goodwill by showing concern.

```
We tried to serve you well in our Emergency
Department. Since only you can evaluate our
services, however, we would appreciate your taking
a few minutes to fill out this questionnaire. Your
comments will help us improve our service and
reward members of our staff when deserved.
Your replies will be kept completely
confidential.
```

By being alert to conditions, keeping informed about what is happening to your fellow workers and your clientele, you'll see plenty of opportunities for goodwill messages. This short treatment is only a springboard for your thinking and practice rather than an extensive catalog.

In fact, opportunities for helpful goodwill messages are so numerous and varied that there is no checklist for them. You'll do well, however, to

1. Express orally or in writing all you can of these messages you don't have to send but should. The subheads in this chapter provide you some starting points for thinking of appropriate situations.

2. Make them specific enough to fit and be meaningful even when you use forms.

3. In these most personal of business messages, be especially careful to get names, addresses, and facts right when you individualize them.

4. Avoid gushing in tone or length.

5. If you are writing within a corporation, note whether you are writing up or down the corporation ladder.

## Questions and Exercises

1. You are offering *Business America* at a special price. Where would be the most effective places to put the price in your letter?

2. In answering an inquiry about fire sprinklers for homes, how would you describe them psychologically to a prospective buyer?

3. If you have to include some negative information about a product, where do you put it and how do you phrase it?

4. In one sentence, write a reference to an order card that is stamped, addressed, and enclosed.

5. Write a four-part action ending selling a modern camera to a dealer.

6. Write a resale sentence on a product you are presently using.

7. Write a statement that has adaptation to
   a. Parents of a two-week-old baby.
   b. An executive who has bought one of your condominiums at Siesta Key, Florida.

8. Should you write a letter of congratulations to someone who has been appointed to a position over you whom you don't like, don't trust, have found inefficient? The person (whom you have worked with two years) got this promotion because of being a smooth talker and operator—a real politician. If you write it, what do you say?

9. One of your superiors dropped dead suddenly. You know the family of the superior slightly, and you admire the spouse considerably; but the superior was unreasonable, difficult, mercurial, explosive, deceptive. Should you write the spouse a sympathy note? If so, what can you say?

10. A team of five executives at your corporation prepared a report for you; but you suspect that one of them, Sarah Mayberry (hardworking, dedicated, intelligent), did most of the work. Should you write a memo of thanks to all five or to just Sarah? If you write all, should you praise Sarah especially?

11. An executive under you has written an unclear, inaccurate report to be presented to the board of directors next week. Should you write a memo spelling out all the faults, or should you call in the executive and go over the report orally? Should you give a reader-benefit reason for taking such action before you give the bad news? What reader-benefit reason can you give?

12. Can you think of any kind of goodwill message that should or should not be expressed orally or in writing?

13. Can you remember any goodwill message that you have received?

14. What are two important general considerations in messages of congratulations?

15. Should you reply to a letter of appreciation from a customer?

16. In a letter of sympathy, should you spare the reader's feelings by avoiding any direct references to death?

17. What would be the three major topics in a letter announcing a price increase, and in what order should they appear?

## Chapter Outline

# 7
## Disappointing Messages

Unless you recall clearly (from the first section of Chapter 5) the suggestions about handling bad-news messages, turn back and quickly review them. The guidelines there are important as a basis for this whole chapter, and especially in international communication. (People from other cultures generally expect even more gentle and gracious presentation of bad-news messages than do people in the United States.)

## Refusing Requests

Most people are disappointed, irritated, or downright angry when told they can't have something, can't do something, or can't expect you to do something—unless you *first* give at least one good reason.

When you deny someone something, therefore, you give a reason first. Then you give something else to compensate for the loss when you can, and you try to extend some gesture of friendliness.

Simply stated, the desirable plan for refusals is therefore

- A buffer beginning (establishing compatibility; defined and illustrated below).
- A review of facts (reasons).
- The refusal itself, subordinated, *or* A counterproposal that implies the refusal.
- An off-the-subject ending.

Before studying this suggested structure, however, read the following refusal, which follows the plan:

> While we are primarily manufacturers of extruded plastic products, as members of this community we also recognize a share in the responsibilities for its well-being.
>
> Each year we therefore actively support the United Way. One of our chief officers usually

```
serves on the Board of Directors, as our Vice
President of Finance presently does. For the past
five years both our employees as a group and
Martin Plastics as a corporation have contributed
our fair share to the United Way each year.
```

```
Since the United Way divides its receipts among
the various charities, we are thus able to
contribute to all at one time. We strongly feel
that the United Way is the fairest way of
fulfilling our charitable obligations and making
the biggest possible contributions.
```

```
Next year when the annual United Way drive is on,
we shall take comfort in knowing that your
charity, Homes for Homeless Pets, will again
receive its portion of the money to continue its
valuable work for the animals that depend so much
on us--and in knowing that we have done our part.
```

## The Buffer Beginning

Since people don't normally ask for what they don't expect to get, a reader opening your reply to a request almost certainly expects pleasant news. If you present a refusal immediately, or even reasons pointing that way, you appear to ignore those feelings and are likely to arouse a negative reaction, causing a mind closed to anything else you say.

To prevent such deadlocks, you need to indicate some form of agreement or approval of the reader and/or the subject. Frequently you can agree with some statement made in the request. At least you can say something to establish compatibility, even if nothing more than that you have given the proposal serious thought. This is your buffer.

*Six warnings* about writing buffers, however, deserve attention.

1. **Don't** appear to be granting the request. Such a beginning as this would mislead most readers:

```
You are right, Mr. Kolb, that abandoned pets
deserve help from each of us personally.
```

*In fact, anything you say in the buffer that seems inconsistent with what you say later will produce more resentment than effectiveness.*

2. The *second* warning is against beginning so far from the subject that the reader isn't even sure the letter is a reply. The buffer beginning must clearly identify the general subject. This beginning is irrelevant:

```
I well remember my first pet, a small white dog
with an irresistible sense of humor.
```

3. The *third* warning is against recalling any disappointment too negatively—for example, answering a claim with "We regret your dissatisfaction . . . ."

4. *Fourth,* you need to be careful about buffer length. Don't make the buffer too short to get in step with the reader or too long to suit an impatient reader.

5. *Fifth,* you need to make a smooth and natural transition to the next part (your explanation).

6. Although many writers begin refusals with "I really wish we could . . . ," this is stereotyped, sounds insincere, and worse, establishes the refusal before showing any reason.

To sum up, we can say that a good buffer will be *equivocal, relevant, pleasant, concise, and transitional.*

## Reasons Rather than Apologies

If you will apply the positive thinking and phrasing under Positive Statement and Success Consciousness near the end of Chapter 5, you will not apologize in a refusal, *especially in the beginning.*

In most cases when you have to refuse, that refusal depends on good reasons. *Those reasons—not some apology or policy—form the bedrock of your explanation.* For example, the following letter from a manufacturer refusing a dealer's request for samples stresses reader benefits in every paragraph after the first:

> Congratulations on your 25 years of service to your community!
>
> Through continued association with retailers, we know that their long-range success depends on sound managerial policies and services.
>
> We have tried to help in these successes by cutting costs whenever possible and passing these savings on to retailers in the form of lower prices. This aim led us to eliminate the high (and often unpredictable) manufacturing and shipping costs of special samples. You and hundreds of other druggists have benefited from these cost reductions over the years.
>
> Our favorable prices on quality products plus national advertising and help with point-of-sale promotions are the best ways we've found to increase your Walwhite sales.
>
> If you'll fill in and mail the enclosed card, Mr. Robert Abbott (your Walwhite representative) will be glad to arrange a special Walwhite exhibit that

> will attract many customers to your anniversary
> sale and well-deserved celebration.

To attempt to apply such reader-benefit interpretation in every case, however, would sometimes result in artificial, insincere talk. Better than that is a thorough, logical explanation that is friendly and positive. The following letter refusing a request for permission to reprint some sales letters of a mail-order house is quite acceptable, though (justifiably) self-protective:

> You can count on a large, interested readership
> for your article about the importance of sales
> letters.
>
> In our company, as you know, we depend on such
> letters exclusively for sales. Of necessity, then,
> we have tested extensively to find the most
> effective procedures. Our highly paid writers are
> continually revising, sending expensive test
> mailings, and comparing the returns. The best
> letters represent a considerable investment.
>
> In the past, rival companies have used some of
> our standard letters without consent. Because that
> use decreased the letters' effectiveness for us,
> we now copyright all our sales forms and confine
> them to company use. Should we release them for
> publication, we would have to incur the same
> expenses again.
>
> Doing my best to help, therefore, I'm sending you
> some bulletins and a bibliography that may help
> you with your article. Will you let me know the
> issue of the magazine your article appears in?

If you establish such good reasons, you have no cause to apologize for protecting your self-interest.

## The Derived, Positive Refusal

Ideally, your explanation and reasons so thoroughly justify you in refusing that anyone would infer the turndown. Thus prepared, your reader is far more likely to accept your decision calmly.

But you cannot always depend exclusively on implication. The refusal must be clear; but even when you have to state it, it need not be brutally negative. In fact, it need not be negative at all. You may have noticed, for example, that the writers of the sample refusals in this section *established the idea of what they were not doing by a statement of what they were doing.*

| Not | But |
|---|---|
| We don't contribute to individual charities. | . . . the United Way is the fairest way . . . of fulfilling our charitable obligations . . . . |
| We do not supply special samples to retailers. | We . . . help . . . by cutting costs . . . and passing these savings on to retailers in the form of lower prices. |
| We cannot let you have samples of our sales letters. | We copyright all our sales forms and confine them to company use. |

When you incorporate the limiting words *only, solely, exclusively* (even phrases like *confine to* and *concentrate on*), no doubt remains.

Saving some of your reasons until after establishing the refusal, or offering other ways of helping, enables you to **embed** the disappointing news and thus reduce the impact of the refusal. In any event, you certainly want to clear up the refusal so you can leave your reader on a more pleasant note.

## The Pleasant, Hopeful Ending

In some refusals you can do little but reassure the reader that you are not utterly indifferent. Good wishes for the success of the project, the suggestion of other sources, possibly the suggestion of being helpful in other ways—all of these are possibilities for ending your letter with a friendly gesture.

Sometimes you can suggest an alternative action. In many instances it can both imply the refusal and furnish you with the positive ending you seek.

Prudential's employees and clients will no doubt benefit materially from the reports manual you are planning, Mr. Lee--especially if it is of the same caliber as the letters manual your staff prepared.

I'm sure many college teachers would be glad to furnish you illustrative material. And I am no exception. In the past 25 years of working with business and college people to improve the quality of their reports, I've collected much HOW NOT TO and HOW TO teaching material.

For most of this I have only my single file copy, which I use in teaching a report-writing course three times a week and which I carefully keep in my office.

I'm sure my student assistant would be glad to photocopy it for you during off-duty hours at the

## Checklist for Refusing Requests

1.  Your buffer opening must pleasantly establish compatibility.
    a. Keep the emphasis on your reader, not on how pleased or flattered you are.
    b. Don't appear to be on the verge of granting or refusing the request.
2.  Your transition must follow coherently and logically from your buffer.
    a. To avoid sounding selfish, keep the emphasis on the reader.
    b. Keep it positive—avoid *although, however, but,* or *yet.*
3.  Give at least one good reason before even implying the refusal.
    a. Emphasize unselfish reasons if you can—not "our policy . . . ."
    b. For believability, you need specificness; but stick to the plausible.
4.  The refusal itself should be
    a. A logical outcome of the reasons given (reader-interpreted).
    b. Presented positively—in terms of what you can do and do do.
    c. Preceded (and preferably followed) by justifying reasons.
    d. Unmistakable but implied or subordinated (as by a counterproposal).
    e. Written without negative words or apologies.
5.  Continue your helpful attitude in the ending.
    a. Your ending must be positive and relevant.
    b. Be wary of the expression "If I can help in other ways, please let me know." It can produce some sarcastic reactions.
    c. Follow through specifically with any wanted action.

regular rate of $4 an hour. Since the job involves no more than 50 or 60 pages, I feel reasonably sure that securing the material this way would cost you only $8-10.

I shall be glad to make the necessary arrangements if you would like me to. I'm sure I can have the material to you within four or five days after hearing from you.

Please note again that this writer does not resort to negative phrasing or apologies.

## Refusing Adjustments

A letter refusing an adjustment is obviously a bad-news message requiring your psychology of saying no. For your buffer, look for something relevant and pleasant; but get to your explanation fairly early.

Several special techniques are important to rebuild goodwill. You already know better than to hide behind the word *policy* or to give no reason at all. But neither can you merely tell what a guarantee states.

Since you are refusing, you *have* to give the basic fact(s) on which your refusal depends. Doing so, of course, makes the reader guilty; but don't accuse directly.

In fact, if you arrange your reasons and explanations carefully, they will probably make the negative answer clear by implication. If not this way, at least you subordinate the refusal by embedding it (that is, putting it in the middle of a paragraph where it doesn't stand out unduly). If you still feel that you must state it, your best technique (for this special situation) is to fall back on the passive, impersonal presentation (something "was not done" instead of "you didn't")—rather than accuse.

After the refusal, you may do well to add some more explanation in support (thus embedding and further subordinating the refusal). Be sure you say enough to make your refusal clear and justified.

Your ending then attempts to get agreement or the reader's acceptance of your refusal as justified. That is, you write with as much success consciousness as seems reasonable about the future outlook, but don't ask whether your action is all right.

Often the best ending assumes that the preceding explanation and decision are satisfactory and talks about something else. Rather than looking backward, it may be *better to look forward to the next likely relationship between writer and reader.* Notice how the following letter explains thoroughly but without direct blame.

> Your customers certainly do have a right to demand that all Neenah monogrammed stationery be perfect. One of the reasons we specify that all orders be typed or printed is to accomplish this aim.
>
> For that same reason, on the rare occasions when a shipment is not exactly as ordered, we print and ship corrected letterheads without question and without charge. To be sure your Neenah customers get exactly what they want, however, we need your careful help. If you'll check your orders of the past two months, you'll see that we have replaced six. A similar check of the enclosed photocopies will show clearly that we followed the original directions exactly on this seventh request.
>
> A corrected shipment for Mr. Washburn reading "Freemont" instead of "Fairmont" and for Miss Wentworth reading "Montevallo University" rather than "Montevallo College" will nevertheless go out to you within two days after we receive your approval of our two-part plan: (1) We'll debit your account for the new shipment at the usual prices, subject to our usual terms; (2) for

```
greater profit for both of us, we ask you to again
instruct your sales personnel to type or print all
orders and verify with each customer every letter
and every number to appear in the final printing.
You can then rely on our providing you exactly
what you order.
```

The accompanying checklist reviews the highlights of refusing adjustments.

# Compromising on Adjustments

When you decide to seek a compromise—usually because of divided responsibility, or uncertainty about responsibility or correction for the trouble—you may use either of *two* plans.

In the *first* you follow the refused-adjustment plan exactly down *to* the refusal. There you make your proposed compromise instead, explicitly. In effect, you are refusing the adjustment requested and are making a counterproposal—a compromise. When you ask acceptance of it, your success will depend not only on (1) how well you have presented facts and reasons to justify the compromise but also on (2) your success consciousness in presenting it and on (3) your phrasing it to encourage acceptance.

The following letter in answer to a strong request for removal of a heater, cancellation of the remaining payments, and refund of the shipping and installation charges illustrates the points. You will notice that it offers to compromise to the extent of canceling the remaining payments but proposes another action instead.

```
You are right in expecting your Warmall to heat a
large area such as your entire office. That is
what it was designed to do.

To do so, the Warmall requires careful
installation. It must be located so that the air
currents can carry its heat to all parts of the
room. Our engineer reports that it was installed
in the proper position but that later remodeling
of your office has blocked circulation of air with
a half partition.

Your heater can be all you want it to be if
relocated; so removing it would be useless. That
```

# Refused- and Compromise-Adjustment Checklist

1. Make your buffer relevant, pleasant, equivocal, and transitional.
   a. Reflect pleasant cooperation (try to agree on something).
   b. Don't imply that you're granting or refusing the request yet.
   c. Avoid recalling the dissatisfaction more than necessary.
   d. Early resale in the trouble area bluntly contradicts.

2. Make your facts and reasons courteous, thorough, and convincing.
   a. An immediate "our guarantee" or "our policy" is abrupt.
   b. Don't accuse or preach. Explain impersonally.
   c. Even intimating refusal before reasons is bad psychology.

3. Make the refusal logical, subordinate, and impersonal but clear.
   a. Give it little emphasis. Consider implying it, impersonally.
   b. Reader education or a counterproposal may imply the refusal.

4. Make your ending pleasant, positive, and success-conscious.
   a. When you need reader action, ask for it positively.
   b. Adequate explanation makes apologies unnecessary reminders.

For the COMPROMISE ADJUSTMENT, use these for Items 3 and 4:

3. Make your counterproposal without parading or belittling it.
4. Ask permission; give necessary directions.

would mean losing your down payment and what you have paid for shipping and installation, although we would of course cancel the remaining payments. Moreover, you must have heat, and the Warmall will do the job.

We have absolute faith in our engineer's judgment, but your satisfaction is more important. So we want to do what is fair to us both.

At your convenience we can move the heater to the position our engineer suggested; and if it does not heat to your satisfaction, we will remove it and not charge you another cent.

Will you suggest the most convenient time for the change that will make your whole office area warm and comfortable?

We can do the job so quickly and efficiently that your business can continue as usual.

For a checklist following this plan of compromise-adjustment letter, see the Refused-Adjustment Checklist.

A *second* method of compromising—usually called the full-reparation beginning compromise—sometimes works better. You follow the plan for *granting* an adjustment at the beginning, through the explanation. The facts, of course, will indicate divided or uncertain responsibility. Your resale talk will indicate that the repaired product (or a replacement up to par, in case the original was beyond repair) will give the service the customer wanted.

Since the original desire for that service presumably still exists, you ask the customer to make a choice—the refunded money or the product. And of course you encourage choice of the product, because that way you have a customer satisfied with your product as well as your fair-minded practices.

Your main purpose is to restore goodwill and confidence. Again your success depends on three things: (1) a start that offers everything requested and thereby pleases the customer, (2) your explanation showing the justice of a compromise, and (3) your fair-mindedness in allowing the choice. The danger—not a very serious one—is that some people might try to keep both the money and the product.

Attached to this letter is a credit memorandum for $93.75, which we cheerfully send you for the five Bear Mountain hunting jackets. It is an indication that Bowen's will always treat you fairly.

Under the assumption that these jackets would find a ready sale at a reduced price despite slight imperfections (a button mismatched, a crooked seam, or maybe a little nick in the fabric), we offered them "as is" and priced them at $18.75 instead of the regular $27.75. We felt that marking them "as is" indicated special circumstances.

Generally we follow the accepted business custom of making all such reduced-price sales final for an entire lot. But as we evidently did not make the situation perfectly clear, we are leaving the decision up to you. If you feel that you're entitled to the adjustment, it's yours.

Many of your customers, however, would probably be glad to get nationally advertised Bear Mountains at perhaps $46 instead of the standard $56. And even if you sell these five at, say, only $37.50, your percentage of profit will be about the same as if you sold perfect jackets at full price.

## Checklist for Compromise with Full-Reparation Beginning

1. The disarming beginning giving everything asked for is basic.
   a. Carefully avoid unnecessary negative reminders.
   b. You have to show reasons before compromising.
2. The explanation must show that the claimant is expecting too much.
   a. Do not directly accuse; show blame impersonally.
   b. Establish the facts to show your reasonableness.
3. Show your service attitude and fair-mindedness in your proposal.
   a. Recall the reader's original desire for the service.
   b. Continuing the reader-benefit interpretation, state your proposal.
   c. Don't parade your generosity in the loss you take.
4. The ending should give a choice but encourage yours.
   a. Tell what you want done: accept your proposal.
   b. End with a short suggestion of reader satisfaction.

As they are, these jackets are still ready to stand a lot of hard wear. They are made to suit hunters' needs, with ample pockets for shells and with comfortable tailoring. Selling them should be easy, especially at a discount.

So if you'd like to reconsider and want to offer these jackets at a saving, just initial the face of this letter and send it to us with the credit memo. We'll absorb the return shipping charges. The decision is yours, but we think you can make a good profit on them at the special price.

Applying the checklist for compromises with a full-reparation beginning to this letter will show that the letter is pretty good and will review the principles for you.

## Requests for Credit Information

Many applications for credit do not give all the information you must have. You therefore write for the needed information—normally using forms in routine situations.

The major problem is to avoid arousing the reader's indignation because you have not approved credit right away. In such a case you write a special bad-news letter with careful explanation and tone not possible in a form.

To soften the effect of the delay in approving credit, begin with a buffer, stress the benefits of complying with the request, show that you treat all applicants alike, make action easy, and promise quick action. If character is not in question, be sure to say so. And to encourage response, use resale or sales promotion to embody your explanation.

The following letter is typical in referring to ". . . the usual financial information that all our dealers furnish us . . ."—an appropriate covering letter for the form.

> Corone fishing gear is a good line to handle. Tackle dealers throughout the country report the favorable reaction of anglers. And our advertising in Field and Stream and Sports Afield continues to create demand for Corone dealers.
>
> We're just as eager as you are to have your Corone sales start; so will you supply the usual financial information that all our dealers furnish us, along with the names of other firms from which you buy on credit? Most of our applicants use the enclosed form, but if you prefer to use your own, please do.
>
> This confidential information will enable us to serve you efficiently--now and in the future.

Because most requests for credit information from customers are simply modifications of direct request, we run no checklist or cases.

## Credit Refusals

In the light of poor standing on any or all of the four C tests of credit (Chapter 6), you will have to refuse some credit applicants. The most likely reasons are unfavorable reports from references (character) or an unfavorable financial position (capital). In the case of an old customer it may be a refusal of a credit-limit revision.

*Whatever the reason, you have to establish it;* but you certainly do not want to close the door irrevocably (except possibly to deadbeats). A poor account now may be a good one a year later.

For that reason, most good credit refusals establish good feeling in a short buffer, show the reasons in an analysis of the circumstances, identify the deficiency, refuse in positive fashion, suggest how the customer can remedy the deficiency, and invite a later application. *The best ending is an attempt to sell for cash.* After all, the reader wants your goods and possibly can't get them on credit elsewhere either.

In the following instance the retailer quickly responded with a financial statement and references in response to the request for them. Since the references reported that payments were good enough during normal times, the credit writer sought to cultivate potential business (based on the references) while declining the account at present (based on the most impersonal and palatable spoiler—conditions):

> Your large order for Stalwart coveralls suggests the prospect of an early strike settlement in your area. We're glad to hear that.
>
> When the miners go back to work, the steady revival of business will no doubt help your collections so that you can reduce both your accounts receivable and your accounts payable. In that way you can probably quickly restore your current ratio to the healthy 2:1 we require. Such an improvement will enable us to consider your credit application favorably. Will you please send us subsequent statements?
>
> You'll probably need your Stalwart coveralls sooner than that, however; they're a popular brand because they wear well. Workers like the reinforced pockets and knees. They'll easily outsell other lines you might carry.
>
> You can stock this popular brand and thus satisfy present demand by paying cash and taking advantage of the liberal discount we can give you. On this order, for instance, the discount at our regular terms of 2/10, n/90 would amount to $14.08--enough to pay interest for three months on a $500 bank loan.
>
> Or you might cut your order in about half and order more frequently. But with a $200 bank loan at 15 percent and a stock turn of 12--which is a conservative estimate, Mr. Wolens--you'd make . . . .
>
> Since we can have your Stalwart coveralls to you in about five days, just attach your check to the memo I've enclosed and mail both of them to me in the enclosed envelope to handle the order in this profitable way.

Usually you can specifically isolate the shortcoming(s) (in one or more of the four C's) in an industrial or wholesale situation (as underlined in the preceding letter) and use impersonal, positive phrasing to suggest the remedy and leave the way open for future negotiations.

In consumer letters involving a retail customer, however, the usual reason for the refusal is the customer's failure to take care of obligations.

This is a highly personal reflection, one in which many credit people invite the customer to come in and talk.

An alternative is the forthright credit refusal in the usual sequence of buffer, reasons, positive refusal, forward look, and counterproposal in the form of a bid for cash business. The following letter refusing credit to a young man just out of college and with unsteady, low-income employment talks concretely and sensibly; it's a good credit-education letter. Note how the writer stresses the idea that character (the most ticklish element) is not the basis for refusal.

> When you wrote last week asking for credit, as a member of the Illinois Credit Union we automatically asked the Union for your record. You can well be proud of the report we received.
>
> Such a complimentary report on your excellent character indicates a promising future. The fact that you have never defaulted or delayed in paying an account means that you will be able to get credit easily when your income becomes steady.
>
> We could extend credit to you on the basis of your personal record alone. If some unforeseen expense should come up, however, you probably could not pay your account. As a cooperating member of the Credit Union, we would then be compelled to submit your name as a poor credit risk. Such a report would limit your chances of obtaining credit in the future.
>
> For your own benefit you'll be better off to stick to cash purchases now, but we shall look forward to the time when you can comfortably and safely contract for credit with us.
>
> Meanwhile you can make your dollars reach further by buying from Bowen's for cash. We buy in quantity, save on shipping costs, take advantage of discounts, and pass these savings on to you in the form of lower prices.

Letters limiting the credit of an established customer are no different from refusals to new customers; they just adapt the talking points. As in any good refusal, these letters do not apologize or remind of the refusal in the end. The accompanying credit refusal checklist incorporates the major suggestions.

## Credit Refusal Checklist

1. Your best beginning talks about something pleasant.
   a. Beware the selfish, misleading note of "We are glad to receive . . . ."
   b. To prevent buying elsewhere, get to resale early.
   c. References to the order, if there was one, should come in incidentally.

2. For your explanation and refusal:
   a. Give some justifying reasons before the refusal.
   b. Do not begin your explanation with writer-interest reasons.
   c. Make clear whether character is or is not the reason.
   d. Avoid a negative, nosy tone; state your reasons as helpfulness to the reader, with just enough facts to show that you know.
   e. Be sure you've made clear that you will not now approve credit.
   f. Without promising, leave the way open for credit extension later.

3. Your counterproposal (in conditional mood):
   a. As help to the reader, introduce a cash, reduced-shipment, or other plan.
   b. If you propose cash with a discount, figure the savings for a year.

4. Your ending:
   a. Leave no details uncovered in your proposal.
   b. In action-ending style, drive for acceptance; and get approval before taking action.
   c. Your last picture should show the reader's benefits.

## Acknowledging Problem Orders

Any firm that sells by mail will receive some orders that it can't handle as the standard ("all's well") acknowledgments discussed in Chapter 6. Some orders will be incomplete or vague, or for goods temporarily out of stock, or from people to whom you cannot sell, or for something a little different from what you have, or for several items involving a combination of these difficulties.

In acknowledging these varied problem orders to keep the business they offer, you need to know how to keep the picture as bright as possible. You need resale to keep reader interest. Adaptation becomes important because of the varied and special circumstances. And since you often must ask the reader for a change of mind or for further action, you need all the principles of persuasion.

When you get an *order that is incomplete* (and therefore vague), you can either try to guess what the customer wants and thereby risk extra costs and customer dissatisfaction, or you can ask for the needed information. Usually you write.

Since it is a *bad-news* message, you will wisely use a buffer. Resale, thanks, and (if a new customer) a hearty welcome are all good buffer material for beginning the letter. A problem here is to avoid misleading the customer into believing that you are filling the order.

Very early—perhaps by starting to interweave some of it into the first part of the letter—you should stress the *resale* element to overcome the drawbacks of additional trouble and delay. Although small bits of it may appear throughout the letter, at least some of it comes before the reader learns the bad news—to bolster the original desire in the moment of disappointment. It can be very short:

> Modern, efficient offices everywhere are using Castellan workstations like the ones you ordered, not only for their wide color choice and modern styling but also because of their people-oriented design and their durability.

When you have thus prepared the reader psychologically, *asking for* the needed information will reveal the bad news. Thus you save words, weaken the bad news by putting the reader's main attention on complying with your request, and avoid any goodwill-killing accusations. More specifically, your technique at this important crux of the letter is: *In one key sentence beginning with a reader-benefit reason for your request, ask for the information.* For example:

> So that we may be sure to send you exactly the workstations you need, will you please specify your color choice?

Now, if you add a touch of satisfaction-resale to motivate the requested action, do what you can to help the reader decide, and promise speed, you'll probably get the information you want, without irritation:

> Coming in harmonious shades of black, walnut, blue, and sand, Castellan workstations blend in well with any decor.
>
> Just use the handy return card, and you'll be enjoying your new workstations within two weeks after we receive the information.

For requesting additional order information in business-building fashion, apply the suggestions in the checklist for acknowledging problem orders.

Sometimes the problem in an acknowledgment is that you *can't fill the order right away.* In the absence of a specified time limit, try to keep the order on the books if you feel the customer would prefer to wait rather than cancel the order. After a buffer, tell when you can fill the order and (usually) assume that such an arrangement is acceptable.

# Checklist for Problem-Order Acknowledgments

1. If you're sending anything, say so quickly and cover details.

2. If *not,* acknowledge while keeping the picture bright with a positive, service-minded, and reselling buffer-like lead into the trouble area.
   a. Avoid negative terms like *forgot, delay, out of stock, wrong merchandising channel* or *don't handle,* and *substitute.*
   b. Remember, too, that emphasis-control methods (discussed in Chapter 3 and under **Emp** in Appendix C) can also soften the impact of necessary negative ideas.

3. The four problem-order situations require different explanations.
   a. Though the incomplete order is the orderer's fault, use a "best service to you" lead and *avoid accusing* by asking ". . . which size/color/model . . . do you want?"
   b. Though the back-order situation is your fault, you can probably explain better than to admit that you are an asleep-at-the-switch seller or to lie about the (assumed) booming sales.
   c. You should also have a respectable explanation for needing to rechannel an order or fill it with a substitute.

4. Likewise, the problem-order situations require different endings.
   a. While making your questions clear, avoid making the incomplete-order writer feel too stupid.
   b. While covering your own shortcomings as best you can in the back-order situation, try to keep the business offered by making clear what you can do/are doing now.
   c. Try to keep the business offered (or at least the goodwill) by explaining and reselling the rechanneling plan.
   d. The ending of the substitute-selling letter is like any other sales ending (Chapter 8)—plus avoiding implications of reader stupidity for ordering the wrong thing.

If the date is so far off that doubt arises (even within the 30-day maximum that federal law allows for consumers), ask instead of assuming. In either case the wise business writer will acknowledge the order promptly.

Again your main problem is keeping the order, despite the delay. Your main element is resale—to convince the reader that the product is worth the wait. It may include both resale on your organization and resale on the goods. If the order is the customer's first, resale is even more important and more extensive.

Your plan and technique are the same as for the acknowledgment of an incomplete order, at least through the first paragraph and some resale talk.

```
Your order No. 5E361 (dated July 19) for 24 No.
536 boron nitride standard 1/2-inch triangular
```

inserts represents a wise purchase. This new
material will let you operate at higher speeds and
take deeper cuts than you ever have before. The
resulting increase in productivity will mean
increased profits for you.

Then the explanation should picture the goods on their way (and imply receipt of them) in the first part of a sentence that ends with a clear indication that this does not mean now (usually by giving the shipping date):

By going onto double shifts, we are confident
that we will have our new sintering machinery set
up and operating in time to get these inserts, in
the quality you expect, to you by the end of
August.

As always, explaining in positive terms what you can do, have done, and will do is better than telling in negative terms what you can't do, haven't done, or won't do. As the writer of the preceding paragraph did, a good letter writer will avoid such unnecessary negatives as "out of stock," "cannot send," "temporarily depleted," "will be unable to," "do not have," and "can't send until."

Only a poor business manager gets caught short without a justifying reason. A good one will have a reason—and will explain it to customers to avoid the impression of inefficiency. Often it is basically strong resale material if properly interpreted. For example:

By performing our own sintering operation, we can
exert a higher standard of quality control and
give you inserts that have uniform density
throughout, with no weak spots, and with increased
resistance to fracturing. We have given your order
priority and are sure that by the end of August
you will have your inserts.

More resale may follow the explanation to help make the reader want the product badly enough to wait. Because it has such an important job to do, it is probably more important in the back-order acknowledgment than in any other. It should be short, specific, and adapted to carry its full effect.

We're sure you want only top-quality tooling that
will perform to specifications--and that is what
we insist on supplying you.

The ending of the back-order acknowledgment may go either of two ways:

1. You may ask outright whether you may fill the order when you have said you can. This plan is preferable if you seriously doubt that the customer will approve.

2. You may phrase it to complete the contract unless the reader writes back a cancellation. Your assumption (that your plan is acceptable) will hold more frequently if you never suggest the thing you don't want your reader to do—cancel.

The following letter illustrates the handling of a back-order problem:

The women's white tennis dresses you ordered April 7--

4 dozen Style No. 16J7 women's tennis dresses, 1 dozen each in sizes 8, 10, 12, and 14 @ $300 a dozen; terms 2/10, n/30

--are leading the summer sportswear sales from Maine to Hawaii.

We are increasing production on this model and have booked your tennis dresses for rush shipment by air express April 27.

The unusual preseason popularity of this trimly cut tennis dress owes much to its shimmering polyester and cotton fabric. When we used up our stock of the genuine combed cotton material, rather than use a substitute we shut down production on this model. A large stock of Glachine cotton fabric is already en route here from Wancrest's famous North Carolina mills, however; thus we are able to promise your shipment by April 27.

For this chance to prove once again Tropical's continuing fashion superiority, we thank you sincerely.

Much of the back-order acknowledgment technique is the same as that used in standard and incomplete-order acknowledgments. The checklist brings out similarities and additional considerations.

Only three reasons are likely to make you *decline an order:*

1. The customer has asked for credit, and you are not willing to sell that way. In that case the problem is a credit problem (discussed earlier in this chapter).

2. You don't have the goods (or a suitable substitute), and you don't expect to get them in time to serve the customer. You then explain the situation, tell where to get the goods (if you know), maybe present resale on your company and sales promotion material on any other goods that seem likely to be of interest, and end appropriately.

3. You don't market your products in the way proposed. Most of these problems arise because (*a*) the orderer is an unacceptable dealer or (*b*) you sell only through regular merchandising channels and the orderer (usually a consumer or retailer) does not propose to go through those channels.

The following letter illustrates declining an order for the second reason:

> Your order for us to repair your Keller 5,000-hp electric motor is evidence that you have been satisfied with our repair work--and we appreciate your confidence.
>
> At present we are equipped to rebuild just about any electric motor up to 500 hp. This is the capacity of our armature lathes and rewinding machinery. As you know, working on motors the size of your Keller is highly specialized work requiring large machines.
>
> We suggest you try Charles Lindgren & Co., 4018 Greenleaf St., Evanston, IL 60202. Lindgren specializes in repairing large electric motors and has the necessary equipment. Because of its good name in the trade, we can confidently recommend Lindgren.
>
> Thanks, however, for offering us the job. For prompt, expert service on your motors up to 500 hp, you can still rely on us.

*A dealer may be unacceptable* because (1) you sell only through exclusive dealerships and you already have a dealer in the territory or (2) because the orderer does not meet your requirements for a dealership. For example, the dealer may insist on consignment sales or unacceptable discounting.

The first part of the declining letter would be the same in each case and (except for the omission of resale) the same as the beginning of other bad-news acknowledgments. In the first case your explanation (usually beginning in the second paragraph) would be how you operate and why you operate that way plus the simple fact of the existing dealership. In the second case it would be a simple explanation of your requirements, with justifying reasons. The ending for the one would be a purely goodwill ending of "keeping in mind" in case you should later want another dealer. The other would end with an offer to reconsider if a change or additional information shows that the dealer meets your requirements.

Some buyers think that all manufacturers or producers should sell to anybody who has the money and omit jobbers, wholesalers, and retailers. They also complain when a producer does not make goods available in local outlets. Both methods of merchandising have advantages and disadvantages. Obviously, however, a producer has the right to sell in any legal way and can explain that way to a consumer asking for goods from a wholesaler or producer or to a retailer attempting to bypass the wholesaler.

Your bad-news letter begins in the same way as those acknowledging incomplete and back orders: with a buffer, including resale to help keep the customer interested in the goods (on which you do make a profit, of course, wherever you are in the marketing channels). As before, you are careful not to mislead.

After this beginning, you explain how you merchandise your goods (not how you don't, except by implication) and why you operate this way. As far as possible, you explain the *why* in terms of benefit to the customer (you-viewpoint)—not the benefits to you. At least a part of the reader-benefit *why* should come before the part of the explanation that conveys the bad news (by implication) that you are not filling the order.

If your explanation is good, the reader will decide that yours is the best way. If your resale talk has been good, the desire for the product will still be there although the purchase has to be elsewhere. You tell exactly how and where to get it, and you give a last touch of resale to encourage ordering the way you suggest.

If you have several equally convenient outlets, you name them all to give a choice and to be fair to all. This letter follows the directions:

> Karsol shower curtains like the ones you saw advertised will give you the wear you want for your motel units.
>
> So that you will be able to select personally the exact patterns you prefer (from eight different designs offered), we have set up a marketing plan of bringing Karsol shower curtains to you through local dealers only. This way you will save handling, shipping, and COD charges.
>
> You can get your curtains at the White House, 300 Main Street in Boulder, thus speeding your purchases and avoiding unnecessary delays.
>
> We have recently sent a large shipment of Karsol shower curtains to the White House, and you will be able to see for yourself that although these waterproof curtains are of exceptional strength and durability, they are soft and pliable.
>
> Stop by the White House and select your favorite pattern of Karsol shower curtains that will satisfy your customers.

If you are really a good business manager, you will notify the retailers, so that they can write or call the interested prospect who doesn't come in (especially if the order is for a big-ticket item).

Many times you will receive orders you can't fill exactly because you *do not have the special brand,* but you have a competing brand or something else that will render the service the customer obviously wants. You know that in most cases people buy a product not for the name on it but for the service they expect from it. If you think your brand will serve (and ordinarily you do, or you wouldn't be selling it), you remember your service attitude and try to satisfy the orderer's wants.

As a point of business ethics, you should not try to sell a substitute unless you sincerely believe you can truly serve by saving the customer time, trouble, or money in getting wanted products or by giving service at least comparable to what is available elsewhere in terms of cost.

Once you decide that you are ethically justified in selling the substitute, you need to remember several working principles:

1. Don't call it a substitute. Although many substitutes are superior to the things they replace, the word has undesirable connotations.

2. Don't belittle the competitor's product. Doing so is not only questionable ethics, it criticizes the judgment of the orderer.

3. Don't refer to the ordered product specifically by name any more than you have to. You want the would-be buyer to forget it and think about yours. Conversely, stress your product, perhaps repeating the exact name several times.

Except that *the identification and resale are in general terms broad enough to encompass both the product ordered and the substitute,* your beginning is the same as other buffers for bad-news acknowledgments. If you phrase the beginning well, you'll have no trouble making a smooth transition to further talk about the substitute.

```
Your repeat order of September 10 for 60 regular-
duty batteries suggests that you find your battery
business profitable. We're glad to hear it, but we
think we can show you how you can do even better
in the coming season.
```

You arrange to introduce at least one sales point favorable to the substitute *before* revealing that you can't send what was ordered. You need to convey the negative message fairly early, however, to keep the reader from wondering why all the talk about the substitute. Your best technique is the standard one for subordinating negative messages: Tell what you *can* do in a way that clearly implies what you can't.

```
In our continuous effort to provide you the best
automobile accessories and equipment at reasonable
```

prices, we have found that the new Acme battery
excels others of its price class in power,
endurance at full load, and resistance to
cracking. Because of those desirable qualities, we
decided two months ago to stock the Acme line
exclusively. Although Powell in Dayton still has
the Motor King, we think your customers will be
ahead in service and you'll make more profits with
the Acme.

Once you are over that rough spot, clear sailing lies ahead. You continue
your sales talk, concentrating on the substitute and what it will do for
your reader, not on why you do not carry the ordered product.

A good test of the adequacy of your sales talk is whether it tells all
you would want to know if you were being asked to change your mind
about the two products.

Because of its 115-ampere power and its endurance
of 5.9 minutes at full load, your customers will
like the fact that the Acme keeps a hard-to-start
engine spinning vigorously and increases the
chance of starting. They'll also like the tough
new plastic case that performs its tough job
better than any other material we know.

Sometimes your price will be higher than that of the product ordered.
If so, presumably you think your product is better. Your method of
meeting the price competition, then, is to sell the advantages and then
point to them as justifying the price.

When you explain the advantages the Acme has over
its competitors, you usually justify at least a $5
higher price in the customer's mind--and you
usually produce a prompt purchase. The Acme
battery will back you up, too, in the customer's
long experience with it. It carries the usual 36-
month pro rata replacement guarantee. And the fact
that it wholesales to you at only $2 more means an
extra $3 profit to you on each sale.

Sometimes you will have to admit (tacitly) that your product is inferior
but adequate. Your technique then is to sell its adequacy and the fact
that it is a good buy because of the price. If the customer had ordered
a higher priced battery than you now sell, for example, you could replace
the three preceding paragraphs with others stressing lower price, higher
sales volume, and higher total profit.

Usually, however, quality and price are about the same; and you simply sell the product on its merits and as a service or convenience because it is available.

When your selling job is done, you are ready to try to get action. You can do either of two things:

1. You can ask the orderer whether you may fill the order with the substitute, or you can ask for a new order specifying it.

2. You can send the product and give the orderer the option of returning it at your expense—that is, you pay transportation both ways. Thus no question of ethics arises.

The first way, you would have an ending something like

> May we help you increase your battery profits by filling your order with 60 of these new Acmes in the same sizes you ordered?

The second way will sell more goods if you word the offer carefully to avoid any high pressure. You should use it, however, only in an attempt to give the best service you can—for example when the customer indicated pressing need, transportation costs are small, and you are reasonably sure of acceptance. Indeed, a recent Supreme Court decision may relieve the receiver of any responsibility for returning or paying for unordered goods.

If you do send the goods on option, you can greatly affect your chance of having them accepted by the wording of your offer. Note the difference between these two ways:

> We believe you will find the Acmes satisfactory. Therefore, we are filling your order with them. If you don't like them, just return them to us collect.

> Because we are so thoroughly convinced that you will like the Acmes, we are filling your order with them on trial. When you see how they sell and satisfy your customers, we believe you will want to keep the whole shipment and order more.

The second way puts the emphasis on the customer's accepting the merchandise, where it should be; the first, on returning the goods. The second way will sell more.

In acknowledging orders, you may find one for several items, of which you can send some but not others. To answer such a *combination order,* you have to combine the principles discussed for different types of acknowledgments and produce a *combination acknowledgment.* For it, the only new instructions are to (1) *apply the appropriate checklist points,*

(2) *treat the topics in descending order of estimated acceptability,* and
(3) *put any substituting last.*

## Questions and Exercises

1. What are your main methods/techniques for subordinating/de-emphasizing unpleasant points you have to make?

2. As a useful technique in bad-news letters and memos, what does "embedding" or "sandwiching" mean?

3. Of the nine kinds of messages discussed in this chapter,
   a. For what kind(s) would "I really wish we could . . ." be a good beginning?
   b. For what kind(s) do you not need a buffer?

4. Of the four C's of credit,
   a. Which is the most destructive of goodwill as a basis for refusing credit?
   b. Which is the least hurtful?

5. Suppose you have an order for five items, *a–e,* and
   a. You have to back-order,
   b. You don't sell but will refer to a source,
   c. You can send right away,
   d. You'll send a substitute, and
   e. You have to ask what size (or color). Put the *a–e* in the best sequence for the letter.

6. How can you improve these messages turning down a job applicant?
   a. We have reviewed your background and credentials with great interest, and we are particularly impressed by your scholastic honors and offices. The latter suggest leadership ability, which we always seek in our employees. However, at this time we have no opening. Perhaps at a later date something will open up.
   b. If it disappoints you to learn that we have selected another candidate to fill the position for which you applied, we want you to know that this reflects no unfavorable assessment of you or your excellent qualifications.

      We hope you will apply again when another opening will possibly occur.

# Chapter Outline

# 8

## Persuasion in Selling Goods

Although you have read the basic principles of persuasive messages in Chapter 5, this chapter goes into depth on advertising and selling by mail and telephone.

Two out of three adults—or about 100 million Americans, according to the Direct Marketing Association—sometimes purchase by mail and telephone. Today such direct marketing accounts for 14 percent of all retail transactions; and since catalog orders are growing faster than in-store purchases, that figure should reach 20 percent before the end of the decade.

Part of this growth comes from the increased convenience of mail-order shopping through 1–800 telephone numbers and credit cards—further encouraged by decreased shopping time for today's two-income families and worry about parking problems and crime on parking lots.

A larger part, however, in the growth of direct marketing stems from its cost-efficiency. The cost of an in-person industrial sales call, for example, today averages about $200—and closing a sale often requires five calls.

*Telemarketing* services to retailers, mail-order merchants, publishers, and even industrial manufacturers is an invaluable tool for reducing such costs and for creating a data base. The computer can record requested market data before the caller leaves the phone line.

Computer technology enables any marketer to classify any person and therefore reach the right person, with the right product, at the right time, with the least wasted motion. Marketing people can thus identify consumers as to sex, age, type of dwelling, education, career, product ownership, credit record, purchasing habits, number of children, and their ages and sexes (called *target marketing*).

As *videotex* becomes more developed and more popular, consumers can select merchandise from pictures on their TV screens. Consumers or dealers can get comparison information on any desired service or product. With the growing importance of satellite communications, simultaneous multilingual communications will be more and more possible.

Imagine a dealer sitting in front of a console ordering perfumes from Paris, Danish furniture from Copenhagen, Italian shoes from Rome, bone china from England, . . . .

Whether you are using direct marketing or marketing through the TV screen, you usually attempt to complete a sale by having the prospect give you an order, make an appointment for a sales representative, or authorize a service. This chapter, however, deals mainly with direct marketing messages that ask for the order.

# General Sales Strategy

Whether you sell by mail, telephone, telex, or in person, your procedures are essentially the same. You seek to gain attention, arouse interest, convince your prospect that your proposal is worthwhile, and confidently motivate the action you want.

In some cases you already have favorable attention, as when you answer an inquiry. In those cases your job is to marshal your sales points and adapt them in a message that satisfactorily answers questions, convinces, and gets action. You've already learned to do this in your study of invited sales (Chapter 6).

But in prospecting—or "cold turkey" selling—you have the preliminary job of getting attention and then arousing interest so that your prospect will be eager to learn what you have to say.

The surest way to get your prospect to read or listen, and ultimately to buy, is to *stress some benefit from what you have to sell.* To construct this benefit theme, you must know a good deal about your product or service, its uses, and the kinds of people who can benefit from it (your prospects). From analyzing your product and your prospects comes the selection of the appeal to emphasize. And from a knowledge of marketing methods and people's buying habits comes the decision of what you want your prospect to do.

## Analyzing the Product

Successful sales executives know that a thorough knowledge of the product is essential to successful selling. You will have a hard time convincing someone to purchase something unless you know it well.

Begin your analysis with some questions. Why was this product or service created? What was it designed to do? Was the product created to satisfy a need that existed and was recognized? Or was it created to satisfy a need that is unrecognized? In either case you must figure out how the product meets the need.

Get to the designers and engineers, if applicable. What was the reasoning behind their overall design? What problems did they meet, and how did they overcome them? What are the product's outstanding features? Get all the information you can. The more you have, the better (and more easily) you'll do your job.

Now you can answer the most important question in marketing any product or service: *What will it do for people?* How will it make their lives better or their jobs easier, add to their security, improve their status, or otherwise satisfy a need or desire? This question is the same whether you're selling to consumers or to businesses.

Although you need to know a great deal about the physical characteristics of a product (overall size, shape, color, . . .), physical description of the product will not sell it. *The psychological description—interpretation of physical features in terms of benefits—is the effective part of selling.*

A portable disk case, for example, has a rugged plastic outer shell, foam padding cushions, an aluminum valance with tongue-in-groove interlock, a padded shoulder strap. So what? The case enables a business executive to take disks home in the evening or on weekends or to take floppies or rigid disks, mag tapes, or disk packs on the road or in an airplane. Trimly styled, the case is comfortable to hold and small enough to slide under an airplane seat.

Insulation is not just pellets or batts of certain sizes and materials. To a true marketer it keeps houses warmer in winter, cooler in summer— and conserves energy, reducing heating and cooling costs. It also deadens outside noises. Since it is fire resistant, it reduces the chances of fire and also decreases damage if and when fire breaks out. Thus insulation adds to the resale value of a house.

Such analysis identifies the promises you can make your reader, the benefits you can point out. Such psychological description helps the reader see your offer in terms of benefits to be received. That's what turns a prospect into a customer.

Psychological description is interpretation, which deserves primary emphasis. Physical description is specific detail, evidence incorporated *subordinately* to bear out the promises established in psychological-description phrases and passages. Though physical description is necessary for conviction, subordinate it to psychological description—interpretation in terms of pleasure, increased efficiency, increased profit, or whatever benefits you can promise your prospect.

### Finding the Prospects

True prospects are people who (1) need your product or service, (2) can pay for it, and (3) do not have it. In selling by mail, determining who these people are and their addresses involves making a mailing list. Of course, you can easily get names and addresses; but are all those people prospects?

Some people who appear to be prospects will already be enjoying the benefits of your product or service—or one like it. But unless you know for certain, you need to find out. And the inexpensive way to find out is to try to sell them.

If you are selling a product everybody needs, all you have to verify is your prospects' ability to pay. But few products are useful to everybody (and direct mail is not the best way to sell those that are; direct mail is a selected-*class medium* rather than a *mass medium* like TV, radio, or newspapers).

In determining need, you have to start with logical analysis. For instance, you wouldn't try to sell snowblowers in Puerto Rico. Nor would you try to sell a central heating unit to apartment dwellers or baby carriages in a retirement community.

Sex, age (and a close corollary, physical condition), family and dwelling status, vocation, geographic location, and financial situation are some of the more significant considerations in determining whether someone is a logical prospect for your product. In some cases you will need to go further than a logical analysis and make a marketing survey.

Logical analysis, and a marketing survey if necessary, will give you a list of the characteristics that describe the most likely prospects for your product or service. If enough people share these characteristics to make it practical to approach them by sales letter, you have target marketing for direct mail.

Most sales letters have to go out in large numbers to secure the volume necessary for profit. But even when they go out by the thousands, you send them to a *selected* mailing list.

Assured of a direct-mail market, you next need a good mailing list. That means names and addresses that are accurate (no waste on incorrect or obsolete addresses), pure (all true prospects), and homogeneous (having the desired characteristics in common—the more the better for adapting your letter).

To get such a list, you can make your own, buy one, rent one, or—if you've already made one yourself—trade for one, sometimes even with a competitor. Making your own list may be the best way if you know how and can afford the time and money.

The obvious place to start compiling a list of prospects is your list of people who have already bought from you. If your marketing plan includes advertisements, especially in trade magazines, inserting coupons in them offering free literature on the product or service will bring in names and inquiries of interested people.

Several directories (Dow's, Poor's, and others) classify names of companies by type of business and areas of operation. The Yellow Pages are a fertile source of prospects, especially if you are restricting your effort to a limited geographic area.

Like many other activities, however, making and maintaining a good mailing list requires not only more time and money but also more know-how and facilities than most people can and will devote to the job. Therefore, unless you are going to study the subject to learn the procedures and techniques, and spend the money for the tools of the trade, you will do better to buy or rent your list from one of the many firms that specialize in such lists.

Hundreds of companies make, sell, and rent lists. Most of them have catalogs of the lists they offer, giving the selection criteria, the size, and the cost of each list. If they do not have the list you want, they will build it.

As a rule, the price of a list depends on the difficulty in compiling it. A major factor affecting the price is the number of common characteristics you specify. The same factor, however, affects the desirability and purity of the list. This last is important; it refers to the percentage of names that are likely prospects.

Another big problem is the list's accuracy, the percentage of correct names and addresses. About 19 percent of the people in this country change their addresses each year.

Whether you buy, rent, trade for, or compile your list, however, for sales effectiveness it must contain the correct names and addresses of people or companies with enough desirable characteristics in common to make them a group of likely prospects. Only then can you adapt your talking points and your references in persuasive fashion, as discussed in Chapter 5.

## Choosing the Appeal

From the analysis of your product will come your sales points. Your next step is to select for emphasis the central selling point—the one big theme around which to build your letter. Answer this question: *What one feature or characteristic of the product or service is most likely to induce the prospect(s) to buy?* Your other sales points you can interweave, relegate to an enclosure, or leave for a subsequent mailing. In selling completely by mail, one incidental point that you may need to make clear (by explicit statement or implication) is why the reader should buy by mail instead of locally.

People buy for many reasons: to make or save money, to build or protect their reputation or status, to preserve health, to save time or effort, to protect themselves or their families, . . . . If you want to, you can find a multitude of buying reasons listed in countless books on psychology, salesmanship, sociology, advertising, and marketing.[1] Pride, love, beauty, acquisitiveness, self-indulgence, self-preservation, cu-

[1] Abraham Maslow's *Motivation and Personality* (Harper & Row, New York, 1954) provides the best classifications: (1) physiological needs, (2) security and safety needs, (3) social needs, (4) ego needs, and (5) self-actualizing needs.

riosity, and sometimes fear play their parts in inducing interest and stimulating the final action—making the purchase.

People are both rational and emotional. They need a rational foundation to support an emotional desire for something. In writing good sales letters, if you remind your reader of a need your product will meet and supply evidence to back up your promise (stressing the most important reason why the particular group of readers will buy), you won't need to worry about whether you are employing rational or emotional techniques. You'll be using both. And that's as it should be.

You may, however, need to vary the division of emphasis according to the kind of thing you're selling. Goods that are durable, tangible, expensive, and essential call for major emphasis on *rational* appeals. Conversely, things that are ephemeral (quickly used and gone), intangible, inexpensive, and nonessential (luxuries) call for more emphasis on *emotional* appeals.

**Why Consumers and Resellers Buy.** Certainly effective adaptation is necessary. One of the most obvious differences that affect your choice of theme is that between consumers on one side and manufacturers and dealers on the other.

Consumers buy for the various benefits the product or service will render. Manufacturers buy for the ultimate profit they will make by using the product or service to improve their manufacturing or other activities. Dealers and other resellers buy for the profit they will make on reselling. That depends on the number they can sell and the markup, less any expense and trouble necessary in backing up guarantees with replacements, repairs, and service calls.

The logic of selling to resellers lends itself to a formula statement as $P = VM - C$ (profit equals volume of sales times the markup, minus operating costs).

You can't always be certain, either, about your choice of theme. Testing two or more different letters on a part of your list in a preliminary mailing (about which we'll say more later) may help you arrive at a choice, but sometimes even testing does not solve your problem.

For example, in selling steel desks and chairs to fraternity houses, two writers came up with two different themes. One played up comfort and subordinated appearance; the other stressed appearance over durability and comfort. A letter addressed to the appropriate purchasing agent for the dormitories might have stressed still another theme—holding down maintenance and replacement costs.

## Identifying the Specific Goal

You may know, before you begin your prewriting analysis, exactly what you want your reader to do. But you'll want to be sure that the action you request your reader to take is logical in the light of purchasing conditions, which are governed by the nature of the product, the circumstances of the customer, and authorized, organized marketing channels. You should identify these conditions specifically before you begin to write.

# Writing the Prospecting Sales Letter

After thorough study of your product and prospect, selection of your theme, and decision on your specific goal, you develop your theme following some adaptation of the line of thought that underlies every selling situation: Attention, Interest, Conviction, and Action, or Promise, Picture, Prove, and Push.

But don't think of a presentation in terms of four or five or even three parts. In a good letter, smoothly written for coherence and unity of impression, you can't separate the parts cleanly. Although we analyze the writing of a sales letter in terms of getting attentive interest, establishing belief and trust, overcoming price resistance, and confidently asking for action, the final version should be smooth because of its coherence and persuasive because of its singleness of purpose (giving it unity) and progression of thought.

If there is a key to selling, it is this: *Help your prospects imagine themselves successfully using your product or service.* Your readers must clearly picture how your product or service will contribute some benefits wanted—status, well-being, self-satisfaction, and so forth.

You help your readers imagine themselves successfully using your product or service through psychological description in dramatized copy. (If you don't remember how to dramatize, look back at Chapter 5.) To help them justify acting to get the benefits you have made desirable, you interweave (or follow up with) physical description and other evidence that they can get the wanted benefits.

## Getting Attentive Interest

If you believe in your product and what it can do for the reader, you'll have no big problem starting a sales letter effectively. All you need to do is *hold up the promise of the big benefit your product can contribute to the reader.* If it's a genuine benefit and your message is to a real prospect, you'll get attention.

Yet because of the clamor for attention that many advertisers talk and write about, many advertisements and letters put on a show with the bizarre, the irrelevant, and the irritating to make the reader stop and listen.

You'll read much and hear much about tricks, stunts, and gadgets for sales letters. Good-luck pennies, four-leaf clovers, keys that open the door to everything from business success to a happy home life with your dog, rubber bands (which most of the time only stretch the reader's patience), cartoons, faked checks in window envelopes, simulated hand-written messages—all of these and many others may distract from your sales message rather than assist it unless they enable you to *cut through quickly to the benefit your product can render.*

Relevance is essential. Without it, your trick or gadget will be only a distraction and a detriment rather than an assist to your sales effort. But *unless it leads naturally, plausibly, and shortly to what your product can do for your reader, it's not worth the effort and expense.*

If you can phrase an opening that is deft, novel, and catchy, use it—provided it paves the way quickly and naturally to the introduction of what your product can do for your reader. If you can't, forget about it.

The benefit-contribution-product beginning is always applicable and always good. Associate the benefit with your reader, then bring in the product as the provider of the benefit, and you have a good opening.

A business-reporting service used the following successful opening in a letter to contractors:[2]

```
A lot of money spent
now and later
on new construction

in your area—

—is going to wind up in somebody's pocket . . .
and it might as well be yours instead of your
competitor's!
```

A mailing to 7,000 dealers brought an average of 15 orders a day for the next two weeks or so for the following letter:

```
ARE YOUR WAGELESS CLERKS HUNGRY?
Because Morgan point-of-sale displays (free with
an order of tools) do such an exceptional job of
selling tools, they can aptly be called "wageless
clerks."
But you can't do business from an empty display,
and to make it easy for you to order refills,
```

---

[2] Many large-volume sales forms having no inside address and salutation use this facsimile or faked layout to look like the usual letter and reduce readers' missing those parts.

```
we're enclosing an order blank with attached
postpaid return envelope.
Take a minute to check your displays--fill in
what's needed on the order blank and shoot it back
to us. We'll send you the needed tools right away.
Glowing reports on the New No. 1020 TOOL
MERCHANDISER come from all over. . . .
The Bright Paint Corporation, Los Angeles,
reports:
"Your new MERCHANDISER has more than doubled our
tool sales."
There's a mountain of proof the colorful No. 1020
TOOL MERCHANDISER is the most vigorous sales-maker
of its kind in the entire tool field.
If you don't yet have a No. 1020 TOOL
MERCHANDISER, it will please you to know it
doesn't cost a single cent. The deluxe self-
service Display, with its natural finished wood
bins and sturdy metal frame, is FREE with a small
tool assortment costing you, the dealer, only
$150, and the tools have a retail value of $250.
This year ACCURACY MORGAN tool sales zoomed to a
record high . . . and it's our hope we can help
you boost your own sales this fall season.
Delivery is prompt.
```

Note that in these quoted openings *the lead is simply a reminder of a need that the product comes in shortly to satisfy.* They do not challenge. They do not begin with talk of the product itself ("Now you too can have Andrea perfume!") or the company ("90 years of doing business . . .").

Good openings positively, specifically, and vividly, but believably, say or imply, "As help in handling this specific problem, I suggest. . . ." They get attentive interest through psychological description of the product in use benefiting the reader. Thus they cause the reader to want more information, especially on how the product can fulfill the promise.

### Establishing Belief and Trust

Having made the promise, a letter must quickly supply explanations and evidence to back it up. If the opening is successful, it has established interest and tentative approval or agreeableness rather than serious doubt. The next part of your sales letter tells how your product does meet the need and gives specific information that will make your reader believe you. You thus maintain and continue the agreement you establish in the start of the letter.

Explanations and descriptions of the product or service in use are how you handle this part. Word pictures of how it works and how it is made, performance tests, testimonials of users, statistics of users, facts and figures on sales, guarantees, free-trial offers, offers of demonstrations, and samples are some of your most common devices.

```
Picture yourself, Mr. Yu, on your next vacation
in a place like--

--An elegant villa in the Virgin Islands, perched
above a crescent, palm-fringed beach, the warm
waters of the Caribbean just steps from your
patio.

--A villa on the timeless Greek island of Tinos,
an ideal base for sailing excursions in the Aegean
Sea. It overlooks a village with intimate tavernas
and quaint shops.

--A chalet just outside Colorado's Arapaho
National Forest, complete with redwood sauna and
some of the best skiing and trout fishing
anywhere.

Having your next vacation in an unspoiled and
affordable location is possible if you join the
90,000 satisfied travelers who subscribe to
VACATIONWAYS GUIDE, the unique showcase of
individually owned vacation homes rented directly
from owners to you.

Timed for your vacation planning, VACATIONWAYS
GUIDE will come to you three times each year.
Thumb through its picture-filled pages that offer
you an ever-changing panorama of unique vacation
homes in all price ranges. A typical issue
includes over 200 listings of very special, very
private vacation properties in the United States,
the Caribbean, Europe, and other international
vacation areas. Read about yacht charges, country
inns, and small private resorts. You'll see
pictures of the properties and read detailed
descriptions--location, setting, accommodations,
furnishings, access to beaches, recreational
facilities, local attractions, rental fees,
availability, and name, address, and phone number
of owner.

You'll also receive the quarterly newsletter
supplement with the latest listings, interviews
with renters, and news on special travel
```

opportunities available only to VACATIONWAYS subscribers. You'll lean how to rent or exchange your own vacation home.

To ensure that your next vacation is the most enjoyable, most memorable ever, VACATIONWAYS has some comprehensive services such as:

--Toll-Free Telephone "Hot-Line."  If you have any questions--from how to charter a yacht to the etiquette of renting a vacation home--just phone and an experienced, friendly staff member will help you.

--Convenient Travel Planning Service. To help you arrange car rentals and in-transit hotel accommodations, and to make all travel arrangements needed to get you to your vacation destination in comfort, just use our service.

--Reduced Airfares. If you are renting in the Caribbean, we can usually save you hundreds of dollars on airline tickets by packaging your rental with "ITX" tour fares.

--Subscriber Money Savers. These are VACATIONWAYS' "perks" and include our South Pacific Pass, one of the best values in vacation travel. You can sample several islands, staying at luxurious private condominiums with daily maid service--for as little as $59 per day.

To join those who have already discovered that a vacation is much more than just a trip, Mr. Yu, subscribe now to VACATIONWAYS GUIDE for just $39.50. This annual subscription includes three seasonal issues and the quarterly newsletters. Simply fill out the enclosed card or call toll free 800-843-3344.

So whatever your vacation dreams and budget are--a villa overlooking Montego Bay, a townhouse in the middle of New Orleans' historic French Quarter, or a chalet in the Rockies--we guarantee you'll find what you want in VACATIONWAYS.

Best wishes,


Michael W. Shaw
President

OUR GUARANTEE: Should VACATIONWAYS GUIDE not live up to our promises or to your expectations, return

your first issue for a full and prompt refund. We
are able to offer you this no-risk subscription
because we know that those who try VACATIONWAYS
love it.

## Prospecting Sales Checklist

1.  Get started effectively and concisely.
    a. Suggest or hint at a specific reader need/benefit.
    b. Concentrate on a positive, distinctive central selling point at first.
2.  Back up your opening promise with a persuasive description.
    a. Subordinate and interpret physical features in terms of benefits.
    b. Specificness in description is necessary for conviction.
    c. Eliminate challenging superlatives and useless history.
3.  Develop the most appropriate central selling point adequately.
    a. Provide adequate conviction through selected methods.
    b. Introduce any enclosure stressing what to do with it or get from it.
    c. Check for any unintentional promises of safety or warranty.
4.  Unless using a recognized-bargain appeal, minimize price.
5.  Forthrightly ask for appropriate action (and tell why to buy by mail).
    a. Avoid high-pressure bromides: "Why wait?" "Don't delay!"
    b. Refer subordinately to ordering aids (blanks or envelopes).
    c. End with a reminder of what the product will contribute.

Dear Mr. Swartz:

$2,500 at your fingertips.

No application is necessary for this $2,500. Your
SYC Bank MasterCard and/or Visa is being held in
your name--with a preapproved credit line of
$2,500.

Just return the attached acceptance certificate
before May 1, 198-, and we'll mail your card to
you immediately. You get much more than just
worldwide buying power:

· Access to more than 4,000 CIRRUS network
  automatic teller machines across the United
  States.

· $1,000 Cash Advance--If you request a $1,000
  cash advance, we will send you a cashier's
  check by return mail.

- $150,000 Common Carrier Travel/Accident Insurance, automatically covering you when you buy your airline, train, or bus tickets with one of your SYC Bank cards.
- Accidental Death Insurance, paying up to $1,000 toward the balance on your account.
- Card Liability Service, offering protection if one of your cards is lost or stolen.

Simply return the attached acceptance certificate before May 1, and enjoy your SYC card benefits.

Although the following letter has the question/answer-type opening and simulated inside address, it pulled well for an account executive of a large brokerage firm in Houston.

Have you ever wondered why so many people do so poorly with their stock investments?

They simply refuse to follow the stock market adage "Buy low and sell high."

Since the market is currently depressed and reaching new lows, many investors are either liquidating their portfolios or altogether shunning the stock market.

Now is the time to take advantage of their distress (without hurting them) and invest in certain attractive situations. These same investors will be around when the market reaches new highs to purchase your stock from you.

As you know, besides capital an investor needs good analysis, patience, and common sense to be successful. To help you with your investments, our research department has recently recommended a small number of stock situations that appear to have minimal downside risk and considerable upside potential in the next 12—18 months.

To learn about these situations and how the winning attitude at XYZ can help you become a successful investor, simply return the enclosed card or call me at 654-7744.

## Overcoming Price Resistance

You've already studied effective ways of handling dollar talk (back in the discussion of the invited sales letter in Chapter 6). The principles are the same here in prospecting sales.

## Asking Confidently and Specifically for Action

Similarly, the preceding chapters (especially Chapter 6) have already told you about action endings (and illustrated them for you) repeatedly— indicate confidently what you want your reader to do and how to do it, make it easy and make it sound easy, and supply a stimulus to prompt action in a quick reference to the contribution the product can make to the life of the reader. Furthermore, the accompanying sales checklist itemizes the points specifically.

# Adapting to Groups

All good sales letters follow the basic procedures advocated in the preceding pages. Only in their talking points and in their interpretation and references do they differ as they go to farmers instead of bankers, to lawyers instead of engineers, to consumers as opposed to dealers or manufacturers.

The major adaptation in sales letters depends on whether you're selling to a **consumer** (user) or to a **reseller** (who buys to resell at a profit). As an illustration of how tone and talking points differ, study the following two letters. The first is to a **homeowner,** the second to a **dealer.** In both cases the product is a special kind of lawn mower that eliminates hand clipping.

```
Lawn-Mowing Time
Extra Time for
Summer Rest and Fun!

You can cut your lawn-mowing time in half with an
easy-operating Multimower because you can
eliminate the hand clipping and trimming and the
raking. The Multimower gathers all the grass it
cuts.

You can cut your grass flush against fences,
trees, and flower beds. The interlocking rotary
cutters enable you to mow tall grass and tough
weeds with no more effort than it takes to cut
short grass. And you handle only the minimum
weight when you use this 58-pound mower. It's
```

light enough for almost any member of the
household to use.

Still you have a precision mower of sturdy
construction and strength-tested materials. The
drive shaft runs on free-rolling, factory-
lubricated, sealed ball bearings that keep dirt
and water from rusting these parts. And the
cutters are self-sharpening. So add gas and your
Multimower is ready to go.

Many of the 80,000 enthusiastic Multimower owners
have been using theirs for over two years. Some of
their statements, along with illustrations and the
details of our 90-day structural guarantee, you
can read on the two inside pages. You'll see, too,
that we pay shipping charges to your door.
Multimower is available only by mail at the
economical price of $139.95.

Use the handy order mailer to send us your check
or money order. Within a week after you mail it,
you'll be able to cut, trim, and gather up the
grass on your lawn in only one easy, timesaving
Multimowing.

The *letter to a dealer* stresses the same points, to show why to expect
high-volume sales to customers; but it does so more rapidly and concisely,
in order to concentrate on sales aids, price spreads, promptness and
regularity of supply, and service as parts of the profit-making picture.
Remember the formula $P = VM - C$. And since V (volume of sales)
is usually the main variable, give it the major attention it deserves by
pointing out how the features of the product will appeal to buyers.

Still the approach is the same as in any sales letter: It seeks the answer
to the ever-present question "What will it do for me?" To a dealer the
answer is always "profits," but profits depend on salability (the features
of the product that cause people to buy), on serviceability, and on markup.
Since salability—features attracting buyers—is usually the main point,
the psychological description becomes *interpretation of those features in
terms of consumer appeal.*

A dealer is also interested in your promptness and regularity in filling
orders, in guarantee and service arrangements, and in (if you provide
any) advertising or other selling aids to help sell more—as in the following
letter:

When you show a customer a Multimower--a lawn
mower that cuts, trims, and "rakes" a lawn in one
operation--you have a quick sale, a satisfied
customer, and a $46.65 profit.

> Your customers will like the Multimower because it gives them more time to spend in enjoyable summer recreation. It cuts right up to walls, fences, trees, and flower beds, eliminating hand trimming. Its easily adjustable and self-sharpening cutters slice down the toughest kinds of grass and weeds for a trim, neat lawn in half the usual time.
>
> Its light weight--only 58 pounds--means easy handling. The quiet operation of the interlocking cutters has won the approval of 80,000 Multimower users. They like it, too, because it is permanently lubricated and self-sharpening. With a minimum of care it's ready for use. So normally you just put in the gas and it's ready to go.
>
> No doubt many of your customers have been reading about the Multimower in the full-page, four-color monthly ads that started running in Homeowners and Vacation magazines in March and will continue through July. Note the testimonials and conditions of our guarantee on the next page--and the favorable guarantee and servicing arrangements.
>
> In these days the $139.95 retail cost will be popular with your customers. Our price to you is only $93.30--a $46.65 profit.
>
> By filling out and returning the enclosed order blank along with your remittance today, you'll be sure to have Multimowers on hand when your customers begin asking for them.

In looking for differences that adapt the two versions of the Multimower letter to users and dealers, did you notice that the main differences are in the psychological description, while the physical description is essentially the same—and subordinated?

The helpful dealer sales checklist summarizes significant points to keep in mind for selling to dealers.

## Legal Considerations

Whether writing to a user or a reseller, a sales writer must keep in mind legal responsibility for what the message says. Recent court decisions have firmly placed product liability squarely on the manufacturers and designers of products. And they may still bear the responsibility even if an injured user admits reading and understanding the instructions supplied with the product. Clearly the ancient doctrine of *caveat emptor,* "let the buyer beware," is changing to *caveat venditor,* "let the seller beware."

Warranties and guarantees are an area in which writers of sales letters are even more likely to get into trouble unwittingly by (1) implying a warranty where no warranty exists or (2) overstating a warranty.

## Dealer Sales Checklist

1. Devote at least the beginning to the reader and benefits to come.
   a. Picture the act of selling and the product's consumer appeal (maybe even price if a bargain).
   b. Stress a distinctive point; avoid general copy and exaggeration.
2. The first point to develop is salability (volume).
   a. Explain the product's points in terms of customers' reactions.
   b. Talk about the dealer's selling—not using—the product.
3. Refer to whatever dealer aids you have (advertising, displays, mats, . . .) as promoting inquiries and sales.
4. Price is usually best handled late, as you ask for an order.
5. Make the reference to any enclosure carry a sales point too.
6. Make the action ending brief and businesslike too.
   a. Exaggerated superlatives are out of place.
   b. Name the specific action you want.
7. Check for any unintentional promises of safety or warranty.

An *implied warranty* might be made if you, the seller, know that a buyer intends to use your goods for a particular purpose and that the buyer is relying on your judgment as to the suitability of the goods. Then you have implied a warranty of fitness for this particular purpose.

If you, the seller, make a promise or affirm a fact to a buyer about the grade, model, or description of the merchandise you are selling, such a promise becomes an *express warranty* in the contract even though you don't use the term *guarantee* or *warranty.*

A federal law of 1975 requires that warranties on products costing $5 or more disclose the terms in simple and readily understood language. The warranty for products costing over $15 must be labeled "full" or "limited." The seller must repair or replace products without charge within a reasonable time if there is a defect for all "full warranty" products. If a warranty is limited, the limitation must be obvious so that buyers are not misguided.

Words to watch out for when you are writing sales messages are *always, never, whenever, all, perfectly, trouble-free, simply, unbreakable, lifetime,* and others like them. They signal that you may need to reword what you said, or qualify it.

## Tests and Testing

Testing a mailing to predetermine the returns (or the pull or the pulling power) of a letter is serious business among high-volume mailers. Testing means simply mailing the letter to a portion of the names on your list to see whether you can get a profitable percentage to take the action you want. You can see why a business executive would be wise to test a mailing before risking the money to send 10,000 letters, especially if the mailing pieces are expensive.

Suppose your mailing pieces cost 50 cents each (not unusual in a mass mailing) and you make $5 on each sale. Obviously, you have to make sales to 10 percent of the list to break even. Now suppose you have a 90 percent accuracy factor (that is, the percentage of correct addresses). Each 100 letters have to bring 10 orders from every 90 people who get them. Further suppose the purity (how many names on the list are likely prospects instead of deadwood) is 70 percent. Your 100 letters then have to bring 10 orders from every 63 good prospects (70 percent of 90). This requires about 16 percent pulling power from your letter ($^{10}/_{63}$).

Other significant reasons for testing are to find out which of two or more messages has the greater pull or which of two times (day or week or month the mailing piece arrives) is more profitable.

You can test one color against another; but if you also vary size, copy, or time, your test doesn't mean a thing. You can test one lead against another; but if the rest of the copy and the time of arrival are not the same, you still have no basis for saying that one lead is better than the other. You can test only one factor at a time!

You usually expect only 5–10 percent pulling power. But especially effective copy, carefully selected mailing lists, or unusual offers often increase these percentages.

Even such apparently insignificant things as the time of arrival are important. Experience has shown that sales letters should not arrive in an office at the beginning or ending of a week or month or at the homes of laborers or farmers in the middle of the week. Around Christmastime and April 15 (income tax time) are especially bad times of the year to mail to consumers, and the fall and winter months (especially January) are better than the spring and summer months. Of course, seasonal appropriateness of the goods and geographic locations can easily affect this. Even temporary local conditions may.

By keeping careful records on tests and on entire mailings, through the years users develop a considerable quantity of experience data that may help guide them in future work.

# Writing Sales Series

The sales letters already discussed are lone efforts to produce or promote sales. Because single sales letters frequently cannot do all the work a series can, probably just as many sales letters go in series as singly. Usually they are obviously processed (form) letters, sent out in large numbers by third-class mail. For further economy they often use some simulated address block instead of an inside address and salutation (like some of our examples). By careful phrasing, however, a skillful writer can *make the one reader of each copy forget the form and feel that it is a well-adapted message that certainly fits personally.* Where the mailing list is small, individualized letters and first-class mail are the rule.

Whether a letter is a single sales letter or one in a series makes little difference in the techniques or preliminary planning, but in one of the two types of series (wear-out and campaign) the letter's organization is more complicated.

## The Wear-Out Series

Probably the most widely used of sales series is the wear-out. In it each mailing is a complete sales presentation on a relatively inexpensive product (usually not over $50). The product almost has to be inexpensive, because one mailing cannot hope to succeed in persuading most people to buy expensive items by mail from a complete stranger.

After the market analysis, preparation or purchase of a mailing list, and preliminary planning comes the writing of the letter. Probably you and several other executives, and perhaps a letter consultant, will spend hours preparing the letter, or several versions of it. These first few copies may cost several hundred dollars in time and consultant's fees.

Then you test your list, and perhaps several versions of the letter. If one of the letters seems to have a high enough pulling power to make it profitable, you run off hundreds or thousands of copies and mail them out at a carefully selected time. Now that the big investment divides among so many, the cost per letter is not so big.

After an interval, usually of one to three weeks, you remove the names of purchasers (unless the product has frequent recurring demand) and send another letter (or sometimes the same one) to the remaining names on the list. Sometimes the third or fourth mailing brings better results than the first, even with the same letter, because of the buildup of impact. You continue to repeat the mailings until the returns no longer yield sufficient profit to continue. Those left on the list are the "hard cases" that apparently won't buy no matter what. The list is worn out—hence the name.

## The Campaign Series

The theory of the campaign series is that people and businesses buy some (usually inexpensive) items quickly, without much thought; but before buying certain other types of items (usually more expensive), most people and firms ponder for a month or more and talk over the situation. To send one letter that first introduced such an item and, after only two minutes of reading time (as in the wear-out series), asked for the decision on an order card would be to pour money down the proverbial rathole. Instead of the wear-out, you would use the campaign series for such a situation.

Your preliminary planning is as different as the price involved. You decide approximately how long most people on the mailing list would want to think over your offer before making up their minds. Then you decide how frequently they should be reminded to keep them thinking about your product or service. On that basis you decide the length of the series—in time and number of mailings.

The essence of planning the series of letters (whether two or a dozen) is to make the whole series cover the parts of a complete sales presentation and knit them together. In any case the first letter will try hard to get attention and start working at interesting the prospect. Further letters will strive to develop interest in buying until the last makes the strongest drive for action. As people respond, you remove their names from the list.

The last letter is not the only one, however, to which a reader can easily respond. Sellers by mail know that they will not usually get any action from more than half of their prospects. But they also know that in almost any large group some people will be sold on the first contact. Consequently, they usually provide order forms with almost every mailing.

## The Continuous Series

Both the wear-out and the campaign series are usually complete sales presentations that try to bring in orders. The continuous series rarely does. The users of the continuous series are most frequently department stores, special stores (jewelry, furniture, drug), oil companies, credit card organizations, and mail-order establishments. The mailing list is usually the firm's charge customers. Since the series generally rides free with the monthly statements, it costs little.

Perhaps the biggest distinction is the rigid planning of the campaign series as compared with the more freewheeling nature of the continuous series, which commonly includes special mailings on holidays but also on almost any other special occasion. It does not run any set length of time or for any definite number of mailings; and it may promote a great variety of products while the campaign and wear-out series are selling one.

## Questions and Exercises

1. How might target marketing help a savings and loan association in your area?

2. What are some questions you might be asked through telemarketing?

3. What might be some disadvantages to buying exclusively with video-tex?

4. Describe a motorcycle in terms of psychological description.

5. Describe a motorcycle using physical description.

6. What are some advantages of selling by mail rather than through sales representatives? What are some disadvantages?

7. Name some products that would be better sold by direct mail than by mass advertising (television, radio, newspaper). Why better?

8. What appeals would you use to sell:
   a. New clothes for extra-tall people (through a special-order house)?
   b. A $99 computerized thermostat control with a built-in microprocessor?
   c. A $59 RainMatic computerized water control unit that screws in between faucet and hose and can be programmed up to eight different watering periods for each day of the week?
   d. *The Wall Street Journal* subscriptions to business school graduates?

9. What are some different ways you might test a sales letter from *The Wall Street Journal* to a mailing list of recent business school graduates?

10. If you were going to use a sales letter campaign to sell a word processing machine, where and/or how would you get a list?

11. Write an action ending to your letter selling a word processing machine to a list of office managers of small companies in the Northeast.

12. Write some phrases or a sentence or two describing the image that comes to your mind when you see the following words:
   a. sunset
   b. bride/groom
   c. designer clothes
   d. sports car

13. For each of the products or services listed below, write one or two opening sentences that you feel will create a desire in
   *A mailing to users selling:*
   a. phone for car
   b. week in Hawaii
   c. new kind of tennis racket
   d. condominium on oceanfront
   e. weekend at a ski resort
   *A mailing to dealers selling:*
   f. new kind of government-approved fertilizer
   g. sunscreen that keeps insects out and the cool in
   h. word processor

# Chapter Outline

# 9

# Effectively Selling Ideas and Services

Like sales messages, four other kinds of business communications—special requests, claims and policy complaints, collections, proposals—are basically persuasive messages. In this chapter you will learn how to get favorable responses from people who initially feel no built-in reasons to respond as you desire.

This kind of situation requires more ability with psychology and language than selling goods does. Such ability, however, is one of the most important you can develop—for both your business and nonbusiness use. **It is a major reason some people are leaders, managers, and administrators, while others (often with equal or better general abilities) are their followers and employees.**

## Special Requests

In enlisting the cooperation of others—which is basic to management—you need to realize that no one ever has enough money or time to give either of them spontaneously and unquestioningly. No one is willing to reveal certain kinds of information without knowing its intended use and deciding that the purpose is good. To put the question directly in these cases is to get an immediate turndown. So the special request has to be persuasive.

Like the simple inquiry (Chapter 6), the effective special request is specific and concise; but it is not direct. The secret of successful persuasive copy is to

1. Secure interested motivation first by offering, suggesting, or implying a benefit—the you-attitude as explained in Chapter 5 and under **YA** in Appendix C—or at least talking about something of interest;

2. Justify the request by interweaving necessary information with explanations and reminders of the benefit(s);

3. Foresee and preclude or minimize objections; and

**4.** After giving the necessary information and persuasion, confidently ask for the desired action.

## Securing Interest

To strike the appropriately persuasive theme, you need to analyze the situation to select the most pertinent and forceful motive as the beginning.

Money being what it must be in business thinking, the strongest appeal is one that holds out the prospect of sales, of saving money, or of promoting goodwill with an audience wherein sales may ultimately materialize. Such potential-dollar themes offer the most concrete form of benefit and are responsible for this opening to an advertising manager of a manufacturing company:

> What would it be worth to Field's to add some
> 8,000 potential customers to its prospect list?

and this opening to the circulation manager of a magazine:

> Who will be your subscribers 10 years from now?

If you can apply such reader-benefit themes appropriately and remain within the realm of good taste (avoiding the suggestion of bribery), you undoubtedly have the strongest appeal you can make.

In many instances, however, such dollar-minded talk would arouse indignation or would not apply. But you need not despair of finding a point that will stress the reader's benefits or interests rather than your own. The letter beginning

> How often have you received--even from well-
> educated people--letters that are not worth your
> attention?

clearly proposes a benefit.

Indirect benefits may serve too. When you can show how your project will promote the welfare of a group in which your reader is interested, you can make a strong appeal. On this basis you might persuade a public accountant to speak to a college accounting club, an alumnus of a professional fraternity to take on a responsible office, or a correspondence supervisor to address a group of teachers or students of business writing.

The following letter written to the founder of the successful *Direct Marketing/Mail* magazine got results (the founder came to Gainesville and talked to two groups of students):

> What can I do with students who consistently turn
> in sales letters with the same old overused and
> misapplied tricks as the dominant message?

Year after year I lecture to my students in Business Communications on how to write a good sales letter. I require reading the textbook, give them outside readings for additional help, and still a few repeatedly miss major points.

Don't you agree that all of them would benefit and more thoroughly understand the techniques of writing sales letters if they could hear an explanation from a specialist with a flair for speaking to groups and winning their attention?

A week from next Monday (February 26) at 1:20 P.M. and 7 P.M. I have scheduled the first of two 50-minute lectures on sales letters to the two groups. I can always count on the attendance of at least 200 students in each group; and with the announcement of a guest speaker who is a specialist in this area of communications, I'm certain their enthusiasm would soar.

Since they received their assignment last week, they will have been exposed to the material in my book before the Monday lectures, and I will be able to notify them in their discussion classes of your arrival. Of course, I'm looking forward to having you as my overnight guest, and my wife is a splendid cook. (She's been looking forward to meeting you for years.)

The students respond particularly well to visiting speakers. Won't you call or write me before the end of next week to let me know I can expect you on Monday? I would appreciate having my students hear from an expert before they become tomorrow's sales letter writers.

Although many such special requests appeal to friendship, interest in a particular field, or altruism, in most business situations you will do better if you select and emphasize direct-benefit talking points.

As you look back at the beginnings quoted so far in this chapter, you will note that in addition to highlighting benefits (or at least supposed interest), these openings are questions. You will note, too, that the questions are rhetorical (asked not to get their answers but to promote thinking and encourage reading on).

Not all persuasive requests must begin with a question. But a question beginning commands greater attention than a declarative statement, is never as challenging as some statements are, can be subtly flattering, and more readily leads to thinking about your suggestion. In phrasing such questions, however, you will be on safer ground if you eliminate the possibility of either a yes or no answer, because such an answer stops thought about the mentioned or implied benefit. To promote thinking about the circumstances that will lead up to the request, each of the preceding openings employs the strategy.

Though you usually should avoid yes or no questions, if the answer leaves an intriguing wonder about how to get the mentioned benefit, you've achieved your purpose of leading into interested contemplation of your message. The following opening addressed to a national retailer contemplating entering the Texas market, for example, is certainly a good one:

```
Wouldn't you consider the respect and attention
of some 200 key Texas retailers a valuable
opportunity to test the true business conditions
in that state?
```

The mental response to such a question is positive and pursuing.

The danger lies in getting an irritated answer—whether that answer is a yes or a no or any of the variants of "So what?" The employee who invited the head of an accounting firm to speak to an in-service group and began with

```
Do you believe in preparing for the future?
```

apparently gave little thought to the probable reaction.

Of greater benefit implications is this one:

```
What does it cost when you have to dismiss a
well-grounded junior accountant because of poor
personal characteristics?
```

Study of the preceding beginnings will show three other advantages that come from question beginnings implying reader benefits: (1) they are more likely to keep the reader in the picture, (2) they keep you from beginning with uninteresting explanation, and (3) they make the transition to the explanation easier.

## Justifying the Request

Having secured interest with a beginning that holds some promise of benefit, you usually need to devote the greater part of your message to explaining what your project is and what good comes of it—particularly the good (benefit) coming to the person you're trying to persuade.

In almost any request, details concerning who, what, when, where, why, and how need clarification; but they do not deserve first place.

Even in this second section (where they belong) you need to subordinate them to reminders of potential benefits.

In inviting a speaker, for instance, you need to tell the nature and size of the audience, the time and place, the facilities available, the amount of time allotted, and the topic (if you are assigning one). Sometimes knowing about other speakers who will precede and follow would be helpful. But even after a benefit-oriented beginning, such details should come in subordinately as much as possible.

The purpose of the following letter was to get a big-name speaker for a retailers' group of 50 to 100. In *Time* the week before, an article about one of New York's biggest retailers explained that Mr. Hoving (fictional name) was considering branches in the Southwest.

> What was your final decision regarding the installation of an employee bonus system in your stores, as mentioned in last week's Time?
>
> Leading Texas retailers are eager to hear how you solved this problem and others like it. And you'd get a very accurate reflection of Texas retail conditions if you'd talk to the group from 2:00 to 3:00 on the 29th and then lead a half-hour's informal discussion when the 50—100 members meet for the 25th annual Texas Business Conference at the Lakeway Inn just outside Austin on the 28th to 30th this month.
>
> Your ideas on sales promotion, ways to meet the competition of discount houses, and personnel-management problems would be eagerly received, shared--maybe even contested if you care to invite a vigorous discussion. And they'd certainly bring you more than usual appreciation because our members are fully aware that our prominent speakers appear at their own expense--that the pay they receive is the benefits of sharing experiences and viewpoints.
>
> To help us get the desirable publicity for your appearance, will you write us by the 10th that you'll be with us? We anticipate your "Yes" with gratitude and enthusiasm--and we're certain that you could pick up some useful ideas and information about a section of the country that is expanding rapidly.

The well-chosen appeal, taken from the *Time* story, is the chance to learn more about Texas business waters before coming in. Of particular note is the skillful way of telling Hoving he gets no fee.

Conversely, nobody would be enthusiastic over a beginning like this:

As a master's candidate at Harvard University, I am planning a thesis on industrial robots. Professor A. R. Hopper of our industrial engineering department has suggested that I write to you to find out the results of your experience.

Notice in the following copy how the student not only changed the opening to an interest-arousing question but also subordinated the necessary but uninteresting details of the original opening:

Just what economies are you experiencing from your installation of industrial robots?

Are they as great as my limited experience and study have led me to believe?

Regardless of your experience in using robots, your comments in answering these questions could contribute materially in making a worthwhile, authentic, down-to-earth thesis of the one I am preparing as partial requirement for an M.S. degree. Too, the finished thesis may well be of practical interest to all users and potential users of robots.

Perhaps you have some printed material that you can simply enclose in the stamped, addressed envelope I've included. If not, will you take a few minutes to tell me your experiences with robots?

Although I don't have to, I'd like to be able to quote you; but I'll handle the material with whatever degree of confidence and anonymity you specify.

Since I have to assemble material and start writing by June 1, I'd be most grateful if you'd let me hear from you before that date.

Why—besides the interest-arousing question beginning and the subordinated facts justifying the request—did seven copies of that letter bring five detailed replies? Did you notice the reminders of the reader's possible benefits? Did you notice how clear and specific the writer made the requested action and how easy it seems? And did you notice the reassurance against any fears as to how the information might be used? And how the writer avoided seeming to push the reader around by justifying the request for action by a necessary end date?

Any one of these points may make the difference between your getting nothing and your getting what you want in a persuasive favor-seeking situation.

## Minimizing Obstacles

Even though your interest-arousing first sentence and justifying explanation may have supplied good reasons, in most circumstances you have a negative factor to overcome. It may be a sum of money you are asking for. Then you break it down into several payments. It may be that you can offer no fee or a smaller fee than a program speaker is accustomed to receiving; then you cite other (perhaps intangible) rewards. It may sound like a lot of trouble or work (say, a questionnaire). Then word it to sound as quick and easy as possible. It may be that you're asking for secret information. If so, give assurance that you will do all you can to protect the reader's interest.

Regardless of the circumstance, you can usually find some positive corollary to the drawback.

As added inducement, you want to make the job sound as easy and as pleasurable as possible. That is why most questionnaires are fill-in or checkoff forms and why a return-addressed reply device requiring no postage ordinarily accompanies such requests.

## Positively Anticipating Acceptance

After establishing the reader's benefit or contribution, making clear exactly what and why (along with reminders of the benefit), and minimizing obstacles, you should confidently ask for the response you want, as discussed under Success Consciousness in Chapter 5. Hesitant, apologetic expressions belittle the request itself and have the disadvantage of suggesting excuses as reasons for refusal. Such expressions as the following hinder rather than help:

```
I realize you are very busy, but . . . .
I'm sorry to trouble you for such an apparently
insignificant matter; however, . . . .
I hesitate to bother you with such a request
. . . .
If you consider this a worthwhile project, . . . .
```

Eliminate such thinking (maybe by rereading the discussion on Success Consciousness in Chapter 5) and forthrightly name the specific action you want. Although you may have referred to it earlier, be sure to ask for it or at least refer to it near the end.

## Special-Request Checklist

1.  Your opening should stress something of reader interest.
    a. When you can, develop a benefit theme.
    b. Though a rhetorical question is usually best, one with an obvious yes or no answer stops rather than starts consideration.
    c. Don't appear to suggest a bribe or depend on obvious flattery.
    d. Explanations do not arouse interest; put them in the middle.
2.  Keep the addressee(s) involved as you shift to your explanation.
    a. Give necessary details to justify your project.
    b. But subordinate these details to reminders of benefit(s).
    c. Adapt your message; when you can, personalize it.
    d. Don't phrase the exact request until after most of the benefits.
    e. Make participation sound easy.
3.  Any potentially negative element requires a careful treatment.
    a. Minimize negatives by positive statements and embedded position.
    b. Maintain a tone of confidence.
    c. Don't supply excuses for nonacceptance.
    d. Give assurance that you will handle confidentials properly.
4.  After justifying it, ask confidently for the desired action in a last punch line on the available benefit(s).

## Persuasive Claims and Policy Complaints

Sometimes you need to be rather persuasive to get results on a claim. Your reason may be that you know the other person to be reluctant to grant claims, that your case is subject to some question and you need to make as good a case as you can within the facts, or (most frequently) that you have already tried a direct claim (as explained in Chapter 6) and have been turned down.

Whatever the cause, you use persuasive organization and psychology. Some of the main appeals (more or less in ascending order of force and objectionable tone) are to the desire for (1) customer satisfaction, goodwill, and favorable publicity; (2) a continued reputation for fair dealing; and (3) legal meeting of a guarantee.

Again your message divides rather distinctly into three parts, but their contents are somewhat different from those of the direct claim:

1.  You begin by stating and getting agreement on a principle that is the basis of your claim.
2.  You explain all the facts in detail, as in any claim. In it you show clearly the other's responsibility.
3.  You apply the facts or minor premise to the principle or major premise so as

to draw a conclusion. The conclusion will point clearly to a certain action. You
then request that action.

The following illustration is a persuasive claim written after a first claim
brought a proposal to compromise. It got the money, the full amount
without compromise, by appealing to fair-minded analysis of the facts
(and hence the injustice of compromise in the case).

```
Claim No. 070—6289

Do you think a sales representative for the XXXX
Casualty Company would sell me a policy if I
offered to pay half the premium requested? I
don't. That would be a compromise on the value of
the policy.

Compromises in the adjustments on policies
likewise are for cases involving doubt about
responsibility or about the amount of damage done.
In my claim no doubt arises about either.

Mr. Hall ran up behind me so fast that he could
not control his car and hit the left rear part of
the side of my car. Clearly he was responsible.
Three reputable repair shop estimates of the
repair job make sure of my having a fair appraisal
of the damages. The lowest of the three is $286.
So no doubt exists about the damage.

Therefore I am returning the Release and
Settlement form you sent and asking that you send
another based on one of the estimates I formerly
sent in. That is the only fair settlement.
```

Whereas claims ask restitution for mistakes, damage, or unsatisfactory
products, policy complaints request correction of poor service or unsatisfactory policies and practices. A policy complaint may be like a direct
claim or a persuasive one, but it is more likely to be persuasive, as in
the following example:

```
Am I right in thinking that Racine Motors wants
its policy on direct-sale commissions and
cooperative selling campaigns to promote long-
range goodwill and increased sales in this
territory?

I think so, but recently one of our sales
representatives called on a prospect in our
territory and found "the prospect" already
enjoying a 20-hp Racine motor, which we normally
stock. Investigation revealed that you sold the
```

```
motor directly at a price below our selling price.
Yet we have received no dealer's commission on
this sale. This is one of several occasions
brought to my attention in the past year.
```

```
We and you should quote uniform prices, and we
should get our dealer's commission on any direct
sales. That, I thought, was the intent of the
exclusive-dealership contract you signed with me.
```

```
We have been contemplating an expansion of our
stock to include your 60-hp motor, which would
play an important part in our sales program.
Please give us a definite working policy so we
will know where we stand.
```

# Collections

Another category of letters selling ideas is the collection letter—selling the idea of "Pay up!" Today the thinking credit management executive accepts the fact that every sale turned down for credit reasons is a lost chance for more profit and approves sales to some marginal credit risks. Collectors remember that they **not only must collect the money but must also retain the goodwill of customers** or see them drift away as fast as the sales department can bring them in.

Indeed, modern credit theory stresses selling not only to good risks but also to marginal risks as a means of increasing sales and profits. If a business firm follows this theory, it will have collection problems— but they will be expected and manageable.

Even the smallest organization today can afford a computerized information processing system that can automatically pick out past-due accounts and type programmed collection letters to them—if a human tells it to. That is what this section is about—**what human beings must do in the collection process:** make the decisions about the number, types, timing, and especially the wording of collection efforts, whether they be communicated through mail, phone, personal visit, Mailgram, or telegram.

### Keeping Proper Attitudes and Objectives in Mind

The trained collector takes the attitude that the debtor should pay because of a promise to do so by a certain date but also realizes that people and organizations pay because of benefits to themselves rather than sympathy or any other reason. The collector therefore not only associates the obligation with the goods through resale talk but also points out the benefits of paying now.

The modern collector's thinking is quite analytical:

- Avoid a tone of exasperation and self-righteousness.
- Avoid a curt tone. Be understanding and cooperative but firm.
- Avoid an injured tone.
- Some delinquents withhold payment because they are dissatisfied with the goods or charges. The job is one of adjustment, not collection. (Federal law prohibits sellers to consumers from even trying to collect on customer-disputed goods or billings of $51-up for purchases within the state or 100 miles of home. The law applies equally to a holder in due course—for example, a credit card company that has bought the original seller's rights in the accounts.)
- Some will have to be persuaded to pay. Use the you-attitude.
- A few, but only a few, are basically dishonest and will have to be forced to pay or marked off as losses. Forcing payment does not include even threats of physical violence, extortion, or rumor-mongering (all of which are illegal). Civil court suit, the only legitimate forcing method, is so destructive of goodwill that you should not even mention it until you say (and mean, according to present law) it is the next step.

Most important of all, the modern collector recognizes the true nature of the job and expects collection letters and phone messages to do two jobs:

1. They must collect the money, promptly if possible.
2. They must also retain the goodwill of the customer if at all possible.

By adding the second job, the collector hopes to retain the customer, prevent the unfavorable word-of-mouth publicity that is inevitably carried by a disgruntled former customer, and make each message more likely to succeed in its first job—that of collecting. In many cases the second job is more important than the first. Certainly to collect $9.50 and consequently lose the goodwill of a customer who has been buying hundreds of dollars' worth of goods a year is stupid.

For effectiveness in both collection and goodwill, the modern collector cooperates with the sales department and may even inject some sales promotion material into early collection letters to a good risk when it might be of interest to the customer. It not only promotes future sales, but it shows confidence in the debtor and willingness to sell more on credit. Thus it is a subtle appeal to pride that helps save the reader's face and goodwill. If used at the end of the letter, it relieves the sting and solves one of the correspondent's touchiest problems—how to provide a pleasant ending for a letter in which some element is displeasing.

You probably remember your pleasure and pride when you saw the rich, dark wood and the gracefully proportioned design of the Ambassador office furniture arranged in your office. That furniture is the finest we have ever sold, and we were well pleased--as we thought you were--when you selected it for your office.

At the time, we were glad to arrange convenient credit terms so that you could have your furniture while paying for it. Now if you will look over your bills, you will notice that those for October, November, and December have not been marked paid. The sooner you take care of them, the more pride you will retain in your furniture because you will subconsciously remember that you are up to date on your payments.

If you come to our store to make your payments, be sure to see Ambassador's new matching line of receptionist's and secretary's furniture: desks, chairs, cabinets, credenzas--everything to furnish a modern, efficient office. And of course we still carry the most complete inventory of office supplies in the area, usually available to you the same day you call.

## Maintaining Collection Series Characteristics

In trying to collect and retain goodwill, the efficient collector classifies delinquent accounts and prescribes the best treatment for each. The method is like a process of repeated siftings or screenings. Classification determines which and how many screenings each debtor will get. The procedure is a series of letters, phone calls, telegrams, and/or Mailgrams.

To do its two jobs best, the collection series should have the following characteristics:

*1. Promptness.* Credit and collection people know that the sooner they start trying to collect after an account becomes due, the better the chance of collecting.

*2. Regularity.* Systematic handling of collections increases office efficiency and has a desirable effect on debtors.

*3. Increasing Forcefulness.* To retain the goodwill of the customer as well as collect the money, the collector starts with as weak a message as is likely to work. Like the doctor who uses stronger and stronger medicine or resorts to surgery only as the need develops, the good collector applies more and more forceful methods and goes to court only after weaker methods fail.

*4. Adaptation.* Not all credit and collection people classify their customers into neat categories of good, medium, and poor risks; but all competent ones vary their procedures according to the quality of the risk (as well as according to the general bases of adaptation already discussed). Usually the poorer the risk, the more frequent the mailings and the more forceful the messages. Whereas three months might pass before anything stronger than a few statements goes to a good risk, much less time might run a poor one through the whole sifting process and to court.

*5. Flexibility.* The collection procedure has to be flexible to take care of unusual circumstances.

## Planning Standard Collection Procedures

Collection plans and procedures vary so much that only a specialized book could discuss all of the variations. Also, various collection theorists and practitioners use different terms to mean essentially the same things. Many of the differences are only minor ones of mechanics, however, rather than significant ones of substance. Most well-planned series apply essentially the logic and psychology explained in the next few pages to a screening process somewhat like the six-screen one shown in Table 9–1.

Of course, you would send only one mailing at each of the notification, inquiry, or ultimatum stages. The nature of the messages makes repeating them illogical. The number and frequency in the other stages vary from firm to firm, and often within firms according to class of customer and other circumstances, such as the type of business (retail or industrial) and the type of sale (open account, installment).

In general, the better the credit risk, the greater the number of mailings and the longer the intervals between them. A typical retail series might be two to four reminders, two or three appeals, and one urgency letter.

**Notification (usually a form telling amount, date due, and terms).** On or about the due date, you send a statement. Most people will pay in response to form notices—the first sifting. Such forms have the advantage of avoiding insults and saving lots of money.

**Reminder (usually forms giving basic information and adding a push).** If the notice brings no response, the collector gives the customer the benefit of the doubt, assumes oversight, and sends one or more

**Table 9–1**

| Stage | Assumption | Nature | Gist |
|---|---|---|---|
| Notification | Will pay promptly | Usual statement | Amount due, due date, terms |
| Reminder | Will pay; overlooked | Statement, perhaps with rubber stamp, penned note, or sticker; or form letter or brief reference in other letter | Same as above, perhaps with indication that this is not first notice |
| Inquiry | Something unusual; needs special consideration | One letter or phone call | Asks for payment or explanation and offers consideration and helpfulness |
| Appeal | Needs to be persuaded | One or more letters or phone calls | Selected appropriate and increasingly forceful appeals, well developed |
| Urgency | May be scared into paying | Letter, sometimes from high executive or special collector | Grave tone of something getting out of hand; may review case; still a chance to come through clean |
| Ultimatum | Must be squeezed | Letter, Mailgram, telegram | Pay by set date or we'll report to credit bureau (or sue, now illegal to threaten and not do); may review case to retain goodwill by showing reasonableness |

reminders—the number and frequency depending on the circumstances. Avoiding offense while giving the necessary information (amount, what for, due date, and terms) is an important concern.

Reminders are usually forms, in order to save both money and the customer's face. The form may be an exact copy of the original notice, or a copy plus a penned note, a rubber stamp such as "Second Notice" or "Please Remit," or a colorful gummed sticker. Effective examples are "Don't delay further; this is long overdue," "Your prompt remittance is requested," "Now is the time to take care of this," "Prompt payment ensures good credit," "Prompt payments are appreciated," "Don't delay—pay today," "Remember you agreed to pay in 30 days," "Have you overlooked this?"

Up through the reminder stage in the collection procedure the assumption is that little or no persuasion is necessary. Thus forms or incidental reminders can do the job more cheaply and avoid the sting that personalized, full-length collection messages would carry.

A phone call or an individual-sounding letter solely about collection is another type of reminder. For greater force in the last reminder, or to poor risks, or about large amounts, the collector may decide to phrase a message that talks collection all the way and seems to be individualized.

Since most delinquents have so much in common, it still may be a relatively inexpensive fill-in form if the writer watches the tone and content carefully.

The following letter for a wholesale concern, for example, adapts easily to a large number of customers. With only one fill-in (for the underscored part, conveniently placed at the end of a paragraph) besides the inside address and salutation, it will serve for a large mailing list. It has a touch of pride appeal along with the reminder to reduce the sting of the apparently individualized message.

> As owner of a successful business, you know what a good credit reputation means. You have one.
>
> That's why we immediately extended you 30-day credit on your recent order. We know that the reports of your good credit reputation are correct. And we likewise know that you'll send us payment as soon as this letter recalls the fact that you owe $85 due November 15 for . . . .

For the later stages of the collection procedure the collector has ample information to adapt an individual letter.

**Inquiry (giving the debtor a chance to pay or explain; offering help).** When the collector has made enough phone calls and sent enough reminders to decide that oversight is not the cause of delay, another assumption comes into play. With a new customer or a poor risk it may be that persuasion or force is necessary—and this may lead to skipping a stage or two in the usual procedure.

With an old customer who has paid regularly, however, reason says that unusual circumstances must be the cause. The collector still has confidence in the customer (based on past favorable experience), still wants to retain goodwill, and is always willing to be considerate of a person temporarily in a financial tight spot.

The letter below illustrates the technique for the inquiry stage.

> I wish I could sit down and talk with you for a few minutes about the circumstances that leave your January and February charges on the books.
>
> But because of the distance, I can only study our past experience with you, and various kinds of credit information. Your past record of prompt payment leaves me wondering what's wrong now.
>
> Please either make immediate payment of the $157.47 balance due or drop me a note today telling just how you intend to handle the account.

**Appeals (basically reader benefits, made increasingly forceful).** The delinquent who does not respond to a friendly inquiry evidently is taking the wrong attitude toward the indebtedness. The collector's new task is to persuade the debtor to pay.

*Basic Considerations.* The appeal stage is the collector's main work. Four important points are guidelines:

1. For persuasiveness, use individualized messages. The earlier inquiries will have collected most of the accounts (the easy ones). The remaining few will require individualized (or at least individual-sounding) messages rather than forms because of the need to be persuasive. By using information in the credit records, the collector can send individualized messages that are specific and therefore persuasive to a degree impossible in a form.

2. Develop only one or two points. Scattering shots weakens the message too much to reach the remaining hard-to-collect delinquents. The better procedure concentrating on a few points usually means longer letters because they must be specific and say enough to make the point emphatic.

3. Retain goodwill as far as possible. Because they are full-length collection messages, appeal stage letters necessarily carry some sting. You want to be firm without being harsh—by skillfully stimulating the customer's desire to pay.

4. Select a reader-benefit appeal. Successful collection involves showing that the debtor will get something wanted or avoid something not wanted—in other words, using the you-attitude.

Basically, people want

1. To get the service the product supposedly gives.
2. To have self-respect and the approval of others.
3. To avoid loss of the things they have and add to them.

*Resale Appeal.* Touches of resale belong in every collection letter, but resale may also be the theme of a whole appeal letter. Essentially it goes back and almost repeats the points made in selling the product. The debtor will see the good value received. That can motivate payment as the way to clear a conscience.

> Now that Asbex and Asbar have had time to prove their profit-making ability to you, can you say that they are a good selling team for you?
>
> When you followed up your original Asbex order of April 15 with the April 27 order for 20 gallons each of Asbex and Asbar, you showed that you thought the fire-retarding twins would move

quickly together. Although your payment of $130
for the first shipment, invoice BT-41198, is now
10 days overdue, you can keep your record intact
by sending us a check in the next mail. If you
make the check for $390, you can also pay for the
second shipment, invoice BT-41390, on its net
date.

From all reports on the way business is in
Ardmore, you'll be sending us repeat orders before
long. We'll be looking forward to serving you now
that you have learned that Asbex and Asbar fill a
recurring need of your customers.

*Pride Appeal.* Often resale talk joins a subtle appeal to pride, or the
appeal to pride may be more or less independent. In either case the
writer uses practical psychology to know when to encourage pride by
sincere compliments, when to needle it, and when to challenge it. The
essence of success with the pride appeal is to *encourage the debtor toward
prideful actions.*

Your choice of 18 Dustex coveralls for a total of
$449.10 shows your concern for maintaining a dust-
free environment in your plant for your employees'
health and comfort.

We feel sure that you have the same concern for
maintaining your preferred credit rating. Drop
your check for $449.10 in the mail today, and your
account will be paid in full.

To help keep your "clean room" and the employees
in it working at top efficiency, look at the
matching Dustex hoods, gloves, and shoe covers on
page 18 of the enclosed catalog. They will help
keep your people cool and comfortable while
preventing contamination of your clean room
environment.

*Fair-Play Appeal.* By using slightly different wording, you can turn the
basic pride appeal into an appeal to fair play. The wording may recall
the debtor's feeling of duty to do as promised. It develops the feeling
that the debtor should carry out the buyer's part of the bargain, since
the creditor has been fair in carrying out the seller's.

On the basis of your urgent need for drive
rivets, and because you supplied us with
references, we were happy to fill your order

February 6 for eight gross of our "Stellar" 1/2-inch-diameter drive rivets.

When we filled your order, we explained that our terms on open accounts call for payment within 30 days. Our suppliers have faith that we will pay them on time, and we have faith that our customers will pay us on time, enabling us to do so.

You know that your account is now past due more than 60 days.

When we shipped you the drive rivets, we had faith that you would do the fair thing and pay for them promptly. Won't you renew our faith?

Make out a check today for the amount past due--$921.60--and mail it in the enclosed stamped and addressed envelope. That's the fair thing to do, isn't it, Mr. Spiegel?

*Appeals to Economic Self-Interest.* Even those who have no sense of pride or of fair play in treating decent people fairly will probably pay if their own economic self-interest is clear. You may therefore write forceful collection appeals to a debtor's desire to retain the valuable credit privilege. In fact, this is the main appeal in commercial and industrial credit collection.

Why is a prompt-pay rating like money in the bank?

Both are able to command goods and services immediately when you want them.

On the basis of your ability to pay and your reputation, we extended credit immediately when you asked. Now we ask that you send your check for $898.76 to cover your August shipment of small jewelry.

Then look through the enclosed booklet. Notice the color pictures of things you'd like to have in stock for Toledo's Christmas shoppers. The heavy hollow silver plate described on page 3 is a line for moderate budgets. It's durable as well as handsome, since it's triple-plated silver on copper.

Should you care to order on our regular terms, enclose a check covering your balance of $898.76 and order the new stock. You can then use your credit as if it were another check drawn on money in the bank.

**Urgency.** When the regular collector is getting nowhere with appeals like those in the preceding messages, the next step may be stronger messages, perhaps from a higher executive taking over.

Actually the letter sent over the signature of the higher executive is usually a forceful development of one of the appeals already discussed. Or it may go a bit further on the economic interests of the debtor and talk about the cost of facing suit (since the debtor would have to pay the bill and court costs); but usually not—especially since it has become illegal for professional collectors to threaten lawsuit unless really intended.

Any executive knows, too, that mentioning a court suit drives customers away. Even now the firm is still interested in goodwill. So the executive more frequently plays the role of helper who allows a last chance and still does not turn the screws all the way down by setting an end date.

> When you began your business, a good reputation in Ardmore made it possible for you to get loans, and your prompt payments got you credit on your purchases.
>
> This reputation is more important to you now that credit agencies are becoming more and more strict in their policies.
>
> We have not received your check for the $260 for our invoices 69507, covering our shipment of 10 gallons of Asbex on April 10, and 76305, covering the shipment on April 20 of 10 gallons of Asbex and 20 gallons of Asbar. Some arrangement for this settlement is necessary right away. We are willing to accept your 90-day note at 12 percent for this amount so that you can retain your credit rating without lowering your cash balance.
>
> Of course we would prefer to have your check; but for the benefit of your business, your customers, and your creditors, please settle your account some way with us today.

**Ultimatum.** If the executive's offer of still another chance does not get the money, the collector will give the screw its last turn—saying calmly and reluctantly but firmly that on a definite date, usually 5 to 10 days later, the account will go to a lawyer to institute suit—unless payment comes before that time. (The tendency of some collection agencies to use this approach as an insincere threat is one of the abuses the 1978 law stopped.)

Though the language of the ultimatum should be firm (and sincere), it should not be harsh. To minimize resentment, the collector commonly reviews the case at this point.

> When we sent your first credit shipment on
> December 4, we took the step all stationery
> wholesalers take and verified your good credit
> reputation with the National Stationery
> Manufacturers Guild, of which we are a member.
>
> When we received a second order on January 26, we
> were happy to serve you again by shipping $42
> worth of Valentine cutouts and art supplies, under
> invoice CB-345. Since then we have tried to be
> both reasonable and considerate in inducing you to
> pay by our usual collection procedures. Now we
> shall be compelled by the terms of our membership
> agreement with the Guild to submit your name as
> "nonpay" unless we receive your check for $137 by
> April 15.
>
> I ask you to consider carefully the privileges
> and conveniences you can retain for yourself by
> making that payment--and don't forget that you
> will save the extra costs of a court suit to
> collect, in which you would pay not only the $137
> but the court costs.
>
> We want to help you keep your present privileges
> so that you can continue to stock your shelves on
> credit. Mail us your check for $137 by the 15th
> and retain those advantages.

If an ultimatum like that does not bring the money, the only remaining letter to write is a courtesy letter, telling the customer of the action taken. Then the case is out of the collection writer's hands and in the hands of a lawyer.

The trouble with that arrangement is that your public relations went with the case—into the hands of the lawyer.

## Collecting Unearned Discounts

A special problem is that of collecting unearned discounts (that is, discounts taken when sending payment after the end of the discount period). Usually the first attempt to collect is to add the unearned discount to the next bill with a note like "Unearned discount taken on previous payment (date)." If that doesn't work, a more or less standard procedure goes into effect.

The fact that the amount is usually small complicates the problem. Moreover, some large purchasers know the collector would think twice before losing their $200 or $200,000 orders to collect an improper $4 or $4,000 discount.

Fortunately, the collector usually has some advantages too:

1. When the occasion arises, the debtor is almost certainly an experienced person who will understand a reasoned business analysis showing that the end result will be a revised system with no possibility of discount.

2. The sizable purchaser has almost certainly investigated various sources of supply and might be as reluctant to change suppliers as the collector would be to lose a customer.

3. The fair-play appeal can include playing fair with all the collector's other customers. That is, you cannot well allow one to take the unearned discount while requiring others to pay according to terms.

Armed thus, the collector is ready for the taker of unearned discounts. First assuming a little misunderstanding of the terms is a reasonable start. Then make the terms clear, and overlook the improper deduction the first time.

If neither misunderstanding of the terms nor failure to check dates is the reason, the collector has a real letter-writing job. Although well armed—with justice, legal advantages, and some psychology on their side—some collectors are afraid to go ahead. The almost inevitable result is chaos in the collection department, or at least in the discount system. Word gets around.

The bold do better. Their appeals are items 1 and 3 above. Often a good letter combines both, as in the following illustration:

> From your letter of May 25 we understand why you feel entitled to the 2 percent discount from our invoice X-10 of April 30. If some of our creditors allowed us discounts after the end of the discount period, we too might expect others to do the same.
>
> The discount you get from us when you pay within a definite, agreed-on period is simply our passing on to you the savings our creditors allow us for using the money we collect promptly and paying our bills promptly.
>
> It's certainly true that your discount of $9.14 is small; but large or small, we would have allowed it if we had had your payment in time to use in making a similar saving in paying our own bills.
>
> The only solutions besides following the terms are (1) stopping all discounts, (2) taking the loss on all our sales, or (3) being unfair to our many other customers by making exceptions and showing favoritism. I don't think you want us to do any of those things, do you, Mr. Griggs?

## Collection Letter Checklist

1. Follow a reasonable philosophy and adapted procedure.
   a. Associate the specific goods with the obligation to pay.
   b. Always identify how much is due and when due.
   c. Except in the first two stages and the ultimatum, the points in b and a are not good beginnings.

2. Fit the tone carefully to the circumstances and collection stage.
   a. Avoid seeming to tell the reader how to operate.
   b. Nasty, curt, injured, scolding, or harsh tone doesn't help; it turns the reader against you instead.
   c. Show confidence that the debtor will pay.
   d. Avoid (1) accusations, (2) apologies, and—except in the reminder and inquiry stages—(3) excuses invented for the reader.
   e. To increase the force, use more collection talk (less sales promotion).

3. For persuasiveness (after the first two collection stages):
   a. Stress what the reader gains by doing as you ask.
   b. Select an appeal appropriate to the circumstances.
   c. Individualize your message for stronger effect, even in forms.

4. Guard against the legal dangers.
   a. Reporting the delinquent except to those requesting information because of an interest to protect is dangerous (so seal the envelope).
   b. Don't threaten physical violence, blackmail, or extortion.
   c. Be careful about your facts, and show no malice.

5. Adapt your drive for action to the stage of the collection.

When you mail us your check for the full invoice amount of $457.14, we know that you will do so in the spirit of good business practice and fairness.

Thank you for your order. You will find that our merchandise and attractive prices will always assure you of a more-than-average profit.

Because collection letters vary so much, they have few universal truths suitable for a specific checklist. The broader suggestions provided, however, will be helpful as a partial checklist.

### Collecting through the Telephone and Telegram

Telephone calls can be effective and inexpensive ways of collecting overdue accounts, especially at the reminder, inquiry, and appeal stages. (For some help on general telephone techniques, read the discussion in Chapter 12.)

Also, you should be aware that some states have restrictions on the number of calls about a debt and the times when the calls are allowed. Using the telephone to frighten, torment, or harass anyone is also in violation of the Federal Communications Commission's Public Notice 70–609. Specifically prohibited are

- Calls to debtors at odd hours of the day or night
- Repeated calls
- Calls asserting falsely that one's credit rating will be hurt
- Calls demanding payment for amounts not owed
- Calls stating that legal process is about to be served
- Calls to one's place of employment.

Telegrams are useful only in the last stage of collections because of the high expense, because wording the appeals is limited, and because Mailgrams have urgency and prestige but at much lower cost. For domestic telegraphic service, you select full-rate telegrams or overnight telegrams. If you send many telegrams, you should get a copy of Domestic Telegraph Service Rules for help on how to count words, figures, forms of money, symbols, and punctuation.

## Business Proposals

A business proposal is a written presentation of facts and reasons intended to convince the reader(s) that the proposer's services are the best available for fulfilling a need.

Three reasons make proposal preparation an important business skill today:

- The increasing complexity and technical content of work in both the public and private sectors;
- The greater sophistication of sources and selection techniques; and
- The more complex requirements from customers or clients in procurement and purchasing.

Because higher-technology products and services are abounding in the marketplace, analytical approaches and detailed information on the characteristics and prices of those products and services are necessary. Individuals, businesses, industries, and governments as buyers of those products and services demand documented evidence that they are getting the highest quality for their money. The written business proposal provides that evidence.

As with sales presentations, a proposal may be *unsolicited* (like the sales letters discussed in Chapter 8 and the justification reports discussed in Chapter 13) or *solicited* (like the invited sales discussed in Chapter 6). Most unsolicited proposals are about comparatively small matters, whereas solicited ones usually involve large projects—and competitors.

Because you can handle the smaller proposals as justification reports or from learning how to handle the big ones, this discussion will cover only solicited (and big) proposals. Since the U.S. government is the biggest customer in the world and has developed and tested a rigorous system of calling for proposals before large purchases, the procedures here are mostly its procedures.

Don't forget, however, that state and local governments and industrial and commercial firms use essentially the same procedures. Likewise, universities and other scholarly, professional, and scientific organizations now advertise many available research grants—each requiring a winning proposal.

The U.S. government seldom does its own research and development, especially for manufactured goods. Instead, it usually relies on industrial/commercial firms for this function. So-called specifications for a new armored personnel carrier, for instance, may be more a list of what the vehicle should be capable of doing than specifications of how to manufacture it.

Rather than asking for a bid, therefore, the government (like other big customers) usually issues an RFP (request for proposals—the government's are published in the *Commerce Business Daily* and the *Federal Register*). The notices include the department issuing the RFP and identifying numbers or other information. They also indicate contractors (if any) who have already won a bid and plan to subcontract portions of the work.

## Planning Your Response to an RFP

Writing a proposal in response to an RFP is a complicated business with a great deal of art to it. Your aim is to build reader confidence in your organization and get the contract.

A good start in planning a proposal is to identify all the discriminators in the competition—anything that could distinguish you from competitors. Basically, discriminators are what the customer sees as strengths or weaknesses (which don't have to be real; but if the customer thinks they are, then you must pay attention to them). To find the discriminators, you'll have to put yourself in the customer's shoes; take on the customer's hopes, fears, and biases; and look at what you can offer as compared to what somebody else can offer for the same requirements.

One technique is to list the approaches and characteristics of all your competitors, including yourself. The characteristics might be background, past performance, size and location, and related programs. The approaches might include technical know-how, manufacturing facilities and experience, management, plans, and personnel. You'll list everything that could matter in relation to the competition.

When you have your list of characteristics and approaches, then you apply your customer's evaluation criteria (not your own) to determine perceived strengths and weaknesses.

In showing how you as the supplier will meet the specifications, the proposal should show that you completely understand the customer's needs, know how to satisfy those needs, and are qualified to do so (in terms of facilities, equipment, and personnel). Finally, the price should be reasonable. Price is frequently less important, however, because ability to fulfill the contract is more important to most customers. Especially in dealing with the federal government, the most successful organizations are not necessarily those best equipped to meet needs but those that best convince the potential customer of their competence and dependability.

You cannot expect to write a winning proposal unless you know as much as possible about what the customer wants. The criteria for evaluating proposals are especially important.

Your proposal must be **complete.** Respond specifically to every specification in the RFP. Provide all the information requested. Establish that you can meet the schedule or deadline for completing the project. Make sure that your staff meets the RFP's specifications and (if specified) that it is made up of permanent employees. Show that you can solve the customer's problem, but do not do it in the RFP's words—don't quote the customer's language in your proposal. To neglect anything, fudge on a specification, or fail to meet any requirement will make your proposal "nonresponsive"—a government term that equates with "kiss of death."

While you're thinking about writing your response, also remember that good writing will help your cause. Good organization is the necessary starting point for good writing. You certainly won't look good if your proposal wanders around the subject, and evaluators won't appreciate having to find their way through it. Clear, correct language not only makes their job easier, it makes you appear professional. Some RFP's are page-limiting; so you need to be specific but concise.

## Organizing Your Proposal

**Understanding the Need.** Despite the information in the RFP, you still have to define the customer's need. In fact, the RFP may very well describe symptoms, leaving it up to you to determine what the problem is.

Writing a successful proposal requires that you glean all the information you can from the RFP and solicitation package in order to demonstrate that you understand the problem the customer wants solved or the need you are to satisfy.

**Making Your Plan or Program to Satisfy the Need.** Once you have identified the customer's need, developing your program or plan to satisfy it is usually the major step in preparing to write a proposal. (If you cannot devise a good plan, you logically cannot submit a proposal.)

Your plan or program must address the problem and be feasible—possible to carry out. If what you propose does not promise to solve the problem or is something that nobody can carry out, it is nonresponsive. Either case will cost you any chance at getting the business.

**Analyzing Your Capabilities.** Once you have shown you understand the customer's need and have presented a feasible plan to satisfy it, you must show the customer that you have the capabilities to carry out the plan. You demonstrate your capabilities by describing your staff, facilities, experience, and financial resources—all the things about your organization that will convince the proposal evaluators that you should get the contract.

Provide résumés on all the members of your organization who will do important work. Be sure that each résumé emphasizes the person's experience necessary for this particular job.

Show that you have the necessary plant facilities, equipment, and other resources to do the job. If what you propose requires specialized equipment, say that you have it or prove that you can get it. Don't overlook transportation: Can you efficiently ship things if that is part of the job?

Experience satisfying similar needs for other customers is a very strong selling point and can be described in terms of the similar needs of current customers.

You must also show that you have the necessary financial resources to buy needed raw materials and special equipment—or that you have the credit standing to borrow needed funds.

Proving that you understand the customer's need, that you have a plan to satisfy it, that you have carried out similar plans in the past, and that you have the means to carry out your plan demonstrates that your firm is the logical one to get the contract.

Though the customer may tell you what plan to use, the usual four parts of a proposal are Introduction, Discussion, Proposed Plan, and Qualifications. Your major job of organizing therefore becomes the job of fitting the four logically arranged kinds of content (preceding paragraph) into the four standard divisions organized on a different pattern.

## Writing the Major Parts

A proposal strikes a balance between marketing/selling principles (Chapters 8–10) and the evidence/believability of a report (Chapters 13–16). If you have studied the applicable sections in this book, you will be prepared to strike the balance.

**Introduction.** The Introduction is crucial since it sets the tone for the rest of the proposal. A poorly written Introduction can ruin the image of capability you need to get the contract. Remember that you have competition (other organizations will be submitting proposals), and you want your proposal to get the best reading.

As with a sales letter, a good start is to promise a benefit (to satisfy the customer's need). This idea you can best convey, not necessarily by stating the promise, but by stating the customer's problem as you see it in good, clear, simple English. Do not repeat the wording in the RFP!

Though you may have identified the problem as the first step in preparing to write the proposal, you will be wise to write the Introduction after you have finished the other three parts of the proposal. (The Introduction is usually an abridgment of the next section, the Discussion.)

Clear, easy-to-understand writing is necessary in a proposal and absolutely essential in the Introduction. First of all, you must identify clearly what RFP you are responding to (a customer may have a large number of them out). To avoid wasting your first paragraph for the identification, you may wish to use a header at the top of the first page of the Introduction, something like "A proposal in response to RFP AB–12–345–6789–CDE to prepare documentation for 'Project Fountain,' a new data base management system."

Most proposals begin the Introduction by explaining who the proposing organization is. If you choose this approach, quickly show how you are the logical firm to do the job; don't just say that you are the "C. W. Jones Division of Proposers, Inc., a subsidiary of Gigantic Corporation, which can do anything." Much better would be something like

```
X Company is an experienced group of writers,
most of whom (as documented later) are familiar
with programming and software through ownership of
personal computers. This broad experience means
that we not only have the personnel capabilities
to prepare superior documentation for the CP/M
version of "Project Fountain" but that we can
later write alternative versions for other
computers and operating systems as needed.
```

**Discussion.** While Introduction might do as the title for that section (but you will think of a better one), Discussion is not what you want to call the second major section of your proposal. In the Discussion you will present the logical arguments to convince the customer to award you the contract.

A proposal is a sales effort; and as such it follows the logic of all good sales efforts. The Introduction should get the evaluator's attention, and the Discussion should arouse interest.

The problem or need is the first item for discussion. In your Discussion you convince the customer that you understand the need or problem and all its ramifications. Now is the time to explore all the side effects and secondary problems.

Next discuss what is required to solve the problem or satisfy the need. You want to demonstrate that you have thoroughly thought through what needs to be done and how to do it.

Go into anticipated problems, and suggest ways to avoid them or solve them. Don't be afraid of making the job sound too difficult or of sounding defeatist. The customer will take your foresight as evidence of your thorough planning, and suggesting solutions in positive language will prevent any hint of defeatism.

List and discuss the possible ways of solving the problem. Show the good and bad points of each. This analysis should lead you logically into the next part (like conclusions and recommendations in a report), the heart of your proposal.

**Proposed Plan.** Your program for solving the problem is the heart. You need to show exactly how you propose to carry out your recommended program.

Whatever you call this section (Our Program is obviously unsuitable), it should also protect you against possible future disputes, especially over the changes the customer may want to make after you have begun the contracted work (often a troublesome point).

Most successful proposal writers begin their thinking with the plan or program to be presented, then construct a chain of logical arguments to prove that the plan or program is the best one. Frequently the nature of the problem and the proposed plan to solve it will provide the organizational framework for this section.

Perhaps the most important part of any program is the people who will carry it out. This section of your proposal should thus contain résumés of all the key people (directors, managers, supervisors, and professional personnel) who will work on carrying out your proposed program.

Anyone who has worked a number of years has probably developed a number of specialities. A COBOL programmer may also be proficient in RPG II and ADA, just as a professor may teach in several related areas. Thus a standard résumé designed to fit all proposals fits none of them well. Each proposed program requires a different set of specialities, and you will profit if you take the time to write new résumés for each proposal—emphasizing the specialities your people have that qualify you for that specific program.

Unless the RFP specifies the form and content for résumés, take the opportunity to sell by presenting each person in descriptive writing. Avoid giving education and personal details (or put them at the end if you have to include them), unless the RFP makes it clear that these details are important to the customer.

Give the person's name, title, proposed position if you get the contract, and a description of the person's experience emphasizing what applies to this proposal. List things successfully done that are similar to what the person will do for your program.

Often the RFP will contain a schedule for solving the problem or satisfying the need, and at least it will specify an end date for completion of the project. You should present in this section your schedule for carrying out your plan or program. It will of course fit into the framework of the schedule specifications, but usually it should be much more detailed.

Supplying your own schedule is further evidence of your thorough planning. If you vary from the customer's schedule, be sure to sell your version by giving your good reasons for doing so. (You should have laid the groundwork for this in the previous section.)

You can avoid future trouble by (1) being clear whether you mean calendar days or working days and (2) scheduling completion of each step a certain number of days after completion of the preceding step. This second device will protect you against, say, the customer's taking a month for a one-week review period (during which you suspend work until the review is done) and still insisting on completion by the contracted end date.

If your program requires special facilities or equipment, now is the time to announce that you have them and to describe them. For instance, manufacturing battle tanks for the army could require high-capacity overhead cranes. You might want to list them, say whether they are operator controlled or remote controlled, and tell how modern they are. Similarly, if you will need a computer, you would want to show that you have one with the necessary capacity and the software to run it.

**Qualifications.** The qualifications part of your proposal should show that your organization has the experience to carry out the program you propose. Essentially you want to show that you are the best choice for the contract and that you are dependable, with a record of success in similar projects.

Whether the RFP requires it or not, plan to include here a list of past contracts on which you have performed well. As with résumés, don't prepare a standard list to tack onto every proposal you write.

Instead, review your list for each proposal so that you can list jobs similar to the one you are seeking and so that you can emphasize the points important for this proposal.

Give the names of past customers, names of references at each customer, and a history of what you did for each customer. In these histories describe exactly what you did, the dollar amount of the contract, whether you completed the job within the budget or not, and anything else that will show your organization's dependability. You may want to itemize everything but the description, making that a narrative paragraph. Keep the histories fairly short, though—you don't want to run on and on extolling your virtues through past job after past job.

This section of your proposal is also where you can point with pride to any special accomplishments.

If you didn't fully describe your facilities and equipment earlier in the proposal, do it now. And if you are a division or subsidiary of another organization, explain it here. Such information leads logically to talk about your financial picture, especially your soundness and responsibility, if you didn't adequately cover this subject earlier.

Something else you might include in this section is letters of appreciation from satisfied customers. Such testimonials are powerful selling tools.

**Providing Good Format and Special Parts.** Many proposals, especially big ones, use appendixes to present matter that is not essential to every reader and might slow down reading. Examples are tables of statistics, drawings, and other supporting material, and documentation from previous successful contracts. (By cross-references at appropriate places, you can point attention to these supplements for readers who want to see them.)

In appearance your proposal should be as professional as you can make it. Submit each copy in a quality binder or other container (unless the RFP prescribes how the customer wants it). The typing, photocopied documents, and technical and engineering drawings should be clean. Any other graphics (graphs, charts, etc.) should look professional. Hire a commercial artist if necessary; it will pay off.

The cover should carry some identification of your organization as well as at least the RFP your proposal answers—as a convenience for the customer who has proposals coming in on a number of RFPs.

Include a title page that identifies you and the RFP as well as the date you are submitting your proposal. You may also want to put a statement on it that the information in the proposal is proprietary and may not be released for any use unless you get the contract. (You may need to see a lawyer for the appropriate wording.)

Some proposals include an abstract of the proposal (sometimes called Summary or Executive Summary) for people who want a quick summary of the major points of your proposal. If you provide one, make sure your abstract sells persuasively. The people who make the final decision commonly don't read proposals but rely on evaluators to weed out the bad ones and recommend the potential winner or winners. It is desirable to keep your abstract to one page, but telling your story well is more important. Take whatever space is needed (but keep the abstract concise).

A useful item in a proposal is a response matrix (a table of the things the RFP specified for the proposal, and where to find them—much as a contents table does). The usual format is the name of the item ("Equipment," "Personnel," etc.) followed by a page reference to the RFP, then the page the item begins on in the proposal, and perhaps some remarks. The primary purpose of a response matrix is to help evaluators quickly find the points they want to go over in your proposal. Anything that makes the evaluators' job easier deserves your consideration.

A letter of transmittal is mandatory. Proposal readers expect it, and it gives you a fine opportunity to do some initial selling. The letter of transmittal goes to the contracting officer as a separate document accompanying the proposal, but you should bind a copy into the proposal for other readers.

The contracting officer is usually concerned primarily with cost; so make your quoted cost and its justification a part of the letter unless the RFP specifies a separate cost proposal. You might also want to say that the signer is authorized to enter into a binding contract, tell who else might answer questions (if the signer is not available), and say how long your offer is good for (though the RFP may have specified this).

You can say what you will charge for the proposed work anywhere in your proposal—but, as you've seen in Chapter 6, several possible factors may influence your decision. Many writers do it in the letter of transmittal—especially in the copy to the contracting officer. If your price is high, you might be inclined to delay quoting your price until you have made your big selling points; *but some government evaluators of proposals won't stand still for this.* They want to know (up front) what the cost is, and you have to cater to them.

RFP's from government agencies and numerous commercial firms specify that a separate "cost proposal" accompany your proposal, and the federal government supplies forms for this.

Basically, break your cost down and show how you arrived at it. Give your direct labor costs, your overhead rate, other direct costs, administrative costs, and your profit. Account for material costs, subcontractors, travel, testing time and costs, and anything else that influences your price. A cost proposal can be very complicated, and most organizations have their accountants prepare them.

Unless your proposal is very short, also put in a table of contents and, if justified, a list of illustrations. Remember that you want to make your proposal as easy to read as possible, and a table of contents is a big help.

If your proposal is extraordinarily large, you might consider including an index. Preparing one is a big job, but it can pay off by helping evaluators find the items they want.

For more information on format, and especially on using heads, subheads, graphics, and special parts, see the chapters on report writing (especially Chapters 14 and 15).

## Questions and Exercises

1. In what ways is a special-request message more difficult than a direct request?

2. How would you handle the negative material in the following special-request situations?
   a. A request for $200 for a worthy cause.
   b. An important questionnaire that will take time to complete.
   c. A consultant's fee less than the consultant generally gets.

3. What appeals would you use to
   a. Raise money for a charitable program in your city?
   b. Urge your representatives and senators to help the starving people in Africa?
   c. Get your school to give you a scholarship?

4. Why and in what ways are the sales tactics in proposals different from those discussed in Chapter 8?

5. To help you understand discriminators, imagine you are answering an RFP for a thousand rowboats and there are only two competitors—you with a fiberglass rowboat and Company XYZ with aluminum rowboats. Make a list of discriminators showing the strengths and weaknesses.

6. Why would you want to include résumés in a proposal?

7. Of the five characteristics of a collection series, which three do you think are most important? Why?

8. Of the six stages a collection series may go through,
   a. In which would you send no more than one mailing? Why?
   b. In which one are you most likely to get into trouble?
   c. In which one are you most likely to send more than one message?

9. What reader benefits might a collection writer use to collect delayed payments from
   a. A car owner to make payments for last month and the month before?
   b. A recent college graduate to pay back a student loan?
   c. An owner of a new spa who owes $4,000 (60 days past due), has a good location, and works hard (but the manager says business is off)?

# Chapter Outline

# 10

# Selling Personal Services (Résumés and Applications)

## Evaluating Yourself, Employers, and Jobs

Sometime in life almost every educated person will write letters to get work: a summer job; an internship; a job launching a career upon graduation; a change of jobs for more money, for a better location, for work that has greater appeal.

Whether you send out letters and résumés or go directly to an interview, an inevitable part of job seeking is job analyzing.

When you seek work, you are selling; and as in any sales situation, you are simply marketing a product (in this case your services) to prospects (firms that can use your services).

In some cases firms *invite* your applications through advertisements, word of mouth, placement agencies, or recruiting personnel. Then you'll write them an invited sales letter (Chapter 6). In other cases you'll have to write a prospecting letter (Chapter 8). Both must convince someone of your ability and willingness to do something; the big difference between the two is in the approach.

The *prospecting application* is the logical first choice for learning because you will write better applications of any type as a result of thorough analysis and writing of this kind. Moreover, in the job market the prospecting letter has these advantages over the invited application:

- You have a greater choice of jobs and locations, including jobs not advertised.
- You don't have as much competition as for an advertised job; sometimes you have no competition, as when you create a job for yourself where none existed before.
- Often it is the only way for you to get the exact kind of work you want.
- You can pave the way for a better job a few years later after having gained some experience.

Of course you need to *know what kind of work you want to do* before you ask someone to let you do it. To choose the best job for you now (and to successfully change jobs later), you need to analyze yourself *and* possible jobs.

## Analyzing Yourself

If you are going to sell your services, you will do so on the basis of *what you can do* and *the kind of person you are.* Your skills are marketable products and deserve careful analysis. The *education* you have, the *experience* you've had (which is not so important in many instances as college students assume it to be), and your *personal attitudes and attributes* are the qualifications that enable you to get along with and do something for someone by using the skills you've developed.

**Attitudes and Attributes.** Early in your career, especially, attitudes and attributes may be the most important of the three. If you don't like a particular kind of work, you probably won't be successful in it. *Of all the surveys of why people lose jobs, none has ever cited less than 80 percent attributable to personal maladjustments rather than inability to do the work.*

Because your attitudes play such an important role in determining whether you will get the job you want, you might look at the reasons some interviewed people are not hired (given in Chapter 12).

No one but you can decide whether you will like a particular kind of job. Consider, among other things, whether you like to lead or to follow, whether you are an extrovert or an introvert, whether you are content to be indoors all your working hours or must get out and move around, and whether you want to work primarily for money or for prestige.

After you have had several years of work experience, you will know better under what conditions you work best and what kind of work you prefer. If you have yet to establish such preferences, the accompanying checklist on your abilities, skills, and interests may help you clarify your thinking about yourself (and at the same time give you some advice). The more checks you can *honestly* put in 1c–f, the more desirable you are as an employee—almost anywhere.

**Education.** For most readers of this book, education is already a matter of record or soon will be. You are laying a foundation of courses pointing to job performance in some selected field. While graduation is a certification of meeting certain time and proficiency standards, the individual courses and projects have taught you to do something and have shown you how to reason with judgment so that you can develop on the job. You will want to find work that makes good use of your valuable educational investment.

## Checklist on Your Abilities, Skills, and Interests

1. Read the statements below, and think before checking the one(s) which most accurately fit you.
   a. I prefer a job requiring: __ physical work; __ brain work; __ both.
   b. I would like to work: __ indoors; __ outdoors; __ both.
   c. I like to: __ work with things, tools, or equipment; __ work with people; __ work with ideas; __ work where I can think my own thoughts; __ work alone; __ work as part of a team; __ express my ideas; __ help others; __ see the results of my work; __ take on new duties; __ keep everything in good order; __ look for other jobs that need doing when my own work is finished; __ learn new things; __ fill requests fast and accurately; __ stay with a job until it is well done; __ keep a good appearance; __ do better than others performing the same work.
   d. I have: __ the ability to make friends easily; __ a good sense of humor; __ a strong sense of responsibility; __ a cheerful outlook.
   e. I am: __ energetic; __ a fast learner; __ good with words; __ good with figures; __ good with my hands; __ accurate with details; __ easy to get along with; __ careful to follow directions; __ dependable and prompt; __ neat in work habits; __ cooperative with others; __ not a clock-watcher; __ willing to do extra work; __ self-disciplined; __ imaginative.
   f. I want to: __ obtain more training after work hours; __ move ahead on the job; __ make my own opportunities; __ do an outstanding job for my employers; __ contribute to the support of my family.

2. Write down about five courses in school (or other learning) that you liked best and/or disliked most.

3. List any nonacademic activities that you particularly like and any accomplishments that made you feel proud.

4. Jot down any kinds of tasks that you have done well or really liked in the past—at home, school, the military service, or elsewhere.

5. Write down, as best you remember, good things that people have said about you.

**Experience.** Experience, likewise, is already partially a matter of record; you've held certain jobs or you haven't. You may have skills to sell learned through volunteer or organization work, even though you weren't paid for the work.

When you are young, then, you sell hard your education (learned skills), basic abilities and personality, creativity and talent, and long-range potential.

To come to a specific vocational decision—because your learning may apply equally well in many different lines of work and because you probably don't know as much about job possibilities as you could (most people don't)—you should do some research.

For an overview, read a description of job opportunities, requirements, and rewards in the kind of work you are considering. Publications like *Occupational Briefs* and other job-outlook pamphlets (Science Research Associates, 155 N. Wacker Drive, Chicago, IL 60606) and *Occupational Outlook Handbook* (Bureau of Labor Statistics assisted by the Veterans Administration) will help you. If you check in *Readers' Guide, Applied Science & Technology Index,* and *Business Periodicals Index* or *Public Affairs Information Service,* you may find other leads.

You may want to consult some guidance agency for tests and counseling. Most colleges and universities have facilities for testing vocational aptitudes and interests, and they are usually free. So do U.S. Employment Service offices and Veterans Administration offices. And in practically any major city you can find a private agency that, for a fee, will help you in this way. Reading and talking with other people—professors, friends, parents—can help you, but only you can make the choice.

Having chosen the particular kind of work you want to do, you should make an organized search for those who can use your services.

**Personal Profile.** Before you start looking for a job, however, you need to firm up or crystallize your own self-analysis into a concisely written, precise, and memorable form.

A written personal profile will serve best. For that, take five sheets of paper and write one of these headings on each: I. Education; II. Work Experience; III. Affiliations and Cocurricular Activities; IV. References; V. Goals and Qualifications. Now fill in each page with significant details:

I. Schools attended (in chronological order) with dates, diplomas/degrees, and major fields of study, credits, and grades. You might add honors and marketable skills, such as machines you can operate and languages you can read and/or speak.

II. Work experience (in chronological order), including after-school, summer, and military duties. Give duties, dates, employers, and maybe pay, location, and reasons for leaving.

III. Affiliations and cocurricular activities. Include significant precollege as well as college, community, hobby, and travel activities.

IV. References. List three to five (at least one professor in your major and your immediate supervisor on any significant jobs) with full names, addresses, telephones.

V. Goals and qualifications. Prepare at least three-item lists for each of your significant learned skills, accomplishments, and evidences of leadership, communication effectiveness, adaptability, strong/weak personal qualities, the kinds of firms you'd like to work for, short-term/long-term goals.

## Surveying Work Opportunities

The next two steps in a wise job search are surveying work opportunities and analyzing companies of interest.

One way of checking your previous self-analysis and relating the findings to appropriate work opportunities is the information interview. This is not an interview for a job but an interview about you, your career plans, and your job-search plans. The purpose is to check your own thinking and to get information and advice from a practicing professional on the kind of job to fit you, where to look for it, and how to get it.

First, read in Chapter 12 about interviewing. Then make an appointment to talk with a recruiter or other personnel representative of a convenient business firm—a person who knows the job market well, whether a possible employer for you or not. Do make clear that you're not asking for a job—though information interviews sometimes lead to job offers.

While awaiting the appointment time, (1) phrase your career goals precisely and concisely, (2) write up the brief autobiographical sketch explained later, and (3) think of two–five places that you consider the most favorable places where you might find a job.

When you go in for the appointment, you'll want to explain (1) your purpose (to tap the recruiter's knowledge and advice on suitable career plans and job prospects for you) and then (2) (concisely, from memory) the essence of your autobiographical sketch. That should start an interesting and informative interchange between the two of you. Do remember that you've asked for someone's time—don't expect too much. Information interviews used to pressure recruiters often backfire.

Professor Kerr[1] found that people who have information interviews impress recruiters very favorably by their extra initiative and interest, their implied respect, and their demonstrated assertiveness. Such interviews are among the very best means of initial contact with potential employers—partly because they tap the hidden job market (the high percentage of available jobs not advertised or even recognized until a well-qualified worker shows up).

Furthermore, through information interviews you can quickly develop a geometrically growing network of informed friends in strategic positions who will be keeping you in mind.

In your job search, don't overlook the possibility of working for Uncle Sam. You should first locate the Office of Personnel Management nearest you by checking in the phone book under United States Government or by getting OPM pamphlet BRE–9. You can also get help from private job-listing services not affiliated with the government because they keep up with what's happening in the federal job market. If you know what

---

[1] Daryl L. Kerr, "Effectiveness of Information Interviews: A New Approach to Job-Seeking Strategy," *Proceedings,* ABCA Southeast Regional Meeting, Atlanta, 1982, pp. 123–41.

federal agency has the job you want to do, you should apply directly to that agency.

Meanwhile, of course, you will be pursuing your job search by other means, such as in the following *print sources.*

Analysis of major industries
—the annual Market Data and Directory
  issue of *Industrial Marketing.*
—Standard & Poor's industry surveys.

Vocational needs
—*Dictionary of Occupational Titles* (U.S.
  Employment Service).
—*Occupational Outlook Handbook* (see highlights in Chapter 15).

Individual fields
—*Fortune* and *The Wall Street Journal* run special
  issues; *Savvy* and *Working Woman* have good career articles.
—trade journals in a specific field (the monthly *Business Publications* edition
  of Standard Rate & Data Service lists these by field).
—Catalyst has a series of pamphlets about jobs for women.

Specific organizations
—*The College Placement Annual.*
—*Career Employment Opportunities Directory.*
—*Career, the Annual Guide to Business Opportunities.*
—annual reports, recruiting brochures.

## Analyzing Companies

The more you can find out about an organization, the better you can decide whether you'll be happy there and the better you can write or interview specifically about how your preparation fits its needs. And remember, that's what you have to do in a successful application—*show that you can render service that fits somebody's need.*

Using your printed sources, you can find out about a company's history, financial and organizational structure, home office and other geographic locations; relative size in the industry (number of plants and/or other operations; array of product lines and services); growth picture (sales for the past five years; potential for new markets, products, or services; competition; growth in per share earnings and stock prices); and the corporation as an employer (ages of top managers, typical career paths in your field, nature of developmental training, average time in nonmanagement assignments, relocation policies, pay scales and—often more important—fringe benefits such as medical and life insurance, stock-purchasing plans, tax shelters, and retirement benefits).

Trade magazines are a basic way of learning about the field you are interested in. Another source you should investigate is associations in that field. Such trade associations abound, and they are the medium for exchanging information about new developments, who's who and where, and who has job openings or is looking for a new position.

If you have pretty definitely settled on the field you want to work in, you can do some invaluable spadework by joining the appropriate trade association, especially if you are still in school. Most trade associations welcome student members (often at reduced dues); and many run matchmaker services to get employers and prospective employees together. You can find the one you want in *National Trade and Professional Associations of the U.S. and Canada.*

If you want to get a head start on your competition, tell the officers of the association that you want to get involved actively, perhaps by working on some committee. Associations need *active* members, and you are pretty sure to be welcomed with open arms. Such association work is generally not too demanding, and it will have the immediate benefit of giving you information useful in pursuing your major. But most important, people working with companies will get to know you. They can provide entrée to job opportunities you might otherwise not learn about—and may serve as references.

From whatever source you can find, learn as much as you can about what the company does, how it markets its products or services, the trends at work for and against it, its financial position, its employment record, what kinds of employees it needs and what it requires of them—plus anything else you can.

## Fitting Your Qualifications to Job Requirements

Actually what you are doing when you analyze yourself in terms of a job is running two columns of answers: What do they want? What do I have?

The answers to both questions lie in three categories: personal attitudes and attributes, education, and experience—but not ordinarily in that order of presentation! In fact, as explained in greater detail in the section Compiling the Résumé, you will put yourself in a *more favorable light if you follow an order emphasizing your most favorable important qualification in the light of job requirements. But remember that desirable attitudes and personal traits and habits are basic equipment in any employee (and for writing a good application). Without them no amount of education and/or experience will enable you to advance in a job.*

One way to maximize the benefits of your personal traits, education, and experience in preparing your résumé (and preparing for an interview) is to write an autobiographical sketch, starting with your earliest years. Tell about where you grew up, your parents, your interests and hobbies and how they changed over the years; about your hopes, goals, satisfactions, your feelings regarding remembered events and situations, and about "special" people you remember and how and why you remember them. Account for your early work experience, school experience, and (if any) military experience. Write down your reasons for your college choice and curriculum interest. Try to formulate your career and personal goals. Try to recall dates, and organize your autobiographical sketch for clear continuity.

*Most of this material will not, and should not,* appear in your résumé. If you summarize the content into a one- or two-page summary, you'll be prepared if an interviewer asks you, a week or so later, what many of them do ask: "Tell me a little about yourself" or "Tell me your life story in two minutes."

You will know how to stress attitudes and interests, education, experience, and goals. In an interview you will be selective rather than chronological, of course.

**Showing the Right Work Attitude.** A company, other organization, or individual puts you on a payroll because you give evidence of being able and willing to perform some useful *service.* That means work. The simplest, easiest, and most effective way to think, talk, and write about work is in terms of doing something for someone.

Without a desirable outlook toward work and working conditions, competence can be a secondary consideration. Before you can ever demonstrate competence, you have to gain the approval of other people. You can be good, but if you don't get along well with people, your superior abilities won't be recognized. Even if recognized, they won't be rewarded.

One of the most frequent criticisms of college graduates is that they have overinflated ideas of their abilities and worth. Confidence in yourself is essential, but so are reasonable humility and modesty. You can achieve a successful balance if you imply both in a specific interpretation of how your education, experience, *and disposition* equip you to perform job duties.

In analyzing any job, therefore, estimate what you think are the two or three most important personal characteristics and plan to incorporate evidence that will imply that you have them. You have to show that your education and experience are adequate in selling yourself to a potential employer.

**Enhancing Your College Preparation.** With the desirable work-for-you attitude, you'll think in terms of job performance. If your reading has not given you a good idea of the duties you would be expected to perform on a particular job, you'll profitably spend some time talking with someone who has done the work. You cannot hope to anticipate everything you might be called upon to do on a given job (nor would you want to talk about everything in your application); but if you anticipate some of the *major* job requirements and write about your studies in a way that shows you meet these requirements, you'll have enough material for conviction.

Although recruiting ads often stipulate a level of academic attainment, your academic status (units of credit) or a diploma does not enable you to perform a useful service. *What you learned in earning them does.* To satisfy the arbitrary advertised requirement, you'll need to establish quickly your graduation (or whatever the requirement is). But the *primary emphasis in your presentation needs to go on those phases of your education that most directly and specifically equip you for the work under consideration.*

Similarly, in planning your application (but not in writing it), you should list, as specifically as you can, job duties you can be reasonably sure you'll have to perform and, in a parallel column, the background that gives evidence of your ability to do them.

An applicant for work in a public accounting firm knows that the job requires analyzing financial data, preparing working papers, assembling financial statements, and presenting a report with interpretive comments. The direct evidence of having learned to do these things is experience in having done them in advanced accounting courses and/or work experience.

The applicant must also communicate findings intelligibly and easily to clients, and (as evidence of ability to do so) should cite training in report writing (and letter writing) as well as in speech. If the applicant assumes that pleasant relations with clients are a desirable point to stress, citing study of psychology and sociology might be useful.

If you are interested in sales as a career, your specific work in direct selling (both oral and written), market analysis and research, advertising principles and practice, and report writing needs emphasis (along with any other specifically desirable preparation that you know about).

In all instances applicants need to be selective, concentrating on the study that most nearly reflects the most advanced stage of preparation. For example, a person who cites evidence of training in market analysis and research will certainly have studied marketing principles. Similarly, the successful completion of an auditing course implies a background of beginning and intermediate principles of accounting. Careful selection of the most applicable courses precludes the necessity for listing prerequisite courses and thus enables you to *place desirable emphasis on the most significant.*

**Making the Most of Experience.** Any job you've ever held that required you to perform some task, be responsible for successful completion of a project, oversee and account for activities of other people, or handle money is an activity you can cite with pride to a prospective employer. You may not have been paid for it; that doesn't matter a lot.

The college student who directs a campus unit of the United Way drive gets a workout in organization, delegation of authority, persuasion, systemization, persistence, punctuality, responsibility, honesty, and accuracy that is good work experience. Such experience is more valuable than that of the student who operates a supermarket cash register four hours a day—and nothing else, though that indicates experience in responsibility for money and customer relations. Especially if both students are aiming at managerial work or some kind of contact work, the one who has earned no pay but has had more experience working with people and assuming authority and responsibility is more desirable.

Even the person of limited experience can interpret it in relation to job requirements, giving the most significant part the emphasis of position. The most directly related phase of experience is the one most nearly preparing you to do something. For example, if a supermarket checker had also been a fraternity or sorority house treasurer (involving handling and accounting for money), an application for accounting work would want to emphasize the treasurer's duties over the checker's job; but an application to do selling would make the checker's job more significant.

Whatever experience you elect to present, you want to show as directly and specifically as possible that as a result of this experience you come equipped with the skills to do the job or at least to learn how quickly. The surest way to present this information about yourself in the *most favorable light is to describe past-experience job duties related to the job you're seeking.*

You will strengthen your application if you interpret the experience to show what it taught you about important principles, techniques, and attitudes applicable to the hoped-for job. Evaluating work experience is the same as evaluating education; it's matching up as far as possible the answers to "What skills do I have?" with the requirements under "What do they want?"

You will rarely, if ever, meet all job requirements; and you will always have some points that are stronger than others. Outright lack of a specific point of preparation or below-average standard are negative points to be handled in the same manner that any good writer handles them: embedded position and corollary positive language.

**Determining a Favorable Order of Presentation.** After you have listed the necessary and desirable qualifications for the job and your own specific qualifications (personal qualities, education, and experience), you will need to decide on an order of presentation that is most favorable to you.

If your strongest point is thorough preparation, that is your start; if it is experience, begin with that. And within each of these categories, arrange your qualifications so that the best comes first (as any good seller does). Write your qualifications in *an order that stresses your strong points.*

For this comprehensive presentation, a résumé (often called a personal record sheet or—recently—a qualification brief) is the preferred form.

## Compiling the Résumé

You should prepare your résumé *before* you write your letter. Making the necessary self-analysis and job analysis helps you recognize your assets and see yourself realistically in relation to requirements and duties in the job you want. Organizing your data also usually shows you what to stress in your letter, discussed later in the chapter.

The purpose of a résumé is *to help sell you to a prospective employer.* You will find that a well-prepared résumé can help you gain appointments for interviews and serve as a useful tool during interviews. If several people are to talk with you at the job location, send a copy for each to whoever arranges your schedule. You might even give copies to friends and relatives to hand to their associates where jobs might be available.

*Caution:* Though we encourage you to make your résumé a selling presentation, we caution you equally against overselling.

Don't think for a moment that you can get by with lying. Many employers are now using the services of the National Credential Verification Services. In one situation NCVS reported falsification of facts in 86 percent (113 out of 131) of the résumés college graduates submitted in applying for a good job. Recruiters would then not even talk to any of the 113. Other employers verify education and experience by calling college records offices and previous employers. Another twist in the verification process is to have applicants *sign* an application, because applications contain a statement about the truth of the information given, and thus falsehood is automatic grounds for dismissal.

Your résumé can accompany either a prospecting or an invited application letter—and often serves to start off an interview favorably. It tells your complete story—the little details as well as the big points—thus *enabling your letter to be shorter and to concentrate on showing how the high spots of your personal qualities, education, and experience equip you to do good work.*

As one authority said, a résumé gives your life's history in two minutes, indicates your organizing and language ability, and leaves your letter free to sell. It is a tabulation of your qualifications, giving pertinent, specific details concerning your education and experience, and sometimes supplying the names, addresses, and telephone numbers of references who can (and will on request) verify what you say about yourself.

## Dividing and Phrasing Well

Since the résumé must carry a wealth of detail and condense the material into a small space, it uses the space-saving devices of tabulation and noun phrases (rather than sentences and conventional paragraphs).

To facilitate rapid reading, you should use headings, some capitalization, and uniform indentions for rows and columns of information. Parallel construction in phrasing requires special care. (If you stick to noun phrases, you'll eliminate this problem.)

Impersonal style, without opinions and comments, is usually best for this concise, basically factual presentation (but be careful not to fall into unnatural, stuffy, pompous phrasing).

Though *no one* form and set of divisions is right and all others wrong, usually the desirable tabulation form will be in three to five parts. *First,* you need an *identifying heading.* The most effective practice is to put your name all in capital letters (or larger print or overstrike) to make it stand out more than any other part of the résumé.

One other possibility, if you have a word processor, is to use an individualized heading and type a separate résumé for every job you apply for:

<blockquote>
(your name)'S QUALIFICATIONS FOR (kind of)<br>
WORK WITH (company name)
</blockquote>

Be careful of appearing to oversell with adjectives on your résumé, particularly in conservative fields like accounting. Rather than using headings like "Effective Work Experience," use a more general heading—"Work Experience"—and let your reader emphasize what you've done rather than how you describe it.

If you use your name as the major heading, you'll need an Objective section, discussed next.

To get the necessary information of your address and telephone number (with ZIP and area codes) on the page for easy finding but without undue emphasis, put it single-spaced and centered under the heading or at the left margin. If some of an extended series of letters or calls might come when you are at different places (home versus school or office, for example), you might well give both, one to the left and one to the right, labeled and with dates if known.

*Second,* most career counselors and placement office workers expect an *Objective* or *Job Objective* section. Stating your career plans and goals clearly and concisely gives recruiters a chance to interview you for an appropriate job. Try to write an objective that is descriptive but not confining, and avoid clichés about "meaningful work" and "career advancement." Some objectives are included on the sample résumés later in the chapter.

One successful applicant, who knew the receiving company well, used simply "Objective" as the heading with a statement that fit specifically but also applied broadly:

```
To work in a marketing line or staff job. To
handle projects and assignments concerned with the
various aspects of marketing and offering cross
training into other major functional areas. To
gain additional business knowledge, experience,
and judgment necessary for advancement.
```

If you use one, your statement of job or career objectives should be specific enough to show that you know where you want to go. Too broad a statement like "I want to use my talents and abilities in the best manner to advance myself and my employer" will present a damaging appearance of self-interest, immaturity, or naïveté. For optimum effectiveness (if you can do it briefly enough), you might make your statement a summary or abstract of your qualities, experience, and accomplishments in terms of their benefit to the potential employer. By implying the jobs/titles you qualify for, it could help an organization immediately to match you to a job assignment it may have.

*Third,* for most college students ready to go on the job market, their *education* is usually the topic deserving treatment next. Then any significant experience can follow. For applicants with extensive related experience that would weigh heavier than their education, the reverse would be true.

In presenting your education, call the section Education or Professional Education. Then list, in reverse chronological order, your colleges and possibly your high school if it's pertinent to the job or the area you want to work in.

For each school, give

Name of school, major or college

Degree, date

GPA *if* yours is high or you are an accounting major
applying for a job in the Big Eight

If the location of the school isn't obvious, put the city after the name. If your minor is important for the job, list it. Only accounting majors are required to list a GPA (and should usually list both overall *and* accounting GPA). Other majors should list GPA only if it is one of their selling points. GPA can be in upper division courses only, the major only, or overall. Indicate the system if it is not the 4.0 system.

For emphasis, underline the name of the school and double-space between information on different schools. *If* you have taken special electives that are pertinent to the job, list them. *Don't* list courses all students take—it looks like you're trying to fill space.

*Fourth,* if you put education as the third part (after the title and job or career objective), will come *experience* (if any). In some very rare cases experience may combine with education. For instance, a successful applicant to a college-textbook publisher for a job as book representative (getting professors to adopt company books) wisely used a double heading, "Education and Teaching Experience." The reason was that the only relevant experience (too little to deserve separate-section listing) was two years of part-time teaching of beginning courses while getting the MA.

Again, the heading could carry justifiable qualifiers such as: "Work Experience Requiring Accuracy" (an accounting applicant); "Experience Working with People" (a public-relations applicant, who stressed extensive leadership roles in campus activities); and "Business Experience Requiring Accuracy and Judgment" (the mature marketing applicant whose objective you read earlier).

List your *work experience* in reverse chronological order, to stress the most recent, most advanced, and usually most relevant. Items to cover in each job listed are beginning and ending dates (month and year), job title, name and place of employer, and duties performed—with emphasis on what you actually did (thus implying *skills,* the important element).

In this section particularly, remember that the less experience you have to list, the more important even seemingly irrelevant work experience is if it taught you anything (good work habits, dealing with people, . . .). Even small jobs such as part-time work while in school can carry impact on the important points of leadership and honesty, for example, if you had responsibility for directing other people or handling money. Similarly, though mere membership in a campus organization amounts to little, election to and significant accomplishment in officer roles in campus activities show two desirable qualities: general approval by others and leadership.

Together the dates given for your education and experience should cover your life since high school. If not, an alert interviewer may wonder if you're hiding something.

In describing your experience, you want to show potential employers progress in your accomplishments.

When talking about any experience you have had, the key ideas to get across are *responsibility* and *accomplishment.* Evidence that you have been responsible also implies honesty, maturity, punctuality, and other virtues.

Writing in noun phrases rather than in sentences will have the desirable effects of shortening your résumé and simultaneously making it clearer, more concise, and more effective:

Tobias & Olendorf, Inc., 520 N. Michigan Ave.,
Chicago, IL 60611 (312/555-7575), 12/81-5/85.

* Responsible for media research and internal
  traffic functions; later promoted to copy
  contact on major accounts.
* Prepared marketing plans, developed marketing
  research procedures, oversaw production and
  directed preparation of print, radio, and
  television advertising.
* Supervised media scheduling.
* Conceived, presented, and implemented improved
  reader/viewer response techniques.

Note the heavy use of action verbs that imply creative, managerial, and customer-relations work—*prepared, developed, oversaw, directed, supervised, conceived, presented,* and *implemented.* These are the kinds of words you should strive to use realistically in talking about your experience. Not only will you present yourself in a good light, but consciously using such vocabulary will keep you thinking in terms of management, professionalism, creativity, and, most important, *doing.* To help you, here is a partial list of such words:

| | | | |
|---|---|---|---|
| administered | directed | judged | regulated |
| advanced | discovered | launched | reshaped |
| analyzed | employed | led | resolved |
| applied | enlarged | managed | restored |
| approved | established | negotiated | revised |
| arranged | evaluated | opened | scheduled |
| assigned | executed | operated | served |
| awarded | expanded | ordered | settled |
| began | extended | organized | shaped |
| commanded | governed | originated | solved |
| conceived | guided | oversaw | stabilized |
| conducted | handled | planned | started |
| controlled | headed | prepared | steered |
| coordinated | implemented | presented | straightened |
| corrected | improved | produced | (out) |
| created | inaugurated | progressed | superintended |
| decided | increased | published | supervised |
| delegated | initiated | raised | systematized |
| designed | installed | ran | trained |
| determined | introduced | recruited | |
| developed | invented | | |

**Final Sections.** The rest of your résumé (after education and experience) requires less skill but even more discretion.

Traditionally, résumés used to include a section on "Personal Details," usually with photo attached. Since federal regulations now make it illegal to consider such information in making employment decisions (unless demonstrably related to the job), employers now generally prefer not to have the facts—for fear of later accusations that the information counted (illegally) in the decision. You'll see that the illustrations, therefore, do not include a personal details section or anything about race, religion, sex, marital status, age, or health. A few people include personal information on a first job résumé (to fill space) and drop the section as their experience takes more space to describe. A personal section doesn't appear often today, however.

Yet you should realize that if a particular personal feature will clearly affect performance in the wanted job, you should (wisely and safely) put it in your application; and an employer can wisely and safely count it in the employment decision.

**References.** Again, traditionally, the ending of a résumé used to be a list of about three "References" (people able and willing, on request, to write or talk evaluatively about you to interested employers). Though two illustrations show that practice, many people now omit the list and add only "References gladly furnished upon request" (with or without the heading "References"). If you don't have enough material to fill a page nicely, references can serve because they're a logical, positive way to finish the page.

Merely offering to provide references may be wise in a solicited application. The prospective employer may have so many applicants to evaluate that getting information from all the references (if listed on all the résumés) would be too big a job. Even in the early stages of negotiating, however, where you have no idea whether the prospective employer is interested, you should have your references ready for presentation. Unless you've presented them before, any interviewer who is getting interested in you will probably request references. Your references are not likely to receive inquiries, however, until your prospective employer is considerably interested.

The thinking of an employer considering a recent university graduate usually goes about like this: (1) I hope to get a good employee who will stay on the job a long time. (2) Adding the recruiting and training costs to the employee's salary and fringe benefits for 40 years (more or less), I expect to spend well over $1 million. (3) Wise decision making calls for me to get all the information I reasonably can to select a good employee worth the money. (4) That means getting information not only from the applicant but from other people (references).

Whether you will list them on your résumé or have them available for a follow-up session, here are some helpful pointers on references:

1. Select three or four people who (at least collectively) know well your personality, your education, and your job performance (if any).

2. The more accomplished or prominent they are (as their titles show), the better; but don't make the mistake of listing a corporation or university president who barely knows you instead of a low-level supervisor under whom you worked three years (or a professor or dean who knows you only from a one-term, once-a-week, big lecture group you attended instead of an assistant professor who taught you the three most advanced courses in your major).

3. Avoid any reference who is biased. That rules out (except for very unusual circumstances) relatives, associates from social or church organizations, and law enforcement officers. The best references are former or present employers, fellow workers, and teachers—who also do a better job of describing the character traits that are important.

4. When you've settled on your best references, get their permission. That is not only the courteous thing to do (because you *are* asking a favor); but it gives you a chance to help them, the employer, and yourself, by telling them the main criteria for the job (points to cover in their responses). Give each reference a copy of your résumé.

5. List your references with names, titles, and addresses and telephone numbers (with ZIP and area codes). Unless other information in the résumé (such as a reference's title and address) at least implies the relationship with you (such as former employer or teacher), make the relationship clear.

## Providing Favorable Appearance

Having finished with the content, organization, and style of your résumé, you still have to decide on its general and specific appearance before you put it in final form. Until you get an interview, it is your representative. Make sure it has a quality appearance—like you.

Naturally, you will consider the quality of the paper and type, the margins and line balance for good layout, and the form and spacing of the section and subsection headings.

The big question is whether to use a word processing machine, to type each copy individually, or to type one and print many copies. Modern word processing equipment allows you to provide each prospect with what is in effect an individually prepared résumé, as illustrated earlier. You can revise, rearrange material, and justify (even up) the right-hand margin if you wish.

As a practical matter, however, you may have to run off multiple copies—because you don't have the time or money to type or have typed all the copies you need. Do not use carbons, photocopies, or mimeographed or dittoed copies. Instead, to be sure your résumé represents you fairly, get the *best* reproduction you can afford—to look as near as possible like the original neatly typed copy. Do *not* type in anything on a printed copy, as you can never satisfactorily match a typewriter (even electric with a onetime carbon ribbon) to printed material, and the resulting poor image can affect your chances of getting an interview.

## Learning from Illustrations

The following five illustrations vary considerably in content and form. Study them thoughtfully. Notice how the varied illustrations all still follow closely the suggestions for form and content.

In designing your résumé, gather all the examples you can (from placement offices, professional clubs, texts like this one)—and then write your own, *not* a copy of any particular example. Your final effort should be conventional in form without copying inappropriate headings, wording, or sections.

The first illustration (Figure 10–1) gives a lot of information in a readable, emphatic layout. Because her activities showed wide interests and responsibilities, Jennifer Corrigan used them before work-related experience. Accounting firms today are looking for recruits with people skills because of increased need to market their accounting and consulting services.

Figure 10–2 is a good example of a person with both related experience *and* experience that shows initiative and good time organization (since Nancy Ross was both working and in school most of the time). To avoid omitting relevant information, you can use two pages. In this field, listing computer specifics is a selling point.

In Figure 10–3 Carlos Anaya makes the most of volunteer and paid experience in managing people. Because he hasn't enough past jobs to fill the page, he uses references to fill the space. Notice that the references include full mailing addresses, phone numbers, and where needed, identification of the reference's job relationship.

These three examples also illustrate various heading placements: marginal, centered, and side heading position can add or subtract space for your presentation, as you can see.

Figure 10–4 shows excellent layout that puts many pieces of information on little more than a page. Notice the emphasis on skill areas and accomplishments related to the job objective.

Figure 10–5 is an example of a résumé for a later job (not just right out of school). Notice the use of bullet format and subheadings to emphasize work accomplishments. Donald Stockman arranged his qualification brief by skill category more than by the more traditional chronological arrangement. In the Education section, he listed additional courses to show his full range of related knowledge.

**Figure 10-1**

JENNIFER L. CORRIGAN                          2117 Lake Forest Road, No. 49
                                                    Lakeside, CA 92129
                                            Telephone:  (619) 000-0000


OBJECTIVE          To work in many different aspects of accounting leading to
                   certification.


EDUCATION          **SAN DIEGO STATE UNIVERSITY,** San Diego, CA.
1982-1986          Degree:  Bachelor of Science, Accounting, May, 1986.
                   Other areas of Study:  Spanish, Economics.


ACTIVITIES &
ORGANIZATIONS      **NATIONAL ASSOCIATION OF ACCOUNTANTS.**  Active Member Status.
                   Communications and Professional Development Committees.
                   Initiated explanatory literature for the student chapter.

1984 to            Projects Director AIESEC (International Association of Students in
Present            Economics and Business Management).  Maintained relationships with
                   other internationally oriented groups, presented programs, educated
                   others, and promoted San Diego High School's Magnet Program.
                   National Conference delegate with full voting status, Atlanta,
                   Georgia, 1985.

                   Student member, WORLD TRADE ASSOCIATION OF SAN DIEGO.
                   Increased visibility of San Diego State University
                   and personal knowledge of international commerce.

1985 to            99's (INTERNATIONAL ORGANIZATION OF WOMEN PILOTS).
Present            Licensed Private Pilot.  Attended National and Regional
                   Conferences in St. Louis, MO, and Santa Monica, CA, in 1985.


AFFILIATIONS       World Affairs Council of San Diego, Lancer Aviation Flight Club,
                   and Institute on World Affairs.

WORK
EXPERIENCE         **Assistant Manager,** Jamison Apartments.  Administration,
1979-present       management, financial activities, customer relations,
                   coordination.

June -1982         **Full Charge Bookkeeper,** Dr. T. A. Bailey, O.D.,
Sept. 1984         Mission Viejo, CA.  General journal entries, accounts payable,
                   accounts receivable, payroll.  Also dispensed contact lenses
                   and served as buyer of frame inventory.

Sept. 1980-        **Bookkeeper,** William P. Peinado, Capistrano Beach, CA.
Sept. 1981         Accounts payable.  Also did legal secretarial work, was
                   responsible for office, typing legal briefs, and greeting clients.


REFERENCES         Available upon request.

**Figure 10–2**

NANCY G. ROSS

3284 Talbot Street
City, State
(000) 000-0000     (000) 000-0000 (messages)


<u>Objective</u>

To work as a programmer or systems analyst and sell the
company's services through proposals and presentations.


<u>Education</u>

State University, Information Systems major, May 1986.

Coast College, AA degree, January 1984.


| <u>Computer Languages</u> | <u>Hardware</u> |
|---|---|
| BASIC | VAX 11/780 |
| FORTRAN | CYBER 750 |
| COBOL | IBM 360 |
| CP/M | IBM PC |
| dBASEII | |
| Pascal | |

<u>Honors and Activities</u>

Deans's List:  Fall 1981 and Fall 1984
Grade Point Average:   3.68 (4.0 scale)

Director of Programs, Spring 1985 – Data
Processing Management Association (DPMA)
Member of DPMA, Fall 1984
Member of Women In Business

<u>Information Systems/Mathematics Experience</u>

1/85 –       <u>State University Computing Center</u>
present      Lab Assistant:  Help students with programs in
             BASIC, FORTRAN, COBOL, Pascal, and other languages
             that run on the CYBER 750 and the VAX 11/780.

11/84–12/84  <u>Software Products International</u>, City
             (Independent Contractor)  Validated business
              applications (testing new software; temporary job).

**Figure 10–2** *(concluded)*

Nancy Ross, page 2

9/84 - present    Self-employed Math Tutor

3/84 - 6/84       Coast College, City
                  Student Assistant III:  Tutored math, graded
                  exams, kept Math Lab filing system in order.

7/80 - 9/80       Jensen Associates, City
                  Draftsperson for a mechanical engineering con-
                  sulting firm:  updated plumbing and heating plans
                  using skills acquired in high school drafting.

Other:            Cashier, bank teller.

                  **Marketing/Management Experience**

7/83 - 8/84       Self-employed Housecleaner
                  Bid on, scheduled, and performed domestic
                  cleaning jobs.

Restaurant experience:  Cocktail waitress, The Halcyon, San Diego
                        Busperson, TGI Friday's, San Diego.
                        Hostess, Gulliver's, Inc., Irvine.
                        Food waitress, Denny's, Inc., City

                        **References**

            Mr. John Garcia, Professor of Mathematics
            Math Lab Coordinator
            City College
            City, State, Zip
            (000) 000-0000

            Ms. Victoria S. Wilson
            Associate Professor, Information Systems Dept.
            College of Business
            State University
            City, State, 92182-0127
            (619) 265-5316

            Ms. Marjorie Cohen, Draftsperson
            Professional Community Management
            P.O. Box 2220
            City, State, Zip
            (714) 951-2403

**Figure 10–3**

CARLOS ANAYA
14 Swift Court
City, State, Zip
(000) 000-0000
(000) 000-0000 (messages)

OBJECTIVE        To work effectively in a management trainee position.

EDUCATION        State University, 8/84 - Present
                 Business Administration major, sophomore
                 City Community College, 9/81 - 6/82
                 25 units of general education

AIR FORCE ROTC   Technical Sergeant, NCOIC GMC Plans; Color Guard
                 Sergeant; Arnold Air Society, 1st Lieutenant,
                 Air Force Association Liaison; Honor Flight,
                 drill team, Dining-In committee member.

EMPLOYMENT

   Police Cadet, Beach Police Department, 6/82 - 8/84
        Received training and experience in government, public, and
        press relations; also in research and development, training,
        report writing, patrol procedures, investigations, public
        safety.

   Coast YMCA, 6/81 - 6/82:  Counselor in youth programs; front
        desk staff.

LEADERSHIP EXPERIENCE

   Advisor, Orange County Explorer Presidents' Association,
        9/83-8/84.  Training, advising, and supporting Association
        Board members in their training, communication, and program
        assistance to County Explorer post officers.

   Associate Advisor, Beach Police Explorers, 6/82 - 8/84.
        Training and advising post officers in successfully managing
        law enforcement Explorer post.

REFERENCES

   Chief James L. Evans               Mr. Michael S. Wilson
   Beach Police Department            Executive Director
   P.O. Box 7000                      Coast YMCA
   City, State, Zip                   City, State, Zip
   (000) 000-0000                     (000) 000-0000

   Mr. Frederick Johnson
   (Explorer Advisor)
   870 Stevens Drive
   City, State, Zip
   (000) 000-0000

**Figure 10-4**

KAREN ANN ASSENTI
6767 E. Amherst Street
City, State, Zip
(000) 000-0000

| | |
|---|---|
| OBJECTIVE | A challenging management-trainee job leading toward hotel restaurant/catering management. |

PRESENT RELATED
EMPLOYMENT 1986

INTERNSHIP—CATERING CLERK - HYATT HOTEL
Initiated Hyatt Internship Program to work 15 hours a week. Responsibilities include: arranging and booking meeting rooms and menus, handling and writing prospectuses and letters to clients, cold-calling for potential sales, and client servicing.

MANAGEMENT
SKILL AREAS

Developed and initiated business plan for an Entrepreneurial/ Venture class . . .designed and presented brochure promotions for a local firm . . .created financial plans, bookkeeping, policies and procedures, promotions, sales representation and monitoring for another local business . . . Analyzed structure and recommended changes for organizational makeup of multi-sensory company.

EDUCATION

Bachelor of Science Degree, May 1986
State University
    MAJOR - Management
    MINOR - Classical Humanities

Leith's School of Food and Wine, London, England
    Graduate Introductory course, 1982.

EXPERIENCE
1984 - 1985

Administrative Assistant for Communication
    Associated Students/State University
    Developed, coordinated, and implemented banquets, reunions, political forums, committees for $5 million student corporation.

1984

Writer/Clerk--DAILY JOURNAL, State University
    Wrote weekly Restaurant Reviews. Responsible for office organization.

1983 - 1984

PERSONNEL STAFF--STUDENT EMPLOYMENT CENTER
    Associated Business Students
    Handled and arranged job interviews for business students.

1983

VICE PRESIDENT OF BUSINESS AFFAIRS--STUDENT ALUMNI CHAPTER
    Designed and developed fund-raising projects for the 80-member alumni auxiliary student club.

1982 - 1983

COCKTAIL WAITRESS/HOSTESS - HOUSTON, TEXAS
    Food and drink services for nightly jazz club.

**Figure 10-4** *(concluded)*

Karen Assenti, page 2

UNIVERSITY/COMMUNITY SERVICE

Member PI BETA PHI Sorority
Member Sigma Iota Epsilon--
  Honorary Management Fraternity
Member Women in Business Club
  One of five members for
  University Program Review Team
New Student Orientation Program Leader
  1984, 1985, 1986
Coordinator for Dorm Hall Activities
  1983.

ACHIEVEMENTS/HONORS

Dean's List--ABCD
Who's Who among American Colleges
  and Universities, 1985-86
ABCD Student Service Award, 1985
Associated Students--Outstanding
  Employee Award, 1985
PI BETA PHI--Adele Taylor Alford,
  Outstanding Junior Award, 1985
Student Employment Center--Staff
  Person Award, 1984.

INTERESTS        Restaurants, eating, traveling, people, all sports.

REFERENCES       Available upon request.

**Figure 10-5**

DONALD STOCKMAN'S QUALIFICATIONS FOR
REPRESENTING BEARLES RADIOGRAPHICS

2277 Greenleaf Street                                    (205) 555-3456
City, State, Zip

### Work Accomplishments

Medical--    * Represented X-ray Division of E. I. Du Pont,
             Nashville, Tennessee, July 1981-January  1985.

             * Assumed territory with 72% penetration and $1.4 million in
             sales.  Ranked 4th in region in net gains the first year.

             * Consistently realized $250,000 in net gains annually.
             Final penetration of 92% reflected over $25 million in sales.

             * Served and sold to radiologists, hospital administrators, chief
             technologists, nuclear medicine departments throughout Southern
             Kentucky, Middle Tennessee, and Northern Alabama.  Principal
             products included medical imaging, film processing, and film
             handling equipment.

             * Designed departments for seven major hospitals to incorporate
             Du Pont equipment sold.

             * Appointed as Equipment Coordinator for district in 1984.

             * Authored three technical presentations for customer and field
             training.

             * Originated an extremity exposure technique that formed the
             basis for Dr. Ray Drew's article on arthritic studies.

             * Introduced three technical representatives and two service
             representatives into the field.

             * Serviced Kodak and Du Pont equipment routinely.

Industrial--* Represented Betz Laboratories from January 1985 to present.

             * Sold water treatment to engineers in paper, tire, ammonia,
             and chemical plants.

             * Improved customer relations at Reichhold Chemicals, General
             Tire, Southern Natural Gas, and Gulf States Paper by thorough
             investigation of existing treatment programs.

             * Formulated water treatment guidelines for these plants as well
             as Demopolis, Union Camp, Hunt Oil, B. F. Goodrich, and Car-Ren.

             * Drafted successful proposals at all listed accounts.

**Figure 10–5** *(concluded)*

### Work Accomplishments (cont'd)

Military--
* Commissioned second lieutenant, 1977, discharged as first lieutenant, 1979.

* Served as platoon leader over 44 men and six E-6 sergeants. Duties included those of supply officer, pay officer, motor pool officer, dispatcher. Became Brigade Legal Officer advising all Fort Lee company commanders.

University--
* Worked under Dr. Wendell Hewitt as graduate assistant.

* Organized class presentations, lectured, graded class work.

Additional--
* Worked for summer without absenteeism on shift work as summer laborer at Gulf States Paper Corporation, City.

* Worked part-time after high school as a sales representative in retail store for two years.

* Mastered Dale Carnegie course while working for Du Pont.

### Professional College Education

Master of Business Administration, 1980, University of X with 2.5 average (3.0 scale).
Some courses that instilled practical sales skills: business communication, financial analysis, statistics, accounting, economics, management, marketing, report writing.

B.S. Chemistry/Mathematics, 1978, University of X.

Electronics (by correspondence), completed May, 1985, Bell & Howell School, Chicago, Illinois. The course objective: learn modern electronic principles for field repair.

### Community Activities

Boys' Club of America--President of local advisory board, 1983 - present

City Chamber of Commerce--committee on service businesses, 1982-84.

City Symphony Board--fund-raising committee, 1980-82.

### References

Will be furnished upon request.

## Checking the Product (a Checklist)

1. Begin with your name all in capital letters.

2. State your objective clearly and concisely.

3. For appropriate emphasis, ease of reading, and space saving:
   a. Give your address(es)—and phone(s) if likely to be used—in minimum space below your name.
   b. Balance material across the page in tabulated form.
   c. Use difference in type and placement to affect emphasis and show awareness of organization principles.
   d. Centered heads carry emphasis and help balance the page, but take more space.
   e. Capitalize the main words in centered heads, and underline the heads.
   f. If you have to carry over an item, indent the second line.
   g. Remember to identify and number pages after the first.

4. Lead with whatever best prepared you for the particular job, but account for the chronology of your life since high school. When extensively experienced, such complete coverage is less necessary.

5. Education details should point up specific preparation.
   a. Show the status of your education: degree, field, school, date.
   b. Highlight courses that distinctively qualify you for the job.
   c. Give grade averages in an understandable form.
   d. Avoid belittling expressions like "theoretical education."
   e. Consider a chronology that emphasizes your most relevant information.

6. Experience: for jobs listed,
   a. Give job title, duties, firm or organization name, full address, specific dates, *responsibilities,* and immediate superior's name.
   b. If experience is part-time, identify it as such.
   c. Consider reverse chronology to emphasize the most relevant.
   d. Use noun phrases and employ action verbs that imply duties and responsibilities.

7. List or offer to supply references. When you list references,
   a. Give the names, titles, addresses, and telephones of references for all important jobs and fields of study listed.
   b. Unless obvious, make clear why you list each reference.

8. Remember these points about style:
   a. A résumé is ordinarily a tabulation (noun phrase); avoid paragraphs and sentences.
   b. Items in any list should be in parallel form (**Para** in Appendix C).
   c. Keep opinions out of the résumé; just give the specific facts impersonally.

# Writing the
# Prospecting Application

Since application letters are sales letters in every way—sales letters selling your services—writing good ones requires self-confidence and positive thinking.

Sometimes getting a job may be harder than doing the job you get. Even organizations that advertise for employees sometimes neglect common courtesy and don't always give a warm welcome to applicants. In applying, you may have trouble getting through a wall of protective secretaries to make an appointment. Promised "will calls" or your unanswered letters may keep you dangling for days or even weeks.

Though such treatment is not usual, it can test your patience—and your spirit of self-confidence—unless you're prepared. That is one of the reasons you should prepare a good résumé *before* writing your application letter. Realistically assessing your strong points through preparing a good résumé can be a big step toward retaining and increasing your self-confidence and optimism. You are then in much better shape to write an application letter—a sales letter selling your services.

At times you may want to send a prospecting letter without a résumé; most personnel people, however, prefer to receive one. Part of this chapter will help you write your application letter. But don't slavishly follow the points and style of our or other people's illustrations. The good model application letter doesn't exist—so be smart and write your own. *A good application letter must be an accurate reflection of the writer's personality as well as aptitudes and skills.*

Before sending your prospecting application to a company, find out the name of the person it should go to. If you want to work in the purchasing department, address your letter personally to the vice president of purchasing or the director of purchasing. Don't just address the letter to the personnel department.

## Securing Favorable Attention

As with sales letters, the infallible way to secure interest in your application letter is to stress serving the reader. Your central selling point may be an ability based on education, experience, or personal qualities—or a combination of them. A student just graduating from college got favorable attention with this:

```
Because I have had an unusual five-year
educational opportunity combining the study of
engineering and management, I feel sure of my
ability to do efficient work in your industrial
engineering department and to steadily increase in
usefulness. I could conduct a time and motion
```

study with a technical knowledge of the machines
concerned or work on the problems of wage rates
without losing sight of the highly explosive
personnel situation involved.

To state the central point, a more mature and better-educated writer
with more experience began as follows to a textbook publishing company:

With my college background of undergraduate and
graduate work, my teaching experience, and a
temperament that helps me adapt easily to college
people and circumstances, I believe I could do a
good job as a field representative for you.

Those openings have nothing tricky about them. They just talk work—
and the education, experience, and/or personal qualities that point to
doing a good job.

Concentrate on rapidly and naturally establishing your qualifications,
with the attitude that you want to put them to work for the reader in
some specific job. Having held out such a promise, you need to back
it up.

## Supplying Evidence
## of Performance Ability

Your evidence in your application letter is simply a job of *interpreting*
your qualifications—the highlights of your opening and résumé. For persuasiveness, you phrase it in terms of skills that point to "doing something
for you."

An applicant for an apprenticeship in an architectural firm wrote a
short letter, but it's packed with statements of accomplishments as evidence of desirable skills. Notice how it establishes interest through qualifications, supplies details, and then asks for action.

At this point in my career, I have two main
qualifications to offer you: my job experience and
my bachelor's degree in architecture from the
University of Nebraska. My practical experience
covers six years of part-time work with the same
architectural firm, Mosely Architects. Projects I
worked on ranged from $40,000 houses to $5 million
office buildings, with banks, churches, and small
condominiums completing the spectrum. While
working on these jobs, I had the opportunity to
associate directly with mechanical, electrical,
and structural engineers, in addition to the six
members of the firm itself.

> Of course I could not have developed and advanced that way without furthering my education. I graduated in the upper 5 percent of my class from the five-year program in architecture at Nebraska. Please refer to the enclosed résumé for information on my awards and extracurricular activities.
>
> I would like to show you my portfolio of school and job work and would be grateful if we could set up a time at your convenience. Please call me at 555-6360 so that we can talk about my working as an efficient apprentice for your firm.

The frequent problem of *overcoming deficiencies* is a difficult function of the letter, not the résumé. In almost any application situation you'll have one or more. If you feel that a deficiency is so important as to merit identification and possibly discussion, embed it in your letter and endow it with as much positiveness as possible.

The applicant wanting to be a publisher's representative knew that the company tended to favor liberal arts candidates from Ivy League schools. The following paragraph met the issue head-on and capitalized on it:

> The fact that I have studied business at Oklahoma rather than liberal arts at any Ivy League school may actually make me a better representative, Mr. Dayton--especially if I'm assigned to the Southwest, where I already know the territory. I could serve happily as your representative in any district, however; I've traveled over most of the United States (and in Europe and the Far East while in the Navy) and can adapt readily to the people and country one finds everywhere.

*Talking the special language* can also help convince your reader of your performance ability. In the examples you've probably noticed that each incorporated specific references to conditions or products or activities peculiar to the given job. Such references certainly further the impression that you are aware of job requirements and conditions.

From your research you can readily establish such references. If significant enough information, they may be good choices of talking points for your beginning, especially if they show knowledge of the company and its working conditions and requirements, along with a desire to serve:

> Lions International's growing membership no doubt makes planning the annual conventions an

increasingly complex job. My major in business administration and my minor in hotel/restaurant management lead me to believe that as a member of your convention planning department I could quickly be effective in helping choose hotels and other facilities at convention sites.

The regular Saturday night reports your retail dealers submit show consumer trends that I want to help you translate into continued Whirlpool leadership--as an analyst in your sales department.

Just as each of these candidates continued to talk the terminology peculiar to the job, you want to show such knowledge of company activities, working conditions, and job requirements. But if you state it in independent clauses (obvious or flat facts that the reader already knows), you'll sound wooden and dull.

The desirability of *emphasizing qualifications instead of analysis* will be clearer to you through comparing the following original letter with the revision.

| **Original** | **Revised** |
|---|---|
| Your financial department is probably expanding. I am to be graduated from the University of X in May. Please send me an application for a position in your financial department. | The combination of a challenging undergraduate program at the University of X and work experience will enable me to work effectively and be productive immediately. I can perform the duties expected of accountants in your expanding financial department. |
| I have taken cost accounting and international finance. I have also taken all prerequisite accounting courses and electives in finance. | My advanced studies in cost accounting will equip me to analyze and communicate financial information that may benefit top management. Through my studies in international finance, I have learned many things that may be incorporated into your increasing involvement in overseas projects. |

| | |
|---|---|
| I worked as a summer intern for Deloitte Haskins & Sells, one of the Big Eight accounting firms. In this job I worked on audits and helped with costing procedures. | My work experience has enabled me to apply my education to actual working conditions in accounting. As a summer intern for Deloitte Haskins & Sells, I was able to participate in audits and deal with numerous problems in costing procedures. |
| I will call you in the next week to see if I can have an interview to discuss a position with Texaco. | At a time convenient for you, I would be most grateful for an opportunity to meet and discuss with you ways in which I could best serve Texaco. |

The original, you notice, is almost painful in its flat, obvious statements. Note how the revision eliminates the flatness and preachiness through subordination, implication, or incidental reference.

Although the revision is a little longer, it accomplishes a good deal more: It establishes qualifications in a good lead; it talks the special language of the reader; it establishes more qualifications.

## Asking for Appropriate Action

Whatever action you want your reader to take, identify it as specifically as possible and ask confidently for it. Ordinarily, it is to invite you in for an interview.

Remember that the reader is under no obligation to see you, that giving you time is doing you a favor, that the time and place of the interview are to be at the reader's convenience, and that you should be grateful for the interview.

The full-fledged action ending of the sales letter thus requires slight modification for the application letter. You cannot with good grace exert as much pressure. For this reason, most employment counselors and employers do not advocate using any reply device. But your application action ending should still *suggest a specific action,* try to *minimize the burdensome aspects* of that action through careful phrasing, *establish gratitude,* and *supply a stimulus* to action with a reminder of the contribution you can make to the firm.

You've already seen several action endings in this chapter. Here are some others.

A Red Cross applicant definitely planned a trip to Washington for job-hunting purposes; so the letter logically and naturally ended with:

> When I'm in Washington during the first two weeks
> in August, I should be grateful for the
> opportunity to come to your office and discuss
> further how I may serve in filling your present
> need for Red Cross club directors. Will you name a
> convenient time?

The industrial-management applicant ended in this simple fashion:

> Please suggest a time when you can conveniently
> allow me to discuss my qualifications for work in
> your industrial engineering department.

The publisher's-representative applicant was in a slightly atypical situation. Lack of both the money and the time right then prevented asking directly for an interview in New York. Here is the solution:

> After you've had a chance to verify some of the
> things I've said about myself in this letter and
> in the résumé, will you write me frankly about the
> possibilities of my working for you?
>
> Possibly I could talk with one of your regional
> representatives in this area as a preliminary
> step. Or I can plan to go to New York sometime
> this summer to talk with you further about my
> successfully representing your firm.

One other item that you should consider is whether to include an *availability date* in your prospecting application. If you are now working for someone, you would want to give proper notice, and you can tell a prospective employer this in your résumé: "Available to come to work for you one month after giving my present employer notice." The other common reason for not being immediately available is pending graduation: "Available to come to work for you immediately after graduation on June 10." Otherwise, we do not recommend that you mention availability. To say "Available immediately" implies that you are out of work, something you would not want to mention.

If you mention availability in your résumé, you should also mention it in your letter as a point in good communication (clearing up all questions between you and the reader). Even if you feel that a stated graduation time implies an availability date, by skillful and brief wording you can reemphasize your knowledge of the company and add mild urgency to your letter with it. For example, suppose the publisher's-representative applicant had changed only the last sentence to:

```
Or I can plan to go to New York this summer--in
time to get in on this year's training program--to
talk with you further about my successfully
representing your firm.
```

Such letters as have been suggested in the preceding pages can open the door for an interview and further negotiations. To make yours do all it can, review the checklist of suggestions.

# Writing the Invited Application

Often a firm makes its personnel needs known by running an ad or simply by word of mouth. As you probably know, most large companies also list their needs for college-graduate personnel with college placement bureaus and have recruiting personnel visit campuses.

Situations where the prospective employer actually goes out searching for new employees give you one drawback (you'll have more competition) and two advantages in writing a letter: (1) you don't need to generate interest at the beginning, and (2) the ad will give you the job category and principal duties.

If the ad identifies the employer, then you should learn something about the organization and its products and services before you apply and indicate why you are interested in the company.

## Organizing Appropriately

When you hear of a job through other people, or an ad, your source will usually identify requirements in some order indicating their relative importance to the employer. If you are equally strong on all points of preparation, you have no problem. You simply take up the points in the order listed.

Most often, though, your best talking point is not the most significant requirement, and usually you'll be deficient in some way. Employ the same strategy you did in writing the invited sales letter: Tie in your strongest point of preparation with something the reader wants done; embed your weakest points in the middle position of the letter, and attempt to correlate them with some positive point.

# Prospecting Application Checklist

1.  The prospecting application must generate interest from the start.
    a. Establish early your central selling point of education or experience or both, in terms of doing something for the reader,
    b. Avoid didactic, flat statements.
    c. Avoid telling the reader how to run the business.
    d. Make clear that you are seeking specialized work.
    e. Be realistic; talk work and doing, not "forming an association with" or *position, opening, vacancy,* or *opportunity.*
    f. You need verve and vigor, not stereotypes like "Please consider my application . . ." or "I should like to apply for. . . ."
    g. Don't let your biography drown out what you can do *now.*
    h. Don't give the reader an opportunity to shut you off negatively.
    i. Mere graduation (rather than learning) is a poor start.
    j. Eliminate selfish-sounding statements or overtones of them.

2.  Interpretation and tone are important from the start.
    a. Maintain a consistent, acceptable tone.
    b. For conviction, use specific points of education or experience.
    c. Generalizing and editorializing are out of place: "invaluable," "more than qualified," even "excellent."
    d. Avoid needlessly deprecating your good qualifications.
    e. Project your education or experience right to the job.
    f. Use enough *I*'s for naturalness, but avoid monotony.
    g. Show your research and thought. Address the letter to the appropriate individual if at all possible; talk about company operations and trends in the industry.

3.  Your education and experience are your conviction elements.
    a. Talk about your experience, schooling, or personal characteristics in terms of accomplishing something.
    b. The emphasis should go on a phase of work connected with the job.
    c. Refer to education as work preparation (in lowercase letters) rather than exact course titles.
    d. You need specific highlights rather than details.
    e. Your résumé supplies thorough, detailed coverage. Refer to it incidentally, in a sentence establishing some other significant idea, just before asking the reader to take action.
    f. A one-page letter is desirable, but tell your story in the most effective way for you even if it takes longer.

4.  Reflect your personality in both content and style. Refer to your significant personal characteristics affecting job performance.

5.  Ask for appropriate action in the close.
    a. Name the action you want; make it specific and plausible.
    b. Don't beg and don't command; just ask for an appointment.
    c. Clearly imply or state that you will be grateful.

d. Show success consciousness without presumptuousness.

e. A final reminder (perhaps tied to an availability date, if appropriate) will help strengthen the impression of what you can contribute.

**For Writing Invited Applications**

6. When writing an application in response to an ad or at the suggestion of an agency or friend:

a. Don't send *just* a résumé, even when asked.

b. Emphasize putting your preparation to work for the reader. But since your reference to the source is an automatic way of securing attention, you should identify it early and *emphasize it if it carries an implied recommendation.*

c. Avoid stating what the reader would infer ("I read your ad").

d. Don't ask questions or phrase assumptions that are clear pushovers: "If you are seeking X, Y, and Z, then I'm the right person."

e. Postpone salary talk until the interview if you can. If the phrase "state salary required" is included in the description, your reply of "negotiable at interview," "your going rate," or "your usual wage scale" is acceptable to any firm you'd want to work for.

Since the beginnings in the prospecting and the invited applications do differ somewhat, however, here are some suggestions that will help you write good invited sales letters.

Your beginning should *mention your main qualifications, identify the job, show a service attitude,* and *refer to the source of the information* (subordinately unless it is significant).

The reference to the ad, or the bureau, or the person who told you about the job, is an automatic attention getter that favorably reinforces the reader's willingness or even eagerness to read your letter. One good sentence can accomplish all four functions and point the trend of the letter.

*The opening of the following letter puts emphasis on service through work, clearly identifies the specific kind of work sought, and desirably subordinates the reference to the source.* Note that after the opening the letter reads much the same as a prospecting application (indeed, if you omit the lead in the faked address block and the first two lines, it could be a prospecting letter). Note also the adaptation of talking points—the stress on experience rather than on formal education.

```
Five years experience
Plus technical training in
Insurance and sales
Would aid me as
```

The aggressive sales representative you
advertised for in today's Express.

As a pipeliner in Louisiana, I made friends with
the kind of prospects to whom I'd be selling your
policies. I had a chance to study people, their
hopes and fears and desires for protection and
security, while doing casework for the Welfare
Society in San Antonio. And while working as a
waiter both in high school and in college, I
learned how to work for and with the public.

The same perseverance that earned me B's in Life
and Health Insurance, Property and Liability
Insurance, and Personal Sales Principles will help
me find leads, follow them up, persuade, and close
a sale. I know an insurance representative makes
money personally and for the company only by
sticking to a schedule of calls. But I'm equally
aware of the value of patience and the necessity
for repeat calls.

As you see from the enclosed résumé, my school
activities have resulted in my knowing people from
all sections of the state. I would be grateful for
your telling me a convenient time and place when I
may talk with you further about my qualifications
for being the hardworking sales representative you
want.

Frequently your source—especially if an ad—gives you an effective entering cue and provides you with useful reference phrases throughout the
letter. From the key phrases you can almost reconstruct the ad answered
in the following letter:

Because of my college education in accounting and
my work experience, I believe I can be the quick-
to-learn junior accountant for whom you advertised
in the May Journal of Accountancy.

Having successfully completed down-to-earth
studies in tax accounting and auditing while
earning my degree, I should be able to learn your
treatment of these problems quickly.

My natural aptitude for analysis and synthesis,
strengthened by special study of the analysis of
financial statements and reinforced with a broad
background of economics, law, and statistics,
should enable me to handle the recurring tasks of
compiling comparative statements of earnings and
net worth. And my training in writing reports will

> help me tell the story to my supervisors as well as to clients.
>
> Will you study the diversified list of courses and the description of my internship listed on the attached résumé? Note also, please, the wide range of activities I took part in while maintaining an A average. Then I would be most grateful if you will write or call me so that we can talk further about my qualifications for beginning a career of immediate usefulness to you.
>
> I can start to work anytime after graduation on June 4.

A variation of source doesn't affect your procedure—except that you *emphasize a source that would be influential in your getting the job; otherwise, subordinate the source.* If you learn of the work through an agency or a third person, the procedure is still the same, as the following two examples show:

> I'd like the chance to prove that my education and personal characteristics closely parallel the description of the desirable management trainee that you gave to Dr. Morley, head of our placement bureau, when you visited the campus last week.

> When I talked with Ms. Sarah Lomer this morning, she assured me that I am qualified by experience and professional training for the duties of a field auditor with your firm.

Start writing in terms of doing something for the reader: what you can give instead of what you hope to get.

## Beating the Competition

Avoid assuming that you don't have much of a selling job to do. Because many others will apply, you'll have to write a superior letter to be chosen for interviewing.

In fact, the reader could face so many letters that yours may not even get read. To assure a reading:

1. You may want to have a complete, well-written letter and résumé in the employer's hands hours or even days ahead of other candidates. Your letter (if it is good) becomes better in the eyes of the employer as poorer ones come in.

2. As an alternative strategy, wait 10 to 16 days after an advertisement appears before sending in your application, because roughly 82 percent of the answers

to a job advertisement will come in during the first week. (For maximum effect, mail so that yours arrives on Tuesday or Wednesday.)

3. If you are in the same town, deliver the letter yourself, with the request that it be turned over to the appropriate person.

4. If you insert your letter and résumé in an envelope large enough to accommodate 8½ by 11-inch pages without folding and you add a piece of cardboard to keep the edges smooth, the contrast between your application and all the others that have been folded may call attention to yours.

But none of these devices will make much difference if you do not write from the viewpoint of contributing to the firm through effective, efficient work.

### Handling Special Problems

While an advertisement or other source of information usually gives you some advantages in writing invited instead of prospecting applications, ads often give you one or more of three special problems.

1. When the ad asks you to "state salary expected," "give salary history," or "give salary on last job," don't do it. You hurt your chances if you aim too high or too low. Instead, say something like "your usual salary range" or "negotiable in the interview."

2. Ads often say, "Send résumé." Again, don't do *only* that. These ad writers want to save time by screening only factual résumés; and they are not interested in selling you on the job, but *you* are interested in selling yourself. An interpretive letter is a much better selling instrument than a résumé alone.

3. You can assume that you must be available immediately (or very soon) and should give the earliest date you can start work (which can eliminate any of your competition who cannot start that soon).

As you already realize, most of the items in the Prospecting Application Checklist apply equally when you write an invited application. Study them again, and add the following items, which are appropriate for only the invited situation.

## Continuing the Campaign

Regardless of the results from your application, you have some follow-up work to do. Since some of that work often calls for skills with strategies explained and illustrated in Chapter 6 (good-news messages) and Chapter 7 (disappointing messages), you may need to refresh your memory of the principles given there.

If you get an invitation to an interview, you know how to handle it. Accept promptly, pleasantly, and directly (if that's your decision), as suggested in Chapter 6. Just remember to continue your job campaign by indicating continuing interest. If within a reasonable time you do not hear from the person or firm you've applied to, you'd probably better send a follow-up letter indicating continuing interest.

## Follow-Up Letters

A good salesperson doesn't make one call and drop the matter if that doesn't close the sale. Neither does a sales-minded job applicant. Election to an office or an honorary society, a research paper that has taught you something significant to the job, and certainly another job offer are all avenues of approach for reselling yourself and indicating continuing interest.

Even if you receive the usual noncommittal letter saying that the firm is glad to have your application and is filing it in case any opening occurs, you need not hesitate to send another letter two, three, or six months after the first one. It should not be another complete application (yours will still be on file); it is just a reminder that you are still interested. An acceptable one is this:

> I know that many organizations throw away applications over six months old.
>
> Because that much time has elapsed since I sent you mine (dated April 15), I want to assure you that I'm still interested in working for you, in having you keep my record in your active file, and in hearing from you when you need someone with my qualifications.

Only a lackadaisical applicant would end the letter there, however. You could bring the information up-to-date and perhaps stimulate more interest in the application with just a few more words:

> Since graduation I have been doing statistical correlations at the Bureau of Business Research here at the University. I've picked up a few techniques I didn't learn in class, and I've certainly increased my speed on the computer keyboard and calculator.
>
> I still want the job as sales analyst with your firm, however.

## Thank-You Letters

Following an interview, whether the results seem favorable or unfavorable, your note of appreciation is not only a business courtesy; it also helps single you out from other applicants and to show your reader that you have a good sense of human relations.

Even when you and the interviewer have agreed that the job is not for you, you can profitably invest about two minutes writing something like this:

> I surely appreciate the time you spent with me last Friday discussing employment opportunities at Monitor and Wagner.
>
> The suggestions you made will help me find my right place in the business world.
>
> After I get that experience you suggested, I may be knocking at your door again.

When you are interested in the job discussed and feel that you have a good chance, you're wise to write a letter expressing appreciation and showing that you learned something from the interview.

> Your description of the community relations program of Livania has opened new vistas to me, Ms. Lee.
>
> The functions of the public relations department in your company as you described them made me much more aware of the significance and appeal of this work.
>
> As soon as I returned to the campus, I read Mr. Fields's book that you suggested and the pamphlets describing U.S. Steel's program.
>
> Many thanks for your suggestions and for the time you took with me. I shall be looking forward to hearing the decision about my application as soon as you can make it.

Remember that thank-you letters must be prompt to be effective.

## Job-Acceptance Letters

When an employer offers you a job and you decide that it's the one for you, say so enthusiastically in a direct good-news letter. Just remember to seal the contract by brief accepting references to (not flat repetition of) the terms—or by filling out and returning supplied contract forms, as in the following:

```
I certainly do want to work with Franklin &
Franklin--and I don't need a week to think it
over, Mr. Bell, although I appreciate your giving
me that much time to decide.

I've filled out the forms you gave me and
enclosed them with this letter. Anything else?

Unless you tell me differently, I'll take off two
weeks after graduation. But, as you asked, I'll
call you on Friday, June 11, to get report-to-work
instructions for Monday, June 14.
```

## Job-Refusal Letters

Sometime in your life you'll have to tell somebody that you don't want to accept an offer. You may feel that it's routine, that it doesn't mean anything one way or the other to a busy person who interviews many applicants and has many other people available. Remember, though, that a human being with pride and ego is going to read your letter. So make yourself think "I don't want that job *now,*" for you may want to reopen negotiations at some future point.

To wind up negotiations pleasantly and leave the way open for yourself, write a bad-news letter (as discussed in Chapter 7) with a pleasant buffer of some favorable comment about the company or the work, some plausible and inoffensive reason, the presentation of the refusal as positively and subordinately as you can phrase it (possibly with the statement of where you are going to work), and an ending expressing good feeling and appreciation or both. The following letter is a good example.

```
Meeting you and talking with you about working
for Bowen's was one of the more interesting job
contacts I have had.

As you will remember from our discussion, I am
still primarily interested in product research.
Since I think that that work will best use my
abilities, I am going to work for [a company] that
has offered me such employment.

I shall certainly continue to watch your
company's progress with interest, and I shall look
forward to reading or hearing about the results of
your new prepackaging program.
```

## Letters of Resignation

The way you quit a job is just as important as the way you get one. It can have powerful repercussions on you later. So leave with style and grace by following a few simple, basic rules.

- Explain your decision orally to your immediate supervisor, and then write a letter explaining your reasons for leaving and saying something pleasant about your work with the company or with the superior or both.
- Be cooperative and work hard right up to the last minute.
- When possible, offer to allow additional time for the company you are leaving to replace you (though two weeks' notice is standard procedure except for high-level jobs).
- Train a person who will succeed you (if asked to do so).
- Keep all confidences to yourself.
- Don't brag to fellow workers about your new job (maybe, don't mention that you are going to leave).
- Clear up all financial debts, and return all company property.
- On your new job, talk positively (or not at all) about the company you left.

Resignation letters, like job-refusal letters, are modified bad-news letters. You want to stay in the good graces of the individuals who have assisted you in your career.

When you have worked for a firm, you have benefited in some way (besides your pay). Regardless of how you feel at the time, remember that you can say something complimentary about how things are run, about what you have learned as a result of your experience, or about the people with whom you have associated.

In many circumstances your resignation can be oral. And in many circumstances it may be better that way. But when you need to write a letter, consider adaptations of the following:

In the past 18 months I've certainly learned a great deal about . . . from my work as . . . at . . . , and I shall always be grateful to you and the other people who have helped me to do the job and to prepare for a more challenging one.

You will perhaps recall that when I had my interviews with you before starting to work, I stressed my interest in working toward a job as . . . Since I now have such an opportunity at . . . , I am submitting my resignation. Apparently it will be some time before such an opportunity is available for me here.

> Would terminating my employment here in two weeks
> be satisfactory? I can make arrangements to work a
> little longer if doing so would help you.

Often when another offer comes your way, you'll discuss the opportunity with your current employer before making a final decision. Such a conference has possible advantages for both employee and employer. Often a counteroffer results that satisfies both and the job change doesn't take place. If, despite a counteroffer, you still decide to make the change, you can resign in good grace with a letter somewhat like this:

> Your recent offer is one I appreciate very much,
> and it made me give serious thought to continuing
> at. . . .
>
> I have appreciated the cooperation, the
> friendliness, and the helpfulness of everyone with
> whom I've been associated here.
>
> After considerably more evaluation, however, I
> believe I can make a great contribution and be a
> more successful business manager by accepting the
> position offered me by. . . .
>
> I hope that I can leave with your approval by
> (specific date). I feel sure that all my current
> projects will be complete by that time.
>
> You'll hear from me from time to time--if for no
> other reason than that I'll be interested in how
> the new credit union works out.
>
> But I'll always want to know how things are going
> for . . . and the many friends I've made here.

When appropriate, a possible talking point is the suggestion of a successor to you; often this is a big help. A constructive suggestion, phrased positively, implies your continuing interest in the organization.

Letters of resignation written by college students who resign after having agreed to work for someone but before actually reporting for work are quite different—something we take up with reluctance. Many personnel people regard them as breaches of contract.

Don't make the mistake of grabbing the first job offered you, only to have something infinitely more to your liking come along later. Also, never let yourself get caught in the position of being committed to two employers at the same time. If you have agreed to go to work for a firm and then you have a later offer that you want to accept, don't accept it until you have been released from the first contract. To the second potential employer, reply something like this:

I certainly would like to accept your offer to come with your firm. Attractive as your proposal is, however, I must delay accepting it until I can secure a release from the Jenkins firm in Blankville. After my interview with you, I accepted this position, which at the time appeared to be the most promising available.

Can you allow me enough time to write the Jenkins personnel manager, explaining my reasons and requesting a release? This problem shouldn't take longer than a week to settle. I appreciate your offer, regardless of how things work out.

If necessary, phone the second potential employer, explain frankly, and get approval to wait.

## Two Useful Modifications of Applications

The following two letter possibilities for helping you get the job of your choice are *not here with the implication that they will take the place of the complete sales presentation* we have suggested to you. Only because they may help you sometime do we even remind you of them.

### The Job-Anticipating Letter

Most personnel people are willing to give advice. Most of them are also pleased with a show of interest in their companies and evidence of long-range planning on the part of a student. With that in mind a number of our students have sent letters like the following, in the junior year of college:

A course in the operation of automated office machines under Mrs. Lora Osmus in the Statistics Department at school gave me skill in their operation and showed me the tremendous possibilities of such equipment for business use.

After comparing X and ABL equipment that was on exhibit on Commerce Day and talking with the X representative in charge of your display, I am coming to you directly and frankly for some help.

Since I have completed almost all the courses required for the B.S. in business administration, I am free to elect practically all the courses I shall study next year before June graduation. On the attached sheet I've listed the courses I've completed and those I'm contemplating. Will you please rank the ones you consider most beneficial for a prospective sales representative?

Naturally, I will regard your suggestions as off-the-cuff assistance that implies no commitment. I'm just trying to equip myself as well as I can to meet the competition for the first available job with your company after I graduate.

I shall be most grateful for your comments.

## The Telescoped Application Inquiry

We realize that good applications take time. They're worth the time, however. But we also know that sometime, somewhere, you may need to send some inquiries in a hurry and simply won't be able to write a complete one. In such a situation you may be able to make profitable use of the services of your college placement bureau in a letter, as one student did. The applicant was too busy writing a thesis and sitting for graduate examinations to prepare a thorough application. So six firms received the following request and reply card:

With completion of an M.S. degree in accounting at the University of North Carolina and two years of retail merchandise accounting experience, I believe I could make you a good accountant with a minimum of training—and be able to advance more rapidly than most of the accountants you could hire.

I am not just an accountant: A well-rounded background of finance, transportation, economics, and other related subjects will enable me, in time, to do managerial work as well.

May I have the Placement Bureau here at the University send you a transcript of my college record together with a detailed record of my experience, faculty rating statements, and names and addresses of former employers?

I shall be happy to furnish any additional information you may want and to be available for an interview at your convenience later if you will check and return the enclosed card.

All six firms replied, but only one of the replies resulted in an interview. This kind of quick note may be a stopgap measure sometime. But this person's experience simply reconfirms the fact that you must tell a complete story if you expect to get a show of effective interest.

## Questions and Exercises

1. What significant points could you add to the checklist on abilities, skills, and interests? What points would you delete?

2. What kind of information do you need about a company before applying? List your top three choices, and rank them on the basis of this information.

3. Give at least five reasons why you might change jobs or not change jobs.

4. Which of the five résumé illustrations in this chapter appeals to you most for your possible future use? Why? Be specific.

5. If a person has never worked on a regular job for pay, what might that person put in place of work experience in the résumé?

6. What are some uses of résumés besides as supplements to applications?

7. What techniques can you use to make résumés easy to read?

8. What three people (specific name and/or position and relation to you) would be good references for you when you finish your intended schooling, and why would you select them?

9. How should a C student handle that fact in the résumé? In the application letter?

10. Before you write your application letter and résumé, write a memo to your instructor answering these questions:
    a. What are your career plans?
    b. What training, attributes, or attitudes do you need for the job you want?
    c. What will you be required to do?
    d. What is the job outlook in your field now? What will it be in 5 years? in 10 years?
    e. What company or organization would you like to work for? Why?
    f. What do you need to know about it before applying? Where would you get this information?

11. To find out about the kind of work you want to do and what a particular company does, ask for an information interview in your area. Often this type of interview leads to summer employment, an internship, or promise of a job upon graduation. Before you ask, read about the company and have good, appropriate, and meaningful

questions about the work and the company. (Keep in mind that this is not an employment interview.)

12. Suppose you've worked for the same company every summer and have been promoted several times. How can you efficiently and emphatically show that on your résumé?

13. Suppose your most recent jobs were low-paying because they were part-time. How could you put them on your résumé along with full-time, better-paying jobs?

14. How does the beginning of the prospecting application letter differ from that of the invited application letter?

15. How is the ending of a sales letter different from the ending of a prospecting application letter? How are they similar?

16. Think of one of your weaknesses. How would you handle it in your prospecting application or invited application letter?

17. Suppose you never had a paying job but have worked in student government. What might you tell in your application letter about such experience?

18. You applied for an accounting job that you really want at a local firm and had a promising preliminary interview. In the meantime, a bank that you also applied to offered you a job and wants your response in writing right away. How would you phrase a letter of delay to the bank?

19. How should you follow up
    a. An interview?
    b. An interview and visit on invitation at a company where you want to work?
    c. A statement from an interviewer that you would hear from the company three weeks ago?

20. Visit your campus career placement office, talk with some of the employees there, and gather some of the forms they give out. Write a memo to your teacher describing your experience, with emphasis on answering the same questions as in Question 22.

21. Visit a plant or company and get an application form, fill it out, and analyze it from the applicant's point of view.

22. If you were an employee responsible for revising the form in Question 21, what about it would you keep? What would you change? Why, specifically?

23. What is your central selling point for an application letter that you're most likely to write?

# Part Four

## Oral Applications
## of Principles

# Chapter Outline

# 11

# Speaking and Listening

The preceding discussion of letters and memos has constantly reminded you of the important part that oral communications play in business, industry, government, and other sectors of our society. Indeed, repeated studies of executives and managers show that they spend more of their communication time speaking than writing.

To manage well, then, you must be effective in both written and oral communication. Whatever the form, a skilled communicator is better able to get subordinates to follow instructions, to get useful information and ideas to and from others, and to report information to superiors.

For three reasons, this book has first given you a thorough treatment of the main kinds of written business communication and now will help you apply the important principles in effective oral communication:

1. Communication shortcomings that employers complain about in their employees nearly always concern the inability to *write* well.

2. Writing is better not only for teaching and learning the basic language skills of clearness, conciseness, and correctness but also for learning to apply the important principles of organization and psychology for effective business communication.

3. The transfer of learning from written to oral application is much easier and more effective than going the other way.

Training and practice in writing, however, are not complete substitutes for training and practice in speaking. So the selective treatment here concentrates on *business speaking* and *the oral application of effective business communication principles* developed in the earlier parts of this book. The purpose is to help you transfer the principles and give you additional pointers applicable to the main kinds of oral communication you are likely to need in business—oral reporting, interviewing, dictating, conferring, and telephoning. First, however, you need to consider some basics of effective speaking that are applicable in all kinds of business communication.

# Preparing for Effective Speaking

### Getting Rid of Bad Habits

You have been talking longer than you've been writing—and you probably have some poor speech habits that can hurt you in various ways if you don't correct them.

1. Carelessness and bad habits about validity, precision of statement, economy of wording, and grammatical propriety are all harmful to business communication. *Solution:* Practice giving care to these aspects of your speech as in your writing; improvement in each will reinforce the other.

2. Slovenly or incorrect pronunciation and enunciation may cause misunderstanding (or *not* understanding) and (when you write) misspellings that strike most people as unsightly warts on your competence. *Solution:* Notice how well-educated speakers place accents, assign sound qualities to vowels, and say distinctly all the syllables in key words. If in doubt, check a dictionary.

3. Inattention to the principles of good organization in sentences, paragraphs, and longer statements often causes wordiness, incoherence, and even confusion. *Solution:* Carry over into your speaking the principles of organization you have learned in becoming a good writer.

### Recognizing Similarities to and Differences from Writing

Certainly successful speeches have central themes, adequate and reliable facts, coherent and compact organization, clarity and vividness of phrasing, and other style characteristics of good writing as explained in Chapter 3 and throughout this book.

Though written and oral business communications have many similarities, they also have some major differences that influence what you say (or *should* say) and how you say it.

| Written | Oral |
|---|---|
| A reader can turn up the light or get glasses if the print is illegible. | Few people will ask a speaker to slow down, enunciate, or speak up. |
| A reader can (if desired) reread unclear or difficult passages. | Except in dyadic (two-person) or small-group situations, a listener must understand the first time or not at all. |
| A reader's immediate reaction is unknown—no direct feedback exists. | Immediate listener reaction is known—direct feedback does exist, even in large groups. |

| Written | Oral |
|---------|------|
| The reader sets the pace. | The speaker sets the pace. |
| Attention span is usually longer in reading than in listening. | An audience's attention span is limited (though usually increasing with maturity). |
| A written record exists (permanent). | No record exists (ephemeral) unless recorded. |
| A writer must spell, punctuate, and paragraph. | A speaker must enunciate clearly and pronounce, inflect, and pause appropriately. |

## Preparing the Speech, the Setting, and Yourself

Of course your major job in making a speech is preparing what you will say and how you will say it. Both the what and the how, however, depend on other factors (such as the purpose, topic, audience, length, and circumstances). This discussion therefore comes with specific adaptation to the main kinds of business speaking.

Whether you initiate the whole thing or accept an invitation to talk, you need to know at least the date, time, place, and kind and size of audience. Also helpful is knowledge about whether your presentation is a one-shot, one-speaker affair or one on a panel or in a series. If other speakers are in the picture, certainly you need to know the general topic, theme, and purpose as well as who the others are, their parts or angles or slants, and who precedes and follows you. Having determined those influencing factors, you must decide what topics or points to cover and do any necessary research for reliable facts.

Your purpose—whether it's to inform with good news, inform with bad news, or persuade (as explained in Chapter 5)—will determine the way you organize and phrase your speech.

Unless the program planner or the nature of the situation does so (say a debate), you will have to decide on whether to write out and read your presentation or to talk from outline note cards (usually the better way). The intellectual level of the topic and the audience, rather than your own, should determine the depth of what you say and the ease/difficulty of your language. (In case of doubt, shoot for solid content and ease of language.)

Since a good speech (like a good orchestral performance) involves many elements, for an important speech you will do well to hold a few practice sessions. Only that way can you coordinate for full effect the content, style, gestures, and other body languages that *will* show up—*in* or *out* of step and/or tune.

Preparing the physical setting may be wholly, partly, or not at all your responsibility, though usually you will have some say about at least any audiovisual aids you need. Whether you are primarily responsible or not, you will be wise to check in advance on seating (adequate capacity?), stage settings, temperature controls, lighting, audiovisual facilities, amplifying system (if wanted), and even whether the doors will be open in time for you to set up.

If you will use projection equipment or an amplifying system, who will control them? Try them out in advance—you don't want any surprises when you are speaking.

Preparing yourself for making a speech involves your voice, physical appearance, and mental attitude. Look neat, clean, and properly combed and clothed for the occasion and your audience.

To get yourself in the right mood, you may have to remind yourself of how well you are prepared, that you *can* do it—in short, psych yourself up. Your body language—posture, gait, how you hold your limbs—will signal to your audience how you really feel. And since these signals are almost impossible to control consciously, you will do better to remove the causes of adverse body language. So think positively.

Having prepared well, let the mental attitude you convey by eye, posture, and gait calmly reflect confidence and competence. You *are* prepared; perhaps you've practiced your speech before a mirror and timed yourself until any earlier feelings of insecurity are gone. You know more about the subject than the audience does or you wouldn't be speaking in the first place.

## Getting into Speaking Position Favorably

If the game plan calls for you to walk in and take over, do just that—at the scheduled time and place, confidently but not arrogantly.

If, however, you are to wait in front of your audience for an introduction, sit comfortably relaxed. Let your speech and your clothing alone now, or you will create a bad impression that you came unprepared.

If you feel a little tense when you first face an audience, an excellent way to release tension is to exhale. Just empty your lungs. Don't gulp a lungful of air and then give a great sigh; merely breathe out all the way and you'll feel more easy.

After the introduction, walk erectly and confidently to your speaking position, thank the introducer, and move right into your subject. The more poise, confidence, and efficiency you show in these short maneuvers, the greater audience respect and support you will get.

On whether you should sit or stand, if in doubt, stand. And if you can arrange it, do not use a lectern or podium. A lectern is useful only for holding your notes and, if needed, a light. (Beware, by the way, of lecterns with microphones on them. Your voice will bounce off the surface of the lectern as well as go directly into the mike, sometimes causing a distracting echo.)

## Giving the Speech

Good speaking is a combination of many elements—the thought content, the style (mainly word choice, sentence patterns, and the organization and transitions), the voice in all its manifold variations, gestures, all forms of facial expressions and other body language, and the metacommunications (the *milieu,* as the French say, meaning the total of surrounding circumstances).

In preparing your speech, the physical setting, and yourself, you will have taken care of the first two and the last one. You could have wisely given some prior attention to the others too, but you couldn't have firmed them up completely beforehand—even by writing out the speech with fully orchestrated markings for voice variations, gestures, and other body language. You would, at best, look and sound like a ventriloquist's puppet.

Like an accomplished conductor rehearsing an orchestra, you need to have practiced with your orchestra of words, voice, gestures, and so on, so that in your speech you can (without a musical score) call upon the various instruments to come into play at the right times and for the best effect. Here are a few specific suggestions.

### Your Voice

Your voice is the major instrument in your orchestra and must be well tuned and played. Try to speak naturally and easily. Your normal, natural voice is the best.

What reads well on paper is usually awful when read aloud. Instead, use note cards, listing *only* the points you want to cover (perhaps with subheads) and any appropriate figures and quotations too long to memorize easily.

When speaking to people, you have only two seconds to break eye contact to look at your notes. Any longer and you lose and must re-create rapport with your audience. So the best notes are two- or three-word phrases, just enough to trigger your memory for what you want to say next. You'll be much more natural and far more interesting to listen to.

If you are forced to read a speech (say for a speaker who couldn't come), overemphasize changes in the tone and pitch of your voice. Also exaggerate your gestures and expressions. In short, overact a little since you want to break away from "reading aloud" to "talking" what you are reading.

When speaking to a large audience, you must project your voice. But projection does not mean shouting. Your volume should be sufficient for your farthest listener to hear you without straining but should allow you some volume left over to use for emphasis. (You might well check with people on the back seats.) If you cannot easily make yourself heard without straining, use a public address system.

In a speech you will have to use more variation in the pitch of your voice than for normal conversation. Be on guard, however, against the tendency to raise the pitch too much and become strident or screechy as you project your voice.

Oral reporting and formal speaking require more than normal attention to pronunciation and enunciation too—no slurring and certainly no "asides." Speak slowly, and distinctly pronounce all the parts of words, especially the ends, leaving no uncertainty about what you said.

## Posture and Movements

When speaking, be yourself, be natural. Your posture should be erect, alert, confident, relaxed, and natural. Your shoulders should be down and loose, not hunched and tense-looking. Your feet should be a comfortable distance apart, with your weight concentrated on the balls of your feet.

Let your hands hang naturally at your sides, and don't move them unless you are going to turn a page in your notes or gesture for emphasis. Never put your hands in your pockets or clasp them in front of or behind you. Standing comfortably erect may feel awkward at first, but look at yourself in a mirror. Don't you look more authoritative, commanding, and assured?

Just as you walked calmly and deliberately to a place in front of your audience, move calmly and deliberately around the stage while talking. You should use walking around for emphasis sparingly, however; like all emphatic devices, it loses its effect from overuse. Generally, the more audiovisual aids you use in giving a talk, the fewer movements you should make. The important thing is to direct your audience's attention to what you want. Moving around can sometimes retrieve an audience's attention, but too much distracts from what you're saying.

Keep gestures restrained and natural unless the situation requires some overacting. When you do gesture, be aware of what you're doing. Gestures are strong reinforcements to language; but the meanings of many of them are not definite, especially to people from other cultures (as explained in Chapter 4). As rough rules, the more formal the occasion, the more restricted your gestures should be; and the larger your audience, the more exaggerated, so that people far away from you can see them clearly.

When you describe something, hold your hands up and apart to show the size. Use your hands to help show spatial relationships, motion, and direction. You can reinforce abstract points by holding up an index finger or pounding a fist into your hand. You can emphasize something by pointing at your audience, making a punching motion, and the like. If you are making a number of points, for emphasis (and for clear transition) hold up the appropriate number of fingers as you tick off each point. You will be wise, however, to try out your gestures before a mirror before you try them out on an audience.

Keep your facial expressions under control, using them only to reinforce what you are saying. Be animated: frown, look sad, outraged, puzzled, whatever you need. You should give the impression of being warm, alert, bright, assured, animated, confident, but not arrogant. And don't forget to smile; an audience responds most favorably to a happy, confident smile.

The only way to tell what reaction you are getting is to look your audience in the eye. So make eye contact with members of your audience on a random basis, moving your eyes from side to side within but not around or over the heads of your audience—and certainly not fixing them on the far wall or your notes (except for momentary glances).

## Your Language

In speaking as in writing, you must adapt your language to your audience. Before speaking, decide on the level of formality you want to use. But be aware that most untrained speakers use far too formal and ornate language in an effort to overcome a deficiency (usually imaginary) in position or authority.

High rhetoric has long been out of style; so keep your language natural. You will get immediate feedback from your audience if your level of formality is inappropriate, and you can quickly adjust (another good reason for speaking from notes instead of a complete text).

Restrict your use of jargon. Its occasional use is desirable to indicate that you are "with" the audience; but too much is hard to understand, even when your audience knows the meanings. Also avoid emotionally charged words. They are generally too highly exaggerated for a business situation, and your audience will recognize them for what they are—and mistrust you.

Nobody is perfect, and in front of an audience you may make a slip. Don't panic. If you handle the situation right, your audience can remain unaware of your problem; and if it does show, you'll have sympathy.

If you forget what comes next in your speech, keep looking thoughtfully at your audience or move about the stage contemplatively until you gather your thoughts. Audiences are not so critical as you may think. In the general run of business speaking they do not expect a professional presentation unless listening to a professional speaker. Your audience will, however, expect you to know your subject, be prepared to talk intelligently about it, and come to a conclusion—requirements you should easily meet when the time comes.

If possible, keep a talk to no more than five or six major points—more are hard to assimilate. Make the transitions clear by any or all means as you shift from one point to another. (The suggestions on **Coherence** in Appendix C and in Chapter 14 may help.)

## Special Attention Tactics

At the beginning of your talk, get your audience's attention immediately. Don't begin uselessly with an egotistic expression like "I'm pleased to be here" or a plea for sympathy like "I'm not used to speaking; so I hope you'll overlook my weaknesses." The best beginning for a speech is the subject—or the conclusion if you think your audience will be in favor of what you are going to say. If not, you may want to begin with your arguments before coming to the conclusion. Some specific ways of beginning a speech, roughly in order of effectiveness, are:

1. A rhetorical question.
2. An illustration that leads logically into your subject.
3. A fact or opinion that sets up the first point you want to make.
4. An apropos quotation.
5. A humorous anecdote (which sometimes makes seriousness hard to achieve later).

People's attention spans are short, rarely more than 15 to 20 minutes unless stimulated. You will know when you are losing your audience by the glassy eyes. Here are some preventatives and remedies for an inattentive audience:

1. Slow down your delivery for hard-to-understand material and speed it up for more easily comprehended matter.
2. Provide clear transitions between subjects and show how they *relate* to each other ("coherence" again). One of the best ways to lose an audience is to shift topics unannounced. You will befuddle and anesthetize with what seems to be nonsense because it does not relate to the topic you *were* talking about.
3. Eliminate distractions. Curtain off windows that have attractive views; screen off any movement behind or to either side of you.
4. Use language your audience readily understands. When in doubt, remember to KISS (keep it simple, stupid).
5. Be animated, energetic. Don't stand like a statue, but gesture, vary your facial expressions, move around some.

6. Talk directly to individuals, changing from one to another, from side to side, and from front to back of the audience (as with eye contact).

7. Use visual aids: slides, chalkboard, an object you hold up. . . .

You can regain an audience's wandering attention by:

1. Changing the volume of your voice, keeping in mind that a low voice is better than a shout.

2. Making a change in the level of formality if it fits naturally with what you are saying and you can logically use it for effect.

3. Directing a question to a member of the audience you point to (and awaiting the answer).

Still your best way to handle inattention is to **preclude** it by making your presentation interesting. For that purpose, visual and audiovisual aids can be very helpful if you have the skills, time, and facilities for preparing and presenting them.

## Visual and Audiovisual Aids

Even a chalkboard on which you can write topic headings and rough graphics can be a godsend to you as a speaker and to an audience for interest, clarification, and memory value. Still slides and audiovisuals can serve much better if the situation provides favorable answers to the four inherent questions:

1. Does the *occasion* justify preparing and using audiovisual aids? For instance, if you are going to sit down with one person and informally deliver your report, would slides or a flip chart be appropriate?

2. Will the benefits justify the *costs* in time and money? Does your budget have enough in it to pay for preparing audiovisual aids?

3. Do you have sufficient *time* before giving your report or speech to prepare audiovisual aids? Slides, for example, require a photography session, a photographer, subjects or objects to be photographed or charts or graphs, developing the slides, sorting to pick the best, and arranging them for projection.

4. Are the necessary *facilities* available where you will speak? Projector? Screen? Projector stand? Power source?

In order to hold your audience's interest, use only about eight slides per minute (six might be acceptable). Omit all weak slides, and limit slide shows to 10 minutes—at most 15. If you must use word slides, limit them to 10 percent of the slides. To help you communicate an idea quickly while the visual is on the screen, learn to write copy in poster style. If a chart has to stay on the screen while you speak several sentences, then it's too complicated. You can sprinkle an occasional statistic in copy for variety; but if you overdo statistics, your audience will forget the few important ones you want them to remember.

In preparing better overheads, here are seven suggestions that will help you: *(a)* Have just one topic or concept for each transparency. *(b)* Limit your copy to six lines per transparency and to six words for each line. *(c)* Select simple typefaces. If you use a typewriter, use only primary-size type (other type should be at least a quarter-inch high). *(d)* Use lowercase letters for most of your material because they are more legible than all caps. *(e)* Choose tinted films to reduce lamp glare— and colored markings to achieve good emphasis. *(f)* Avoid mixing horizontal and vertical formats. (Some experts suggest using horizontal visuals for maximum visibility.) *(g)* Pay attention to copyright laws, but you can consider clip-art books for illustrations.

## Public Address System?
## Chalkboard?

Use audiovisual aids only to help your audience better understand what you are saying. Audiovisual aids play the same part in oral reports that graphics do in written ones: mainly they help make quantitative data clear and quickly and easily comprehensible. You can also use them to highlight the main points of your speech.

Some common audiovisual aids are: slide projector, overhead (transparency) projector, motion-picture projector, opaque projector, videotape player, flip chart, chalkboard, felt board, actual object, model of an object, poster (large drawing, picture, etc.).

The two basic rules for visual aids are: (1) they must be clearly visible, and (2) they must be quickly comprehensible.

Generally, when a visual aid fails to do its job, the fault is due to either (1) too much information or (2) information presented too small or too densely to be seen, or both. Common examples are charts with too many lines on them, charts whose lines are too fine or light to be seen, and illustrations that are too small.

When preparing visual aids, constantly keep in mind that presenting information is wasted effort unless the audience can readily comprehend it. When you use a visual, explain it to your audience.

Be careful, however, not to block the view of a visual aid from any members of your audience. If, for instance, you want to point to something on a chart or a projected image, use a poińter and keep well to the side of the screen or chart. Talk to your audience, not to the visual aid you're using.

### Ending the Speech

Some people have as much trouble ending a speech or oral report as they do ending a letter. As with a letter, the time to quit talking is when you have finished saying what you planned to say. Avoid the natural temptation to close your speech with any expression of hope that you have done well or a hesitant declaration that you think you have finished.

If a question-and-answer session is to follow, then you may have to announce that you have finished: "That concludes my report. I'll be glad to answer any questions." Otherwise, here are five ways to signal unmistakably the end of a talk:

1. Summarize the points you covered.
2. Challenge your audience to meet the objectives outlined.
3. Appeal to your audience to do what you want.
4. Wrap up the major point you want to make with an apt illustration, anecdote, or quotation.
5. State your intention to do whatever you advocated.

## Making Oral Reports

Oral reports are important applications of the preceding principles for effective speaking. They serve the same purpose as written reports: to help the receiver make decisions by providing needed facts and/or ideas. They also answer the same questions as written reports (Is something feasible? Should some action be taken? What's the best way?) and share the same characteristics (they are management tools; they are usually assigned jobs; they are delivered to superiors; they are directed to a specific and usually limited audience; they give more than normal attention to organization; they make use of devices for clear communication; they are expected to be accurate, reliable, and objective; and they follow the form, content, and length best suited to their particular function).

An oral report may be as informal as a conversation between two people or as formal as a full-scale presentation to a large audience, complete with audiovisual aids. Where in this range a particular oral report will be depends (as with written reports) on the occasion, the kind and amount of information transmitted, the relationship between reporter and listeners, and so on. In general, oral reports tend to be shorter than written reports simply because detailed information is hard to communicate orally and because listeners have shorter attention spans than readers.

You go through exactly the same steps in preparing an oral report that you do in preparing a written one (as explained in Chapter 14). You plan your attack, get the facts or evidence you need, organize your material for coherent presentation, analyze it for interpretation and solution to the problem, and then present it clearly and concisely in appropriate style.

Indeed, a frequent kind of oral report is a synopsis of a long written report. The author of an important report (now speaker/reporter) may now synopsize (orally) for a group of high-level executives and answer their questions. Thus the oral report often becomes the start of a conference (discussed in the next chapter) to decide on what to do about the reporter's recommendations.

If you feel you need more help on preparing an oral report, read Chapter 14, which deals primarily with written (and incidentally with oral) reports. Virtually all of what is there applies to oral reports, with a few differences:

1. In a large audience, some members may be there against their wills; so retaining their attention may be a special burden for the speaker.

2. In oral reporting you communicate through many more means. Body language (including eye contact, facial expressions, gestures, stance) and your voice (quality, pitch, enunciation, pronunciation, pace and pauses, . . .) are all tools. Even the usually desirable use of audiovisual aids is a greater problem for the oral reporter (especially in large groups) than their counterparts (graphics) are for a report writer.

3. Though the procedures for researching and phrasing major written reports (Chapters 14 and 15) are the same for oral reports, you cannot expect an audience to follow and understand the detail, precision, and length of the kinds of reports assumed there.

In other words, to make a good oral report, you need to (1) learn how to prepare the particular kind of report by studying Chapters 13–16, plus what appears above on the present topic, Making Oral Reports, and (2) present the report as explained earlier in this chapter.

A listener sees and/or hears only your presentation of your speech or oral report and can judge it, therefore, only by what you say. The checklist for speeches and oral reports is therefore from the audience's point of view to help you keep your listener(s) foremost in your mind as you prepare to talk.

## Speech and Oral Report Checklist

1. Were the speaker's overall *(a)* appearance, *(b)* walk-on, and *(c)* prespeech platform stance and actions appropriate and effective?
2. Was the speaker's voice *(a)* clearly audible and *(b)* expressive?
3. Was the speech *(a)* well organized and coherent, *(b)* well phrased, *(c)* well reasoned and documented?
4. Was the language level appropriate for the topic and audience?
5. Were the speaker's *(a)* gestures and *(b)* eye contact adequate, appropriate, and effective?
6. Did the speaker *(a)* use audiovisual or other graphic aids effectively? *(b)* do anything distracting?
7. Did the speaker *(a)* summarize? *(b)* come to a logical conclusion? *(c)* adequately signal the end? *(d)* exit properly?

## Listening Effectively[1]

Just as speaking is the initiating or encoding phase of oral communication, listening is the receiving or decoding phase. *And,* when you think about the interplay of these skills, you realize three important points:

1. Neither is worth anything without the other.
2. The oral interplay of speaking/listening accounts for about three times as much of your communication time as writing/reading does.
3. Considerable skill in all forms of communication (for both sending and receiving messages) is vital for an effective business manager in today's civilization.

Learning to listen well is the single biggest thing you can do to improve your personal relations. When you really listen to someone, you take a big step toward avoiding conflict by *understanding* that person. Further, when you listen well, you help others to work out their problems (listening is, after all, the basis of counseling and psychiatry). Good listening will lead others to communicate full information to you, and fuller information will help you to be more successful. Finally, as you demonstrate good

[1] See Eastwood Atwater, *Listening Skills to Make You a Better Manager,* Prentice-Hall, Englewood Cliffs, N.J., 1981; Ralph G. Nichols and Leonard A. Stevens, *Are You Listening?* McGraw-Hill, New York, 1957; Ralph G. Nichols and Thomas R. Lewis, *Speaking and Listening,* Wm. C. Brown, Dubuque, Iowa, 1965; Robert L. Montgomery, *Listening Made Easy,* AMACOM, New York, 1981; Thomas E. Anastasi, *Listen! A Skill Guide for Business and Industry,* CBI Publishing, Boston, 1980; and J. Sims and P. Peterson, *Better Listening Skills,* Prentice-Hall, Englewood Cliffs, N.J., 1981.

listening, you will lead others to improve their listening practices, resulting in an overall improvement in communication.

## The Task of Listening

Listening effectively is not easy. The spoken word is gone immediately unless stored in the hearer's mind, which must adapt to the speaker's pace.

We talk much more slowly than our minds can comprehend when we hear. Since our minds operate so much faster than our mouths, when someone is talking, we tend to think about what we are going to say next and we cease to concentrate on what the other person is saying.

Spoken language also complicates communication with a greater variety of sentence length and style, more personal references, more informality, and often complex nonverbal signals (gestures, facial expressions, and voice inflections, pitches, rhythms, and volumes).

Even in one-on-one conversations and interviews, many people exhibit certain bad habits that prevent effective listening—

- playing with pencils, cleaning fingernails, . . . .
- looking around or out the window instead of at the other person
- finishing or interrupting sentences
- reading, writing, staring, ignoring the speaker
- making irrelevant side comments, objections, or premature questions.

## Learning to Listen (and Getting the Emotional Impact)

You learned at a very early age that your mother's (and others') smiles, pats, hugs, and cooings meant love and approval (and their frowns and "Tsk, tsks" meant the opposite). Unless you are unusual, however, you have not developed that kind of attention, sensitivity, and understanding for the emotional content in much adult talk.

Of course you get the point if your boss says "I want it *tomorrow,* and I want it *right* this time, dammit"—or if your assistant says "Your careful explanation saved me a lot of time in setting up and interpreting those complicated tables in the report." But, do you notice the force or meekness, word choice, context, and body language of a conversationalist or platform speaker? Together or separately their connotations often confirm or almost deny a literal translation of the words—and to miss them is to miss the point.

## Learning to Listen (and Listening to Learn)

Though learning effective listening is not easy, an intelligent and interested person can do it and become a better performer in any way of life.

Although in everyday living you will listen and learn in interviews, lectures, conferences, and conversations, the principles and techniques of listening show up best in listening to speeches and lectures.

**Identify the Subject and Plan.** Most speakers will deliver planned talks organized in the traditional pattern of introduction, thesis, body, and conclusion.

Though many speakers will tell a story, quote from some authority, or say something startling first to secure attention, *the essential time for concentration is when the speaker announces the subject, why it is pertinent, and the plan of presentation.* If you are not tuned in for this thesis statement, you are going to have difficulty following the rest.

**Stay Tuned In.** The body of the speech (the longest part) includes the several points that support the speaker's thesis. The evidence may be statistics, testimony, stories, and/or explanation and logical analysis.

Major points and the evidence supporting them may come in *deductive* order (usual if the purpose is only to inform). This is, stated very simply, generalization followed by supporting detail. If the purpose is to persuade, an *inductive* order (generalization after evidence) will be better—and more likely if the speaker is a good one.

Obviously, this is the part on which you should exercise your concentration and your critical faculties. *The questions of completeness, validity, appropriateness, and recency are significant here.*

You will find this part easier to follow (and more interesting) if you check the speaker's announced plan against delivery and *stay on the alert for transitions*—those statements signaling a change of point. The points or principles (the *ideas*) fill in the blueprint of the plan and establish the final structure. The *facts* supporting the principles are subheads.

If the speaker announces no plan, try to anticipate what is coming. If your guess proves right, you'll feel pleasure—and probably reveal it in feedback to the speaker. And if you're wrong? Never mind, you'll have concentrated better and benefited from the mental exercise.

Good speakers (and good writers) build up their points or principles step by step. In an informative speech the conclusion is often very short. It may be no more than a quick recap of the main points and a brief statement of how the subject is significant. The conclusion of a persuasive speech may be a little longer. The persuasive speaker may not reveal a stand until the end. In addition to establishing the real objective, some speakers may use strong argument. Question and challenge mentally, but reserve judgment until you've had the time to sift and reevaluate.

When you're the trapped victim of a speaker who indulges in harangue, cajoling, or bombast (especially if backed only by scant, prejudiced, one-sided, or unsound facts or logic), tune out; you're entitled to stop listening.

**Be Sensible—Control Your Note-Taking.** The temptation to record a speaker's words *verbatim* is too great for many listeners—unfortunately. This kind of note-taking causes listeners to lose significant ideas, to become confused, and to give up on note-taking—and usually on listening also.

Most speakers and lecturers agree that good listeners take good notes—and that those who take good notes *listen a lot and write a little.* Keep your notes brief and clear during listening (complete thoughts for major points; just words and short phrases for supporting details). You can expand and review later.

Rarely does an introduction merit recording. Even the thesis is better not written down when first stated. (Write it down after you've heard enough to state it precisely.) Even the brief outline or plan (if the speaker gives you one) is better recorded point by point as you go along. Strive to understand each main point your speaker makes. If you're preoccupied with catching errors or taking notes, you won't get the message. Withhold your judgments until you have reviewed the main ideas and thesis.

*Careful distinction between fact and idea* leads a listener to note-taking that is economical and efficient. Divide your paper into two columns, one for principles and one for facts. You'll have difficulty determining which is which sometimes. But the effort will help you concentrate and will provide enough useful reminders for later review. You'll have more entries in your facts column than in your principles column. If you have to slight the recording of one, slight the facts; concentrate on the principles.

The sooner you can review your notes after the speech, the better. As you listened, you should have mentally questioned for completeness, adequacy and appropriateness, authenticity, recency, and omission of data. An even more fruitful time to do this, however, is shortly after the talk—in a review arriving at an evaluation.

**Avoid the Main Stumbling Blocks to Good Listening.** To begin with, accept the fact that listening demands patience and an open mind—a considerate, even charitable, mind. (The temptation to tune out and escape to reverie or daydreaming is ever with us.)

Sometimes you may be prone to pretend attention when your mind is not receiving any ideas. No speaker with much experience gets fooled. If you fall into such habits, wake up—and learn.

Another stumbling block is undue attention to the speaker's appearance, voice, or speech characteristics. Don't shut yourself off from learning because of a person's physiognomy, size, dress, or voice characteristics. The mind may have a lot to contribute.

All too often we abruptly reject or dismiss a speaker and subject because we consider them dull or difficult. Remember that the dull speaker is probably doing just what the assignment was—to give you facts and ideas—and refusing to insult your intelligence, or take pay under false pretenses, by entertaining you instead. Be selfish: Take for yourself what is meaningful and useful. Very few uninteresting speeches are devoid of something useful.

As for rejecting the difficult discourse, remember that this can become a pattern of progressive mental deterioration. The more you do it, the flabbier and more superficial your mind becomes. The way to growth is a continually renewed determination to hear the speaker out and a planned effort to tackle uninteresting as well as difficult material.

Another stumbling block is the tendency of listeners to let physical surroundings distract them. Airplanes, buses, trains, thunder, and other outside noises are sometimes loud; but you can easily ignore when you want to (during a favorite TV program, for instance).

Usually you can control physical circumstances. Windows and doors close as well as open. Heating mechanisms turn off as well as on. If you can't control the distraction, enlist the aid of the speaker.

A reminder of something already said will summarize the key point: In your listening, concentrate on principles, not detailed facts presented in support of principles. Emphasis on facts makes you lose principles, which are the most significant parts of speeches; emphasis on principles makes you not only get the principles or ideas but also helps you remember many of the facts that support them.

## Questions

1. Of the special attention tactics for speakers, which one appeals to you most/least as a speaker/listener?

2. Based on your experiences in listening to speeches, do you agree with the suggestions about reading from a manuscript versus talking from memory or notes? Why or why not?

3. Of which of the three categories of bad speaking habits are you most guilty?

4. Have you distinguished between fact and idea in your notes from a recent lecture? If not, could you?

5. Of all the speech stumbling blocks named, which ones bother you the most?

# Chapter Outline

# 12

# Special Forms of Oral Communication

In addition to making oral reports, you will certainly use other forms of oral communication in your jobs from the time of your first job interview. Later on, you may interview new employees or have evaluation and exit interviews with your staff. You may interview sources for information as well.

You'll dictate either to a person or a machine (because you'll save time and money by not writing all messages out yourself), participate in conferences from department meetings to international conventions and seminars, and sometimes even take part in an electronic conference via telephone or television. You'll use regular telephone service daily.

These special forms of oral communication are mostly commonplace but important nonetheless. Good techniques in all these forms of oral communication can help you get—and keep—your job, your staff, and your customers.

## Interview Procedures

### Nature, Importance, Kinds

Interviews are a widely used and important tool in business and industry. Like many tools, however, interviews can be very productive or very damaging.

Four traits characterize most good interviews:

1. They are not group communications but are usually dyadic (on a one-on-one basis).
2. They are not like a random conversation but have a specific purpose and concentrate on a specific subject.

3. They are not (at least not usually) interrogations but are conducted with the willing consent of both parties and have none of the accusatory atmosphere of an interrogation.

4. In interviews, as in good conversations—instead of monologues or long-winded pontifications—half the job of each participant is listening.

Because of the last point, remember the discussion of listening in Chapter 11. You can become a better interviewer or interviewee by becoming a better listener.

The common types of interviews in business and industry are:

1. Personnel interviews
   a. Employee screening and hiring. (And now, closely related, the getting/giving of career and job information and advice through information interviews— as explained in this chapter and under "Surveying Work Opportunities" in Chapter 10.)
   b. Orientation, instruction, and training of employees new to a job.
   c. Review of employee progress.
   d. Discussion of employee grievances, firings, resignations, and problems.
2. Research—making plans, determining what has been done/discovered, possible uses, next steps, and so on.
3. Exploratory—determining the existence, cause(s), and cure(s) of a problem with an employee or activity.
4. Opinion sampling—Surveys in Chapter 14.

Whatever type of interview you engage in, the basic structure and purposeful nature of interviews allow three general plans for conducting one:

*1. Directed.* A directed interview is completely planned from start to finish. Often the interviewer will have a checklist of questions to follow, especially when an interviewer is not thoroughly trained or when sampling is the purpose. In personnel work, organizations use directed interviews when different interviewers screen different applicants for the same job or jobs. Directed interviews minimize the effects of any interviewer bias on the results and interpretations.

*2. Nondirected.* In a nondirected interview the interviewee can set or at least influence the subjects covered and the directions of flow in the interview. As a way of eliciting information, the interviewer plays a much more reactive role than in a directed interview. The nondirected approach is useful in grievance, counseling, and exit (resignation or termination) interviews and forms the basis of both information interviews and psychoanalysis.

*3. Stress.* Conducting a stress interview involves intentionally putting the interviewee in a hostile situation, under artificial stress, to see the reaction. Such an interview has little justification unless such stress is an essential part of a job. You may establish the interviewee's irritation or anger threshold but lose a potentially good employee, who will probably feel contempt for your questionable practices.

But because you should recognize immediately if someone subjects you to a stress interview, here are the six usual devices for conducting one: The interviewer will (1) criticize or ridicule your appearance at the start, (2) take and maintain a threatening, unfriendly tone, (3) deliberately interrupt you repeatedly as you are about to make a point, (4) criticize or ridicule any opinion you express, (5) ask you very personal (perhaps insulting) questions, and (6) purposely allow long silences to develop and try to force you to end them.

The commonest kind of interview in business and industry is the directed personnel interview. Here is a guide that will help you conduct or take part in successful interviews. To be specific, for both parts, interviewer and interviewee, the guide assumes a job-application interview.

## The Employer (Interviewer)

**Preparing for the Interview.** Have available all the information you will need about the job: rank, salary, duties, location, hours. . . . Before you call in an applicant, set the stage: clear your desk, check your own appearance, alert your secretary to intercept any phone calls or visitors, close the blinds to avoid silhouetting yourself, and review the applicant's application or résumé.

**Beginning the Interview.** To relax the applicant, be friendly and welcoming as you shake hands and offer a seat. Sitting on facing chairs or on a couch rather than behind your desk removes a physical barrier and reduces the formal office atmosphere. Taking another minute or two to review the applicant's résumé gives the applicant a chance to settle down and look around.

The first question you ask is critical since it sets the tone. Remember that you need to hire someone; so be in a positive frame of mind and treat every applicant as a potential employee. A common opening is "Tell me about yourself," but the question is so general that most applicants don't know where to start and the interview begins on a nerve-racking basis. A better way is to begin with a shared interest—a hobby or a personal or business experience. Then proceed to your first question.

To get the applicant to open up, begin with questions that the applicant should be able to answer positively. Examples are whether the applicant satisfies the job's educational requirements, whether the applicant is physically able to perform the job, or whether the working hours are acceptable.

At the beginning avoid falling into the trap of giving more information about the job than just enough to get the applicant answering you easily and naturally. Once you start giving a sales pitch on the job and your company, getting the interview back on the track with the applicant giving you information will be very hard.

**Getting Information.** Once the applicant has begun to open up, you can go about your task of learning whether you have a desirable prospect. Try not to ask questions answerable yes or no, which tell you little. Instead, ask questions calling for comment. For instance, rather than asking "Do you like purchasing?" ask "What activities do you like best about being a purchasing agent?" Try to make each question (or its answer) lead logically into the next.

In asking questions about former jobs, try to avoid a mere chronological listing by asking questions that bring out more important points—things like any upward progress and special likes, dislikes, and accomplishments or successes. Whatever answers you get, be sure not to show any disapproval or disbelief, even if you feel that way. Keep the applicant talking openly while you listen and watch carefully for symptoms of uneasiness, casual remarks, or lapses of memory.

When a period of silence develops, you can wait for the applicant to end it by saying something—often very revealing information—if you don't allow the silence to last too long and undo all your efforts to create a natural and relaxed atmosphere.

You'll need to take some notes—which are more accurate than memory and more encouraging to the applicant than just listening. But don't write all the time or whenever the applicant is saying something personally unfavorable or discussing a negative topic. Even so, be sure to cover your notes so that the applicant cannot see what you are writing—or better, use the item number only of a preplanned checklist and jot down by each number your coded evaluation on the point.

**Interviewing People from Other Cultures.** As you read earlier, people from other cultures often view a situation in their own special ways—especially in employment interviews. They bring their backgrounds with them and, unless they have been in our country for some time, will act as they would in a similar situation at home.

In Japan, for instance, a person's background (family, studies) is most important. In that culture job applicants are supposed to be modest about their abilities and should outwardly show appreciation for being considered for jobs. An American interviewer's straightforward questions may embarrass a Japanese, and the answers the Japanese gives may appear evasive and suspicious. To the Japanese the American may seem crude and poorly informed by asking background questions.

Some people from India, when being interviewed, because of their cultural background will agree with anything the interviewer says, no matter how outrageous or contradictory it may make them seem. And what to a German might seem forceful and mature may appear arrogant to an American. You can see that successfully interviewing non-Americans often requires a good deal of tact and understanding on the part of the interviewer.

**Giving Information.** Once you have heard all the information you need, you should have a pretty good idea whether the applicant is worthwhile. If not, terminate the interview as graciously as you can.

We recommend that you never turn down an applicant face-to-face. If you do, it will generate the natural question "Why?" If you trap yourself into explaining, you may be in for an argument and possibly anger or tears. Reject the applicant later in a carefully worded, considerate disappointing letter (Chapter 7).

If, however, you have a good prospect, now is the time to sell your organization and persuade the applicant to join it. You can describe your organization's structure, what it does, and what the opportunities are for advancement (without firm promises!). You can tell more about the job: duties, promotion possibilities . . . .You may want to describe how you choose new employees, what criteria your organization uses in its selections. If necessary to persuade the applicant to sign on, you can go into fringe benefits (hospitalization, pension plan, profit sharing, vacation policy, and the like). Otherwise, leave discussion of fringe benefits until after the applicant has agreed to come to work for you.

**Ending the Interview.** The thing to avoid is an awkward, indefinite, and disorganized ending, especially if because of an interruption from outside (phone, visitor, . . .) that makes you look disorganized. You can maintain your image of competence if you follow a planned sequence of events to wind up the interview. A good first step is to ask if the applicant has any questions about the job, your organization, or the interview. Next, summarize what the two of you have discussed. The applicant's acceptance of or comment on the summary tells you how clear things are and signals that you are bringing the interview to a close. Both you and the applicant should be agreed on what actions each is to take following the interview.

One way to give (as an employee) or get (if you're an applicant) specific information about a particular job is to use the company's job description.

## Writing and Reading
## Job Descriptions

Whether you are looking for a job, are training and developing in a job, or are a manager looking for people who fill jobs, you are most certain to need some acquaintance with job descriptions.

A job description is a statement of the duties, qualifications, and responsibilities of the job, based on information obtained through job analysis. Its purpose is to identify the job, define it within certain established limits, and describe its scope and content. A job description may include information on working conditions, tools and equipment used, and relationships with other jobs.

Job descriptions vary widely, ranging from very brief (no more than an occupational title definition) to extremely lengthy and detailed with much supplementary information. The trend, however, is to one-page job descriptions that are accurate, specific, concise, complete, impersonal, positive, and precise. Present tense, action verbs, and simple sentences should dominate.

Even though there's no ideal format that will work in every situation, the most widely used formats have the following sections: Job Identification, Job Summary, Job Duties, Job Specifications. Sometimes a section called Accountabilities describes the expected end results. In lower-level jobs this section states to whom the incumbent is accountable in carrying out the duties and responsibilities that have already been outlined.

The Job Identification can have just the job title, or it can be more detailed and include the name of the department or division, date, job code (the six-digit numerical code of the Department of Labor published in DOT—*Dictionary of Occupational Titles*), name of person to whom the person in the job reports, name of person who wrote the job description, and name of person who approved the description.

The Job Summary must have enough information to differentiate the major functions, responsibilities, and activities of the job from those of other jobs.

In outline or paragraph form the Job Duties section should encompass those duties related to major performance requirements: not only regular day-to-day duties and duties at irregular intervals but quantity and quality of supervision received, amount of human interaction needed (teaching, counseling, training . . .), responsibility for keeping records for company funds, requirements for following orders/instructions, degree of accountability for human and material resources, operation of office machines/equipment, and other unusual physical or emotional demands.

Figure 12–1 provides an illustration of a job description.

**Figure 12–1 / Sample Job Description**

JOB TITLE:      Statistician for Southwest Insurance Company

DATE:            May 10, 198—

JOB SUMMARY:  To accumulate, compile, tabulate, and provide all kinds of statistical data covering company operations.

JOB DUTIES:

1. Accumulates company-wide statistics in any area requested or required; sets up tabulation procedures; establishes feasible use of information for company officials.
2. Cross-checks and balances controls with affiliated departments.
3. Writes management reports that are beyond the skill or capacity of other departments.
4. Reviews tax forms to determine procedures.
5. Analyzes data, makes suggestions, shows trend indications to superior.
6. Resolves tabular differences between home office and regional offices for loss premiums input.
7. Helps senior statistician.

JOB SPECIFICATIONS:

Education:   College graduate or equivalent experience

Experience:  Three years statistical experience

Knowledge:  Insurance Accounting
              Insurance Principles
              Knowledge of company tabulations, formats
              Systems—Unearned Premium and Loss Reserves
              Calculations—Taxes

Position from which an employee could be promoted into this position: Statistical Clerk, Senior
Contacts:   Internal within own, affiliated departments and regional accounting:
              10% of time
           External with pools and association: 5% of time

Working Conditions:  Office environment; regular hours

Source: *How to Write Job Descriptions—The Easy Way,* Bureau of Law and Business, Stamford, Conn. 1982, p. 84.

## The Applicant (Interviewee)

**Preparing for the Interview.** As a job applicant, you have only one objective in an interview: to convince the interviewer that you can successfully do the job and become a desirable part of the organization. Since most employment interviewers have pretty definite ideas about the kinds of people they want to hire and the kinds they don't, preparing for the interview may well start with study of things that might hurt your chances or even disqualify you.

Professor Frank S. Endicott, longtime director of placement at Northwestern University, has compiled the following list (in order of frequency) from a survey of 153 companies:

### Why Some Employment Interviewees Aren't Hired

1. Poor personal appearance.
2. Overbearing, conceited, or know-it-all attitude.
3. Inability to express self clearly (poor voice, diction, grammar).
4. Lack of planning for career (no purpose and goals).
5. Lack of interest and enthusiasm (passive, indifferent, or lazy).
6. Lack of confidence and poise.
7. Overemphasis on money, best dollar offer.
8. Poor scholastic record, just got by; marked dislike for schoolwork.
9. Unwilling to start at the bottom; expects too much too soon.
10. Makes excuses, hedges.
11. Lack of maturity and decisiveness.
12. Lack of courtesy (ill-mannered, tactless).
13. Condemnation of past employers.
14. Fails to look interviewer in the eye.
15. Loafs during vacations.
16. Friction with parents.
17. Sloppy application.
18. Merely shopping around.
19. Lack of knowledge of specialty.
20. No interest in company or in industry, or never heard of company.
21. Emphasis on whom one knows (not what).
22. Unwillingness to go where sent.
23. Cynical or radical attitudes.
24. Intolerant (strong prejudices).
25. Narrow interests.
26. Spends much time with movies, TV.
27. No interest in community activities.
28. Inability to take criticism.
29. Late to interview without good reason.
30. Asks no questions about the job.

Research shows that people who have high levels of social-communicative anxiety have fewer job offers than people who have low levels of anxiety.[1] People with high levels of social-communicative anxiety are more inhib-

---

[1] Steven M. Ralston, "Social-Communicative Anxiety and the Personnel Selection Interview: A Review and Synthesis," presented at the International Convention of the American Business Communication Association, Salt Lake City, Utah, October 19, 1984.

ited, awkward in conversation, nervous, have less eye contact, allow longer silences, make more negative and irrelevant statements. Because of such behavior these people appear to be less competent and successful on the job and to have greater difficulty in establishing and maintaining good relationships with co-workers.

Programs on interviewing skills may help people who have high levels of social-communicative anxiety. Some of the programs have an individual identify the irrational fears of the apprehensive communicator and get that individual to replace the irrational thoughts and beliefs with rational or nonthreatening statements. Role-playing using videotape, participating in workshops, and training in muscle relaxation can help some interviewees.

To achieve your objective of getting the interviewer's favorable evaluation, you need to know three things so that you can make a good appearance and sell your qualifications.

1. You must know exactly *what you want to do* (see Chapter 10). To enter an interview (presuming you get one) and tell the interviewer you aren't sure what you want to do is a sure sign of immaturity. You are mistaken if you think that because you say you want to work in a specific job, an organization will not then consider you for anything else. Remember that the organization called you in because it thinks you can fill a need. In reality, it will consider you for all the openings it has at the time.

Suppose that, between the time an organization invites you for an interview as a technical writer and the time you come in for it, the sales department announces that it has a critical need for a representative. Human nature being what it is, the organization will look at *everyone* who comes in, regardless of specialty, as a potential sales representative. So you see, indicating exactly what you want to do often gains you an interview and opens up opportunities that would have been closed had you made some weak, general statement about your career desires.

2. You need to *know about the organization* and the field it operates in before you can undergo an intelligent interview. You should already have done most of the research before sending in your résumé. When the organization invites you for an interview, you need to know much more about the organization's structure, its problems, needs, activities, plans for the future, and the like. Most of this you can get from annual reports, brokerage house reports, *Standard & Poor's* and *Moody's* manuals, and articles in periodicals (check the periodical indexes in your library). You want to build up a stockpile of facts about the organization that you can interweave into your presentation during the interview, showing the interviewer that you are interested in the organization and its activities and that you have prepared yourself for the job and the interview.

3. You must know specifically *what you can do for the organization.*

If the interview results from your reply to an advertised job opening, you will know. But even if you come in as a result of a prospecting application, the organization will tell you before the interview what job it is considering you for.

You will therefore want to arm yourself with as much information as you can about the job in question. What are the usual duties of someone doing that job? What is the customary salary range? What career paths does the job generally lead to? You can get the answers to these questions by consulting government publications describing various jobs, talking to people who work in such jobs, and talking with professors who teach in that area.

All of this is the necessary background information you should have for the interview. But your primary objective in the interview will be to describe yourself and your qualifications so as to convince the interviewer that you are the logical choice to fill the job. To do that, you'll need your information well organized in your mind and ready for prompt use. Interviewers' average decision-making time is 8–10 minutes;[2] so the interviewer is in process of making the favorable/unfavorable decision from the first glimpse of you and from your first word. This means that you need to start and keep building up a favorable impression from the first by being well prepared.

*First, prepare a list of the points about yourself that you want to cover in the interview:* applicable training, important prior job experience, personal traits, and so on. Now commit these to memory. They are the absolutely essential items you must discuss with the interviewer.

*Next, think of and organize for telling two or three success stories.* These should deal with problems you met and solved, recognized successes, earned promotions, and the like. The stories may come from earlier jobs or from your education experience. Have them ready to use at appropriate times in the interview.

*Third, project what questions the interviewer might ask.* At this point you need to do some important thinking. Tough questions should not appear to you as threats designed to trip you up and cost you the job. (The interviewer may be applying some mild stress, but bear in mind that questions reflect the organization's need to learn enough about you to make an intelligent evaluation.) Look at questions as opportunities, even invitations, for you to sell yourself.

Most interviewers' questions fall into six categories. While you needn't prepare answers for whole lists of questions, be sure you can give ready

---

[2] N. L. Reinsch, "When Does the Interviewer Decide? A Critical Review of the Literature," *Proceedings,* Southwest ABCA Spring Conference, 1981, pp. 149–60.

answers (ones that sell you and your skills) to questions in at least these categories. (A few suggestions for answers follow some of the questions.)

### Sample Questions—Academic History

Tell me about your education.

If you could do your college years over, what might you do differently? Why?

How was your education financed?

What elective courses did you take?

Why did you choose these particular ones?

What appealed to you most about the subjects in your major?

What motivated you to seek a college degree?

Why are your grades so low?

What are your plans for graduate study? (The key here is to indicate a willingness to study further while clearly understanding that the job and the organization come first: "Though I expect to devote most of my time and energies to [the job], I hope I will have occasion to continue my studies.")

### Sample Questions—Work History

Tell me about your previous jobs, starting with the first one and working up to the present.

Give me an example or two of your ability to manage or supervise others. (If you are a new graduate, don't apologize for not having been a manager in business—no one would expect you to have been one. Point proudly to whatever leadership functions you performed while in school, since they are a good indication that you will achieve similar positions in the world of work.)

What are some things you would like to avoid in a job? Why?

To what extent is your progress on the job representative of your ability, and why?

What have been your most satisfying/disappointing work experiences? (Or *school* experiences.)

Describe one or more situations in which your work was criticized.

How do you know whether you've done a good job?

Why do you want to change jobs? If the company is family owned and no further promotions are open to outsiders, say so. Or if your company has been absorbed or gone out of business, say so. When there are touchy problems, never badmouth, because your talk will boomerang and it will make you look like a troublemaker.

    Disguise the difficulties of your other job in positive language. If the work was stupid, repetitive, with no future, say you learned all that was possible from the job and are looking for an opportunity to apply your skills to new challenges. Instead of telling what's wrong with your foulmouthed tyrant boss, move the conversation to what attracts you about the new people or job.

What do you think management could do to help you function better as an employee?

### Sample Questions—This Job

Why do you think you will be successful in . . . ?

Why do you want to work for us? Give some specific examples. (Answering will be easy if you did your research beforehand.)

Why should we hire you? (*This* is what you came to the interview to tell! So tell it.)

What can you do for us now? (The job in question, of course. Describe those things about you that will indicate that you can perform the job right away and with a minimum of training.)

How long will you stay with us?

What geographic location do you prefer? Why? (Unwillingness to move is among the major reasons otherwise qualified applicants do not get jobs with big companies.)

What salary do you expect? (For a full discussion of this subject, read on a few pages to the section Talking about Salary.)

### Sample Questions—Goals and Ambitions

What are your long- and short-term career goals? (You have to have some, and they should be realistic in view of your age and present progress.)

Have you established any new goals recently? (A trick question, since your answer is subject to the interpretation the interviewer places on it. Not having established any goals recently can mean that you are either immature for not revising your plans or unimaginative and stodgy for the same reason! You will have to answer in light of the interviewer and how the interview is progressing.)

What do you plan to be doing in 10 years? How do you plan to get to that point?

Who or what in your life would you say influenced you most with regard to your career objectives?

Have you done anything to improve yourself in the last year?

### Sample Questions—Self-Assessment

Tell me all about yourself. (Two suggested answers, depending on the atmosphere of the interview, are: "Surely. Would you like me to start with my last job, my education, my . . . ?" or "On my last job I had an experience which I think shows that. . . ." Such a general question is a direct invitation for you to sell yourself; so start with your strongest point.)

How would you/your family/a friend/a professor/your boss/a colleague describe your personality? (Again, stress your strengths. This may sound like a "no-win" question, but it is really an excellent opportunity for you. Remember that you will be hired for your strengths, not your weaknesses. Don't make the mistake of admitting to a small weakness just to appear human. Say something like "I believe I am ambitious, tolerant, patient, sympathetic—all qualities you would want in a . . ." and continue selling yourself.)

Basic traits are useful to mention such as "I'm healthy; rarely miss a day" and "I work well with a wide variety of people." Instead of a long list of self-described talents, vary your statements with quotes from others: "My supervisors tell me I am quick to learn/a hard worker/good at delegating."

For traits that are important to the position, give some brief examples. Claiming to be good at solving human-relations problems becomes much more convincing when you comment, "My boss asked me to analyze our high turnover. I did and recommended remedies that were used. Turnover dropped 50 percent."

What are your strongest/weakest personal qualities? (About the only "weakness" you can safely admit to is an impatience with people who repeatedly fail to do their job. Through your research and through listening to the interviewer's reaction as you proceed, you should have an idea of what the company *needs*. Answer this question accordingly.)

What would your obituary say if you died tomorrow?

What things give you the greatest personal satisfaction?

What things frustrate you the most? How do you usually cope with them?

What kinds of personal crises have forced you to miss workdays? (Often this question is an attempt to circumvent the equal-opportunity laws that forbid questions about marital status and children. Rather than fall into the trap, mention some onetime crisis not related to your children, such as trouble with your car or your teeth. You are under no obligation to say whether you are married, single, divorced; or whether you have children. If you have no children and do not plan to have any in the near future, you might want to tell the interviewer. If you have children, you might want to answer the unasked question by explaining that you've had excellent child care for years.)

What are some of the basic factors that motivate you?

Which types of decisions are easiest for you to make? Which ones are difficult?

**Sample Questions—Outside Interests**

Some people think that student involvement in many campus activities infringes too much on valuable study time. How do you feel about this?

What do you do in your spare time? What is particularly rewarding about this activity? (Choose parts of your life that the interviewer wants to know about. Refrain from saying that you spend every free moment building a political network because you hope to get into politics. The interviewer will visualize you on the phone and in the halls politicking on company time. Nor do you want to talk about climbing mountains in lone wildernesses, because the potential employer will see high medical benefits in case of a mishap.

Describe interests that enhance your value to the company, such as your activity in park redevelopment or Little League baseball where you're on good terms with several of its good customers. Keep to something neutral such as that you jog or swim regularly to keep fit.)

In what ways have your outside activities and interests better prepared you to meet the challenges of your life?

What has your chief contribution been to any group with which you have been involved?

What have you learned from your activities outside of work or school?

**Probe Questions—(to follow up on something you've mentioned)**

What was the most challenging aspect of that, and how did you handle it?

In your role as a leader, what was the most difficult interpersonal conflict you encountered? How did you solve it?

How might that experience help you in the future?

Who helped you the most in that situation?

How did you happen to . . . ?

What prompted your decision to . . . ?

What would you do if . . . ?

Remember that your goal is to sell yourself and your skills to the interviewer. When you're given open-ended questions (like "Tell me all about yourself"), talk about your strong points for the job in question. Stress your strengths, and admit only to such weaknesses as being too critical of your own performance.

Armed with a knowledge of the organization and what it does, a memorized list of your strongest selling points, and ready answers to questions like those above, you are mentally well prepared for the interview. Only the physical preparation, packaging the "product," remains.

The cliché that the best physical preparation for an interview is a good night's sleep is still absolutely true. If you are well rested, you will perform at the top of your abilities, as you want to do.

You must make a good appearance. As in most situations, how you look will be the basis for the first impression; and an interviewer's unfavorable first impression will set up an obstacle that you will spend most of the interview trying to overcome. The image you want to present is therefore of someone the interviewer can easily visualize successfully working for the organization.

Dress formally enough to *suit the occasion*. While for some jobs a sport coat and slacks or a sweater and skirt may be suitable, a suit is more likely to present the image you want. Bear in mind that dark, subdued colors are more sincere and serious. Coordinate your accessories to your clothing, but don't distract from a professional look with too much jewelry. A well-tailored suit is a good investment for both men and women.

Good grooming is, of course, a must. You should be clean and clean-smelling. Shine your shoes, trim your nails, have your hair cut, shave, and go easy on the after-shave or perfume. Strive for a clean, well-groomed, *natural* appearance.

**Before the Interview.** When you go to an interview, carry an attaché case. It will give you a businesslike air and let you carry extra résumés, paper, paper clips, and anything else you find necessary.

Arrive for an interview 5 to 10 minutes before the scheduled time, no earlier and no later. If you arrive too early, you will appear overanxious. Besides, the longer you have to sit and wait, the more nervous you may become, leading you to make mistakes. Never, of course, arrive late for an interview.

You may be asked to fill out an application form while waiting for the interview (but only for a low-level job). Before filling out the form, ask if you can take it with you, fill it out later, and mail it in, explaining that you will have plenty of time to give all the information wanted. This tactic can keep you from having to scribble away in the waiting room, making you appear clerical.

When you fill out the form, do so legibly and in ink. Leave no empty spaces, writing "not applicable," "to be discussed in interview," or "see attached résumé" when you do not want to give information on the form. Do not fill out the part of the form asking for your history of jobs. People apparently design such forms to make it impossible for you to present your work experience favorably. Instead, attach your résumé to the form and refer to it.

The organization may very well interview you at lunch or invite you to lunch in the course of your visit. If so, *do not drink,* even if invited to do so and if your host does. Explain that you want to keep your head clear for this most important time. No one will criticize you for that.

Now that you are mentally and physically prepared for the interview, go in there and *sell your qualifications.*

**Beginning the Interview.** Your guiding principle during an interview is that time is limited (most interviews do not go beyond 30 minutes) and you have to develop your sales presentation on yourself.

A typical campus recruiting job interview, according to personnel experts, goes something like this:

| | |
|---|---|
| 4–5 minutes | Interviewer reviews résumé and establishes rapport with general and easy-to-answer questions ("Why did you decide to study at _____?"). |
| 16 minutes | In this information-gathering phase, the interviewer tries to find out your motivation, attributes, accomplishments. This is your time to sell yourself with specifics. |
| 5 minutes | Here the interviewer answers your questions about the organization. |
| 1 minute | Now the interviewer summarizes and closes the interview and lets you know when and how you'll hear from the organization. |
| 4 minutes | The interviewer writes up the interview as soon as you leave. |

Obviously, interviewers and interviews vary widely, but trained campus recruiters often follow a pattern similar to this one. As you can see, you haven't much time to make the points you need to make that you decided on earlier. Thus you will want to exert some control over the directions the interview takes.

Your job will be easier if you can adjust the usual superior-to-subordinate relationship of interviews to a more equal footing between you and the interviewer. You can begin to do this as soon as you enter the interviewer's office if you strive to present a confident, self-assured image— but not a cocky or arrogant one. Whether you are a man or a woman, shake hands *firmly.* You needn't crush bones, but holding out a hand as limp as a dead fish makes a poor impression. After you are seated, do not smoke. Even if the interviewer lights up and invites you to, refrain. Nobody looks good when smoking. And of course you will not chew gum.

If the interviewer follows the usual practice of beginning with four–five minutes of small talk to put you at ease, swing the conversation onto your strong points as quickly as you can. If, for instance, the interviewer comments on your hobby of playing golf, you can remark that the game has certainly taught you patience and how to deal with frustration, and this has stood you in good stead in . . . .

That puts the interview on the track you want—dealing with you as a potentially good employee. If the interviewer submits you to a stress interview (and such tactics may be unintentional), your behavior is to remain calm, patient, reasonable, and gracious. *Never get angry!* Simply keep steering the interview back on track until the interviewer realizes you will not succumb to stress tactics.

**During the Interview.** To understand your attitudes and motivations, the interviewer may commence a depth interview—probing with broad, open-ended questions to get you to reveal your feelings and attitudes. Generally these will be why and how questions. Remember, this information-gathering part of the interview lasts only about 16 minutes.

"How did you get the promotion to assistant sales manager?" "How do you feel about Sanders after working for him for three years?" "Why was that experience so important to you?" If you have prepared yourself as recommended above, such questions should not trip you up. Just keep thinking of every question as an opportunity for you to talk about yourself and your strong qualifications.

Keep your voice moderate, clear, and expressive as you talk to the interviewer. Equally important, maintain eye contact all the way through. You don't want to get into a staring contest; but to fail to look the interviewer in the eye, especially when discussing something less than favorable to you, will unavoidably make an impression of dishonesty and/or weakness. (If you have trouble looking into the interviewer's eyes, concentrate on the bridge of the nose, or look at the space directly between the eyes.)

When the interviewer asks you a question that does not let you lead into a discussion of one of your strong qualifications, answer as briefly and positively as you can. Remember that you won't have much time to present your sales pitch; so minimize time spent on (for you) nonproductive questions and answers. When you make a point, stop. Try not to ramble on, especially just to fill a silence.

Try not to brag or boast; doing so never makes a good impression. You should be able to talk positively, assuredly, and self-confidently about your successes, especially if you have prepared your answers ahead of time. Keep the interview on your good points, resisting any interviewer efforts to get you to talk about your weak ones. A reply something like this will usually do the job: "Yes, I might have handled that differently, and now I would; but the important things I accomplished then were. . . ."

When confronted with a wrong interpretation on the part of the interviewer, or an untrue assertion, don't deny it; that appears argumentative and defensive. Instead, respectfully and positively correct the interviewer. Finally, never say anything bad about a past employer. You will only make yourself look bad and warn the interviewer that in the future you may bad-mouth this organization too.

Constantly during the interview you will be gauging the feedback you get from the interviewer: expressions, remarks, gestures, body language. . . . You will quickly know when things are not going well, and you can take steps to improve the tone of the interview. Above all, however, you must listen. If the interviewer ever thinks you are not listening, you may very well find the situation deteriorated beyond saving.

**Talking about Salary.** Salary discussion is important in the hiring process; so you need to give it special attention.

Ideally, as an applicant you want to avoid any talk of money until after the organization has offered you a job, or at least until after you have completed your sales pitch on yourself. In any case, the longer you can postpone it, the more information you will have about the organization and the job and the better you will be able to negotiate.

Remember that salaries are almost always negotiable. The first figure you hear from the organization should be your base for negotiating. If you state the first figure, the organization will surely see that as the base for negotiations.

You want the organization to state the first salary figure. The organization naturally will want you to be the first to quote an amount. This situation often results in a "You go first—No, you go first" routine that would be amusing if so much were not at stake.

If the interviewer asks you about your present or last salary, dodge as gracefully as possible to avoid giving it. If you cannot get out of it, give the total compensation figure, including all fringe benefits, such as vacation, medical plan, retirement or pension plan, profit sharing, and the rest.

If the interviewer brings up the question of salary too soon in the interview by asking what salary you want, reply that you think the salary basis should be what you can contribute to the organization and resume selling yourself. If the interviewer presses you, be indefinite: "The customary for this job." "Your usual range for such work." "In the 30s." If you have done your homework, you should know about what the job should pay before you go in for the interview.

If you are forced to quote a dollar amount, and you think the top salary for the job is, say, about $22,000, overlap it on both sides and say, "$19,000 to $25,000." This, you hope, will begin the negotiations at the top end of the scale. If you have no real idea what the job should pay, as a last resort quote a figure 20 percent above your last salary.

When you change jobs or you can otherwise choose between two jobs, you may well get 20 to 30 percent more pay in one than in the other. Once in a job, however, you'll be lucky to get more than half that in any one increase. Your big raise, therefore, comes from negotiating at the outset. Remember, however (before bargaining too hard on salary), that many other things about two jobs may make one the better choice at several thousand dollars less, such things as

- Doing the kind of work you enjoy.
- Keeping your family together (especially if your spouse has a job).
- Living in a climate that appeals to you.
- Living in a low-cost area (for which statistics are readily available).
- Saving on moving expenses and perhaps on the cost and trouble of selling and buying a home.
- Living in the kind of state, city, or culture or among the group of friends that appeals to you.

The better you have sold yourself, the stronger your bargaining position will be. Negotiate your salary based on, in order of preference, your real worth to the organization, your need for the top of the salary range, offers from other organizations, your interest in furthering your career, and your needs. Not many people have ceased being considered for a job because they asked for more money than the organization first offered. If the organization is unwilling to negotiate, the answer will be "No, that is as much as we will pay," and you can then accept or refuse the offer.

**Ending the Interview.** Usually you'll have about five minutes to ask questions toward the end of the interview. Be sure to have some current and relevant questions about the company and the job. According to campus recruiters, you may appropriately ask about salary and fringe benefits if the interviewer hasn't mentioned them yet in the interview.

When you sense that the interview is approaching its close, you want to accomplish four things, in this order: (1) summarize your strongest qualifications for the job in a final statement, (2) express your enthusiasm for working for the organization, (3) thank the interviewer for an interesting interview, and (4) make sure both of you agree on what the next step will be.

After you have said good-bye, leave. Don't remain in the reception room or elsewhere around the offices, for you will appear to be indecisive or at a loss about what to do next.

**After the Interview.** As soon as possible after leaving the organization's offices, write down the names of the people you met and any other information you learned. Don't trust this to memory—it is vital that you have everything correct and the names spelled right. Note what strengths and weaknesses about yourself came out in the interview, what went well, and what didn't.

You must, the day after the interview or as soon thereafter as practical, write a thank-you letter to the person who interviewed you. For help on future interviews and in writing thank-you letters, Chapter 10 gives you recommendations on how to handle this kind of message. Unless you go back for further interviews, this is your last chance to sell the organization on hiring you; so don't overlook briefly touching on your strong points.

## The Information Interview

Sometimes you'll be able to talk informally with a potential employer in order to get information about jobs in that company's field. Or you may be able to interview a person in a professional organization who can guide you in choosing a career. Here are some helpful questions to ask in such cases:

1. What are the entry requirements?
2. What training is necessary?
3. What are the job responsibilities?
4. What career advancement opportunities are available?
5. What kinds of companies use this type of job?
6. What is the salary range—entry level? experience?

**7.** If you had to do it over, what would you do the same? differently?

**8.** Who else do you suggest I talk to about this kind of job?

Remember, an information interview isn't a veiled request for a job. It's a way to gain helpful information and future contacts.

## Dictation Skills

Dictation is easy to learn. Without some study and practice, however, you probably will not make the most effective use of this common office procedure. (You should be aware that dictating by machine is four times as fast as writing in longhand and twice as fast as dictating one-on-one to a secretary.) Machine dictation also is considerably less expensive. (Machine dictation costs $6.08 per letter, as compared to $8.10 for a secretary dictation letter. No wonder 46 percent of executives use machine dictation.) To help you be more efficient and effective in dictation, whether you dictate directly or through a telephone and/or dictation equipment to your secretary or a typist in a word processing center, here are some tips.

### Getting Ready to Dictate

Besides learning how to compose good business messages before you start dictating, you have some other preparations to make. Don't put yourself in the position of having to stop dictating (especially if directly to a secretary) to get something you should have had at hand to begin with. Get together all the information you will need: letters you need to answer, invoices you have to write about, files on matters you want to cover . . . .

Plan what you are going to say and how you will say it in each letter, memo, or other piece you are going to dictate. Make notes to yourself (perhaps right on the papers you are going to talk about), work up outlines . . . in other words, organize first. (An increasing practice that saves time for everybody involved stems from making notes on papers to be answered. Often by expanding the note a little, you can really give all the answer you need to, especially in internal communications. All your secretary has to do is make a photocopy to file and return the original as an answer.) But never make the time-consuming mistake of writing out your dictation in longhand and then reading it to a secretary or dictation machine!

If you are going to use a dictation machine, know what its capabilities and limitations are. Learn where all the controls are and what they do. Spend some time practicing with the machine, at home if necessary, so that when you begin to dictate you will feel relaxed and comfortable. You might well play back some of your dictation so that you will know how you sound.

## Dictating

Whether you dictate direct or use a telephone and/or dictation machine, dictation is dyadic communication; it involves two people, you and a secretary or typist. Regardless of the setup for your dictation, remember that a live human being will be on the other end whether you can see the person or not.

If you work with a secretary, you and your secretary must respect each other and know each other well enough to work calmly and efficiently together. You can help your secretary by setting aside a period for dictation at about the same time each day. Making it routine will help your secretary more efficiently plan a day's activities. Dictating in the morning is the best since your secretary will have the remainder of the day to transcribe the dictation, rather than waiting until the next day when shorthand notes may have cooled off.

Minimize interruptions while you're dictating. Cut off your phone and close the door if you need to. To further conserve your secretary's time, minimize your use of rough drafts. Rough drafts double or triple the time spent on a piece of writing. If, however, you have access to word processing equipment, you can often have as many rough drafts as you desire, making changes all along the way—especially useful when preparing long, involved reports.

The time to give a secretary or typist instructions is *before* you begin to dictate a message, not after you have finished. Nothing enrages a secretary more than to type a three-page message only to find at the end that you wanted a letter instead of a memo! So here's a list of things you may want to give instructions about before beginning to dictate:

1. Identify yourself if you are dictating to a machine in a word processing center or stenographic pool or in any other situation where the transcribers might not know who you are.
2. Give any special instructions: rush job, airmail, certified mail, and the like.
3. Specify the form of message you want: letter, memo, draft, whatever.
4. Specify the stationery: letterhead, memorandum form . . . .
5. Specify the number of carbons or photocopies.
6. Specify the names and addresses of those your message is to go to. (An efficient system in answering correspondence is to number the incoming messages with

matching numbers on the dictation, letting the transcriber get the names and addresses from the messages you answer.)

**7.** Fully describe any enclosures.

Much of the success of your dictation will depend on how well the transcriber hears and understands you. To begin with, talk directly toward your secretary or the microphone—not to a window or to the top of your desk.

*Talk naturally.* If you're acquainted with the person you're writing to, try to visualize the face. Even if you are not personally acquainted, a careful look at a letter you're answering will often enable you to visualize the face behind it. Your dictation will just naturally sound more empathetic if you do. But remember that you're dictating a written message. Using natural speech patterns will help signal pauses for punctuation, clauses, sentences, and so on. Natural speech will also help you avoid dictating in a monotone; it's deadly to listen to and can cause your transcriber's mind to wander, resulting in mistakes.

*Enunciate clearly* to the point of exaggeration (it won't sound exaggerated to the transcriber). Spell out words that sound alike, such as *accept* and *except,* and the names of people, places, and products unless the spelling is obvious or you are sure the transcriber knows. Spell out any unusual words and especially jargon or technical terms. Taking a few seconds to spell out something is far easier than making your secretary or typist question you about it or try to guess what you meant.

Your secretary can take your dictation easier, too, if you remain seated and resist the temptation to pace around your office, smoke, or chew gum. Some people dictate too fast and some dictate at almost a snail's pace. You can make it easier for your transcriber if you vary your speed, slowing down for difficult parts. And try not to be nervous about dictating. Nervousness is contagious.

While you should try not to dictate what the typist doesn't need (because dictating simple spelling and punctuation, for example, would imply ignorance), too much is better than not enough. If you know who will transcribe your dictation, you will know, for instance, how much punctuation to dictate. If you are unsure, play it safe and dictate any punctuation that is complex or doubtful. Do not assume that whoever types your messages will take care of spelling, punctuation, grammar, diction, and syntax for you; you will seldom have such a paragon working for you, especially early in your career.

Don't include jokes and extraneous comments when dictating. They often leave the transcriber wondering whether they belong in your message—and they slow down the transcription process.

Most authorities wisely say you should *dictate paragraph breaks.* Paragraphing is an integral part of the writing process, and as an author (even of a memo) you should bear the responsibility for it. Signal a paragraph break by saying "paragraph" or "new paragraph." Many successful dictators number each paragraph when dictating to help the transcriber and to provide clear references. (The numbers do not appear on the final document, of course.)

When you want to capitalize a word, such as *computer,* say "capital computer" or "cap computer." If you want something typed in all capital letters, say "all capitals" or "all caps."

If you dictate a quotation, indicate the quotation marks by dictating "quote" and "unquote." You know the names of all the punctuation marks, and should dictate punctuation when the proper punctuation is not obvious. Two marks that often present problems to transcribers are the question mark (?) and the exclamation point (!). To avoid uncertainty, you should always dictate these two.

While dictation direct to a secretary is still in use, most people recognize that dictation equipment is more efficient and economical because (1) interruptions don't waste time while a secretary waits for the dictator to resume dictating after looking up something or answering the telephone, (2) recorded dictation doesn't cool off as shorthand notes may overnight or over a weekend, (3) a secretary can do other things in time otherwise spent taking dictation, and (4) most people dictate faster to a machine than to a person.

If you use dictation equipment, make regular use of the indicator so that your transcriber will know the approximate length of your messages. A practiced transcriber who is familiar with your dictation style will know roughly how much typed copy a given spread between your indicator marks will make and can turn out a centered, balanced message on the first try.

When you make a mistake, correct it immediately. Otherwise, you may mislead your transcriber to forget to make the correction. Announce that you are going to make a correction by saying "correction," use the correction indicator to further alert your transcriber, identify what you are correcting, and dictate the corrected matter.

You can also help your transcriber by announcing the end of a message with "end of letter," "end of memo," or whatever is appropriate, as well as marking it on a machine indicator.

## After Dictating

First of all, turn off your machine when you are finished. You don't want it to record anything embarrassing or confidential.

When you get back your transcribed message, *read everything carefully before you sign it.* Remember, as dictator you (not the typist) are responsible for any errors.

When you must correct a typing error, be diplomatic and considerate:

even the best of secretaries (or word processing machines) have off days now and then. Try to make it a learning experience for both you and the typist. Don't unnecessarily mark up a letter or memo so that it requires total retyping. Use a pencil *lightly* so that the typist can erase your marks and white-out the errors without having to retype the whole page.

And—in the same vein of being a diplomatic and considerate (and wise) employer—when your secretary or typist does good work, give the deserved compliment. A compliment or a thank-you may not replace a salary raise, but it does wonders for morale.

## Telephone Tips

One other very common type of oral communication you'll use every day in business is talking on the telephone. With good telephone skills, you can build personal and business relationships. Bad telephone habits, on the other hand, can lose you both customers and goodwill with your colleagues. Here are a few tips for successful communication by telephone:

- Try to answer your calls on the first ring—it makes you seem alert and helpful.
- Be sure to identify yourself when answering the phone. Your name and department may be enough if you don't usually answer calls from the public. If you need to answer someone else's phone, say "Marian Davis' desk."
- Keep paper and pencil by your phone so that you can take messages and notes without fumbling for materials.
- Put a caller on hold if you must ask a colleague a question, since an open line can be embarrassing at worst and noisy at best.
- Let your receptionist or office partner know when you leave, and pick up and return your messages when you return.
- Keep a list of frequently called numbers to save time.
- Place your calls yourself, and try to sound like yourself on the phone. Be natural and helpful. Imagine the caller, and put expression into your voice.

Think of times you've talked to someone on the telephone who seemed rude, tired, or uninterested in helping you with your problem. Those images alone should help you develop a friendly, personable telephone manner.

## Conference Management

Conferences are oral communication situations among people, not speeches *at* them. The free interchange of ideas that ideally characterizes conferences is absent in speech/report situations and the seeking and giving of information in interviews.

Conferences are popular in virtually all kinds of organizations because they provide an environment for two-way communication and immediate response from both management and lower-level people.

Whether conferences are impromptu meetings or formally scheduled and conducted discussions, they share three attributes:

1. *Three or more people.* If fewer than three attend, it is a conversation or an interview.

2. *A leader.* Without a planned or natural leader, a conference will degenerate into a bull session or an argument.

3. *A specific objective.* Without a specific objective, a conference will be only an unstructured, time-wasting discussion group.

Business conferences usually fall into one of three categories. The first is information-giving upward, usually a report to superiors. The second is information-giving downward, which gives directions, instruction, or information to subordinates. The third is information-seeking, in which management looks for information or advice.

Any conference is a team effort and when run properly will avoid the faults of conferences that have given them a bad name in some organizations. Too many conferences are time killers and lead only to further conferences. Others, because of ego trips or bad planning, take more time than their objectives or results justify. In the end, poorly planned conferences waste an organization's time, personnel, and money. Therefore proper planning is essential to successful conferences.

## Planning the Conference

When planning a conference, ask yourself (1) *whether a need exists* to justify one and (2) *whether a conference is the best way to handle the situation.*

If you are convinced that a conference is justified and is the best approach, your next questions are (3) *how to define its objective* and (4) *whether the objective is attainable.* If you cannot define a conference's objective, you can hardly expect others to contribute to meeting it.

Next, consider (5) *what topics* the conference should cover (the agenda), (6) *in what order,* (7) whether *one conference* will be *sufficient* to cover all of them, and (8) *what kind of conference* to hold (information-giving, information-seeking, brainstorming . . .).

If you have fixed the conference's objective, agenda, and type, you are ready for the next step, (9) *picking the participants.* Ideally you should never invite people to participate in a conference just to keep them informed or because they might be hurt or insulted if not invited.

The participants in a conference should be only those directly concerned with the problem or situation under discussion. Like most ideals, this one is hard to achieve; but the more directly each participant is involved, the more successful your conference is likely to be.

Next, you must take up what is probably the most important question about any conference: (10) *who is to lead it.* Just as a good leader can stimulate participants to achieve the objectives, a poor leader can make a conference futile. Basically, the best leader is one who talks little but stimulates others to talk. The leader should not necessarily be the highest-ranking participant—who might inhibit free interaction among the other participants.

Now nearly ready, you still have two related groups of questions to answer: (11) *who is going to take notes* or make and distribute a record of the conference. (Don't make the mistake of the man who handed a pad of paper and a pencil to a woman at a conference with instructions to take notes, only to have her caustically inform him that she was the treasurer of the corporation!) If you plan to tape-record the conference, will the presence of the microphone inhibit anyone? Remember, too, that tape recordings must be transcribed, a lengthy and therefore costly process.

As the final step in planning, you will need to (12) *consider the location,* the physical setup, and interruption-control measures. Usually you will want a conference room or an office large enough to hold all the participants. In any case you will first have to reserve the room for the time you will need it. Be sure of enough chairs. And if the meeting is large, you may want to set out name cards telling everyone where to sit.

While you are arranging for the conference room, decide whether you should furnish pads of paper and pencils at each seat, whether to set out ashtrays (no ashtrays serve as a useful deterrent to smoking in a closed room), and if carafes and glasses are present, remind yourself to have them filled. Now is the time to arrange for audiovisual equipment. Finally, if the conference will be long enough to justify a break, do you want to have coffee or other refreshments available?

Controlling the temperature in a meeting room is often a problem since you must compensate for the heat generated by bodies (and a lot of bodies in a room will generate a lot of heat). An overheated room makes people drowsy, while one that is too cold keeps people thinking about their discomfort instead of the conference. A good compromise, if you can arrange it, is 68° F.

Because messages and telephone calls are common disruptions of conferences, ideally you should forbid any interruptions except in cases of extreme emergency. However, you will probably not be able to do more than unplug the telephone and ask everyone's secretary not to interrupt the conference unless really necessary.

For an informal meeting, you may simply call the participants on the phone to tell them about it. For a bigger or more formal conference, send each participant a memo or an electronic message. In either case, inform people early enough so that they will have sufficient notice to schedule time for the conference.

The more you tell participants before the conference starts, the better they will be able to prepare for it and the more likely they are to contribute successfully. To that end, announce the objective of the conference and list the agenda. This information will help participants to gather materials they will need and also help the leader during the conference to keep the discussion on course.

Cover also the essentials of the date of the conference, the time it will begin and the projected time it will end (to help participants plan their other activities), and exactly where the conference will meet. You may, if addressing subordinates, let them know things you want them to review beforehand. So everyone will know who is coming, you might well include in your memo a list of all the participants.

## Leading the Conference

A successful conference depends on effective leadership. Without direction, most meetings quickly degenerate into argument at the worst and into wasted time, indecision, or inaction at the best. Though resorting to the more esoteric rules of parliamentary procedure is usually unnecessary, a leader does need to know enough to keep the conference running smoothly by giving everyone an equal chance to contribute.

To begin with, the leader must respect the participants in the conference. Otherwise, whether superiors or subordinates, they will react angrily and turn from contributors to obstructionists. A wise conference leader, then, will never threaten, embarrass, ridicule, or insult anyone.

A conference that yields useful results comes from maximum contribution by the participants. To encourage participants, the leader should try not to dominate the conference. That is one good reason for the leader to sit with the participants, not to stand looking down at them. Anything that tends to separate or elevate the leader is counterproductive. Even a U-shaped table is a poor arrangement. An oval or rectangular table is much better; but the wise leader will sit in the middle of one of the longer sides, not at the end.

Everyone in a conference should feel free to contribute; open intercommunication is what transforms a meeting into a conference. A protracted monologue or dialogue that excludes others discourages them from getting into the discussion. In fact, the leader who allows such a monologue or dialogue to develop implies approval of it.

Basically, then, leading an effective conference is a matter of successfully dealing with people. Here are some of the more common problem types and situations you may run into and some suggestions for handling them as a conference leader:

*The nonparticipant.* Unless you think it will overly embarrass the person, try directing a question to the nonparticipant to break through the shell and bring out a contribution to the conference.

*The violent argument.* When two or more participants get into an argument, allow one side to finish stating its case, then give the other side equal time. Do not allow interruptions; your goal is to help each side clearly understand the other side's position.

*The private conference on the side.* Ask the people involved to share their conference with the rest of the group. If this doesn't work, ask them nicely to hold their own conference later so that you can get this one back to its task.

*Leader of the revolution.* If a participant tries to take over your leadership job, a useful technique is to place the revolutionist on your immediate right or left where your eyes won't meet. If this person tries to interrupt other participants, you can effectively squelch such interruptions by a hand motion or by whispering a request to be quiet until recognized.

*The timid soul.* Place a shy or introverted participant directly opposite you, thus allowing responses to you rather than to the entire group.

*The uninvited guest.* The best remedy for people who join your conference without being asked is to tell them to leave. If an uninvited guest is your superior, however, you may be able to do little about it except try to prevent undue interruptions.

*The late arrival.* Regardless of your precautions, someone will usually come late. You can minimize the disruption by making sure that the empty chair is nearest the door. Don't comment on the late entry; it would only disrupt your conference further.

*The chronic arguer.* If one of those people who disagree with everything gets going, don't make the mistake of reacting directly yourself. You will split the conference into two sides, yours and the arguer's, effectively destroying your all-important neutrality. Instead, get the other participants to react to the arguer, using your position as a leader to keep the conference progressing by making the arguer the devil's advocate.

*The contemplative ones.* When participants go into glassy-eyed reveries, direct questions specifically to them. If you get no reaction, just sit there a few moments until the silence does get through.

*The tongue-tied participant.* When someone can't seem to get to the point or is unable to make a point, tactfully state the point back as best you understand it, preferably in the form of a question, "You think the cost of the new pump is too high, right?" If you get agreement, you have helped over a rough spot.

*The surprise package.* If a participant brings up a point outside the scope or agenda of your conference (usually in an attempt to impress a superior or embarrass a competitor), interrupt and firmly get your

**Figure 12-2 / What Is Wrong with This Conference?**

conference back on the agenda (promising to discuss the point after the conference is over, if willing).

## Participating in a Conference

Your progress in an organization may depend heavily on how you show up in conferences. They may be the best means you have to bring yourself to upper management's (your bosses') favorable attention.

As a start, do your homework: be prepared to discuss *all* the items on the agenda, especially the interesting and important ones. A little study of the background of a major problem (causes, losses, past attempts to solve, reasons for failure, proposals for solution) can make you look good in the eyes of all the other participants—some of whom may not have done their homework so well. Take some time to consider carefully any ideas you may have before presenting them to a group.

As a good participant, you will want to both speak and listen; but above all, listen well. In fact, a useful and common technique is to wait until most of the others have said something before speaking yourself, since you will then have more information to work from.

Even if everyone at the conference seems to be employing the technique, you can still turn it to your advantage by waiting until the silence just begins to become embarrassing and then relieving it (and the conference leader) by starting the discussion. The best entering wedge is a question rather than a statement of opinion, since a statement may unintentionally put you into opposition to other participants as they react to you. Beginning with a question is more likely to force them to make statements, which can then be to your advantage.

### Ending the Conference

Before you dismiss the participants, summarize what the conference accomplished so that everyone understands the conclusion(s) or agreement(s) reached.

Afterward, you may want to distribute a summary or the minutes of the conference to the participants and others who should be informed. Put these in outline form, stripped of all the frills (it's no time to editorialize). Distributing the minutes serves to (1) create a written record of what the conference accomplished, (2) assure that all the participants agree with the result(s) of the conference (you will hear if anyone doesn't!), and (3) clarify the participants' assignments, if any.

## Electronic Conference Controls

When people gather for conferences in today's electronic world, they no longer need to be at the same location. As you learned in Chapter 2, you can set up conferences by telephone and by television to include almost any number of people scattered virtually all over the world.

Remember, when you connect participants by telephone, you are *teleconferencing;* when you connect them by television, you are *videoconferencing.*

### Teleconferences

This convenient means of group discussion among geographically separated people is still common, and you may take part in your first teleconference early in your career.

The two drawbacks to teleconferences are lack of visual contact among the participants and the need for the leader to exercise strict control, especially to cut off unwanted conversations between participants.

When people communicate by telephone, they cannot of course see each other, nor can they show things to each other. While this means that they have none of the visual cues to communication we rely on when talking face-to-face, virtually everyone in our society has learned to deal with telephone conversations—though they require that we *listen* harder than in face-to-face situations.

The inability to show things is a more serious drawback to the telephone. Most people in business overcome this by planning, by making sure that all participants have a copy of whatever they will talk about. Even when the need to supply a document to one person on the other end of the line comes up during a telephone conversation, you can send the document in a minute or two by facsimile transmission over another line.

The second drawback to teleconferencing, the need for strict control by the leader, is not really a drawback. As pointed out earlier, the better control you exercise over a conference, the more successful your conference is likely to be. The main danger is that two or more participants will get involved in a miniconference of their own, holding a private conversation and leaving everyone else in the teleconference to listen. If you are leader, you will want to break up such private conversations as quickly as they get started. Fortunately, since people do listen harder on the telephone, you will find it easier to interrupt and regain control. Just break in and continue breaking in until everyone has stopped speaking; then reassert your control.

A lesser danger is that of participants' interrupting you and others while they are speaking—a lesser danger because most people have learned that interruptions in telephone conversations are never as productive as in face-to-face conversations. As conference leader, nevertheless, your job will be easier if you set the rules at the start: *no one speaks without your permission.* Though this may sound heavy-handed, it is essential to successful teleconferencing, especially when many participants are on the line together. (Incidentally, as a general rule the more participants there are in a teleconference, the less participants talk and the more they listen.)

The advantages of teleconferencing are fairly obvious. The first is, of course, cost versus physically gathering the participants together. Even a long teleconference in the middle of a business day (when telephone rates are highest) will not come close in cost to the expense of having participants travel to a common location, incur food and lodging expenses, and return (including the hidden expense of nonproductive time while traveling).

## Videoconferences

Videoconferences are the same as teleconferences except that the participants can see each other over television as well as hear each other. Basically, each group of participants is in a room with a conference table, a camera and microphones, television screens, a graphics station, and a conference easel, as you saw in Figure 2–5.

You can talk normally to the group in the other meeting center, watching them on one screen and monitoring what you are sending them on a second screen. You have complete privacy since the cameras are voice-actuated, automatically switching to the person speaking, and need no operators. You also have manual control over them and can switch at will to a wide-angle shot of all your participants.

A separate camera lets you present 35-mm transparencies, artwork, photographs, documents—even zoom in to show small objects. Facsimile machines are available to transmit documents to and from the other meeting center during a conference. And of course you can videotape your conference if you wish.

Videoconferencing is a very flexible tool and, even at its present high cost, is more economical than having participants physically travel long distances to a central location.

Because of the cost, the need for planning, the relatively small size of the meeting center conference rooms (more than five or six people can crowd the table), and the novelty, most participants are well prepared at videoconferences. If you have to lead a videoconference, you will find that you can easily adapt the suggestions given for conferences earlier.

## Questions and Exercises

1. In Professor Endicott's list of reasons why some interviewees aren't hired, which three surprise you most by their frequency ranking? Which three do you think might have tripped you if not thus forewarned?

2. Do you wholly agree with our suggestions on talking about salary? If not, wherein and why?

3. How should you respond if a job interviewer
   a. Asks you to talk about your former employer?
   b. Asks you to tell about yourself?
   c. Allows a long pause in the conversation?

4. Consider your answers to the following questions currently asked by some interviewers (some are for people changing jobs rather than graduating from college):
   a. Are you generally lucky?

    b. What kind of criticism do you get from your family?

    c. How would you evaluate, on a 10-point scale, the extent to which you've been able to achieve your aspirations so far in your career?

5. What's your worst telephone habit now? How will you correct it?

6. Discuss your answer to Figure 12–2's question, "What's wrong with this conference?"

7. Of the five categories of oral business communications the chapter discusses, which two do you expect to be the most important (not necessarily the most frequently used) in your career? Which do you expect to be the least important?

# Part Five

## Reporting for Management Decisions

# Chapter Outline

# 13

# Reports—Importance, Definition, Classification, and Short Preparations

## Importance of Report Writing

As with memo and letter writing, two basic facts about report writing deserve your preliminary attention:

1. Corporate executives put great value on report writing as an important element in management success. A national survey of *Fortune*-500 executives in 1983 shows 91 percent of vice presidents indicating that reports are important communications in business. So regardless of the work you do (except work for yourself or for wages), your ability to prepare good reports will be an important consideration in whether you get a good job and how fast you move up.

2. Most people who have not studied how to prepare reports do it poorly. The *Fortune*-500 survey found that 81 percent think college programs in business should require a strong course in report writing.

The basic language of good reports differs little from the standard English appropriate in any functional communication. So if you have done well in a good course covering letters and memos (as presented in the preceding chapters of this book), you have a running start on a course in report writing. (If not, you certainly need to study at least Chapters 3 and 4 and the first big section of Chapter 5 prior to studying reports.)

Good reports, however, require more preliminary preparation, a more objective style, and use of certain supplementary communication techniques rarely learned except in reports courses. Indeed, the preparation before writing involves most of the work: making a plan, getting the facts or evidence (research), organizing for meaning and coherence, analyzing this material to arrive at an interpretation of and solution to the problem, and then writing up your analysis as clearly, concisely, and objectively as you can.

Improving your ability to do all these things is an important part of a liberal education and especially the kind of education needed to cope with today's information-oriented world. Study and practice in preparing and presenting reports will help you, therefore, when you're a job candidate and when you're on almost any work assignment.

## History, Functions, and Present Need of Reports

In early history nobody needed reports. Almost everybody operated a complete one-person business or directed a small group of people under an on-the-spot manager.

Later, as society became more complex, some individuals gained power as tribal chiefs, masters, or employers—and found reports essential. When one of these managers sent somebody to scout an enemy tribe, do some work, or captain a second ship to develop trade along a different route, the owner needed reports to make wise decisions about future operations. Thus the ship's log came into being as one early form of written report.

**Specific Ways Reports Serve.** The impossibility of a manager's being in two places at the same time made reports necessary. Overcoming the problem of *distance,* then, is the first specific function reports may serve.

When organizations grew to where the manager could not find time to oversee all operations (sometimes even under the same roof) and some of the processes became so technical that the manager did not have the knowledge to evaluate all of them, reports became more and more widely necessary to solve two more specific problems: *time* and *technology.*

With the increasing complexity of society, *records* became more important too; and as their fourth specific function, written reports provided permanent records.

As managers became responsible for more and more varied activities, the wiser ones realized that they could not do all the necessary thinking about new products, processes, and procedures. They therefore invited employees with initiative to submit ideas in reports. Hence reports began to serve management in a fifth way as vehicles for *creative ideas.*

As managers became responsible for numerous employees, some of whom they rarely saw, they often found that submitted reports were the best indicators they had of how well an employee was doing an assigned job. Thus reports began to serve in a sixth way—as a basis for *evaluating the employees* who presented them.

You see readily that reports have become essential tools of modern management if you bring these trends up to the present world of large and complex organizations, where

- Top management may be thousands of miles from some operations.
- Management cannot possibly find time to oversee all the activities (even in one location).
- Some of the processes are so technical that no one can be competent to decide wisely about all of them without guidance through reports from specialists.
- Numerous records are necessary to keep various involved people informed.
- Competition pushes a manager to use all the creative brainpower of all employees in developing new ideas, through reports and other means.
- Personnel managers may never see employees they have to evaluate for raises, promotions, and (sometimes) the opposite.

**Questions Reports Answer.** In helping managers in those six ways, reports help with decision making by answering one or more of three key questions:

*1. Is the project under consideration feasible?* In thinking about any proposed action that is not obviously possible, the decision maker's only logical first question is whether it *can* be done.

*2. Should we take a certain proposed action?* With feasibility established, decision makers trying to decide on a proposed new product, plant, or other project will want—in answer to a second question—a report showing whether expected benefits will result in higher profits, better quality or quantity, or less time, material, or effort expended. That is the cost-benefits question.

*3. Which is the best (or better) way (or solution)?* Only with the feasibility and benefits established can one logically consider this third question. Then the study and report may consider a choice between or among proposed ways, or it may have to propose and evaluate different ways to lead to a choice—maybe between the present way and a proposed new way, between repairing the old and buying the new, or between or among products to buy for a given purpose (office or farm equipment, line of trucks), financing procedures (buy or lease), or location to seek a job or establish a plant.

Any board of directors, president, governor, manager, superintendent, or department head in any organization—public or private—wants satisfactory answers to all three questions before approving substantial expenditures, changes in operations, or new regulations. Many times those questions lead to the assignment of reports. For this reason, management today expects all employees (except possibly day laborers) to be able to prepare and present reports.

If you need more evidence that learning to present better reports will be a worthwhile activity for you, consider how your study of reports can help you as a student, as a job candidate, and later as an employee.

## Help When You're a Student and Job Candidate

Learning the things necessary for a good report can help you earn better grades. Increased familiarity with sources of information—not just published sources and how to find them in libraries, but also methods of securing original data—enables you to do research more efficiently for papers required in other courses. (Reports are certainly not like term papers in objective or in some phases of treatment, but the information-gathering research behind them is similar.)

Documenting—that is, backing up what you say with factual evidence, citing publications you use as authorities or sources of information, and explaining your research methods to assure soundness—is also similar in reports, term papers, and theses. Certainly you'll profit from the carry-over of organization principles and improved language ability. For these reasons, students who have studied and applied reporting principles usually earn better grades.

When you apply for a job, you'll find that employers put a premium on the services of people who can produce good letters and reports. Because reports play such a prominent role in most businesses, prospective employers often give preference to applicants who have learned how to prepare and present them.

Directors of college placement services report that an increasing number of recruiters ask, as one of the first questions, what grade a prospective employee earned in reports.

## Help When You're on the Job

The reports a trainee on a new job usually has to submit may not only help determine assignment to a division of the company, but they also often determine whether to promote or drop the employee at the end of the training period.

Even after you become a full-fledged employee, typically your superiors will study your submitted reports not only for information and ideas but also for evidence of your ability to communicate clearly, quickly, and easily. Since those who make the final decisions about salary increases and promotions may never have met you, they often consider equally important your immediate superior's evaluation and your *written* reports. Employers often regard reports as the best (and sometimes they are the only) indication of how well an employee is doing the job.

Your study of reports, as you see, can help your grades in school, your chances at a desirable job, and your effectiveness and status in your career. Indeed, a recent study of how top executives got there showed that many of them mentioned their reports as important to their various promotions. You can hardly find a better set of rungs for the ladder to success than a series of good reports.

# Definition and Classification of Reports

The word *report* is such a broad concept that most attempts at one-sentence definition are either incomplete, too general to be useful, or not quite true.

The best *definition* for *report* is this: *A report is a presentation of facts and/or ideas to people who need them in decision making.*

Analysis of that definition involves several clarifying points: A presentation may be oral or written (as reports may be). "Facts and/or ideas" covers the three possibilities—and that statement fits.

Perhaps the most discriminating part of the definition, however, is the last part. As used here, a report does go to somebody who faces a problem of making some kind of decision; and the purpose of the report message is to help in making a wise decision. That rules out such things as term papers and write-ups about books read—things often referred to in academic circles as reports.

Etymology, a frequent part of an extended definition, is another help in defining *report*. One meaning of *re* as a prefix is "back," as in *recall.* The *port* is from *portare* ("to carry"). Hence the executive who explained a problem and assigned a report-writing job quite properly said, "Find the answer, Jim, and bring it back."

Still, the best way to get a clear idea of the meaning of the word *report*—as of many others—is to consider the usual characteristics of reports, along with the special characteristics of different classes. Here, therefore, you find those characteristics.

Usually, but not always:

1. A report is a management tool designed to help an executive make decisions. Thus it is functional communication for the benefit of the receiver.

2. A report is an assigned job. Usually the assigner will make clear the kind of report wanted; if not, the reporter should ask.

3. A report goes up the chain of command. A few reports go between people of equal rank, as between department heads, and some (usually better called directives) go downward from executives (but most of the reports that executives prepare go to still higher authorities—boards of directors, legislatures, . . .).

4. A report is for one person or a group (usually small) unified by a common purpose or problem, and usually having a leader who authorizes (orders) the report and thus becomes the primary addressee (who

may then send a written report on up the chain of command to a few higher executives or reproduce it and send copies to the whole group).

5. A report gets more than normal attention to organization. Because reports are usually expositions of complex facts and ideas for practical purposes and for busy receivers, reporters work harder at organization than most other communicators.

6. A report makes more than normal use of certain techniques and devices for communicating clearly, quickly, and easily.

7. A report should be accurate, reliable, and objective. No executive wants to base decisions on a reporter's errors, assumptions, preconceptions, wishful thinking, or any kind of illogic. Where the receiver might otherwise question the validity, the reporter therefore explains sources and methods of collecting data to show the soundness of the facts presented.

8. Good reports—like good buildings, pieces of furniture, or anything else—vary in design according to their functions and conditions of use.

**Classification.** If a report includes only facts, it is an *informational* report. If it goes further into interpretation (conclusions and/or recommendations), it becomes an *analytical* report. If the person who authorizes a report does not indicate which kind (informational or analytical), the reporter should ask.

Since an analytical report has more in it than one giving the bare facts on a subject, it is naturally longer. Long or short, however, a report may be analytical or informational.

Similarly, since long reports are likely to be somewhat more formal than shorter ones, you often see an analytical report referred to as a *formal* report and shorter ones as *informal.* In fact, no necessary relation exists between the length of a report and its formality. The only legitimate basis for calling any report formal or informal is the degree of formality in its style; and that should be a reflection of the relationship between the reporter and the receiver(s).

On the basis of subject matter you'll hear about business reports, credit reports, engineering reports, and technical reports. Similarly, as the basis changes to frequency, *periodic* reports may be daily, weekly, monthly, quarterly, or annual—with counterparts that are *special* reports. Other obvious bases give you private/public, internal/external, and letter and memo reports.

Two other often-used names of reports (treated later) clearly indicate their bases of classification and refer to true independents. *Progress reports* explain what has been done on a project and usually try to predict the future (both in relation to any preset schedule). *Justification reports* (usually short and sometimes called *initiation reports* because the reporters usually initiate them) propose certain specific actions and provide evidence to show the wisdom of those actions.

The term *research report* may mean merely that preparation required some research (as most reports do). Most authorities, however, restrict the name to mean a report of research done to advance the forefronts of knowledge (often called pure or theoretical research) and perhaps without any immediate, practical applications in mind. To avoid being misled, you have to know who is talking. (When used here, the name carries the second meaning.)

Since this book deals largely with analytical reports (on the principle that anybody who can prepare them can leave out the interpretation and make informational reports), the primary basis of classification is length—*short reports* (usually progress or justification reports in memo or letter form 1–3 pages long) or *short analytical reports* (usually 6 to 10 pages), and *complete analytical reports* (or long reports, usually 10 or more pages).

Much more important than knowing the names and classifications of reports (except the distinction between *informational* and *analytical*) is close attention to the characteristics that reports should have. They should be full of useful information that is *accurate, reliable, and objective; presented in functional rather than literary style; adapted to the receiver(s); carefully organized; and clearly, quickly, and easily understandable.* That relates directly to the preparation of reports—the main concern in the rest of this and the next three chapters.

## Basics of Report Preparation

Preparing an analytical report (short or long) is a five-step process. Because the steps become more complex as the report length increases, this chapter gives you adequate explanation for only short reports. Additional explanation on each step comes where needed—in Chapter 14.

1. First, the reporter *plans the attack* by getting a sharp concept of the problem, breaking it down into its essential elements, and raising questions to be answered about those elements.

2. Then the reporter *collects appropriate facts,* using the most suitable methods and checking for reliability. Often reflective thinking, records in the files, observation or inspection, or a few interviews or consultations will do. If necessary, an experiment, a survey, or library research can come into play (as explained in Chapter 14).

3. Then comes *organizing the facts* according to the most suitable of direct, indirect, or persuasive sequence (Chapter 5), *chronological order,* or *order of importance or location.*

4. While *interpreting the facts* into logical conclusions and workable recommendations (omitted in informational reports), a good reporter

attempts to be objective by avoiding all possible prejudices, preconceptions, wishful thinking, and fallacies (explained in Chapter 14).

5. Finally, the reporter *puts the report into words, symbols, and graphics,* using all suitable techniques and devices to make clear what the problem is, show that the information is reliable by explaining the sound research methods, and present the facts and what they mean. To make understanding the message clear, quick, and easy, a good reporter

a. Uses commonly understood words (uneducated, technical, and educated people all understand them and all appreciate the ease of comprehending everyday English).

b. Chooses specific, concrete, humanized wording that shows how the facts affect people (preferably the receiver).

c. Keeps sentences so direct and short (average about 17 words) that they need little punctuation except ending periods (or the oral equivalents).

d. Keeps paragraphs direct and short (questioning those of more than eight lines because short ones seem easier, are easier, and need fewer transitions).

e. Uses headings, topic sentences, and summarizing sentences to show the reader the organization (that is, where the line of thought is going and where it has been).

f. Itemizes (as here) to call attention to important points and to force concise and precise phrasing.

g. Uses all kinds of nonverbal means of communication (charts, graphs, tables, pictograms, maps) to assist words in presenting ideas clearly, quickly, and easily—thus making the report both clearer and more interesting.

## Preparing Short Reports

The best form for a report depends on the situation—mainly who its recipient is (and the relation to the reporter), its purpose, and its length. Yet the emphasis here is not on learning the forms themselves but on the uses of different forms and the proper information, organization, interpretation, and style in the reports.

Since you have presumably studied letter and memo writing in the preceding chapters (the best background you could have for studying short reports), you already know the two main forms (letter and memo) and most of the desirable characteristics of style. You also know the basic organizational sequences—plans you learned for welcome messages, bad-news or disappointing messages, and persuasive messages (Chapter 5).

You will, however, have to make seemingly minor (though sometimes difficult) modifications of the style you've learned in previous chapters.

1. Start the changes by substituting *convincing* for *persuasive.* Ideally a report is strictly objective and logical in presenting valid arguments. Though no person can be strictly objective, as a report writer you must try by using only validated facts and sound logic. Those things stem from mental processes (not emotions)—and affect the reader as logical *conviction.*

2. Always use a subject line (as the title) in letter as well as memo reports.

3. Make full use of itemizations, tables, charts, graphs, and attachments when they will help the reader get the message more quickly, clearly, or easily. (Because the amount of quantified data is usually greater in long reports than in short ones, the treatment of graphic presentation is in Chapter 15.)

## Letter Reports

Many short reports of one to four pages are in regular business letter form (with a subject line as the report title). Usually they go between organizations rather than between departments of the same organization, where memorandum form is more likely.

Since the letter report is likely to be longer than the usual letter, however, and since it *is* a report, it may take on the following special features of reports:

1. More than usually careful organization.
2. Objectivity (absence of emotional suasion, viewing both sides of the situation, enough interweaving or implying of methods and sources to assure soundness).
3. Use of subject lines, subheads, and itemizations where helpful.
4. Use of tables and graphic devices (often as attachments) where helpful and economical.

Depending on whether the message is likely to meet with reader approval, disappointment, or resistance, the letter report should follow the appropriate plan, as explained in Chapter 5 and illustrated thoroughly in Chapters 6, 7, and 8, respectively.

Although a letter report, like any other, needs to convince the reader that its facts are reliable, usually the best way to validate it is in incidental phrases interwoven right along with the information: "Inspection of . . . reveals . . ."; "Legal precedent in cases like . . . is clearly . . ."; "Microscopic examination shows . . ."; or ". . . , according to such authorities as . . . ." Be sure to avoid plagiarism, though, by giving credit to your sources (though you won't usually use footnotes).

Indeed, letter reports are like other reports except for the form that gives them their name, the limits of length and hence of the topics for which they are suitable, and their usually more familiar style.

Two common types of letter reports are those about job and credit applicants (personnel and credit reports), discussed in Chapter 6. You should study the explanations and the illustrations there. Notice that both illustrations use subject lines effectively. Note, too, that both begin immediately with important information because they face no problem of reader disappointment or resistance.

Personnel and credit reports, however, do have the legal problem of avoiding libel suit by referring to the request for information, trying to be fair to both parties, and asking confidential use of the information. Notice how the two illustrations handle that problem.

These two kinds of reports should be informational, in that they should rely on facts and subordinate or entirely eliminate unsupported opinions—and certainly recommendations. But letter reports may be either informational or analytical. In some cases they are more nearly directives than reports, but directives are more likely to be in memo form.

Here is a typical direct-style letter report from industry:

```
Florida Power Corporation
P.O. Box 1240
Crystal River, Fl 32629

September 29, 1986

Ms. Mary Feezell
Martin Marietta
P.O. Box P
Building K-1007, MS: 58
Oak Ridge, TN 37830


           NEW-FORMAT TERMINATION RECORDS


Dear Mary:

I am sending you our first tape of termination
records. The tape contains records for 366
employee terminations, which represent all
terminations at Crystal River #3 in the six-month
period, January 1, 1986, to June 30, 1986.

The tape records are formatted according to the
NRC Pilot Program File Format Specifications, a
copy of which I am enclosing for your reference.
The specifications for the tape itself are as
follows:
```

<u>JCL Parameters</u>

| | |
|---|---|
| 9 Track | |
| 1,600 bpi | Den=3 |
| Nonlabeled | Label=(1,NL) |
| ASCII code | OPTCD=Q |
| Record length = 80 bytes | RECL=80 |
| One record per block | BLKSIZE=80 |

All internal deposition is reported in nanocuries (code K on record). The following codes identify the critical organs for the Internal Exposure Records (Record Type I):

    50 = Digestive System (Lower Torso)
    28 = Lungs
    96 = Thyroid

A list of department codes used in our computer system is enclosed. These are the numbers that are reported for each employee on record type A in positions 65-67 ("Job Title or Craft").

For documentation purposes I am enclosing a hard-copy printout of the tape contents with this first tape.

Please let me know if you are able to read the tape successfully. We intend to submit a termination tape for each subsequent calendar quarter. If you have any questions, please call me at 904-759-6486 Ext. 403.

Sincerely yours,


Bruce B. Hopper
Chief Health Physics Technician

Because the following message is somewhat bad news and the reader may be reluctant to take the suggested action, the report uses the more convincing indirect rather than the faster-moving direct plan. You will note, too, that it uses no subject line. To do so would defeat the psychological purpose of the indirect plan of getting in the arguments before giving the conclusion.

As you always should when you have a step-by-step procedure or a series of pointed, emphatic principles, qualities, conclusions, or recommendations to convey, this report uses subdividing heads and itemizations effectively.

ROSS AND ASSOCIATES
Certified Public Accountants

October 4, 1985

Mr. Sam Chaska
Sam's Lobster House
1122 Restaurant Road
San Diego, CA 92115

SUGGESTED PILFERAGE-PROBLEM SOLUTIONS

Dear Mr. Chaska:

Since our last meeting on September 15, I have researched possible solutions to your depleted inventories due to pilferage.

Three approaches should solve your employee-theft problem. By implementing the procedures, you should not only decrease employee theft but also provide a more solid inventory base.

Preemployment screening

Cautious hiring procedures should be your first line of defense against employee theft. If your company can establish a thorough screening process, you will be less likely to hire individuals who are prone to thievery.

The main sources of information can be the applicant's references and the initial interview. By thoroughly checking all backgrounds of potential employees, you lower the risk of hiring someone who is dishonest.

Preemployment screening can use three methods:

1. Previous employers and other references.-- Always ask references about any known or suspected dishonesty.
2. Polygraphs and voice stress tests.--Though these tests have the reputation as the most effective way to pinpoint prospective thieves (85 to 90% accurate), Section 432.2 of the Labor Code restricts them to a voluntary basis and the cost is $50-75 per employee.
3. Paper and pencil tests.--Costs for the tests are low, job applicants generally do not feel

threatened, and the multiple-choice questions measure both employment history and attitudes toward theft.

### Clearly established policies and procedures

Establishing a solid foundation of policies and procedures is the second step in preventing pilferage. Discretion is necessary in the presentation to make your procedures clear without threatening.

The few necessary steps in the presentation and continuous maintenance of the program are:

1. Management should establish a clear policy regarding employment theft.
2. Employees should get a clear explanation of this policy, occasional reviews, and constant posted reminders.
3. Any employee detected as stealing should be sanctioned immediately.
4. The policies must be enforced on an equal basis without exceptions for rank.

### Tighter inventory controls

The success of minimizing employee theft also depends on having a tight inventory control system. The current inventory controls are insufficient in preventing employee theft. Too many loopholes make employee pilferage tempting.

To begin a thorough inventory system, a physical inventory count will be necessary to establish beginning figures. Once these figures are established, suitable inventory control software will be necessary. The Peachtree software package seems to be the most appropriate for your EPSON computer. At a cost of $550, this system is relatively easy to set up and use.

Additional steps in inventory control will also be necessary:

* periodic surprise audits of inventory;
* strict controls on cash registers;
* use of ink for all records; and
* spot checks on trash cans and dressing areas.

### Conclusion

Through implementation of these procedures, Sam's Lobster House will have better control of its inventory and will be more aware of any possible employee pilferage.

Any questions regarding this report can be directed to me or to my senior associate, John Peters.

Sincerely,


Susan Ross, CPA
Ross and Associates

Sources
Bullard, Peter D., and Alan J. Resnik, "SMR Forum: Too Many Hands in the Corporate Cookie Jar," Sloan Management Review, 25:51-56, Fall 1983.

Flory, Stephanie, "Pre-employment Test Can Help Retailers Control Internal Theft," Merchandising, 6:60, October 1981.

Hollinger, Richard C., and John P. Clark, Theft by Employees, Lexington Books, Lexington, Mass., 1983.

Kantor, Seth, "How to Foil Employee Crime," Nation's Business, 71:38-39, July 1983.


# Memorandums

Just as letter reports are more likely for communicating between organizations, memo reports are more appropriate within an organization. There they flow in quantity. The headings used in the illustrations of memos in Chapter 2 show the main variations in form.

Except for the differences in form and use, memo reports generally follow the instructions already given for letter reports. They are, however, inclined to (1) be ephemeral and hence less formal (often being handwritten without carbons), (2) make even greater use of itemization (almost characteristically), and (3) become directives going down the chain of command.

One of the most common and effective techniques is itemization. Numbering each paragraph (military style) almost forces a writer into careful organization, precise statement, and conciseness.

Careful phrasing of subject lines helps by indicating the contents con-

# Checklist for Letter and Memo Reports

1. Form. (See Chapter 2.)
2. Organization and coverage:
   a. Bring in your main point (request, conclusion, recommendation, or something else) in the first sentence unless your reader might resist; if so, lead up to it with whatever facts, reasons, or explanations are necessary to convince—especially any reader benefits you can point out. (Chapter 5 explains the psychology.)
   b. Make clear that your information is valid and pertinent by showing what the problem is and how you got your information to solve it (unless obvious); but see 3b.
   c. Effective dates (for directives)—and when necessary, other time limits, places, and people concerned—are important points.
   d. Consider whether you should mention alternatives.
   e. Should you explain more specifically how to carry out your proposal?
   f. Cover all points your reader will need—especially all steps in logic.
3. Style:
   a. Make the subject line (if used) indicate the content accurately.
   b. Emphasize the important and avoid undue emphasis on the rest. Imply or interweave purpose and method.
   c. Be sure your terminology, sentence length and structure, and paragraph length and structure make for quick, clear, easy reading. Itemizations and tabulations may help.
   d. Display significant data, conclusions, and recommendations by increasing white space around them, itemizing, and/or tabulating.
   e. For coherence, precede displayed items with an appropriate introduction.
   f. Don't develop a fever; remain logical and objective.
4. Tone:
   a. Soften commands and recommendations for acceptable tone. "You will . . ." and "You must . . ." are too commanding for most situations. "If you will . . ." is usually too weak.
   b. Direct accusations in independent clauses are always objectionable.
   c. Positive is better than negative phrasing.
   d. Item 2a is an important factor in tone.
   e. Consider whether to write impersonally ("Employees will receive their checks . . .") or (usually better) naturally ("You will receive your checks . . .").

cisely, and capitalizing or underscoring makes them stand out. When an authenticating signature is necessary, the usual practice is for the writer to initial by the name in the "From" line.

The following memos show usual layout, typical direct style, and typical memo-report situations.

MEMO

October 30, 1985

TO:        Maro Folts, Senior Accountant
FROM:      Deborah Rossback
SUBJECT:   Upcoming 1985 Fall CPA Computer Show

Since we are currently in the market for a computer system, I think we might benefit by attending the 1985 Fall CPA Computer Show in New York, November 19-21.

It first came to my attention in reading this month's issue of the CPA Journal. The New York State Society of CPAs and the Foundation for Accounting Education are sponsoring the show, which features the latest equipment available to assist accountants.

Some of the programs available at the show are:

* Low-cost seminars
* "Hands-on" computer workshops
* Latest systems available

Low-cost seminars

The purpose of the seminars is to assist accountants in understanding computer hardware and software. An additional bonus is that you can earn two units of CPE credit for each seminar attended.

"Hands-on" computer workshops

Apple, DEC, IBM, and Tandy are sponsoring four-times-a-day workshops intended to get you familiar with the actual systems.

Latest systems available

Some of the systems featured will be the Apple Macintosh, IBM PC, DEC Rainbow and Micro PDP-11, and the Tandy 2000.

I would like you to attend the show with me. Please let me know as soon as possible if you would have any schedule conflicts in attending. I feel that it is very important that we examine the systems available before investing in a computer system for our company.

Interoffice Memo

Date:        November 13, 1985
To:          Melissa Burrascano, Marketing Manager
From:        Linda Silva
Subject:     <u>MailPro User's Guide</u>

Here is the user's guide for Joe's MailPro
mailing list program. We wrote it with the least
experienced user in mind. It includes the
objectives and format of the manual, an overview
of the program, a guide for preparing the MailPro
diskettes, and a brief explanation of each program
option.

MailPro is extremely easy to use because the
program leads the user through each step. For this
reason, we did not include a step-by-step
tutorial, as is common in most of our user's
guides. Instead, we placed the emphasis on the
overall flow of the program.

Joe looked the guide over yesterday and gave it
his approval. He said it accurately describes the
program.

If you find any problems, please let me know by
Friday, November 16, so that we can correct them
and still get the completed user's guide to the
Printing Department on time Monday.


     Date:    2/10/86
  Memo to:    Mr. J. G. DeWolfe
     From:    R. R. Fortune    *RR 7*
  Subject:    REDUCING ABSENTEEISM

<u>Conclusion.</u>--Our recent high rate of absenteeism
seems to be a result of too low humidity.
Absentees reported colds or other respiratory
diseases as the causes in 73 percent of the cases.

<u>Humidity in relation to respiratory diseases.</u>--
According to the U.S. Public Health Service, the
higher the humidity in buildings, the lower the
rate of respiratory diseases. You can see this
relationship in Figure 1 on the attached pages.

The explanation is that a high humidity prevents
excessive cooling from evaporation of skin
moisture.

Desirable humidity-temperature relationships.--
Although our 68 degrees is considered the best
temperature, it isn't warm enough for most people
unless the humidity is about 40. Ours is usually
about 20. As Figure 2 of the USPHS study shows, a
humidity above 50 makes most people feel clammy
and a humidity below 30 causes them to feel a
dryness in their noses and throats.

Recommended corrective steps.--To reduce
absenteeism, improve the health of our personnel,
and enhance employee relations, I suggest the
following:

1. Arrange some way to raise the humidity to
   about 40.
2. Purchase one temperature-humidity guide for
   each office. Besides providing a constant
   check on room conditions, these meters will
   remind the employees that you have done
   something about their comfort and health.

The prices of temperature-humidity meters range
from $2 to $200. The cheapest ones are likely to
be inaccurate; but the Wechsler at $18.50 carries
the recommendation of Consumer Reports. It looks
like a small clock with two red hands pointing to
temperature and humidity scales. Hardware,
department, mail-order, and specialty stores carry
it in varied colors to fit the decor of any
office.

## Justification Reports

Another kind of short report often using memo form has its own special
name. Of course, any analytical report could be called a justification
report because it draws conclusions (and makes recommendations if
wanted) and presents facts to justify them. But as used in report writing,
the justification report is a special kind.

Almost invariably the writer makes an original proposal, rather than
a requested study, although the proposal may well be the requested full
write-up of a suggestion that you have dropped in a suggestion box.

It is a direct presentation that gives the recommendation immediately,
followed by concise statements of the most important considerations
and conclusions, before giving detailed explanations and supporting facts.
Thus it *quickly* gives all a busy reader needs to know (*if the reader
trusts the writer*). Probably this point is the main reason for the increasing

popularity of the justification report among executives. But if the reader wants to read the whole explanation, the plan is still good. The reader can follow the details better by having already read the conclusions and recommendations.

You will provide good organization and coverage for your justification reports if you set up the five standard headings and do the following in this order:

1. State the purpose in one sentence. The first part, in phrase or dependent-clause structure, should mention a benefit. The second part should be the recommendation in an independent clause. (Make sure you *do* use a complete sentence—"To save us money" *isn't* a sentence.)

2. State the cost and savings (or advantages) in no more than two sentences. Don't delay the fast movement by long-winded explaining here.

3. In a third part called "Procedure" or "Method of Installation" or whatever is most appropriate, cover concisely such things as necessary space, personnel, training, special materials, time, restrictions (rules, regulations), and interruptions of work. Usually one to three sentences will do.

4. Itemize the conclusions, state them pointedly, and keep them to the minimum number that will cover all aspects. One of them has to be on cost and savings. A frequently overlooked aspect is the goodwill of all the people concerned. The conclusions are not always all benefits; some may point the other way.

5. In a discussion section (sometimes called "Discussion of Conclusions" or "Explanation of Advantages"), give all the details supporting the statements already made—itemized to match the itemized conclusions. Interweave into your explanations enough of your methods to answer the reader's question "How do you know?" This point applies particularly to your method of figuring the cost and savings.

The following typical example illustrates both the plan and the technique:

```
American Camp Corporation

March 19, 198-

MEMO TO: Glenn P. Johnston
   FROM: Julian R. Pinckard
SUBJECT: HOW A VIBRATION MONITORING PROGRAM WOULD
         SAVE MONEY FOR AMERICAN CAMP

Purpose.--To save American Camp at least $200,000
in lost production each year, I recommend that we
initiate a Vibration Monitoring Program for the
paper machine bearings.

Cost and Savings.--Sufficient vibration
monitoring equipment would have a onetime cost of
$38,000; a technician to operate the equipment and
```

monitor the bearings would cost $25,000 yearly. Comparatively, catastrophic bearing failures cost $832,000 in lost production last year.

Method of Initiation.--Southern Bearings, which contracts to supply our spare bearings, would supply the vibration monitoring equipment at a 20 percent discount. A Southern vibration expert would conduct a one-week training program for our technician at no extra cost. Southern would also set up a record-keeping system specifically for our program at this time.

Conclusions.--American Camp would gain three benefits by having a Vibration Monitoring Program for paper machine bearings.

1. Save at least $208,000 per year by avoiding only one catastrophic bearing failure per year.
2. Have 1,600 more mechanic man-hours per year available for our work order backlog.
3. Have a permanent record of bearing vibration readings available for predicting bearing failures.

Discussion of Conclusions.--

1. During the past year, catastrophic bearing failures on the paper machine have averaged $208,000 per failure, as the following calculations show:

| Bearing T. D. No. | T38 | T43 | T61 | Average |
|---|---|---|---|---|
| Lost time (hours) | 22 | 14 | 12 | 16 |
| Production (tons/hr.) | 32.5 | 32.5 | 32.5 | 32.5 |
| Selling price/ton | $400 | $400 | $400 | $400 |
| Cost per failure | $286,000 | $182,000 | $156,000 | $208,000 |

Avoiding one bearing failure could save $208,000.

2. Our present bearing monitoring program consists of two mechanics listening to bearings through a metal rod twice weekly. This amounts to 32 man-hours per week, or 1,600 man-hours yearly. These man-hours would be available for use on the work order backlog. A mechanic's hourly rate is $18; we are already spending $28,800 per year for an inferior bearing monitoring program.
3. The vibration monitoring equipment would

> maintain a permanent record of bearing
> vibration readings in the computer part of
> the equipment. This record would be
> invaluable information for predicting (and
> thus precluding) bearing failures.
>
> Conversely, we cannot compare accurately the
> noise and vibration levels our mechanics' ears now
> pick up twice a week at 800 monitoring points over
> a long period.

You might well notice several specifics about the preceding report:

The writer, who *initiated this idea* (usual for this kind of report), moves fast in presenting the basic idea and facts.

The boss, if trusting the reporter, may approve after reading less than the first half; but reading further provides details if wanted.

The clear, concise, and prominent (by underlining) but easily typed heads serve as guideposts to the reader.

The matched pair of itemizations helps the reader relate pointed conclusions with supporting facts and explanations.

Deserved emphasis justifies the inevitable repetition of cost and saving—the reason you make such proposals, though neither has to be in dollars and cents.

Perhaps most important of all, notice how the writer *concisely but subordinately interweaves* only enough methodology to answer the reader's question "How do you know?"

Although the form of justification reports is commonly memo, it may be letter or some other form such as that illustrated. In letter or memo form the title would serve as the subject line. Of course, the five division heads may be centered heads or sideheads above the text if you prefer. In any case you can easily adapt the Checklist for Letter and Memo Reports for use here.

## Progress Reports

As the name suggests, a progress report tells how you are getting along on a project. It may be a single, special report, but it is often one in a series of required periodic reports. (In a series the last one is the *completion* report.) As a periodic report, a progress report is usually strictly informational. A special progress report is likely to be analytical because of the special problem that called for it.

The general purpose of a progress report is to keep management informed. An owner may want to consider whether to continue as planned, change the plan or methods, or drop the project. A contractor may need to consider such questions as when to order certain materials, whether to increase workers and equipment assigned to a job, and whether to bid on another job.

The basic contents of a progress report are the answers to these questions:

1. Whether the project is on schedule.

2. If the project is not on schedule, why not and what corrective measures are under way or recommended?

3. What will be done next and what the plans and prospects are for completion on schedule.

In answering those questions, a progress report may cover any or all of the purpose and nature of the project (usually the reader already knows), what has been done, the present status, what is now being done, plans and outlook for the future, and unexpected developments. The last may be of major importance if the report is designed to get a decision on a problem that has arisen.

In a series each progress report briefly summarizes former work reported but stresses developments since the preceding report. Progress reports on research projects may or may not include tentative findings and conclusions—depending on the writer's confidence in them and the immediate need for them.

No single plan is always best for a progress report. What is best depends on the whole situation, especially the content, the deserved relative emphasis of parts, and the attitudes and wishes of the reader.

Preferably all the progress reports in a series should follow the same plan. It may be topical by division of the subject (supervision, equipment, materials, and labor; or steps, phases, or divisions of the job); or it may be chronological (by days, weeks, or months; or past, present, and future). One simple plan calls for

1. The transitional elements of background and summary of work already done.

2. The body giving the details of recent progress (since the preceding report, if any).

3. The prophetic or future prospects, in relation to the scheduled completion date.

A more specific but somewhat flexible plan is

1. Quick introduction (purpose and nature of the project, unless known; summary of work to date; status, including any significant results).

2. More detailed summary of earlier progress reported, if any.

3. New progress (work done, methods and personnel, obstacles and what you've done about them) in relation to schedule.

**4.** Realistic forecast (plans in relation to schedule, and recommendations or requests, if any).

More important than *what* plan, in most cases, is that you have *a* plan— a unifying thread to hang your beads on.

Like the plan, the form of progress reports may vary with the circumstances. Short ones usually are in memo or letter form, longer ones in some adaptation of complete report form.

SUBJECT: Monthly Progress Report No. 2 on Orangeville Expressway

Present status

1. Work on the 10.8-mile section of expressway running south to Brownville is on schedule. The final surface is 80 percent complete. We have had no delays during the past month and have regained the two days formerly lost and reported.

2. The 18.4-mile section of expressway running north to Malden remains approximately two weeks behind schedule. We have cleared the right-of-way to Malden, and the roadbed is completed along the first 8.6 miles north of Orangeville.

3. We completed the overpass for U.S. 1 on December 14, ahead of schedule by 18 days.

Expected progress

1. During January we expect to complete the southern link to Brownville except for the drainage preparation and the approaches. Work on them will most likely have to fit in between rains normally expected at this time of year in this area, especially in the valley of Hogtown Creek. Present progress and normal weather expectations suggest that this link will be ready for traffic just before the completion deadline on March 3.

2. During this month we will extend the roadbed along the north section to Malden. The first layer of tar will go on a 5-mile strip, beginning at Orangeville and extending north. Additional workers being hired should ensure completion of this section before the deadline of June 24.

Since progress reports often deal with technical work, you need not be surprised if you fail to understand some things in some of them. If you have trouble with the following, for example, remember that the technical writer did not write for you but for another technical person, who understood perfectly. (The situation accounts for the stiff, formal style.) This report also illustrates a not unusual organization around topics rather than time, while the time sequence and relation to schedule are still clear.

SUBJECT: Progress on Prototype Power Supply for Collins (Job 280)

At the end of three weeks on the two-month schedule for developing a prototype power supply for Collins Radio, the project is two days ahead of the preliminary time estimate. The circuit has been designed and tested for dependability. It is now undergoing final inspection.

1. Results of circuit dependability test.--The test circuit operated within the desired limits of ±2 percent of the desired voltages and currents. Measured by a thermocouple in the 3' × 3' × 3″ base mounting plate of aluminum, the temperature readings (with attendant voltages) ran as follows:

| Hour | Transmit Voltage @ 200 Ma. | Receive Voltage @ 100 Ma. | Bias Voltage @ 65 Ma. | Temperature (Degrees Centigrade) |
| --- | --- | --- | --- | --- |

[No use to waste space in this book on the recorded results.]

2. Printed circuit board.--The basic sketch work for the printed board is finished. The component placement and hookup connections were frozen yesterday. Now the enlarged negative is being drawn. It should be ready for the developer on January 13, five days ahead of the final acceptance date.

3. Chassis design.--The chassis drawings went to Alsfab on January 9. The prototype chassis, with finishes of black anodize on the base and gray enamel on the cover, will be ready on January 14. The dimensions are 6″ × 4″ × 3″ or 2 inches smaller than the maximum Collins allowed.

```
4. Remaining work.--The printed board has to be
   etched and built. It will be tested in the
   small chassis, and the complete unit has to
   be tested for all conditions, including
   vibration, moisture, and temperature. Unless
   now-unseen troubles develop, the present rate
   of progress should continue and the prototype
   should be ready for shipment by February 7.
```

## Credit Reports

A typical credit report, discussed as a letter report in Chapter 6, illustrates those written by individual references about a credit applicant. But various trade associations, credit bureaus, and special credit-reporting agencies have to write so many credit reports that each develops special forms for convenience and the economy of standardization. So no form is standard except within a particular reporting agency such as Dun & Bradstreet (the granddaddy of credit-reporting agencies).

Because the four C's of credit—capital, character, capacity, conditions (explained in Chapter 6)—are the bases for credit decisions, the report invariably covers these topics (but not under these headings). The information includes anything that might have a significant bearing on the credit worth of the subject (individual or firm) and omits anything else—except the legal defenses (as explained in Chapter 6).

## Annual Reports

In accounting to their various publics for their management of funds entrusted to them, corporations and governmental units summarize each year's activities in their annual reports. The mail is thus heavy with these annually from February to May.

Although most annual reports are not short, they are largely factual reporting (informational) rather than problem-solving analytical studies with conclusions and recommendations, discussed in the following chapters. They are periodic reports and are something of a special type and form. Certainly they are the most widely circulated reports (many companies distributing more than a million copies annually), and the writings about them are so numerous that a 10-page bibliography would be easy to compile—and still incomplete.

Since the middle of the 19th century, when annual reporting really started, the number of stockholders has increased greatly. Labor has increased its power and become intensely interested in corporate affairs. Management has seen that its publics include stockholders, the financial community, employees, customers, government officials, and the general public. It has realized that many of these people are interested in more than strictly financial data. They want to know about wages, fringe benefits to workers, products (and research and development of new products), and overall policies—especially company ecological policy.

Annual-report writers today, therefore, try to write so that everyone can understand; and they try to cover topics of interest to all publics. Realizing that people are inclined to take a dim view of things they don't know about, management has shifted to the attitude of telling as many people as possible as much as possible.

Indeed, today the annual report is a major part of the public relations programs of most corporations. They therefore make their reports available to anybody who asks, and some go to considerable expense to make their reports appealing, readable, and informative.

Some have gone so far that the reports seem more like propaganda than objective reports. But the usual annual report is highly informative and quite reliable.

Usually the letter from the president or top executive is both an introduction and a synopsis. And in some cases it is the entire report, running to 10, 12, or more pages.

Most annual-report writers adapt all the devices already mentioned here—readable style, liberal use of meaningful headings, graphic illustrations—to make reading easy and interesting. Mostly they are specialized journalists with the necessary full authority to squeeze any kind of wanted company information out of any office or any person in the firm. Without that authority, you could not write an annual report even if you knew how.

You can find a tremendous volume of material about annual reports (including examples) in a good library, as mentioned in Chapter 10 on application letters, and you can get examples by writing to almost any corporation. The annual report of a company and the 10-K form are sources of information that anybody should read before investing in a company's stock or applying for a job with that company.

## Questions and Exercises

1. For our time and place, arrange (in order of logic and/or importance) the three questions reports answer.

2. Give any other changes (additions or deletions) you think proper in the three questions reports answer.

3. Of the five steps listed in preparing an analytical report, which do you expect to cause you the most trouble?

4. Of the seven things this chapter says a good report writer does for clear, quick, easy reading,
   a. With which do you expect to have the most trouble?
   b. Which do you consider most important and which least important?

5. Justify or disapprove each word in the chapter's one-sentence definition of *report*.

6. For present-day society, arrange in order of importance the six specific ways reports serve.

7. Give any other changes (additions or deletions) you think appropriate in the named six specific ways reports serve.

8. Assume (unless you truly believe) that study of report writing will not help you in the ways explained, and justify your viewpoint.

9. Apply Question 5 to the general function of a report given in this chapter.

10. Play the devil's advocate further by attacking one or more of the eight listed characteristics of reports.

11. Now apply Question 10 tactics to the treatment of names and classes of reports.

# Chapter Outline

# 14

# Preparing Major Managerial Reports

Having learned in Chapter 13 what a major analytical report is, you should be ready to learn *how to prepare one.* You should realize, too, that a good course in business reports is a course in research procedure, in the organization of ideas, in logic, in practical English composition, in supplementary communication devices, in organizational behavior and communication, and in human relations—all in a current and *practical* setting.

Since this chapter is about major analytical reports used as bases for management decisions, you need to realize that such reports involve much learning that shorter ones do not. Though today's efficiency-minded organizations make much more frequent use of the short reports discussed and illustrated in the preceding chapter, the longer analytical reports explained and illustrated here and in the next two chapters are necessary for big decisions.

Furthermore, you need to be aware that only those employees who can prepare these longer and more demanding reports are likely to get on the fast track of the promotion line in almost any business firm. The starting point is a sense of planning.

Preparing a major analytical report is a five-step process: (1) planning the attack on the problem, (2) collecting and documenting the facts, (3) organizing the facts, (4) interpreting the facts, and (5) presenting the report in appropriate form and style. This chapter explains the five steps before the next two chapters explain and illustrate proper style and different forms.

## Planning the Attack

Whether a report is oral or written, planning the attack involves six procedures:

1. Get a clear view of what the central problem is. This procedure requires reflective thinking. It may also require a conference with the

person who needs the report. As a check, you can try writing a *concise* and *interesting* title that *clearly indicates the content and scope.* If you can also put in one sentence a precise statement of the purpose, clearly indicating what problem you are trying to help solve, you have the necessary clear view.

2. Consider conditions that influence the report—the attitude, degree of interest, knowledge, and temperament of the reader or audience; the use to be made of the report; and its importance.

The reader's or listener's temperament and knowledge of the subject have considerable influence on how much background and detailed explanation you need to give, and whether you can use technical terms. Your reputation as an authority and the reader's or audience's attitude will influence how persuasive you need to be. Any known biases and special interests may influence what you should stress and whether you must use impersonal style. Your relationship to the primary receivers will indicate how formal or informal the style should be.

In considering use, remember that reports commonly go up the chain of command for approval and maybe stay in the files for future reference. Therefore they need to be clear to various people years later.

Limitations on time, money, or availability of data may affect how thorough you can be and whether you can use costly plates and charts.

3. Divide the central problem (the *text* of your report) into its elements, the main divisions in an outline of the topic. At this point you merely need a starting guide to what kinds of facts to collect.

The dividing process is a job of finding the natural divisions of the whole. Since an introduction will be Part I in your final outline, for now you can skip it and begin listing your criteria or other major divisions as II, III, IV, . . . or 2.0, 3.0, 4.0, . . . .

If the problem is one of deciding between/among two or more things, the *criteria* are usually the best major division headings. For example, if you are trying to decide which of several jobs to take, on what bases (criteria) do you decide? Maybe

| | | | | |
|---|---|---|---|---|
| II. | Kind of work | | 2.0 | Kind of work |
| III. | Location | | 3.0 | Location |
| IV. | Beginning pay | or | 4.0 | Beginning pay |
| V. | Chances for advancement | | 5.0 | Chances for advancement |
| VI. | Working conditions | | 6.0 | Working conditions |

Some topics common to many business problems are: disadvantages of present system, advantages of proposed system, costs and means of financing, taxes and tax effects, personnel required, effects on goodwill, transportation, method of installation, utilities available and their costs, materials required, time involved, safety, increases or decreases in quality, market, competition, convenience, and availability of land.

4. Raise specific questions about each element. These questions further divide the problem, lead to subheads in your outline, and point more directly toward collecting data for answers.

Put down all you can think of in this planning stage. But so long as you have three to five major divisions between the introduction and the conclusions, don't worry too much about completeness. As you do your research, you'll think about (and add or combine) other major and/or subdivision topics for completeness in the final outline.

If cost is one of the elements in a problem, for example, you want to ask what the costs are for operating one way and what they would be under a revised system. And you might do well to break the questions down further into first costs, operating costs, and depreciation; costs for personnel, for upkeep, and for power; and the like. Specific questions on goodwill might include those about customers, stockholders, workers, and the general public.

5. Take stock of what you already know. You may pose a hypothesis, but don't let it close your mind to other possible solutions. Don't assume that you know the answer until all the facts are in. *You certainly don't want to start out to prove a preconceived notion.*

Get a clear concept of the assumptions you are willing to make. Clearly indicate information gaps you need to fill, and jot down what you think tentatively are the best sources and methods for getting the missing data— company records, experts, books and articles, and maybe the person who faces the problem you're helping to solve.

6. Make a working schedule. Assign estimated time blocks for each of the remaining steps in producing the report: collecting remaining data—and organizing it, interpreting it, and wording the final report. If you plan a survey, remember that mail requires time and that people don't always respond to questionnaires immediately. For any except the most routine kinds of reports, be sure to allow some time for revising early drafts to put the final report in clear, interesting, and inconspicuous style and form.

The first item on the working schedule is the next step in report preparation—collecting the facts.

## Collecting the Facts

For collecting complete and reliable facts, you may use any or all of five approaches. (1) For most problems, careful study of the company records is the most logical, fastest, and cheapest start. Beyond that you have (2) data bases and library research (reading), (3) observation, (4) experimentation, and (5) surveys.

Item 2 provides secondary (secondhand) data, and the others provide primary (firsthand or new) facts. In most cases you should use at least the first two of the methods in such a way as to get at the essential facts and assure their reliability.

## Computer and Library Research

While many (even most) reports in business and industry are short ones (discussed in Chapter 13) dealing with day-to-day operations and not making much use of research beyond company records, high-level managements making major decisions nearly always depend partly on major reports. For them, computer and library research is almost invariably a part.

Indeed, study of various data bases, published books, articles, theses, brochures, speeches, and other reports is the most universally useful method and is *usually the best first step.* When you face any problem of consequence, somebody else has probably faced the same or a closely related problem and written something worthwhile and relevant to your problem.

Besides being the quick and easy way to collect facts, reading may also give a bird's-eye view of the whole problem, acquaint you with terminology and methods you may not have thought of, refer to other good sources, show formerly overlooked natural divisions and aspects of the problem, and in general help you revise your tentative outline and plan of attack.

Reading about almost any topic, however, can be so extensive as to bog you down. To avoid that pitfall, remember that a report is a practical communication concerned with *currently and foreseeably pertinent* data. *It is not* a compendium, an encyclopedia, or a definitive treatment. Hence you can and should be *selective* in your reading for a report—ignoring the long ago, faraway, outdated, or otherwise irrelevant. A good start is to weed out data-base and bibliographic materials by looking at their dates.

To be most helpful in your research, the information here is selective on the basis of dates and on other bases. It gives you the *essence of computer and library-research procedures* or approaches and the main *keys* (guides) to finding what you need. With them—plus a little effort and help when needed from reference librarians—you can find what you need for your report.

Today most large libraries have computer bibliography search help with major retrieval systems. You are able to get fast, current, comprehensive, and precise bibliographic citations and numerical data, sometimes at little or no cost. After you and the librarian arrive at the appropriate data base(s), you enter the terms that describe your topic. The computer can respond on call with a printed bibliography (often with abstracts).

INFORM and MANAGEMENT CONTENTS—perhaps because of their broad scope—are probably the most often used data bases in business research. More specialized ones are PsychInfo (with psychological emphasis), ORBIT (accounting), and Microcomputer Index.

DIALOG (an information retrieval service on science, technology, engineering, social sciences, business, and economics) can be expensive (at $73/hour) for on-line retrieval; but a researcher can keep the costs down by (1) choosing only a few key words for the search, (2) having off-line printouts mailed, or (3) using the evening-hour subscription service for Knowledge Index or BRS/After Dark.

THE NEW YORK TIMES ON LINE provides the full text or abstracts of *Times* articles, and THE INFORMATION BANK offers abstracts of *Times* articles about current affairs and business, economic, and political information.

NEXIS offers worldwide information on banking, finance, and management science.

DISCLOSURE II provides extracts of various reports to the U.S. Securities and Exchange Commission: 10-K and 10-Q (financial), 8-K (corporate changes), 20-F (financial reports, proxy statements, management discussions, and new registrants).

STANDARD & POOR'S NEWS offers news on more than 9,000 publicly owned U.S. companies—earnings, management changes, contracts, mergers, acquisitions, bond descriptions, and corporate backgrounds, subsidiaries, litigations, and officers.

Another helpful device is the cumulative Business Index on computer output microfilm. You can sit in front of this machine and find current sources of information under either subject or author.

Besides these machines and their constantly updated data bases, libraries nearly always have at least three broad categories of materials—reference books, books in the stacks, and periodicals. Chapter 15 digests the most pertinent parts of one annually updated book of particular interest to *students and others interested in career planning and job opportunities*—the 1984–85 *Occupational Outlook Handbook* (U.S. Department of Labor, Bureau of Labor Statistics), with projections on the jobs outlook to 1995.

Some other main categories of regular reference books are:

Encyclopedias *(Americana, Columbia, Encyclopaedia of the Social Sciences, Encyclopedia of Science and Technology,* and the definitive *Encyclopaedia Britannica*). (For any rapidly changing topic, check the publication date.)

Collections of generally useful, up-to-date statistical and other information, surprising in variety and amount (*The World Almanac* and *Facts on File*).

Census reports (U.S. government censuses of agriculture, business, government housing, manufacturing, population, minerals, and other breakdowns. Remember that the U.S. Census is decennial; so the information you read in 1985 is really 1980 data.)

Yearbooks of various countries, trades, and professions (commerce, shipping, agriculture, engineering, and others).

Atlases (especially those by Rand McNally, *Encyclopaedia Britannica, National Geographic,* and Hammond).

Dictionaries (*Webster's Ninth New Collegiate Dictionary, Webster's Third New International Dictionary* [unabridged], and [for etymology particularly] the *Oxford English Dictionary*).

Directories (such as Thomas' for American manufacturers and Ayer's for newspapers and magazines).

Who's who in various fields (including the *Directory of American Scholars, American Men of Science, World Who's Who in Commerce and Industry,* and Poor's *Register of Corporations, Directors, and Executives*).

Statistical source books *(Statistical Yearbook, Statistical Abstract of the United States, Survey of Current Business, County and City Data Book).*

These are just a few main examples of the numerous reference books that are usually in a library. Constance Winchell's *Guide to Reference Books* (recent editions revised by Eugene P. Sheehy) tells about them and many more. Other helpful guides are Herbert W. Johnson's *How to Use the Business Library,* Robert W. Murphey's *How and Where to Look It Up,* Gale Research Company's *Encyclopedia of Business Information Services,* and Rae E. Rip's *United States Government Publications.*

For reports, often the best up-to-date printed sources are periodicals (pertinent articles found through appropriate periodical indexes). Fortunately, one or more of the numerous periodical indexes, both general and specific for almost any field, cover most periodicals. Table 14–1 describes the main current indexes; but if you do not find one for your specific field, look around and/or ask the reference librarian. And if the abbreviations or the system of indexing is not immediately clear to you, the preface always explains.

Whatever library key you use, you need to develop resourcefulness. Often when you look under one topic (say "Business Letter Writing" or "Report Writing"), you will find little or nothing. Don't give up. You have to match wits with the indexer and try to think of other possible wordings for the topic. "Business Letter Writing" might be under "Business English" or "Commercial Correspondence," and "Report Writing" under "Technical Writing" or something else.

When your resourcefulness brings you to a book or article that seems to be useful, a look at the table of contents may quickly tell you whether it will be helpful.

If it seems pertinent, check its *reliability.* Remember that no decision maker wants to base decisions on unsound data, yours or anybody else's. Consider whether (1) the material is outdated, (2) the textual evidence and the reputation of the publisher and of the author reveal any possible slant or prejudice, and (3) the author is a recognized authority in the

**Table 14–1 / Main Current Indexes**

| Title | Coverage | Publication Facts (Most Frequent Issue and Cumulation) |
|---|---|---|
| Accountants' Index | International; technical books and magazines | Quarterly, annually |
| Applied Science and Technology Index | Scientific, engineering and technical American and international magazines | Monthly except July; annually |
| Biological and Agricultural Index | International; books and magazines | Monthly except August; annually |
| Business Periodicals Index | Business, industrial, and trade magazines | Monthly except August; quarterly, annually |
| Chemical Abstracts | International; all phases of chemistry | Biweekly; semiannually |
| Education Index | Professional literature | Monthly except July and August; annually |
| Engineering Index | Domestic and international literature on engineering | Monthly; annually |
| Index Medicus | International; medicine and related fields | Monthly; annually |
| New York Times Index | The news in the paper | Semimonthly; quarterly, annually |
| Predicasts, International | International business activity | Weekly; quarterly, annually |
| Predicasts, U.S. | U.S. business activity | Weekly; quarterly, annually |
| Public Affairs Information Service (PAIS) | Periodicals and government documents and pamphlets of general, technical, and economic interest | Monthly; quarterly, annually |
| Readers' Guide to Periodical Literature | General American magazines | Monthly; annually and/or biennially |
| Science Citation Index | Sources, Citation, Permuterm Subject, Corporate indexes | Monthly; annually |
| Social Science and Humanities Index | Emphasis on history, international relations, political science, and economics | March, June, September, December; annually |
| Social Science Citation Index | International multidisciplinary index to literature of social, behavioral, related sciences | Quarterly; annually |
| Wall Street Journal Index | Corporate and general business news | Monthly; annually |
| Work-Related Abstracts | Labor activities and problems | Monthly; annually |

field. Reading a review in a related journal can help in judging the worth of a book.

If the material (including its date) meets the tests for reliability and relevance, take notes—*a separate card or sheet of paper for each important note.* If you put more than one note to the card, you will have trouble in arranging the cards later because the different notes on a card will not all fit at the same place in the report.

To save time later in arranging notes, at the head of each card put a notation indicating where the information fits in your plan. It may well be the heading in your outline or the divisional symbol from your outline, say Section 3.3.

Of course, if you take a needed note on some topic not in your tentative outline, you make a card for it and add the topic to your outline. Using cards for your notes gives several advantages:

1. They encourage taking concise rather than wordy notes.
2. You can handle them better than sheets of paper—and move them around better for adding to, subtracting from, or reorganizing your original (tentative) outline.

When in doubt, take fuller rather than scantier notes than you think you need; it's easier to omit later than to come back for more.

Some notes you may want to take as verbatim quotations, but usually not. Good researchers do not use many direct quotations—only (1) to gain the impact of the author's authority, (2) to be fair by stating exactly before criticizing, or (3) to take advantage of the conciseness, exactness, or aptness of phrasing. If you do quote, be sure to quote exactly and not change the original meaning.

In most cases you can save words and express the idea better for your purposes if you paraphrase. When you paraphrase, however, be sure not to change the original meaning.

Whether you quote, paraphrase, review, or abstract the article or book, you must list in your bibliography *all* printed sources used directly in the preparation of the report; so you need to take the necessary bibliographic information while you have the book or magazine in hand.

Although bibliography form is not the same for all fields, the usual information is author's name (surname first, for alphabetizing), title of book or article and magazine, publisher and place of publication for books, edition if not the first for books, volume and inclusive page numbers for magazine articles, and the date. For use in citations in the text, record the specific pages used for each note. (A later section, Documenting Your Research, will explain the exact forms for use in your bibliography and notes.)

## Observation

The second method of collecting data—observation—includes not only its usual meanings but also investigation of company records of finances, production, sales, and the like. As such, it is the main method accountants and engineers use for audit, inspection, and progress reports.

The job of collecting data by observation usually involves no particular problem of getting at the facts. The important part is more likely to be *knowing what facts to consider.* This problem requires keeping in mind what your purpose is, so as to notice everything relevant and to relate each pertinent fact to the whole situation.

Observation has the advantage of being convincing, but it has the disadvantage of not getting at motives. That is, it may answer *what* but not find out *why.* For instance, an observer stationed in the aisle of a supermarket may tabulate which brand of detergent each shopper chooses, but that will tell nothing about why each shopper made that choice. And an observer who is not careful may put too much stress on a few isolated cases or may ignore factors (weather, place, time of year, month, week, or day) influencing what was visible for recording.

## Experimentation

For the most part, experimentation is useful in the physical sciences rather than in business and the social sciences. And of course, the methods used vary almost infinitely according to the particular experiment to be done. The basic requirements for reliability in experimentation are four:

*1. Accurate equipment (if used).* If a laboratory balance is inaccurate, or if a tachometer or thermometer misrepresents the facts, the results of an experiment using them will be unreliable.

*2. Skilled techniques.* A technician who doesn't know how to set a microscope won't be able to see an amoeba and, if unable to pipette both accurately and fast, will be no good at Kahn tests. Skilled techniques also include proper selection of specimens for study.

*3. Sufficient controls or repetition of results.* If an experimenter takes two specimens just alike and treats them exactly alike except in one way (perhaps inoculates one, keeping the other for a control), different results (say one gets a disease and the other does not) make a strong start toward convincing us. If repeating the experiment produces exactly the same thing every time (100 percent), only a few repetitions are thoroughly convincing. For very much drop from 100 percent, however, the experimenter has to multiply the number of tests many times to produce similar faith in them through statistical probability.

*4. Testing only one variable at a time.* If soil, seed, and temperature all change in two runs of an agricultural experiment, you cannot attribute different results to any one of them. If you clean your tank and refill with different gasoline, repair your carburetor, and adjust your ignition system all at the same time and your car runs better, you won't know what caused your troubles before.

Experts in certain phases of business can use experimentation that closely parallels laboratory methods if they are careful about their *equipment, techniques,* and *controls.* For example, marketing specialists can test the comparative effects of different advertising campaigns and media, sales promotion devices, prices, and packaging. Their problems of equipment and technique may be more psychological than mechanical and manual, and their controls can be difficult to set up to make sure that only one element changes; but experts can manage all three to assure reasonable reliability. (See Tests and Testing, late in Chapter 8, on testing sales campaigns.)

## Surveys

Often the quality to be tested is not subject to exact laboratory-type examination—the sales appeal of a new car, for example. The only place to get an answer to that is from people. In fact, the survey for fact and opinion is a major method of collecting data for business and social science reports. It is particularly useful in discovering *why* people do certain things and in *forecasting* what will happen (both frequently important jobs of business reports).

Regardless of which of the three kinds of surveys you use—mail questionnaire, personal interview, or telephone interview—research by survey involves certain basic problems, principles, and techniques.

*Determining what people you will survey* is the first problem. In some cases you may decide that the opinions of a few experts will be worth more than the answers of thousands of the general public, as they will be if the problem is technical or professional (say medical or legal). In that case, Chapter 9 and the Interviews Procedures section of Chapter 12 will help you more than the discussion of sampling here. If the whole group involved (called *the universe* by statisticians) is small, you may decide to ask all of them. But in most cases you take a sample.

*How large a sample* you need for sound results then becomes your next problem. The answer will depend on the degree of accuracy required and on the variety of possible answers. For instance, if plus or minus 10 percent is close enough, your sample can be much smaller than if you have to be accurate within a range of 1 percent. And if you have to forecast election returns only in terms of Democratic, Republican, and other votes, your sample can be much smaller than if you have to forecast the purchases of the 50 or more makes and body styles of cars. As an even simpler illustration, you can certainly better predict the fall of a coin (only two choices) than of a pair of dice, with 11 possible readings.

Although a full treatment of sampling theory would require a complete book, statisticians have provided some *simple devices for determining adequate sample size*. The simplest is the split-sample test. You break your sample arbitrarily (that is, to avoid any known differences) into two or more parts. You then compare the results from the various parts. If the results from the partial samples are acceptably close together, the results from the total sample will be acceptably reliable.

More precise checks on the adequacy of sample size require only a little mathematics and procedures explained in any beginning book on statistics. Judgment, a study of statistics, and observation of professional pollsters' accuracy based on surprisingly *small* samples, however, show two things: (1) most people think a sample must be larger than it (statistically) needs to be, and (2) most people give too little attention to the other equally important requirement for a sound sample—stratification.

*Assuming a stratified sample is basic.* Even your adequate *sample must be stratified* (sometimes imprecisely called *representative*) or your results can go wild. That is, *each segment of the universe must appear in the sample with the same percentage as in the universe.* According to sampling theory, this will be the result if you take a large enough *random* sample (one in which each item in the universe has an equal chance of getting into the sample). In practice, however, you often have trouble making sure you really have a random sample. Unsuspected selective factors may work to produce an unstratified (and hence unsound) sample.

To avoid such a possibility, you can (as professionals usually do) use stratified sampling if you have data showing the proportions of different segments in your universe. Fortunately, you usually do. Just as a college registrar's office knows the number of students in different classes, majors, age groups, grade-point groups, and the like, the statistical sourcebooks provide breakdowns of people in nearly every imaginable way. Whatever group you may want to sample, you probably can find the proportions of the different segments making up the universe.

The U.S. Census Bureau, for example, similarly breaks down its population figures. Remember, though, that the Bureau's real head count is every 10 years (those ending in 0—1980, 1990, . . .). Figures between those years are only estimates—but good ones. If 50 percent of your universe are farmers and 70 percent telephone subscribers, half your sample must be farmers and 70 percent telephone subscribers.

*Adequate size and stratification together make a sound sample.*

A sound sample can still produce unsound results, however, unless your techniques of getting answers from it are also sound. If you start out by surveying a minimum sound sample but get answers from only half of it, the sample of actual answers is unsound because it is too small. If you survey more than enough and get a large enough sample of answers, but 100 percent of one stratification group answers and only half of another group answers, your returns are not stratified and hence are not reliable.

*How can you induce people to answer survey questions?* Sometimes a respondent is already so much interested, because the benefit is obvious, that you can begin directly with the request. At other times you have a selling job to do, as in persuasive requests (Chapter 9).

Whether you are using a mail questionnaire, a personal interview, or a telephone interview makes little difference in the approach. But to make a direct inquiry when you need a persuasive request may result in decreased returns and hence an unreliable sample.

Fundamentally, your persuasive method is the same as in persuading people to do anything: *Show them a benefit to themselves.* It may be a gift or reward, direct payment of a fee, or appeals to pride and prestige (but not obvious flattery), appeals to their desire for better service or more efficiency in their kind of work, or the possibility of their getting answers to some questions or solutions to problems.

The last two are frequently the best (because they avoid suggesting a bribe or being too mercenary, as the first two might), and they are more immediate and tangible than the others. For instance, personnel officers who read lots of poor application letters are likely to answer a textbook writer's or a teacher's questions about preferences in application letters—because of the possibility that they may as a result get more good applications and thereby make their work easier. A frequent method of inducing answers is the offer of a copy or digest of the survey results.

A big point to remember in making persuasive requests is to show a benefit *before* making the request. Then if you explain who is making the survey and why; make answering as easy, quick, and impersonal as possible; assure respondents that you will honor restrictions they put on use of the information; and tell pointedly just what you want them to do, enough people will usually do it to make your results reliable. Skilled approaches, both oral and written, often bring percentages of answers that surprise the untrained who have tried their hands and failed.

Chapter 9 explains in detail how to induce people to respond as you wish. If you feel more adept at talking on the phone than at writing a persuasive letter, you might consider calling people in your selected sample. If you do, the principles in Chapter 9 apply to the oral persuasion too.

The approach you use will be a major factor in determining your success, but *the questions you ask will affect both the percentage of returns and the worth of the answers.* For that reason, **writers of questionnaires and people planning interviews need to keep in mind the following main principles professionals use:**

1. Ask as few questions as you can to get the necessary information. Don't ask other people for information you should have dug up for yourself. (One kind of duplication is permissible: Double-check questions that get at the same information from different approaches as a check on the validity of answers.)

2. Ask only what you might reasonably expect to be answered. Requests for percentages and averages are either too much work or over the heads of many people. Questions requiring long memory may frustrate and bring erroneous results. And most people don't even know *why* they do many things.

3. Make your questions as easy to answer as possible (perhaps by providing for places to check); but provide for all likely answers (at least the "no opinion" answer and perhaps the blank to be filled as the respondent wants).

4. Make your questions perfectly clear. To do so, you may sometimes have to explain a bit of necessary background. If you ask "Why do you use X peanut butter?" you may get "It is cheapest," "A friend recommended it," and "I like its smooth texture and easy spreading" from three respondents. If you really want to know how the customer first learned of X, you should phrase the question in such a way as to get answers parallel to the second. If you are interested in the qualities that users like (as in the third answer), you should ask that specific question. Also, double-barreled questions ("Did you see X, and did you like it?") frustrate the reader.

5. Carefully avoid leading questions—questions that suggest a certain answer.

6. Insofar as possible, phrase questions to avoid the "prestige" answer—the respondent's answering to make the best impression.

7. Try to avoid unnecessary personal prying. When personal questions are necessary, make them as inoffensive as possible (for instance, by asking which named *income* or *age* or *educational group* the respondent falls in).

8. Arrange questions in an order to encourage response—easier or impersonal ones at first, related ones together to stimulate interest and aid memory.

9. Insofar as possible, ask for answers that will be easy to tabulate and evaluate statistically; but don't sacrifice shades of meaning or intensity of feeling. Often the most helpful answers a survey brings are those to open-ended questions; but they will reduce your returns.

Often *scaled* answer forms can bring responses desirably showing intensities of feelings that are still easy to tabulate and evaluate statistically.

For example, a form asking for students' evaluations of professors might use a labeled continuum, thus: "On (a certain aspect of teaching), how would you rate Professor X?"

| Excellent | Very Good | Good | Average | Poor | Bad | Terrible |
|-----------|-----------|------|---------|------|-----|----------|
| +3 | +2 | +1 | 0 | −1 | −2 | −3 |

***Which type of survey and on what bases?*** After you have decided on the questions you want answered, your next problem is deciding whether to use mail questionnaires, personal interviews, or telephone interviews. No one type is always best. The main *bases for your making a wise decision* are:

*1. The kind and amount of information requested from each respondent.* People are more willing to *tell* you personal information—and more of it—than they are to put personal facts in writing or to do very much writing. On the other hand, factual information (especially statistics, percentages, and averages) that the respondent may not know at the moment would come best in writing because the respondent can take a little time to dig up the information for a mail questionnaire.

*2. Costs.* Two facts about the survey example affect the choice of method on the basis of cost—its size and its dispersal. Within one telephone exchange, if your group is not large, the telephone is the cheapest method; but if long-distance charges are involved, they become prohibitive unless the group is small. The mail questionnaire has the advantage of wide geographic coverage at no additional cost; and the bigger the group, the greater the advantage, because duplicating and (even two-way) mailing of copies of a good set of questions cost little. The personal interview is almost always the most costly method (mainly in interviewer's time) unless the group is both small and close together.

You need to consider cost per return, however; and since the mail questionnaire usually brings in the lowest percentage of returns, its advantages may not be so great as at first thought unless a good covering letter and set of questions mailed at an opportune time induce a high percentage of answers.

*3. Speed in getting results.* If you must have the answers today, you can get some of them by telephone (and by personal interview if your sample is not too large and the people are close together); but you can't get them by mail.

*4. Validity of results.* Each of the three kinds of survey has advantages and disadvantages in terms of validity. Either the personal or the telephone interview can better clear up any confusion about questions and thereby get appropriate answers. In addition, the personal interviewer may pick up supplementary information (such as the general look of economic conditions around the home and incidental remarks of the talker) that will provide a check on answers given.

On the other hand, in personal and telephone interviews people may give you offhand answers to get rid of you because the time of the call is inconvenient; and they may answer according to what they think is your view (playing the prestige-answer game). Moreover, high-pressure personal selling, obscene phone calls, and other abuses have made many people wary of personal and telephone calls, thus making oral surveys increasingly difficult and complicating the job of keeping samples stratified (and thus valid). Also, certain segments of the population have fewer telephones than others and thereby skew a telephone sample—just as the fact that certain kinds of doors (maybe apartment dwellers'), being especially hard to get into, skews samples for personal interviewers.

Perhaps the biggest advantage' of mail questionnaires is that people can choose the most convenient time to answer and are therefore more likely to answer thoughtfully. That includes taking time to check records for information.

Moreover, everybody has a mailing address where a mail questionnaire can get in; so in view of costs and time, the mail questionnaire is less likely to be limited to a too-small group or one that is geographically or economically limited. But those who choose not to answer may be a special group (say the less educated who don't like to write) and may thereby unstratify your carefully planned sample.

5. *Qualifications of the staff.* Some people who can talk well and thus get information may not be able to write a good questionnaire and covering letter; and, of course, the opposite may be true. Even some good talkers have poor telephone voices that discourage that method. And others have appearances that discourage personal interviews.

If you select an adequate and stratified sample, induce people to answer by showing a benefit, ask good questions, and use the type of survey most suitable for your situation, surveys can get you a great variety of valuable information for your reports.

## Documenting Your Research

Since a major report is usually the basis for an executive decision that may be costly if it is wrong, business executives rightfully expect reports to answer at least two, important questions: What are the facts? How do you know? In an analytical report, two more questions arise: What do you make of (conclude from) these facts? Then what do you recommend that I do?

The second question means that the report must provide evidence that the information is trustworthy. Usually you do that by explaining your sources and methods of research as a basis for judgment about the report's soundness. The only exceptions are in the reports of unquestionable authorities (whose word would be taken at face value) and in cases where the methods and sources are obvious.

In short reports usually you can best explain the sources and methods in incidental phrases along with the presentation of data, as in the following:

> Four suppliers of long standing report him as prompt pay and . . . .
>
> Standard quantitative analysis reveals 17 percent carbon . . . .
>
> Analysis of the balance sheet reveals . . . .

Notice how the illustrative short reports in Chapter 13 interweave the references to methodology of research and to published sources—right within the text of the report.

In major managerial reports, though the introduction explains methods and mentions printed sources in general, the bibliography, footnotes, and/or other citations in the text explain more specifically. Such explanations and citations are basic for two important reasons: (1) to back up or validate your information and (2) to avoid the accusation of plagiarism or stealing another person's ideas and/or words.

At least, any report writer except the recognized authority precludes what one reader expressed as "the distrust I have of those people who write as if they had a private line to God."

Since you often use some published materials and/or special research methods in collecting data for major reports, citing those sources and/or explaining those methods is an important part of assuring your reader about the soundness of the facts. By paraphrasing or quoting a recognized authority, you add support for and impact to your statements.

When you use another author's special ideas, facts, or wording, however, to avoid plagiarism you have a moral (and in some circumstances a legal) obligation to give credit where it is due. Though you do *not need to cite* your source for information (as distinct from the exact wording) that is "in the public domain"—information that is (1) common knowledge, (2) obvious, or (3) readily available in many sources of the kind (such as dictionaries and encyclopedias)—otherwise you cite your sources by one of the somewhat varied but established systems.

Unfortunately, *bibliography* forms are not standardized. For the past 50 years the trend in documentation forms has been toward simplicity and efficiency, especially in business, industry, and the sciences.

This statement does not, however, mean less documentation, but more efficient forms. *So unless you are sure that both you and your reader(s) understand and prefer other generally accepted forms used in your field (in the main professional journals, for example), you should use the following content and form.*

Readers generally expect a bibliographical entry to give the author's name, the title (of both an article and the journal), and (for books) the edition (if not the first), the publisher and place of publication, and the volume (if more than one); the volume number (if on the magazine) and all page numbers for magazine articles; and the date of publication for anything (noting n.d. for "no date" when you can't find it).

Preferably the pieces of information are in that order. Some people omit the publisher of a book or put it in parentheses with the place of publication. In some specialized fields even the date or title may come first. Usually the several entries in a bibliography appear in alphabetical order by author's name, which is inverted for the purpose.

Unless you choose to follow the well-established form of your special field, you should be up-to-date and enter books as

```
Wilkinson, C. W., J. H. Menning, and C. R.
Anderson (eds.), Writing for Business, Third
Edition, Richard D. Irwin, Homewood, Illinois,
1970.
```

Even in this simple entry, you have three somewhat unusual items:

1. Three people worked on the book, but the name of only the first needs to be inverted for alphabetizing.

2. Since the "authors" were editors rather than writers of the book, you see eds. right after their names.

3. Because the book is not the first edition, the entry tells which it is. Some writers would add, at the end, 369 pp., $9.95—two pieces of information usual in reviews of new books but not in bibliographies.

The recommended form for magazine articles is

```
Gallagher, William J., "Technical Writing: In
Defense of Obscurity," Management Review, 55:34-
36, May 1985.
```

If you want to be more helpful to the reader, you may annotate your bibliography with brief notes indicating the content and your evaluation of the book or article:

```
Darlington, Terry, "Do a Report on It," Business,
94:74, 93, May 1985.
Good treatment of report functions and short,
simple, direct approach for report writing.
Especially good on five-point plan for organizing.
```

You need to note two points here:

1. Enclose titles of parts like magazine articles and book chapters in quotes; but underscore titles of whole publications (italics in printed copy) with the first word and all others except articles *(a, an, the),* prepositions, and conjunctions capitalized.

2. Listings of magazines do not include the publisher and place but do include the volume number (if available) and all page numbers, hyphenated for inclusive pages and separated by commas for jumps in paging.

If no author's or editor's name appears on a book or article, the entry usually appears in the alphabetical list by first word of the title (not counting *a, an,* and *the*). Sometimes, however, a writer chooses to alphabetize by publisher instead—especially pamphlets, booklets, reports, and the like put out by corporations and governmental agencies. Thus you will see entries like

```
"Are Your Memos on Target?" Supervisory
Management, 9:39-40, August 1984.
Texaco, Inc., Annual Report of 1985.
U.S. Department of Agriculture Bulletin 1620,
Characteristics of New Varieties of Peaches,
U.S. Government Printing Office, 1985.
```

(Note, in the first illustration, that when a comma and a stronger mark—question mark or exclamation point—need to come at the same place, you simply omit the comma.)

At those points in the report text where you make use of printed sources, you also tell the reader about them by specific references or citations. One way of doing so is *footnoting,* which is decreasing in use (especially in business and technical writing) because footnotes heckle readers. A better method for most situations, now coming into wider and wider use, is to interweave the minimum essentials of a citation subordinately right into the text, like this:

```
Wilkinson says ("The History and Present Need of
Reports," The ABCA Bulletin, 19:14, April 1982)
that reports . . . .
```

Still, footnote citations (indicated by raised numbers in the text and matching numbers before the notes) may be necessary in some cases to keep long, interwoven citations from making the reading difficult. Remember, however, that footnotes at the bottom of the page (or worse, grouped at the end) are more interruptive to a reader than parenthetical citations.

The first footnote or interwoven citation, plus whatever bibliographical information may appear in the text, is a complete reproduction of the bibliographical entry with two minor changes: The author's name is in the normal order (given name or initials first), and the page reference is the specific page or pages used for that particular part of the report. Accordingly, first footnote references to a magazine and a book would be as follows:

[1]H. R. Jolliffe, "Semantics and Its Implications for Teachers of Business Communication," Journal of Business Communication, 1:17, March 1983.

[2]C. W. Wilkinson, Dorothy C. Wilkinson, and Gretchen N. Vik, Communicating through Writing and Speaking in Business, Ninth Edition, Richard D. Irwin, Homewood, Illinois, 1986, p. 469.

Later references to the same works can be shortened forms with the specific page number(s) and just enough information for the reader to identify the source. Usually the author's surname, the title, and the page(s) will do, whether interwoven in the text, put in footnotes, or divided between the two. Thus later references could be as shown below:

Jolliffe ("Semantics and Its Implications," p. 18) makes the point that . . . .
Wilkinson et al. (Communicating . . ., p. 29) discuss letters in three broad categories:. . . .

The old practice of using Latin abbreviations (such as op. cit., ibid., and loc. cit., to mention only a few), which have long confused many people, is disappearing along with footnotes. Except in scholarly writing for other scholars, the usual current practice is to use English words and a few standard abbreviations like p. for page and pp. for pages—preceding page numbers that do not follow volume numbers.

The newest and probably the best bibliographical citation system—coming into wider use, especially in science and industry, probably because of its efficiency—involves these steps.

1. Numbering the listings in the bibliography after you've arranged them in the usual way.

2. Using these numbers and the specific page number(s), usually separated by colons and enclosed in parentheses, at the points in the report requiring documentation—usually just before the periods at the ends of sentences, like this (4:39).

3. Explaining the system at its first use, by a footnote or parenthetical note something like "(4:39, meaning p. 39 of Item 4 in the Bibliography)."

*Letters, speeches, and interviews used as sources of information do not belong in a bibliography.* The method for citing them is by footnoting or by interweaving in the text the information about the giver and the receiver of the information, the form, the date, and any other pertinent facts.

Although these are the main points about documentation, several large books and many smaller ones, plus numerous pamphlets, deal extensively with this subject. As further illustration of bibliography forms, and as sources of more detailed information about them, footnotes, and other details of form, here are the major publications:

American Psychological Association, *Publication Manual* (Third Edition), Washington, D.C., 1983.

*A Manual of Style* (Thirteenth Edition), University of Chicago Press, Chicago, 1982.

*The MLA Handbook,* Modern Language Association of America, Washington, D.C., 1977.

*U.S. Government Printing Office Style Manual* (Revised Edition), U.S. Government Printing Office, Washington, D.C., 1973.

Turabian, Kate L., *A Manual for Writers of Term Papers, Theses, and Dissertations* (Fourth Edition), University of Chicago Press, Chicago, 1973.

\*    \*    \*    \*    \*

Beyond that, the preparation of a report depends on the particular form to be used; and the form you choose should be the one best adapted to the situation. (The cases for major reports of different kinds are all in Appendix A.)

## Organizing the Findings

However you collect and record the necessary facts for your report, you have to organize them for interpretation (in an analytical report) and for presentation. At this point, however, you need concern yourself only with *organizing the text* of the report. (Company and/or standard plans—as explained and graphically illustrated in Chapters 15 and 16— will take care of the contents and organization of the other parts and the overall organization.)

Because the text is the essence of the report, *you do not have a section heading for it.* The title of the whole report serves that function. The divisions of the text, then, usually constitute sections 2.0, 3.0, 4.0., and so on—where you present all your facts, explanations, and reasons leading to your conclusions and recommendations. According to the instructions in an earlier section (Planning the Attack, items 3, 4, and 5), you should already have set up the organization of your text as a tentative and probably incomplete plan to guide you in collecting data. If you didn't read and follow those instructions, you need to do so now.

That preliminary plan is the starting point for doing the present job—making a final outline as a guide to interpreting and presenting the facts.

Basically, organizing (outlining) is the process of putting related things into groups according to common characteristics *and your purpose* and then putting the groups into a desirable sequence. In the process you may find that you need to revise your tentative outline because the information classified according to your first plan is not logically or psychologically arranged for good presentation. For instance, you will want to *make sure that things the reader or audience needs to compare are close together.*

Certainly you need to check your tentative plan before going further. You may now be able to see enough interpretations of your data to make a sentence outline, as you couldn't earlier, because sentences require you to *say something about* the topics. If you can, it will be easier to follow while wording the report, it will force more careful thinking, and it will give the essence of your report (not just the list of topics discussed but the key statements about those topics). Because of its helpfulness in phrasing the report, you may want to make a full-sentence outline (like a lawyer's brief or a précis) for close-knit logical wording, and then change it to one of the less cumbersome forms (later discussed) for final presentation.

**Grouping for Outlines.** Whether you use full sentences or noun-phrase topics, close adherence to the following principles is necessary for a good final plan (outline):

1. *Stick to the one basis of classification* implied in your title and purpose as you break down any topic (such as your text) into its parts. For example, on the basis of credit hours earned, college students are freshmen, sophomores, juniors, seniors, or graduates. You can't logically classify them as juniors, Protestants, and Democrats. Such a procedure shifts bases in helter-skelter fashion from credit hours earned to religion to politics. You would have overlapping topics, whereas *the divisions of an outline should be mutually exclusive.*

If your title is "Reasons for (or Why) . . .," the major divisions of your text can't logically be anything but the list of reasons. If the title is something like "Factors Influencing . . ." or "Ways to . . .," each major division of the *text* will have to be one of those factors or ways. The title "Market Factors Indicating Why a Rexwall Drugstore in Savannah Would Sell More than One in Charleston" commits you to show for each subject—Charleston and Savannah—market factor evidence supporting your thesis. (This does not forbid giving the introduction, conclusions, and recommendations similar major-division status and numbers, though they are not parts of the text you're organizing.)

Your proper basis for dividing the text will depend on the nature of the problem. It may be the parts of a whole, the factors to be considered, time periods, space areas, and many others. Cost-benefit and before-after analyses sound good but are too simplistic, and they defeat juxtaposition too much, for good report writing about more than simple problems. Organizing on the basis of how or where you got the information is never desirable—except possibly in a simple comparison study to evaluate the method or source. Even then, however, you have a better way.

*In outlines of comparison leading to a choice*—which are the major kinds of major managerial reports—*use the criteria* (bases on which the choice depends) rather than the subjects (the things between or among which you must choose) *as the major divisions*. Your criteria are the things on which your choice will stand or fall, and hence they deserve the emphasis.

In evaluating a Cadillac and a Lincoln, for example, you should use both names frequently in your organization scheme, but neither would be a major heading as such. Your major headings would be the tests you decide to apply: *costs* (initial and operating—and possibly trade-in value), *performance, comfort, safety,* and *appearance.* Under each head you would have to analyze each subject (Cadillac and Lincoln).

2. *Follow one good system* to show the relationship of all the parts. The increasingly used system in business and industry is the decimal system. It has become popular because it immediately tells exactly where a reader is in a report and (since it developed in the physical sciences) because some people think it lends an air of scientific authority. The older Roman system of outline symbols still appears in business use, however, and is still popular in many areas of education.

| **Decimal** | | **Roman** | | |
|---|---|---|---|---|
| 1.0. | | I. | | |
| | 1.1. | | A. | |
| | 1.2. | | B. | |
| | 1.3. | | C. | |
| 2.0. | | II. | | |
| | 2.1. | | A. | |
| | | 2.1.1. | | 1. |
| | | 2.1.2. | | 2. |
| | 2.2. | | B. | |
| 3.0 (etc.) | | III. (etc.) | | |

You can use the decimal system without indentation—but the time and space you save yourself cost readers in speed and ease of reading; so they prefer indentation. Many writers and readers also prefer to use only the first decimal point.

3. *Cover all categories*—that is, all the divisions at any level must add up to the whole indicated by your heading over those divisions.

All the Roman-numeral divisions together must add up to everything covered by the title, and all the capital letters under Section II must total the II data (and the same if you use decimal notation).

4. *Use no single subdivisions.* If you start to divide section 2.1 by putting a subhead 2.1.1, you must logically have at least a subhead 2.1.2; you can't divide anything into one part.

5. *Use parallel grammatical structure for parallel things.* All the Roman-numeral divisions are parallel things; all the capital-letter divisions under one of them are parallel, but not necessarily parallel with those under another Roman-numeral division. They may all be complete sentences, all nouns or noun phrases (probably the best), or all adjectives.

6. *Consider the psychological effects (reading ease) of the number of parts* in any classification. Three to seven is the optimum range.

7. *Organize for approximate balance.* That is, try not to let some of your divisions cover huge blocks of your subject and others almost nothing.

**Sequencing Effectively.** Put the parts of each breakdown into the sequence most appropriate for your purposes and the situation. The *overall sequence or plan of a report* is usually one of the following:

1. *Direct (sometimes called deductive), giving the big, broad point first and then following with supporting details.* This plan arouses more interest than some other plans because it gets to the important things quickly, saves the time of the busy person who wants only the big idea, and provides a bird's-eye view that helps in understanding the rest more intelligently. It is therefore desirable if the report's conclusion is likely to be welcomed or if the reporter is an authority whose unsupported word would be readily accepted, at least tentatively. But it is psychologically unsound where it risks the danger of objections at first and continued resistance all the way through.

2. *Inductive (sometimes called scientific), giving a succession of facts and ideas leading up to the big conclusions and recommendations at the end.* The inductive plan is slow and sometimes puzzling until the conclusion tells where all the detailed facts lead; but it is necessary in some cases for its strong logical conviction, especially when you expect opposition to the conclusions and recommendations that are coming.

3. *Narrative (usually chronological accounts of activities).* If no good reason argues against it—but usually one does—the chronological sequence is both the easiest to organize and the easiest to follow. The main objections are that it doesn't allow you to stress important things (it may have to begin with minor details, and the biggest things may be buried in the middle) and that it doesn't allow you to bring together related things that have to be seen together for clear significance.

The somewhat similar spatial arrangement (from top to bottom, front to back, left to right, or by geographic area) is usually the obvious choice if it is appropriate for the material.

4. *Weighted (that is, according to importance).* The weighted plan's basic advantage is that it enables you to control emphasis by putting the most important points in the emphatic positions, first and last.

For certain kinds of material and conditions, arrangement according to difficulty or from cause to effect (or the reverse) may be the wise choice. Similarly, some kinds of things almost have to appear in a definite order for the necessary logical sequence (the way proving a geometry proposition does).

Whatever the plan of organization, in the final presentation you will need to use meaningful headings and subheads, topic sentences or paragraphs, standard transitional words and sentences, and summarizing sentences to indicate organization, to show the coherence of parts in the organization, and to tell the hurried or half-attentive reader or listener the essence of the sections. The summarizing sentences, however, grow naturally out of your interpretation of the facts.

## Interpreting the Facts

If the report is just informational, you are ready to put it in final form when you have organized the facts; but if it is to be analytical, you have to study the facts and interpret them into conclusions and/or recommendations.

Interpretation is probably the hardest part of report preparation to teach—or to learn. Realizing six points, however, can help:

1. Without substantial, verifiable facts, you have nothing worthwhile to interpret. The solution is to go back to the data-collecting step and get the facts.

2. A fact alone is not worth much. Significance comes only from relating two or more facts. *Seeing* formerly unknown relationships requires *imaginative intelligence* and *careful analysis of two or more different sets of facts at the same time.* Whether the analysis is simply logical reasoning or mathematical (usually statistical) figuring, a necessary ingredient is imagination.

For example, consider how George J. Van Dorp, water commissioner of Toledo, developed his method of determining the public interest in TV programs. As a fan of a very popular TV program, Van Dorp noticed that pressure in the water mains ran consistently high during the program. When commercials interrupted the show, the water pressure dropped appreciably—for about the duration of the ads—then went up again when the show returned to the screen.

Many people seeing the changes in water pressure *and* the beginning, interrupted, and ending times of the program would never have *seen* a relationship between the two sets of clear facts. Van Dorp had the *imaginative intelligence* to *see* the relationships—to interpret facts.

3. Since the report user wants a sound rather than a prejudiced or illogical basis for decisions, one consideration (beyond the ability to see relationships) is *objectivity in making the interpretation*. Since you are a human being, your whole background and personality influence your thinking; you therefore must strive to be as objective and logical as possible and to avoid the temptation to stretch the truth a bit for dramatic effect. The following two basic kinds of attitudes require attention if your report is to be unbiased:

a. *Preconception*. A reporter who jumps to a conclusion and closes out other possibilities before collecting and evaluating the facts will, under the influence of that preconception, overlook or undervalue some facts and overstress others. Such is the danger of working from a hypothesis—unless you check results by pursuing a directly opposite hypothesis.

b. *Wishful thinking*. If you have a strong desire that the investigation turn out a certain way (because of a money interest or any other kind), you will find it hard not to manipulate facts to make them lead to the desired result. Such attitudes can also lead to unintentionally slanted wording, since they will (even subconsciously) affect your choice of phrasing.

4. You must avoid the pitfalls of logical thinking (called *fallacies*).

a. Avoid using sources (both books and people) that may be unreliable because of basic prejudice, because they are uninformed, or because they are out of date. Further, your sources may have misquoted or misinterpreted *their* sources—a common occurrence. Although you should have checked these things in collecting your data, you might well examine them again in the interpreting process.

b. Avoid making hasty generalizations—that is, drawing conclusions on the basis of too little evidence (maybe too small a sample, too short a trial, too little experience, or just too few facts). Remember that sometimes you can draw no logical conclusion from the available facts.

c. Avoid using false analogies. True analogies (comparisons of things that are similar in many ways) are effective devices for explaining unknown things. You simply teach the unknown by comparing it to a similar known. But be sure you are really comparing similar things, or the truth may slip out through a small hole of difference.

d. Avoid stating faulty cause-and-effect relationships, such as

(1) Assigning something to one cause when it is the result of several. Comparisons that attribute the differences to one cause need careful controls to be valid. Otherwise, some unseen (or intentionally ignored) cause may deserve much of the credit for the difference.

(2) Attributing something to an incapable cause (for instance, one that came later).

(3)  Calling something a cause when it is merely a concurrent effect—a symptom, a concomitant.

e. Avoid begging the question—just assuming, rather than giving evidence to support, a point that is necessary to the conclusions drawn.

f. Avoid using emotional suasion (usually characterized by strong and numerous adjectives and adverbs, or any kind of emotionally supercharged language like that of a defense attorney pleading with a jury) to win your point.

g. Avoid failing to distinguish, and make clear, what is substantiated fact, what is opinion, and what is merely assumption.

5. Another important *consideration* in making your interpretation is discovering the really significant things to point out. State them pointedly, and itemize them if they run to more than three or four. You can then turn them into practical recommendations that are general or concrete and specific, according to the instructions you get with the report assignment. Itemization will usually help make the recommendations desirably pointed too.

Causes, symptoms, effects, and cures are always important. So (in terms of graphic statistical data) are high points, low points, averages, trends, and abrupt changes (especially if you can explain their causes). Without going into disturbingly technical statistics, you can probably hold interest with such measures of central tendencies as the mean (call it average), median (midpoint), and mode (most frequent item). Sometimes you might well use indicators of dispersion, such as standard deviation, range, and the *-iles* (percentiles, deciles, quartiles).

Appropriate comparisons can often give significance to otherwise nearly meaningless isolated facts. For instance, the figure $7,123,191 given as profit for the year has little meaning alone. If you say it's 7 percent above last year's profit, you add a revealing comparison; and if you add that it's the highest ever, you add another. If your volume of production is 2 million units, that means less than if you add that you're now 4th in the industry as compared with 10th two years earlier.

Breaking down big figures into little ones also helps make them meaningful, especially if you also humanize/individualize them. For instance, you may express capital investment in terms of so much per employee, per share of stock, per stockholder, or per unit of production. The national debt becomes more meaningful if you give it per citizen; the annual budget makes more sense as a per-day or per-citizen cost; library circulation means more in terms of number of books per student.

Often a simple ratio helps, such as "Two fifths (40 percent) of the national budget is for defense." A pie chart showing the percentage going to each category in the whole budget would be especially meaningful.

6. Whatever the analysis reveals, you need to state it precisely. Guard carefully against stating assumptions and opinions as facts. And select graduations in wording to indicate the degree of solidity of your conclusions. The facts and analyses will sometimes (but rarely) prove a point conclusively. They are more likely to lead to the conclusion that . . . , or indicate, or suggest, or hint, or point to the possibility, or lead one to wonder—and so on down the scale. Usually you can do better than stick your neck out (by claiming to prove things you don't) or draw your neck in too far (with the timorous last three of these expressions).

\* \* \* \* \*

But phrasing the ideas well is a problem for the fifth and last step in preparing and presenting a report—writing it or speaking it.

You should understand clearly that everything said so far is applicable to both written and spoken reports. The steps in preparing the report are the same. You must plan your attack, collect the facts you need, organize your findings, interpret the data if appropriate, and finally put your report in the proper style. Only in this last step do written and oral reports begin to differ materially.

So don't think you should put an oral report in fully written form and read it. As Chapter 11 points out, reading a speech is usually the worst kind of oral presentation. As you develop your outline and assemble notecards, you will be generating the notes from which you should speak. In fact, your speech notes should be all of your divisions and subdivisions, with enough information on each so that you will remember all you want to say.

## Questions and Exercises

1. a. Briefly identify a two- or three-way decision somebody (preferably you) has made or now faces and the three main criteria.
   b. What main kinds of new information were necessary?
   c. What methods and sources did the decision maker use to get the new information?

2. What is the main danger in using population figures from the U.S. Census?

3. a. If you were considering changing your major and/or your career plans, what one printed source would you go to for the best information on the immediate-future picture in your new field(s) of interest?
   b. If you wanted to use the term in an important course paper, to what book would you go to determine whether to write *data bases, data-bases,* or *databases?*

4. In collecting data for a report,
   a. What are the four requirements for a valid experiment?
   b. What are the two requirements for a valid sample of people for a survey?

5. In documenting your research,
   a. What five pieces of information (in order) do you give in your bibliography about a book you used?
   b. What six pieces of information (in order) do you give for a magazine article?

6. In organizing the text of major reports, what main sequences are useful for the major divisions between I (Introduction) and the Conclusions?

7. For information on a current topic, would you start looking in the card catalog or in one of the indexes?

8. You have many indexes to choose from to find information, but which one would you be most likely to use for the following topics?
   a. News story for doctors about a breakthrough for a cancer cure.
   b. A story about a liquor company's buying an oil company.
   c. A new experiment in the Miami schools about protecting teachers from student abuse.
   d. The write-up by P. N. Zeiss, Vienna, Austria, of his experiment of grafting a dogwood on a redbud.

9. Arrange the following entries (a–d) for a bibliography in the preferred up-to-date form suggested in your text:
   a. The entry for this textbook,
   b. *Communications for the Executive* by Robert Duggin, 1986, Harper & Row Publishers, New York,
   c. *Changing Times,* vol. 39, February 1985, pp. 37–40, "Jobs for New College Grads," and
   d. "Education Careers by Mail," by Christiane Bird, *Working Woman,* vol. 9, September 1985, pp. 45–46.

10. What methods of research would you use to solve the following problems:
    a. To determine the reasons why the sales of one of your branch stores have been down for the past two years.
    b. To find out what university teachers of business communication consider important areas to cover in their classes.
    c. To help you decide which city would be the best for starting a dental practice.

11. Make up two questions that would
    a. Probably lead to prestige answers.
    b. Encourage answering in a certain way.

    c.  Pry unduly into personal affairs.

    d.  Put unrealistic demands on memory.

12. Which type of questionnaire would be best to use
    a.  If you have unlimited time and money and you need the information in order to write a paper in which your information must be documented?
    b.  If you work at a state adoption agency and you need personal information as to how well adopting families have adjusted for the past two years?
    c.  If you wish to investigate the smoking habits of a selected group of students on your campus (for use in a paper for a marketing class)?

13. Make suggestions to improve the following partial outline:

    1.0.  City Y's Favorable Attitude toward Gulf States Saw Mill

        1.1.  Attitudes mixed toward labor policy

    2.0.  Labor Supply Limited

        2.1.  Not enough skilled labor

        2.2.  Wage problems

            2.2.1.  Union threatens strike

            2.2.2.  Rates for longevity unequal

            2.2.3.  Why rates are unfair

14. Your boss at First Federal Savings and Loan has implied, several times, that he thinks you (the marketing manager) are wasting time and money giving gifts to new customers and previous customers (who have come back). After a great deal of research investigating the past five giveaway campaigns, you have information that refutes his implications and will write the report. Which sequence or plan will you use, and why?

15. Which plan would be best if you want to control emphasis in your business report?

16. To be sure you understand the Roman and decimal systems of outline symbols, illustrate each system through five levels below the title, which is the first level.

17. Assume that you are writing a report on whether to live in a dormitory or an apartment. Draw up a tentative outline.

18. Using the citation system recommended by your textbook, how would you cite a reference to page 90 of the sixth bibliographical entry?

19. In a report you want to cite an interview with Professor Erin Bloch, head of the computer science department at Y University. What are two ways you can cite this interview?

# Chapter Outline

Basics of Effective Report Style
Headings and Subheads
Objectivity in Presentation
Presentation of Quantitative Data
Graphic Aids as Supplements to Words
Questions and Exercises

# 15

## Presenting Major Analytical Reports Effectively

Your final phrasing of your report will not be difficult if you have done well the preceding four steps of preparation. You will notice that the suggestions here relate more to the *effectiveness* than to the *correctness* of your style, for two reasons:

1. Correct spelling, grammar, punctuation, sentence structure do not assure effectiveness—though you should have pretty well learned these aspects of your language before studying reports. (If you haven't, a more basic study of composition—or a careful review of Chapter 3 and Appendix C or some other good handbook—may be advisable.)
2. Effective presentation presupposes reasonable correctness of language as well as information but also requires that you help your reader or audience to get your message clearly, quickly, and easily. How to do this is your next concern.

## Basics of Effective Report Style

Because almost everything about style in Chapter 3 applies to report style—and the few exceptions are obvious—you should read that material carefully before going on to the special points about report style.

As you have already seen in Chapters 13 and 14, effective reports use various techniques and devices for communicating clearly, quickly and easily: commonly understood words, short sentences so direct that they require little punctuation, short paragraphs so direct that they require few transitional words, itemizations, graphics, and headings.

Even though you have read Chapters 3, 13, and 14, several points of basic style and some of the special techniques deserve a bit fuller treatment for preparing reports.

*Adaptation* requires that you consider not only your primary reader but likely secondary ones. Even though some of your important readers may know the background of the problem and the technical terms of the field, others may not. The good report writer must therefore provide explanations necessary for the least informed of important readers.

This duty includes restricting your vocabulary to words they will understand readily. If you feel that you must use specialized terms, you had better explain them. (Usually a parenthetical explanation right after the first use of a technical term is the best way.) But if your report includes many such terms, it should provide a glossary in the introduction or in an appendix.

*Coherence* becomes a greater problem as the length and variety of points in a report increase. Hence as a report writer you need to observe carefully the use of transitional words, previewing topic sentences and paragraphs, and summarizing sentences and paragraphs in the illustration in the next chapter. **Coh** in Appendix C and items S5–7 in the Checklist for Major Analytical Reports (see Chapter 16) should also prove helpful.

A particularly effective means to coherence in report writing is the use of informative and interesting "clipped-sentence" headings. J. H. Menning (a coauthor of the first five editions of this book) named them "talking heads." Here is how one writer helped keep readers on the track with good talking heads, topic statements, summary paragraphs, and transitional ideas. (For economy of space, the quoted item is only some of the *transitional* parts from various places in the 27-page report. The bracketed parts are our commentary.)

### II. NASHVILLE'S LARGER MARKET AREA

```
Since women often will travel long distances to
buy clothes, the secondary area surrounding the
metropolitan area is important in determining the
location of a Four Cousins retail store. [After
this topic lead-in, several paragraphs followed
identifying for both Nashville and Knoxville
principal communities and the number of people in
them.]

Even though 370,000 more possible customers live
within the market area of Nashville, most of the
sales will come from the people within the
immediate metropolitan area. [Summarizes II and
makes transition to III.]
```

### III. BETTER POPULATION FACTORS IN NASHVILLE

```
The total population and its rate of growth,
number of women, and number of employed women show
more clearly the potential buyers of women's
clothing. [This topic statement preceded A, B, and
C headings of subsections giving the facts about
and the interpretation of the topics as
announced.]
```

Even though Knoxville has a larger population and about the same growth rate, Nashville has more women and a significantly larger number of employed women. Thus it furnishes the kind of customer Four Cousins sells to. [Indicates what A, B, and C add up to.]

Potential customers are buyers, however, only when they have sufficient buying power. [Clearly foreshadows a topic coming up and why.]

### IV. MORE BUYING POWER IN NASHVILLE

Effective buying income (total and per capita), income groups, home ownership, and automobile ownership give estimates of ability to buy. [The information as presented then follows in four sections.]

[This summary statement comes at the end of the section.]

The Nashville shopper has more dollars to spend, even though home- and auto-ownership figures imply more favorable financial positions in Knoxville families. Higher expenditures for homes and cars in Knoxville explain, in part, why Nashville merchants sell more.

### V. GREATER RETAIL SALES AND LESS COMPETITION IN NASHVILLE

[The writer continues the use of these coherence devices throughout the report.]

(Though illustrated here only as major heads, such talking heads are equally effective at any or all heading levels.)

*Parallelism* is a special pitfall of the unwary report writer because reports so frequently involve series, outlines, and lists. The breakdown of anything must name all the parts in similar (parallel) grammatical form—usually all nouns or noun phrases, adjectives, or complete sentences.

*Timing of the verbs* (tense) in reports also often trips a careless report writer. One simple rule answers most questions of tense: *Use the present tense wherever you can do so logically.* The present tense applies to things that existed in the past, still exist, and apparently will continue to exist for a while (the universal present tense). Otherwise, use the tense indicated by the logic of the situation. Thus in talking about your research activity, you say that you *did* certain things, such as conducted a survey (past tense in terms of the time of writing). But in reporting your findings, you say "70 percent answer favorably, and 30 percent are opposed." The universal present tense implies that the findings are still true.

*Ten common faults* listed in American University Professor William Dow Boutwell's study of government reports (and printed in the *Congressional Record,* Vol. 88, Part IX, p. A1468)[1] occur frequently in business and industry reports too:

1. Sentences are too long. Average sentence length in poor government writing varies from 65 to 80 words. . . . In exceptionally good government writing . . . average length is from 15 to 18 words per sentence.

2. Too much hedging; too many modifications and conditional clauses and phrases . . . . Psychologists say that "conditional clauses cause suspension of judgment as to the outcome of the sentence, and therefore increase reading difficulty."

3. Weak, ineffective verbs. *Point out, indicate,* or *reveal* are the weak reeds . . . overuse of the parts of the verb "to be" . . . sentences with *was* or *is* as the principal verb . . . .

4. Too many sentences begin the same way, especially with *The.*

5. An attempt to be impersonal, which forces use of passive and indirect phrases . . . .

6. Overabundance of abstract nouns. Such nouns as *condition, data, situation, development, problem, factor, position, basis, case* dominate . . . . How bright and real writing becomes when picture-bearing nouns take the place of vague ones. . . .

7. Too many prepositional phrases . . . ("of the data," "under the circumstances," etc.) add to reading difficulty.

8. Overabundance of expletives. "It is" and "there are" and their variants ruin the opening of many good paragraphs.

9. Use of governmentish or federalese . . . technical, office terms.

10. Tendency to make ideas the heroes of sentences . . . : "Refusal of employment of older workers continues."

## Headings and Subheads

Because written reports are sometimes long and because readers may want to recheck certain parts, good report writers use headings and subheads, in addition to topic and summarizing sentences, to show their organization and coherence. And, you have seen in Chapter 11, a good oral reporter will use the oral equivalents for the same purposes. Also, for the same purposes, headings are an important element in this book.

---

[1] An AP Newsfeature, "Gobbledygook: Language of Government," by Richard E. Myer, September 5, 1971, stresses many of the same points; and books like Don Miller's *The Book of Jargon* (Macmillan, New York, 1981) and Jason Brown's *Jargonaphasia* (Academic Press, New York, 1981) are still doing the same thing.

If you have not thought about them already, for illustration flip back through some parts of the book with which you are well acquainted and see if they don't serve these purposes.

Skill in using heads and subheads can be a valuable technique in your presentations, not only of reports, but of anything else that is very long—even long letters. It can even help you in school in writing essay exams. The only reasonable test of how far to go in putting in subheads is this: Will they help the reader get the message? If so, put them in.

Despite the fact that headings and subheads are often great helps, no single system of setting them up is in universal use. More important than what system you use is that you *use some system consistently* and that the reader understand it. Most readers understand and agree on the following principles:

1. A good heading is a title for its section. As such, it should clearly indicate the content below it, should have reader interest, and should be as brief as possible without sacrificing either of the other two requirements.

Trying to keep titles too short, however, frequently leads to sacrifice of exactness and/or helpfulness. Note the difference, in examples from annual reports, between "Profits" and "Profits Up 8 Percent from Last Year," and between "Position in the Industry" and "Position in Industry Changes from Eighth to Fourth." Particularly in reports where some readers might only skim, you can help them by *using talking headings to tell the big point about the topic instead of just naming the topic.*

2. The form and position of the head must make its relative importance (status in the outline) clear at a glance. That is, headings for all divisions of equal rank (say the Roman-numeral heads in an outline) must be in the same form and position on the page, but different from their superiors (of which they are parts) and from their inferiors (their subdivisions). Putting heads of different levels in the same form and position is confusing; it misrepresents the outline.

3. Centered heads are superior to sideheads in the same form (compare second- and third-degree heads in the following illustration); heads in capitals are superior to those in caps and lowercase; and heads above the text are superior to those starting on the same line with the text (compare third- and fourth-degree heads in the illustration).

4. You should not depend on headings as antecedents for pronouns or as transitions. The one word *This* referring to an immediately preceding head is the most frequent offender. Transitions between paragraphs and between bigger subdivisions should be perfectly clear even without the headings.

5. In capital-and-lowercase heads capitalize the first word and all others except articles (*a, an,* and *the*), conjunctions (for example, *and, but, for,* and *because*), and prepositions (such as *to, in, of, on,* and *with*).

The following not only illustrates one good system but further explains the principles. Note that *above* second- and third-degree heads the spacing is one more than the double spacing of the discussion.

## FIRST-DEGREE HEADINGS

The title of your whole report, book, or article is the first-degree heading. Since you have only one title, no other head should appear in the same form. As illustrated here, the title uses the most superior form and position (as explained in Items 2 and 3 above). If you need more than this five-level breakdown for your report, you can type the first heading in spaced C A P I T A L S and move each level of heading up one notch.

### Second-Degree Headings

If you use solid capitals centered on the page for the first-degree heading (title), a good choice for the second-degree headings is centered caps and lowercase. Preferably, in typewriter face they and any other uncapitalized heads should carry underscoring to make them stand out. If you do not need the five-level breakdown illustrated here, you could just start with this form.

### Third-degree headings

To distinguish third-degree headings from their superiors, you may put them at the left margin above the text, underscore them to make them stand out, and write them in initial-cap form (as here) or in cap and lowercase (which would require capitalizing the D in Degree and the H in Headings).

Fourth-degree headings.--For a fourth level, you may place headings at the paragraph indention on the same line with the text and write them as caps and lowercase or as straight lowercase except for capitalizing the first word. These headings definitely need underscoring and separation from the first sentence, preferably by a period and dash, as here. Some people drop the dash or the period.

Fifth-degree headings can be integral parts (preferably beginnings) of the first sentences of the first paragraphs about topics. Underscoring (italic type when printed) will make them stand out sufficiently without further distinctions in form.

# Objectivity in Presentation

Clearly a report user expects a writer to be as nearly objective as is humanly possible in collecting the facts, in organizing and interpreting them, and finally in presenting them.

That does not mean, however, that you must use impersonal style (which some people erroneously call *objective* style). You can be just as objective when saying "I think such and such is true" as when saying "Such and such seems to be true" or even "Such and such is true." The second and third versions mean only that the writer/speaker thinks something is true. The only sound objection to the first version is that it wastes two words, not that it is *natural* style.

The only real justification for recommending impersonal style in reports, as many books do (meaning no use of the first or second person—i.e., pronouns referring to the sender or receiver of the message), is that methods and results are usually the important things and therefore they, rather than the person who did the research, deserve emphasis as subjects and objects of active verbs.

But since most things happen because people make them happen, the most natural and the clearest, easiest, most interesting way to tell about them is to tell who does what. A report about research the writer has done therefore naturally includes *I*'s; and if it keeps the reader(s) or audience in mind properly, it also naturally includes *you's*. To omit them is unnatural and usually dull, because it leaves out the most basic element of an interesting, humanized style—*people doing things*.

Actually, more destructive to objectivity than the use of a natural style is the use of too many or too strong adjectives and adverbs. Such a heightened style—using emotional connotations, fancy figures of speech, and other techniques of oratory—has its place where the author feels deeply and wants the reader to feel deeply about the subject; but it leads to distrust and is inappropriate in reports anyway, where both parties supposedly think hard rather than emotionalize.

Simply put, then, the best advice on natural versus impersonal style is this: Find out whether your primary reader thinks reports have to be in impersonal style. If so, accept the burdensome restrictions and do the best you can by

1. Avoiding "It is" and "There are," especially as sentence beginnings (**Exp** in Appendix C).

2. Putting most of your verbs in the active voice (**Pas** in Appendix C).

3. Picturing people, other than yourself or the reader/listener(s), of course, taking the action of as many as possible of your verbs. But anytime your primary reader/listener(s) will let you, *phrase your report naturally but calmly and reasonably.* Where the natural way to express an idea involves an *I* or a *you,* use it. Don't let anybody talk you into referring to yourself as "the writer"—or "the speaker."

Except for the fact that letter style allows more use of emotional suasion than report style does, the discussion of style in Chapter 3 applies to reports as well as letters.

In addition, reports also make more extensive use than letters of certain other techniques of presenting ideas clearly, quickly, and easily: using headings and subheads, presenting quantitative data skillfully, and using graphic and visual aids to effective communication.

## Presentation of Quantitative Data

Most reports make considerable use of quantitative data. Consequently, you need to know how to present these figures for clear, quick, and easy comprehension. Most people will want the figures on the measurable topics you discuss; and unless they have made clear that they want only the facts, they probably will want your interpretations showing what the figures mean (conclusions) and what you think should be done about them (recommendations). Even if those people have the ability to make the interpretations themselves, they probably will want you to make them—for possible ideas they might not see and for economy of their time.

The following brief suggestions will help you present quantitative information the way most people want it:

1. Make sure your figures are reliable by checking your sources and derivations of them. And when you present an average, make clear whether it is the mean, the median, or the mode.

2. Write isolated quantities in one of the standard ways explained under **Fig** in Appendix C.

3. Present key figures as simply as possible. Usually some ratio, rank, difference, or correlation is more important than the raw data. Instead of a gross of $2,501,460.70 and expenses of $2,124,101.40, the simple figures $2½ and $2⅛ million tell the story better. The ratio 1:7 or about 15 percent for the net certainly reads easier than $377,359.30 and is probably the more important figure. Moreover, except in bookkeeping and highly technical research, such rounded and simplified figures are precise enough for most purposes.

4. Another way of increasing readability is to break big figures down into so much per . . . (whatever is an appropriate divider). If the divider is the number of persons involved (employees, students, or citizens, for example), you also gain interest by humanizing the presentation.

5. Insofar as possible, avoid cluttering your paragraphs with great masses of figures. Tables are better if you have many figures—say more than six, as in a table of two lines and three columns (or vice versa).

Ordinarily, however, extensive tables are not necessary to clear understanding of the text but are in a report to show that you really have the facts. In that case put tables in an appendix and refer to them specifically in the introduction or text.

6. Put necessary statistical information as close as possible to the place in the text where it is most pertinent. Readers will probably refuse to flip pages back and forth to find a table, or at least will resent having to do so; and their concentration (and comprehension) will suffer.

7. Small tables (usually called spot tables), perhaps using key figures based on extensive data in an appendix, are not only easy to read but can appear close to the relevant discussion on a page. Use them freely.

8. Help your reader by pointing out (in terms of line graphs) highs, lows, averages, trends, ranges, and exceptions or extremes. They are not always readily apparent, especially to the many people who are not accustomed to analyzing statistical data; but they are usually important, especially if you can also explain their causes and/or effects.

## Graphic Aids as Supplements to Words

Just as tables are useful for presenting large amounts of related quantitative data clearly, concisely, and precisely, various graphics can present small amounts (often the key figures from tables) even better. Their strengths are in presenting information for clear, quick, easy, interesting, and memorable reading (though usually not with precision).

For these reasons, various studies have found that graphic aids (and visual aids in oral communication) help readers/listeners understand and remember. Though the impact (or remembrance of information) varies with kinds of people and kinds of material (quantitative data versus ideas, for example), the rounded figures go about like this:

|  | After 3 Hours | After 3 Days |
|---|---|---|
| Read or hear | 70% | 10% |
| See | 72 | 20 |
| Both | 85 | 65 |

Since reports so frequently treat quantitative data, designs, organizational plans, and the like, you often almost have to use charts, graphs, pictograms, drawings, and maps as well as tables to present your information well, especially in oral reports—and, as the little table shows, graphics greatly increase the impact.

But in most cases these devices *only assist, not replace, words.* And since interpretation of graphics is not one of the three R's everybody learns, most graphics help explain and/or support the text *only if the text helps them by telling how to look at them and what they mean.* Good communication therefore often involves care and skill in *interplaying* words and graphic aids.

If you haven't already done so, you could and should learn much about using graphics effectively by observing them in current use as you read other books, newspapers (especially *USA Today*), and newsmagazines like *U.S. News & World Report* and *Newsweek.* Still, this book's explanations and illustrations of the commonly used types will help. They give enough related text to show how to interweave the graphics as assistants to words.

As you study the explanations and illustrations, look not only at the graphics; but notice what kinds of information call for them, whether the graphics really help, and how the authors *interrelate them and words* so that each aids the other. Besides that key point of interplaying graphics as aids, keep in mind the five other most important points about using them:

1. A graphic device should not call attention to itself until *after* an introduction to it (some discussion of the point and reference to the graph); in most cases it would otherwise only confuse and break continuity of thought.

2. The existence of the graphic aid, or where it is, is not the important thing and does not deserve the emphasis when you refer to it. So refer to it *subordinately* and use the main clause of your sentence to make the significant point. "Twice as many men as women like X, as Table 2 shows," is one good way.

3. Insofar as possible, place graphic aids close to (usually between) comments on the point. In written reports, that means (preferably) right before the reader's eyes. Unless the device is staring the reader in the face when you mention it, tell precisely where it is—*subordinately* (for example, "As Fig. 1 on the next page shows, X goes up as Y goes down").

4. Carefully label each graphic device (unless obvious) as a whole (title and easy-reference number) and by parts, and provide a key (legend) if necessary. Variations in color, shading, cross-hatching, and kind of line (solid versus broken, for example) are common means for distinguishing the different kinds of data in lines, columns, bars, and the like.

Where precision of quantified data is important, help the reader by using grid lines (such as on graph paper) and by labeling significant points with the exact figures. *And remember that percentages or other ratios are often more important than the raw figures from which they come.*

Avoiding two kinds of possible distortion deserves particular caution.

a. *Be sure to start at 0 as the base.* If, for example, you use 0 as the base and the first year presented has a volume of 50 and the second

60, the second year will look like what it is (10 points or a 20 percent increase, from 50 to 60). If you start at base 40, however, the second year appears to have doubled the first (20 above the base 40 and thus twice as high on the scale as the 50 of the preceding year, which was only 10 above the base).

Because you must begin at base 0, you have a problem if all your quantities going on a scale (usually the vertical or Y scale) are high. To avoid both leaving large open spaces at the bottom and distorting by ignoring the 0-base logic, you may begin at 0 and make a scale break as fair warning to a reader (see Figure 15–1).

**Figure 15–1 / An Illustration of How to Show a Broken Scale**

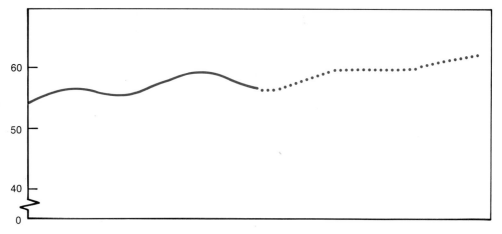

b. *Select both the vertical and horizontal scales to produce a slope that looks and feels right for the situation.* Readers generally view a graph line rising at anywhere between 0 and a 30° angle as a normal slope. Similarly, a slope of 30° to 45° seems a little threatening; and a steeper slope seems treacherous.

5. Interpret your graphics (usually right after them) unless doing so would be insulting because the meaning is so obvious. Generally, try to make at least one summing-up comment, as what seems obvious to you may not be obvious to a reader seeing the graphic for the first time.

To begin seeing illustrations of graphics, start flipping the pages of this book from the front. You'll notice that they illustrate (more or less in order) special layouts such as the title page, table of contents, boxed checklists, outlines of chapters, photolike reproductions (of letter, envelope, and memo layouts), parallel-column presentations, symbolic drawings (of message strategies), résumés, regular tables—and literally dozens of other special arrangements on the page that help you see the information.

You'll also notice that the best procedure in using graphics begins by (1) introducing the topic and the key point, (2) subordinately referring the reader to the graphic aid at the point where it will be helpful, (3) using the best type of graphic for the purpose, and (4) further commenting on (interpreting) the graphic device.

To illustrate the most commonly used graphics, besides three others, here are five from an article in the most recent *Occupational Outlook Handbook* (U.S. Department of Labor, 1984–85) and enough of the text paraphrasing to interplay further instructions about graphics with the best available information on job prospects from now until 1995.

*Bar charts* are among the easiest graphics to make and to interpret. In their simplest form you set up a row of bars (usually on a horizontal base of time periods; but it may be on a vertical base and represent time or any other function). The varying lengths of side-by-side bars show changes in the other variable (as in Chart 1).

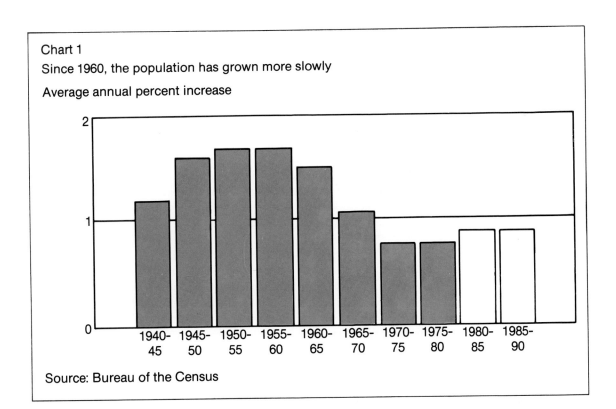

Chart 1

Since 1960, the population has grown more slowly

Average annual percent increase

Source: Bureau of the Census

The *Handbook* writer probably chose wisely not to provide more grid lines (because the data were not precise) and (to avoid distraction from the main point) not to segment the bars (by different shading) into percentages of males and females in each bar. Notice the standard graphic-language code for distinguishing known data (solid lines for line graphs or for boxing-in bars) from projections (all lines broken).

Chart 1 shows clearly the baby boom that increased U.S. population 1945–65, the small population increase in the 70s, and the projected (predicted) slow rise of about 0.9 percent or less a year in the 80s and 90s. Interpreting that chart by putting its bare facts with others (not presented yet, but some well known) would suggest several likely consequences:

1. That more women might come into the work force in the 70s as fewer births let them and as the boom babies became old enough to operate without constant maternal care;

2. That the work force would start booming about 1965 (causing strong competition for jobs) as the boom babies began reaching their 20s;

3. That growth in the labor force would slow down in the 80s; and

4. That the 1990s would offer more jobs than the available new workers (born in the low-birthrate 70s) could fill—hence little competition for jobs and high pay.

You recognize that drawing a line connecting the exposed corners of the bars in Chart 1 would produce another simple and widely used kind of graphic—a *line graph* or *line chart.* In this case it should be a *faired* (smoothly curved) line—a truer representation of the given facts—because the data change more or less smoothly (instead of in jumps at intervals, which would call for stepped straight-line connections between the jumps).

You should recognize, too, that like the simple bar chart, the simple line graph can present projections (broken lines such as - - -, — —, or . . . .) and several concurrently changing kinds of data (distinguished by colors) on the same base. (You should limit their number to the range of easy comprehension/comparison.) (See Chart 4 and Figure 15–2).

A frequent two-line business chart pictures one line labeled *costs* and the other labeled *income*—where they cross being the break-even point.

Though the *Handbook* does not show it, given statistics do provide data (as Chart 1 had given bases for speculative interpretation) for another use of a faired two-line graph—of men as a decreasing and women an increasing percentage of the people coming into the labor force. That's what you would have if you removed the walls and left only their upper-front edges from Chart 2. (We modified the chart design slightly—to make a faired two-row bar chart—for ease of reading.)

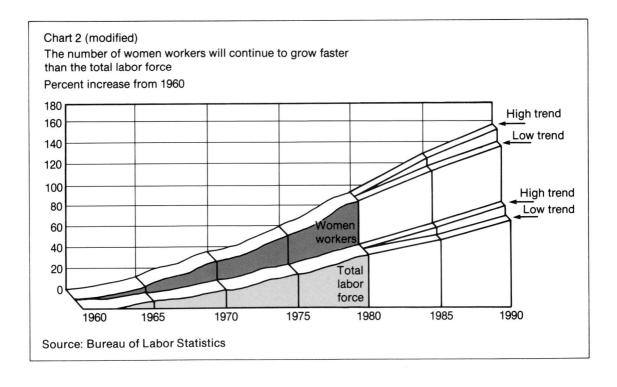

Chart 2 (modified)
The number of women workers will continue to grow faster
than the total labor force
Percent increase from 1960

Source: Bureau of Labor Statistics

To show the percentages of different kinds of workers employed in each category, the *Handbook* wisely uses the standard (and best) graphic form for breaking down wholes—the *pie chart.*

*Pie charts* are specialists in showing the parts of a whole—preferably with different colors or shading to distinguish the parts, labels to identify them, the raw figures for precision, and (usually the most important figures) their percentages for quick, easy comparison. Even they, however, can broaden their service by showing more than one breakdown. Chart 3, for example, might be better as one pie with different cross-hatching to distinguish the two broad categories.

Since pie charts are stationary rather than moving partitioners (i.e., pictures breaking a whole into its parts at a given time), they cannot well present projections. The authors of the *Occupational Outlook Handbook* article we're paraphrasing therefore could have turned to two better ways of presenting such information—a line graph (two lines, projected, for the emphatic picture) and words for precision and details—to trace

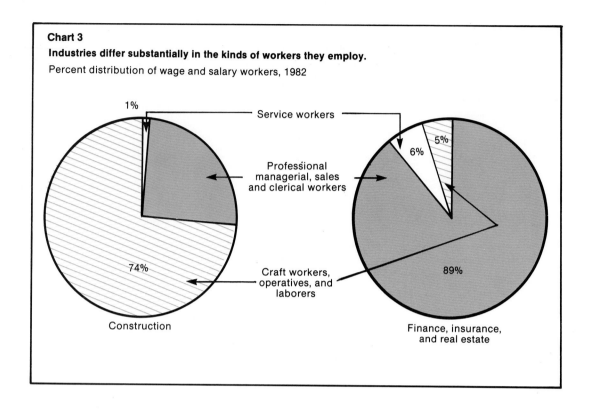

**Chart 3**

**Industries differ substantially in the kinds of workers they employ.**

Percent distribution of wage and salary workers, 1982

1%

Service workers

Professional managerial, sales and clerical workers

74%

Craft workers, operatives, and laborers

Construction

6%     5%

89%

Finance, insurance, and real estate

the expected trends of all the subgroups. They use this approach in Chart 4.

Chart 5, a bilateral beginning/ending bar chart, forecasts (for 1982–95) changes in employment (in millions) among industries. As you see, agriculture remains on the negative side and the big gainers (manufacturing, trade, and services) go up from about 3.5 to 10.0. Smaller gains of 1 and 2 million each will occur in the construction, transportation, and finance areas. Mining and government will have small gains, from less than half a million to under a million.

Chart 6 shows an interesting comparison between *rate* (percent) and *number* of new jobs. Notice how the comparison is reversed when changed from percent to number (while the *rate* of growth for computer service technicians is large, the actual *number* of jobs is greater for auto mechanics).

Though the preceding explanations and illustrations give you a good look into graphics, the following suggestions on the uses of different graphics may be helpful as a kind of summary/reminder.

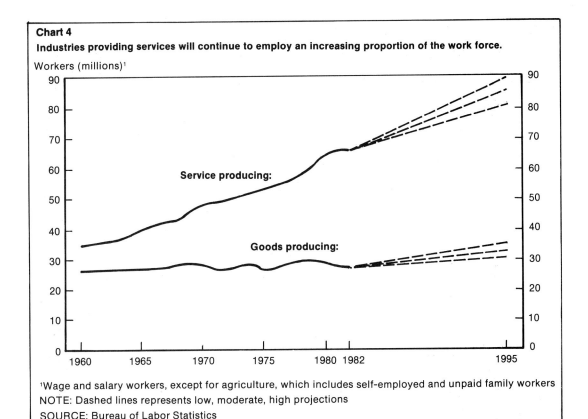

**Chart 4**

**Industries providing services will continue to employ an increasing proportion of the work force.**

Workers (millions)[1]

Service producing:

Goods producing:

1960    1965    1970    1975    1980  1982                          1995

[1]Wage and salary workers, except for agriculture, which includes self-employed and unpaid family workers
NOTE: Dashed lines represents low, moderate, high projections
SOURCE: Bureau of Labor Statistics

1. A *table* is usually the starting point for quantified graphics of other kinds. We don't illustrate tables here because you've already seen many in use. If you want to see more, however, flip through the report illustration in Chapter 16.

2. Use *line graphs* (perhaps marking the tops of columns in a bar chart) to represent trends according to time. Usually the perpendicular axis should represent volume of the subject treated and the base (or horizontal axis) should represent time. Two or more different kinds or colors of lines can show relative quantities as well as the absolute quantities of several subjects at any given time.

3. Use *segmented bars or pie charts* (preferably moving clockwise from 12:00) to represent the proportions in the breakdown of a whole. Usually the color or shading of sections distinguishes the parts (which should

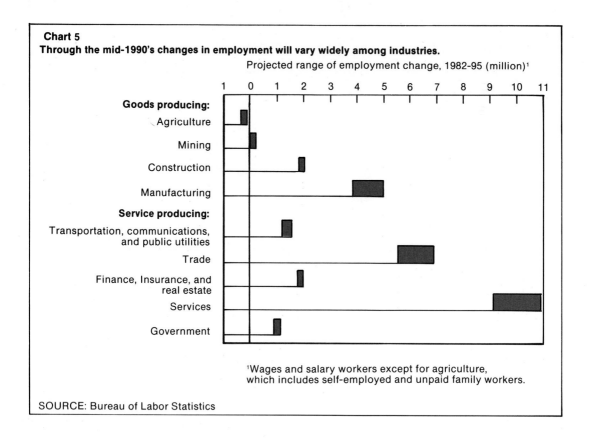

**Chart 5**
**Through the mid-1990's changes in employment will vary widely among industries.**

Projected range of employment change, 1982-95 (million)[1]

Goods producing:
  Agriculture
  Mining
  Construction
  Manufacturing
Service producing:
  Transportation, communications, and public utilities
  Trade
  Finance, Insurance, and real estate
  Services
  Government

[1]Wages and salary workers except for agriculture, which includes self-employed and unpaid family workers.

SOURCE: Bureau of Labor Statistics

not be confusingly numerous). They should carry labels of both the raw figures for precision and (usually the more important point) the ratio or percentage of the whole for easy comparison. After beginning at 12:00, place pie chart sections clockwise in order of descending importance.

4. A kind of hybrid showing the partitioning characteristics of multi-line graphs, segmented-bar charts, and pies is the *belt chart* in Figure 15–2 (also called the cumulative line chart and the component-part line chart). Intended to give only an impressionistic (rather than precise) picture of 6½ decades, it gives a pretty good idea without any precise figures. (This figure is from an earlier edition of the *Handbook;* omitting date and source helps concentrate on the design and use.)

5. Use *maps* for geographic distribution of almost anything; *organization charts* of rectangles arranged and connected to show lines of author-

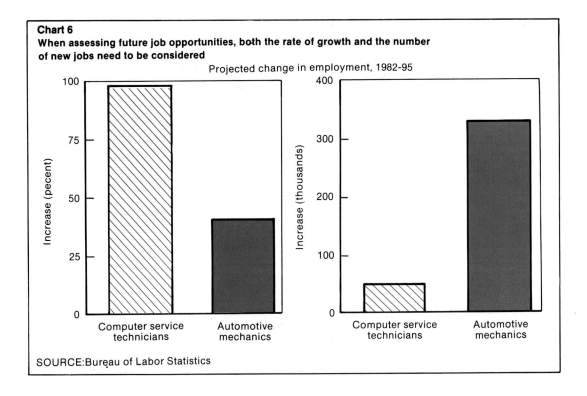

**Chart 6**
**When assessing future job opportunities, both the rate of growth and the number of new jobs need to be considered**

Projected change in employment, 1982-95

SOURCE:Bureau of Labor Statistics

**Figure 15–2**

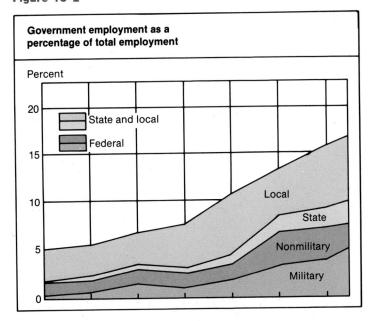

**Government employment as a percentage of total employment**

ity and communication; *flowcharts* showing movement and stages in processing; *blueprints* giving precise sizes and relationships; and *photographs* picturing accurate size, texture, and color. All are useful graphic devices in their places, which are sometimes in engineering, architectural, and other professional/technical work instead of in business. In any case you need to keep them simple enough for easy reading and concentrated on the point under discussion.

6. Use *symbolic pictograms* (such as little people representing workers or bags of money representing profits) to add interest, especially for nontechnical presentations, when you have the time and money and are preparing a report in enough copies to justify the cost.

But *keep all the little characters the same size* (though each may represent any quantity) and vary the number of them to represent different total quantities (usually lines of them making bar charts). Otherwise, you mislead because the volume in the pictogram involves a third dimension (depth perspective) not shown in the pictogram. Of two cylindrical tanks representing oil production, for example, one actually twice as big as the other looks only slightly bigger because of the unseen third dimension. (If you remember from your geometry that the volume of a cylinder is $\pi r^2 h$, you'll see why.)

Though it might appear to be a contradiction to the *number/not size* rule for showing quantity in pictograms, the map in Figure 15–3 (using side-by-side piles of sales contracts as bar charts, with percentage figures for the two years covered) is particularly effective for showing shifts in regional sales. One of the reasons is that the one chart involves multimedia—map, bar chart, and just a hint of pictograms—and the piles of sales contracts are bars in a bar chart showing the quantities.

As a weekly newsmagazine wanting to report current quantified data interestingly, *U.S. News & World Report* makes frequent use of pictograms, purely for their interest value, while the figures appear in other forms. For instance, in a thorough article on inflation it used eight pairs of bars to present (in black) the current costs of eight cost-of-living items and (in red) the costs five years later (assuming continuation of the current rate of inflation). Along with the cost figures at the top of each bar was (above each pair) a clever little symbolic drawing: a hospital bed for a day in the hospital, a pack of cigarettes, an ivy-covered tower, an apron (maid service), and so on. *USA Today* also uses imaginative graphics.

7. A *flowchart* (Figure 15–4) can show steps in a process and decision results. Flowcharts use both words *and* pictures to show simply the

**Figure 15–3**

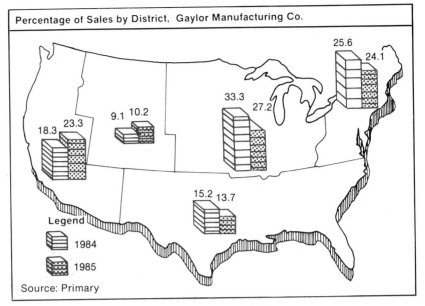

Percentage of Sales by District, Gaylor Manufacturing Co.

25.6
24.1
33.3
27.2
9.1 10.2
18.3  23.3
15.2  13.7

Legend

1984

1985

Source: Primary

structure of a problem or process. Constructing a flowchart will help you make sure you've covered all parts of a potential decision. Usually flowcharts flow vertically and emphasize the final actions (or products in a manufacturing or processing flowchart).

8. If you have to provide multiple copies of your report, consider whether your graphics are reproducible. What may be fine for offset printing may not work in some kinds of photocopy processes. *Computer-generated graphics,* increasingly common, often pose problems. A computer printout or a photograph of a visual display may be of such poor quality that you would lose important details in reproduction, necessitating expensive and time-consuming tracing or redrawing.

One other danger you need to be aware of is that when you first start working with computer graphics you'll be so involved with the colors and ease of preparation that you may lose sight of the primary purpose of graphics—to help your audience understand your information. Be sure to *label, introduce,* and *discuss* all the graphics in a report, no matter how you create them. Also be careful to limit the number of colors used and the amount of information covered in one screen, just as you would for any good visual.

**Figure 15–4 / Income-Averaging Requirements**

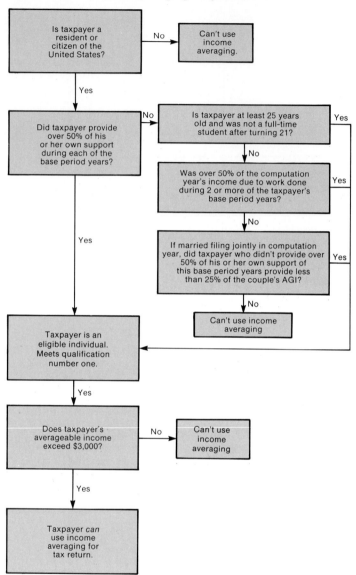

9. Graphics and other visual aids (usually flip charts or slides) for oral presentations pose problems peculiar to speaking situations, and we deal with these in Chapter 11.

Careful study of the illustrations, warnings, and instructions of graphics given here will enhance your ability to use these effective devices to become a better report writer. At the same time you will have had an up-to-date insight into the current job picture and some valid bases for projective thinking about career planning to 1995.

## Questions and Exercises

1. To adequately discuss the figure below, what other information do you need? Write two or three sentences describing the data you have.

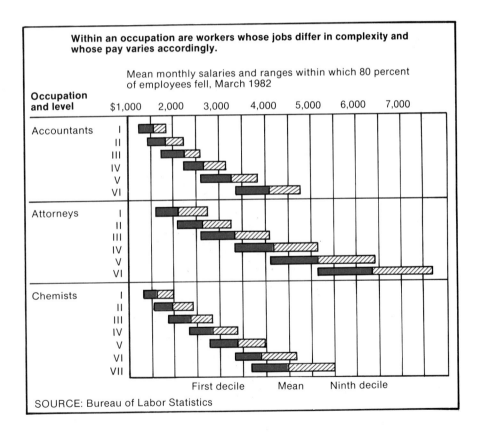

Within an occupation are workers whose jobs differ in complexity and whose pay varies accordingly.

Mean monthly salaries and ranges within which 80 percent of employees fell, March 1982

SOURCE: Bureau of Labor Statistics

2.  What caption would best describe the following graph about book-keepers' salaries?

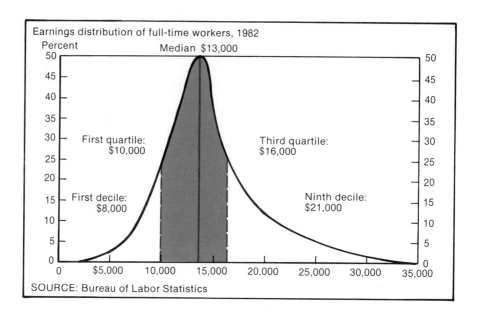

3.  Using the next three charts, describe the impact of the census figures on hiring opportunities in education. What would be useful titles for these three graphics?

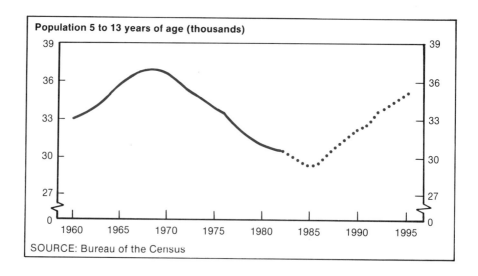

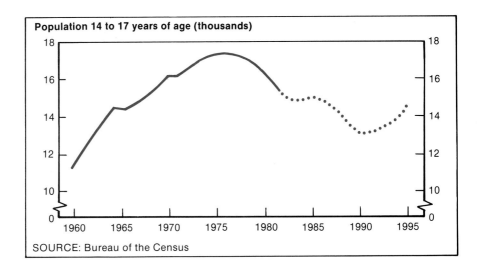

Population 14 to 17 years of age (thousands)

SOURCE: Bureau of the Census

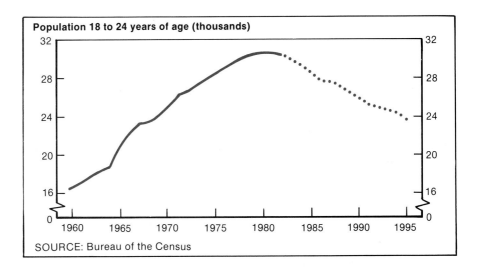

Population 18 to 24 years of age (thousands)

SOURCE: Bureau of the Census

4. Discuss the impact of the statistics in this bar graph on women in the work force.

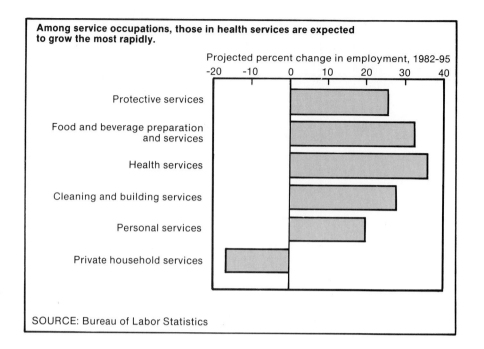

Among service occupations, those in health services are expected to grow the most rapidly.

SOURCE: Bureau of Labor Statistics

5.   Write two paragraphs discussing these tables.

**Best Bets for the Next Decade
Fastest Growing Jobs**

| JOB | % JOB GROWTH, 1995 |
| --- | --- |
| Computer Service Technicians | 97 |
| Legal Assistants | 94 |
| Computer Systems Analysts | 85 |
| Tool Programmers, Numerical Control | 78 |
| Computer Programmers | 77 |
| Electrical Engineers | 65 |
| Electrical and Electronics Technicians | 61 |
| Occupational Therapists | 60 |
| Health Services Administrators | 58 |
| Physical Therapists | 58 |
| Mechanical Engineers | 52 |
| Podiatrists | 52 |
| Engineers | 49 |
| Registered Nurses | 49 |
| Nuclear Engineers | 48 |

Source: Bureau of Labor Statistics. (Civilian employment in occupations with 25,000 workers or more, actual 1982, projected 1995).

**Worst Bets for the Next Decade**
**Slowest Growing Jobs**

| JOB | % JOB GROWTH, 1995 |
| --- | --- |
| Postal Clerks | −18 |
| College and University Faculty | −15 |
| Compositors and Typesetters | −7 |
| Stenographers | −7 |
| Butchers and Meatcutters | −6 |
| Mail Carriers | −5 |
| Communications Equipment Mechanics | 3 |
| Air Traffic Controllers | 4 |
| Stationary Engineers | 4 |
| Drafters | 5 |
| Farm Equipment Mechanics | 5 |
| Health and Regulatory Inspectors | 7 |
| Plasterers | 7 |
| Boilermakers | 8 |
| Telephone Operators | 8 |

Source: Bureau of Labor Statistics. (Civilian employment in occupations with 25,000 workers or more, actual 1982, projected 1995).

6. Write the following statements in first-degree heading (one statement), second-degree heading (one statement), third-degree heading (two statements and two headings), fourth-degree heading (two statements and two headings), and fifth-degree heading (two statements and two headings):

   The Super Suds Company should change from radio to TV advertising; TV gives better coverage; Nelson survey shows high TV rating, Belle survey gives TV high rating; a 1983 study in Southwest, a 1983 study in Northeast, random sample shows . . . ; possible error of 3 percent suggests . . . .

7. Which type of graph is best for:
   a. Showing Americans how their tax dollar is spent for government costs.
   b. Showing population growth during the past 25 years.
   c. Showing the growth of men and women in the labor force.
   d. Showing an uninterested audience (subscribers to a newsmagazine) figures on inflation in the Northeast, Midwest, Southeast, and Far West of the United States.

8. Which heading talks?
   a. City Y's Attitudes toward Industry.
   b. City Y's Attitude toward Gulf States Saw Mill.

     c.   Population Growth Greater in Austin.

     d.   Population Growth in Phoenix.

9.  Which is the best/better way of handling figures? Why?

     a.   (1)   Y Company increased its profit over last year's by 10 percent (almost $9 million).

           (2)   Y company increased its profit by $8,996,496.46.

           (3)   Y company increased its profit.

     b.   (1)   The Department of Defense spent X dollars in 198_.

           (2)   The 198_ cost of defense in the United States comes to X dollars per year or X dollars per day per person.

# Chapter Outline

# 16

# Analysis and Illustration of Major Analytical Reports

## An Overview of Report Format

In details the makeup of major analytical reports varies with the organizations sponsoring the reports.

Yet in the larger aspects of report parts and their interrelations, agreement far exceeds disagreement. This chapter explains and illustrates major report makeup with emphasis on the generally acceptable main points.

The illustrations may not be perfect reports, and certainly are not here as wording for you to copy. They do, however, show acceptable content, form, and general style for their particular situations as starters to your thinking—not as solutions to all your problems.

### Layout and Pagination

Most major analytical reports include three broad categories of several parts each. The parts marked with asterisks in the following list normally do not appear as separate parts except in long, formal reports; but the others are almost universal—and in the order listed.

Preliminaries
- Cover*
- Title fly*
- Title page
- Letter of authorization*
- Letter of acceptance*
- Letter of transmittal
- Table of contents*
- Table of illustrations*
- Synopsis* (but may be in transmittal)

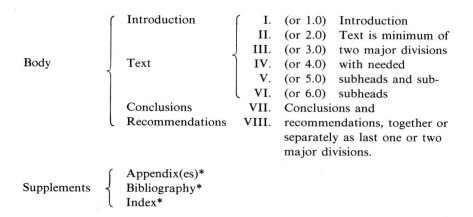

The following specifics will help in layout and pagination:

1. Generally each of the listed parts except text, conclusions, and recommendations begins a new page; otherwise, only the filling of one page calls for a new one. If used, the table of illustrations may go on the same page with the contents if space allows without crowding. Each appendix begins on a new page and should be separately titled.

2. Counting the preliminary pages begins with the title fly, if used (but the numbers, in lowercase Roman numerals, do not appear until *after* the title page). Pages in the body and supplements take Arabic numerals. The first page number of any part beginning a new page goes at the center bottom of the page; others appear (preferably) at least two spaces above the end of the first line. No page numbers need adornments such as parentheses, hyphens, periods, and underscores.

3. For bound reports, the "bite" of the binding requires typing with an extra-wide margin where the binding will be so that the binding will not hide any writing and margins will be proper when the report is open.

### Optional and Minor Parts

Now, before the parts that require full discussion and illustration, let's clear out the no-problem parts and the optional parts marked with asterisks in the preceding list.

The *cover,* much like the cover of a book but generally useful only for reports of 20 pages or more, is there to hold the report together and protect it. But unless it is transparent or has a cutout revealing the identifying title page, it needs to carry at least the title (perhaps in shortened form) and the author's name. (It may carry the rest of the title-page information too.) The cover should lie flat when opened, and the binding should be securely attached.

The *title fly* is a full page carrying only the title. Whatever its use in printed books, it is only excess paper in typewritten reports. If used, it counts as the first of the preliminary pages (lowercase Roman numerals), although the page number does not usually appear on it.

When the person who authorizes a report makes the assignment by a *letter (or memo) of authorization,* a copy of it should appear in the report. This situation is most likely when the assignment is a big one, especially if it is a public affairs problem or the report writer is an outsider working on a consulting basis. By showing what the assigned job was, the letter enables any reader to judge the adequacy of the report. To make sure of getting a useful report, the writer of the authorization needs to state the problem precisely and make clear the purpose, scope, and limits on time, money, and the like. Asking specific questions and, if known, suggesting sources, methods, or approaches may help further, and also save money. Including the letter of authorization in your report makes clear where you were limited in expenditures and allocation of resources.

A *letter of acceptance*—rarely included—is the answer to a letter of authorization. Together they constitute the working agreement or contract.

A *table of illustrations* will help if some of the tables and graphics might be useful to a reader independently of the discussion around them. In table-of-contents form it lists separately the tables, charts, and figures in sequence by their identifying numbers and titles—and gives the pages on which they appear.

An *index* would serve little purpose in most reports both because they are not long enough to need one and because readers do not use reports as reference books. Ordinarily, the table of contents adequately helps a reader find a certain point.

## Standard Short Preliminaries

### Title Page

The title page is usually the first of the preliminary pages (counted as lowercase Roman numbers down to the introduction), but the page number does not need to appear on it. Four other blocks of information usually do: the title itself, the name and title of the writer, and the place and date. In many instances the name of the organization where both writer and reader work is desirable information. When needed, a brief abstract, a list of people or departments to receive copies, project or serial-number identifications, and classifications for secrecy ("Confidential," etc.) may appear also.

*Phrasing the title well is usually the main problem.* First, a good report title, like any other title or heading in functional writing, should be *precise* in indicating clearly the content and scope. Secondarily, a good report title should be *interesting*—at least to the intended reader. As a third desirable quality, a good report title should be *concise*—have no wasted words like "A Report on . . . ," "A Study of . . . ," or "A Survey of . . . ."

An example will make clearer some frequent false steps and final solutions to the problem of writing *precise, interesting,* and *concise* report titles. A student proposed a report on "A Study of the Compensation of Executives." Discussion with the professor quickly led to omitting the first four words and then changing to "Executive Compensation" for a further 33 percent reduction in words. That adequately solved the problem of conciseness.

Further discussion soon revealed, however, that the student never intended to write about all executives but only about high-level ones in corporations. Despite the emphasis on compensation, the student wasn't even interested in the executives' basic salaries, having already seen evidence that up to $600,000 annually didn't keep executives from leaving jobs. The student revealed that the real topic of interest was evaluation of several new means some corporations were beginning to use to keep their top executives. Traditional means—high salaries, stock options, bonuses, and retirement programs (the things most people would envision from the word *compensation*)—were only tangential to the main topic.

The next title was "New Methods Corporations Use to Retain High-Level Executives"—but the assigned report was to be an *analytical* report, and this title suggested a mere presentation of undigested facts.

Assuming assignment by Pow Chemical Company to study the problem and write a report on what the corporation might do to reduce executive turnover, the student arrived at a different title: "Pow's Possible Benefits from Applying Some New Means Used by Corporations to Retain High-Level Executives." That title narrowed the topic and then zeroed in on the real problem. It said precisely what the report was to be about (no more, no less) and implied an analytical rather than informational report. (You might note that it doesn't even—and doesn't need to—contain the key word of the original, *compensation.*) The first three words could not help *interesting* Pow officials, the intended readers. But is it concise—not short, or brief, at 16 words—but concise? Are all the words *possible, applying, some,* and *used by corporations* worth their space? What do you think?

Since an analytical report is about a specific problem of an individual or group, its title should indicate that specificness, often to the extent of naming the person or group as well as the problem. You can't answer such a general question as "Should Spot Radio Advertising Be Used?" The answer would be sometimes yes and sometimes no. For that reason, one student phrased a title as "Why the P. L. Lyon Company Should Discontinue Spot Radio Advertising."

That title, however, was a *final* title, written *after* the writer had done the research and made the analysis. Knowing what the decision was, and knowing that the key point would be readily acceptable, the reporter reasonably chose to tell the reader directly—as in a direct strategy letter. To have phrased it that way *before* doing the research, however, would have been to act on a preconception that could have prevented the writer from facing facts fairly.

With the title well done, you should have no more trouble with the title page. In looking at the illustration later in this chapter, note how the writer grouped information into four parts and used balanced layout (each line centered) for good appearance.

## Letter of Transmittal

Following the title page—unless the report is an extensive and formal one, including such things as a copyright notice, title fly, letter of authorization, and letter of acceptance—page ii (counted, but not necessarily physically numbered) is a letter (or memo) of transmittal. (In a formal public affairs report with a large number of indefinite readers, a typical preface often replaces the personalized letter of transmittal.)

Written after completing the report, in regular letter or memo form and in a style appropriate to the circumstances, the letter of transmittal *must* do at least two things: transmit the report and refer to the authorization (if any). In informal situations one sentence can do both: "Here's the report on fish poisoning you asked me to write when we were talking on May 10." Usually it needs to be a little more formal than that, but you need not use phrases like "As per your request, . . ." and "In accordance with . . . ."

*Do* subordinate the reference to the authorization to avoid a flat and insulting sound—seeming to tell about the request for the report as if the reader doesn't remember. In the rare cases where no authorization happened, instead of the reference to it the writer tells enough background to arouse interest.

Despite the importance of conciseness and the possibility of doing in the first sentence all it *has* to do, a letter of transmittal will say more, if for no other reason than to avoid a curt tone. Some appropriate additional things to talk about (but not all in any one letter) are

- A highlight particularly significant in affecting the findings, or a reference to special sections likely to be particularly interesting to the reader.
- A summary of conclusions and recommendations (or even an interwoven synopsis if the reader is likely to be sympathetic and unless a synopsis two or three

pages later says the same thing). Even then, the letter can give very briefly the general decision but not supporting data.

- Side issues or facts irrelevant to the report but supposedly interesting or valuable to the reader.
- Limitations of information, time, and/or money if they are true and not a part of the introduction, where they naturally belong—and provided that they do not sound like lazy excuses.
- Acknowledgments of unusual help from others whom you have not cited later as sources.

The letter may appropriately—almost always *should*—end with some expression indicating your attitude toward the significance of the report and/or appreciation for having the opportunity to work on it, because

- If you are in the business of making such studies, you surely appreciate business.
- If you're within the company, you certainly should appreciate the opportunity to demonstrate your ability and to learn more about the company.
- An important report assignment is a chance to make a good impression (and be marked for promotion). The value of that chance and a good report could easily suffer, however, if you do not express your appreciation for the chance. Be careful of weak tone here, however. Don't sound as if you learned about your topic writing the report.

## Table of Contents

The next part, usually page iii (with the number centered at the bottom, as always on a page with extra space at the top because of a part heading), is the table of contents (or simply contents)—often omitted in short analytical reports because a good set of internal headings does the job. It sets out the major, if not all, headings of the report and their beginning page numbers. Thus it quickly shows the organization and serves as a handy guide for the reader, especially the busy reader who may want to check only some parts. In the absence of an index, for long reports it needs to be adequately detailed for the purpose.

To list in the table of contents the table itself and those parts that come before it would look a little odd; the reader would have already seen them. You therefore list only those divisions (with subdivisions down the scale as far as you think helpful) following the table. Remember, however, that the *preliminary parts down to the introduction are not parts of the outline and do not get outline symbols,* such as I and A (or 1.0 and 1.1) but only their names and page numbers (small Roman numerals). If a separate synopsis comes immediately after the table of contents, for example, you list it flush left without an outline symbol, as the first thing on the list.

Then comes the real outline of the report—the headings and subheads. In most reports you may well give all of them, reproduced in exactly the same wording as elsewhere (but not in different styles of type). Preferably you should put the outline symbols before them—in the decimal system or in capital Roman numerals for the major divisions (including the introduction, conclusions, and recommendations) and capital letters for their subdivisions. *(Remember that Roman numerals, like Arabics, line up on the right.)* If any heading is too long for one line, break it at least seven spaces before the page-number column and indent the carryover. After each heading is a leader line of *spaced* periods (with a space or two before and after) leading to the page-number column. For proper appearance (vertical alignment), make *all* those periods while your machine is on either even or odd numbers on the scale.

Supplementary parts such as appendixes and a bibliography continue the Arabic page numbers of the body copy, but they do not carry outline numerals to the left in the table of contents because they are not logical parts of the discussion being outlined.

The table of contents may be single- or double-spaced, or single-spaced within parts and double-spaced between, whichever makes the best appearance on the page; but double-space at least between the parts and major divisions.

## Synopsis and/or Abstract

Written after you complete the report proper, the synopsis is a condensed version of the whole report (preliminaries, introduction, presentation of facts and the interpretations of them, and conclusions and recommendations). It is the report in a nutshell—usually reduced somewhere between 10:1 and 20:1. In most cases you reduce the introduction even more and the conclusions and recommendations less because they deserve the main emphasis as the report's reason for being.

While putting the synopsis or executive summary early reveals your conclusions to the reader, the reader benefits of having such a summary override the psychological objections to direct style. Neither psychologically nor practically can you hold an impatient reader away from the conclusions long enough to read a long report anyway, the way you can on a short one or a letter. Even in a long report that needs to convince, the synopsis serves important purposes:

1. It saves time in many cases by giving all a busy reader wants.
2. Even for the reader who goes on through the whole report, the synopsis gives a brief view that helps in reading the rest more easily and more intelligently, because already knowing the final results makes clearer how each fact or explanation fits.

3. Often the synopsis also serves as the basis for a condensed oral presentation to a group of important readers such as a board of directors (as explained in Chapter 11).

4. Sometimes a number of readers who do not get the whole report but need to know the essence of it get what they need from reproduced and distributed copies of the synopsis.

Particularly for the first and last uses, many executives now insist that major reports coming to their desks have *one-page* synopses up front—an increasing trend. You should therefore try to keep synopses down to one page, even if you have to single-space within paragraphs (but of course double-space between).

For an example of a good synopsis, read the detailed one below. It specifically and concisely synopsizes a report of six major divisions (besides the introduction and the conclusions and recommendations) running to 27 pages. Desirably, it focuses on a quick presentation of results (the conclusions and implied recommendation) in the first paragraph, while also making clear the purpose, the readers and authorizer, and the writers. Then it summarizes the six data-filled sections in the same order and proportionate space given the topics in the full report. It includes the headings of these sections for reference ease.

Synopsis

Savannah people are likely to buy more at a Rexwall Drug Store than Charleston residents are, according to this market evaluation prepared for the Chairman of the Board, Rexwall, Inc., by Factseekers, Inc.

Population and Buying Units
Though metropolitan Charleston merchants serve 11,000 more customers from the shopping area, Savannah retailers can expect some trade from almost twice as many out-of-town buyers (340,000 versus 184,000). Savannah's 1,000 more family units more than compensate for the fact that the Charleston family averages 3.62 people, while the smaller Savannah family averages 3.4.

Buying Income
Savannah individuals average $85 more buying income, but the larger Charleston families average $35 more per family for a total of half a million more annual buying income. With less first-mortgage money to do it, 2,800 more people in Savannah have built homes in the past four years; but 17,000 more Charlestonians own automobiles.

### Retail Sales

The higher income of the individual Savannah buyer and the larger number of customers from around Savannah explain why $2.5 million more passed through the hands of Savannah retailers last year. Individually, Savannah residents spent $75 more; the small Savannah family, however, spent only $55 more.

### Drugstore Sales

Though five years ago Charleston druggists outsold those in Savannah by an average of $3,000, last year the 61 Savannah drugstore managers and owners collected about $5 million--$170,000 more than 62 Charleston druggists--for an average of $4,000 more per drugstore in Savannah.

### Overall Business Factors and Stability

Overall business factors also point to Savannah as the choice. Savannah's estimated business volume of $989 million is almost twice that of Charleston. Since a significant part of this difference is attributable to the 10 million more tons of cargo handled by the Savannah docks, Savannah consumers and retailers will feel the pinch of recessions and strikes more than Charlestonians.

The extra $36 million Charleston manufacturing added, however, is almost as uncertain in the stability of that city as the effects of shipping are on the economy of Savannah. Charlestonians benefit from $35 million more of the relatively stable wholesale business, but $32 million more agricultural income from farms averaging $4,000 more in value helps bolster the Savannah economy.

### Business Activity

Certainly Savannah's business activity has been consistently better than Charleston's in the past four years. Though the trend continues up in both cities, construction has averaged $12 million more annually in Savannah. Bankers in Savannah have consistently received about 10 percent more deposits than their Charleston counterparts have--for $150 million more in commercial accounts and $12 million more in savings.

In both cities postmasters have collected about 8 percent more each successive year, but Savannah citizens have steadily paid for $200,000 more postage than Charlestonians have.

Since a synopsis derives exclusively from the report itself—which has adequate illustration and documentation—it needs neither graphics nor citations. But you do need to give the main supporting facts. This is one reason for using the term *synopsis* rather than *abstract.*

Abstracts are of two kinds—topical (giving only the points discussed) and informative (giving the findings about each topic, with emphasis on conclusions and any recommendations made). A synopsis is like an *informative* abstract, emphasizing results, but is usually fuller and more helpful.

# Content and Form of Major Parts

## Introduction

The introduction to a major analytical report serves primarily to answer the second of a report reader's two inevitable questions: How do you know? Rarely does it answer any part of the first question: What are the facts? If that question needs a brief and early answer (before the text gives all the facts), the synopsis does the job. Unless a synopsis or informative abstract is a part of the introduction, therefore—as in some forms of reports—the introduction is no place to put your data.

Since the introduction begins the *body* of the report—which also includes the text (the facts and analyses), conclusions, and recommendations if the reader wants them—the title of the whole report appears at the top of the page. Remember to set up that title exactly as on the title page, superior over all other headings in content and in form. (Number the page 1, centered at the bottom on a page with extra space at the top because of a heading there.)

The first real problem in writing an introduction (often best done after the other parts) is selecting a heading for it. The stock term *introduction* is neither a precise nor an interesting preview of the contents. One of the best we've ever seen was "The WHY and HOW of This Report," but you don't need to use its wording. In fact, you should not copy anybody's word patterns in a title or anywhere else, especially if they are unusual. You should look at illustrations for ideas and principles of communication—then express your thoughts in your own way.

In explaining how you know your forthcoming facts are reliable, you need to state your *purpose, methods,* and *scope* so that the reader can judge whether the research would produce information that is sound and adequate for the purpose. Clear and explicit statement of the purpose is essential. No reader can judge a report without knowing what the writer set out to accomplish. Similarly, unless the research seems basically sound (in methodology and scope) for the purpose, the reader naturally discredits the whole report. The introduction, then, is an important part of the conviction in the report and therefore deserves careful attention from both writer and reader.

The section headed Purpose may take several paragraphs for full explanation, especially if it includes history or background of the problem; or it may be short. Long or short, it should contain some *one* sentence that is a pointed, concise statement of the problem you set out to solve. That sentence should come early, too. Then use the flashback method to follow quickly with clarifying background. As another alternative, you may relegate any very long background story to an appendix and refer the reader to it—especially if it is nonessential for most readers.

*Methods and scope* can come under separate headings or (because they are often nearly inseparable) under a combined heading. Your reader does want to know, however, what you intended to cover (scope) and how you got and analyzed your information (method—that big question again, How do you know?). In a study involving a choice or evaluation, for example, the introduction needs to explain the *criteria* or *standards* used, as a part of method and scope or as a separate part. In fact, since the criteria in such a report should become the major subdivisions, explanation and justification of them should be an important duty of the introduction.

How thoroughly you need to explain your methods depends on two major points: (1) how new and questionable your methods and findings are and (2) your reputation as a researcher. On both bases nobody questions the audit report of a reputable auditing firm that says no more on methods than the following: ". . . in accordance with generally accepted auditing standards, and accordingly included such tests of the accounting records and such other auditing procedures as we considered necessary in the circumstances." Most report writers, however, cannot depend so completely on either such standardized procedures or their reputations to convince their readers that they used sound research methods.

A frequent question is how much methodology to put in the introduction and how much (if any) to relegate to an appendix or to interweave along with the presentation of findings. No simple answer fits all cases and relieves you of thinking. A general answer is that you explain your methods at the best place(s) to show that your facts have a solid basis in valid research. Your reader will want at least a general idea from the introduction.

If specific details of research procedure, special materials and apparatus, or technique are too difficult for your reader(s) to remember and associate with the later resultant findings, you had better omit the specifics from the introduction and interweave them with the presentation of findings. (A specific question with its answers from a questionnaire is a good example.)

Like long and unnecessary background, certain details of methodology may sometimes go in an appendix, but only if (1) they would interrupt or unduly slow up the fast movement of the report proper and (2) most readers of the particular report would not want or need them. (Detailed explanations of unusual statistical procedures are good examples.)

Besides the standard parts (purpose, method, and scope), an introduction may take up one or more (rarely all) of several other possible topics:

- *Limitations* of time, money, or availability of data, for example.
- *Glossary* of explanation of technical words or certain terms applied in a sense unfamiliar to some likely readers.

The last part of the introduction should be a concise statement of your *basic plan*. Remind the reader of the major steps in your organization and logic—usually naming, in order, the topics from II (or 2.0) to the conclusions in your table of contents.

Usually one effective sentence can chart the way through to the end, like this: "As bases for determining the more favorable market conditions, this report examines—in this order—population characteristics, buying power, retail sales and drugstore sales and the attendant competition, stability of the economy, and the current business outlook." If you compare this statement of plan to the separate synopsis presented earlier, you will see that they both reflect the careful organization of the same report.

## Text

You have two major problems in presenting the text: (1) showing the reader the organization carefully worked out as the third step in report preparation and (2) phrasing well the findings of the second step (collection of data) and the interpretations made in the fourth step. Satisfactory solutions to both are necessary if you are to give your reader the reliable information wanted.

Your main methods for showing the overall organization, the relations between parts, and the relation of each part to the whole are headings and subheads, topic sentences, and summary and anticipating statements.

The *headings and subheads* grow directly out of your attack on the problem, where you broke it down into its elements and further subdivided it by raising questions about each. Now that you are presenting the facts that provide the answers, you need only phrase these elements and questions into headings and subheads. Remember that good headings, like functional titles, are indicative, interesting, concise, and (in some cases preferably) informative to the extent of telling the most important findings about the respective parts. (Notice the heads in the illustrative report.)

Just as a well-phrased heading may tell the main point about the section over which it stands, a topic sentence can give the essence of a paragraph and clearly foreshadow what the paragraph says. The topic sentence puts the big point across fast, arouses the reader's interest in seeing the supporting details that follow, and makes reading easier because of the preview. Although the resulting deductive paragraph plan is not the only one possible, it is the most useful for most kinds of writing, including report writing.

Reversing the plan produces a paragraph that presents a series of facts and arguments leading to a summarizing and maybe a concluding sentence at the end.

Both plans may apply to larger sections as well as to paragraphs. In fact, both a paragraph's topic sentence and the first part of a larger section may reflect, summarize, or provide a transition from a preceding part, as well as give the essence and preview of what is to follow. And endings of both paragraphs and larger parts commonly summarize them, show the significance of the just completed part to the whole problem at hand, and foreshadow what is to follow in the next section. (Look again at the example of coherence and transitions in Chapter 15 (the Nashville-Knoxville report).

Also consider this pair of examples illustrating bad and good report style (described more fully in Chapter 15).

Here's a flat example that is short only because it forces the reader to dig in its Figures 1 and 2 for the information:

> The greatest majority of the students interviewed showed their preference for buying at home in place of buying in the larger cities of Birmingham or Tuscaloosa. The overall percentage for the entire body of male students represented by the sample was 78. The freshmen showed an even greater tendency for home buying by their percentage of 84.
>
> Figure 1, below, gives a picture of the place of purchase of the entire group without regard to the nature of the group. Figure 2 divides the group according to the students' rank.

This rewrite is more informative, emphatic, and readable:

> When University of Alabama men are ready for a
> new suit, they buy at home 78 percent of the time.
> Although 4 out of every 100 will buy in Tuscaloosa
> and 7 in Birmingham, as shown in Figure 1, these
> 11 atypical cases do not warrant extensive
> advertising.
>
> The Alabama man, although never weaned from
> hometown buying in the majority of cases, does
> slowly shift his clothes-buying sources from home
> to Birmingham to Tuscaloosa. The gain of only 13
> out of every 100 purchasers over a four-year span,
> however (Figure 2), only confirms the suspicion
> that Bold Look advertising dollars in Tuscaloosa
> would be wasted.

Unless the logic of the situation clearly dictates otherwise, you'll do best to use the present tense throughout the text. When a reader reads it, your report analyzes, presents, takes up, examines, establishes, and finally concludes (all present tense). Of course, you'll have to assume that your most recent information is still applicable; hence, even though last year's sales figures are a historical record of what people bought, you are justified in saying, "People buy . . . ," meaning that they did buy, they are buying, and they will buy.

With your well-organized, clearly presented, and sharply summarized facts and analyses at the ends of sections, you will have led the reader to your statement of conclusions and (if wanted) recommendations.

## Conclusions and Recommendations

When you put your conclusions and recommendations into words, they should not be surprising—and they won't be if you have done an adequate job in the preceding part. There you should have presented all the evidence and analysis necessary to support your conclusions. *No new facts or analyses should appear in the conclusions or recommendations.*

Whether you separate conclusions and recommendations into two parts makes little difference. Some people prefer separation because, they say, the conclusions are strictly objective, logical results of what the report has said, whereas the recommendations are the individual writer's personal suggestions of what to do about the problem. Whichever point of view and plan you use, the important thing is to be as objective as possible in stating both conclusions and recommendations.

As evidence of that objectivity in your conclusions, and as a means of saving the reader the trouble of looking back into the text to see that you do have the data, you will do well to lift basic figures or statements from the earlier presentation and interweave them into the conclusion sentences. The writer of the previously illustrated synopsis knew that the reader could not possibly retain the 200 or more facts and figures given as evidence in 27 pages of analysis. In reminding the reader of the significant evidence affecting the decision in the conclusion, shown below, that writer wisely attached a specific figure to every fact. Note, too, the specific wording of that ending section—as well as the selectivity and brevity.

### VII. THE PREFERRED CITY: SAVANNAH

```
Although a Charleston druggist enjoys the
advantages of

--a population with a half million dollars more
buying income annually and families with $34 more
to spend

--11,000 additional potential customers

a Savannah drugstore would probably sell more
because of these advantages:

--$170,000 additional drugstore sales and $4,000
greater sales per drugstore

--$2.5 million more retail sales and $162 more
per person spent in retail stores

--1,000 more families and per capita income $87
higher

--four-year trend increases of 8 to 10 percent in
construction ($12 million more), bank deposits
($150 million more), and postal receipts ($200,000
more).
```

Both conclusions and recommendations need to be as pointed and positive as the facts and the writer's judgment will allow. (Itemization helps here.) Since the reader retains the right of final decision, present your recommendations as definite suggestions but certainly not as commands. The example just cited—phrased specifically in terms of the objective of the report, to select the city that is likely to be the more profitable scene of operations—avoids indecision on the one hand and its equally undesirable opposite, imperative command.

## Standard Supplements

### Appendix

Although the report reproduced as an illustration in this chapter didn't need an appendix, many reports do. The key to the decision is this: Use an appendix for material that the reader does not *need* to see to understand the text but that some readers may *want* to see to be sure your textual statements are clear and valid.

Frequent uses of appendixes are for survey questionnaires; for extensive formulas and statistical calculations; for extensive history, or detailed experimental methodology too long for the introduction; and for large maps, diagrams, or tables of figures that may be the basic data of the whole report but do not belong at any particular place in the text. Often the best way is to put a big table in the appendix and use appropriate figures from it as spot tables at key places in the text.

### Bibliography

On almost any big problem somebody has published something relevant. After finishing your research, you must tell what your sources are, to avoid the accusation of plagiarism and to provide your reader with places to get fuller information.

Your footnotes and/or internal citations in the text give the specific references. But at the end you list—in alphabetical order of authors' surnames (or titles of unsigned sources)—books, magazines, and other printed sources. If you need to cite letters, lectures, speeches, interviews, or other oral communications, usually you cite them by references within the sentences or in footnotes. If you want to list them at the end, you may use a heading like "Sources Used" or "References." "Bibliography" means list of *books*.

For illustration, we present the following bibliography from a 20-page report on a problem in intercultural business communication. After arranging the items alphabetically, this author also provided item numbers for concise, specific citations in the text (as explained in Chapter 14). The spacing is the preferred form of single within items (except when preparing copy for a printer) and double between them.

PUBLICATIONS CONSULTED

1. Condon, John C., and Faithi S. Yousef, <u>An Introduction to Intercultural Communication</u>, Bobbs-Merrill Educational Publishing, Indianapolis, 1975.

2. Graham, John L., "A Hidden Cause of America's Trade Deficit with Japan," Columbia Journal of World Business, 16:5-13 (Fall 1981).

3. Mason, R. Hal, Robert R. Miller, and Dale R. Weigel, International Business, Second Edition, John Wiley & Sons, New York, 1981.

4. Morris, Desmond, Manwatching: A Field Guide to Human Behavior, Jonathan Cope, London, 1978.

5. Terpstra, Vern, The Cultural Environment of International Business, South-Western Publishing, Cincinnati, 1978.

## Short Analytical Reports

Though this chapter and the preceding one have discussed major analytical reports, you will often write short analytical reports that condense the format somewhat, as explained here.

1. The short analytical report usually omits all the preliminaries except the title page, letter of transmittal, and (possibly) the synopsis.

2. It often also combines the letter of transmittal and synopsis, omits the table of contents and depends on headings throughout the report, omits the bibliography and provides the full references as footnotes or interwoven citations, and interweaves the essential parts of possible appendix material right into the text.

3. It may (but rarely does) also put the title-page information at the top of the first page and move right into the next part on that page; combine the essentials of authorization, transmittal, and synopsis as a summary right after the title-page information; and omit the introduction as a separate part and interweave its essentials into the text. It could thus have only three sections—the title-page information, the summary, and the text.

When you prepare either a long or short report, use the following checklist before final typing. Although the checklist is primarily for complete analytical reports, many of the items apply to shorter ones. Those that may not apply to short analytical reports have an asterisk at the end. For greatest usefulness, the sections appear in the order of presentation in the final report. Remember, however, that this is only a checklist. If you need fuller explanation of a point, use the index to find it in the appropriate chapter or in Appendix C.

# Checklist for Major Analytical Reports

*\* (An asterisk means not necessary in short reports.)*

**Preliminary Parts and Mechanics (PPM)**

1. If you use a *cover,* be sure it carries at least the title and author's name (or reveals them from the title page).*

2. The *title page* needs at least four items: *(a)* the title (phrased for precision, interest, and conciseness), *(b)* the authorizer's name and title, *(c)* the author's name and title, and *(d)* the place and date (in that order and centered or in some other pleasant design). It may also have the organization's name, a brief abstract, a distribution list, and/or a project- or serial-number identification, and/or a secrecy classification.

3. A *transmittal letter* or *memo,* in regular letter/memo form:
   a. Starts by transmitting the report and, naturally and subordinately, referring to the topic and authorization.
   b. May reveal briefly only the general decision or may synopsize the report (unless a separate synopsis comes later).
   c. Ends expressing appreciation (and perhaps willingness to help further.)

4. The *table of contents* (or simply contents) lists the later successive parts and body sections of the report, with beginning page numbers for all and (optional, but helpful) outline symbols before the body sections.*
   a. A separate synopsis (if used), as the next page following the contents table, is the first item listed (with no outline symbol, flush at the left margin, and with the first of your vertically aligned, spaced-period leader lines between items and the page number column).*
   b. The greatest part of the table of contents shows the organization/outline of the body.
      (1) Use of outline symbols is your option.
      (2) Wording (not the type form) of heads here and in the report must be identical.
      (3) Break too-long lines to leave at least seven spaces between them and the page-number column, indent the carryover(s) and subdivisions, and make leaders of at least three spaced periods, with a space before and after.
      (4) Double-space between at least the parts and major divisions, and systematically single-space elsewhere only to keep to one page.

(5) Page numbers and Roman outline symbol numbers line up on the right.

c. Supplementary parts (i.e., optional appendix and bibliography) do *not* have outline symbols but do continue the Arabic page numbers of the text.

5. A separate *synopsis* (SY) or *informative abstract* is usually single-spaced with double spacing between paragraphs.*

a. Make the first paragraph stress the problem solution (or its main part) and subordinately reveal enough about the authorizer, purpose, and preparer for extra copies of the synopsis used alone to be clear.

b. Compactly and specifically present for each major division, in order and preferably in proportion, your main supporting facts and figures, while subordinately interweaving any necessary background, method, and scope.

c. Emphasize findings, not analysis—preferably in present tense. Rely on sequence and only short transitional words for coherence.

6. Give attention to *report mechanics* (layout and typing) and, if needed, the generally applicable points of mechanics. (See **TM** in Appendix C):

a. Double-space the body and make its bottom and side margins 1–1½ inches, top slightly less, plus extra space for the bite of any binding used.

b. Start a new page only to (1) start a new part (the body is all one), (2) leave a bottom margin, or (3) allow for at least two lines of copy below a heading.

c. Starting with the title fly, if used, count preliminary pages down through the synopsis and (beginning with the table of contents) number them in lowercase Romans.

d. Give all later pages Arabic numbers, *without decorations*, two or more spaces above the right ends of lines (except centered at the bottom on first pages of report parts).

e. Vary the placement, spacing above and below, and type form of headings to show different levels. Underline any heads not in solid capitals, and double-space centered heads of more than one line.

### Organization/Outlining (O)

1. Phrase your title to indicate the nature, purpose, and limits of your study and to provide a basis of classification; then make the text's major divisional headings on that basis (usually comparison or partition).

2. Use no heading for your whole text and no single subhead anywhere. The major divisions of your report (symbolized by 1.0, 2.0, 3.0 . . . or I, II, III . . .) are first the introduction, then the logical divisions

of your topic (the text, in two or more parts), and your conclusions and recommendations (together or separate).

3. Phrase each heading to cover all of its subdivisions.

4. In phrasing, placing, and sequencing all division headings at all levels, make clear the relationship of each part to its whole and its function in your interpretation. Outline symbols may help.

5. Maintain parallelism of grammatical form among headings of the same class, using synonyms where necessary to avoid monotony of wording.

6. Try to make your headings informative (preferably "talking"—not just topical) as well as precisely indicative of what they include.

7. Use enough headings to help show your organization.

8. Use placement and type variations in headings (and maybe outline symbols) to show their status in the outline, and relations to others.

### Introduction (I)

Clear presentation of the *purpose, method, scope,* and *basic plan* is the main duty of the introduction.

1. Put the exact report title at the top of the first page of the body.

2. Then, for this first major division, try to phrase a more meaningful title than the stock term *introduction.*

3. Though you need several paragraphs, *(a)* be sure your *purpose* is compatible with your title and organizational plan and *(b)* provide one particular sentence that is a pointed, concise statement of your problem.

4. Give a short *history* of the problem only if needed as a lead-in to purpose (details, if helpful, can go in a later flashback—or maybe an appendix).

5. Explain your *methods* of gathering data specifically enough to show thoroughness and be convincing, but significant details beyond a reader's ability to remember (like questions in a long questionnaire or settings and measurements in a laboratory experiment) can best come later with the data.

6. As part of *scope,* clearly show any limits of coverage not made in the title; but justified (not excuse-making) limits of time or money are more appropriate in the letter of transmittal.

7. You might include a glossary for a large number of necessary unusual terms; for only a few, preferably explain each parenthetically just after the first time it comes up.

8. Try to cover the required elements of the introduction without breaking it into too many pieces (more than *purpose, method, scope,* and *plan*), especially if the parts are short.

9. In a "Basic Plan" section at the end of the introduction, brief the reader on the sequence of major topics coming.

10. Keep findings, conclusions, and recommendations out of the introduction. If you want to get them to the reader early, a synopsis or even the letter of transmittal is a better place.

### Style (S)

1. Remember that a natural style is clearer, easier, and more interesting than impersonal style for both writer and reader.

2. Enliven your style and increase readability by *(a)* using commonly understood words and short, direct sentences and paragraphs, *(b)* making people (not things) subjects and/or objects of many if not most sentences, *(c)* using mostly active voice, *(d)* eliminating "It is" and "There are" sentence beginnings, *(e)* using discrete (but not overlisted) itemizations for pointed, concise statements like conclusions and recommendations, *(f)* putting the emphasis where it belongs (see **Emp** and **Sub** in Appendix C), and *(g)* presenting quantities in easily read and remembered forms (ratios, fractions, rounded numbers, simplified percentages, rankings). Remember that the relative status of something (percentage, ratio, or rank) is often more significant than the absolute value.

3. To avoid seeming prejudiced, state plausible assumptions made, give immediate and specific evidence to support points, give all the same kind(s) of information about each compared subject, and avoid emotionally persuasive passages and disclaimers like "objective," "unbiased," "impersonal."

4. Use the universal present tense to indicate continuing existence for things and tendencies that existed in the past, exist now, and are likely to continue.

5. Don't use headings as antecedents of pronouns; your text should read coherently *without* the heads.

6. Make clear, by topic statement at the beginning of each big section, the topic and any subdivisions (in the order of later treatment).

7. At the end of a sizable section, sum it up with emphasis on its significance to the overall problem (and preferably with a transitional forward look to the next topic).

8. Interpret key points from graphics in relation to your objective, *emphasizing the message* and (by parenthetical, midsentence, or

nonsubject mention) *subordinating the reference to the graphic and its location.*

9. By evidence, explanation, and logic, lead the reader to foresee likely conclusions and recommendations coming; but (ordinarily) leave explicit statements of them until the end.

## Graphics (GR)

1. Use graphics whenever helpful; but omit useless ones.

2. Choose the best kind of graphic for the kind of data.

3. Lead in with discussion of the point and proper introduction of the graphic (emphasizing what to see in it), tell *subordinately* where it is if not in sight, and (usually) follow with necessary key points of emphasis or interpretation.

4. For reader convenience, place graphics near the discussion (small ones may be on graph paper on the same page, larger ones on the next page).

5. Give graphics proper titles, numbers (charts and tables in separate consecutive series), labeled parts, and credit sources of published ones.

6. Give reliable dates of graphic information (not always the date of publication), maybe in parentheses after the title.

7. For easy reading and close relationships, consider small spot tables closely associated with different points, though they may all come from one collective source table (appendix material) that buries key points.

## Documentation (DOC)

When you use others' material (except as explained in Item 1 below), you must give credit (to avoid plagiarism) and you want to cite the source as support for your point. The usual means for citing published material are a bibliography and specific citations in the text, source indications on graphics, and possibly footnotes.

1. Put in your bibliography publications from which you used special ideas, facts (including graphics), or quotations. *Special* excludes information that is *(a)* common knowledge, *(b)* obvious, or *(c)* widely available in many sources of the kind.

2. Make specific citations (at the points you used others' materials) in the simplest way. Remember that to promote continuity and ease of reading, interweaving citations into the text is preferable to footnotes.

3. Avoid repeating complete citations (except for different page numbers) as long as you're drawing from the same source, but make very clear what you borrowed.

4. For convenience, number footnotes (if used) anew on each page.

5. Cite the basic circumstances in the text or a footnote where you use information from interviews, speeches, and letters (which do not belong in the bibliography); explain questionnaires, observations, and experiments as sources in the *methods* section of the Introduction (plus necessary specific questions, conditions, or procedures, along with the findings in the text—I-5 above).

6. Use no source citations for the synopsis, conclusions, or recommendations; they all derive from the text, where needed citations must appear.

7. Unless restricted by assignment, be sure to use an established, clear, and consistent documentation form and *get it exactly right*—in content, capitalization, sequence, and punctuation.

### Conclusions and Recommendations (C/R)

1. Introduce no new facts in the terminal section; it derives from, maybe quickly recaps, and interprets information presented before.

2. Put conclusions and recommendations (together or separately) in their order of logic or importance.

3. State conclusions and recommendations pointedly (specifically and concisely, with key supporting facts and figures), as firmly as your information justifies (rarely involving "prove"), and (preferably) itemized.

4. Take a stand (including "My findings prove nothing," if necessary).

5. Make sure your conclusions and recommendations derive from facts and explanations already presented.

6. You may conclude and suggest action but not command.

## The Illustration

The following illustration of a complete analytical report (which one of our students wrote) is on a typical business/industrial problem. **[We've single-spaced the body—contrary to Checklist point 6a—solely to save about five pages in the book.]**

In compiling and analyzing information on such a topic, the report writer considered the site, market trends, local regulations, and a large amount of cost and financial information. Notice especially the varied graphics and clear presentation of technical information, important features of a major analytical report.

WHY REDEVELOPMENT OF STRAUSS COMPLEX

IS NOT NOW ADVISABLE

Prepared for

Richard Strauss, Owner

Strauss Complex

Rachel Garcia, Manager
Property Research Division
Garcia Commercial Mortgage
3607 Louisiana Street
San Diego, California 92104

April 3, 1985

April 3, 1985


Garcia Commercial Mortgage
Property Research Division
3607 Louisiana Street
San Diego, CA 92104


Mr. Richard Strauss, Owner
Strauss Complex
2233 El Cajon Boulevard
San Diego, CA 92115

Dear Mr. Strauss:

Here is the report you requested, determining the
advisability of redeveloping the industrial park into
office buildings at your complex.

The report shows that the proposed plan is not advisable
at this time for economic reasons. The existing park will
continue to generate more revenue until lease rates rise
in the Kearny Mesa area or operating costs decline.

I am glad I had the opportunity to prepare this report
for you and would be happy to serve you again.


Sincerely yours,

GARCIA COMMERCIAL MORTGAGE




Rachel Garcia, Manager
Property Research Division


RG:sar
Encl.

Contents

## Executive Summary

### Recommendation

Strauss Complex will provide a greater rate of return if
you retain its present use, rather than redeveloping it
to an office complex.

### Investigation

Site Analysis. Strauss Complex (SC) is located on the
south side of Clairemont Mesa Boulevard just east of
Highway 163, within 10 minutes of downtown San Diego. SC
enjoys easy access to all modes of transportation,
including air, all (major) freeways, shipping, and rail.

Market Trends. Kearny Mesa continues to change from an
individual use to an office use. Its combination of
competitive lease rates ($0.58-$1.45/SF) and a relatively
low office vacancy rate (18.3 percent) shows that the
demand for office use will remain high.

Building Specification and Cost Analysis. Six three-story
office buildings, similar to the one on-site, were
proposed to replace the existing industrial buildings.
These 61,000-square-foot (SF) buildings would cost $2.3
million each, including all tenant improvements,
landscaping, and parking facilities. The total
construction cost of $13.8 million for the entire project
includes $12,500 for demolition of the existing
buildings.

Financial Information. Financing can be arranged at 12.5
percent over a 30-year period on $11.575 million of the
total project cost of $13.8 million. This package would
require a down payment of $2.225 million and a monthly
payment of $123,535.

The proposed net annual operating income for the entire
office complex amounts to $383,019, based on a gross
income of $2,645,000 less the annual operating expenses
of $779,760 and the loan payment.

The current annual net income for the existing project
averages $532,980, based on a gross income for the entire
project of $696,305 and annual operating expenses of
$166,415. The existing project thus produces $150,000
more per year than would the proposed redevelopment.

## WHY REDEVELOPMENT OF STRAUSS COMPLEX IS NOT NOW ADVISABLE

### I. The Why and How of This Report

This report will consider the advisability of replacing the existing industrial facility with an office complex. It evaluates both the existing and the proposed land uses to determine whether redevelopment seems economically favorable.

We compiled the information for this report from a series of interviews with professionals in the real estate development industry and from industry publications. These sources provided us with the foundation on which we based our report and the necessary details to assist us in drawing our conclusions.

Our recommendation on the proposed redevelopment of this property stems from consideration of the location, market trends, type of building and its construction costs, and financial information.

### II. Positive Aspects of Location and Available Transportation

#### Location

The Strauss Complex (SC), located on the south side of Clairemont Mesa Boulevard just east of Highway 163 (according to its sales brochure), is "within 10 minutes driving time of downtown San Diego; 15 minutes from San Diego International Airport and in a strategic location within the City and County of San Diego" (4, meaning Item 4 in the Bibliography). The vicinity map (Figure 1) shows the central location of the proposed site.

#### Transportation

Garcia Commercial Mortgage determined that SC is within easy reach of five major modes of transportation and within two miles of all major freeways in San Diego County. Santa Fe and Southern Pacific rail sidings are within 10 minutes of the complex. Approximately 75 trucking firms offer local, regional, and transcontinental services. The port of San Diego and the San Diego International Airport are within 15 minutes of the site. Montgomery Field, a small commuter airfield, runs adjacent to the complex (4).

1

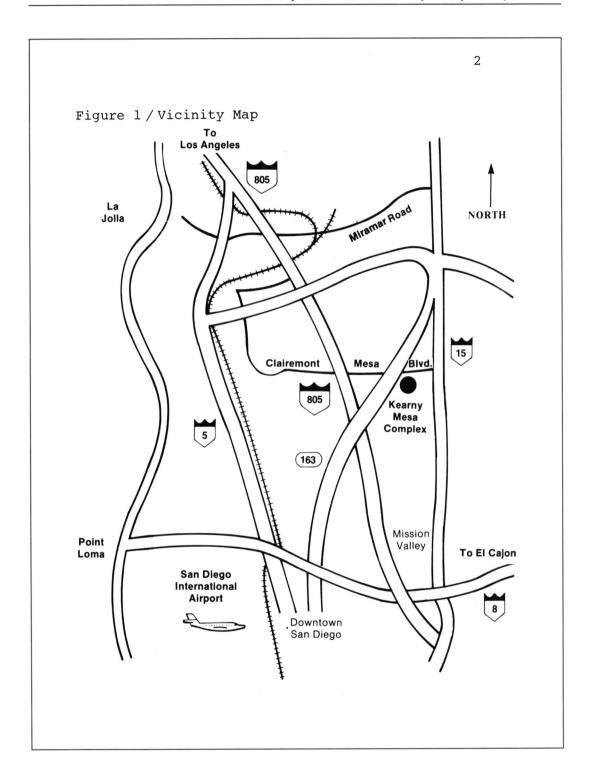

Figure 1 / Vicinity Map

3

## III. Favorable Market Trends

### Shift in Uses

In the past, Kearny Mesa has been primarily an industrial area. With the high cost of office space and the rapid growth of San Diego, many companies are moving to Kearny Mesa. This demand for office space has pushed industry east to lower rent areas and caused an increase in rents in the Kearny Mesa area.

### Lease Comparison

Kearny Mesa's lease rent rates are currently very competitive within the San Diego market. Table 1 shows a comparison of the lease rates of the major areas of San Diego.

Table 1. Lease Rates

| | |
|---|---|
| Kearny Mesa | $0.58-$1.45/SF |
| Downtown | $0.29-$2.92/SF |
| Mission Valley | $0.50-$1.85/SF |
| Sorrento Valley | $0.65-$1.65/SF (1:14) |

The lease rates in the Kearny Mesa area continue to climb. In 1983 the average lease rate increased to $1.03 per square foot (SF), an increase of 10.8 percent over the 1982 average. The current lease rates for office use in Kearny Mesa range from $0.58 to $1.45 per SF (1:24).

Even with the rising lease rates, Kearny Mesa's rates rank below those areas of high office use, such as Downtown, Mission Valley, and Sorrento Valley. As a result, the demand for Kearny Mesa office space will remain high.

### Vacancy Rates

During the past five years, vacancy rates in Kearny Mesa have risen from 16 to 18.3 percent. This change was mostly an increase in vacancies in buildings constructed between 1967 and 1979. In contrast, vacancies declined in newer office buildings (1:24). Figure 2 gives a comparison of some of the vacancy rates in San Diego County.

## IV. Competitive Building Specification and Cost Analysis

We based construction costs, specifications, and building layout for the proposed redevelopment of Strauss

4

## Figure 2 / Vacancy Comparison

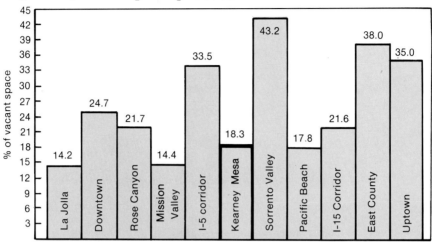

Complex on costs and requirements of the recently
completed three-story office building located there.

The redevelopment will include the demolition of all
existing industrial buildings and the construction of six
new three-story office buildings complete with parking
and landscaping. All new office buildings will be nearly
identical to the existing building. Figure 3 later in the
report illustrates the site plan.

## Specification

Each building will have a gross area of 35,424 square
feet. The total net leasable area is 30,938 square feet
divided by floor as follows:

| | |
|---|---|
| 1st floor | 9,048 SF |
| 2d floor | 10,008 SF |
| 3d floor | 11,882 SF |

Here is a detailed building description from an
interview with the construction supervisor of Garcia
Commercial Mortgage Company:

Approximately 1.40 acres (60,984 SF) of usable land
will be required for each building. This area will
allow for the building pad of 165′ × 75′, parking for
124 cars or four spaces per 1,000 square feet of

5

leasable space, and a smooth blend of perimeter landscaping.

The office buildings will be of steel frame construction with glu-lam beams supporting a 2' × 4' wood floor joist system. The exterior will be constructed of precast concrete panels with tinted reflective glass in painted aluminum frames. The roof will be a built-up composite rock roof.

The floors will be ceramic tile in the rest rooms and carpet and sheet vinyl throughout the rest of the tenant and common areas. The service core on each floor has two rest rooms, one janitorial closet, one electric room, two stairwells, and one elevator.

The elevator is a hydroelectric U.S. Elevator with a capacity of 2,500 pounds or 16 passengers. It has double doors and an average speed of 150 feet per minute. All mechanical equipment except elevator equipment is housed on the roof. The elevator equipment is housed on the first floor.

## Building Costs

We estimate total building costs to be $13,799,994 for the entire redevelopment project. As Table 2 shows, this includes a demolition cost of $12,500 for all existing industrial buildings and a construction cost of about $2,300,000 for each new office building.

The building cost per square foot of net leasable area runs to $64.92 per square foot, which includes all hard and soft costs. This price compares favorably with the average building costs from the 1985 Dodge Construction Systems Cost Manual, which shows a cost of $65 per square foot for a similar type of building (5:33).

Another check using the Mean System Costs 1984 shows a price of $63 per square foot for this location (6:441). Both the Dodge and the Mean prices show that the estimated cost compares very competitively for an office building of this type.

## Building Layout

The arrangement of the proposed buildings maximizes the available space and creates a pleasant working environment for the variety of tenants who will occupy them.

As you can see in Figure 3, on Lot 6 three buildings line up parallel to Complex Drive. Parking is at both the

6

Table 2: Construction Cost Summary

| Item | Cost per Building | Total Project Cost |
|------|------:|------:|
| Hard costs: | | |
| Demolition | n/a | $    12,500 |
| Shell construction | $1,318,005 | 7,908,030 |
| Tenant improvements | 425,912 | 1,703,648 |
| Landscaping | 34,409 | 706,454 |
| Other expenses | 7,625 | 45,750 |
| | | |
| Soft costs: | | |
| Architectural and engineering | 53,825 | 322,950 |
| Civil | 5,174 | 31,044 |
| Soils | 4,194 | 25,164 |
| Testing | 7,464 | 44,784 |
| Printing and reimbursables | 2,628 | 15,768 |
| Title | 5,471 | 32,826 |
| Legal | 1,394 | 8,364 |
| Insurance | 2,151 | 12,906 |
| Permits and fees | 5,247 | 31,482 |
| Leasing commission | 119,546 | 717,276 |
| Marketing | 937 | 5,622 |
| Interest | 98,975 | 593,850 |
| Development fee | 40,000 | 240,000 |
| | | |
| Subtotal | 2,132,957 | 12,797,742 |
| | | |
| Cost adjustment* | 167,042 | 1,002,252 |
| | | |
| Total | $2,299,999 | $13,799,994 (5) |

*Cost adjustment is based on a change of the Consumer Price Index of 7.83 percent.

east and west ends of Lot 6 and behind each office building. Additional visitor parking is in a central parking lot in front of the office buildings. All building and parking lot perimeters have bluegrass lawn and eucalyptus trees.

The building on Lot 2 forms a horseshoe cluster with a centrally landscaped quad area. This arrangement will help attract a large single user for this area, giving the occupant a feeling of having its own corporate campus. Parking around the perimeter of the building cluster allows easy access. Like Lot 6, all building and

7

## Figure 3 / Proposed Building Layout

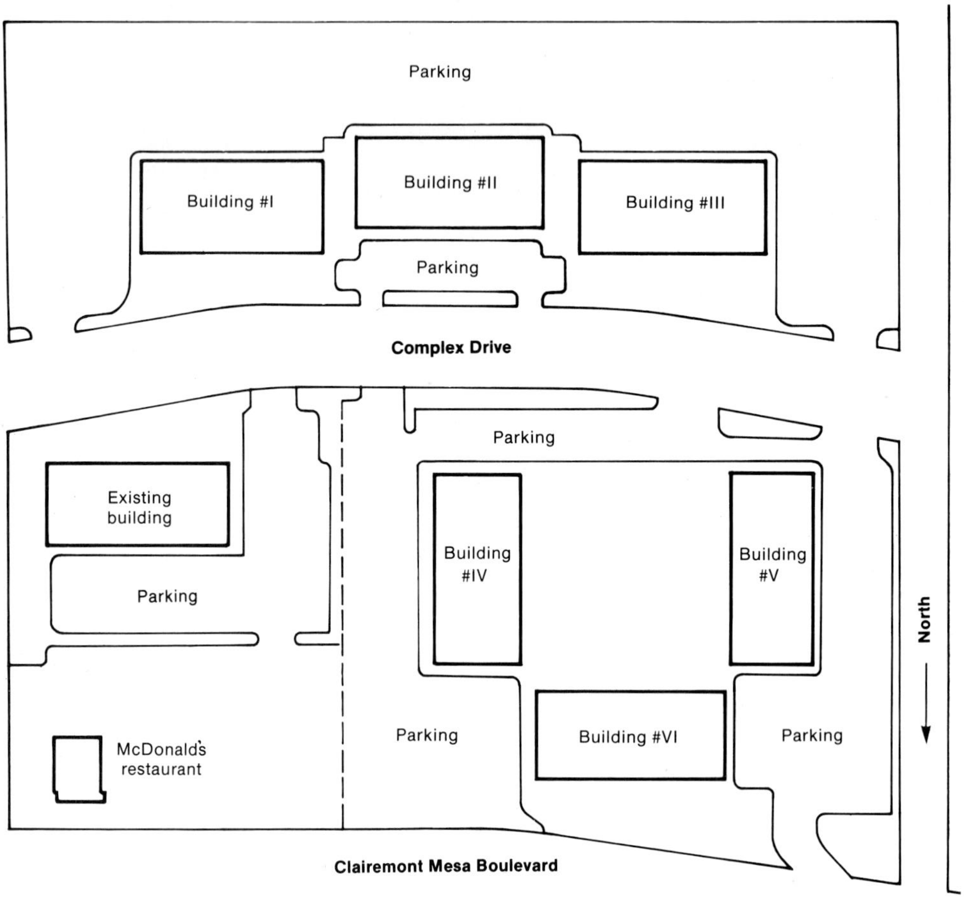

parking lot perimeters will have lawn and trees and will feature automatic irrigation systems.

This layout will help create a pleasant working environment that will make Strauss Complex a desirable place to work.

8

## V. Negative Financial Information

### Loan Package

The total estimated construction costs come to $13.8 million over a four-year period. We can arrange 12.5 percent financing for a construction loan of $11.575 million, requiring a down payment of $2.225 million. The monthly payment for this loan package will be $123,535 based on a 30-year loan compounded monthly. Permanent financing will have to be arranged at the end of the four-year construction period.

### Operating Costs

The projected operating cost averages 35 cents per SF per month (Table 3), or $10,830 per building per month, excluding loan payment.

Table 3: Operating Costs

| Item | Per Square Foot per Month |
| --- | --- |
| Property taxes | 11.5¢ |
| Insurance | 0.85 |
| Maintenance (landscape, water, A/C, parking lot sweeping, windows, etc.) | 4.4 |
| Janitorial services | 4.5 |
| Janitorial supplies | 0.2 |
| Utilities | 10.25 |
| Property management | 3.0 |
| Contingency/miscellaneous/reserve | 0.3 |
| Total | 35.0¢ |

### Operating Income

The projected monthly gross operating income comes to $38,673 per building based on a $1.25 per SF rent. Subtracting monthly operating costs and monthly debt service, the monthly cash income per building is $7,254, or $43,523 per month for the entire project. Table 4 gives a breakdown of projected income.

9

### Table 4: Projected Income

| | |
|---|---:|
| 186,628 SF @ $1.25 per SF × 12 months | $2,784,420 |
| Less: Vacancy allowance (5%) | (139,221) |
| Net operating income | 2,533,822 |
| Less: Debt service | 1,482,420 |
| Spendable | 1,482,420 |
| Total cash in project | $2,225,000 |
| Percent return | 52.3% |

## Current Income

The existing industrial complex currently earns a gross income of $696,305 with operating expenses of $166,415, with a net total income for the year of $532,980. Table 5 shows the comparison between the current income of the existing industrial complex and the projected income of the office complex.

### Table 5: Earning Comparison

| Per Year | Industrial | Office |
|---|---|---|
| Gross income | $696,305 | $2,645,199 |
| Operating costs | 166,415 | 779,760 |
| Debt service | —0— | 1,482,420 |
| Net income | 529,890 | 383,079 |

## VI. Recommendation

The high rate of growth, the location, and the construction outlook make this project seem quite attractive. With lease rates climbing and low vacancy rates in the Kearny Mesa area, a definite market exists for this type of office complex in Kearny Mesa.

Comparing the net income of the existing project with that of the proposed project, however, shows that the existing project will provide a greater return. We therefore think that the redevelopment of Strauss Complex to an office complex is not economically advisable at this time.

10

## Bibliography

1. Chamber of Commerce, 1983 San Diego Office Building Guide, Chamber of Commerce, San Diego Office, 1983.

2. Duncan, Don, "Responses of Real Estate Lenders and Borrowers to Changing Mortgage Money Market Conditions in San Diego County," master's thesis, San Diego State University, 1984.

3. Estes, Jack C., Handbook of Loan Payment Tables, McGraw-Hill, New York, 1976.

4. Garcia Commercial Mortgage, Strauss Complex Sales Brochure No. KMC-C-4/72.

5. Perira, Percival E., "1985 Construction Cost Information," Dodge Construction Systems Cost Manual, pp. 2-33.

6. Smith, Kornelius, "Square Footage Costs," Mean System Costs 1984, pp. 8-441.

## Questions and Exercises

1. Besides usually being longer, what are the main differences between short analytical reports as discussed in Chapter 16 and the short reports discussed and illustrated in Chapter 13?

2. Besides being shorter, what are the main differences you may make between a short analytical report you're writing and a complete analytical report?

3. Try your mind and hand at presenting graphically your answers to Question 2.

4. Give a skeletal table of contents of a short analytical report for each psychological plan of message (direct, disappointing, persuasive—as explained in Chapter 5).

5. What was your answer about the conciseness of the final (?) report title worked out (in the section on Title Page)? Explain.

# Appendixes

# Appendix A

## Cases

### About the Cases in This Book

For clear, quick, and easy case identification and cross-referencing, you will find the following efficient numbering system:

1. All cases in Appendix A carry sequential numbers labeling them by related chapter and individual number, as 6–12, for example.

2. Appendix B provides supplementary cases in eighteen series. Each series carries a Roman numeral, and the related cases in each series carry capital-letter designations. At appropriate places you will see references to these supplementary cases of the same kind with cross-references such as "Appendix B I A; VIII A, D" (meaning Case A of Series I in Appendix B and Cases A and D in Series VIII are three more similar cases).

The cases in this book are disguised and sometimes slightly modified real situations. Mostly they are from among the more difficult communication situations of business. Most names of firms and individuals, however, are fictitious for obvious reasons.

We have tried to give you the basic information needed without complicating details. You are expected to fill in details from your own imagination. But you are not to go contrary to the statements or implications in the cases, and your imaginary details must be reasonably likely.

*The writing in the cases is intentionally not good—nor is the order of points the best—because you would learn nothing from copying from us. So beware of copying our sentences and clauses. Put your ideas in your own words.*

## Cases for Chapter 6

(Good-News and Goodwill Messages)

**6–1.** As company president, you must write a memo to all employees asking them to meet with their supervisors and a member of the personnel staff to fill out a job description questionnaire during the next two weeks.

An up-to-date job description is important because it helps supervisors make proper work assignments and ensures that the employees will not be asked to perform tasks that do not fall within the limits of their skills, experiences, and responsibilities. Workers can know what supervisors expect and can evaluate their own performance in light of the established job objectives. A job description serves as a basis for the annual performance appraisal, helps set appropriate wage and salary levels, helps explain to newly hired employees what the job entails.

Some employees have been dissatisfied with the existing set of job descriptions. Some employees are performing tasks and fulfilling responsibilities that do not appear in job descriptions, while others are performing jobs that do not even have written descriptions. These and other problems associated with job descriptions have made recruiting and hiring more difficult, have complicated grievance handling, and have caused serious problems in performance appraisal. Write the memo asking the employees to prepare the questionnaire as carefully and completely as possible and thus give the personnel staff as much help as they possibly can.

**6–2.** Assume that you are John Hansen, Universitetsforlaget, Box 2977, Tøyen Oslo 6, Norway, and you have a good friend Thomas Rutherford, general manager of ISBN, a large timber company manufacturing plywood, fabricating timber panel products, and merchandising through its own retail outlets. Rutherford will be visiting the UK and staying in London April 17–24 and is interested in observing the method of distribution and merchandising of timber-based panel products, including chipboard, plywood, moldings . . . .

To help Rutherford make contacts, you are writing J. G. Bigham, General Marketing Manager, Global Manufacturers, 37 Queen Street, Henley on Thames, Oxon RG9 1AJ, asking Bigham to look over Rutherford's itinerary in suggesting contacts and giving advice about where he can best see how things are done in London.

**6–3.** Ever since you were a child, you have heard about Lloyd's of London. Now that you are wealthy and want prestige and safety, you think you'd like to be a member of Lloyd's. You don't know, however, how much money you have to have, how much activity it takes, how the annual returns run, what the liabilities are, how you become a member, whether you have to have an agent (and if so, how you get one), how you get out of the arrangement, what the tax arrangements are. Since you like to go to Europe at least every few years, you wonder if being a member of Lloyd's of London would make these trips tax-deductible.

Write an inquiry to Lloyd's Bank International Ltd., Membership Records Department, 40–46 Queen Victoria Street, London EC 4PA EL, UK-England.

**6–4.** From the Medina County Historical Association, 610 First Street, Hondo, Texas 78861, you order and put on your Visa bill a recently published account on the history of Medina County for $57.50. This book is to be a gift to your sister, whose birthday is August 20. You ordered it in May, but now it's August 10 and the book has not come. Your sister lives in Hong Kong. Getting the book to her now will be impossible; so you are canceling your order and asking Visa to make an adjustment.

a.  Write the letter to Visa.
b.  Write the letter to the Medina County Historical Association.

**6–5.** In the last seven years your drink company, Coola-Cola, 1819 Peachstreet NE, Atlanta, GA 30345, has had problems with sluggish overseas operations. Sales volume percentage increase in unit sales of concentrate and syrup to the foreign market was 14 percent six years ago, but now it has dropped to 1 percent. On the other hand, domestic volume growth has been steady (9 percent six years ago and 9 percent this year).

As CEO, you are inviting 35 executives to fly to Jekyll Island, Georgia, two weekends from now to hammer out a strategy to revive foreign sales. The company will pay all expenses for this strategy meeting at the Hilton that will begin Friday at 5 P.M. and continue through Sunday noon dinner.

Coola-Cola will have to urge its foreign bottling systems to increase availability, awareness, and per capita consumption of its drinks. Perhaps the company needs new packaging and bottling equipment and needs to spend more money on marketing. Perhaps it should move into fountain sales and vending machines, which are nonexistent overseas but are lucrative in the United States.

Diet Coola-Cola presently sells in just 42 countries but will move into 15 additional ones by year-end.

Write the memo for the CEO that will go to the 35 executives.

**6–6.** As your CEO directed, you are to write a memo to all employees encouraging them to attend one of the three scheduled sessions with the personnel manager on a possible need for updating their pension and retirement arrangements with your company, Pollafirm Corporation. You are in the Public Relations Division. Pollafirm's average retirement age is 62, partly because of early-out incentives. Only 75 employees out of Pollafirm's 10,500 are over age 65, and only 4 employees have retired at age 70 or above since 1979.

**6–7.** Another memo you are to write from the Public Relations Division of Pollafirm Corporation (preceding case) is to blue-collar workers telling them about the five-week workshops where they can take self-assessment and interest tests and learn more about the company. These workshops will be held in the company library for one hour after each work shift starting two weeks from today. (You found when you worked for a competitor that such programs stimulate an increase in morale and in the quality and quantity of work. You also found that many blue-collar workers made the climb into salaried jobs.)

**6–8.**    Another memo to all employees from the Public Relations Division of Pollafirm (preceding cases) tells them about the redesigned cafeteria menu to aid workers in cutting their intake of cholesterol and sugar. After a pilot study involving 70 workers, you found that the workers cut their intake of cholesterol by 45 percent and their intake of sugar by 34 percent and increased their average intake of 10 vitamins by 11 percent (all medically recommended changes for health and longevity).

**6–9.**    With TV advertising costs rising 10 percent or more a year, more and more companies (including your Finex Corporation, maker of inexpensive but durable watches) have been cramming sales pitches into 15-second commercials. As director of marketing for Finex, you get the idea that you might be wise to have a special Christmas sales campaign on TV and at cinemas telling your prospective customers that Finex makes more than 200 styles of inexpensive watches. Instead of 15-second commercials, you are proposing two-minute commercials in five major cities (New York, Chicago, San Francisco, Dallas, and Miami) promoting a showcase of your watches. In two minutes the ad can feature at least 11 styles. Viewers will stay tuned for special effects that show giant watches doubling as beach chairs and racquetball courts.

Before you go ahead and talk with your advertising agency about this idea of gluing a Christmas catalog to the TV screen, you write a memo to members of the board of directors asking them to come to a meeting in the boardroom next Tuesday morning at 10 A.M. to discuss the proposed advertising.

**6–10.**    When you (Charles or Charlene Todd, 810 13th Street Northeast, Toronto, Ontario, M6S 4G1, Canada) were a child you loved the book *Miss Flora McFlimsey's Christmas Story,* by Andrew Walden. A visitor, however, tore up the book; so you ended that visit with just the covers and a few pages. Now that you have a child of your own, you want to get a copy of that favorite book; so you're writing Olde Book Shoppe, 115 West 45th Street, New York 10036, asking it to find the book. The Shoppe has a special service called Book Chase.

**6–11.**    You are moving to Kowloon, Hong Kong, and want to open an account at a tailor company called Mings, 19-B Hankow Road 1/F,

Kowloon, Hong Kong. Where you have lived before, you have had numerous charge accounts and a bank account. Write a letter to Mings asking for an account and giving references. You are an accountant with the Deloitte Haskins & Sells overseas division.

**6–12.** As director of sales for the toy helicopter manufacturer Red Box Toys, P.O. Box 8764, Boston, MA 02189, write a memo recalling your Combat Copters helicopters from your distributors. The Consumer Product Safety Commission says that at least 30 incidents are on record where the helicopters have flown into people's faces, sometimes causing lacerations. Urge distributors to get consumers to return the toys to the place where they bought them. Company guarantees refunds.

**6–13.** A drug for arthritis called Arment has been on the market for 15 years, and its sales volume has increased each year. The bottles of Arment, like those of a well-known painkiller, were tampered with, this time in two New York drugstores, with the result that five people have died from poison. As Director of Marketing, Allied Drug Products Company, Chattanooga, TN 37400, you must recall all Arment, see that a new tamperproof cap is designed, and then put the drug back on the market. Write a form letter or memo that makes the request to your dealers to return the product to you, but add some resale on Arment (inexpensive, FDA-approved, used 15 years safely, large numbers of users . . .).

**6–14.** As Thornton Matthews, Director of Administration, National Conference of Bar Examiners, 259 North Lake Avenue, Suite 1039, Chicago, Illinois 60600 (Phone 312/540–0876), write an inquiry to Professor Mavis Fish, Y University, X City, State, ZIP, about Richard M. Bremer, who is applying for admission to the bar of Texas.

Bremer, a graduate of State University, was a former student of Mavis Fish in Business Communication several years ago at State University, where he graduated. After leaving State, he received the J.D. degree this May from the University of Virginia. He was employed as a law clerk with Price and Strassburger in Dallas summer before last and last summer with Fairbrother, Burry, Forman, and Murry in Houston.

Since Bremer gave Professor Fish as a reference, you would appreciate her opinion of his integrity, legal ability, and fitness for the practice of law.

**6–15.** As director of sales, you are to notify your salespeople that they must send you a list of slow-paying customers. You're also compiling a list of ZIP codes where the company has had trouble collecting. You'll send all salespeople a list of problem collections. They will need to check the "bad" ZIP code list when they take orders, then check for problem customers within these ZIP codes. This system will work better than address checking (and is done just as fast by computer) because bad credit risks may try to fool you by using several addresses within a single ZIP code.

You need to cut bad orders to a lower percentage to save collection costs.

**6–16.** As senior vice president of American President Companies (1950 Franklin Street, Oakland, CA 94612), write a memo to each member of the board of directors for consideration before the board meeting a month from today.

You want to propose (for board voting) a 3 percent stock dividend in lieu of the next equal-value cash dividend. After deducting cash distributions for all fractional shares, you estimate the retained money at $8,929,605. (This figure is the value of shares to be issued, based on a price of $26 per share—the closing price of the company's stock on the New York Stock Exchange on the latest record date for dividends.) You propose to use the money (instead of borrowing) to improve current operations, salaries, and other investments in the future growth of the company.

**6–17.** Clip (or copy) from the pages of any newspaper or magazine an ad featuring a product or service in which you are interested. Write an inquiry to the manufacturer or distributor asking for details not furnished by the ad. Price, local availability, and servicing are possibilities. Ask four significant questions, *at least one of which requires explanation on your part.* Attach the ad or copy to your letter.

**6–18.** Assume that you have a bright 12-year-old daughter and 14-year-old son who are mathematically inclined but who are not very turned on by their teachers or schools. In the *Houston Post* you see an ad about a computer camp for boys and girls aged 10 to 18 under the direction of Michael Zeiss. According to the ad, a new camp will be in operation next summer in the Houston area. Since you live in Silsbee, TX 77756 (P.O. Box 548), your son and daughter would not have far to go to camp. But you have some questions to ask Zeiss (Computer Camps, Inc., Old Woodstock Road, Moodus, CT 06469): time spent on computers, time spent in outdoor activities, kinds of activities, homework, cost, kinds of computers. (Do students bring their own, and if so, would an Apple II serve?). Add any other likely questions.

**6–19.** As Donald Tate of Olde Book Shoppe (Case 6–10), write Charles or Charlene Todd and tell him or her that you hope to find the wanted book in a month or so. There will be a flat $5 charge for the time and effort (plus the cost of the book) for Book Chase. Add some appropriate resale on the house.

**6–20.** For Donna Miller, Code MC–7, NASA Headquarters, Washington, DC 20546, answer the inquiry from James Herzberg, 4035 North Firestone Drive, Hoffman Estates, IL 60195, about arrangements for his high school physics class to send an experiment on the next space shuttle. NASA charges $500 to reserve a space through its special program for individuals and small organizations, called Small Self-Contained Payload Program (nicknamed the Getaway Special). NASA needs details about the experiment at least three months before launching. For an experiment weighing 60 pounds, NASA charges $3,000 ($5,000 for 100 pounds and $10,000 for 200 pounds). The physics class can share space and costs with more than one party.

**6–21.** As head of the service department of Medalcraft Industries, manufacturer of metal outdoor furniture (300 Fenway Drive, Irondale, PA 15789), you are to answer the inquiry from one of your dealers, Sinclair Furniture, 3345 Third Avenue, Pittsburgh, PA 15231, about refurbishing some Medalcraft furniture sold to a good customer 10 years ago. The furniture has rust spots on all the tabletops (one large round table and three nest tables) and on the legs of all six chairs. Three years ago the customer scraped off rust spots with a stiff wire brush, painted with Rust-Oleum, and sprayed with black and green Medalcraft paint. The furniture looked all right for two years but then went back to its present rusty condition. What can the customer do to make the furniture look like new again?

Write Sinclair Furniture that you can strip the furniture, put it in a zinc bath, then paint it with two finishes so that it will look fresh again. This should last about 10 years, and the procedure costs $35 a piece plus freight (an added $10 per piece). The nest of tables is considered one piece.

**6–22.** As Professor Mavis Fish (Case 6–14), reply to Thornton Matthews about Richard M. Bremer. You well remember this active, hardworking, intelligent former student. He was active in many worthwhile student activities while making an almost A average. As an adviser to the scholarship committee for the Student Government Association, you got well acquainted with Bremer and found him to have strong leadership qualities, integrity, and persuasiveness.

**6–23.** After reading Case 6–18, assume that you are Michael Zeiss, director of Computer Camps, Inc., and that you will answer Mr. and Mrs. Harlan Zabinski's letter asking about your new camp that will open this summer. You plan to enroll 80 youngsters for each of four two-week sessions at the woodsy countryside location near Houston at a cost of $150 per week. Except for Sundays, each morning at breakfast the students sign up for at least two sessions of traditional camp activities such as hiking, boating, swimming, horseback riding (extra cost). But the chief focus of the camp is on computers, and there are three daily 90-minute sessions. Beginners study BASIC and introductory programming; more advanced students take courses in Pascal, assembly and machine language programming, graphics, peripherals, and related subjects. During free time the campers play games on any of the 42 Atari, Apple, NEC, Hitachi, and Commodore computers. After several days of intensive instruction (including homework) the campers choose their own computer project. Students may bring their own computers, but the camp has enough for everyone. Generally about one fourth of the campers are familiar with computers before they arrive. Zeiss feels that in the future those who are not computer-literate will be at a terrible disadvantage. Training kids to work with computers is like training them to read—it's that critical. Besides answering the Zabinskis' questions, send along a colorful brochure picturing the camp (cabins for boys and separate cabins for girls, air-conditioned computer classrooms, swimming pool, horse stables, lake for boating and fishing, crafts cabin, nature trails). There are no tennis, handball, basketball, or volleyball courts.

**6–24.** Answer the writer of the inquiry about Lloyd's of London (Case 6–3) with the following information: Lloyd's members must have a net worth of at least 100,000 pounds (about $120,000 at current exchange rates). Market professionals say, however, that you should have a net worth of at least $250,000.

Members need agents to tell them how much they made—or lost. Big accounting firms usually can make recommendations for getting an agent. The London-based Association of Lloyd's Members should check the agent's performance ratings. Members don't need to know all the intricacies of insurance. A managing agent decides which syndicates one should participate in. Then professional underwriters run the syndicates on a day-to-day basis.

Average annual returns range from 6 percent to 15 percent. Not all syndicates earn money, however. For example, the syndicate that helped underwrite insurance for a malfunctioning satellite had claims of $92 million. Lloyd's members face unlimited liability for any losses their syndicates run up. In a couple of cases, losses have totaled as much as four times the amount of capital committed.

To join Lloyd's, investors require a sponsor who has known the applicant for a year. Several Lloyd's membership groups make regular recruiting visits to the United States to find prospective new members. Once approved, investors pay a membership fee of 3,000 pounds (about $3,600) and commit at least 100,000 pounds in capital. Most new members just use a bank letter of credit.

Trips to London would be tax-deductible.

**6–25.** Study any Internal Revenue Service form carefully and see how you could improve it.

**6–26.** Collect forms from employment agencies, credit departments, insurance companies, businesses, universities, . . . and analyze them as to their good and poor features.

**6–27.** Design a form that your publisher, Richard D. Irwin, Inc., can use for its authors. The authors need to tell about themselves—their other publications, their education, their experience. They also need to evaluate the strengths and weaknesses of their textbook, to be published by Richard D. Irwin, as well as the strengths and weaknesses of three of the major competitors.

**6–28.** As manager of the Order Department in the Compton Printing Corporation—a large company at 30 West 23rd Street, New York, NY 10010, U.S.A., phone (212) 354–9856, telex: 765543, cable: COPRCO—you find that members of your department are writing several identical or almost identical letters every day. These letters, which range in length from 5 to 25 lines, deal with changes in orders that sales representatives of your company throughout the world have requested or have indicated may be necessary.

These letters convey one or more of the following messages:

1. We processed order number such and such.
2. We pulled the order from production for changes in copy. Please send necessary information by (date) to retain the scheduled delivery date.
3. We're sorry not to be able to comply with your request for a change. The order was printed (date) or the goods were shipped (date).
4. We are sending you (or customer) the cut requested.
5. The goods have been rescheduled for shipment the week of (date).
6. Should we continue to hold the order? If so, for how long?

Design a form that the correspondent can fill in with a minimum expenditure of time and thought. Be sure to include company name, division, date of message, place for name of representative, city, state, Zip code, country, order number, name of customer, as well as the date and form of the message (telex, telegram, cable, or telephone call) from the sales representative concerning a change.

**6–29.** Write a letter asking for an exchange of an article you ordered. You make up the names and addresses and the reason for wanting the exchange.

**6–30.** Order five items to be individually gift wrapped and sent to an address overseas. Assume the enclosure of a suitable card, and have the order charged to your American Express card.

**6–31.** From the 51st Street Photo, 67 West 51st Street, New York, NY 10036, order the following:

| | | |
|---|---|---|
| 1 Model BM–510 | Micro Dictator @ | $  224.95 |
| 1 Model PC–20 | Canon Personal Cartridge Copier | 869.00 |
| 1 Model BMC–110K | Betamovie Video Camera/Recorder | 1,799.00 |
| 1 Model 285 | Vivitar Flash | 54.95 |

Ship UPS (estimated handling and insurance $15.50). Charge to Visa.
  You saw the ads for these products in *Photography* magazine. You don't have a catalog or order blanks.

**6–32.** In a popular fashion magazine you see a $200 outfit that really appeals to you in the Neiman-Marcus ad. To order the fashionable clothes, you write Neiman-Marcus, P.O. Box 2896, Dallas, TX 75221, and ask to open an account so that the outfit can be sent to you. (You are to fill in details.)

**6–33.** Assume that you are working for a large U.S. corporation and living in Puerto Rico (129 Paradiso, Rio Piedras, PR 00926). So that your children will have some popular toys for Christmas, you order from Toys-R-Us, 1098 Molman Avenue, Hartford, CT 06105. (You make up the kind of toys you want to order and the prices you found in an old catalog of the company.)

**6–34.** As manager of 51st Street Photo (Case 6–31), acknowledge the order, charge to Visa, and ship UPS. (You make up the name and address of the buyer.)

**6–35.** Assume that you are the personal shopper for Neiman-Marcus and acknowledge the order described in Case 6–32. Enclose a Neiman charge card. Add resale and sales promotional material.

**6–36.** Acknowledge the order to the corporation executive who lives in Puerto Rico (Case 6–33).

**6–37.** For Constructive Playthings, wholesalers, 1987 West 119th Street, Grandview, MO 64030, acknowledge the order from a retailer, Kiddie Korner, 208 West 103rd Terrace, Leawood, KS 66206. You are sending a truck shipment of toys, Invoice # 56987, dated today, amounting to $3,546.98 (includes trucking costs) on terms (2/15, n/45). Kiddie Korner was a customer of yours three years ago, but for some unknown reason you stopped getting its business. Welcome KK back and add appropriate resale/sales promotional material.

**6–38.** As Credit Manager, Constructive Playthings, 1987 West 119th Street, Grandview, MO 64030, reply to The Christmas Store, 5314 West Lincoln Avenue, Skokie, IL 60076. This small company purchased toys from you and paid cash with the order. Now it sends you an order for $4,000 of assorted toys. The references check out, but two of them have done credit business with The Christmas Store only once. Approve credit for the order on hand and explain your terms: 2/10, n/30, shipments UPS or freight collect, 18 percent annual interest charged on overdue accounts (1½ percent per month).

**6–39.** Since you are the credit manager for Holland Bulbs, Dorpstrat 119, Harmelen 3481 EC, Netherlands, grant credit and send $2,546 worth of bulbs to Brennans, 6329 North Galena Road, Peoria, IL 61625. The price includes ocean freight, duty, insurance, and inland shipping to Peoria. Brennans sent Karen Marietta to Holland Bulbs to select special plant food and the finest giant Dutch tulips, daffodils, hyacinths, alliums, crocuses, irises, amaryllises, and narcissi. As you told Ms. Marietta, your bulbs are carefully packed and then placed in a special temperature-controlled container and rushed across the Atlantic to Peoria. Welcome Brennans as a new customer with "Special Bericht vanuit Holland" (Special Greetings from Holland).

**6–40.** After getting a report from the Credit Bureau on Franklin Office Supply Company, 1610 High Street, Cape Girardeau, MO 63710, and after talking with Britt Tanner, your sales representative, you are going to grant credit on terms 3/10, n/60 with a $1,500 limit. Carey Franklin, the owner, started the supply store two years ago. With some savings and some borrowing and the repayment of small amounts, he has managed to stay in business. Weatherford's Office Supply and Kyle's, old established stores, located within a mile of Franklin, furnish strong competition.

Tanner says that Carey Franklin is energetic, hardworking, and progressive. On the other hand, the Credit Bureau reports that he is slow in paying his personal bills. The business climate around Cape Girardeau seems favorable. You are going to grant Franklin credit for $1,250 in office supplies; but you carefully and specifically remind him of the due dates and the advantages of cash discounts. Work in the idea that he earned the credit on the basis of his going firm. Tell him about some of your various services, sales helps (envelope stuffers, sales representative), and other merchandise. Because transportation is good between him and you, the wholesaler (Illinois Office Supplies, Inc., 1908 Lake Street, Chicago, IL 60675), he'll have fast deliveries that will keep him from carrying a big inventory.

**6–41.** Assume that you are Yoshiko Usui, owner of Mings, 19-B Hankow Road 1/F, Kowloon, Hong Kong. You received the credit information you requested from the United States on George Wright, an accountant with Deloitte Haskins & Sells, 220 Kashigaoka, Kowloon, Hong Kong (Case 6–11), and you are granting him credit and inviting him to your tailor shop to select materials for new suits.

You have the finest in silks, wools, ultra suede in an assortment of colors, textures, designs. Generally a suit can be made in 24 hours as long as you have two fittings. Prices are much lower than in the United States, and the workmanship is finer.

Invite Mr. Wright to come by your tailor shop, have a cup of tea, and look over your selection. Four tailors can serve him.

**6–42.** Assume that Sally Cobb, City Furniture Company, 809 15th Street, Y City 39876, ordered $3,500 of furniture from your wholesale supply house, Americana, 907 Valley Road, X City 54987. Along with the letter she sent references. Grant the credit, state your terms, and include resale and sales promotional material.

**6–43.** As credit manager for Crown Music Company, Highway 22 North, Y City, X State, ZIP, you will write a credit grant letter to Mr. Kelly Gene Johns, 219 Radburn Way, Prattville, TX 76574, who at age 16 wants to buy a Sonory stereo system and wants it shipped UPS. For credit references Kelly listed his supervisor at the Prattville Machine and Welding Company and two high school teachers.

Along with his credit application he sent a down payment of $50. Under Crown's billing system, Kelly will receive a statement on the 1st of each month, with payment due by the 10th. There will be five equal payments of $50 each with a 1½ percent monthly finance charge on the unpaid balance.

**6–44.** As Credit manager, Charles Knopf Publishers, 597 Fifth Avenue, New York, NY 10017, write a credit-granting letter to Ellen Weaver, The Book Mall, 642 Poplar Street, Denver, CO 80220, and send the books she ordered totaling $375.56. Your terms are 2/10, n/30. Even though Weaver has not had retail experience, she chose an excellent location for her store, has inherited money, has a husband with a good job, and is bright. Your sales representative, T. F. Pail, reports that she graduated with honors from Smith College 30 years ago. She got into the book business because she was bored with country club life and because she had always wanted a bookstore. In checking Weaver's accounts, you found that she lived in a paid-for $100,000 home, had an excellent credit rating, and was well thought of as a leader in the community, as was her husband. By complimentary comment on the high intellectual level of her book selections, related to her personal background (including lack of business training or experience), try to hint that some Babbittry might be good business. In other words, as an analogy, a wise fisherman (though he loves steak) will use worms (not steak) for bait—because fish prefer worms. So push some lower-brow, more popular books.

**6–45.** You (Jim or Jane Spann, Rt. 9, Box 78, Battesville, MS 38543) were foolish enough to rent a stereo set for $17.95 a week with a purchase option after 72 weeks from Robert Hobbs, Stereo Warehouse, Oxford, MS 38677. Much to your surprise you later realized that the stereo was a used one that had been refurbished and that had probably been repossessed. Under the contract you'll owe $1,292 for a set worth only $500 new. Some rental agreements disclose the total price of the item leased, but you did not have such a clear agreement with Mr. Hobbs. Also, your state has not brought rental purchase under its regular consumer credit laws (which set usury limits on interest rates and require full disclosure).

After 40 weeks of paying $17.95 for a used stereo, you want to call a halt to the deal. Write Hobbs a letter asking for permission to stop the payments. You want Hobbs to let you keep the stereo.

**6–46.** While you were visiting relatives in a city 1,000 miles from home, you had an appendectomy. Today you receive a bill for $300 from the surgeon. The surgeon's secretary told you that your health insurance policy would cover the surgery. Therefore, you think you should not have to pay the bill.

**a.** Write a letter to the surgeon.

**b.** Write a letter to your health insurance company.

**6–47.** You and your spouse were set to enjoy a great vacation at your favorite resort. And then, because orders increased, your company (Cramin Paint Co.) asked you to postpone your vacation. You did so, but in the process had to cancel your reservations at the resort and lost your $60 deposit. Write a memo to the director of employee relations asking that Cramin reimburse you for the $60.

**6–48.** When you had to use City Ambulance to take a friend to the local hospital (cost $100), you had a run-in with the ambulance driver, who was ugly, demanding, and unreasonable. The City Ambulance paramedics, on the other hand, were most cooperative, thorough in their handling of your friend, and pleasant. The driver demanded immediate payment, but you put off paying and obtained forms that allowed your friend to pay three months from the day the ambulance was called. Now that three months have passed, your friend is ready to pay the bill but wants you to write a complaint letter about the driver's attitude. Write the letter.

**6–49.** For two months you have been having trouble with your mother's bill at the Fairmount Health Care Center in Jefferson City, Missouri. The bookkeeper, Warren Carl, blew his top when you asked questions about the bill. He said he did not have the time to fool with you but that the bill should be $456. The bill that came for your mother's retirement home was for $910. Carl blamed the computer for the mistake and said that he would write headquarters again. The statement the previous month also had you incorrectly billed for $910. The parting remark foaming out of Carl's mouth was that he could not issue you a corrected bill. This is not the first time you have crossed swords with Warren Carl. You've talked with several other patrons about the retirement home and learned that they too have received incorrect bills. Because you want to get a correct bill and because you feel that the president of Fairmount Health Care Centers, 1609 N. 14th St., St. Louis, MO 63106, should know about Carl's behavior, you write a letter.

**6–50.** Assume that you are Day Lee Snow, owner of an exercise salon, 3028 Williamsburg, Ann Arbor, MI 48104. From Spencer's catalog you ordered a partly assembled 34-pound bike with no standard or deluxe consoles for $99.99 to replace a five-year-old bike that customers had worn out. When you tried the bike out, the bike post sliced through the plastic seat. Although you were not hurt, you were scared, concerned that your customers could have had this bad experience, and disgusted over the shoddy merchandise.

You write Spencer's Department 157, Chicago, IL 60627, and separately send the seat. In your letter explain what happened and demand a new seat immediately.

**6–51.** SBC (a large television network that competes with ABC, CBS, NBC) is one of the investments of your company (Capital Management, a unit of Equitable Life with 747,034 shares). The problem is that an undesirable character named Daniel Roddy wants to take over SBC and says he'll bid $5.4 billion for all of its shares.

You (director of capital management) are asked to write a letter protesting (on the basis of Roddy's character and questionable financing) SBC's letting him negotiate such a deal. You do not think it wise to do as Roddy wants, which is to turn over SBC's present shares for some of Roddy Broadcasting System, Inc. stock and high-yield and high-risk "junk bonds" with a face value of about $5.4 billion. The merger with his company and a divestiture of all of SBC's nonbroadcasting properties would follow Roddy's hostile buyout of the network.

Roddy has been charged with hypocrisy for preaching family values and then appearing drunk in public and for criticizing the networks' TV "garbage" while boasting to *Playboy* magazine that he has photographed nude women. He talks hard-line conservatism but seems genuinely concerned about such pet liberal issues as overpopulation, world hunger, and nuclear proliferation. Although he presides over a major news organization, he says he limits his newspaper reading to the sports section. He professes to admire the social proprieties, yet treats his senior executives like servants.

Roddy loves publicity and is willing to sacrifice his dignity to win. You feel that his offer is a proposed hostile leveraged buyout, and you don't want to be a part of it. You have been pleased with SBC's management, and you don't want to exchange your stock for a series of debt instruments.

To protest the takeover of SBC, write a letter to Virgil Turner, president of SBC, Rockwell Center, New York, NY 10019.

**6–52.** Continental Manufacturers, 2756 Peachtree Avenue, Atlanta, GA 30365, engaged a Fartran Inc. truck for use by an employee (Mark G. Dykema) to move from Atlanta to Miami. At Baggett's Truckstop in northern Florida the 22-foot Fartran would not start, stranding Dykema and a friend until a mechanic arrived the next day to fix it.

Before the end of the trip the truck needed a new battery. On Interstate 75 the trailer hitched to the rear of the truck came unfastened and Dykema's belongings were jostled and damaged. As a grand finale, the old truck—with more than 90,000 miles—stalled in the street in front of his new home in Miami and the cargo door jammed. Dykema paid a local mechanic $27.50 (receipt enclosed) to replace the badly corroded and broken battery cable.

Assume that you are Dykema and that you are writing Fartran's Atlanta office (3450 Peachtree Avenue, 30365) telling of your problems and asking for a settlement of money to fix up your damaged furniture. A reputable furniture-repair shop estimates that the damage comes to about $2,000. Of course getting the furniture fixed does not compensate you for your frustration and for the time you lost getting from Atlanta to Miami.

**6–53.** The past year you've made one or two trips per month into O'Hare International Airport (Chicago) and you've rented a car from Chicago Budget Rent-A-Car Corporation, with headquarters at 9575 W. Higgins Rd., Rosemont, IL 60018. Your plan has been to drive to Belvidere, Rockford, and sometimes Beloit, and then back to O'Hare the next day. The cost of the car rental has varied from $30 to $60, depending on the make and model rented. But when you turned in your rented car (Contract 13835774) yesterday, the charge was $110.04. You were overwhelmed by this charge, but the attendant on duty merely said that the charge was $110.04. By letter ask Chicago Budget Rent-A-Car Corporation to check into the situation and issue an appropriate credit to your American Express Account 3675 359826 31009.

**6–54.** As Product Specialist, Tagmay Company, Newton, IA 50266, you are to send a check and a letter today to Mrs. Della Colburn, P.O. Box 125, Samona, CA 95467. Mrs. Colburn had trouble with her clothes dryer and had it repaired in Samona; but since it was still in the warranty period, she wrote you and told you her problems. The company will pay her the suggested list price of the motor ($109.96) to repair the appliance. The shade-tree mechanic in Samona charged her $120 (motor and labor).

**6–55.** For Vera Bailey (Case 7–46), send a check for $134 to the state Medicaid Agency and explain that you did not realize that you were to take the initiative in reporting the $16.75 increase that started January 1 of this year. You were aware of this increase because you take care of your mother's bank account (a simple chore since there's not much to balance). Add the goodwill-building idea that you are glad that Medicaid is checking on its numerous accounts. You have been reading about the terribly wasteful expenditures in the federal government, such as people collecting Social Security payments of dead people . . . .

**6–56.** After you read the problem in Case 9–19, pretend you are Albert P. Ginchereau, Jr., adjustment manager of Ozment Manufacturing. You will take back the defective food processor and replace it with another one again. Make up the details for explanation and points of resale.

**6–57.** As claims manager for Sohn Laboratories, Townhall Rd., Belleville, IL 62221, draft a form letter to answer claims from retailers about your defective batch of insect repellent Bitex in 6-ounce spray cans. Somehow cans of Skunk Here were mislabeled Bitex—something of a surprise to the people who thought they were spraying an insect repellent on themselves! Hunters use Skunk Here to make themselves smell like skunks so as to cover the betraying human odor. It is pungent, to say the least! Ask retailers to take one can of Bitex from each carton they have in stock and aim a quick spray at a piece of paper. If the can contains Skunk Here, they will know immediately. Ask them to return all such cartons to you, freight collect. If they send the enclosed postage-paid return card to you filled out with their names and addresses, you will immediately send them a carton of Bitex, and you will replace the rest of the defective cartons when they arrive at your plant.

**6–58.** As general manager for Chicago Budget Rent-A-Car Corporation (Case 6–53), write a letter to Emerson Mills, 401 Forest Lane, Lawton, OK 74078, and explain that he was charged time and mileage rates rather than the corporate rate he was entitled to. Remind Mills to present his corporate rate ID or sticker in the future so as to prevent any overcharge. His charge should have been $32 per day plus tax and fuel, or a total of $51.57. The American Express account has been credited for $58.47, but he must allow four to six weeks for the credit to appear on the statement.

**6–59.** As Steven Heine, Adjustment Manager, Spencers, Chicago, IL 60627, send Day Lee Snow a new seat for the exercise bike (Case 6–50) and explain that the bike had apparently been misassembled. From now on, the company is putting warning labels on all its bicycles and providing kits to secure the seats on affected models. With the seat, you are sending instructions and a kit. Add resale such as adjustable handlebars, roller brakes (help regulate pedal load), and low cost.

**6–60.** As president of the six Fairmount Health Care Centers, answer the complaint letter of Mrs. Barbara S. Spinks, 987 Hickory Dr., Jefferson City, MO 65101 (Case 6–49). You are enclosing a corrected bill for $456 for the preceding month. Apparently the confusion stems from three months ago, when Barbara's mother spent 26 days in the nursing-home part of Fairmount, yet reserved the room in the retirement-home part of Fairmount. Since there were four other available rooms left vacant at this time, the manager, Ron Smith, decided not to charge Barbara for holding the room in the retirement part of the home. As for Warren Carl's behavior toward Barbara, you have no reason or explanation. Carl's family built the first Fairmount Health Care Center, and he was given a job as bookkeeper and receptionist because of his family connection. He has been at this job now 12 years.

**6–61.** Write Jullian Pickett of West Texas Dairy Supply, Box 456, Monahans, TX 79756, congratulating him on being certified to sell and service the InFARMation line of farm computer products. The line includes a computerized feeding system, which adjusts a cow's feed during the lactation period. You are head of the Chamber of Commerce in Monahans.

**6–62.** As a banker, you've been involved with Atlantic Southeast Airlines, based in Atlanta. You have just read that it bought 10 Embraer Brasilia aircraft, and you want to write a note of congratulations to the airline and its president, George Williams. The Brasilia offers an ideal combination of speed, passenger amenities, low operating costs, and financing. The 30-passenger aircraft is pressurized and will operate at speeds of approximately 325 miles per hour. It has Pratt & Whitney engines. Atlantic Southeast will use the new planes to serve small cities in the Southeast. Write George Williams a goodwill letter.

**6–63.** As public relations officer for the First National Bank, 717 Travis, Houston, TX 77002, you want to please the 400 clients who keep $100,000 or more on deposit. Write a letter to them telling them about your new VIP program.

These customers bypass teller windows in the lobby and head straight to a plush lounge on the third floor, where they get prompt service and refreshments of their choice. If they want to retrieve valuables from their safe-deposit boxes, an attendant escorts them to a room with an Oriental rug and crystal chandeliers.

Another privilege is the use of a six-passenger, twin-engine airplane. First National owns the plane and employs the pilot (but the customers pay for the fuel). Since the plane is in almost constant use, customers need to put in their requests early for its use.

**6–64.** A prominent citizen, Lecil Bevill, died, and you are to write a sympathy note to his wife. Lecil served on the state Mental Health Board, the Hospital Board, was a former county probate judge, then federal court monitor of the state mental health system. He helped organize the Western States Life Insurance Company and served as vice president. You assume that you worked with him successfully at one of these activities.

**6–65.** Write your representative in Congress thanking that person for voting for a bill you favored. You make up the name of the representative and select the bill.

**6–66.** You are General Marketing and Sales Manager of International Bondware, 8987 East Northwest Highway, Palatine, IL 60067 (312/349–8700). You offered to sell your company to the Fort Maynard Paper Company, and word of the negotiations leaked out. The deal fell through, and International began making some organizational changes. Seizing upon this combination of circumstances, your competitors—and a couple of recently terminated employees—began spreading the word that your company was on the ropes, about to be closed, and shaky.

To counter this debilitating flood of rumors, write a letter to all of your customers and prospects. You want to lighten the gloominess but deal with the serious situation. Admit that you will cease production of China-Therm paper plates, close your plant at Millville, New Jersey, and reorganize your sales group. You are ready to provide the quality and quantity of paper disposables the customers require through your Chicago and Shelbyville, Illinois, plants.

Your concentration of facilities and product lines will increase your ability to serve the customer by improving inventory control and shipping. New programs are already under way to enhance capacity, to meet delivery schedules, and to provide customers with accurate order-tracking information.

**6–67.** As president of Richard D. Irwin, Inc., 1818 Ridge Road, Homewood, IL 60430, write a form letter to all Irwin authors announcing that Dale Creamer has joined the firm as vice president—editorial after a three-month recruiting effort. He comes from Davis Publishing Company, where he had a most successful career in all facets of college textbook publishing. Fourteen years ago he started as a sales representative in the San Francisco area and subsequently became field manager for the San Francisco District. Five years later he became accounting editor and went on to become editor in chief for social science and humanities, the largest of Davis's four College Division editorial groups. And six years later he became editorial director of its College Division. Since joining Irwin, he will be visiting a large cross section of campuses across the country and will be attending many academic conventions this year. He wants to meet authors and other leaders in the business/academic community. (He values a strong working relationship with authors and wants to be a good team player.)

(Add other details you think important.)

**6–68.** As one of the vice presidents for international marketing for Coola-Cola (Case 6–5), write the CEO saying that you'll be interested in attending the strategy session at Jekyll Island and adding any other appropriate comments and/or suggestions—for example, trying a Coola-Cola D(ecaffeinated).

**6–69.** At a cost of almost $4,000, you had to have (and pay for) a funeral for a relative 1,000 miles from home. The funeral director, Horace Wilkins of Dawson and Wilkins, was very businesslike, helpful, considerate. Much to your surprise he even credited you with $200 for the shipping case that you had to purchase from the local funeral director and he allowed a $155 credit since you had no visitation. To show your appreciation and to encourage good business practice, write Wilkins and the firm a thank-you note for their good service.

**6–70.** As the head of the Chamber of Commerce in your city, you read in your local paper where the president of the United States gave an award for promotion of exporting to an industrialist in your city named Roby Phifer, president and founder of Phifer Wire Products. Presentation of the E award was this morning at the White House.

Phifer Wire Products has been exporting for 30 years and sells in all 50 states. In the past four years the company has added 300 jobs. The award was an adaptation of the World War II E pennants awarded to industrial plants for superior production. Now the award is based on a substantial increase of exports over a sustained three-year period, including breakthroughs in particularly competitive markets, the introduction of a new product into U.S. export trade, or the opening of a trade area previously closed to American-made products. Ten years ago Phifer exported to 34 countries, but that has increased to 110 today, including customers in Europe, South America, Asia, and Africa. It is the world's largest producer of insect screening.

Write a sincere letter congratulating Roby Phifer on winning the award.

**6–71.** Now play the role of Roby Phifer and acknowledge the letter from the head of the Chamber of Commerce in the preceding case. Phifer might give credit to the company's dedicated employees and to the cooperation from the Department of Commerce in Washington and from state and local officials.

**6–72.** As Mary Carter, chief inspector for Studio 3 Associates (manufacturer of plastic seat covers), you get a copy of the buyer's letter to the Better Business Bureau in Chicago (Case 9–20) and you phone the customer, Ted Shapiro, to make a date for picking up the plastic seat covers, but you also write a letter to keep his goodwill. Write the letter for Mary to Ted.

**6–73.** Telephone credit card fraud is still a problem to some of the 50 million Americans who carry telephone credit cards. Some people steal or find the cards, or overhear holders reading the numbers to an operator. Once a number gets out, lots of people can use it. College students and military base personnel are groups of young people living away from home and making frequent long-distance calls.

Don Nixon, Florida spokesman for Atlanta-based Southern Bell, says that students have taken out ads announcing telephone credit card numbers and the fact that they are useful for "free" calls. (In California stolen numbers bring from $2 to $10 each on the black market.) Credit card fraud cost Southern Bell millions during the first nine months of last year. Besides causing the company to lose money, the floating numbers produce problems in tracking down some callers. To help stop credit card fraud, Nixon will send a notice in the monthly statements to telephone users urging them to give their numbers to operators in a voice that can't be overheard and (when possible) to use push-button phones that allow the codes to be entered without being spoken.

Your assignment is to write the message for Don Nixon. In your message point out to the telephone subscribers some of the benefits of local and long-distance phone service, but stress the importance of keeping their credit card numbers to themselves.

**6–74.** The board of Finex Corporation liked your idea (see Case 6–9), so you went ahead with your plans with your ad agency. Write a goodwill message to the CEO thanking him or her for supporting your idea.

**6–75.** As the president of a chain of nursing homes in Illinois, write a form letter from your headquarters (Fairview, 178th St. and S. Kedzie Ave., Hazel Crest, 60429) to your patient (or to the sponsor if the patient is unable to function). This letter is to welcome patients to your nursing home and to ask them to complete a questionnaire about your services. The patient or sponsor would receive this mailing a week after entering your nursing home.

**6–76.** Mortan Leach, Pearce, Finnel & Smith, Inc., Suite 1000, The First National Bank Building, Birmingham, Alabama 35280 (205/645–9876), will introduce its equipment leasing and corporate cash management programs at the Birmingham Industrial Show May 11, 12, 13. The show will be at 2065 Alpine Village in Birmingham and costs $5.

As a goodwill gesture, you, Keith Mintz, financial consultant for Mortan Leach, Pearce, Finnel & Smith, are sending two complimentary tickets to two customers who have strayed from dealing with you (Dr. and Mrs. Clayton Monpere, 4103 Thornhill Drive, Montevallo, AL 35113). Along with the complimentary tickets, write a note to the Monperes.

**6–77.** As personnel manager for National Paper Company, 4570 Lavallet Road, Pensacola, FL 32566, write a goodwill letter or memo to James Sponseller, who has just joined your maintenance department. Along with your letter you'll send an annual report.

**6–78.** Auditron Ratings Survey, 4310 Avon Road, Batesville, MD 20732, asks you to write a form letter for the signature of Vince Morris.

The letter is to tell the receiver (Donald C. Peterson) that Evelyn Moody of your interviewing staff will be telephoning and making a survey of Peterson's television viewing. You are writing the letter before Mrs. Moody calls, because people are often suspicious when anyone starts a telephone call with the phrase "I'm conducting a survey . . . ." If any doubts arise about any research organization that telephones, the receivers can call the business information offices in their area to verify the caller's reputation. Auditron Ratings and other legitimate research companies have nothing to hide.

If Peterson wants to ask any questions before Mrs. Moody calls, he can telephone toll free 800–654–6987. The results of the survey will be useful to the television stations who are trying hard to provide the kind of television programs Peterson enjoys.

Write the form letter for Auditron.

**6–79.** Assume that you have just returned from a convention of your profession and will write a cheerful, positive note congratulating the person who was in charge. Be specific in telling about the arrangements you liked, the highlights of the program . . . .

**6–80.** When you took over as manager of a large department store, you felt that you had to change the policy of giving discounts to your employees. The policy favored the high-ranked employees and was unfair to clerks and maintenance workers. For the higher the rank of the employee, the greater was the discount. This practice also was time-consuming to figure out at the point of purchase. The new system will be to give a standard rate of 20 percent discount on all goods, as your competitors (Lord & Taylor and Filene's) do. You and your top managers feel that this will be fair and will take less time in figuring discounts.

Write a memo that will be inserted in pay envelopes next payday.

**6–81.** Play the role of Ward McMillen, director and owner of Northgate Shopping Center in X City. Because of the recent crime in your shopping mall (teenager shot to death in mall restaurant as customers watched in horror, woman abducted from parking lot of shopping mall), you are taking some steps to make customers, managers, workers feel safe. You are hiring police during their off-duty hours to protect the mall, and you are giving the police force headquarters in the northwest corner of the mall. You are installing closed-circuit television to spot shoplifters, and stationing officers on the roof to watch for auto tampering, assaults, and other crimes.

Recommend that salesclerks leave together and escort each other to their cars so that they won't be easy prey for criminals who may follow them from work. Keeping close track of how many items clothing buyers take into fitting rooms and rigging garments with sensors that set off electronic alarms if shoppers attempt to leave the store without paying could help in keeping down shoplifting.

Ask for everyone's cooperation in making Northgate Shopping Center the safe place to shop, as it was just a year ago.

**6–82.** Assume that you work as president at a defense-related firm called TWR, Livermore, CA 94550. In your business you have many reasons to talk with important defense administrators in Washington, DC. Up to this point you have had conversations on just regular telephones that were not spyproof. But now for just the cost of $2,000 per telephone, the company can buy spyproof phones—the kind high government officials use for secret conversations. These phones, a National Security Agency spokesperson said, will have a small computer device in the sending telephone that would change voice sounds into rapid beeplike pulses, using a digital code. A computer in the receiving telephone, equipped with the same code, would decipher the signal and turn it back into voicelike sounds.

The feeling today is that Soviet electronic eavesdropping is on the rise, because such spying is made easier by the increased volume of voice communications transmitted through the air rather than through wires and because new technology makes it more feasible to encode and decode conversations at a reasonable cost.

In your memo to the general manager, Patton Hartzell, you recommend that TWR do a study to see how many telephones should be spyproof and also to see what company (AT&T, GTE, ITT, Motorola, or RCA) would have the best product at the lowest cost.

**6–83.** Assume that you work in market research for Safewell Grocery chain and that your recent assignment was to see how well generic products are moving at Safewell. You have found that sales of generics fell 4.1 percent, to $2.58 million, for the year ending May 25. You also found that generics have not penetrated any new product categories.

With the inflation rate down, probably more erosion of generic brands will come. The double-coupon policies at some stores have encouraged shoppers to buy name brands for less than generics.

Write the good news to Sales Manager Doris Miller, Safewell Grocery, 549 Inlet Road, Chicago, IL 60632.

**6–84.** As the manager of Rayfers, a large department store at Northgate Shopping Center in X City, you (like the mall director and owner) have become concerned about the safety of your salesclerks and customers.

To help protect both groups, you'll write a memo to your salesclerks telling them to park close to elevators, stairs, or the plaza entrance—at night, under a light. They should watch for loiterers everywhere, but especially near bank machines. Have them urge customers to have packages sent home or to leave them hidden in the car. Always accompany children to public rest rooms. Never leave children unattended—not even in arcades or theaters. Women should carry small purses and not put them down in rest rooms or when paying for purchases. Women should keep from wearing gold chains or ropes around their necks, because someone can grab the necklace and throw them down. No one should carry large amounts of cash or more credit cards than needed.

Besides taking these precautions, they should know that you have hired a security guard who will escort any concerned worker, customer, or child to safety.

**6–85.** Holm Corporation, a leading manufacturer of telecommunications equipment based in Santa Clara, California, was started in 1970. Under Maxwell Orr and Jerry Oldshoe, the two founders (electrical engineers from Texas's Rice University), Holm developed a corporate culture that might clash with that of IMB, the large corporation that recently paid $1.25 billion for Holm. Holm doesn't have a dress code or set working hours, and employees who stay with the company six years get a 12-week paid sabbatical. The company's headquarters are in a campus setting with landscaped streams and wooden walkways. A gym and a swimming pool are on the grounds for employees' enjoyment.

Orr and Oldshoe spent time yesterday with some Holm officials in question-and-answer sessions, assuring them that they intended to preserve Holm's culture. Perks such as profit sharing and stock options will undergo changes, but the details have not been worked out completely yet. A few of the officials at the meeting were dubious about the prospects of a happy marriage between IMB (a huge company that is famed for its buttoned-down, highly regimented managerial style) and the free-spirited Holm of Silicon Valley.

Now assume that you are Mr. Orr, president of Holm, and have the job of writing a memo to *all* the employees to assure them that your new bosses at IMB recognize the need to preserve Holm's culture and informal style. Employees will continue to set their work hours. They can still enjoy the million-dollar recreation center and earned sabbaticals. The competitive market spawned by divestiture prompted Holm to seek an alliance with IMB. The opportunities for growth are better with IMB than without it.

**6–86.** As director of marketing for Finex Corporation, maker of inexpensive but durable watches, you have approval from the accounting office to budget $400,000 on TV ads promoting your watches. The ads will be around a miniseries.

CBS has 27 percent of the nation's evening TV audience, while ABC has 24 percent. For a 30-second commercial on a high-rated show in prime time, CBS charges $102,000, while ABC charges $95,000. Both stations are featuring miniseries with well-known actors next season running Sunday, Tuesday, and Wednesday; but the one on CBS lasts nine hours and the one on ABC runs six hours. Neither station will permit 15-second commercials around the miniseries.

You are to decide whether to run the ads around the miniseries that plays on CBS or the one that runs on ABC. Write your decision in memo form to the CEO, telling what you are going to do and why.

**6–87.** Coola-Cola has a market share of 70 percent in the area of the international market where you are in charge. You feel that the name of the game isn't to increase market share but to increase the market, to take shares from juices, milk, coffee, tea, and beer. The company will have to try to instill new drinking habits in consumers in your area. You've had trouble, however, with the company's low-calorie soda and lemon-lime drink called Sprint. Because of a previous engagement to help a company manager in Mexico, you can't attend the strategy meeting; but you want this memo to get to Angelo Goizueta, chairman of the international division.

**6–88.** For more cases on direct inquiries, see Appendix B VI J; IX H, I, J; XII A, C; XV A. For direct replies, see XII B, D; XV D. For requests, see X E; XI B; XIII C, D. For general good news, see II E; III B; VI A; VII D; IX K, L; XI D, F, G, H; XIII G; XIV E; XVI B. For goodwill, see I C, D; II B, D, F, G; X D; XI E; XIII B; XVII C, D, G.

# Cases for Chapter 7

(Disappointing Messages)

**7–1.** As Newell Metzler, Martin Street, Fort Worth, TX 76190, write a refusal to Noel Poindexter (Rt. 1, Box 292, Kinta, OK 75451). As senior vice president of the National Cattleman's Association, you cannot promote Poindexter's Custom Cattle Care service (a kind of cattle boarding house) when you address the Cattleman's Association, because there are other CowBelles and Cattlemen who are in the same kind of business. These competitors would resent your promoting Poindexter's business.

**7–2.** Although you want to leave the area where you now work and move to an area where you think you would be happier, you have decided (after weighing all the facets of living) to turn down a job offer in a desirable location because you don't feel you can work with the present person who would be over you. If you took the new job, you would have a 10 percent raise in salary; but you are afraid that you and your superior will clash. Basically, you feel that this head plays dishonest and sneaky games. You don't want to be in that camp. (Add details and write this sensitive message.)

**7–3.** As one of the vice presidents for international marketing for Coola-Cola, write the CEO a memo explaining why you cannot attend the strategy session at Jekyll Island two weekends from now (Case 6–5). (You make up the reason.) Offer to send Creighten Stewart, the person under you. You've got lots of confidence in Stewart's intelligence and ability.

**7–4.** Charter Company (owners of *Ladies' House Journal, Redlook*) has to decide whether to buy a 134-year-old newspaper, the *Gazette,* in Y City for $30 million. Readers and advertisers have left the cities for the suburbs. Large advertisers have spread their dollars around buying space in both city and suburban papers and time on television. Instead of taking ads in all city papers, advertisers have gravitated to the only other paper, the *Herald,* which has a circulation of 424,000, or 27,000 higher than that of the *Gazette.* The aging *Gazette* physical plant needs new equipment. Also, it has operating losses and severance obligations ($12.5 million). For all these reasons, Charter is not going to buy the *Gazette.* Under the signature of Mark S. Case for Charter Company, write the board of directors at the *Gazette* the turndown letter.

**7–5.** Your university has supported a recreation area and lodge called Ann Jordan for the past 30 years. The lodge is used by groups of active and retired faculty, staff, administrators, and trustees. As director of public relations, you have to turn down the request of the Disabled Veterans in a nearby city, who want to use the lodge the first weekend in June. At that time a management seminar from the university will be using the lodge. Also, the veterans would not fit into the classification of who is eligible (see below).

**7–6.** (*Modification of preceding case*) Assume that the lodge is available at the time the Disabled Veterans wish to use it but that the Disabled Veterans do not qualify (according to the terms specified when the benefactor gave the lodge to the university).

**7–7.** When you lived in Southwest Miami, Florida, you bought a desirable piece of property on Red Road. Today you get a request from Father Byron Hughey, Saint Thomas Episcopal Church (also on Red Road—9865, with ZIP 33156), asking you if its organized Little League teams can use your lot to practice baseball. Parents will furnish lights, bleachers, backstop, and trash containers. You don't have any immediate plans for the large lot right now, but you don't want children, their families, and their friends tearing up the grass and messing up the appearance of your lot. Also, you wonder about your possible legal involvement if some child should be seriously hurt while on your property with your permission. (Can you suggest an alternative to Father Hughey?)

**7–8.** This year the committee on admissions to the law school at your university has a limit of 300 candidates from 2,500 applicants. Those applicants who scored 600 or above on the law school aptitude test will now have interviews and careful scrutiny of their reference letters before the final decision.

For the law school's dean of admissions, you have the assignment of writing the turndown letter to those who scored below 600. They might well consider some other law schools that do not receive such a large volume of applications.

**7–9.** As head of the Search Committee at your university or college, you have interviewed three candidates from three other schools for a particular job in one of your departments. (You make up the names, addresses, kind of department.)

Fortunately, the candidate your committee wanted was the one who accepted the job. But now you have the assignment of writing to the two other candidates turning them down.

**7–10.** As Martha Devine, Manager, Data Processing Center, Sunshine Oil Company, P.O. Box 876-A, Tulsa, OK 74129, draw up a letter to turn down Robert F. Pfeiffer, Kirksville Road, Durant, OK 74710. You have had an incredible number of applications and have tried to give the most careful consideration to each one. Naturally, you appreciate the applicant's interest in your company but have filled the job with one whose qualifications seem specifically suited to your needs.

**7–11.** When you checked into the Biltless Hotel, Madison Avenue and East 43rd, New York, NY 10036, two weeks ago, the desk clerk first told you that the hotel had no room for you—even though your secretary had made reservations for you a month earlier. After much discussion, however, the desk clerk assigned you a room. You were to officiate at a trade show, so would not be in your room much anyway; so the small size didn't bother you too much, but you did resent paying the same price ($100) as your fellow worker Jim Price paid for a much nicer and larger room with a lovely view.

Although you phoned Jim several times during your four-day stay at the Biltless, you did not use the phone any other time. On checking out, however, you faced a huge phone bill with calls to Denver, St. Louis, London, Mexico City, and New Orleans. You protested, argued, and tried to persuade the stubborn hotel operator that you didn't make any of those long-distance calls and in fact were at the trade show at the times of some of them. Still, the calls were on the bill for your room—1104. Because you were in a hurry to catch a plane, you put the hotel bill on your VISA card and said that you would write the hotel and VISA later and straighten out the bill.

Now you are back in your office of Medical Systems Division, General Selectric, 3098 Parkway, North Hampton, GA 30491, and you have your work log in front of you along with the list of billed phone calls you did not make. At the time of the calls to Denver and London you were working at the trade show (as coworker Jim Price can verify). At the time of the call to Mexico City you were entertaining two radiologists (prospects for some of your equipment). From your work log you can show that you were having breakfast at the time of the listed calls to St. Louis and New Orleans, though the only proof is that you met Jim Price both those mornings for a quick meal at the Grill before going to work at the trade show.

Before you write VISA and the Biltless, you therefore call Jim Price and ask him to send you a memo showing where and when you and he had breakfast the two mornings April 11 and 12 and your on-duty time the four days at the trade show. Jim agrees to write and send the memo.

Now with Jim's memo copied for the hotel and VISA, you still have a letter to write refusing to pay the unjustified charges. Write one letter that can go to both VISA and Hotel Biltless.

**7–12.** *(Oral assignment)* Instead of a writing assignment, the preceding case can be an oral assignment.

**7–13.** Employees are making far too many personal calls during the business day at your insurance office. Your brother-in-law has asked the phone company to help out at his company with a similar problem—the phone company can just lock out certain outgoing calls such as long distance, joke and weather lines, and 900 numbers.

Some of your agents need to make long-distance calls, of course.

You want to fire people who make too many personal calls, but your lawyer says you can do that only after you have put a statement to that effect (and made the limits specific) in the new edition of the employee handbook, due out next July 1.

It would cost quite a bit (you have 23 phones), but you could buy locks that cover either the dial or push buttons on phones. You might also invest in a computerized system that gives you a printout of all calls, times, and phone lines. This plan would give you proof enough to fire people.

Before you resort to these rather drastic measures, you would like to convince your employees to behave more responsibly. (You would save a lot of money this way, both on calls and antitheft measures.) You could:

1. Install pay phones in employee rest areas (and make some money on employee calls instead of losing it).

2. Put a "Business Phone: Keep Personal Calls Short" sign on all phones.

3. Stop issuing company telephone credit cards and get employees to bill you for itemized out-of-town calls on their own credit cards.

4. Rearrange the layout so that employees share phones and offices and monitor each other's phone use.

5. Send employees a memo on phone use with a three-minute egg timer (to remind them to keep calls short).

Write a memo to employees telling them what you have decided to do.

**7–14.** Assume that you have the desire to travel and that on a recent trip to Guam you visited the health department and accepted the position of medical records coordinator for the Health Department in Agana, Guam.

Before you left for Guam, however, you had applied to a large hospital in your area to work in the medical records department. Now you are offered a job at this large hospital but will turn it down because you prefer to work in Guam.

**7–15.** About two weeks ago Miss Molly Johnson, 9870 Southwest 66th Avenue, Miami, FL 33156, ordered three famous-name record albums at $8.98 each from Holland Music, 300 Fenway, Boston, MA 02114, and included a money order sufficient to cover the price and mailing. Today you receive a letter asking whether she can send the records back and get her money. You have to refuse her; all record sales are final. Each record has been auditioned critically. She was the first to play her records. And she has saved by ordering direct from Holland. The script and language of her letter indicate that she is a high school student. For desirable specificness, make plausible references to current hits and popular entertainers.

**7–16.** Mrs. Steve Leprevost, 860 Pheasant Drive, Athens, GA 30604, ordered a box spring (called the foundation) and mattress (60 × 80) for $879.99 from The Sleep Shop, 675 Ponce de Leon Avenue, Atlanta, GA 30376, two months ago. Today she writes and wants you to take back the queen-size bed and send her a king-size bed (76 × 80) that sells for $1,179.99. Even though you'd be making a larger sale for this extra-large bed, the state laws forbid you to exchange mattresses, as described in detail on page 754 of your catalog. Sign the letter as the adjustment manager.

**7–17.** The letter you must answer today is from Lucia F. Mintz, 324 Spring Oak Road, Memphis, TN 38113, requesting that you (AARP

Pharmacy Service, 4567 24th Street, North, St. Petersburg, FL 33723) credit her mother's account (membership number 7982309—Mrs. Floyd R. Mintz) for the $122 in drugs that you sent Mrs. Mintz two weeks ago. Lucia Mintz says that her mother used some pills out of each bottle but then had to go to the hospital for tests. Shortly after all the tests were run, Mrs. Mintz died. Because of federal law, you cannot accept medicine back nor can you credit the account for the $122.

**7–18.** As adjustment manager of the Flick Company, Box 9877, Minneapolis, MN 55435, maker of electric shavers, you have a claim letter from Dayton Chase, 876 Mourning Dove Court, Gaithersburg, MD 20865, and his shaver, asking for the replacement or repair of the shaver under your guarantee covering any defect of workmanship or materials for 90 days.

Examination reveals that the shaver was dropped or otherwise given a hard knock. Your guarantee specifies normal use; but it does not cover careless handling. A new head and black plastic housing are needed. You have to have a check for $17.99 before you will put the shaver in first-class condition and renew your guarantee. Or you'll repair the shaver and return it COD. In a resale plug, remind Chase that his new Flick Rotomatic has three floating steel heads with 36 steel blades.

**7–19.** Six months ago, while the Charles Shellabargers were in their Florida home (9793 Midnight Pass Rd., Siesta Key, Sarasota), they had you replace a self-framed Thermopane glass window next to a glass door (cost $109.55). Although you could not tell exactly, you felt that something had hit the glass (bird, rock, air rifle shot). Three days ago you got a letter from Shellabarger from his summer home, 1105 Country Club Dr., Warsaw, IN 46580, telling you that the neighbor who regularly checks on his home in Florida found that the very same glass was cracked again and bulging out. Shellabarger asked you to examine the glass and replace it at your cost. A neighbor, Mrs. Gordon Lloyd, would let you in to examine the glass. When you looked at the glass, you figured that this time pressure had made the glass crack. You do not feel that the fault was in the glass, nor do you feel that your installers were at fault. You can replace the glass for $109.55, using a different type of insulation so that the new glass will have more room for expansion when the temperature is high. Your company is Pittsline Glass, Buttonwood Dr., Sarasota 33580.

**7–20.** As president of Bartech Computers, 1023 Troy Ct., Troy, MI 48084, you have a letter from Oscar Asher, 91 N. Lincoln Road, E. Rochester, NY 14445, complaining that his Bartech Apollo microcomputer has stopped working and that the Bartech dealer in Rochester, The Data Shop, refuses to fix it. A phone call to The Data Shop gets you the rest of the story. Asher attempted to modify his Apollo to show lowercase letters on its screen (it shows only uppercase, resulting in a very big cost saving for Apollo customers who don't need both upper- and lowercase), following a series of articles in a popular computer hobbyist magazine.

In his attempt, according to The Data Shop, Asher overheated a memory chip and burned through the foil on the board at several points while soldering in jumper wires. The Data Shop pointed out to Asher that his attempt to modify his Apollo voided the warranty. It offered to replace the ruined chip and repair the board for a total parts and labor charge of $78 (not unreasonable). Write Asher explaining that The Data Shop told him the truth: his warranty is void, and he will have to pay to have his computer fixed. He will probably want to when he sees all the new programs just made available for his Bartech Apollo and described in the enclosed brochure, especially the new Casino software that lets him duplicate all the Las Vegas casino games almost exactly.

**7–21.** When Judith Mitchell (750 Holly Avenue, Salt Lake City, UT 84121) bought her Bartech Mercury computer from your factory store in Salt Lake City (now closed), she thought she was getting a high-grade piece of equipment, according to her letter to you (president, Bartech Computers, 1023 Troy Ct., Troy MI 48084). After having used it only four years in her pharmacy, she is getting "keyboard bounce" (some of the keys are hitting and bouncing, causing them to hit again and register two or three impulses instead of the intended single impulse). Since she keeps all of her customer and prescription records on her Bartech, she wants you to send her a new keyboard right away.

First of all, her warranty expired three years ago. Second, the Mercury was designed strictly as a home computer for playing simple computer games and learning basic computer programming—it was never intended for commercial use, and Mitchell has worked something of a minor miracle in programming it to do the work it is doing. You no longer produce the Mercury, and in addition the manufacturer who supplied you with the keyboards for them went out of business.

Offer Mitchell a commercial-quality keyboard, as good as those on the best electric office typewriters, ready to wire into her Mercury, for $129.50—you will pay shipping. Or perhaps she might be interested in trading in her Mercury on your new Bartech Mark XVII business computer, which will handle all her paperwork: inventory, payroll, taxes, bookkeeping, invoicing, past-due billing, ordering, as well as keep her customer/prescription records. You'll be glad to have your representative in her area call on her if she is interested in a Mark XVII.

**7–22.** *To:* Oeste Office Supply Co., 160 Granite Springs Road, Yorktown Heights, NY 10598. *From:* Stewart's Computer Supplies, 194 Meadow Street, Agawam, MA 01001. You no longer carry the Diablo HyType II Multistrike ribbons, part #24160. Retail for those is now $8.95 per cartridge. Instead, you now stock NordskComp ribbons (from Norway).

Ribbons are equal to or better in quality than Diablo ribbons. Cartridge is less bulky, and reinforced sockets for rollers help prevent ribbon from jamming. NordskComp #3006 replaces exactly the Diablo #24160, and like it will work in all Diablo printers except the 1200 series. Retail price is $4.95 each. But Oeste might want to consider the NordskComp #4009, the high-capacity version of the #3006. Same high-quality Mylar ribbon, same carefully engineered cartridge, but 360,000 impressions instead of the #3006's 220,000 impressions. Retail price of #4009 is $5.95 each.

Can you substitute NordskComp for Diablo ribbons, and would Oeste like to order the #4009 instead of the #3006? Oeste ordered six dozen cartridges.

**7–23.** As customer service representative for Stewart's Computer Supplies (see preceding case), write to J. C. Zacharias, Zacharias Office Equipment, 2 Pine Street, Wheelwright, MA 01094. Zacharias ordered six Lester #2 copyholders @ $137.50 each. The copyholders stand on a desk and hold copy: typewritten sheets, continuous form computer printouts, whatever. Metal bar across copy under line being read. Operator presses foot pedal, and copyholder pneumatically rolls copy up one standard typewriter line. Used for copying text or data by hand (typing or keyboarding) since operator can advance copy without removing hands from keyboard. Lester #2 is obsolete; you haven't carried in six years.

Now carry Sunnie Automatic Copyholder: quiet, easy to operate. Looks like a typewriter roller, with knobs, on a stand. Single-line display not only highlights line of copy to be read but magnifies and also illuminates it with an 8-watt fluorescent light (included) to reduce operator eyestrain. Operator uses foot control switch for start, stop, forward, and reverse movement; can roll copy back and forth a line at a time or continuously. Copyholder swivels 360° and can be raised or lowered on its stand for operator convenience. Place behind or to either side of keyboard. Holds single sheets, continuous forms (with or without pin feed holes), or text up to ¼″ thick. Heavy-duty steel construction. Tough baked-on enamel finish. Rubber-covered base. Three-prong plug. One-year guarantee. Maximum form width: 18½″. Comes in putty, tan, black, blue, or dark brown. Cost is $151.75 each. Sell the substitute.

**7–24.** You are the credit manager for Lane Furniture Company (manufacturer of porch furniture), 7314 Hanover Road, Dearborn, MI 48197.

It's the middle of June, and the following letter arrives from a new customer, City Furniture Company, 943 Oak Street, Winnetka, IL 60037:

> The summer furniture I ordered early February for delivery May 1 came today--too late for me to sell before clearance sales July 4. About all I can do with this furniture (24 chairs, 6 umbrella tables, 6 stacked tables, 6 umbrellas) is sell it at no-profit prices, store until next spring (which I don't intend to do), or return it to you, charges collect. Unless you are prepared to make a significant price concession, that is what I'm going to do. I'm returning your invoice and have instructed the freight people to hold the shipment until I hear from you.

City Furniture (and its owner, Paul P. Young) doesn't realize that your company had a strike and that you've had to hold up orders. You wrote your regular customers but apparently overlooked Young. He has every right to return the shipment (392 pounds), but that would be expensive. Rather than lose a new customer because of misunderstanding (and pay shipping charges both ways), you grant the price reduction to encourage him to keep the furniture. You'll knock off a 20 percent discount on the $1,400 total wholesale cost if he'll keep the furniture. Enclose a revised invoice with your letter. You might have to use some resale talk to convince Young that he should keep the furniture.

**7–25.** Slip into the role of Patricia M. Bennett, adjustment correspondent for Sax Manufacturing Company, P.O. Box 87654, New Orleans, LA 70187. You have to acknowledge the following claim from Yvonne Bohara, Casual Corner, University Mall, Hattiesburg, MS 38401:

> Six weeks ago I ordered 2 gross of women's casual dresses at one of your special prices. Counting on these as one of the special attractions, I advertised heavily. The day of the sale, lots of women came in--but no dresses! Today the dresses arrived. I can't use them. How do you want me to return them to you?

Your truck did carry the shipment of women's casual dresses, but the truck caught fire in an accident and a few of the dresses were damaged. By the time you discovered what had happened, it was simply too late to get a new shipment to Yvonne Bohara. The only thing you see to do is offer her a credit memo for the full amount ($2,880), then explain what happened, then offer to let her keep the dresses for $9.50 each instead of the $10 originally agreed upon. Enclose a second credit memo for the $144 and try to convince her of the worth of your proposal.

**7–26.** Paul Mueller, 1296 Ada Avenue, Idaho Falls, ID 83401, is pretty mad at you, Meta Kart Company, 1012 County Hwy AA, Nekoosa, WI 54457. In the spring he ordered one of your Spartan gasoline-powered golf carts. Says he had no trouble assembling it and it worked fine. But this weekend, only the fifth time he had used his Spartan, the brakes failed on the 15th hole and the cart rolled downhill and into a tree, bending the front of the body pretty badly as well as the front suspension and steering. The Polaroid photographs he enclosed show the damage graphically. They also show the protective shipping covers still on the front brakes. Those covers should have been removed before using the cart, as your instructions clearly state. Leaving them on causes the brake linings to overheat and glaze and the brakes to fail. Mueller has a $176 estimate for repairs from his local auto body shop and wants you to agree to pay the bill. You can sympathize with him, but he should have read your instructions more carefully (in which case he would not have put the canopy on backward as the pictures show). Offer to send him new brake linings and a new steering rod (needed to complete the repairs) without charge, but that's as far as you'll go. Good resale could help Mueller look more favorably on his dependable Spartan, which (with its brakes open to the cooling air) will give him the service he expects.

**7–27.** Franklin Office Supply Company, 1610 High Street, Cape Girardeau, MO 63710, sends an order amounting to $2,500.94 to Illinois Office Supply, Inc., 1908 Lake Street, Chicago, IL 60675. The firm sold this customer for three years on its regular terms with a $1,500 credit limit. The books show $800 now due. Because of the amount still on the creditor's books, it will not be advisable to refuse the order outright. Because of the long history of delayed payments, the amount now due, and the large increase in the size of the order, it will not be wise to grant the full credit. Sit in for the credit manager and write Carey Franklin, the owner, suggesting that the order be cut to $1,000.

**7–28.** As credit manager for Friendly Computers, 12374 Garden Grove Boulevard, Garden Grove, CA 92643, you are refusing to fill an order for Bret Monpere, Computerland, Northwood Shopping Mall, Madison, WI 53722, for computers amounting to $15,000. He owes your firm $3,000, 45 days past due. Acknowledge Monpere's order, but refuse to fill it. He can pay cash for this order or, better still, clear up the account before buying more.

**7–29.** Your company, Goldberg-Stein, Inc., 439 West Broadway, New York, NY 10021, gave Pier One Imports a $2,000 credit limit. The store exceeded the credit limit twice recently, and you allowed it. However, on the second occurrence, about a month ago, you called Vera Barton, the store manager, and urged her to keep within the limit. Now Barton sends you an order for $2,588.79, which (with outstanding bills) brings the amount owed you to $3,250. None of this is past due. Write her that you are processing the order but that before sending the goods, you want a check for at least $500. Perhaps the business has outgrown the present limit. If Barton will send the store's latest financial statements, you will take up the matter of increasing the limit.

**7–30.** Leonard Mignot, 2400 Oakland Avenue, Abilene, TX 79687, asks for too much credit for his own good and your company's safety. He plans to open a small television repair (and sales) shop; and he's sure he can make a go of it, especially if he can get some extended credit right at first.

He grew up in Abilene, worked there as a clerk in Miller Electric (selling TV sets), studied business at the University of Texas, and joined two civic organizations in Abilene. His order to you (Electronics Incorporated, P.O. Box 601, Houston, TX 77098) is for $1,500 worth of supplies, for which he proposes to pay $300 down and the rest in six monthly payments. He plans to begin with $7,000 worth of stock—and you assume that he is making the same proposal to other potential suppliers.

You have to refuse because your terms are definitely 2/10, n/30. The mortality rate among TV repair shops is high. But since you'd like to have him stock your equipment now and in the future, you point out to him the benefits of getting more capital to start with, offer him a 5 percent discount for cash with order, and try to build longtime goodwill and immediate cash business. Assume that you are the credit manager at Electronics Incorporated.

**7–31.** As credit manager of Weatherford Office Supply Co., 626 Broadway, Cincinnati, OH 45202, you have to acknowledge the order for three Viscount III word processors for Hector Mfg. Co., 900 Victory Dr., Portsmouth, OH 45662. A credit check shows that Hector's 10-year-old business is related to the building trade and that because of high interest rates there has been little building recently. The company owes $50,000, about half of it overdue, and it has been laying off workers. At this time you feel that Hector is too big a risk to take on a debt of $15,000 for the word processors.

**7–32.** Because of existing debt and slow payments, Allen and Jemison Lumber Company (6742 Blackheath Avenue, Joplin, MO 63141) must decline credit to Lloyd Wood (49 Oak Street, Neosho, MO 64850) for $1,500 worth of lumber. You rate credit applicants on an ABC basis. Wood's credit report shows A for employment certainty, residence, character, and reputation; B on income amount and payment habits; and C on income commitments—giving a total average of B.

Wood is a good citizen who earns a fair salary as a bank clerk, but he has already obligated himself to pay as much each month as he can manage. He is paying $200 a month on an old home he bought a few months ago, with plans to fix it up. The Credit Bureau reports that two of his debts involve rather large amounts that should have been paid several months ago. One, you learn, is a plumber's bill for a new bathroom; the other, a hospital bill for an addition to his family. If Wood will concentrate on clearing up his present indebtedness, he would make you a good credit risk in the future. Show him how it is to his advantage to pay cash for the present while reducing these old debts.

**7–33.** You are the credit manager for a company that makes computers. One of your regular customers, a small Mom-and-Pop store called Computing Products Center, has placed an unusually large order for computers. Even though CPC has always paid on time, doing so has been a real hardship.

You believe that the store has overextended itself. Write a letter recommending a smaller order in line with the amount the store usually spends each month and suggesting a wait-and-see attitude about reorders. Recently the computer business has been having difficulty because so many new kinds have flooded the market. All this flooding causes customers to be confused.

**7–34.** When you (Manager, Meta Kart Co., 1012 County Hwy. AA, Nekoosa, WI 54457) took on Libby Lawn & Garden Supply (3512 Pinemont, Houston, TX 77018) as a dealer for your line of golf carts and garden tractors, you agreed on a $12,000 limit on carts and tractors and a $2,500 limit on parts and accessories. Since you made the agreement, Libby's business has remained fairly static and you have no reason to expand the agreed-on credit limits. Since Libby presently owes you $1,988.43 for parts and accessories, you must refuse to accept a new order for another $823.69 in parts on credit.

**7–35.** Video Circus, 1225 Boston Avenue, Longmont, CO 80501, has sent you (Sales Manager, Techtel Corp., 6805 Lincoln Avenue, Lincolnwood, IL 60646) an order for 12 of your Model 3 cordless, remote telephones, 3 each in beige, white, black, and yellow. Unfortunately, you cannot ship the telephones until you find out how many Video Circus wants with dials and how many with pushbuttons. Write and find out.

**7–36.** As president of Stop-Fire Manufacturing Company, Industrial Park Area, New Brunswick, NJ 08945, you find that your company is short of coiled sheet steel because of recent strikes. You need the steel to produce your fire extinguisher, and so you are looking into foreign sources from which to buy it. In the meantime, write a form letter to customers in the United States telling them that their orders are back-ordered.

**7–37.** Mrs. Franklin Randall, who lives in Germany, where her husband is stationed, wants to order several Christmas gifts from your catalog (make up the kinds of gifts). Assume that you have to back-order one of the gifts because of its popularity; for another gift, there's a missing piece of information (color, size, where the gift is to be sent, etc.). You are also on your own to add the necessary resale. Mrs. Randall's address is 461–72–8160, 596 Maint. Co., APO NY 09175.

**7–38.** As an employee in the College/University Department of Eastern Publishing Company, 1890 Ridge Road, East Amherst, NY 14098, write a personal letter to Dr. Heinz Fohr, P.O. Box 28901, Sunnyside O, 32, Pretoria, South Africa, telling Fohr that two books (*Megascopes,* copyright 1985, and *Writing for Excellence,* sixth edition) are due from the printer in June. Fohr's name has been placed on the follow-up list; so he should receive a copy of each of these publications as soon as they are available.

**7–39.** Your job is director of sales for Borg, Inc., 1534 W. Van Buren, Phoenix, AZ 85007. Decline to accept an order from United Supply Company, 290 W. Middle Turnpike, Manchester, CT 06040, for 60 Fitz-All lawn mower blades. Your exclusive dealer in Connecticut is Ludwig Tool and Garden on Fairland Drive in Huntington. Your dealers have protected territories to ensure their profits. You're happy with Ludwig, but who knows what the future holds? Maybe United can arrange to get the blades from Ludwig. You'll keep United in mind.

**7–40.** You, district manager for McGowan and McGrath, 470 E. Green Bay Avenue, Saukville, WI 53080, have to refuse a first order from Wimberly Tools and Machinery, 48 S. Main Street, Bainbridge, NY 13733, for one 4″ × 4″ cross-feed table and three dozen No. 4 BA plug taps. The best source for the cross-feed table would be Palm and Green Mfg. Co., 165 Granite Springs Road, Yorktown Heights, NY 10598; you can recommend P & G products. You don't carry any cross-feed tables that small. You don't know who would handle BA (British Association) taps, or even whether they are available in this country; they are used primarily by hobbyists.

**7–41.** *To:* K. L. Hansen, Buyer, Faithful Office Supply, 4160 Youngfield Avenue, Wheat Ridge, CO 80033. *From:* You, Order Dept., P. A. Bargh Co., 7822 Myers Lake Avenue, Rockford, MI 49341. Faithful ordered six Royal 110 Series Print/Display Calculators. Does Hansen want No. 114PD 10-digit display (dealer net $55.97 each) or No. 116PD 12-digit display (dealer net $62.83 each). Faithful ordered two #8251 Brother Charger II All-Steel Portable Typewriters (dealer net $62.97 each). Bargh is out of stock at present, will have in three weeks, will back-order them. Faithful ordered 12 Panasonic three-Cell Waterproof Flashlights. You do not carry these, but Hansen may be able to get them from Knight & Walsh Sales, 425 Faith Road, Salisbury, NC 28144. Faithful ordered four No. 100HUR Heuer MultiFunction LCD Stopwatches (dealer net $18.96 each). You no longer carry this model, now carry No. 1000N Heuer Microsplit MultiFunction Stopwatch (dealer net $22.50 each). Has same features as 100HUR (six-digit LCD display; $\frac{1}{100}$-second reading; split-second feature up to 59 minutes, 59.99 seconds; functions as a watch showing hours, minutes, seconds and month, date, day; quartz accuracy $\pm 0.0004$ percent; water resistant; color-coded push buttons; black plastic case with lanyard). Push buttons are twice size of those on 100HUR; LED display is brighter and larger. How will you handle selling the substitute?

**7–42.** For P. A. Bargh (see preceding case), acknowledge an order from J. W. Barnes, 1365 Logan Avenue, Costa Mesa, CA 92626, for one #RWK160B ITC Man's LCD Watch with AM/FM Radio ($24.96), one #LW601BK Casio ¾-Size 50-Metre Watersports Alarm LCD Watch with Stainless Steel Band ($25.96), and one #JT100BK Casio Pace Runner Jogging Watch ($35.96). Barnes OK'd charging the order to a MasterCard account. You can send the #RWH160B watch with radio right away. The #JT100BK jogging watch is out of stock; you will send it when you get some in. The #LW601BK watersports alarm watch is now priced at $28.96; you will send it at new price.

**7–43.** As the customer service representative for Chef's Bazaar, 616 Chestnut St., So. Charleston, WV 25309, acknowledge the order from C. R. Hirsch, 5776 Grant Ave., Cleveland, OH 44105, for a Combo Starter Set of Phalcalon cookware and the check for $342. Pots made of cast and machined aluminum, anodized with a finish 30 percent harder than stainless steel. Cast-iron handles tin-plated and riveted to pots with ¼-inch-diameter rivets. Used by world's leading chefs since 1966 because of superior cooking performance, ease of cleaning, durability. Pots' surface will not crack, chip, rust, or peel; once seasoned, virtually stick-free. You are shipping set today except for the 5-quart saucepan and the 8-inch omelet pan. You have these items on order, and when they come in, you will send them on to Hirsch. Unfortunately, Hirsch ordered from your advertisement in an old magazine; the price of the Combo Starter Set has gone up to $362. Get Hirsch to send you a check for the difference.

**7–44.** As the Olde Book Finder, 806 Desale St., Vienna, VA 22180, write to Edmund George, 3405 Magnolia St., Texarkana, TX 75503. From your fall list George ordered the copy of Robert P. Elmer's *Archery,* published in 1926 (good condition, $110). By the time his order (with check) arrived, you had sold and shipped the 1926 *Archery.* However, you have just acquired a copy of Robert P. Elmer's *Target Archery,* published in 1946 (very fine condition, with dust jacket, $65). You are holding this later edition for George and are holding the check pending his decision. You will either refund the difference or, if George prefers, you will send both *Target Archery* and a copy in very good condition of James Duff's *Bows and Arrows* in the 1927 first edition (a $55 value) for $110.

**7–45.** As Ward McMillen, director and owner of Northgate Shopping Center in X City, you have been most successful in renting space and managing for the past 20 years. But your overhead has increased (maintenance, higher wages for cleanup crews, higher light bills, more safety precautions), so you are going to have to raise the rent for each business 50 cents a square foot. Write a form letter that will be processed so that it looks personal. Point out some of the good things about the mall (central location, ample parking, freedom from crime, spacious walkways, piped-in music, vast cornucopia of goods for every taste). The increase will go into effect the first of the year.

**7–46.** As director, Fiscal Division (name D. P. Oliver) of your state Medicaid Agency, 2700 Fairway Drive, Capital, State, ZIP, you write the patron or sponsor (Mrs. Vera Bailey, 6822 Woodcrest Drive, nearby city in same state) about her mother, Mrs. Anna Marie Stern (Social Security number 335–38–9297), a patient in Glen Acres Nursing Home.

Annually Medicaid examines the bank records of every Medicaid patient. When you received Mrs. Stern's record from the First National Bank in her town, you noticed that her annuity from the one life insurance policy her husband left her had increased from $143.59 to $160.34 a month starting in January of this year. Her husband died 44 years ago. Mrs. Stern had never worked outside the home. Her only income is the annuity from this life insurance policy and $125.60 from Social Security. Medicaid pays all her expenses at the nursing home beyond this now-figured $285.94 income.

Mrs. Bailey should have reported the income increase immediately to Medicaid. Since she did not, Medicaid has overpaid $134. The error must be corrected by a reimbursement to Medicaid for $134 ($16.75 times eight months) within 15 days from the date of this letter. If Mrs. Bailey's records do not agree, she should submit written information within 15 days. If she has any questions, she can write the state Medicaid office or phone (--- --- ----). Write the letter for D. P. Oliver.

**7–47.** For 10 years Ralph Bowie was a reliable employee of West Coast Electronics, of which you are the production manager. He started as an assembler, was promoted to foreman, and eventually (five years ago) became a supervisor (of Assembly Line 3).

Two years ago his wife died of leukemia just about the same time that his two children left home. This family breakup apparently led to his becoming a rather hard drinker, and the drinking, in turn, led to *(a)* a 60 percent increase in his rate of absenteeism; *(b)* a surliness of temper, complained of by several members of his work force; and *(c)* a decrease in the productivity of Assembly Line 3 from highest (of all four lines) to lowest.

You sent Ralph several memos tactfully calling his attention to the decline in productivity and asking his opinion of the reasons for it; he did not reply. You called him in for an informal chat, during which he offered a number of specious reasons (a large number of new trainees, a batch of defective components that had to be returned) but persistently shied away whenever you tried to suggest that he might have some personal problems he'd like to discuss. Two months after that, he got into a brawl with one of his assemblers. You called them both in; accusations of name-calling were exchanged; you excused the other worker and tried again to get Ralph to admit that he was in need of psychological counseling. He quit, calling you a "busybody" and saying that the company could "take their job and shove it."

Today you received the following letter:

```
            McKENZIE AIRCRAFT CORPORATION
                 100 Industrial Plaza
                 Cincinnati, OH 45229


      Mr./Ms. (use your own name here)
      Production Manager
      West Coast Electronics
      1546 Occidental Blvd.
      Los Angeles, CA 90019



      Dear Mr./Mrs. _____;

      Ralph Bowie, formerly employed by your firm, has
      applied for work with McKenzie Aircraft. Can you
      give us specific information regarding the
      following aspects of his performance with your
      company:

      1. Was he prompt and reliable in performing
         assigned duties?
```

2. How many people did he supervise?
3. Was he well liked by his fellow workers?
4. Did he show leadership potential?
5. Why did he leave your firm?
6. Would you rehire him?

Answers to the above questions and any other information on the applicant that you care to supply will be greatly appreciated and will, of course, be treated confidentially.

If we can reciprocate this courtesy at any time, please do not hesitate to call upon us.


Yours very truly,



Theodore Pedrolli
Director, Employment Services

How are you going to respond to this letter? You have sympathy for Ralph. Maybe he has straightened out; you just don't know. You are obliged to be honest and specific in your reply; and, of course, you must be careful not to assume knowledge you don't have evidence for.

**7–48.** Answer an inquiry from Rose Dukas, a graduate student in Office Administration at Arizona State College. She asked you about the positive effects you've found at Bank of the Pacific from the new open office. In such offices, partial walls give lots of employee contact and a less constricted, closed-off feeling, she says. She read about your new decor in the *Los Angeles Times* business section.

You've found few positive effects, actually. Because of the partial walls, everyone hears everyone else's phone conversations, interviews, and personal details. Employee conflicts can't be discussed, nor can evaluation interviews be done in such offices. Employees have found themselves to be interrupted more often, and you feel that concentration, production, and performance have been suffering.

You do think that the B of P offices are much more attractive this way, and figure that except for loan and personnel employees, the trade-off of lack of privacy is balanced by lower construction costs, flexibility (the wall modules can be moved), and modern appearance.

**7–49.** Assume that you are a member of the Bureau of Auto Repair, State of California, Sacramento 95876. You have the unpleasant job of warning George Kornasiewicz, Kornasiewicz Auto Repair Service, 27009 Visitacion, San Francisco 94101, and 20 other mechanics in Sacramento and San Francisco about complaints you have received from motorists.

Since you have to write so many letters, you're going to try a form letter that hits on some of the general complaints: mechanics put seltzer tablets in battery to make it foam; mechanic poured oil on shock absorber to make owner think it leaks; worker poured barbecue sauce on alternator to cause a burning smell. Other complaints have been that mechanics quote a low price for repairs (called lowballing), but then they present an exorbitant repair bill. Customers have even complained that their fan belts have been cut with razor blades.

Write the letter to Kornasiewicz warning him of the complaints you have been receiving.

**7–50.** As a tax accountant, write Mrs. Elise Cunninsham, a U.S. citizen who is teaching in Austria (71/1 Tivolgegasse, 1120 Vienna 12, Austria, Europe), that she can't claim an exemption for dependency for her child Alice, who lives with her. She divorced Alice's father in 1984, and he (Albert Cunninsham) pays her maintenance (the fancy new name for temporary alimony) and child support.

The key in support cases seems to be support rather than custody. If she wants the exemption, maybe she can go back to court and get her ex-husband to sign a paper giving her the exemption even though he pays more than half of the child's support. Maybe she should keep better records and prove that she pays more than half.

The most recent tax court case is Alfonso Lorenzo Dillard TC Memo 1984–26. It ruled that the support-paying father got the exemption even though the mother had custody.

**7–51.** As president of Central X Power Company, you have to write the president's letter to shareholders (the standard beginning part) for the annual report. Unfortunately, your batting average in this game has not been good. (Over the past 15 years you have had to explain the closing of three plants that cost $66 million.)

You and your board of directors, however, have tried to avoid the former troubles (cost escalation due to licensing problems, schedule delays, new regulations and accompanying design requirements, construction problems, high inflation, and interest rates).

For reasons (as described in detail concerning the newly built Millbrook plant), the board of directors made a painful decision to cut dividends 29 percent.

On the brighter side, the company has got a rate increase of 3 percent, which should help build financial strength. The company initiated an early retirement program but deferred the yearly merit raises.

Acting upon the recommendation of an independent audit group, the company began a goals and objectives program that ties budgeting and performance evaluation directly with planning and corporate objectives. The company hired several highly qualified people from outside to add perspective and diversity to a strong utility management team. The human resources program was expanded to encourage employees to give their best. Central X Power has an extraordinarily strong and loyal employee group. The service they provide is extremely reliable.

The company survival and vitality depend on exerting every effort to keep the costs of supplying electricity as low as possible, to make its value to customers as high as possible, and to meet the expectations of investors.

**7–52.** As a trainee for the county health agency in your city, you spend time in various departments learning the policies and procedures. Your first assignment is in the inspection department, where your job is to visit different restaurants to see if they comply with the health code. In each case you must inform the manager of the restaurant in writing of any violations. Most of the eating establishments you visit comply with the regulations; but the Golden Ox, 2398 Bentley Avenue in your city, has some serious problems.

You list these infractions in your notebook:

1.  Grease, dirt, and smoke stains on window curtains.
2.  Garbage overflowing in alley.
3.  Men's rest room—no hot water, no soap.
4.  Women's rest room—no bathroom tissue paper.
5.  Smoking in kitchen (head cook).
6.  Cooked food sitting on counters not refrigerated.
7.  Kitchen help not using utensils to handle food.
8.  Pots put away dirty.
9.  Some food kept at unsafe temperature.
10. Roach droppings in storeroom.

The health code states that restaurants in such violation of the health code must be closed within four days and stay closed until another inspection determines that all violations have been corrected. You must inform Grant Crain, owner of the Golden Ox, of the violations of the code.

**7–53.** As a consultant in administration, you have received a point system that one of your clients (Bonanza Air Lines, 5266 W. Pierson Rd., Flushing, MI 48433) plans to establish to determine discipline for excessive absences. You are to make comments and suggestions. Here is the plan:

Employees who have 10 points against their records during any three-month period will receive warnings that failure to improve their attendance record will result in disciplinary action. Points are to be awarded as follows:

For each unexcused and unreported absence    3 points
For each reported but unexcused absence      1 point
For each unexcused lateness                  1 point

Bonanza defines a reported absence as one in which the worker reports the absence before the time scheduled to begin work.

You hate to throw cold water all over this plan, especially as the personnel manager who designed it, S. J. Abrams, is very enthusiastic about it—and tends to sulk when told something isn't great. But, . . . while the plan will take some of the uncertainty out of when an employee will be disciplined, it is still not a clear guide as to when discipline will occur and what the penalty will be.

Even if Bonanza gives points for a first warning, second warning, and so on, suppose an employee does not receive notice of points assessed. And if an employee calls at night, the message may not get through to the proper supervisor, since Bonanza operates with a skeleton staff at night. Further, what arrangements will ensure that messages received during one shift will be passed on to the next shift? Another problem is telling employees promptly that they have reached the 10-point warning level; the system won't do much good if an employee may have accumulated 20 points before receiving the warning.

Write a letter to Abrams detailing, in an organized and considerate fashion, your comments on the proposed plan. Add any other realistic comments you think would help.

**7–54.** Inform your branch offices by memo that you won't be imposing on all old and new clients the new nine-digit ZIP codes they worked so hard to compile. (And the Postal Service will not be enforcing its October 1 deadline either.) Businesses with bulk mail were going to be required to use the old five-digit ZIP codes plus the new four-digit specific codes in order to send bulk mailings.

It's not your people's fault, of course. The Postal Service directory has errors that need to be corrected, and then new real estate developments need to be added. Furthermore, a lot of the mailing software now available can't yet match addresses and the longer codes.

You'll probably be able to use the new codes eventually; so have your staff save the data collected so far and ask new clients for the nine-digit ZIP codes.

(As an alternative assignment, you can write clients who sent you the new ZIP a tactful form card saying that you'll use it later but not yet.)

**7–55.** Security Savings and Loan, 243 North Water Street, Springfield, IL 62525, hired George Shoop in its marketing department five years ago. George had previously held two other jobs that he got through family connections. He has not been satisfactorily productive in those jobs or with your company.

George was asked to review and write a report on the bank and savings and loan competitive interest rates and trends in 12 geographic markets. When his report was turned in a week late, it was poorly written. Another assignment that George failed on was his preparation of weekly reports of Treasury rates and competitive rates in five major markets. Although he failed to do a good job, the company had enough faith in him to ask him to do monthly reports that measure deposit flows, new accounts, transactions, and savings cost for each office, market, and region. As before, George's work was late and poorly done.

As vice president of marketing and product development, you called George in and went over his lack of productivity. In the course of conversation George expressed an interest in helping with the advertising; so you let him develop special direct-mail letters. After several weeks he brought in letters he had written to new customers, inactive customers, old customers . . . . Although he tried to write good letters, he obviously had not studied or learned much about how to write well. You and the other vice presidents felt that you could not use his work. And you had the job of telling George so.

Next you assigned him to the job of promoting IRA deposits with a goal of at least 35 percent increase in retirement savings accounts. Although George said he tried his best, he increased these accounts just 10 percent, while others hit 40 percent.

Next you let George phone holders of maturing CD accounts to see if the customers would reinvest. The two others who did the same job in the department reduced withdrawals 40 percent, but George reduced them just 10 percent. In little memos you gave the results to the two other workers and George.

These are just a few examples of George's lack of productivity. After a meeting with the CEO, you are told to write George telling him of the company decision to discontinue his service. Offer to give him two months to find another job, and offer to give him personal recommendations. Shoop has been honest and pleasant but not hardworking or productive.

**7–56.** For more cases on refusals, see Appendix B II C; VI B, F, G; VII B, E; X F; XI C; XVI F; XVII A. For modified adjustments, see IV B. For substitute, see VI H. For rechanneling, see IV D; VIII E.

For general bad news, see IV E, F (oral); IX A, D, M, N; XVIII E, F; XIV A, B, C, D; XVI D; XVII E, F.

## Cases for Chapter 8

(Persuasion in Selling Goods)

**8–1.** *Company:* Tools for Living, 630 Charles Street, Poplar Bluff, MO 63901. *Mailing list:* Appliance dealers in Midwest. *Product:* Bonneaire fresh air machine removes 99 percent of all particulate pollutants from air—good-bye to soot, dust, animal dander, pollen, cigarette smoke, smog, molds, fungi, hair spray fumes. Newly developed electret filter removes particles as small as $\frac{1}{10,000}''$ (the thickness of human hair).

Bonneaire claims 45 cubic feet of air a minute, the average room three times an hour. Has switchable ion generator—negative ions are well known for their presumed psychological good effects, creating a sense of well-being such as comes from standing next to a waterfall. A switchable fragrance dispenser allows owner to add fresh scent to air. Bonneaire measures $11'' \times 7'' \times 5''$, uses only 45 watts energy, comes in handsomely styled brushed aluminum case, and retails for $130, but only $78 to dealers. UL-listed and one-year warranty.

**8–2.** As an appliance dealer in Springfield, Missouri (The Appliance Store, 2003 East Battlefield Road—65804, phone: 887–1529), you bought a good stock of Bonneaire fresh air machines (preceding case). You've made a mailing list of 108 beauty salon prospects to whom you'll write. Because of all the chemicals they use, many beauticians have serious lung problems; so the air filter could help them breathe easier.

**8–3.** Your mailing to the beauticians pulled 10 percent returns. Now a month has passed, and you'll try your hand at writing a follow-up message with the theme of the pollen pollutant now that spring is here.

**8–4.** Oral assignment: *(a)* Call the places around Springfield where you know there is a problem of smoke-filled rooms (conference rooms at the university, eating and drinking establishments, . . .). *(b)* Call the well-established beauty salons in hopes of selling them an air filter machine. They have already received two of your mailings.

**8–5.** *Product:* The Corporate Tie comes with solid background with company logo woven into fabric or a single logo embroidered at the bottom of a solid or striped tie. Minimum order 60 ties.

*Company:* Travis Ruis, New Haven York Center, West Haven, CT 06500.

*Mailing list:* 5,000 public relations directors at companies, universities, state departments. Assume enclosure with pictures and prices.

*Added sales:* Women's corporate scarves, belts, ties.

**8–6.** Type a letter on a word processing machine that will invite customers to "The Office of the Future" display at the civic center in your city, 9–5 next Monday, Tuesday, and Wednesday. You are head of sales for SYZ Company, 3411 Ninth Street, Philadelphia, PA 19107. Before you can write this case, you'll have to see what the latest is in office equipment. In general, the display will have the latest word processing machines, computers, electronic filing, videotext . . . .

**8–7.** To help stimulate business for your certified and licensed company and workers called Advanced Appliance Service, Inc., you get a mailing list of real estate dealers in Y City and write them a letter promoting your honest, dependable, and expert inspections on appliances. You've been in business 23 years, but you've never offered this particular kind of service.

Before a real estate dealer buys a house, condominium, or building, you can inspect its air conditioning, furnace, appliances to see if there are any problems. Your charge to inspect two appliances is $24.50, additional ones $4. If a central air conditioning system needs to be checked, then the charge is $28.50 plus $4 for each additional appliance.

If any of the appliances need parts or replacing, you handle Kitchen Aid, Magic Chef, GE, Whirlpool, Kenmore, Modern Maid, Tappan, Frigidaire, White-Westinghouse.

**8–8.** Assume the role of president of your university alumni association. On letterhead stationery of your university, write a letter to a mailing list of alumni association members offering them the opportunity of buying an authentic Hitchcock chair (33″ high, 21½″ wide, and 19½″ deep) produced from selected kiln-dried hard rock maple. The chair comes with a handwoven rush seat and features the official university seal. Each chair bears the original Lambert Hitchcock warranty attesting its status as an authentic Hitchcock.

In 1818 Lambert Hitchcock founded a manufactory in which quality and craftsmanship were the cornerstones. Using skills handed down through the generations, the Hitchcock Chair Company's master artisans of today continue to create fine furniture loyal to the founder's exacting standards. Each component is precisely hand-fitted to its specific location. The seat is handwoven directly onto the frame of the assembled chair for maximum strength.

Due to the extensive hand craftsmanship involved, each chair will be produced on a direct commissioning basis only. To get a chair for Christmas, buyer needs to order within the next two weeks. Remittance of $295 should be made payable to The University Chair or charged to American Express, MasterCard, or Visa. Credit card orders may be placed by calling 1–800–345–5243.

Due to the size of the shipping container for the chairs, they must be shipped via motor freight. Since freight charges will vary according to distance, they will be collected upon delivery. Anticipated charges average $30 per chair within the United States. Upon delivery, if not satisfied, buyer may return chair for full refund. Hitchcock Chair Company's full one-year warranty applies.

**8–9.** *Company:* T & J Publishing, Celebrity Keepsake Series, P.O. Box 1071, Lake Geneva, WI 53147 (wholesalers).

*Product:* Birthday greeting cards feature famous people born on the same day as the recipient's birth date. The series of 366 cards lists historical figures, Nobel peace prize winners, popular entertainers, outstanding athletes, prominent entrepreneurs, in addition to the recipient's name under the heading "And One Great Human Being." Suggested retail price is $1.50 to $2.25 per card. The charge to the mail-order marketer is 75 cents per card, including the card and envelope, imprinting of the recipient's name, and shipping to the customer.

Assume that you are to write to the owner of a large gift shop called Little Travelers, 1710 Highway 35, Ocean, NJ 07714 (just one name on your bought mailing list) promoting these unusual cards.

**8–10.** Your large department-store-type firm uses mail, telephone, magazine inserts, on-campus solicitations, and television to promote its goods. It has a dozen different mailing programs targeted to specific lifestyle segments of the population (college students, newlyweds, movers, new mothers, cash customers . . .). Today you have the assignment of writing a form letter to a list of new mothers offering the mothers a free Winnie the Pooh plush toy if they will just submit a credit application you are enclosing. You can make up the names and addresses of the company and a mother.

**8–11.** Your company, Green Care Lawn Service, uses a complete program of fertilizers, weed controls, and preemergents at the proper times for maximum benefit. You also have a shrubbery-pruning service and can create new shrub beds with pine bark or rocks. Besides all of this work you can also dehatch zoysia lawns and scalp back all the turf grass areas. With a mailing list of homeowners in a wealthy part of your city, write a promotion leaflet describing your service. Your firm can give free estimates if homeowners will call 331–1340 anytime Monday through Saturday. Naturally, you'll time your leaflets to arrive at the homes late winter–early spring.

**8–12.** Ingvar Kamprad, of IKEA (rhymes with "I see ya"), sells furniture to 50 stores in nine countries, but not in the United States yet. This year IKEA will print 25 million catalogs bringing more than 10 million customers to stores carrying its furniture, where they will spend more than $3 million. After a prospective customer gets the catalog and selects things of interest, browsing through the store is the next step. Usual shopping spree time: three hours. Children can stay in the playroom, and everyone has lunch at next-to-nothing prices in each store's cafeteria. The clerk picks the knockdown furniture the customer selects, helps toss it in the station wagon or car; then the customer puts it all together when home. The buy-it-by-catalog program works so well that IKEA now controls nearly 20 percent of the home furnishings business in Sweden.

Through a friend Kamprad got the name of Mona Barnes, who owns the Denmark Shop, 6820 Veterans Memorial Blvd., Metarie, LA 70003. In this first letter to President Barnes, send along an (assumed) IKEA catalog and ask whether she would like to handle this top-quality furniture that is easy to ship, to move. Scandinavian styles appeal especially to young people everywhere.

**8–13.** National Geographic Society, 17th and M Streets, Washington, DC 20016, has a mailing list of 9,589,896 members and subscribers but wants to sell for $22.95 a 518-page full-color book called *Journey into China* that has 400 color illustrations. With the book comes a color wall map 2½ feet by 3 feet. Assume an order card, but write a convincing letter selling the book to the subscribers and members.

**8–14.** *Product:* Golfer's gift set includes a solid brass green repair tool and ball marker that can initial balls with three letters. The tool and marker come in an all-leather pocket-size case with brass chain to attach to a belt loop or golf bag. Comes in an attractive gift box. Costs $9.95, postage paid. Money-back guarantee.

*Company:* A. G. Klapperich, Route 1, Cody Road, Mt. Calvary, WI 53057.

*Mailing list:* Golfers in Midwest and Southeast.

*Assignment:* Write a letter for the word processing machine to go along with a reply form and six-page, two-color folder.

**8–15.** *Product:* Speedshredder will shred technical manuals, blueprints, computer report forms—even microfilm and microfiche. Machine has hardened solid steel cutting cylinders that never need oiling or resharpening. Has six-month warranty on parts and labor. Costs $750.

*Company:* Monroe Business Forms, Inc., 1200 Milwaukee Avenue, Glenview, IL 60020.

*Mailing list:* Retailers selling office supplies.

*Assignment:* Write a form letter with faked inside address. Assume an enclosed order card, business reply envelope, and four-page, three-color brochure.

**8–16.** Your company publishes a magazine called *Computing,* P.O. Box 703, Martinsville, NJ 08863. To people on a bought mailing list, you are to write a form letter offering to send a free sample copy and offering a discount of $2.03 if person will subscribe for a year. Customer has 30 days to review the first issue and (if it doesn't please 100 percent) to mark "cancel" on the bill and owe nothing. In plain English *Computing* answers such questions as: What's the best computer for under $1,000? What's the most advanced word processing program on the market today? What new programs and accessories—compatible with your system—will be available in the next six months? Along with your letter you'll assume enclosures of a brochure telling more about the magazine, an order card, and a copy of one of the articles entitled "Ten Valuable Tips on How to Buy Software."

**8–17.** Your university is sponsoring a three-day program called Project Management and the Personal Computer six months from now on the 21st, 22d, and 23d at a cost of $495 per person payable to University Seminars. (Tax-deductible for all expenses of continuing management education, including registration fees, travel, meals, and lodging.) Fee includes cost of all meeting materials used during the course. Teams of three individuals from the same organization receive a 10 percent discount.

The course teaches how to use tools to develop project schedules and budgets, track and control expenses, analyze project costs, update schedules, generate printed progress reports, level resources, evaluate productivity. Course is valuable for executives, managers, supervisors in government and industry who are concerned with effectively managing ventures and projects where the cost, schedule, and performance of programs must meet rigid requirements. Course has AACE, Inc. Certification Board approval for credit toward meeting the continuing education requirements for recertification as a Certified Cost Engineer/Certified Cost Consultant.

Write a sales letter that goes along with a registration card inviting executives, managers, supervisors in government and industry in the area around your university to come to the program.

**8–18.** Foreign patients have long sought medical care in sophisticated U.S. hospitals. But now some U.S. hospitals like yours, facing tighter health-care budgets and dwindling occupancy rates, have started seeking foreign patients.

Often patients make the trip to the United States for major procedures such as coronary bypass surgery, which can cost $20,000. The people who can afford such a trip typically come with dollars in hand, and they pay all the charges.

The way to get more international referrals is to stay in touch with doctors abroad. Foreign nationals trained in U.S. hospitals constitute a global network; and international seminars, in addition to providing scientific exchanges, also help hospitals strengthen referral networks. Your hospital offers annual postgraduate seminars in Miami and Colombia.

For Carlos Ruiz, director of international affairs at Cedars Medical Center, Miami 33186, try to get 3–5 percent international hospital admission (and the added revenue) by writing a letter to foreign doctors reminding them of the good care at your hospital. Write the letter to the doctors who have attended your seminars, stressing the good care that your hospital can provide faster than a financially strained health program in some other countries. The care may even be less expensive if the other country's technology is less developed.

**8–19.** Select a computer or word processor that you would like to promote through direct mail. Assume an appropriate well-defined mailing list as well as promotional ads in news magazines and business magazines and on TV. Select a central selling point and develop your letter around it.

**a.** Sales letter from manufacturer to dealer.

**b.** Sales letter from dealer to individual.

**8–20.** For more cases on persuasion in selling goods, see Appendix B II A; V A, B, C, D, E, F; VIII A, B, C; XI A; XIII A; XV B.

# Cases for Chapter 9

(Effectively Selling Ideas and Services)

**9–1.** Your supervisor, Harriet Hauge, notified you that she failed to get you the 6 percent raise you thought you were entitled to receive; but she did manage to obtain a better-than-average raise for you (3 percent). A committee of three people must review and approve all larger-than-average raises, and she was unable to convince the committee to approve your 6 percent. She promises, however, that she will take your case to the committee again, but only if you write a memorandum clearly stating your position. The committee meets today. You have one hour to prepare your case.

Hurriedly you jot down "reasons" that you think support your case: was not absent or tardy during last year, worked overtime without pay on new projects, was punctual at meetings, served as member of company safety committee, active in United Way drive and blood drive, filled in for supervisor when she had an operation and was hospitalized three weeks, conducted groups of international visitors through the plant and made favorable impression. (Add any other points you can think of that would be logical, and rephrase and reorder the points mentioned.)

**9–2.** In your midwestern office, winter days get pretty gray and bleak. You (office manager) read about the positive effects of a new kind of fluorescent light called Vita-Lite ($15 each), which produces light most like that in real sunlight. Other ways of getting full-spectrum light are going outdoors (hard to do in your winters!) and using windows that allow ultraviolet light to enter (you haven't had time to check costs on this yet, but replacing windows is expensive).

You think that adding the new light bulbs would cheer up employees on gray days, because some doctors have studied the effects of sunlight and found that it adds calcium to bones, reduces stress, raises moods, and may even affect metabolism. Exercise also has these effects. Ultraviolet rays also regulate eating and sleeping patterns.

Write a memo to the building manager asking for installation. Justify the expense. Find or make up some reasonable-sounding evidence.

**9–3.** As head of the Search Committee at your university or college, you have found a professor at another school who meets with the committee's approval. Write a letter inviting this professor to come to your campus on a specified date (at your school's expense) for a job interview with your colleagues.

**9–4.** XYZ Company has made arrangements with the External Degree Program at your university for its employees to take courses by correspondence. The employees have not been too responsive even though you've promoted this program through your house organ and bulletin boards. Cost for one hour of credit is $50—or just $150 for a three-hour course.

Draft a memo, to go along with this month's paychecks, urging the employees to take part in earning college credit a convenient way. The student sets the pace of the course, so is not under any great pressure. Most exams are open-book (convenient and fair). Assume an attractive enclosed brochure describing all the courses available.

**9–5.** As A. L. Lee, you have the job (assigned by the other board members of Makanai Kai condominiums, 129 Paokalani Ave., Paia, HI 96779) of writing a positively worded message that will be framed and placed on the back of the entrance door of each apartment. Many of your linens, dishes, pots, pans, wastebaskets, ice buckets, draperies, and just about everything that isn't nailed down have disappeared from the apartments. The replacement costs continue to go up and up.

Most of your renters are from wealthy backgrounds and can well afford the high rent you charge. But many of them are careless, and the linens, pots, and pans wander off to the beach and to luaus—or are damaged, broken, or taken. If the losses aren't stopped, you'll have to do something to cover the replacement costs. The board is now considering the problem. This message is the first step in the solution (along with a more careful check on the disappearance or undue damaging of furnishings in each apartment). Depending on the results of this step, the board may consider raising rents or requiring a damage/loss deposit.

**9–6.** Even though you are of college age, you are wearing braces and you owe $900 to an orthodontist, Dr. Sarah Arnold, in your hometown. When you had your last checkup, you told the bookkeeper that you would send $100 each month. But after sending one payment, you have financial problems because of your family. Your mother has cancer and has had to quit her job and hire an attendant. Your father lost his job because of the recession. So you now have to send $50 a month toward the cost of the attendant. Write Dr. Arnold from your school address explaining the circumstances and asking her to accept monthly payments of $50.

**9–7.** As a member of the Preservation Society in your city, write a letter persuading the owner of a 14-room Victorian home near downtown not to tear down the home. The Preservation Society does not have the money to buy it; but it could be used for gift shop, bookstore, lawyer's office. Tell the reader about other homes in your community that have been saved from destruction.

**9–8.** As chief of police in Y City, write a persuasive memo to all your local law enforcement officers urging them to attend one of two series of stress awareness seminars starting next Monday (8–9 A.M.) and Tuesday (1–2 P.M.) at Taylor Secure Medical Facility, Hardaway Road, Y City. The King Hubbard Fraternal Order of Police coordinates these stress seminars along with the human resource development at Taylor in conjunction with the human resource development section of the State Department of Mental Health and Mental Retardation.

The first seminar Monday or Tuesday will be aerobic exercising. Aerobic exercising is a good way to release built-up adrenaline that the body produces as a reaction to stress. A buildup of useless adrenaline in the body produces anxiety, and the only natural release is through exercise. One problem today is that the majority of people (even law enforcement officers) get little physical exercise during times when they are experiencing increased amounts of stress.

Write the memo urging your law enforcement officers to attend the seminar either Monday or Tuesday.

**9–9.** After 20 days in Mercy Hospital 60 miles from home following open-heart surgery, you receive a bill from the hospital saying you owe $200 for drugs you don't ever remember even seeing. When you called the hospital, the report you got was that you were knocked out when these drugs were administered. Even though you were in the recovery room for an hour, you can't see how you could have taken $200 worth of drugs in that period. Write a request (and keep a copy) asking the hospital to list in detail all the expenses you had while you were a patient. Your friends have told you that they have had trouble with the hospital just "padding" the drug list so that it could make some money and therefore help pay for so many of the charity cases that it has to serve.

**9–10.** Assume that you work in promotion with Loyal Viking Cruise Lines, 133 East 55th Street, New York, NY 00234, and that your job is to get the names (of potential wealthy customers who enjoy cruises) from 25,000 travel agents in the United States. You have a budget of $240,000, so have had a full-color brochure printed that includes a response form for the travel agent to send the names and addresses of a dozen or so people to you. After you get the names, then you can send your Loyal Viking literature to these people. Today your job is to write a cover letter that goes along with the brochure to the travel agents persuading them to send you the names of these special people.

**9–11.** Assume the role of Father Byron Hughey, Saint Thomas Episcopal Church, 9865 Red Road, Miami, FL 33156. Your church has gone in actively for baseball for children starting at age six. The problem is that you do not have your own practice field and that the fields at all the parks are full with organized city Little League. The playground that you have for your elementary school children is too small. About a block from the church, however, is a large lot owned by Henry and Bell Gallagher, Route 1, Houghton Lake, MI 48679. According to church members, the Gallaghers rarely come to Florida. They bought the lot for speculation. Perhaps they would have the Christian spirit and let the children of Saint Thomas use the lot for organized/supervised baseball starting in February.

**9–12.** As sales manager of World Circle Travel, Inc., 400 Madison Ave., New York, NY 10021, you are to write a memo to the president, Ruth Jarrett, justifying having and promoting a Caribbean cruise just for singles. You recommend the seven-day cruise that leaves Fort Lauderdale January 19 and March 30 and goes to Nassau, St. Thomas, and San Juan.

The singles market is one of the fastest-growing markets in the United States. In the last 12 years there was a 78 percent jump (from 10.9 million to 19.4 million). Fueling the singles boom are a high divorce rate and a trend toward marrying later in life. Almost a third of those living alone have never married. Their ranks rose from 2.8 million to almost 6 million in the last 12 years, in large measure because of an increase in the young-adult population.

To help the millions of divorced, widowed, and never-married people find the companionship they so often crave, a diverse network of enterprises has sprung up—dating agencies, magazines, singles bars, magazine and newspaper ads, and church or temple services—so why not travel for singles?

Entertainment on the cruise could be directed toward the interests and lifestyle of singles. Prices could remain the same as for other cruises.

**9–13.** Because of the problems with unscrupulous mechanics and service people, California has a Bureau of Auto Repair, Sacramento. Just last year state officials received complaints from 35,000 motorists and took some kind of action on 18,000 of them. The bureau issued 5,928 warning letters and 77 notices of fraud and revoked 10 mechanics' licenses.

As a member of the Bureau of Auto Repair, your job is to write a letter to all mechanics in the San Francisco–Sacramento area urging them to take a series of tests of the National Institute for Automotive Service Excellence. Passing the tests brings mention in the American Automobile Association's Approved Auto Repair list and a seal to display at the garage. The tests run the first Thursday and Friday of each month from 8 to 5 and cost $50 a day.

**9–14.** Volunteers for the Rehabilitation Organization will sell pecan halves at $5 a pound, attractively bagged for Christmas giving. Write a form letter to the 60 study and service clubs in your community asking the members to help with this worthwhile cause by shelling, bagging, or selling. Name some of the good things the Rehabilitation Organization does.

**9–15.** Your company, General Selectric, 88 Orchard Road, Princeton, NJ 08540, is having a one-day seminar in Cleveland, Ohio. As director of sales and public relations, you are to invite 46,000 contractors to the seminar to tell them about a new product called Fast Tracker, an energy-efficient lighting system. Fast Tracker gives more light for less watts; thus contractors install fewer lamps and fixtures, doing the same lighting job for less money. If the contractors cannot attend, then they are invited to send for a Profitable Relight Kit that contains sales tools and information on topics covered at the seminar. General Selectric budgets $82,000 for the campaign. Assume that you have already designed a brochure and reply card but have the covering letter to write. Write the invitation.

**9–16.** A newly formed organization called the Women of the Chamber of Commerce has asked you to write a letter to prominent women in your community asking them to join your organization (annual dues, $20) and to serve on various committees such as "Clean City—Clean Up the Litter," "Fix Up the Old Train Station," "Report on the Cultural Advances," "Report on the Growth and Prosperity," "Development of a Slide Presentation to Promote the City," and "Preservation of the Old Landmarks."

For the social and self-improvement parts of the programs, here are some topics the group can discuss: "How to Invest in a Time of Falling Interest Rates," "Succeeding in a Dual-Career Marriage," "Exercise and Diet to Avoid Stress," "Power Politics for Women," "How to Delegate and Make It Work," "Time Management Strategies," and "Career Dressing and Image Development."

**9–17.** Find something your local newspaper is promoting that you do not agree with and write a letter of protest. For example, one newspaper ran a series about the available prostitution business in the local town. The three-part series with pictures upset the community considerably, and the newspaper received many letters to the editors. Or perhaps you could be upset over the local apathy about all the trash that litters the roads, streets, yards, and parks of your community and you want to get your state to pass a bottle act similar to what Michigan has (meaningful fine for discarding a bottle, piece of paper, or other trash on public or another person's property). Or you could be upset about the local toxic waste dumps or nuclear power plant.

**9–18.** For a variation of the preceding case, you could find something in one of the newsmagazines that you disagree with considerably. Write your complaint and mail it to the newsmagazine. (If your letter gets published, perhaps your teacher will give you extra credit.)

**9–19.** Assume that you bought a food processor with a one-year warranty. It never worked properly; so you took it to the nearest repair service, 50 miles away, where it was worked on at no charge. But the blades still did not turn properly and the machine leaked; so you wrote the manufacturer. There was no reply. You contacted a local consumer-fraud bureau and wrote twice again to the manufacturer. The manufacturer sent you a new food processor, but it too turned out to be defective. Write the manufacturer—Ozment, 174 Hawthorne Road, New York, NY 10022.

**9–20.** Ted Shapiro, P.O. Box 27189, Alsip, IL 60543, bought a set of plastic covers for furniture at a cost of $304.95. When they were delivered, he discovered that several of the seams were not sewn. He called the company; the covers were picked up for repair and later returned to him, but the seams still were not sewn. Disgusted and feeling inadequate about his writing skills, he employs you to write the Better Business Bureau, 606 South Cook Street, Chicago, IL 60622, and send a copy of the letter to the firm (Studio 3 Associates, 78 Chestnut Street, Asheville, NC 28801).

**9–21.** Assume that you are a dealer in stationery supplies named Kapalama, Ala Moana Shopping Center, 1450 Ala Moana, Honolulu, HI 96822. Four days after you order $500 worth of supplies from Niagra Frontier, 9870 West Snyder, Buffalo, NY 14208, you get the bill but not the products. In the next two weeks you get two more notices saying that your payment is overdue and that your account will be turned over to a collection agency if you haven't paid within the next six days. Write a letter telling Niagra Frontier that you have not received your supplies.

**9–22.** Before your shipment arrives (see preceding case), you receive another letter saying that your account has been turned over to a collection agency. The letter says that if you want to maintain your "good name," you must send a check, money order, or cashier's check postmarked no later than September 10. You receive this letter September 11. Naturally, you are unhappy; but you want these supplies, for they were at good prices and there's customer demand for them. You have the feeling that no one at Niagra read your last letter. Even though you feel a little less diplomatic, write another letter explaining the situation and asking that Niagra send you the ordered stationery supplies and "call off the dogs."

**9–23.** While you were in Florida during the three-week Christmas holidays, you left a friend to house watch your $300,000 Edwardian-style home at 3411 34th Place NW, Washington, DC 20016. The friend had no problem with robbers but had a problem keeping warm because there was not enough oil to burn in the furnace. The friend called you in Florida, and you promptly called your oil contractor (Hilton Bahniuk) to see why your home was short on oil. Bahniuk of Bahniuk Oil Company, 1987 Milwaukee Avenue, Washington, DC 20018, said that he had fulfilled his contract and that you had received the amount of oil allotted.

When you reported to your friend what the contractor said, your friend told you that the pipes in the upstairs bathroom had broken, causing water damage, and that the house was cold (no warmer than 40° upstairs). You authorize the friend to buy electric heaters and a cord of wood to burn in the three fireplaces. You had left plenty of wood, but the friend had to use it in order to keep somewhat warm downstairs. You call the oil contractor again and tell him about the broken pipes and the water damage, but the contractor gives no promise of delivering oil.

Write a persuasive letter urging the contractor to deliver the oil so that your friend won't freeze to death and so that the pipes and radiators won't break.

You talked with your lawyer, who advised you that because of the high legal fees suing the oil contractor would not be worthwhile.

**9–24.** Your Cannon Electric Company, 5220 Carlinford Ave., Riverside, CA 92504, has been hiring lower-level personnel through a local employment agency, Technical Employment Service (generally called TES), 3859 Main St., Riverside, CA 92501.

Surely Aurora Ignacio (the TES manager) can see some injustice in your paying the full screening fee for an employee who works only two weeks and quits. So, as personnel director for Cannon, you're going to try again.

When Paul Morton came to you two weeks ago (after TES screening), you assigned him to benchwork during the afternoon shift (2 P.M.–10 P.M.)—close to your most experienced worker for the breaking-in period—and all went well. When your every-two-weeks shifting of shifts came today (Monday) and Paul found himself on the graveyard shift (10 P.M.–6 A.M.), he stormed into your office and insisted on one of the other shifts. As his temper rose and you stuck to your calm no, he came out with another argument—the guy assigned to the adjoining bench on that graveyard shift was Paul's bitterest enemy for stealing (during high school days) the best girl he ever had, for winning the first-string quarterback position on the football team, for this, for that, and for the other. Your still firm but calm no brought a huffy resignation on the spot.

You can't tolerate such emotional, must-be-pampered people in your shop—you have a business to run. Does Ignacio think you should pay the full TES fee for the two weeks of breaking-in work you got out of Paul? Try to persuade him to make an adjustment.

**9–25.** As Peter Pappas Paul, Collection Supervisor, World Adjustment Bureau, Inc., 200 Galway Place, Teaneck, NJ 07666, you are to write a form letter for the word processor (so that it can be personalized) to collect money for magazine subscriptions. Your letter will go along with a computer-printed statement telling the name of the magazine, the account number, how much is owed, for how many issues, and where the checks are to be sent.

Your letter should tell the customer that World is a collection agency that operates nationally. The name of the customer will remain in World's files until payment comes in for the magazine shown on the enclosed statement. Once the payment comes in, the customer's name will come off the list and the magazine delivery will start.

**9–26.** Assume that you are employed in the collection department of Wall's Stores (branches in 20 states but home office at 1640 W. Sepulveda Blvd., Torrance, CA 90501). Write a guide letter that Wall's could send in the collection stage your instructor assigns: reminder, inquiry, appeal, urgency, or ultimatum stage. (A guide letter is like a blank key; before it's any good, you have to cut and file it to fit the particular lock/customer.)

**9–27.** Mings, 19-B Hankow Road 1/F, Kowloon, Hong Kong, opened an account for Chester Reed, 1246 Paseo Encinal, San Antonio, TX 78246, based on references in the United States. Two months ago, when Reed was in Kowloon, he purchased three hand-tailored suits for $600 for himself and a lady's ultrasuede suit with matching handbag and shoes for $300. So far he has paid nothing on his bill. You sent him a friendly reminder a month ago.

**a.** Since two months have gone by, you write him a friendly letter.

**b.** Still you do not hear from Reed and two more weeks have gone by. Write him an inquiry letter.

**c.** Another month goes by, and you still have not heard from Reed. Write him an urgency message.

**d.** Apparently something in your letter moved Reed, for he called you from the Shangrila Hotel in Kowloon and told you that he had had lots of trouble with his wife when she found out about his girlfriend (for whom he had bought the suit with matching handbag and shoes). He had been tied up with business affairs and with the lawyer who was getting the divorce for him. Reed asked for extended time of one month, and you agreed to extend the time.

**e.** Now a month later you still have heard nothing from Reed. This time instead of writing him at his home address, write another urgency letter to his business address (1409 Alamo Plaza, San Antonio, TX 78241).

**f.** Two more weeks go by, and still no cash from Reed. Write him the ultimatum that unless he pays something on his account of $900, you will have to turn his name over to the International Trade Association. Once his name is turned in, it will be hard for him to ever get credit in the Orient. He has credit now, and he should protect that privilege.

**9–28.** As Frank Lawrence (Dividend Department, A. G. Edwards & Sons—stockbrokers, One North Jefferson, St. Louis, MO 63103), you must write Joe Grass (4606 Powers Boulevard, Decatur, IL 62521) to collect $81.75. *Basic facts:* On the fourth of last month Grass sold his 75 shares of Diebold, Inc. stock through the Edwards office in Springfield, Illinois. Though the ex-dividend date was the 10th of last month, through an error Edwards paid the $81.75 dividend to Grass instead of the purchaser of his stock on the 4th.

**9–29.** *From:* Pica Electronics, 4590 N. Peck Rd., El Monte, CA 91732. *To:* M. S. Gabel, Wilson Office Machines, 420 Hoefgren, San Antonio, TX 78203. Write an inquiry-stage collection letter over your signature as credit manager. Wilson sells your MicroWriter word processors. In addition to collecting the amount due ($3,600), this letter must also provide a reasonable amount of goodwill for Pica. Wilson purchased three Model 7 MicroWriters three months ago on terms 2/10, n/60, but has not paid anything. You have sent the usual discount-reminder note, then the usual due-date statement, and 15 days later another statement with a penned friendly reminder on the bottom. Wilson has been a regular discounting or prompt-paying customer of yours for six years, but Gabel has been manager just two.

**9–30.** Although you also wrote an excellent appeal-stage letter when the account was 110 days old (50 overdue), Gabel (previous case) did not reply. Now that the account is 130 days old (70 days overdue), write an urgency-stage letter suggesting that Wilson get a bank loan or that it pay you in partial payments ($1,200 spaced over the next three months). Should you have some specific resale on your company and/or on the MicroWriter Model 7?

**9–31.** Since the urgency letter (previous case) still brought no results from Gabel, write a second urgency-stage letter. Use the approach you think will get Wilson to pay up without losing the customer. The account is now 90 days overdue, but you're not ready for an ultimatum to Wilson Office Machines.

**9–32.** Still Gabel (previous case) ignores your letters; so today, when the account is 110 days overdue, you write the ultimatum. Wilson has 10 days to pay or you will turn its name over to the appropriate credit agencies (but don't let this sound spiteful). Stress the positive (pay and keep all the advantages of credit). Show your reasonableness in the past, your reluctance to take the present action, and the justice and necessity of doing so. Word the ultimatum clearly, precisely, and calmly. When its name is listed with all the credit agencies, Wilson will have a difficult time getting new credit—and its old credit sources may dry up unless it waters them regularly.

**9–33.** Kellogs department store chain wants a new line of tennis rackets to sell under its trademark. It serves a broad market of middle- and lower-class America but would like to capture the upper-class market with a quality tennis racket. Primarily it wants an affordable racket that will sell and produce few complaints.

The request for proposals (RFP) is for the purchase of 100,000 tennis rackets. Kellogs will consider any material, including composites, wood, and metal. The preliminary delivery schedule is as follows:

100 test rackets due three months from proposal

30,000 within first month

40,000 within second month

30,000 within third and last month.

Bidders should provide specifications and warranty. Kellogs will consider all rackets from reputable domestic and foreign manufacturers.

*Proposal instructions:* Bidders will submit a technical/cost proposal that describes the tennis racket they propose. Of particular interest are the following characteristics:

 1. Materials, construction, appearance, and durability.
 2. Performance under usual weather conditions.
 3. Performance under unusual weather conditions.
 4. Purchase cost per item.
 5. Service cost.
 6. Cost of parts.
 7. Suitability to clay, grass, and hard courts and for all tennis balls.
 8. Supportability: parts and service.
 9. Producibility.
10. Management of bidder.
11. Financial stability of bidder.

*Evaluation criteria:* Same as the proposal instructions. All items are of equal importance.

Assume that you are the proposal writer and that you are with a leading tennis racket manufacturer. You'll have to find the company, the facts, and the figures to meet the criteria. Also, the company that makes the tennis rackets must have the characteristics that Kellogs wants.

**9–34.** Using the information in Case 9–33, assume that the product is a fishing rod and reel. Obviously, Item 7 under characteristics will not apply to rods and reels, but you can think of characteristics that will apply.

**9–35.** Using the information in Case 9–33, assume that the product is golf clubs (see preceding cases).

**9–36.** The RFP is for buses X City will buy to serve its transportation system. X City will consider sizes that can carry 25–200 passengers, and they can be new or reconditioned buses. Buses must meet standard Department of Transportation safety and environmental standards. Delivery schedule is as follows:

First bus in 6 months.

Buses with seat capacity of 20,000 due in 12 months.

Buses with seat capacity of 40,000 due in 18 months.

An optional number of buses whose additional seat capacity equals 40,000 due in 24 months.

An optional number of buses whose additional seat capacity equals 40,000 due in 30 months.

X City is particularly interested in the following characteristics:

1. Subsystem/system integration: subsystem descriptions, loading, unloading, safety, comfort, fare collection.
2. Performance characteristics: passenger load, speed, range, braking distance to stop.
3. Cost of buses: purchase, service, parts, operation, fuel.
4. Suitability of buses to freeway traffic and intended application.
5. Supportability considerations: service, parts, equipment.
6. Supply of buses.

*Evaluation criteria* (in descending order of importance):

1. Suitability of the buses to commuters, freeway traffic, and intended application.
2. Projected costs per passenger mile and for typical trips.
3. Performance characteristics.
4. Supportability.
5. Passenger comfort.
6. Other factors, including the bidders' ability to support the operation with service, parts, and personnel.

**9–37.** For more cases on persuasive requests, see Appendix B I A, B, E; IV A; VI C, D, E; VII A, C; IX E, H; XI I, J; XIII C; XV C; XVI A, C, E; XVIII A, B. For persuasive claims, see IV A, C. For collections, see XVII B; XVIII C, D, E. For proposals, see IX G.

# Cases for Chapter 10

(Selling Personal Services—Résumés and Applications)

## Preliminaries to Preparing Résumé, Applications, and Interviews

**10–1.** After reading Chapter 10 and the Interviews section of Chapter 12, make an appointment with a personnel director or other hiring decision maker of a firm. Interview that person to determine what the firm feels is vital to include in an unsolicited application letter and résumé. Find out the best methods for securing a job there. Then report your findings to the class in a written or oral presentation (as your instructor directs).

**10–2.** Before you write your application letter and résumé, but after reading Chapter 10, write a memo to your instructor answering the following questions:

**a.**  What are your career plans?

**b.**  What training, attributes, or attitudes does one need to obtain a job and succeed in your chosen field?

**c.**  What will you be required to do on the job? (Give a job description.)

**d.**  What is the demand for people in your field this year? What is the outlook for availability of jobs in your field five years from now? Ten years from now?

**e.**  What company or organization would you like to work for? Why?

**f.**  What do you need to know about this company before applying for a job? Where would you get this information?

**g.**  Give the pertinent information about the company you have chosen.

Since you will be using library materials, refer to Chapter 14 for ways to tell how you got your information.

**10–3.** Write out 10 questions that you feel you should (or could) ask a corporation's campus recruiter who might interview you.

## Prospecting Application

**10–4.** Investigate summer job opportunities in your field. Consider internships, part-time work, work that will give you at least related experience if you cannot find something exactly in your field. Write a résumé and cover letter to the person who will choose people for the job you select.

**10–5.** Assume that you are in your last term of school and near graduation. You want to find work that you like, for which you have been preparing, and in which you could support yourself now and support (or help support) a family later as you win promotions.

Newspapers, trade magazines, and placement bureaus list no job of your choice. So you decide to do as any good seller does: analyze the product (yourself); then appraise the market (companies that could use a person who can do what you are prepared to do); then advertise (send the companies an application letter and résumé). Such a procedure sometimes creates a job where none existed before; sometimes it establishes a basis for negotiations for the "big job" two, three, or five years after graduation. And very frequently it puts you on the list for the good job that is not filled through advertising or from within the company.

To analyze the high points of your preparation, you will need to consider the courses you have had and make plausible assumptions about the courses you will have completed on graduation. (You will have to make a temporary decision about the kind of work you want to do.)

Distinguish between those courses that actually qualify you to do the type of work you are seeking and those that give you background education. If you've had experience directly related to the job you want as a career, that's fine; but any work you've done means qualifications. With these training and work sections mapped out, complete a tentative résumé with appropriate references.

Then study the market, as suggested under the section Analyzing Companies in Chapter 10. Select one company and plan a letter-résumé combination addressed to that company. Adapt it as specifically as possible to the one company. You may or may not be able to find out the name of the specific individual to address it to. If not, address it to the personnel department or to the head of the particular department in which you are interested.

Be sure to choose *a job utilizing your education.* It should be a job geared to what you could reasonably assume will be your level of performance at graduation. Few just-out-of-college folks can expect to be sales managers, chief buyers, senior accountants, copy chiefs, and the like; you'll have to begin at a subordinate level and work up; you'll want to *show in your letter that you realize this fact.* On the other hand, don't waste your time and your instructor's by applying for something that you could readily do if you had never gone to college.

You will sometimes hear advice to confine your presentation to a one-page letter and a one-page résumé; but don't be afraid to go to two pages for either, especially if you have quite a bit of job experience. As in sales letters, some highly successful ones run to two and sometimes even three pages. What is important is that you make your presentation fully, and in the way that is most favorable for you. Take as much space as necessary to present the facts about yourself in the best light.

Do remember, however, that overselling may detract from your good qualities.

**10–6.** Your faculty adviser mentions the forthcoming campus visit of the personnel director of a large local company that will be hiring five people from your field this year. Write an invited letter (send along with résumé) selling your qualifications and asking to be placed on the on-campus interview schedule.

**10–7.** You are a reentry student, aged 30, who has children and a long job history. Write a functional résumé that emphasizes skills and accomplishments over dates. Now write a prospecting letter selling your maturity and breadth of experience to a major corporation that tends to hire fast-track 22-year-olds.

**10–8.** You've decided that you want to earn some money, see some new places, and have some fun this coming summer. So you're going to address an application for summer employment to a summer camp or an inn at a resort (possibly one of the national parks). You'll have to indicate a willingness to do housekeeping duties (including kitchen and dining room work), although if you have enough maturity and the right kind of experience you may be able to get some kind of clerical or even more specialized assignment. Since college students chosen for such jobs are really hosts and hostesses to the guests, stress poise, dignity, and cheerfulness, as well as any talents for entertaining or instructing (maybe in your hobby).

**10–9.** You want to be a counselor at a summer camp for children of any age group at least eight years younger than you. Choose a camp with which you are familiar, or find out about one. Address the letter and résumé to the camp director (by name if you can get it). Note here the importance of understanding and getting along with youngsters, the ability to direct activities, and the emphasis on leadership, athletic, and teaching abilities. Apply to a camp that is not in your home town or your college town; it should be a residence camp, not a day camp.

## Invited Application

**10–10.** Find a want ad in *The Wall Street Journal,* the Sunday newspaper, or a trade magazine in your field that describes a job you could fill upon graduation. (Make sure the ad calls for letter, not telephone, answers.) Copy or clip the ad, and attach it to your letter when you turn it in.

**10–11.** You see an ad in the placement center newsletter for the perfect job for you. Write a letter to the college recruiter selling your qualifications and asking for an interview. Assume that your résumé accompanies the letter.

**10–12.** You have learned of a $1,000 scholarship that is available for somebody with your major who *(a)* has at least a B average, *(b)* can attend a week-long, expense-paid convention in Atlanta during the summer, and *(c)* will write a letter of application. Assume *a, b,* and *c,* and address your letter to the National (your major) Association, 570 Glaspie, Oxford, MI 48051.

The association has several reasons for and restrictions on giving you $1,000 plus another $500–600 in trip expenses:

**a.** It wants to encourage good people to get into the line of work (and, it hopes, the association).

**b.** It wants to help with the professional education of selectees by giving them additional early insights into the ways the professionals work and talk.

**c.** It will spend only about $10,000 a year on the five scholarships to be granted by making them nationally competitive.

The basis of selection is solely the letter you send in (with or without a résumé—your choice, unless your instructor makes it for you).

# Cases for Chapter 11

(Speaking and Listening)

**11–1.** Choose a technical topic, such as how to invest so you could afford to send your children to college. Plan an oral presentation to a group of laypeople, such as a PTA, television audience, or civic group. Your instructor will specify the amount of time involved.

**11–2.** Research and plan a three- to five-minute talk on one of the following topics (or a similar one). Assume that your audience is well educated, but not necessarily in your field.

- The positive effects of exercise programs for executives.
- Why the company should adopt an electronic mail system.
- How to motivate employees by praise instead of by criticism.
- How to succeed in a job interview.
- Why market research is the job for you.
- What kind of personal computer to buy for college course work.

- What was the worst job you ever had—and why.
- What your dream job is—and what you will do in a typical day.

**11–3.** Research and plan an 8- to 10-minute speech, with visuals, on a technical topic (such as what Big Oil Company should do about polluting the ocean near its gasification plant).

**11–4.** After receiving your graded analytical report (or before if time makes it necessary), assume that *(a)* your class is the board of directors that will make a decision on your recommendations, *(b)* you will have 10–15 minutes to make your report to them orally, *(c)* you will use at least one visual aid, and *(d)* the board will be judging you as an employee as well as on your report.

**11–5.** Read a current article on some aspect of business communication and write (as your instructor directs) a review or condensation of the article. In two or three minutes, tell your class about the review or condensed version of the article, using your jottings as speech notes, not a script.

**11–6.** Review the résumé checklist in Chapter 10 and prepare a well-organized written list of incomplete-sentence jottings about yourself for a stranger who is to introduce you as an expert on a topic you are to speak about (this may be you in the future, but be realistic). At random, and with only a few minutes for preparation, have a classmate introduce you using your notes.

**11–7.** As an alternative, assume that the person who was to introduce you in the preceding case could not come. Using your notes, introduce yourself.

**11–8.** Individually or in groups, as your instructor directs, visit a bank, a savings and loan association, and a credit union. Give an oral report on which is the best source of a loan of several hundred dollars to tide you over for a while.

**11–9.** Individually or in groups, as directed, visit one each of a jewelry, sporting goods, clothing, hardware, and drugstore. Report on the differences and reasons for one of the following:

**a.** Main points in their credit policies.
**b.** Their furnishings and fixtures.
**c.** Other areas as your instructor specifies.

**11–10.** When you are a half to three quarters finished with your analytical report, give an oral progress report to your classmates. Is your project on schedule? Why or why not? What will you do next? What obstacles have you encountered, and how have you handled them? Will you finish on time?

**11–11.** You are to assume that you are a salesperson at a sales meeting and you are to give a persuasive oral presentation to fellow corporation members (class members). You may use the product you wrote your sales letter about or you may select another product.

**11–12.** You are to secure a corporate annual report from one company and make an oral report to a committee (the class). You and your instructor can decide how long the presentation will be and what it will be about.

**11–13.** Keep a log of your communication activities for one day. Then compare the amount of time you spend in reading, writing, speaking, and listening.

**11–14.** Have a student partner help you read passages aloud to each other. After the student listens to the material, the reader asks several questions based on the passage.

**11–15.** Attend a lecture and listen for (and list) key words and key ideas. Were there any distractions that kept you from being a good listener?

## Cases for Chapter 12

(Special Forms of Oral Communication)

**12–1a.** With one student playing the role of interviewer and the other playing that of applicant, conduct an employment interview before the class. For realism, this should be for the job the applicant hopes to get upon graduation.

    **b.** Instead of an employment interview, conduct an information interview.

**12–2.** Dictate a solution for a memo or letter-writing case that your instructor selects.

**12–3.** In a conference made up of a suitable number of students, consider any problem of national, local, or school scope, coming up with realistic solutions if possible. The student chosen as leader should be responsible for as much organizing of the conference as is appropriate. The participants may be as cooperative or obstructive as the instructor directs.

**12–4.** You are a marketing research analyst who is asked to do a telephone interview on some everyday product such as soap, coffee, tea, soft drinks, toothpaste, or paper towels. Work up a guide for interviewers to follow to find out such things as preferred brand, uses, package size purchased, monthly amount purchased, who purchases, and whether coupons are used. Be sure the entire interview takes no more than three minutes, including the introductory statements. Assume that the interviewers have limited experience in conducting telephone interviews. Calls will be made by automatic dialing machine.

**12–5.** Divide your class into groups to simulate the telephone interview in the preceding case. Those not engaged in interviewing can evaluate their classmates' performances.

**12–6.** If possible, use the free inter- or intrastate telephone lines to set up a session on teleconferencing with a school away from yours.

## Cases for Chapter 13

(Reports—Importance, Definition, Classification, and Short Preparations)

**13–1.** As office manager of your firm, write a memo to all employees in the international sales division telling them about how to cut their overseas phone costs when they stay in foreign hotels. (You would like to hear about their experiences for a brochure you are planning.) Many hotels now belong to Teleplan, a service that guarantees users phone costs with a reasonable surcharge. Before this service began, hotels added traditional and very large surcharges to foreign calls to cover their costs and then some. (Some hotels did not join the plan and still add these charges; in these cases calls can have as much as a 250 percent surcharge, though 100 percent is more common.)

Since the employees have to call orders and questions home frequently when they are abroad, encourage them to use Teleplan hotels. Or they could telex if time permits; or use lobby phones or post office, railway station, or airport phones and call collect, thus avoiding the larger surcharges. Something has to be done. Phone charges, up 37 percent since last year, have cut deeply into the profits from successful sales abroad of your new line of printers.

Teleplan charges at least are published, limited, and uniform within hotel groups; so your staff can plan costs ahead of time.

If Teleplan is not available, the best plan is for employees to call collect using a credit card or to call the office *briefly* and leave a message to be called back. (U.S.-to-Europe rates are less than Europe-to-U.S. rates, and billing Europe-to-U.S. calls goes by actual length only.)

Employees need to be aggressive and *ask* about hotel phone rates, whether charge cards are acceptable, whether a government phone center is available, and so on.

**13–2.** Presto Corporation has a "dedicated blood reserve" at the local Blood Bank (524 South Seigel Street). Any Presto employee who needs blood in any amount for himself or herself or for members of his or her immediate family can draw on this reserve for free blood when hospitalized. (Hospital/doctor charges for administering the blood go into the hospital bill and come under the group hospital/surgical insurance plans.)

In establishing the reserve, Presto management pledged that our employees would "maintain" it by making voluntary donations throughout the year. Last year brought 184 donations (one pint per donation) but the use of 320 units. Therefore, we have a "deficit" of 136 units in our reserve. The Blood Bank is requesting that we make a serious effort to replace that many units within the next two months.

One reason for many employees' reluctance to donate blood is probably the adverse publicity about AIDS (Acquired Immune Deficiency Syndrome). When this often-fatal blood disorder was first diagnosed, some of its victims were found to have received blood (through blood banks) that carried the virus thought to cause AIDS. This danger no longer exists, as a new screening technique detects any blood sample with AIDS and would-be donors who carry the virus are rejected and advised to see their own physicians immediately. There is no danger of acquiring the disease by *making* a donation. Donors are also tested at the Blood Bank for high or low blood pressure, anemia, hypoglycemia, or other health factors that might make it dangerous for them to donate.

The Blood Bank is open to receive donations from 9 A.M. to 9 P.M. daily, including weekends. A donation takes about 25–30 minutes. Only persons over 65 or under 18 and persons taking certain prescription drugs are ineligible to donate.

Though donations of all types of blood are welcome, at this time the service particularly needs donors whose blood types are A-negative. The *Presto Summary,* monthly company newsletter, publishes the names of employees who make donations.

Assignments:

**a.**   As public relations director of Presto, write a suitable memo to all employees urging them to donate.

**b.** Write a memo to Richard Dawson, general manager of Presto, suggesting any additional measures you believe would help promote blood donations. Use your imagination freely; but remember, there is no direct profit to the company from this; so keep costs minimal.

**c.** Write a letter to Dr. Saul Rosen, Blood Bank director, asking about the possibility of having the mobile Blood Bank unit spend an afternoon at your plant. Suggest dates, possible number of donors you could recruit. Ask for any promotional aids the Blood Bank might furnish. Should you apologize for the "deficit"? Should you discuss prescheduling donors to minimize time lost from work?

**13–3.** You have begun hiring telemarketing people to sell your product (pick a likely one). To avoid training these new hires one at a time, write a memo giving them tips on how to be most successful. Use headings and as personable a style as possible (don't preach at them).

Monday and Tuesday calls get the best results. Before 5 P.M. is better than between 5 P.M. and 9 P.M. Rural areas pull better than cities. December and January proved to be the best months for phone sales (because of the weather?).

Workers should speak slowly, pause to give the customer time to think, decrease volume for emphasis, use a low pitch (sounds less anxious), and overall try to sound pleasant and interested in the other person.

**13–4.** Your boss, Jim Harrelson, has asked you to assemble some information on computer-based training. (He thinks that some of the repetitious training his trucking company has to do might be done other than in class.) You find some current articles and write a report.

Three articles that might get you started are: Nicholas and Elaine Caruso, "Trainer," *Data Processing Digest,* 30:30, February 1985; Jack Levine, "Improve Corporate Management Skills through Computerized Training," *Data Management,* 22:32–33, July 1985; and Lin Olsen and Robert D. Fazio, "The Shoemaker's Children: How Digital Uses Interactive Video to Train Computer Technicians," *Training and Development Journal,* 27:30–32, December 1985.

**13–5.** Because you've had some information leaks of confidential new product information, you consider new office security measures as follows:

- Pay for the installation of executives' home alarm systems. ($500–1,500 per home)
- Tie these home alarms into plant security for better control than a residential system can give. Use a leased telephone line, perhaps, or a radio link. ($15 per month)
- Make sure all the phone lines are secure—including the basement terminal box, even though few employees ever go into the basement. ($45 per terminal)

- Buy paper that makes an all-black copy when someone tries to make copies on an office copier. The paper can be photographed using infrared film, but you figure few people would go to this much trouble. ($0.05–.10 per sheet, depending on security level desired)

Sum up the options for your boss.

**13–6.** As an accounting intern advising a growing landscaping business, write a memo telling the owner how to streamline procedures from the notebook and box of receipts that now make up the record-keeping. As a first step, tell him or her to order multiple-copy sales slips so that the work flow for the crews and records for the part-time bookkeeper can be better organized.

Decide which kind to order, and explain the advantages and costs.

- *Carbon sales slips* (write original only or up to two more copies by inserting carbons)

| 8½ × 8½ | or | 4 × 6¼ |
|---|---|---|
| 8,000 for $155.00 | | 8,000 for $105.00 |
| 4,000 for $ 96.50 | | 4,000 for $ 59.95 |
| 2,000 for $ 60.95 | | 2,000 for $ 35.95 |
| 1,000 for $ 42.95 | | 1,000 for $ 25.50 |

- Prices include your heading printed on each, but no numbering.

- *Carbon-backed sales slips* (carbon-backed paper, two or more colors of printing, no carbons to lose)

| 4¼ × 7 | Two-Part | Three-Part |
|---|---|---|
| 4,000 | $108.00 | $134.00 |
| 2,000 | 61.50 | 76.95 |
| 1,000 | 37.50 | 46.50 |
| 500 | 26.50 | 30.50 |

- Prices include your heading and consecutive numbering.

- *Customized sales slips* (carbonless copies, printed with list of major items you sell, hours, heading, guarantee—whatever you choose)

| | 5½ × 8½ | | 3⅜ × 5⅛ | |
|---|---|---|---|---|
| | Two-Part | Three-Part | Two-Part | Three-Part |
| 8,000 | $253.00 | $365.00 | $109.00 | $168.00 |
| 4,000 | 146.00 | 198.00 | 71.50 | 103.00 |
| 2,000 | 84.95 | 111.00 | 42.50 | 57.95 |
| 1,000 | 48.95 | 64.95 | 26.50 | 35.95 |
| 500 | 31.95 | 38.95 | — | — |
| 250 | 21.95 | 26.50 | — | — |

**13–7.** Building/remodeling your own file space could cost as much as $19,750 annually. On the other hand, you can rent an equivalent space in a commercial record center for $4,025. Assuming that your 500 inactive trans-files would fit in such a space, which should you choose? Can you negotiate a deal for long-term savings? Are the files kept in locked vaults? How and when can you get access?

Write a memorandum to your supervisor recommending a course of action.

**13–8.** Relocation costs have increased enormously lately—it now costs between $35,000 and $40,000 to move an executive. What costs are included in this figure? How can you bring your costs down? Average according to a national moving company:

| | |
|---|---|
| Van line service | $ 4,333 |
| Relocation firms, motels, family transportation | 10,895 |
| Total | $15,228 |

Intangible costs can also be associated with moving stress related to leaving family behind, selling and buying houses, and worrying about a spouse finding a job.

Write a memo advising managers how to plan for the coming relocation.

**13–9.** Find out the latest rules on keeping a travel diary to monitor business use of a company car. Explain these rules (with examples, where needed) to a client of your accounting firm.

**13–10.** Analyze whether to buy accounting software as part of a new computer system and install it yourself or to have your accounting firm or its computer consultants install it. Decide what the advantages/disadvantages of each plan would be, and determine the comparative costs. Write the report to your superior.

**13–11.** Two years ago the Equal Employment Opportunity Commission spanked you (as personnel director) and the CEO of your manufacturing firm (Four-N Company) as WASPs and sexists for your imbalance in hiring (as shown in the Then columns in the table below). Though EEOC did not fine you then, it made clear that it would if you couldn't show reasonable improvement in five years. Meanwhile you must submit biennial reports showing progress or in all levels of employment a reasonable explanation for its absence.

Since the first two-year report is due the first of next month, write the memo report to R. H. Hamilton (your CEO), using the figures in the Now columns.

| Job Category | Male | | Female | | Black | |
|---|---|---|---|---|---|---|
| | Then | Now | Then | Now | Then | Now |
| Officials and managers | 99.0% | 97.2% | 1.0% | 2.8% | 0.3% | 0.9% |
| Professionals | 96.9 | 92.1 | 3.1 | 7.9 | 0.9 | 2.0 |
| Technicians | 88.1 | 85.7 | 11.9 | 14.3 | 2.4 | 4.1 |
| Sales workers | 99.7 | 96.0 | 0.3 | 4.0 | 2.2 | 3.5 |
| Office and clerical | 28.0 | 19.3 | 72.0 | 80.7 | 2.6 | 4.1 |
| Craftsmen | 98.6 | 97.2 | 1.4 | 2.8 | 3.2 | 3.6 |
| Operatives | 60.5 | 58.7 | 39.5 | 41.3 | 6.2 | 6.9 |
| Laborers | 78.1 | 70.3 | 21.9 | 29.7 | 10.9 | 12.0 |
| Service workers | 77.2 | 84.6 | 22.8 | 15.4 | 5.4 | 6.4 |
| All categories | 75.4 | 72.7 | 24.6 | 27.3 | 3.6 | 4.5 |

**13–12.** Car pools just haven't caught on even though getting in and out of the parking lot at your plant is a nightmare at shift-change time.

When you, a traffic researcher at the Blair Company, surveyed a quick sample of workers to find out why more of them didn't take the city or county buses, they noted that buses took longer (for some of them up to three times as long), were less convenient, and didn't run late enough for the night shift people.

A recent Chamber of Commerce study in your town showed that bus ridership might increase if the bus companies extended evening and weekend service and express routes and if they provided park-and-ride lots for working people.

National surveys find that 54 percent of the people who drive wouldn't ride a bus if you paid them, 26 percent would like to ride a bus to work, and 20 percent would ride a bus on certain days when unusual circumstances occurred. Of the people who normally ride a bus, 18 percent say that they have no other means of transportation. The median annual household income for a bus rider is $15,000, compared with $25,000 for nonriders. People who choose to ride the bus (to save money, avoid traffic, take advantage of a convenient route) have a median annual income of $23,000.

Write a memo report to management proposing a solution to your parking problem.

**13–13.** As a new employee in the advertising department, International Airlines, 2300 North Street, N.W., Washington, DC 20037, write a memo with graphics to George Garn, head of advertising. International has been running 30-second TV ads at prime time (between 5:30 and 6:30 P.M.) during the popular news presentations on CBS, ABC, and NBC. The ads up to now have featured mainly businessmen rushing to catch a plane; but already 18 percent of business passengers are women. Your concern is that more women should be featured in the ads in view of their increasing role in employment and in airplane travel.

Women are increasing in the work force at a rate of almost 2 million every year. More than half of the country's 84 million women, including a majority of mothers with school-age children, now work or seek jobs. The management-consulting firm of Sandler & Heidrick, Inc. says that the number of women corporate officers in the 1,300 largest companies rose to 416 last year—a one-year increase of 28 percent. According to the U.S. Department of Labor, 6 percent of the nation's working women are managers and administrators, 1 percent farm workers, 35 percent clerical workers, 7 percent sales workers, 6 percent schoolteachers, 21 percent service workers, 15 percent blue-collar workers, and 10 percent other professionals. Among the approximately 38 million women in non-farm jobs, 87.3 percent are white and 12.7 percent black. Marital status shows 19.0 percent single, 56.4 percent married, and 24.6 percent divorced, separated, or widowed. In addition, millions of other women work at home or in volunteer tasks each year. Mothers working at or seeking jobs represent 53 percent; 47 percent are not in the labor force.

Women also are going to professional schools in record numbers. The Labor Department says that they will comprise 18 percent of all professionals in seven years. About 10,000 are studying engineering—10 times as many as nine years ago. Total earnings of working women seven years ago were $127.4 billion; today they are $254.3 billion (up 100 percent). Working women earning $25,000 or more seven years ago numbered 25,000 and today 217,000 (up 768 percent). Life insurance coverage in force for women ran $200 billion seven years ago and today $380 billion (up 90 percent). Individual women holding American Express cards six years ago numbered 0.7 million; today there are 1.9 million (up 171 percent).

**13–14.** You are a young paralegal assistant working for a young, beginning lawyer. Up to now you have been going around the corner to Kinko's Duplicating Service to make copies at 5 cents a sheet (legal or regular size).

Today a letter from Copox, 1350 Jefferson Road, Rochester, NY 14623, offers its reconditioned Copox 490 for $1,195, or $41.31 a month with down payment of $119.50. If you and the lawyer take Copox up on its 15-day-trial offer, you get (1) free copier stand (31″ high × 18″ wide × 30″ wide with large roomy shelves to store paper, dry imager, developer, and office supplies) that regularly sells for $165; (2) starter supply kit, worth $28; (3) free delivery and installation, worth $64.

The brochure says:

These machines have merely been outgrown by their previous users. We select only the finest copiers from this supply. Copiers have received the meticulous care of skilled Copox technicians throughout their history. We take these "cream of the crop" copiers, carefully clean and disassemble them, and then rebuild them "from the ground up." Defective and worn-out parts are replaced, working surfaces lubricated and adjusted. Once this is done, we run a complete operational check.

The brochure adds that the machine makes 11 copies per minute and that each copy costs less than 1.5 cents for paper and supplies.

Should the lawyer invest in this Copox? The lawyer wants you to write a memo report with recommendations. Last month you finalized 10 wills and in the course of doing so made copies of 50 pages. As a guesstimate, you assume that you use about 20,000 sheets of copy paper every two months. The lawyer pays you $60 a day.

**13–15.** You are the controller at Eagle Transfer in Savannah, Georgia. Your problem: you have 80 trucks and you need to get money to your drivers so that they can get cash discounts on fuel. (If you give the drivers credit cards, they will lose the discounts. On the other hand, if you give each driver cash, it might be stolen. You don't want your drivers constantly under threat of robbery, especially since they drive at night a lot.)

Your choices:

Western Union money orders, available at all Western Union offices (open 24 hours a day); or

Money transfer companies (at least three rival companies nationwide), which give drivers money at truck stops on their routes. These companies serve 4,500–6,000 truck stops and can also provide you with statements of drivers' fuel expenses.

Both types of service have the same transfer fee.

Make the choice and write a memo to all drivers describing how they will pay for fuel beginning the first of next month. They may miss getting the cash early. The money transfer company closest to you is Day and Night Bank Transfer (headquarters in Atlanta). It serves 5,200 truck stops 24 hours a day and provides an itemized statement by driver name once every two weeks.

**13–16.** To save office and mailing expenses, you decide to try a new kind of billing envelope, to be delivered and hung on customers' doorknobs. (A courier can deliver many in a short time in a concentrated, highly populated area.)

The preaddressed envelope will have lines for the customers' return addresses and a "place stamp here" mark. Your invoice is inserted. The customer removes the hanging stub; fills in the invoice number and account name or number; encloses the stub, payment, and invoice in the envelope; and mails the envelope back to you.

Since you mail out 500 bills a month, hand delivery would save $110 a month in postage and costs only about $50 if you hire students to work a few hours at the end of each month.

As the person in charge of billing and collecting, write your superior a justification report.

**13–17.** Assume that you are Herbert Zoellner, a member of the AFL–CIO executive council, the key policymaking group for the federation. To this group you are to write a justification report urging that the AFL–CIO enlist more women into the organization and give them a fair chance at executive positions.

One out of every three union members is a woman, and women account for half of the total increase in union membership in the past 20 years. More than 7 million women belong to unions—up from 4 million 10 years ago.

Ten years after its founding, the Coalition of Labor Union Women (which started with 3,000 union women) has grown from 10 chapters to 75 chapters and has 18,000 dues-paying members.

Women have risen to the position of secretary-treasurer in four major state labor bodies, served as president or secretary-treasurer of more than 100 regional union councils, and held presidencies of hundreds of local unions.

About 350,000 women—among them truck drivers, clerical personnel, health-care workers, and airline flight attendants—belong to the Teamsters Union of 1.9 million members. The Teamsters has a woman president (a graduate of Cornell University's School of Industrial and Labor Relations).

The percentage of women in the labor force (of all those age 16 or older) was 37.7 percent, 1960; 39.3 percent, 1965; 43.3 percent, 1970; 46.3 percent, 1975; 51.5 percent, 1980; 53.4 percent, 1984. Although women now make up more than 30 percent of union members, only 16 percent of all the women in the work force are unionized. In contrast, 28.4 percent of all workingmen are members of unions.

Pay equity is the number one issue that women face today. At one eastern university, for example, union officials say that it is unfair for the university to pay its mostly female administrative assistants an average of $13,500 a year, while the school's truckdrivers, who are mostly male, are paid more than $18,000.

Many unions are discovering that women are ripe for membership. In the last five years the Textile and Clothing Union has won representation elections covering 2,000 workers in Colorado—75 percent of them women.

**13–18.** Move the clock up a few years and pretend that you are working as Assistant Manager, Human Resources (Personnel), Markhall Corporation, Kansas City, Missouri. Although the company has a retirement plan, you think it might be wise to offer the employees a stock ownership plan (ESOP). Employee stock ownership plans are incentives to attract and reward valued employees. Employers can reap substantial savings and tax benefits, also. ESOP plans help employees share in the company's growth.

You are to study three stock incentive plans and write a justification report to Gordon Rosen, the personnel manager, proposing that Markhall adopt one of them. By writing a thorough and interesting report, you may help yourself climb the executive ladder in Markhall.

**13–19.** Sipsi-Cola Bottling Company of Erie, Pennsylvania, needs to purchase 20 new delivery trucks and five service vans. Assume that you are an official at this company and have studied the idea of buying trucks and vans that are equipped to burn natural gas.

East Ohio Gas Company of Cleveland operates the largest compressed-gas fleet in the United States. The utility's 900 vans, trucks, and sedans, all powered by natural gas, use $500,000 less in fuel a year than they would if they were operated on gasoline or diesel fuel, the company estimates.

One of your competitors converted its 14 trucks to burn natural gas at a cost of $1,500 per truck. The company figured, however, that the fuel bill for its fleet of converted trucks and six vans amounted to a saving of $11,000 a year.

There are only three gas-fueling stations in the United States (20 in Canada and 240 in Italy), but that will not be a problem since one of these stations is right in Erie. Also, your trucks and vans serve just the metropolitan area; so there's no danger of running out of natural gas.

Reserves of natural gas are estimated to last more than 100 years. The development of a lightweight aluminum cylinder for storing the compressed gas helps also.

Besides financial savings, compressed-gas vehicles are safer than gasoline-fueled cars, trucks, vans, or buses because compressed gas doesn't explode upon heavy impact.

According to Bill Langer, transportation director for the Creek School District in northeastern Pennsylvania, the 30 compressed-gas buses start smoother and there's no problem when starting in winter.

Sipsi-Cola can purchase the 20 trucks and five vans at the same cost whether they are equipped to use compressed gas or gasoline.

With these facts you are to write the memo justifying the purchase of compressed-gas vehicles to Bryan Walsh, the controller of Sipsi-Cola.

**13–20.** Justify the purchase of a certain brand of word processor for an office of 20 workstations. Go to the library and get cost figures from *Datapro Surveys, Computerworld, Datamation,* and *Modern Office Technology,* among other sources, so that your evidence will be the most current possible. Assume that your office already has a VAX central computer system. Your clerical staff and managers are eager to have workstations. Should the workstations be alike? Should you get dedicated word processors, PCs, or the new workstations that include communications for built-in electronic mail? What about security for information access? Can you do it for $2,000 a workstation?

**13–21.** Assume that you are to evaluate wristwatches to find the best one to give men and women employees on the 25th anniversary of their working with your long-established, nationally known corporation, or on their retirement if that is earlier.

You are to write your report to your boss (make up the name and title and the corporation name). No exact price was set, but you have a range of from $100 to $300 (though the boss added that it could be more). No matter whether it costs $20 or over $2,000, every watch has the same basic features: (1) *time base* (oscillating balance wheel and hairspring, vibrating tuning fork, quartz crystal, or electronic); (2) *counting and converting system* that is controlled by mechanical gear train or integrated electronic circuits; (3) *source of power*—mainspring or battery; (4) *face* with analog (hands) or digital display. You can buy four kinds: mechanical, electrical, digital, and quartz analog. How many jewels? Federal Trade Commission says a watch with less than 7 jewels should not be advertised or sold as "jeweled" but that 17 jewels are sufficient for mechanical watches. Good quartz analog watches have seven–nine jewels. Pin lever watches may run for a year or more; but when they stop, it's not economical to repair them. Consider the composition of the case and band—metal (what kind?) or plastic—for durability and style. Better watches should be water resistant and/or shock resistant. Should availability of service be a consideration? Research the available watches and fully report on your findings, recommending one or more watches to your boss.

**13–22.** You are assistant to the president of C & F Electronics, P.O. Box 19806, St. Paul, MN 55190. Your company has six vice presidents, one at the home office in St. Paul, the other five stationed at regional branch offices in Houston, San Francisco, New York, Miami, and Seattle. The president has some new ideas about marketing a new product and wants a conference.

The president asks you to do some research and write a memo report on whether it would be less expensive to set up a videoconference to last three hours or whether it would be better to fly the five vice presidents to St. Paul for a day and put them up for one night at a hotel. The conference, whatever its form, is scheduled for 9 A.M. next Tuesday. Besides getting the costs of airfares, hotel rooms, meals, and the like, get the costs for a videoconference. What other costs and benefits might figure on either side of the question?

**13–23.** Today just about anybody can be sued in the United States; and with lawyers charging $75 to $150 or more an hour, defense costs may run to thousands of dollars. To minimize the risk, many people are buying personal liability insurance with limits of $1 million or more. Such umbrella insurance is usually (but not necessarily) an adjunct to the liability protection in motor-vehicle and residential insurance. This insurance rises above basic protection and shields the insurer against damages for, among other things, libel, slander, character defamation, shock, false arrest, wrongful entry or eviction, mental anguish, sickness or disease, and malicious prosecution.

Most contracts exclude occupational liability. For example, a politician who slanders another politician could not get an umbrella policy. Some insurance companies refuse insurance to public officials, broadcasters, professional entertainers and athletes, newspaper reporters, editors, and publishers. Most property and casualty companies, including big-name car and home insurers, sell umbrella insurance at premiums ranging from $70 a year for $1 million in protection to $250 for $8 million. To buy an umbrella policy, a customer must have homeowners or tenant liability insurance in amounts that the policy prescribes and must have automobile insurance (if the customer owns a car).

A wealthy uncle and aunt of yours feel that their chances of being sued are great because they have two teenagers (16 and 18) who drive; they own a snowmobile, boat, and swimming pool. Because you are in the School of Business, they think you can do the research and tell them (1) whether you agree that they need the insurance and (2) what company would be best. You are to investigate and compare three companies (total cost, discounts, legal defense costs, people covered, exclusions, and where protected—the United States, Canada, the world). Assume that the aunt and uncle both drive and that they have car and house insurance. Write them a letter report from your school address giving them the information they want.

**13–24.** After you have read about umbrella insurance in Case 13–23, try your hand at writing a memo report. Assume that you are an employee in the insurance and benefit department of a large corporation. Your boss asks you to find out about umbrella insurance for its key people (upper-status employees). Group as well as individual liability protection is available. The board of directors of your corporation likes the idea and has approved investigation. Again you are to research three companies and, based on your study, to recommend which you think is best.

**13–25.** T. M. Maguire, advertising director for Century Car Seats, 5610 North Western Avenue, Chicago, IL 60650, wants to push sales through newspaper supplement advertising in Y City and X County, where there have been many accidents recently. Before Maguire contracts for the advertising, however, he wants to find out if the people in this area are aware of the law that requires children under three years of age to be restrained in a car seat while riding in a car. Recently he made a trip to Y City and X County and observed many cars with toddlers as riders, most of them not restrained in car seats.

Maguire wonders if these toddlers and infants have car seats but just don't use them. Maybe the parents don't know about the law. Maybe they think there should not be such a law. Maybe they use the car seats only when the road is wet or slippery or when they drive in heavy traffic.

To find out the answers to these questions, so that Maguire can slant the advertising in the most effective way, he commissions a reliable agency, Hardy Incorporated, to conduct a telephone survey of people in Y City and X County. Assume that you work for Hardy and that you have the job of writing a letter report based on the following information from four tables of facts. The first survey of Y City involved telephone interviews with a random sample of 551 adult residents, while the second survey was based on telephone interviews with a random sample of 399 X County residents. All the interviews were done between January 31 and February 15 of this year. Statistically, you can be 95 percent confident that the survey results are no greater than 5 percent different from those of the entire adult population of the area.

| | Survey 1 | Survey 2 | | |
|---|---|---|---|---|
| Whole group: | | | | |
| Aware of child-restraint law | 64% | 58% | | |
| Degrees of agreement with law (strong +/mild +/mild −/ strong −) | 32/57/9/2 | 45/42/10/3 | | |

| | Parents | Not Parents | Parents | Not Parents |
|---|---|---|---|---|
| Parents of under-three child: | | | | |
| Aware of law | 83% | 62% | 100% | 54% |
| Not aware | 17 | 38 | 0 | 46 |
| Agree with law (strong +/mild +/mild −/ strong −) | 38/48/12/2 | 32/58/8/2 | 3/51/11/6 | 45/42/10/3 |
| Have car seat | 76 | | 83 | |
| Don't have car seat | 24 | | 17 | |

| Make use of seat (Survey 1/Survey 2) | Always | Usually | Sometimes | Never (including "no seat") |
|---|---|---|---|---|
| For short trips | 51/34% | 15/29% | 11/14% | 24/23% |
| For long trips | 55/62 | 11/9 | 11/3 | 24/26 |
| In heavy traffic | 56/57 | 13/11 | 7/11 | 24/20 |
| For wet/slippery road | 62/53 | 9/12 | 5/15 | 24/21 |

**13–26.** When Dr. and Mrs. Gary Bransway, 904 South Lincoln, Urbana, IL 61890, engaged you, Robert C. Schug (98 Lakeview Drive, Green Lake, WI 54787), as their architect for a summer home in Green Lake (48 Beaver Drive), you promised them five progress reports at these stages: (1) completion of below-ground and foundation work, (2) completion of structural framing, (3) closed-in stage, (4) interior finished, and (5) job completed. After many hours in drawing house plans, you finally got their approval of an attractive home and you also secured Mueller Construction Company as the general contractors.

Assume that you wrote the Bransways a report telling them of the completion of the foundation six weeks ago and a second report telling them of the completion of the basic structure three weeks ago. Today you have to write them the belated closing-in report. (You ran into problems in getting the kind and size of sliding glass doors that open from the great room to the deck. The supplier has had to back-order the oversize doors, but you hope to have them in two weeks.)

Because the Bransways wanted the home to be completed by summer, you are starting on some interior finishing and have some questions about paint selection. Ask them whether they can possibly come to Green Lake in the next week or so to reevaluate their paint selection. The paint they selected for the outside trim will not look good with the outside walls. Also, you have doubts about the selection of wallpaper clashing with the paint for the inside structure. You want them to be satisfied with this expensive second home, and you want to be able to continue writing them favorable progress reports; but you need their help.

**13–27.** Assume that you are Delliah P. Ott, Director of Executive Course Development, Eastinghouse Electric Corporation, 2006 Randolph Avenue, St. Paul, MN 55104. You are to write a progress report to the corporate policy committee on what you are doing to help managers.

You first asked Eastinghouse top managers to develop a list of the essential competencies they needed to perform their roles. You got a list of 125 items, which you grouped into six functional areas: marketing, engineering, manufacturing, finance, personnel, and general management.

Next, you divided these managers into task forces. An experienced and successful senior general manager chaired each task force. Other managers served as advisers and resource people. Each task force had a writer to record and report task force deliberations. The task forces were to determine what and how much a manager needed to know in the specific functional areas.

Three weeks after these task forces met, you invited a guest speaker (Professor Ronald B. Newman, Department of Management, Pennsylvania State University, University Park, PA 16897) to talk about his experience and about his successful books on management.

A week after Professor Newman's talk, you designed a course tailored to developing Eastinghouse managers. This four-week residential course you called "Management for Excellence." At the writing of this progress report, the course has just begun; but the evaluations you received from the first meeting were most rewarding.

**13–28.** Assume that you have a scholarship from the Biltmore Foundation based primarily on industry and seriousness of intent rather than high scholarship. Biltmore does expect satisfactory work and above all diligent effort. As part of your responsibility to the foundation, you must write a report once a year on your progress during the past year. Using the facts of your own record, write in letter form a progress report to Vernice Washington, director of scholarships.

**13–29.** As the person in charge of a general sales meeting for sales representatives of XYZ Company, write a memo that gives a progress report to the vice president about the forthcoming convention.

The convention will be held at the Hilton Head Inn, Hilton Head Island, North Carolina, Tuesday, Wednesday, and Thursday, June 10–12. Hospitality hour on Tuesday 6–7, Courtney Room, third floor, followed by banquet in Regency Room. Conference rooms engaged 9–5 and 7–9, second floor (Royal Blue and Royal Red).

Keynote speaker is Warner Westervelt, well-known author and long-time top salesperson. Other speakers from other companies are: Jane Ray, Ray Cosmetics; Lee Coyle, United Motors; Henry Moore, Public and Gamble. Attached tentative program shows the names of other outstanding business leaders who will lead panel discussions at morning and afternoon sessions.

Breaks for refreshments are scheduled for 10 A.M. and 3 P.M. No evening entertainment is scheduled because of the sessions running until 9 P.M.

Notices about this general sales meeting should appear in house organ. Each sales representative should be told about this command performance by April 1.

You'll attach an estimated and tentative budget.

**13–30.** At this point, you have completed the major part of your course. Review your progress, write down your weaknesses and strengths, and draw a conclusion as to your growth. Submit your discoveries and conclusions about your progress to your instructor.

**13–31.** Assume that you are working on a class project that will require several weeks (say a major report) and that your instructor asks for a progress report to see how you are coming along (in reference to what you should have done by the specified date).

**13–32.** *Problem:* Crab pickers are in short supply in coastal towns because young people shun the tedious, smelly, and not very lucrative work. Most of the hand pickers are women aged 40–70 who use paring knives and fingers to pluck juicy morsels of meat from the tiny, fragile cavities of the blue crab. Pickers have to dissect 100 pounds of whole crabs to get 14 pounds of meat. An average worker can pick just 30–50 pounds of meat a day.

*Product:* A vibrator called Pik Right (the size of a large refrigerator) shakes the meat out of the crab.

*Process:* Cooked crabs travel on a conveyor belt. Saw blades cut through crab shells. Every 12 seconds the Pik Right machine starts its shaking process. Crabs start their journey with a tumble in a grater that snaps off claws and legs. Then they ride one by one, on plastic saddles, through a trimming machine. Inside, rotary saws and brushes remove back shells, gills, and entrails. Clean crab cores emerge, and workers place them upside down in slotted trays that carry 20 at a time through a steam cabinet. The heat loosens the meat, and the meat drops onto the conveyor.

*Disadvantage:* It shreds the larger, more valuable lumps of so-called backfin meat that human pickers leave intact.

*Advantage:* Each machine can pick 225 pounds of meat an hour. Peak season in the Chesapeake Bay and in other shallow, protected waters along the Atlantic and the Gulf Coast is between August and November.

*Assignment:* Assume that Mr. and Mrs. Charles Perry own a cannery in Toddville, Maryland, and that it has always used crab pickers (20 workers at $5 an hour for an eight-hour day during the peak season). They had a difficult time finding workers last year and the year before, and this year they scraped the bottom of the pail and have not been pleased with the workers' production.

The machine costs $250,000. Assume that the Perrys could not agree on whether to buy the Pik Right; so they ask you (their school-of-business son or daughter) to advise them and show your reasoning. They have the money. Write a letter report.

**13–33.** An architect is designing 10 houses for a builder in southern California. According to the building code, he must have R–19 insulation in walls if hot water is conventionally heated, but may use R–11 wall insulation if solar apparatus is installed with a backup hot water system.

The difference between R–11 and R–19 insulation is approximately 22 cents per square foot. The houses will have 1,400 square feet of wall to be insulated.

1.  If R–19 insulation is used, the total interior square feet (floor space) of houses will be reduced (because of thicker studs) from 1,200 square feet to 1,170 square feet.
2.  With solar, the houses may have 4 percent more glass (windows, skylights, etc.).
3.  Dual glazing (double windows) will be required with the conventional hot water source only. Comparable cost per window: $85, single glaze; $175, double glaze.

*Find out:* Cost of solar system for average house and estimated savings on monthly utility bills with solar use in southern California.

The architect wants the builder to decide which way he wants to go—with the solar or with the heavier insulation. He suggests that the builder consider the market enhancement (advertising value) of either option.

**13–34.** As an outside consultant, write a letter report to Max Coe, president of General Scientific, a company deciding how much to allow for car cost reimbursement in the major city locations.

You've been asked to collect information on the costs of owning and operating cars in major U.S. cities. You've found a rental-car survey ranking such costs as follows:

| City | Cost Per Mile (cents) | | |
|------|------|------|------|
|      | 1984 | 1983 | Increase |
| Los Angeles | 60.69 | 56.89 | 3.80 |
| San Francisco | 58.16 | 54.46 | 3.50 |
| New York | 57.25 | 54.55 | 2.70 |
| Miami | 53.47 | 50.07 | 3.40 |
| Chicago | 52.74 | 49.44 | 3.30 |
| Denver | 51.91 | 47.81 | 4.10 |
| St. Louis | 51.57 | 47.57 | 4.00 |
| Seattle | 50.58 | 47.08 | 3.50 |
| Houston | 49.31 | 44.09 | 5.22 |
| Boston | 48.48 | 45.34 | 3.14 |
| Minneapolis | 47.53 | 45.34 | 2.19 |
| National average (all towns) | 49.61 | 45.67 | |

The figures are for a new compact car driven 10,000 miles annually for five years, including the purchase cost of the car, taxes, loan interest, depreciation, insurance and license fees, average repairs and maintenance, and gasoline and other service station charges.

Compact car prices range from $8,955 to $9,321. Insurance, licensing, and fees range from 9.76 cents per mile to 23.53 cents per mile. Interest runs from 8.55 cents per mile to 10.07 cents per mile.

Mr. Coe's company now reimburses employees 25 cents per mile when they use their personal cars for business. The IRS allows taxpayers to claim 20.5 cents per mile for unreimbursed business usage. Tell Mr. Coe what his reimbursement policy should be, citing this chart or other evidence.

**13–35.** As head of the Public Health Service committee, write a report to the president of the United States calling attention to two new studies of children aged 10–17 and recommending more emphasis on school fitness programs.

One survey showed that as many as half of all youngsters don't get enough exercise to develop healthy hearts and lungs. Only 36 percent in grades 5–12 attend daily physical education classes, well below the government's goal of 60 percent by 1990. Physical education programs focus on group sports instead of individual fitness skills that promote lifelong health. Since the 1960s young people have become fatter because of poor diets and "passive" activities such as watching television, using computers, playing videogames.

Two out of three youngsters could not pass basic physical fitness tests. For 12-year-old boys, the tests required 38 bent-knee sit-ups in a minute, 30 push-ups in 2 minutes, a long jump of 5 feet 4 inches, and a mile run in 8 minutes 42 seconds. Twelve-year-old girls were expected to do 33 sit-ups and 40 modified push-ups, jump 4 feet 11 inches, and run a mile in 10 minutes 18 seconds.

Fitness peaks at around age 14 and flattens out or declines from that point on. People who develop poor health habits as children often are overweight and injury-prone when they start crash exercise programs in their 30s and 40s.

**13–36.** Many managers find staff meetings to be time-wasters (about 18 percent in a typical survey). Managers dislike writing memos, too (about 45 percent). You think you can solve both problems by having teleconferenced meetings—bigger meetings rather than lots of small ones scattered in a number of your branches, conveying information orally and visually rather than in writing.

Your supervisor, Jan Cardiff, asks you, a new assistant in the central office, to write a justification letter report (for her signature) to go to all branch managers of the Camden Corporation, St. Louis, MO 63122. You do some research on electronic meetings and discover:

- An average of 20 million meetings a day are held in the United States;
- 80 percent of these last less than 30 minutes;
- 60 percent require only vocal communications;
- 35 percent involve only information exchange;
- 90 percent of air travel in the United States is business travel;
- Teleconferencing would serve 50–60 percent of all meetings, thus reducing travel costs;
- Facsimile machines and an electronic blackboard can add visual aids even to audioconferences.

Your purpose is to show the advantages of electronic meetings and persuade managers to support them. Your department holds two major sales meetings a year (250 salespeople divided among 28 different locations), seven meetings of product development teams from the three R&D offices (8–10 people each, who must see each other's graphics and spreadsheets), and probably 40 short meetings of department members and employees visiting from other branch offices.

**13–37.** This year Ralph Ulmer (67) retired from 25 years of selling with Electroflux vacuum cleaners and took a lump sum of $60,000 rather than monthly retirement checks. Ralph and his wife, Rose (64), ask you (a relative) to draw up a portfolio of recommended investments for them. They live in a modest, paid-for home (21 Elmood Place, Athens, OH 45709), drive two cars, contribute heavily to their church, and are generous with their three children and five grandchildren (to whom they hope to leave some money when they die). The Ulmers want investments that pay well, are safe, and will help them live well and leave a nice estate. They do not want to invest in real estate because they are not good at that type of thing. They have no income except Ralph's Social Security ($560). At age 65 (later this year), Rose can draw Social Security that will be $284 a month. Besides library research on different stocks, bonds, money market funds, and tax shelters, you might talk with different investment brokers and with people who understand the market.

**13–38.** For more cases on memos, see Appendix B VI I; VIII D; IX B, C, F, O. For a letter report, see III C. For justification reports, see III A; IX P.

## Cases for Chapter 14

(Preparing Major Managerial Reports)

**14–1.** Assume that your university wants to recruit the best and brightest high school seniors. Admissions officials at other schools you have talked with say that films allow a more emotional sales pitch than brochures or speakers. Teenagers are also used to videos in their lives.

More than 200 colleges have enshrined themselves on film in the past few years, and some colleges credit the features with a rise in applications. The productions, which average about 10 minutes, generally cost between $20,000 and $60,000.

Your assignment is to discover and give proper emphasis to academic factors pointing to high-quality work and qualifications to emphasize in the film you want to produce to advertise your school. Assume that you are Cecilia (or Charles) Tippin, assistant director of student recruitment in the Office of Admission Services. You are to write your report to the director of student recruitment, Curtis P. Mauter.

**14–2.** You are a recently graduated personnel specialist; so your boss (Ann Johnson, vice president in charge of personnel) asks you to collect information on available pension plans. She suggests that you cover profit sharing, stock bonus, employee stock ownership, and cash or deferred payment plans. She also wants to know the difference between defined benefit and defined contribution plans, and wants to consider only choices that are IRS-qualified, so that contributions and earnings are nontaxable (until the employee retires, of course). Write her an informational report based on your readings.

Readings that might get you started are: Richard Eisenberg, "Rating Your Firm's Retirement Plans," *Money,* November 1985, pp. 186–92; William H. Hoffman and Eugene Wills, eds., *West 1986 Annual Federal Taxation: Individual Income Taxes* (West Publishing, St. Paul, Minn.,

1985); and Glenn A. Welsch, Charles T. Zlatkovich, and Walter T. Harrison, *Intermediate Accounting,* (Richard D. Irwin, Homewood, Ill., 1984), p. 639.

**14–3.** Assume that you are in the Public Relations Department for a city of about 300,000 and have been placed in charge of finding out about the quality of life in your city, because your department is trying to attract new business and industry. Your report is to go to the mayor and the committee for city expansion. Based on the following information, what recommendations can you make in your report?

Your survey on people's views of life in the area represents a random sampling of 411 adults interviewed last month through the telephone. Margin of error is 5 percent (or if 50 percent of those polled answered a question one way, there's a 95 percent chance that 45–55 percent of the entire population, if polled, would answer the same way).

When asked "How satisfied are you with life in the area," people answered: Very satisfied, 26 percent; satisfied, 64 percent; dissatisfied, 5 percent; very dissatisfied, 1 percent; don't know/no answer, 3 percent.

To the question "What do you think is the major problem facing the area at this time?" the responses were: Unemployment, 16 percent; crime—law enforcement, 14 percent; economy—lack of growth, 6 percent; roads-streets, 5 percent; politics-government, 4 percent; race relations, 3 percent; lack of entertainment, 3 percent; size—rapid growth, 3 percent; annexation, 3 percent; schools, 2 percent; transportation, 2 percent; other, 15 percent; don't know/no answer, 25 percent.

Answers about more specific aspects of life in the city appear in the following table:

**How Residents Rate Life in the Area**

|  | Excellent | Good | Fair | Poor | Don't Know/ No Answer |
|---|---|---|---|---|---|
| Overall quality of government | 3% | 42% | 41% | 10% | 4% |
| Police protection | 7 | 48 | 34 | 7 | 4 |
| Treatment of people by police | 8 | 43 | 31 | 8 | 10 |
| Fire protection | 20 | 56 | 13 | 5 | 5 |
| Garbage collection | 15 | 50 | 19 | 8 | 8 |
| Water system | 12 | 59 | 19 | 6 | 4 |
| Cost of utilities | 2 | 22 | 43 | 32 | 2 |
| Amount of air pollution | 5 | 34 | 36 | 21 | 4 |
| Amount of water pollution | 7 | 41 | 32 | 10 | 10 |
| Level of property tax | 7 | 30 | 37 | 11 | 16 |
| Level of sales tax | 2 | 26 | 50 | 18 | 5 |
| Condition of interstate highways | 9 | 46 | 32 | 10 | 3 |
| Condition of your roads and streets | 3 | 36 | 36 | 24 | 0 |

## How Residents Rate Life in the Area (*concluded*)

| | Excellent | Good | Fair | Poor | Don't Know/ No Answer |
|---|---|---|---|---|---|
| Quality of parks and other recreational facilities | 12 | 48 | 29 | 6 | 5 |
| General availiability of cultural activities | 12 | 45 | 28 | 7 | 8 |
| General quality of cultural activities | 12 | 48 | 27 | 5 | 9 |
| Quality of museums | 20 | 52 | 15 | 3 | 10 |
| Quality of theater | 8 | 41 | 25 | 10 | 16 |
| Quality of music and concerts | 19 | 49 | 18 | 4 | 10 |
| Quality of public libraries | 37 | 50 | 6 | 0 | 7 |
| Quality of churches | 40 | 49 | 7 | 1 | 3 |
| Quality of restaurants | 23 | 57 | 13 | 3 | 5 |
| Quality of grocery stores | 23 | 61 | 12 | 2 | 2 |
| Quality of local radio stations | 24 | 56 | 11 | 4 | 4 |
| Quality of local TV stations | 19 | 60 | 14 | 4 | 3 |
| Quality of local newspapers | 16 | 55 | 20 | 6 | 3 |
| The climate | 28 | 53 | 13 | 2 | 4 |
| Friendliness of people | 30 | 48 | 16 | 4 | — |
| Availability of sporting events | 24 | 52 | 14 | 2 | 7 |
| Availability of nightclubs or similar places where people can go for entertainment | 14 | 41 | 20 | 7 | 19 |
| Availability of social activities | 12 | 51 | 24 | 6 | 8 |

**14–4.** As office manager for General Hydraulics, you are considering alternatives to sending your manuals and large mailings out to a commercial printer. (You have read a recent article that said printers are cheaper than copiers for volume of 2,500 copies or more.) Your student intern, when sent to the library and asked to call vendors, supplies the following information.

1. Copiers are more reliable than they used to be, and produce good enough quality for most industrial jobs.
2. Copiers that could be used as printers cost $10,000–100,000 plus, depending on how much volume a month you use them for.
3. Very large or high-grade jobs should go to a commercial printer.
4. Copying costs on your own machine are about 1½ cents per page.
5. Color copiers cost $24,000–40,000, or lease for $300–1,000 per month.
6. Color copiers are getting better all the time, as the technology improves. Right now, color copiers often don't have great colors; and furthermore, the machines have greater maintenance problems than regular copiers.

7. Minicopiers featuring reduction, enlargement, and color are coming down in price as discounts become available.

|         |     | Lists   | Sells |
|---------|-----|---------|-------|
| Aabard  | 100 | $1,695  | $845  |
| Corona  | 20  | 1,095   | 625   |
| Mitchell| 10  | 1,495   | 778   |
| Rhonol  | 9   | 1,330   | 825   |
| Pelham  | 70  | 1,395   | 837   |
| Mack    | 50  | 1,150   | 690   |

Write a report using the relevant information. Decide what printing and copying you should do in-house and what kind of equipment you should buy or lease. You employ 2,000 people at four locations and produce a million pieces of paper a year for personnel and customers. Only about 10 items a year run over 2,500 copies each, however. You produce four color mailings: a brochure on new products (5,000 copies), the annual report (4,000 copies), a recruiting brochure (3,000 copies), and the annual employee award dinner program (2,500 copies). You may want to do more library research on office paper needs.

**14–5.** You are to do the research and write a report to Homer Beveridge (director of sales, General Selectric), recommending three American-made cars that sales representatives can select. Each sales representative gets a new car after three years or after 60,000 miles. Standard equipment includes automatic transmission, power steering, power brakes, AM radio, air conditioning. (Desired extra features are available at the sales representative's personal cost.) The cars can be two- or four-door models. Cost, cost of operation, comfort, maintenance costs, safety are some of the things you'll investigate.

Assume that you are in market research for General Selectric and are in the same building as Homer Beveridge.

**14–6.** To keep Y County thriving despite the closing of several plants, less enrollment at the university, and general recession, the Chamber of Commerce wants to find out about the amount of shopping that residents do outside the county.

Paul Bloom, president of the Chamber of Commerce, authorized you (an employee of Hardy Incorporated) to write a report. Using the information from a survey by telephone interviews with a random sample of 389 adult Y County citizens (giving a confidence figure of 95% $\pm$ 5%), write the report to Bloom. Not only does Bloom want the information, but he wants your recommendations or suggestions of what the Chamber of Commerce can do to keep business in Y County.

When shopping for item, do you go outside Y County?

| | Always | Frequently | Occasionally | Never |
|---|---|---|---|---|
| 1. Clothing | 3% | 13% | 20% | 65% |
| 2. Automobile | 7 | 5 | 20 | 67 |
| 3. Rugs, wallpaper, etc. | 4 | 3 | 11 | 82 |
| 4. Toasters, dishes, etc. | 2 | 4 | 11 | 83 |
| 5. Major appliances | 4 | 2 | 8 | 87 |
| 6. Groceries | 3 | 2 | 4 | 91 |

Major reasons for shopping elsewhere:

Price, 33%; variety, 17%; availability, 16%; trip/visit, 16%; closeness/convenience, 7%; service, 6%; quality, 3%; other, 2%

Country stores/merchants compared to outsiders

| | Better On | Same | Worse On |
|---|---|---|---|
| Prices | 18% | 73% | 9% |
| Quality | 10 | 84 | 7 |
| Variety | 17 | 80 | 20 |
| Repair service | 12 | 77 | 10 |

Age, race, and income related to percent of outside shopping for:

| | Clothing | Major Appliances | Home Furnishings | Automobiles | Household Items | Groceries |
|---|---|---|---|---|---|---|
| Age | | | | | | |
| 18–30 years | 45 | 21 | 28 | 45 | 25 | 12 |
| 31–40 years | 33 | 12 | 21 | 34 | 17 | 9 |
| 41–50 years | 20 | 11 | 14 | 31 | 9 | 6 |
| 51–60 years | 33 | 6 | 10 | 26 | 8 | 8 |
| 61–70 years | 30 | 5 | 5 | 20 | 11 | 5 |
| 71 + years | 12 | 0 | 0 | 8 | 4 | 0 |
| Race | | | | | | |
| White | 38 | 14 | 22 | 38 | 19 | 8 |
| Black | 25 | 9 | 5 | 18 | 11 | 10 |
| Income | | | | | | |
| Less than $5,000 | 30 | 18 | 22 | 27 | 11 | 11 |
| $5,000–10,000 | 23 | 13 | 11 | 17 | 21 | 10 |
| $10,000–15,000 | 38 | 3 | 8 | 25 | 14 | 3 |
| $15,000–20,000 | 34 | 5 | 12 | 28 | 16 | 7 |
| $20,000–25,000 | 33 | 9 | 18 | 38 | 4 | 2 |
| $25,000–30,000 | 41 | 10 | 18 | 33 | 18 | 10 |
| $30,000–35,000 | 22 | 5 | 18 | 48 | 9 | 9 |
| $35,000–40,000 | 54 | 25 | 38 | 65 | 29 | 14 |
| Over $40,000 | 53 | 23 | 32 | 44 | 28 | 11 |

**14–7.** Marjorie Dole, a candidate for reelection to the state legislature, wants to know how people feel about the economic condition in the state. So she hired you to interview voters and give her an analytical report with recommendations. Since you have been making such surveys each spring and fall for several years, you'll give her a report based on the last five. From each telephone poll of a random sample of 554 voters, you can be 95 percent confident that a result from this sample is not more than 5 percent different from that of the entire adult population.

As an employee of McDermott Incorporated, write the analytical report based on the information in the following tables:

| | Spring 1984 | Fall 1984 | Spring 1985 | Fall 1985 | Spring 1986 |
|---|---|---|---|---|---|
| Compared with a year ago, are you financially Better off/Same/Worse off? | 32/22/47% | 30/27/43% | 40/24/36% | 43/26/31% | 46/24/30% |
| A year from now will you be Better off/Same/ Worse off? | 26/55/19 | 34/52/15 | 35/52/13 | 39/51/10 | 35/52/14 |
| During the next 12 months will the country have | | | | | |
| Good times | 23 | 24 | 46 | 44 | 45 |
| Good times ± | 12 | 19 | 18 | 17 | 11 |
| Same | 13 | 12 | 13 | 14 | 21 |
| Bad times ± | 8 | 10 | 4 | 4 | 4 |
| Bad times? | 44 | 34 | 20 | 21 | 18 |
| Are business conditions | | | | | |
| Better | 13 | 12 | 52 | 67 | 66 |
| Same | 5 | 6 | 10 | 8 | 12 |
| Worse | 82 | 82 | 38 | 25 | 21 |
| than a year ago? | | | | | |
| Five-year predictions: | | | | | |
| Good times | (no survey) | 28 | 39 | 39 | 41 |
| Good times ± | | 18 | 18 | 16 | 10 |
| Pro-con | | 9 | 6 | 6 | 8 |
| Bad times ± | | 13 | 8 | 9 | 10 |
| Bad times | | 32 | 30 | 31 | 30 |
| Is now a | | | | | |
| Good time | | 47 | 54 | 56 | 64 |
| Bad time | | 53 | 46 | 44 | 36 |
| to buy major household items? | | | | | |

**14–8.** For the controlling board of a specific state, county, or city school system, write a requested report on whether the buses used should have seat belts. It's a cost-and-savings question, though the savings are not all in dollars and cents.

**14–9.** Should X Company use janitorial service? Find out the cost of such a service and weigh it against the cost of hiring janitors (considering all costs). Also consider the cost of supplies and convenience, but don't stack the cards.

**14–10.** Hardy McDuff is a candidate for election to the state legislature in your state. Drunk driving has been a problem in his community, but many of the people he talks with are skittish about raising the legal drinking age to 21.

Before taking a stand on this issue, he hired you to interview Y County voters and give him an analytical report with recommendations. From your telephone poll of a random sample of 398 voters, you can be 95 percent confident that a result from this sample is not more than 5 percent different from that of the entire adult population of McDuff's state. (Some "no answers" explain why the figures do not always add up to 100 percent.)

As an employee of Hardy Incorporated, write the analytical report based on the information in the following tables:

| | Very Serious | Serious | Not Very | Not at All |
|---|---|---|---|---|
| How serious is the drunk-driving problem here? | 50% | 39% | 11% | 1% |
| Divided by sex (M/F) | 40/57 | 45/33 | 13/9 | 1/1 |

| | Favor | Oppose |
|---|---|---|
| Do you favor/oppose an age-21 law? | 70% | 30% |
| Divided by sex (M/F) | 63/75 | 37/24 |
| Divided by age group | | |
| 18–30 | 58 | 42 |
| 31–40 | 79 | 21 |
| 41–50 | 77 | 23 |
| 51–69 | 69 | 31 |
| 61–70 | 91 | 9 |
| 71+ | 78 | 22 |

| Predicted effect of raising age divided by favor/oppose | | | (Undivided) |
|---|---|---|---|
| Increase problem | 2 | 17 | 6% |
| No change | 39 | 70 | 49 |
| Decrease problem | 59 | 13 | 45 |

**14–11.** Assume (1) that another school (college or university) is looking for a new professor in one of your course areas (current or past), (2) that you are a full professor in the searching department selected to chair the search committee, and (3) that your committee has researched and interviewed three interested candidates, each of whom would move up a notch in rank and salary if selected.

Now you are to write an informational report to your department head categorizing the information (factual and/or imaginary, but *realistic*) that your committee has collected under three–five categories, but *not* in any way showing favoritism toward any applicant.

**14–12.** Assume that your department members have read your first report (preceding case) and asked that your committee give them an analytical report with recommendations, putting the candidates in rank order.

**14–13.** As a marketing research analyst for Rosen and Gross, 3835 Orleans Ln., Minneapolis, MN 55441, you are to write an analytical report to J. D. Maloney, President, North American Stores, 2570 E. 12th Avenue, North St. Paul, MN 55109.

North American is considering building and operating a new grocery store in your city. Maloney wants you to visit three to five different supermarkets and look at 8 to 10 categories of food and grocery items. Draw up a list of the items you will price-shop, including brands and package sizes. Be sure to compare comparable things in each category. (*Warning:* Don't compare a product weighing 1 pound with a product weighing 1½ pounds or of different quality.)

Include your synopsis in your letter of transmittal.

**14–14.** As Mario Tulares, director of advertising, you want to order equipment for filming your own local commercials. You advertise industrial products to commercial clients at trade shows rather than to the general public on television.

Some equipment you think would work for the job:

| | Cameras | |
|---|---|---|
| RVC 3260 × 1 | $1,165 | (The more expensive cameras are |
| RVC 1451X | 1,395 | lighter and easier to carry. The |
| SVC 2400 | 1,100 | S series cameras are color.) |
| SVC 2800 | 1,350 | |

| | Video Monitors | |
|---|---|---|
| MVP 122 | 12″, 21 lb. | $ 450 |
| MVP 91 | 9″, 12 lb. | 345 |
| VCM 1900 | 19″, 69 lb. | 1,200 (color) |

| Betamax Player | |
|---|---|
| BLP 305 (player only) | $1,160 |
| BLO 420 (recorder/player) | 1,340 |

You realize that the company hasn't authorized many extra expenditures this year, but producing commercials yourself instead of having an outside company do it could save a lot of money once you have the equipment.

You think the training department could use the equipment also, and thus help justify the cost. Since you'll save production costs, you figure the payback period at 18 months for the advertising use alone. It costs about $1,000 for a minute of high-quality finished film or tape. If you use one camera and shoot the film at your own plant, it costs about

$5,000; if you use a production studio, figure up to $20,000 for the same film.

Convince Ed Sloan, the controller.

## Cases for Chapter 15

(Presenting Major Analytical Reports) and Chapter 16 (Analysis and Illustration of Major Analytical Reports)

**Whether you are going to use Cases 15–1 and 15–2 or not, you should read them for points that should apply to nearly any major report-writing project.**

**15–1.** Subject to approval by your instructor, choose a topic for your report. Preferably it should be a real problem actually faced by a company, organization, or individual; if not, it should be a problem somebody probably faces somewhere. It should be for one reader or a very limited group of specific readers. A term-theme topic or something like a textbook chapter will not do because it is not a report. If you can't quickly give the name or title of somebody other than a teacher who might ask for such a report, your topic is unsuitable.

It should be an analytical report: the relevant facts plus interpretation and evaluation of the advantages and disadvantages (the pros and cons) of at least two alternatives and the eventual selection of one in your final conclusions and recommendations. In other words, it must be a problem that you help someone to solve. See the list in Case 15–3 for suggestions if you can't readily think of one—perhaps from your own work experience.

It should be a topic for which you can get information in the library *and* (not *or*) through interviews, questionnaires, or your own observation or experimentation.

You should settle on a topic early in the term and should not change topics after midterm for any reason. The kind of problem we're talking about usually takes 10 to 20 pages for the text alone and requires most of the school term. You and your teacher will of course cover regular classwork and the shorter assignments meanwhile.

As your instructor directs, be prepared to submit on one typed page

**a.** A tentative title (not *now* worded to show a preconception of the outcome, but clear, concise and catching).

**b.** A one-sentence statement of the purpose of the report.

**c.** An indication of who the readers are and your relationship (actual or assumed) to them.

**d.** Sources and/or methods of collecting data, including the titles of five items from your tentative bibliography.

**e.** Major divisions (with subdivisions, if you like) of the coverage or body of the report.

Be prepared at any time to give your instructor a progress report in memo form, indicating what you have accomplished, what difficulties you've encountered, what remains to be done, and your plans for finishing. (See Chapter 13.)

At the time directed by your instructor, submit the report with title page, letter of transmittal, contents listing, synopsis, body (including introduction, facts and interpretations intermingled but in two to five major divisions, conclusions, and recommendations), bibliography, and (if necessary) appendix.

As further clarification and suggestion, here are some of the better topics chosen by students in one class:

Comparative evaluation of swimming pool (or goldfish pool) disinfectants under specific conditions.

Comparative evaluation of materials and procedures to reduce black-shank damage to tobacco plants (specific conditions).

Whether X Company should expand (or restrict, or diversify) its product line (or territory).

You'll find a long list of other possibilities in Case 15–3.

**15–2.** One of the requests coming to your desk as director of Research, Inc., NY 10032, is from the president of (name of firm supplied by your instructor). The company is a chain of retail (type of store supplied by your instructor) stores with outlets in most major cities. The chain is now contemplating opening a store in either one of two cities (names of two cities supplied by your instructor).

The letter to you as director, signed by the company president, reads:

Will you please submit in report form your analysis of retail sales possibilities for (specific goods) in (names of two cities)?

Before deciding where our next branch will be, we would like the opinion of a firm of your caliber.

Naturally, we want to know the story on population, buying power, retail sales--with special emphasis on (specific goods)--competition, and current business. But please include other data that will be helpful to us in making our choice.

Your problem is only to determine which city would probably bring us the larger volume of sales. Please do not attempt to cover taxes, wage

scales, real estate costs, or availability of
sites, and maybe crime rates that might affect us.
After your determination, we will require a
shorter report on each of those topics.

Since we plan to have the store in operation
within a year's time, will you please confirm that
you can submit the report no later than (specific
date as assigned), subject to the same rates as on
previous studies?

You can get all the necessary comparative data from secondary library
sources: *Statistical Abstract of the United States; County and City Data
Book; Market Guide of Editor and Publisher;* Rand McNally's *Commercial Atlas and Marketing Guide; Sales Management Survey of Buying
Power; Marketing/Communication*'s studies such as *Sales Planning Guide*
and *Major American Markets;* and *Consumer Markets,* published by
the Standard Rate & Data Service. The foregoing are some of your
more useful sources. But they are not intended to be an exhaustive list.
You will of course want to consult the censuses of population, business,
and manufacturers for (respectively) breakdowns of populations, influence
of wholesaling and retailing on the local economy, and the value added
to the economy by manufacturing. In all cases you will want the latest
reliable data; recency of information is important.

Your entire analysis should focus on the answer to this question: Which
of the two towns is a better market for selling more of the specific merchandise that this store sells? Population is, of course, a factor—size
as well as distribution and character. The retail market area always needs
examining. Income figures are significant (a person with $4 is in a better
position to buy than one with only $2). Retail sales indicate whether
people are willing to spend their money (total retail sales, per capita
retail sales, and retail sales figures in the particular line you're investigating—if you can find them). Sources of business strength are appropriate
considerations (a manufacturing town suffers more than a distribution
center during a recession; a community depending primarily on farm-
ing for its sustenance weathers economic storms more readily than one
heavily dependent on shipbuilding, for instance). And the current business
picture (as measured by construction, postal figures, employment, and
bank deposits) is important for its diagnostic value.

The list of topics above is merely to help you start thinking about
what to include; it is not intended to be inclusive, orderly, or arbitrary.
For instance, no study of this kind would ever omit competitive factors.

*This is assigned:* Exclude any discussion of banking facilities, communications facilities (newspapers, radio stations, advertising agencies), and
transportation facilities. These are adequate in both cities and so would
not affect the decision. Furthermore, the people would have done enough

reading themselves to know where the cities are—and the pertinent geographic and climatic features.

Once you've made the final decision of what factors to include and—just as important—the order in which to lay them out, the analysis becomes a matter of simply comparing the two cities simultaneously to show which city is the better market—more people with more money to spend, and the apparent willingness to spend it, especially for this kind of merchandise.

*Do not* attempt to turn out a chamber of commerce root-for-the-home team piece of propaganda. Impersonally, impartially present the facts about the two cities and make your decision on the total evidence.

An analytical report is not just a compilation of tables and labels. Your report must present the facts in statistical display (graphics primarily, for readability). Without these, your report has no base and, in the reader's mind, no authenticity. But the most significant part of the report is your own expository (analytical) comment, which explains the significance of the data you have gathered.

Of course, your grade will depend partly on physical appearance and mechanical correctness (freedom from errors in spelling, punctuation, and grammar). Counting most heavily, however, will be

1. Organization (the order of points for logic and emphasis).
2. Readability (stylistic factors).
3. Complete, authentic evidence and its reliability, analysis, and documentation.

**15–3.** Parts of this assignment probably are not suitable for a large class in a small community because too many students would be getting in too many business executives' hair. This danger can be less serious, however, if students work in teams, at least on the data-collecting part of report writing. Also, consider the listed topics, which are not report titles, just suggestions to start thinking about what could be an endless list of the same kind of thing.

For your choice of the following topics, assume that you can and will arrange amicably for access to, observation of, or experimentation with the obviously necessary facts (usually available only in a small local firm). Then write the kind of report (form, tone, and length) that the facts and the situation seem to require (or your instructor assigns). Assume that the appropriate person has asked you to do the report, and assume an appropriate position for yourself. In most cases you will probably be an employee; but in some, you might reasonably assume that you are a consultant on a fee basis. Each situation is to involve thorough study of existing conditions and application of well-established, up-to-date principles (learned from courses, articles, books, and/or people) leading to recommendations for wise decision about or betterment of the situation.

Should X City convert raw garbage to energy?

Should X Country Town have house-to-house garbage collection instead of a dumpster system?

Can X City support another hospital?

Can X City support another cemetery?

Can the town of Y support a catering service?

Should your university authorize student evaluations of teachers and/or courses, and if so, how should they be done?

Should X City attract new business, and if so, how?

Should doctors X, Y, and Z incorporate their clinic?

Should the professional cleaning service in X City advertise through newspaper, TV, or direct marketing?

Should X Savings and Loan Association give premiums to encourage new accounts?

Should X Company encourage its sales force through contests?

What about a joint venture for X Company?

Should X Community have separate emergency care units in addition to the units at the hospital(s)?

What is the best organizational form for X Business—sole proprietorship, partnership, C corporation, or S corporation?

Should X Bank have a special program to woo clients who keep $100,000 or more on deposit?

Why should or should not X Community School System have merit pay for teachers?

What is the best compensation plan that will motivate the employees of X Company?

Why should or should not X Company expand to an international market?

Why should or should not X Company have an international joint venture?

Why should or should not X and Y companies merge?

How effective have been antidrinking programs such as MADD?

How effective has been legislation about car seats for children?

Why should or should not X Corporation have an employees' child-care program?

Evaluate and recommend a retirement program for X Company.

Recommend a physical fitness program for X Company.

Besides offering the regular retail charge card, should X Department Store offer VISA, MasterCard, and American Express also?

Should X Grocery Chain stock generic canned goods?

Should X Drugstore stock generic drugs?

Should Mr. X buy a fast-food franchise for his college-graduate son or daughter?

Should X University have a learning skills center with emphasis on basic math, science, writing . . . ?

Could/should your community afford a Wellness Center?

Could/should your community afford a program for the street people (those homeless people who have nowhere to sleep at night)?

Assume that a successful and well-to-do friend of yours wants to get instant stock quotations for his or her office. What would be the best facility to buy, and why?

Since some companies are selling software by encouraging owners to copy it for others, you have to do some research to find out which shareware program would be best (would bring your company the best software at the below-normal prices). Assume that your boss has asked for this report.

Should Y City developers build a conference center?

Should Y City developers build a hotel?

Approved vacation practices in a specific local firm.

Traffic-accident "hot spots" in a town or city (or, if too large, an appropriate area).

A campus bus service? Volume? Pay? Routes? Costs/income? Franchised/school-operated?

Student costs of attending your school (low/medium/high).

Causes for failure in college work (student/school viewpoint).

Justifiable improvements at a specific sorority/fraternity/dorm.

A new (or up-for-sale) riding stable in your town—prospects for success?

Student TV, magazine, or newspaper preferences/habits at your school.

Proper credit (less, same, more?) for this (or other) business communication course.

Best buy in this year's (under 10-hp outboard motors, vacuum cleaners, . . .)?

English errors students make in (first business communication course).

Training needed for writing/speaking done by local business executives in first five years out of college.

Student reasons for choosing to attend your school.

Paralegals—should X Law School train them?

Paramedics—should X Medical School train them?

Needed improvements in X Company's employee motivation.

The absentee-worker problem at X.

Bugs in X's inventory control.

The letter writing done by a small local firm. (Only students who have studied letter writing should attempt this assignment.)

The public relations of a local firm (limited parts, if necessary).

The accounting procedures of a local firm (limited aspects, if necessary).

The advertising program and budget (not copy) of a small local firm.

The advertising copy (not program and budget) used by a local firm.

The physical layout (floor plan) of a local store (same problem a housekeeper works on by moving the furniture around).

The hiring and firing and promoting criteria (or just one criterion) and procedures in X (business firm), related to personnel turnover.

The financing arrangements of . . . .

The stock control procedures of . . . .

The fringe benefits (or just one) or salary scales of . . . .

The materials-handling procedures of . . . .

Pilferage losses and control in . . . .

A time and motion study of some local processing or manufacturing operation.

Any other problem of this type that you think of and can get facts on, and that your instructor approves.

Proposed equipment and procedures for fire prevention and/or fighting in a certain forest, building, or operation.

Should a given company devote some of its lands/efforts to producing . . . (a kind of production or service not now emphasized).

Solution to the problem of poor growth and fruiting/flowering of certain plants on a large lot (or crops on a specific field or farm).

Critical analysis (with suggestions) of the company publications of a comparatively small local firm.

Possible computer applications in a local library (or company).

Suggestions for improving appeal and income at a small fee-charging, publicly or privately operated park and lake.

Would a proposed campground (private, specific location) be a successful business venture?

Analysis of a local company's employee relations problems, with suggestions for improvement.

Would a specific large wood products company be wise to set up a sawmill and/or paper mill in a certain locality where it has some landholdings?

To have or not to have coffee breaks for a given company's employees.

What the people of a 10,000–100,000 community think of their public schools, with emphasis on suggested improvements.

Any of these problems can generate an oral report if your instructor so directs.

**15–4.** Find an organization that grows, makes, or deals in a product that you think might be sold profitably outside the United States and analyze the market potential in one or more foreign markets. After a little preliminary investigation, you should discuss with your teacher (and get agreement on) the kinds of information you are to get and analyze, such as estimated size of the market, kind(s) of customers, methods and estimated costs of advertising and promoting, best ways (and costs) of distributing, and the present and/or foreseeable competition.

Almost any business capable of competing domestically can export, but some products are not appropriate for certain markets and some require modification to be successful.

You can get much useful information in various places:

United Nations' publications such as *Yearbook of International Trade Statistics, Monthly Bulletin of Statistics,* and *Trade Statistics.* If these are not in accessible libraries, write the UN Sales Section, New York, NY 10017.

The U.S. Department of Commerce, *Business America, Commerce Business Daily,* and *Market Share Reports* will be available in libraries or from the Government Printing Office, Washington, DC 20402. The Department of Commerce computer system (identified as DIALOG) also helps find markets. WITS (Worldwide Information and Trade System), a Department of Commerce computerized system, gives information on potential business contacts in the United States and abroad.

*Predicasts, International* is published weekly, quarterly, annually.

Various state agencies may help: state world trade association, district export council, state docks (if any), chamber of commerce, departments of agriculture and industries, governor's office of international development, international departments in state banks, and such centers as the International Trade Center at the University of Alabama.

For background briefings to aid in understanding other people, you can read the section on Adaptations to International Business in Chapter 4.

**15–5.** The president of the small company where you work, Mel Bingham, asks you to compare the IRA and the Keogh plan for possible use for the employees' tax-sheltering retirement plan. Take a small-sized, actual company about which you can get information; assume that Bingham gives you a deadline (the due date your instructor assigns you); and write the complete analytical report your president wants.

**15–6.** Patio homes are the new thing in your area. Managed essentially as condominiums, they are individual homes (one level) with yard in front (that the management keeps up) and yard in back (that the owner keeps up or gardens). You and a friend want to develop some patio homes in your area. Your friend lives 500 miles away, so you must do the research. You need to know what would be the best buy in low-energy appliances (dishwasher, washer, dryer). What is the best heating and air conditioning unit, water heater? Since you'll be selling to some widows, divorcées, retired people, and unattached people, safety is a prime concern. What kind of windows and door locks should you purchase? What other safety precautions should you plan for? After you have gathered your facts, write a report to your friend analyzing your information and proposing (recommending) specific choices.

**15–7.** Evaluate the purchase of used computers for your small company. Look at resale value, service availability, software depth, and operating system compatibility, among other things.

# Appendix B

## Case Series

### I. Alton Medical Foundation Series

Most hospitals need more money so that they can continue to give quality care. Assume that you are to write a series of letters to get tax-deductible money for Alton Medical Foundation, 1415 North Jefferson, Springfield, MO 65890. (You make up the facts about the foundation.)

**A.** Write a letter to each member of the staff asking for a gift of $1 per pay period (amounting to $26 a year). For a full year's participation, the giver will receive a certificate (which can justify a tax deduction).

**B.** Write a letter to people outside the hospital asking them to become associates (for a $50 gift), advocates (for $100), advisers (for $250), diplomats (for $1,000), councillors (for $2,500), or medalists (for $5,000).

**C.** Write a thank-you note addressed to staff members to go with the certificates mentioned in A.

**D.** Write a thank-you note to the people listed in B who gave $50 or more.

**E.** Write a follow-up letter to go out next year to the people who gave $50 or more.

### II. Business Communication Association Series

You are in charge of this year's Association for Business Communication regional meeting in your area (East, Southeast, West, Southwest) six months from now. Choose your favorite city and your favorite place (name the civic center, university center, hotel, motel, or convention center). Part of your job is to

**A.** Write a form letter to ABC members at colleges and universities in the area promoting your conference. (You make up all reasonable details.)

**B.** Congratulate in a form letter. The person you write has a paper accepted for presentation. Urge this person to register and pay the $50 fee. Ask if the presenter will need any audiovisual equipment. Give any interesting and needed detail, and suggest your willingness to help the speaker do a good job.

**C.** Turn down a person who wants to make a presentation. You and your screening committee cannot accept this paper because it is not up to the standards you require. The topic is a misfit. The proposer (a quack) is not competent and wants too much time. Apparently your promotional letter was effective, because you are swamped with proposals from all over the United States and the world.

**D.** Thank each person who agrees to be a coordinator of a session at the conference. You'll want to remind each one to start and stop on time, announce each topic and introduce each speaker (name, place of employment, specific topic), and check ahead to see if speakers want audiovisuals and question-and-answer time.

**E.** Tell the writers of some of the papers that their papers have been selected for the printed proceedings. Make clear that the writers are to put their papers in publishable format (double-space, follow MLA style manual). Two copies of paper should come to you by a certain date. Allotted time for presentation is 15 minutes.

**F.** Write thank-you notes about two days after the convention to all the people who made presentations.

**G.** Write thank-you notes to all coordinators (also after the convention).

## III. Corporate Apartment Series

**A.** You (Bernie Leventhal, as president) think your corporation, XVT, 15700 Drummet Boulevard, Houston, TX 77054 (phone: 713/442-5100), needs a corporate apartment in Washington, D.C. In the past two years your CEO as well as middle and senior management representatives have made monthly visits to Washington and have stayed at expensive hotels and entertained representatives from Congress and business. Besides the cost—which rounds out to an average of $3,000 a month just for executives to stay in hotels, eat, and entertain—there are some other factors to consider. It's much more relaxing to have a client in an attractive, warm, well-decorated atmosphere than in an office or some hotel room.

When you talked with Russel Shaw of ITT, he said that an apartment stimulates revenue-producing "borderline" business trips. If a habitation is already present, a sales executive might take the highly speculative, lead-seeking junket that he might not make if it meant a steep commercial hotel charge rather than simply another night in the flat-rate firm lair. ITT feels that its corporate apartments in Chicago, New York, and Los Angeles have been well worth their expense, Shaw confides.

When you asked about costs in general, Shaw was evasive, saying that ITT had different arrangements in each city. In one city it had a corporate apartment in an exquisite, residential hotel that the company rented, while it bought the apartment in another city and leased the apartment in the third city. The costs of furnishing vary too and can range from $10,000 to over $100,000. The interior designer for the apartment in New York went overboard with good paintings and house fittings, Shaw added.

While in Washington recently, you stayed at the Capital Hilton and ran up the usual high bills for sleeping, eating, entertaining. Between business appointments, however, you called several real estate agencies and learned basically the same general information. No definitive statistics are available, but today there are probably between 3,000 and 4,000 corporate apartments in the United States.

The apartments may be located in residential hotels with fine services available at the push of a button, or they may be located in splendid apartment houses with revered addresses. Some corporate executives like to have available all the services that a hotel provides. Very few apartment buildings (except for apartment hotels) are set up to provide room service. It's important to some corporate executives to have restaurants nearby if the apartment does not have such service. Demand for corporate apartments continues to increase.

Typically apartments in some of Washington's luxury residential hotels can run from $500,000 to well into the millions. In Park Tower, for example, the basis of an apartment is living room with two or three windows, formal foyers (halls), library, marble bathrooms, two bedrooms, living room, dining room, breakfast room, kitchen. The cost runs anywhere between $890,000 and $2,100,000, depending on the size and on how high up the building you are. But one real estate agent, Duran Pogue, told you that at California House on California Street (near the fashionable embassy district and not too far from convenient hotels) there were corporate apartments for sale for $200,000.

Corporations rent, lease, or buy apartments. Pogue said that one of his clients used the corporate apartment in a hotel so little that the corporation made arrangements with the hotel to rent the apartment except for the months of January and February. If a company owns the condo outright, the interest is deductible, but the principal payments are not. Most companies prefer to rent because they don't want to be saddled with the hassles of owning. Pogue notes that the ratio is at least 10 to 1 for companies renting corporate apartments.

Even though you feel that there will have to be more research done in Washington with real estate agents, you think that before you spend more time pursuing your idea of a corporate apartment, you should get the approval of Jasper Brooks, CEO of your corporation. Write a justification report to Brooks.

**B.** As Jasper Brooks, send Bernie Leventhal your approval of the justification report about the corporate apartment. Before writing the memo, however, you talked with Furman Ward, head of accounting, and Ward recommended that the company investigate renting an apartment in a desirable location (preferably near the center of things in Washington and not out as far as Arlington or Fairfax). Since Bernie had this idea and has already talked with some real estate agents in Washington, D.C., you feel that all possibilities should be explored, and the sooner the better.

**C.** After visiting many apartments in Washington, D.C., and its environs and talking with countless real estate representatives as well as executives who have used corporate apartments, you will write a letter report to Jasper Brooks, CEO, from your room at the Capital Hilton, Washington, giving information about the apartments you found available for rent. Because all of the apartments would need decorating and furnishing, you recommend that the company hire an interior designer such as Fran Topol, Atlanta; Francois Azaria, New York; Enrique Ruiz-Fornells, Washington. You have seen the work of all three of these interior designers, and all are good.

1. You found an 800-square-foot apartment in ideal location on California (close to hotels, deli, embassies) in stylish old building for $800 a month plus water and electricity. Entrance to building most attractive (enclosed courtyard). Guard on duty night and day for security reasons. Apartment has one large bay window in front, two windows in the only bedroom, one in kitchen, and one in bath. Narrow hall connects bath, kitchen, hall. Two other corporations have apartments in building (a desirable asset). Apartment on third floor and has stairway (wide and gracious) and modern elevator.

2. Still in the district but 10 minutes from the center of things, there's an apartment (2619 Garfield Street) in a 10-story building, but it's on the eighth floor, is 1,500 square feet, rents for $1,000 a month plus utilities, has no security guard; metro five blocks away. Has most space in living room, small bath, kitchen, one bedroom. No window in bath or kitchen, but large windows in other two rooms. Large closet in bedroom, but owner said no walls could be changed to make for more space. Walking distance to a deli, but no hotels around. Good elevator service.

3. Apartment on fifth floor in old hotel called Fairfax Arms has convenience of maid and food service. No corporate apartments there yet, which is a disadvantage. No hotels, deli, or grocery store near, but metro not too far (about eight blocks). The 2,000 square feet take in a small entry hall (no windows), living-dining area, two bedrooms, breakfast room, kitchen, two bathrooms. Kitchen and bathrooms have no windows, but bedrooms and living-dining area have wide windows with good views. Security guard on duty in hotel lobby at all times. Dining room open 6 A.M.–1 P.M. and 5 P.M.–11 P.M. Cocktail lounge open 4 P.M.–1 A.M. Rent runs $2,000 a month plus utilities.

4. Luxury residential hotel, Washington Plaza, has corporate apartment costing $5,000 monthly (plus all utilities except heat), with 2,500 square feet, including entranceway (wide and impressive), living room, dining room, library, two baths, two bedrooms, kitchen, breakfast room. Guard on duty at all times. Courtyard in back of hotel. View of courtyard from library and dining room. Windows in all rooms except baths and hallway entry. Washington Plaza has good address, near metro, near deli and restaurants. Slow elevators. You met some executives from large corporations while on elevators; and from what you figure, the building is being taken over by corporations (which could be a plus).

Along with your letter report, you are sending your inside and outside photographs of each apartment. Because there's such a demand for corporate apartments and so little selection close in the city, a decision should be made promptly.

## IV. Desk-Pad Series

**A.** *You,* Bill Sikes, Big Town Office Supply Company, P.O. Box 183, Mesquite, TX 75181. *Your wholesaler:* Kyle Office Supply, 10 St. Lucia Park, Tiburon, CA 94920. *Product:* Permex desk chair pads, size 45″ × 53″, in slick, hard acrylic. *Problem:* Big Town bought two dozen Permex pads. Out of the first dozen Big Town sold, you (Bill Sikes, manager) had complaints because the pads cracked and broke after ordinary use. You want to send back the unsold dozen to Kyle and get an adjustment on the ones you sold. These retail for $60 and wholesale for $45. Also, you want a replacement that will not break. Write the letter for Sikes.

**B.** For Kyle, respond to Sikes about the Permex pads. Because of the breaking problem with Permex, you now stock Tenex clear vinyl pads with textured pattern and gripper back (great for deep pile carpets). *Warranty:* Tenex Corporation warrants to the original purchaser that Tenex chair mats will be free of defects in material or workmanship at time of shipment and will not crack or wear through when used as recommended under normal conditions of use. (This warranty does not cover any Tenex acrylic chair mats and is limited to one year for all Tenex static control products.) This warranty does not cover use with metal casters. Tenex mats sell for $60 and retail for $76.

On the boxes that each Permex pad was shipped in, there was a notice that these acrylic chair mats would be free from defects in material and workmanship at the time of shipment, but nothing was said about their cracking or breaking. Kyle cannot refund the money for the dozen that Big Town sold, but it can give credit on the dozen that Sikes did not sell if he'll send them back to you, and you'll replace them (for the difference in price) with the improved Tenex.

**C.** Kyle Office Supply also writes the manufacturer, Permex Corporation, 1850 West Estes Avenue, Elk Grove Village, IL 60008, a "Whatchagonnado?" letter about its troubles with the desk pads.

**D.** Writer, Seagail Friedman, 1625 Lamplighter, Southfield, MI 48075, writes Tenex Corporation, 500 Aberdeen Road, Akron, OH 44352, to supply the home office building for Lincoln Insurance Company, Lincoln, NE 68506, with 50 desk chair pads, 45″ × 53″ in clear vinyl with gripper backs like she saw advertised in *Office* magazine last month. As Bonnie Sharman, director of sales, rechannel her request to the nearest dealer, Weatherford Office Supply, 896 Dearborn Avenue, Denver, CO 80229— and promptly inform Friedman of what you're doing.

**E.** As manager of Big Town, Mesquite, TX 75181, handle the claim of Barbara Stone, office manager of First National Bank, Dallas. First National bought 60 Tenex vinyl pads with textured pattern and gripper back and used them two years. Today, while you were out of the office, Barbara brought one of them by and left it with your assistant. She said that even though the one-year guarantee was up, she didn't think that this particular desk pad should have worn out so fast, because where it was it got little use. The assistant told her that you would examine it and call her later in the day. As soon as you looked at the pad, you realized that someone very heavy had been sitting in a desk chair that had metal rollers. The warranty clearly says that metal rollers should not be used. Phone Ms. Stone and explain what you found. Warn her that the other pads will wear out if metal rollers are used.

**F.** Or you could assume that instead of calling her, you'll write her a friendly note about the situation.

# V. Executive Card Series

**A.** Letterhead:
Melbourne Office: 6th Floor, Trak Centre 445 Toorak Road, Toorak, Australia 3421 Telephone (03) 2400727

*Product:* Black and gold plastic credit card called The Executive Card that earns discounts for members at restaurants, hotels (20–50 percent), movie theaters (two tickets for the price of one). If cardholder orders a dinner, a second main course is free on request. Presently 25,000 Australians are members, and they pay $45 a year for the privilege of having this money-saving card. If any card member goes to any establishment listed in the directory and, for any reason, does not receive the full credit allowed, a letter to you, the president, will bring a check for it.
*Mailing list:* 50,000 prospects in Australia. Those who join receive their cards with their embossed name and an impressive 400-page, four-color directory of service establishments. (A supplementary directory goes to the membership in June, listing new places to visit, stay, and dine and places that are no longer in the program.)
*Message:* The Executive Card is a money saver. The organization takes pride in high standards. Make subscribing easy. Sign your name as Club President. (Add specific information to sell beyond facts in case.)

**B.** When a customer's one-year membership expires, a letter with a new card telling all the changes and additions taking place accompanies an invoice for the new dues. Write the letter as the Club President.

**C.** Write a follow-up letter a month later (preceding case). Remind the people on your list to renew, and give them reasons why and advantages of Executive Card membership.

**D.** Assume another mailing to people on another mailing list you have acquired. You are going to offer a discount price of $35 (a $10 saving) to the next 500 people who sign up and pay for The Executive Card.

**E.** To ex-members who have been out of the program for a year or more, write a letter inviting them to rejoin and offer them a transistor radio premium if they rejoin within 35 days. The radio sells for about $20 retail.

**F.** Again, to a list of ex-members, write a letter with the theme of "Sign up two new members and your next year's membership is free!"

## VI. General Selectric Series

Assume that you are male and in the medical sales division of General Selectric. Three years ago you moved your family (a wife and two children) from Albany, Georgia, to Dallas, Texas (where you are now happily living in a four-bedroom, 2,100-square-foot home that you had to pay $140,000 for in order to be in a desirable school district and a good neighborhood). You sold the house in Albany for $65,000 and have felt strapped ever since because of the $1,000 monthly mortgage payments.

The first year was quite an adjustment period for the children and your wife (especially your wife, for she missed her friends and the slower pace of Albany). Now your son is well adjusted in elementary school and your daughter has just started middle school, where she also is well adjusted.

In Dallas you left sales (where you were in the top 2 percent of all General Selectric sales) for management (a step up the ladder, but down in pay because you have no bonus on the sales of medical equipment such as CAT scanners). You've enjoyed training sales representatives and have been all around Texas to help troubleshoot and to help boost sales.

Because of your good record, the company wants to move you to San Francisco, California, because sales have slipped there and you are needed to work with the sales representatives. When you mentioned the move to your wife, she brought up all the negatives—high-cost area to live; area with different people who have different values and lifestyle; problems of finding good home, school, friends; long way from the family in Texas; the stress and strain of a move; but mainly—she would have to give up her job as a professor at SMU.

You checked around and learned that an employee's saying no to a move used to be the kiss of death for the employee's career. But since you have moved once and have done well in sales and in management, your superiors would probably accept your turndown if you have good reasons. Some of the reasons for not wanting to move are your wife's job and the higher costs of living in San Francisco. On a company-paid trip to California, you found a house similar to the one you are presently living in, but it would cost a lot more. Goods and services you estimate to be more also.

One big concern is that your wife has just gone back to her teaching career and seems most happy with her work at SMU. Finding the same type of teaching assignment in the San Francisco area might be impossible or it might take years. What's more, with the high cost of living plus the even higher costs when the children go to college, you need two incomes. By staying in Dallas, you have many universities not too far away.

Also, even though General Selectric pays for your move, you found that before you still had hidden costs that the company did not pay for. You had to paint and fix up the Albany house so that it would sell. Then you had to paint and redo much of the house in Dallas so that it would be livable. There were also the costs of trips from Albany to Dallas that you paid for before the move.

And even though the children and your wife hated leaving Albany, they have adjusted well to Dallas. The children developed more self-assurance and the ability to adapt to new surroundings. Most of the feelings of depression and loneliness disappeared in six months for you, but it took your wife a year. The children found new friends as soon as school started. You had moved during the summer, thinking that was best because the school term would not be interrupted. Even though the company offered to buy the house in Albany (as it would in Dallas) if you could not sell it, you were able to sell it yourself, and you'd probably be able to sell the Dallas home too. The company will not give any financial assistance in purchasing a home.

Your immediate boss, Howard Keating, assures you that the move to San Francisco is not a lateral move but a move up, that it would be good experience, and that you would be groomed for senior-level management. Presently your salary is $40,000 and your wife's $24,000. If you moved to San Francisco, your salary would be $50,000.

Keating says that you have to put your decision in writing to him and that it would be wise to give your reasons if you turn down the assignment.

**A.** Write a memo to Keating saying that you will move to San Francisco.

**B.** Write a memo to Keating saying that you (will not) do not want to move to San Francisco.

**C.** Write a memo to Burt Knudsen, Keating's and your superior at the home office in Milwaukee, Wisconsin, explaining why you prefer to stay in Dallas until the children are through college (about 10 years).

**D.** Write a persuasive request to Burt Knudsen in Milwaukee asking if the company will give you a cost-of-living allowance that would help with the move from Dallas to San Francisco.

**E.** In considering the move to San Francisco, you discover that you will have to send your children to private schools. Some companies pay the private school tuition. Write Burt Knudsen asking (persuading) General Selectric to help you pay these additional costs of living in San Francisco rather than Dallas. Private school will cost an additional $5,000.

**F.** As Burt Knudsen, turn down the requests discussed in D. The company estimates that to move any executive costs around $40,000. The policy is to buy the mover's house if the mover cannot sell it. No additional financial help can be given at this time.

**G.** For Burt Knudsen, for the same reasons as those given in F, turn down the request to pay for private schools.

**H.** As Burt Knudsen, you've done some deeper managerial thinking and decided *not* to write Memo G—too big a chance of losing a good man (whom you need badly in San Francisco). So, instead, you reason (and explain to him) that paying him a separate cost-of-moving allowance and/or cost-of-private school allowance would be a precedent-setting action contrary to General Selectric policy but that nothing keeps you from bumping the base salary to $55,000 because he is a good man and you want to keep him.

**I.** General Selectric has an overseas assignment for manager in sales training and has narrowed the field to three people. As assistant personnel head, evaluate these people according to the following information: personality (genuine curiosity, patience, optimistic attitude, sense of humor, tolerance for ambiguity, ability to live with temporary setbacks); sales experience; record of sales with General Selectric; age; comments from rating sheets score on Management Potential Test; education.

You make up the names and facts on these three people and then recommend the one you think best for the assignment—but don't make the decision a pushover. Personality as specified makes more difference than the other points listed. Write a memo report to your personnel director.

**J.** Your company, General Selectric, 5830 S. Howell, Milwaukee, WI 53207, plans to have a week-long meeting of top management and sales representatives a year from today in Honolulu on Oahu Island. You have been looking at brochures about Hawaii and have decided that you need more information about three deluxe hotels: Hyatt Regency at Hemmeter Center, Hilton's Hawaiian Village on Kalia Road, and (one of the oldest but finest hotels) the Royal Hawaiian. You need to know the sizes of the auditoriums and conference rooms, whether these rooms are in the hotel or some adjoining area. Since the conference will be a week long—Wednesday through Tuesday (use exact dates)—and last over a weekend, what shows, exhibits, concerts, and so forth are available? Could the hotel provide an authentic luau one evening (preferably the last)? You would like more information about each hotel's tennis courts, swimming pool, and live entertainment. Are golfing facilities available? What about group rates on rooms? Complimentary suite for your president? Banquet facilities, menus? You will have 420 representatives and executives attending.

# VII. Horn Series

**A.** You (Jane or Jim Post) own a travel agency called Little Traveler, 289 Winterdale Drive, Kansas City, MO 64109. Your customers, Mr. and Mrs. Cecil Horn, 700 Haven Hill, Olathe, KS 66061, paid $3,298 each for a 22-day trip to Greece, Crete, Rhodes, Mykonos, Turkey for August 31–September 21 of this year. They did not buy the Tour Cancellation Protection Plan, which costs $25 per person—they assumed that all would be fine.

But Mr. Horn developed a malignant brain tumor, which was not diagnosed until August 5. Obviously, they think they cannot go on this tour/cruise. You've tried to find other people to go in their place but have not found anyone. Today you'll write or call Maupintour to see if it will refund the Horns' money. The Horns have gone to the Orient, Scandinavia, and South Pacific with Maupintour and have been most pleased.

**B.** As secretary to Taylor Maupin, write a letter for his signature to the Little Traveler saying that Maupintour cannot refund the money to the Horns since they had no Tour Cancellation Protection Plan and since it is just about 15 days before departure. With the Tour Cancellation Protection Plan, customers can cancel before the tour begins and receive a full refund of all money paid to Maupintour for land tour arrangements. Customers who must cancel from the tour en route are assured of a full refund for unused tour services. No cancellation penalties would be charged. If customers must pay additional airfare for an emergency return, then they'll be reimbursed for the lowest available fare for a direct return if flights were confirmed by Maupintour. Participation begins when the $25 fee is received by Maupintour. Fee is nonrefundable and valid for applicant only.

**C.** Mr. and Mrs. Cecil Horn came to your travel agency today and convinced you that they could go on the 22-day trip that they paid for. The tumor seems to be a small one, and the doctor will give Mr. Horn papers saying that he is well enough to travel. The Horns ask you, Jane or Jim Post, to write a persuasive letter (or to make a persuasive phone call) asking for permission for the Horns to go August 31. From your observation Mr. Horn looked well, seemed alert, was enthusiastic; but he said little since Mrs. Horn did all the talking. She was unhappy at not getting the $6,596 refund. But she was reasonable when you explained why Maupintour refused. Even though you doubt whether Mr. Horn should travel, you write the letter or make the phone call to Maupintour asking it to let the Horns make the trip.

**D.** Again as secretary to Taylor Maupin, you will reluctantly write a letter to the Horns saying that the Horns can go on the 22-day trip since the doctor said Mr. Horn was well enough.

**E.** Again as secretary to Taylor Maupin, you must write a letter refusing to let the Horns go on the trip. As page 135 of the Maupintour guide says, "Maupintour reserves the right not to accept or retain as a tour passenger any person whose mental or physical condition or general deportment impedes the operation of the tour or affects the rights, welfare, or enjoyment of other tour passengers." Although Mr. Horn seems all right today, he might not be two weeks from now. People with brain tumors can have convulsions, can become confused, can have problems with walking, talking, hearing, eating. You're glad that the Horns enjoyed the other trips with the company and hope that someday they will be well enough to go abroad.

**F.** For variation of the preceding case, assume that Maupintour has a cancellation policy that says that when a person cancels a tour 10 months before departure, the company makes a full refund. There's a 50 percent refund when the person cancels five months ahead but just a 15 percent refund when the person cancels a month (or less) before departure.

## VIII. HVG Series

**A.** As Senior Vice President, Dealer Division, HVG Company of America, 41 Rosewood Drive, Elmhurst Park, NJ 07409, write a sales letter to dealers promoting your new and lightweight HVG VIDEOMOVIE, an all-in-one camera and recorder. Consumers today are enjoying video recording with this easy-to-use product, and dealers are enjoying the profit and the 100 percent markup. VIDEOMOVIE is a full-performance camera that records natural colors with fine sharpness and clarity. Customers can connect it directly to a television set for viewing at home or in a hotel room.

To promote VIDEOMOVIE, you are running ads on CBS, NBC, and ABC before the evening news and half-page ads in *Tempo* and *Lifeo* magazines in October, November, and December (to stimulate Christmas buying). Warranty is for one year from date of purchase. HVG will repair any defect in material or workmanship in the item, free of charge.

Write a personalized sales letter, assume an enclosure, and try to get each dealer to buy from HVG.

**B.** As Senior Vice President, Consumer Division, HVG Company of America, write a sales letter to owners of your HVG videocassette recorders promoting VIDEOMOVIE, an all-in-one camera and recorder. You'll assume an enclosure of a brochure that has pictures of people loading, focusing, and shooting.

The camera and recorder functions include direct TV connection for playback (via provided cable) directly to the terminals of an AV television, or through a tiny RF converter (also provided) to the antenna terminal of regular TV. VIDEOMOVIE can be connected to other recorders and used as a master player for dubbing, editing, or transferring compact recordings to full-size cassettes; or it can be used as an independent camera for direct recording onto full-size cassettes.

In this letter you'll not mention price. The letter is to get interest, to get your reader to read your brochure, visit the local HVG dealer, or write you directly. Add appropriate details.

**C.** As a follow-up letter to owners of your HVG videocassette recorders and to promote VIDEOMOVIE, write another sales letter and include another brochure. But this time include an order blank and an addressed envelope. By ordering direct from HVG Company, the consumer gets the same one-year warranty. HVG repairs any defect in material or workmanship free of charge. Price from the company $750.

Add appropriate sales material based on current information about home video recorders now in use around the world.

**D.** As Director of Sales, HVG Company of America, you write a memo to your senior vice presidents of the Dealer and Consumer divisions and your ad agency account executive asking them to meet in your office next Wednesday at 10 A.M. You need to come to an agreement about the promotion of the HVG VIDEOMOVIE. Because the promotional campaign through television and magazines has not been successful, the company is going to have to change its promotion policy. Production was slowed because of a threatened strike, but that problem has been settled.

In the memo tell the vice presidents and the ad executive to come with plans as to how HVG can make consumers want the VIDEOMOVIE and how it can make the dealers want to sell them.

**E.** A potential customer (Horace Cummings, Rt. 2, City, State, and ZIP) wants an HVG VIDEOMOVIE as a Christmas gift for his family. He saw HVG's ad in the October issue of *Tempo* magazine and orders direct from the company in New Jersey. In his letter dated October 22, he said that he had tried to buy from two nearby local dealers and had been told that all VIDEOMOVIES were back-ordered until about two weeks before Christmas.

Assume that you are Senior Vice President, Dealer Division, HVG, and answer Cummings telling him that the company does not sell direct to consumers. Resale talk plus talk of the advantages of buying from a local dealer are most important.

# IX. IMB Series

**A.** Your company (IMB, a conglomerate, P.O. Box 1250, Westbury, NY 11595), will have to go up 5 percent on product prices and 10 percent on maintenance charges. Your job (as director of marketing) is to write a memo to customers who have your products and who plan to have you service them. Stress the idea that IMB gives quality service on quality products.

**B.** Write a memo to sales representatives telling them about the price increase.

**C.** Quickly write a memo to middle managers reminding them that IMB's policy is for them to take annual vacations and for them to make their plans known to headquarters by March 15.

**D.** A colleague of yours at IMB asks your opinion of an after-dinner speech he is making to a group of managers a month from now. You feel that the speech is too serious, too long, too scholarly. How are you going to tell your friend and colleague that this speech would be better as an article in a scientific journal than as an after-dinner speech?

Your friend's topic covers too broad a subject because it is on Major Methods of Job Evaluation: Ranking, Predetermined Grading, Point

Method, Factor Comparison, and Guide Chart-Profile Method plus other methods such as (1) the time span of discretion approach, (2) maturity curves, and (3) the guideline method.

**E.** As leader of a team with three other colleagues at IMB, you are working on an important project that is due two months from now. Today you learn that one of the main workers on the project, Donald D. Collins, has plans for a vacation for the first week of next month. His absence will make it impossible for the rest of the team to make progress. The other two colleagues on the team ask you to write Collins a memo requesting that he change his vacation plans so that the project can be completed on time. Could you suggest that the team work on Saturday or after work hours?

**F.** The board of directors of IMB wants to change the purchasing procedures. Assume that you are the vice president for materials management and that you are to write to plant purchasing managers about this change at IMB. From now on, you are to be notified about contracts in excess of $30,000 two weeks before contract signing and your office has to approve all contracts.

**G.** Each member of the class should write a letter or memo proposal on a project of his or her choice on a subject of special interest or knowledge. Address the proposal to an appropriate member of IMB management or to a prospective customer. For this assignment, you should have four main divisions: *(a)* introduction (objective, background information, description of general approach to doing the work), *(b)* discussion (what you intend to do, how you intend to do it, why you intend to do it that way, how long it will take you to complete it), *(c)* capabilities (background and knowledge to do work successfully, facilities and tools needed, time and help required), *(d)* conclusion (advantages of buying IMB product, why product is important to buyer, what buyer is to do, and when buyer should do it).

You can assume a one-page section that would have a summary of the hours it will take to complete the work (in dollars/hour), a list of the materials and their associated costs, overhead expenses (including transportation if appropriate), and profit.

**H.** IMB has to cut costs because last quarter's sales were 40 percent below average. The board of directors voted to curtail production, but it asked you to write a memo to all employees asking them which of the following cost-cutting methods they considered most satisfactory. IMB can close the plant for two weeks, ask for volunteers to take payless leave, shorten the workday to six hours, or lay off the last employees who were hired. As vice president in charge of public relations, you are to write the memo and tabulate the results. The tabulations will be presented to the board of directors next week. You will be glad to share the results with any employee who is interested.

**I.** As vice president in charge of public relations for IMB, you have been asked to write another memo to all employees asking them whether they would like to begin work at 8:30 instead of 9 and work until 4:30 instead of 5 for June, July, and August.

**J.** Another version of the preceding case could be that employees asked to get off at noon Friday and suggested that they begin each day at 8 A.M. instead of 9 A.M. In this way the plant could shut down at 12 noon Friday and employees would have a longer weekend than before. Many companies are doing this today. Do the employees want this plan?

**K.** As Joyce Tabtabai of the Industrial Relations and Personnel Department of IMB, invite all personnel to come to the cafeteria a week from Tuesday for free flu and pneumonia shots. Last winter absences due to flu and pneumonia increased 4 percent over the previous year.

**L.** IMB is going to give free health exams to all employees under age 40 who have been with the company a year. Employees just come by the Industrial Relations and Personnel Department and pick up the official health examination form. Examinations are not compulsory, but recommended. Doctors must be board-approved.
   Write the memo for Joyce Tabtabai.

**M.** You, Joyce Tabtabai, received a request from Sam Day, band director of the local high school. Day wants IMB to allow the band members to sell boxes of candy two weeks from now among the employees and on the premises of your plant. The proceeds from the sale will go for new band costumes and music. Company policy forbids such soliciting, and IMB's liability insurance policy does not cover such solicitors. Write a letter refusing Sam Day.

**N.** Another message you have to write today as Joyce Tabtabai will be a personal-sounding form letter that goes to people who have been writing IMB about not receiving gifts of $8\frac{1}{2}'' \times 11''$ reproductions of famous art paintings that hang on the walls of the company. Each year for the past 10, IMB has sent out free copies of some famous paintings to friends and customers. These reproductions have become most popular and have increased in cost.
   The cost of just providing the boxes and labor for packaging and mailing has doubled in the past eight years. Because of the high costs, the board of directors decided to discontinue the practice and asked

you to write the letter. Instead of the art package, IMB will mail New Year's cards. All of this sounded like a good idea until the company got many inquiries from customers and friends. Write the letter for Joyce.

**O.** As Eric Antonakes, personnel manager, IMB manufacturing plant in Springfield, Missouri, write a memo to your plant supervisors asking them to come to a meeting in your office next Wednesday at 4 P.M. to discuss the problem of workers who get injured on the job.

In the past 10 years the costs for disability coverage at IMB have quintupled. There must be a way to control the runaway costs. A major reason for the cost run-up, according to the National Council on Compensation Insurance, is that more workers are protected against a greater array of occupational hazards than ever before. Also, benefit levels have risen by more than 50 percent in the past 10 years. Two years ago (the latest year for which totals are available) claims paid under workers' compensation by insurance companies alone reached $8.6 billion—up from $2.2 billion 10 years earlier. IMB has been paying $2.43 for every $100 of payroll to cover workers against occupational hazards.

To help cut these costs, you feel that IMB should work to get workers back to jobs rather than continue them on disability pay. Often the disability pay approximates income received previously, because the benefits are tax-free. And because of the tax savings, injured employees have few incentives to "get well" and return to work.

**P.** Assume that you are a manager assistant in the personnel office at IMB headquarters and that you feel that the other people in personnel at the company's many plants and offices should be aware of the problems associated with the way women feel and should take some creative steps to meet these problems.

IMB has many female executives. According to a recent Gallup Poll survey of 722 female executives with the title of vice president or higher, many women feel that their roles in the male corporate world are often very difficult.

The survey shows that being female affects personal/social behavior: 61 percent say they have been mistaken for secretaries at business meetings; 60 percent feel cut off from social conversations or activities among male colleagues; 44 percent feel that older executives patronize them; 33 percent feel that the presence of female executives makes male executives more appearance conscious; and 24 percent feel uncomfortable about socializing with male colleagues because it would not look right.

According to the survey, being female affects job performance and evaluation also: 70 percent feel that they get less pay than men of equal ability; 60 percent have the impression that in certain areas their views get less respect than men's views; 41 percent feel that male subordinates feel threatened by female bosses and resist taking orders from them;

37 percent feel that their dress and appearance count more in evaluations of them than men's do; 29 percent feel that their personal lives get more scrutiny than men's; 20 percent feel that legal and social pressures to promote women often accelerate their professional advancement; and 7 percent feel that their bosses often pit them against other women in competition for a token top job.

Asked how they would like to see their work circumstances altered, 20 percent said that they would like more money or support for their department and 34 percent said that they would like more clout.

A majority of these female executives say that they meet regularly with other women to share information, discuss problems, and offer each other support. Networking is particularly common among the young, lower-level women (68 percent). Four out of five of these female executives say that they feel a responsibility to help their younger female colleagues up the corporate ladder.

With this information, write a justification report asking for suggestions of what IMB can do to help women executives adjust to the corporate world.

## X. Investments Series

**A.** Assume that you have been out of school long enough to have quite a bit of money to invest and have been using a broker in a nearby city who is with a long-established investment firm, Murial-Leach-Smothers, and Barney. You live in a small town, so must depend on brokers away from where you live. Your broker, Harold Baker, has been "hungry," so has been churning your account even though you did not give him discretionary authority. In the past six months he bought seven stocks (five losers) and sold seven stocks (six winners). Also, the interest payments from a municipal bond did not get into your account but apparently got into someone else's account.

When you called Baker and reported these facts, he said that he would not buy or sell anymore until he heard from you and that he would find the missing interest payment on the municipal bond. But a month after you talked with him, he still had not found the missing interest and he took money out of your Ready Assets account and bought Annon (forecast to be a leading oil stock).

Still disgusted, you called Baker again; but he convinced you that he had made the right move in buying Annon and that he and the firm would find the missing interest. He said that it had to be a human or computer error.

Another month goes by, and you are still dissatisfied; so you write a letter to the Regulation and Surveillance Unit of the New York Stock

Exchange, 11 Wall Street, New York, NY 10005, explaining your situation.

**B.** Still another month goes by, and you have heard nothing from Baker or the Regulation and Surveillance Unit; so you write another complaint letter (even stronger) to the Market Surveillance Department, National Association of Securities Dealers, 1735 K Street, NW, Washington, DC 20036.

**C.** Again these letters fail. So a friend of yours, Professor Virginia Hines, who teaches finance in a university nearby, told you that the SEC will be interested in a complaint, particularly if it involves fraud or violations of securities laws. You now write Consumer Affairs and Information Services, Securities and Exchange Commission, Washington, DC 20549.

**D.** Write Professor Hines (you make up the address) and tell her that you appreciate her kindness and information about record-keeping of your stocks. Since talking with her, you have heard from Consumer Affairs and Information Services. Harold Baker, former broker, is no longer with Murial-Leach-Smothers, and Barney; so you have a new broker (Sally Medberry) and have a new system of keeping your accounts straight.

**E.** As time goes along, you continue to lose money in the stock market; but even worse you frittered away some money on trips as well as on some horses at the Kentucky and other derbies. The crushing blow, however, was when your job was phased out and you've not been able to get another job until three months from now. Never did you think you would be out of money. Can't pay the rent and can't borrow from family or from the bank (because you do not have a good credit rating). In desperation you write your professor friend, Virginia Hines, and ask for a $1,000 loan until you start work in three months. Offer to pay the going rate of interest on the loan. Be frank in telling your story like it is.

**F.** Virginia Hines has to turn down the $1,000 loan because she has the responsibility of nursing-home payments for her father, house payments, and college expenses for her son. University salaries have increased 4 percent from last year, but that's not enough to help her meet her increased expenses. The money she made on the market will help, but she's faced with increased income taxes. Can you, as the writer for Virginia Hines, think of any source where the high-living friend might get some money for three months? The loan sharks should be avoided!

# XI. Management Series

**A.** Write a form letter individually addressed on a word processing machine to 7,000 executives in such firms as IBM, Borg-Warner, PPG Industries inviting them to attend a five-day seminar for $1,650 in Clearwater, Florida. (The sessions will be at the Bobo headquarters daily 9–12 and 1–4, leaving time for golf, tennis, swimming at the many recreational places. You can add details that are appropriate.)

Leader of the seminar will be Robert Bobo, 57, the leading evangelist of quality in the United States and author of five books about successful management. Bobo acquired his management insights on the factory floor, starting in 1953 as a $75-a-week inspector of radar equipment. By 1961, while a quality manager of the Pershing missile program at Martin, he conceived the Zero Defects policy, which urged workers to sign no-flaw pledges and recognized those with perfect performances.

Later Bobo became director of quality at TII; and with slogans like "Make Certain" and "Buck a Day" and "We Can Make It," he created a system of quality managers throughout TII that has been used by other large corporations. Seven years ago he left TII to start his own firm (Bobo, Inc., 500 Bayview Avenue, Clearwater, FL 33515), which now has more than 100 employees and revenues of $23 million for last year.

**B.** For background information, read the preceding case. Assume that the university where you go to school received a $2 million grant from RMB, a leading manufacturer, and set up an Institute for Manufacturing and Automation for engineering and business students. The feeling is that universities of the future educating the people are necessary to factories for the future. Three months from now your school plans a conference on manufacturing for the 600 students in the program and possibly 1,000 executives. You've read about Robert Bobo and read his philosophy in his popular book *Can Quality Be Free?* (which has attracted almost a cult following among managers since its publication three years ago). Write Bobo a persuasive letter asking him to be the keynote speaker (9–10 A.M.) at your conference. You name the specific place and dates. You will have his five books on display and will have someone in charge of selling the books. Your school has no money to pay him an honorarium.

**C.** As an assistant to Robert Bobo, write a refusal to Catharine Crosby, explaining that Bobo cannot be the keynote speaker at the conference of the Institute for Manufacturing and Automation three months from now. At that time Bobo will be directing a three-day seminar for executives in Mexico City. Perhaps Bobo could come to the campus at another time and be the keynote speaker. Bobo appreciates being invited and having his books promoted. (You'll make up other details and the address of Catharine Crosby.)

**D.** As Robert Bobo, write an acceptance to Catharine Crosby to be the keynote speaker at the conference of the Institute for Manufacturing and Automation.

**E.** Play the role of Juan Durate, 6 Rhin, Mexico DF. You just attended the three-day seminar for executives in Mexico City and feel you learned a great deal about quality management from Robert Bobo of Bobo, Inc. After the seminar you have had several meetings of the workers at your plant and have put into practice some of the Bobo philosophy. Write a goodwill letter to Robert Bobo.

**F.** As Bill Rosenblatt, production manager for one of GPP Industries, you are to write a memo to your boss, Harvey Mappin, reporting on your five-day seminar that cost the company $1,650 plus another $1,000 for travel, hotel, and meals. Before going to the seminar in Clearwater, you had read all five of Robert Bobo's books. Most of the seminar came from Bobo's best-seller *Can Quality Be Free?* Bobo, a showman, had lots of razzle-dazzle and pizzazz with colorful slogans, banners, video-tapes, slides, movies, pamphlets, and other handouts. In the buzz sessions you learned that most of the managers were aware of the need to increase efficiency and reduce costs.

Deere has changed its slogan to "Nothing runs like a Deere factory"; and in its new plant in Waterloo, Iowa, it is using computer-controlled assembly techniques to turn out many tractor models, bearing as many as 3,000 options without costly plant shutdowns for retooling.

AT&T Technologies in Richmond, Virginia, has computers that receive complex instructions from a dozen Bell Laboratories design centers in the United States. Instructions are used to turn out on demand a limitless variety of circuit boards containing hundreds of parts. The company can change designs overnight without interrupting production.

Companies are using computer-driven robots, lasers, and ultrasonic probes. For example, GE invested $38 million to modernize an outdated dishwasher factory in Louisville. Now central computer panels, sometimes monitored by just one person, check the full range of production and part supplies. The manufacturing process cuts down on waste of steel, plastic, and rubber hoses. Controls can be quickly reprogrammed to make any of 15 dishwasher models.

Even though you enjoyed the seminar, you really didn't learn anything that was not in Bobo's five books. Should you tell your boss this? Recommend that the company buy Bobo's books for the company library.

**G.** As Harvey Mappin, of GPP Industries, acknowledge the memo report from your production manager, Bill Rosenblatt, and tell him that you have ordered Bobo's five books for the company library. Now the problem will be to get production managers to read the books. Also, you would like to talk with Rosenblatt about using computer-driven robots; so suggest a time and place for a conference.

**H.** A few weeks after the preceding memo, Bobo's five books arrive and are placed in the company library. Now it's Mappin's job to write a memo to all managers urging them to read the books—especially the best one, *Can Quality Be Free?* After the managers have time to read the books, you plan to call a meeting to discuss the books and to see how GPP Industries can apply some of the philosophy.

**I.** Time passes, but only several managers at GPP Industries check out Bobo's books. For Harvey Mappin, write another memo to your managers urging them to read Bobo's books. You plan to have a meeting to discuss the Bobo philosophy and its application in 10 days in the company boardroom from 5 to 6.

**J.** Well, you (Harvey Mappin) had the meeting in the boardroom and all GPP managers attended, but just a few had read Bobo's main book, *Can Quality Be Free?* You felt that the meeting was a flop even though you got Bill Rosenblatt to talk about Bobo's philosophy and about the seminar he attended in Clearwater. You still want to get the managers to think of new ways to increase efficiency and to cut costs. So for Mappin write another memo pressing for input from the managers. Again urge them to read Bobo's books and come up with ideas and philosophies for GPP.

## XII. New Zealand

**A.** As Nelson Barns (110 Vista Drive, Redondo Beach, MD 21229), divorced and father of Winston Barns (age 10), you have the problem of sending Winston to private schools at Christchurch, New Zealand, so that he can be near his natural mother during the next year. You don't feel that your divorced wife (Winston's mother) has very good judgment about schools; so you will write the superintendent of education at Christchurch and ask for help in finding Winston the best school. You want Winston to have a good foundation in the basics as well as in foreign languages. He tests high on all achievement exams.

**B.** Professor Thomas C. M. Ford, 9870 University Drive, Christchurch, New Zealand, highly recommends three schools to Nelson Barns because of their outstanding faculties, sound programs, academic achievements: St. Andrew and St. Christopher (both Episcopalian schools) or Stillman (Presbyterian). All three schools require that students wear uniforms and that they include a foreign language starting in the third grade.

**C.** For Nelson Barns, write one letter to each of the three schools Professor Ford recommended. What are some specific things you will ask? Since Winston likes school and has a high IQ, you want him to go to college and be well prepared for the competitive international world. You feel that being good in math, science, English, foreign languages is most important in today's global society. Cost enters in, too.

**D.** As Timothy McClaren, headmaster, St. Andrew Preparatory School, 220 Cambridge Street, Christchurch, New Zealand, answer Nelson Barns with the following information: language choice for elementary grades is French, German, and Spanish; for other grades, Chinese, Japanese, Russian as well as advanced French, German, Spanish. Students write compositions in English starting with third grade. By the time they are out of the elementary grades, they are ready to do research papers.

Not only do the students have a sound foundation in math, but they are ready for computer science by their junior year. Courses in political science, anthropology, psychology, sociology, geography, astronomy, physics are available along with the regular program of 12 years of English, 4 of Latin, 8 of history, 12 of math, science as shown in the enclosed catalog.

Students can live at home and attend school or they can board at the school. Cost varies accordingly. All 500 students wear uniforms and attend daily short church services. For enrichment, there are courses in music, drama, and art. Concerts, plays, art shows go on all year at St. Andrew.

For sports, students have the choice of swimming, track, cricket, soccer, fencing, rugby (but not football, baseball, or basketball). St. Andrew has competitive games with St. Christopher and Stillman.

Students are tested for academic achievement in 3d, 6th, 8th, and 12th grades. If a student scores high on a math test in the third grade, for example, that student will not stay with the average third-grade math class but will move according to ability and achievement. The same goes for other courses. All teachers have at least the master's degree, and many have Ph.D.'s.

**E.** After you get the helpful letter from Headmaster Timothy McClaren, St. Andrew, you write him a thank-you letter for Nelson Barns. You plan to be in New Zealand next month to get Winston for his annual visit to Maryland; so you will stop by the school and look over the campus and talk with some of the teachers.

# XIII. Shopping Center Series

**A.** As _____, manager of a regional strip shopping center (30 stores and offices), you have the job of explaining to a prospective tenant how your lease works. Different for each store, it's what is called a triple net lease, the same kind used by 90 percent of all shopping centers, regardless of their size. On top of a base rent, each tenant pays a pro rata share of the community expense, such as parking lot cleaning, snow removal, and lighting of the outside of the building and the parking lot. Each tenant also pays a similar proportion of the real estate taxes and of the fire and casualty insurance.

The share of the expenses paid depends on the square footage of the store or office divided by the 175,000 square feet total in the shopping center. The prospective tenant wants to lease 10,000 square feet. It's an old drugstore that he could turn into an appliance store. You'd like to add an appliance store to your tenant mix; so persuade him that the lease is a good deal. Base rent is about $2,000.

**B.** As _____, send a memo or letter to each of your tenants informing them of a summer tabloid advertising section that is available to them. All tenants must belong to the Merchants Association (it's in the lease), which arranges for shopping center advertising, promotion, and special events. The board of directors of the Merchants Association met and decided that the cover of the tabloid section would have a football weekend theme because it's the high school's homecoming weekend. The tabloid will have eight pages altogether; just the cover will feature the shopping center name, logo, general ad. Individual stores can pay for their own ads inside. Members of the Merchants Association pay about 7 cents per square foot a year for such group advertising. The front page will cost $400. Let members know deadlines for placing individual ads and offering suggestions for the group ad.

**C.** Rumors have been flying around your small town that the shopping center is to be sold. The previous owners are getting to retirement age and, in fact, spend the cold winters in resort areas that are warmer. The three of them are all local people, though, and the tenants fear an owner from the nearby city, who will probably be a shrewd businessperson, an outsider, and one who squeezes them for profits. The average tenant in a shopping center pays 5–10 percent of gross sales for rent, in addition to paying a share of expenses. For example, a drugstore pays 5 percent; a jewelry store, 8 percent; a dry cleaner, 10 percent (no merchandise cost, just the franchise and chemicals); a grocery store, 1.5 percent; and a ladies' ready-to-wear store, 7 percent.

As manager of the shopping center, call a meeting for 7 P.M. next Wednesday (after most of the stores close). All managers and owners are supposed to be there. How will you tell them that you plan to stay in your job, that the new owner (who *is* a successful businessman from a large city) plans to change nothing now but hopes to make improvements later? He wants a one-on-one relationship with his tenants. Add details you think appropriate to convince the tenants that the change is positive.

**D.** As Mary Robbins, president of the Smoky Hills Summer Playhouse, write to Toby Richardson, owner of the Smoky Hills Shopping Center, and ask him to be on the playhouse board. The playhouse presents five plays between June 1 and August 30 every summer. You've been in operation for over 50 years and offer opportunities for local college students and actors to appear in productions. You can afford to use only a few Equity players (who command higher salaries), but the operation is financially sound. You've even found enough money to build a new dormitory in the woods for the students who come for the summer. You think it would help the theater raise money if successful business owners got involved on the board.

**E.** As manager of the shopping center, you negotiate the snow removal contract every year in September. You contract the job out because the equipment is very expensive. You pay an average of $80 an hour for payloaders, dump trucks, and road graders; and all removal must be done between 9:30 P.M. and 8 A.M. If the snowfall is 3.5 inches or over, the snow removal crew goes to work. Because the last two years have been very cold and snowy and hard on the contractor's equipment, he's raising his rates to $90 per hour. You must pass the increase on to tenants as part of their pro rata maintenance share. Tell them the bad news.

**F.** As the owner of the chain of grocery stores that is represented in the shopping center, notify the manager that you will not be renewing your lease. In fact, you're moving out six months early because the grocery business is so low margin that you're going out of business because of the new superstores in town. Your lease expires December 31, and you're notifying the manager on June 1. (Your lease requires six months' notice.)

**G.** As manager of the shopping center, you now have 20,000 square feet that will be empty. You'll also have six months' rent on the empty space (preceding case), but a new store would earn even more money for you. Go to your prospective tenants file and write a letter to the ones who've expressed interest who could use that much space. (For example, a typical dime store takes 11,000 feet; a coffee shop, 1,900; a department store, 40,000; a liquor store, 10,000.)

**H.** As _____, manager, write a sales letter to Kiddie Korner, 302 West 87th Street, New York, NY 10024, inviting it to locate one of its branches in your mall. Space rents for average $1.50 square foot. You have no children's shop to compete, but you have a vast cornucopia of goods for every taste. Assume an enclosure with pictures of the mall and a map showing where Kiddie Korner could locate. Space has 4,000 square feet, area just redecorated. Stores on each side of the area do large volume of business.

**I.** A local drugstore owner writes to you, the shopping center manager, and says he wants the space you have vacant. He'll move his existing store in your center (10,000 square feet) and also move in his liquor store from the north end of the shopping center (3,200 square feet) plus his liquor store in your competitor's center directly across the street. The grocery store space will need $125,000 of remodeling to hold the new operation. He wants you to pay. Assume that you will grant his request.

**J.** The only way you as manager can see to pay for the remodeling is for the drugstore owner to accept an increase of $1 per square foot in his lease and to take a 10-year lease. (Most leases are for five years.) Once the $125,000 plus the interest of prime plus 1 percent is paid off, the rent will go down a dollar, of course. The drugstore owner doesn't want to use his money for the remodeling because he needs it for inventory. He needs to add a rear entrance ($30,000), new heating and air conditioning units ($52,000), a new ceiling ($20,000), floor covering ($15,000), and additional electric wiring ($8,000). Persuade him to see it your way.

**K.** You're the owner of a decorator shop, and you want to move into the space left by the moving of the liquor store (3,200 square feet). Your country cottage theme requires that you paper all the walls, insert a small-pane effect into the large front windows, and build a plank floor that extends into the sidewalk of the shopping center. The landlord is responsible for the exterior walls of the center, the roof, and the foundation of the building. Tenants are responsible for their own sidewalk maintenance and cleaning, maintenance on the heating and air conditioning of their stores, interior improvements, and their own security. All interior changes must have the shopping center manager's approval. Get his approval.

# XIV. S. P. Rand Series

**A.** As vice president of employee relations for S. P. Rand, Inc., manufacturers of paper products (with 5,000 workers at this plant at Lake Bluff, Missouri), you have the job of writing a message to each worker on the problem of the rise in benefit costs in the past 30 years. If the company adds any more benefits, some of the previous ones will have to be taken away.

Benefits this year cost $7,187 per employee—up 8.5 percent from last year. Ten years ago the average fringe benefits per worker were just $3,230; 10 years before that—$1,431; and 10 years before that—$720. Fringe benefits now cover Social Security (employer's share averages $1,274); life, health insurance, $1,274; pensions, $1,040; paid vacations, $902; paid holidays, $553; paid rest periods, $532; unemployment compensation, $269; workers' compensation, $258; sick leave, $244; profit sharing, $218; other (moving and termination pay), $632.

A few of your 5,000 employees are pushing for dental insurance. Management feels that employee benefits must be curtailed rather than expanded. From the employee's standpoint, many of these benefits are not subject to taxation and thus are a very cost-effective way of providing the employee with real income. Write the message telling the workers the benefit story.

**B.** Using the information in the preceding case, write a memo to all workers telling them about a new policy that they will not like; so you'll have to phrase it as positively as possible. The paid rest periods (such as lunch breaks) are costing the company $532 per employee. Many workers have been taking too long for lunch (20 to 30 minutes beyond the scheduled time). Starting the first of next month, you will omit this paid rest period.

**C.** Assume that the company decides to omit all benefits for moving in order to keep the costs of fringe benefits reasonable. Write the message as positively as you can.

**D.** Now the workers want dental insurance, which would add too much money per worker to the total fringe benefit package. All workers get fringe benefits as stated in A except the paid rest periods and moving costs. Business is still slow nationally and internationally despite all the predictions that the recession will soon be over. Refuse the workers free dental insurance.

**E.** Now it's a year later and business has improved, sales are up nationally and internationally, and the recession seems put to bed. You have the good news to tell your employees that now they can enjoy another fringe benefit—dental insurance for themselves but not for the family. Remind them of all the benefits they have in working for S. P. Rand, Inc.

# XV. Technical Business Machines Series

**A.** As Harry Wright, assistant to the sales manager for TBM, 1800 Industrial Drive, Detroit, MI 48208, write to the sales manager of one of the following inns in Cleveland, Ohio, asking questions and giving explanations. You are looking for facilities for a small sales meeting (25), May 20–21, but rooms for two nights, May 19–20. You do not know how many singles and doubles you'll need. Any specials for group rates? Want one lecture room with projection screen both days (8:30–5). Want coffee served in lecture room about 10 A.M. and 2 P.M. and would like sweet rolls if price is reasonable. Want lunch May 20 and 21 and dinner May 20 plus a cash bar before dinner. Is there a charge or minimum for cash bar?
*Inns:*

Downtown Plaza Motor Hotel, 314 Broadway, Cleveland 26501

Hampshire House Motor Lodge, 1135 Hamilton Parkway, 26515

Merritt-Meyer Motels, The Cleveland Downtowner, 919 Washington Avenue, 26508

Travelers' Inn, 11234 River Road, 26558.

**B.** Reply to Harry Wright for one of the inns that appeals to you (or your teacher assigns) and invite him to visit.

1. Downtown Plaza (10 miles from airport) has corporate rates $47 single or $56 double (two twin beds) per night. Luncheon menu prices $4.65–6.25. Dinner $11.50–13. No charge for cash bar. No charge for projection screen, but lecture room costs $50 for two days. Coffee and croissants or sweet rolls add $75 per day. All prices include taxes and gratuities.

2. Hampshire House has corporate deal for one person $43 or $51 for two people. Meeting room (seats 30) for two nights and two days costs $30. Dinners cost $17 (including $1.75 for dessert that can be

omitted). Luncheons vary from $4.50 (soup and salad) to $6.50 per person. No charge for coffee, but croissants are $1.50 per person per service. Orange juice sells for $0.75. All meeting rooms have screens but no projectors. To set up cash bar, have to have $100 minimum. Another arrangement is to have waiter from lounge (40 feet away) take drink orders. Close to airport.

3. Merritt-Meyer, 12 miles from airport, has block rates for single rooms if there are 15-room reservations ($40 single, $48 double). Regular commercial rate is $49.50. All prices include gratuities and tax, as do lunch and dinner prices. Luncheons cost $6.60 per person, and dinners $15.40. Coffee break service twice per day costs $4.50 per person and includes sweet rolls in morning. Soft drinks may be substituted. Small meeting rooms already booked for May 20–21, but have combined dining and meeting room, with folding door partition at no charge. Have no projector or screen. No fee or minimum charge for cash bar, but soft drinks are $1.50 each, and mixed, $2–2.50. Wine served with dinner runs $7 per liter.

4. Travelers' Inn has meeting rooms with projection screens and equipment, rent $20 per day. Block rate (for 10 rooms or more) runs $32.70 per night (including taxes and gratuities). Luncheons (salad, hot rolls, soup, dessert choices) cost $7 (buffet style). Full smorgasbord for dinner costs $13. Changes in or additions to standard menu can be arranged with highly rated management at Gatepost Restaurant. No charge to set up cash bar. Drinks run $2. Coffee bar service available at $0.70 per cup (coffee or tea); $0.50 per glass of fruit juice or canned beverage; sweet rolls, $0.50 each; bagels and cream cheese $0.35 each.

**C.** As Harry Wright, consolidate all the data and write a memo report to your boss, Peter Santos, recommending one of the inns. You inspected all the inns and find the rooms very clean, comfortable, tastefully decorated. All offer limousine service at airport for either $2 or $2.50 (one way). Most of your salespeople prefer to drive, and the freeway approaches are good for any of the four inns.

Providing your own projector or screen would be no problem.

Latest sales meeting bills indicate that each sales rep would consume, in addition to meals, four cups of coffee (or other beverage) per day, 2.5 drinks, two sweet rolls. (At cash bar, reps pay for own drinks, and drinks are not allowed on expense account.)

**D.** Mr. Santos agrees with your choice and instructs you to write, for his signature, a letter to the inn you recommend. You will want to be explicit about any additions or changes you want the inn to make in accordance with suggestions that others offered but that were not specified in the bid. You will expect the inn to send or bring you a formal contract within a week.

## XVI. Trendy Computer Series

**A.** As CEO of Trendy Computers, P.O. Box 7654, Cupertino, MA 05141, you've been aware since 1979 that some companies are giving sabbaticals to some of their employees. If Trendy decides to offer sabbaticals, who should get them, how long should they last, should the employees vote on having them, should employees submit an application with an outline of what they intend to do while on a sabbatical, would sabbaticals help executives get rid of burnout? Realizing that you should not make such a decision yourself, you call a meeting of your board of directors. Write the memo for the CEO, encouraging the directors to bone up on the question and attend the called meeting.

**B.** After several meetings and extensive investigations as to what other companies were doing about sabbaticals, you (the CEO) and your board of directors agreed to let all of your 4,000 U.S. salaried employees be eligible after four years with the company for a six-week sabbatical in addition to normal accrued vacation time. Employees will have to apply for the sabbatical six months before it starts, and they should indicate in their application what they intend to do (such as pursue a serious interest in a project that they wouldn't be able to pursue during regular work). Employees do not have to (but are encouraged to) write a follow-up on what they did while enjoying this personal growth period.

The CEO has turned the job of writing the memo and the sabbaticals policy statement over to you, the personnel director.

**C.** One of your key employees (55-year-old Richard Seidel) hit all the beaches in Hawaii, Fiji, the Caribbean, and Mexico. After such an enjoyable eight weeks (two weeks accrued vacation and six for sabbatical), he wants to retire next year. Since his wife just came into a sizable estate, money is no problem. But you, the personnel director, have the problem of trying to persuade him to stay on with the company. Write a memo giving him valid reasons why he should stay. (You'll have to make up the reasons.) Write the memo for the personnel director.

**D.** Now assume that you are Richard Seidel and that you have the job of refusing the request of John Richards, the personnel director, for staying on beyond next year with Trendy Computers. You've been with the company steadily since it was founded 14 years ago. You've worked long and hard and helped put the company on its feet with your mind, body, and even some of your money (when things were rough). Your personal reasons of enjoying your wife and children and your love for travel are the main reasons you are retiring early. You'll always be interested in the company and will watch it from some beach somewhere. You found out that you really didn't miss the company, the 9–5 job.

Write the refusal for Richard Seidel to the personnel director.

**E.** Now assume that you are a key employee, Carey English, age 36, who has been with Trendy Computers three years. You are experiencing stress, nervousness, burnout, lack of creativity—and feel you need a six-week sabbatical. You took your one-week vacation six months ago and got some relief, but not enough. Even though you have not been with the company four years, you want to persuade it to let you take leave now. For Carey English, write the persuasive memo to the personnel director.

**F.** As personnel director, you took Carey's persuasive memo in to the CEO, and he and you agreed that the company could not start making exceptions to the sabbatical ground rules. One year from now, when Carey has completed four years with the company—then the sabbatical rewards Carey. Write the refusal for the personnel director.

## XVII. West Mill Road Series

**A.** As a real estate developer (Selfridge's), P.O. Box 987, Winston-Salem, NC 27198, you have to write a client, Mrs. Atley Jeffrey, CLU, P.O. Box 7654, Charlotte, NC 28290, clearing up a misunderstanding. Jeffrey, an insurance representative, rents 865 square feet at a monthly rent of $500 in an attractive building at 3640 West Mill Road.

Jeffrey's office called you and asked that you clean its carpets. You explained that your rents are normally structured to anticipate cleaning only at the beginning or on renewal of a lease but that some tenants elect to have their carpets cleaned at their own expense during any such term. The lease started December 20 two years ago and is due for renewal in one year, but you have no renewal provision. You spent about $10,000 in redoing the hall areas and in repainting the exterior of the building in hopes of making the vacant space more leasable and of retaining the goodwill and continuity of tenancy of existing tenants.

When Jeffrey saw that you had recarpeted some offices across the hall, she wrote you and asked you why you didn't recarpet the space in the insurance suite. Explain in a letter that you are leasing this recarpeted area for $8.22 per square foot. The recarpeting of that space was part of a renegotiation that increased the rent from $6.50 per square foot. Offer to renegotiate Jeffrey's lease for an extended term at a higher rate—with improvements of her choosing "factored in."

**B.** Apparently your letter to Atley Jeffrey satisfied her and she continued to rent your space on West Mill Road, but she failed to pay last month's rent; so you sent a reminder and phoned. She promised to get a check in the mail soon. Said she was just swamped with business. Another month goes by, and you made a personal visit and found her not in, but you talked with a bookkeeper who said that Jeffrey was thinking of moving but assured you that you would get the check.

You have a difficult message to write because you want to keep Jeffrey in your building and you want to collect the money for the two months' rent ($1,000). Write the letter.

**C.** Two and one-half months beyond the due date, you get Jeffrey's check. Write a thank-you letter with touches of resale on the desirable location, good parking space, nice neighbors in the other rented offices.

**D.** Even though you wrote a good letter that brought a compliment from the receptionist at Jeffrey's office, you still get a feeling that you must do some selling to keep Jeffrey in your building. She's been there 2½ years and her lease is up in six months. Offer to renegotiate her lease and to redecorate the insurance suite (see A). Offer to come to Charlotte and work out the details at her convenience.

**E.** Jeffrey told you when you went to see her that she would like to continue to rent from you and that she preferred to skip the redecorating. She added that business was off; so she didn't want to increase her basic rent. Two months after that discussion (but still with no renewal contract), you find that you have to go up on your rents. Her increase will be to $7.45 per square foot annually. Write the bad-news letter to Jeffrey.

**F.** John Chandler, manager of Business Consulting and Research, has been renting from month to month (since 1984) two separate areas in your West Mill Road building. He has paid $7.45 per square foot for 759 total square feet; and for a storage area (510 square feet), he's paid $2.50 annual rent per square foot. He's been a faithful tenant (paid on time), but you know from your many conversations with him that he's been having a struggle getting his business established. You would like to persuade him to have a renewal provision, and you want to keep him as a satisfied tenant. You also have to tell him that there will not be an increase in the rent of the storage area but that there will be an increase in price of $0.60 to $8.05 per square foot for the 759-square-foot suite. Write Chandler a letter using persuasion and bad-news strategy.

**G.** As real estate developer of Selfridge's, write a form message in memo form telling your six tenants that you are glad to have them at West

Mill Road, that you hope their businesses are thriving, and that you are going to replace the roof and put new wallpaper in the two lavatories in two weeks.

# XVIII. Republic Series

**A.** Your company, Republic Co., Glenford Road, Farmingdale, NY 11735, builds military jet aircraft. Absenteeism averages 5.3 percent of scheduled working time. Disputes between supervisors and employees have led to shouting matches on the plant floor, and often these arguments are settled through fistfights in the parking lot. You and other officials feel that shop-floor bosses are a key to the company's problems because workers are being made shop-floor bosses with little or no preparation, and some tend to bully those underneath their control.

You (supervisor of training and development) have read about Zenger-Muller, 1010 Brighton Way, Bakersfield, CA 93309, a consulting firm that has sold to 250 companies since 1980 its 15-week courses that include role playing and studying videotapes of typical contacts between bosses and workers. You talked with several executives at Honeywell and American Can who said the course was most beneficial to their companies because the morale of supervisors improved. The 15-week course is a three-hour session every other week. Participants memorize lines like "Calmly describe X's (the employee's) behavior which concerns you" or "Express support and reassurance for X."

Write a memo to your superior, Harvey Sonora, vice president—industrial relations, suggesting that Republic send 93 supervisors from the plant through the course. Cost per supervisor runs $750. But as Linda Dodson (director of employee relations for Republic) says, "You pay for personnel training programs in one way or another. They cost you either in money up front or in lost productivity in the end."

**B.** As supervisor of training and development for Republic, write a memo to the 93 supervisors (shop-floor bosses) who were selected to attend the Zenger-Muller 15-week course. The supervisors will be learning through example, through role playing, and through using videotapes. They will be exposed to typical contacts between bosses and workers. Their course meets for one three-hour session every other week in the Conference Room at the nearby Holiday Inn (Fivepoints East) starting two weeks from this coming Monday. Republic pays for the course and pays the employee's wages while the worker is at the course. Each supervisor will be released from work to attend the course at the time on the enclosed card.

Convince the supervisors that their jobs will be easier, that morale should improve, that absenteeism should be reduced as a result of this course. More than 750 corporations have used similar methods with excellent results.

For more information about the Zenger-Muller course, invite these supervisors to a meeting next Tuesday, 10 A.M. or 2 P.M. in the company cafeteria.

**C.** *Your company:* Zenger-Muller. *Company that owes you:* Republic Co. *Amount owed:* $69,750. *Past due:* 60 days. *For:* Zenger-Muller Training Course for 93 shop-floor supervisors held at Holiday Inn Fivepoints East, Farmingdale, NY 11735. Course was for 15 weeks, with one three-hour session every other week, starting October 10. Course included learning through example, role playing, videotaping. The 93 supervisors wrote evaluations at end of sessions, and these were sent to vice president Harvey Sonora and Linda Dodson, director of employee relations for Republic.

You sent a statement 30 days ago, but it was ignored. Send a personal note with resale on the course. According to evaluations, the supervisors were/are most enthusiastic, morale is good, behavior should be changed as a result of the course.

**D.** Write a middle-stage collection letter to Republic to collect the $69,750 now 120 days past due.

Because you heard nothing from your persuasive collection letter when the account was 60 days old, you phoned the accounting department at Republic when the account was 90 days old and got a promise from Sarah Day that a check would be in the mail. She did tell you that the company won an Air Force productivity award for its work on the A-10 Thunderbolt II jet fighter and that Harvey Sonora circulated a memo congratulating the workers and praising the shop-floor supervisors. Harvey told her that he thought the course of Zenger-Muller was mostly responsible for the improved working conditions. Sarah talked about layoffs, high costs, but insisted she'd have a check to you in a week.

No check came, so you phoned again a week later. Again Day reported that a check would be mailed. You sent another statement with a note on it in your handwriting that the company had not received payment (when the account was 104 days old) but got no response.

Since your company feels that Republic has the money (revenues last year of $1.4 billion), write an appeal letter now that the account is 120 days past due.

**E.** The appeal you wrote from Zenger-Muller to Republic got no results, and now the bill is 150 days old. You phoned Harvey Sonora when the account was 127 days old and talked with him about the Air Force award and tried to find out why your company wasn't paid for the supervisors' course. Harvey said that accounting was not his department and he knew nothing about the business it did. He did give you the name of the head of accounting (J. S. Raymond) and suggested that you write Raymond directly.

The letter you'll write Raymond is much more forceful, an urgency letter, and you'll review all your previous collection efforts.

# Appendix C

## Concise Writer's Handbook

This alphabetical list of short, easy-to-remember **symbols** will save teachers time in marking papers and will help students by giving brief explanations of many writing problems.

The **symbols** (the **boldfaced** part of each entry) are easy to learn because they are nearly all abbreviations of already familiar grading or proofreading terms. Even the few unalphabetized ones at the end are mostly standard proofreader's marks.

The list includes the suggestions most students will need for improving their English.

**Ab** Before using an abbreviation, make sure it is appropriate, understood, and standard (including capitalization, spacing, and punctuation—though *Webster's Ninth New Collegiate* allows some choices).

**Ac**curacy Get facts, names, addresses, and statements right.

**Accus**ations See Chapter 4.

**Ad**apt to your reader's interests, reading ability, and experience. See Chapter 5.

**Adj/Adv** Be sure you use the right form of a word for its function in the sentence. For the comparative and superlative forms, see **Cpr** 3.

**Ag**reement of subjects with their verbs and of pronouns with their antecedents is essential to clear, inconspicuous communication. Don't be confused by other words that come between two that are supposed to agree.

1. Notice that the first sentence about agreement is an illustration of the first point: *agreement* (singular) is the subject of the verb *is;*

643

but between them is a prepositional phrase with four plurals. As other illustrations, consider

Selection of topics *depends* on the reader's knowledge and interests.

Lee also tells how important the arrangement of the records offices *is.*

*Part, series, type,* and other words usually followed by plural phrases are frequently pitfalls to the unwary writer:

The greatest part of their investments *is* in real estate.

A series of bank loans *has* enabled the firm to stay in business.

2.  *Any, anyone, each, every, everyone, everybody, either,* and *neither* all point to singular verbs (and pronouns)—except that in an either-or situation, with one noun singular and one plural, verbs and pronouns agree with the closer noun.

Any of the women in the group *is* willing to give some of *her* time to helping the group when asked.

Either board members or the president *has* power to act on the point.

Neither the mayor nor the council members *are* allowed to use city-owned automobiles in transacting *their* own business.

3.  Two separate singular subjects combined by *and* require a plural verb or pronoun; but when combined by *besides, either-or, together with,* or *as well as,* they take a singular:

Mrs. Davis and her secretary *do* the work in the central office.

Considerable knowledge, as well as care, *is* necessary in good writing.

But note:

The honorary president and leader of this group *is* Mr. Anderson (one person, two titles).

4.  Be sure your pronouns agree in number and gender with their antecedents (words they stand for).

Find out whether Coronal Supermarkets is dissatisfied—without emphasizing its (not *their*) possible dissatisfaction.

The benefits students get from studying the practical psychology, writing skills, and ways of business in good courses like letter writing and report writing will help *them* throughout life.

5.  Relative clauses beginning with *who, that,* or *which* require verbs agreeing with the antecedents of those words.

The manager is one of those *persons who* expect unquestioning loyalty.

The *actions* in the life of any animal *that* interest a biologist are those concerned with food, shelter, protection from enemies, and procreation.

6.  Plural-sounding collective subjects take singular verbs and pronouns when the action is that of the group but plural verbs when the action is that of two or more individuals in the group:

The board *is* having a long meeting. (Board acting in unison.)

The board *have* been arguing and disagreeing on that point for months. (Board acting divisively.)

7.  Beware of letting the complement tempt you to make the verb agree with it instead of the subject:

Our main difficulty *was* errors in billing.

The biggest cost item *is* employees' salaries and wages. (In most such situations, however, rewriting would be better.)

8.  Certain words deserve careful attention because their form is an uncertain or misleading indication of their number:
    a.  The meaning of the whole context determines the number of *any, all, more, most, some,* and *none.*
    b.  *Acoustics, economics, genetics, linguistics, mathematics, news, physics,* and *semantics* are all singular despite their look and sound; *deer* and *fish* are both singular and plural; and *mice,* like *men,* is plural.

9.  Beware of words whose forms are in transition, like *data.* The original forms, from Latin, were singular *datum* and plural *data.* In modern usage, *datum* is disappearing and *data* is coming into use as both the singular and plural form.

All the data are in.

All the data is in (commonly seen in modern usage).

**Amb**iguous—more than one possible meaning and hence not clear. Usually you can clear up the temporary confusion by (1) correcting a faulty pronoun reference (see **Ref)** or (2) rewording to straighten out a modifier so that it can modify only what you intend (see **Mod).**

He took over the management of the business from his father when he was 55. (When his father reached 55, Carl took over management of the business.)

We agreed when we signed the papers that you would pay $100. (When we signed the papers, we agreed that you would pay $100 *or* We agreed that you would pay $100 when we signed the papers.)

**And** is a strong coordinating conjunction—one of the most useful and most troublesome of words.

1. It should connect (in the sense of addition) only things of similar quality and grammatical form. Used otherwise, it produces faulty coordination between an independent and a dependent clause, misparallelism, or sentence disunity. See **Sub, Para,** and **Unit.**

   > The plans call for a new four-story building, and which will cost $4.5 million. (Omit *and;* it can't connect an independent clause to a dependent one.) See **Coh.**

   > In this course you learn the ways of the business world, the principles of practical psychology, and to write better. (The infinitive *to write* is not parallel with the nouns *ways* and *principles.* Make them all the same form before connecting them by *and.*) See **Para.**

   > We feel sure that the saw will serve you well, and we appreciate your order. (The two ideas are not closely enough related to appear in the same sentence—probably not even in the same paragraph.) See **Unit.**

2. *And* is properly the most-used connective, but don't overuse it to connect a series of independent clauses into a long, stringy sentence. If the clauses deserve equal emphasis, you can make separate sentences. If not, subordinate the weaker ones. See **Sub.**

   > The consultant first talked with the executives about their letter-writing problems *and* then took a sample of 1,000 carbon copies *and* classified them into two groups *and* 45 percent of them were for situations that could just as well have been handled by forms. (After talking with the executives about their letter-writing problems, the consultant classified a sample of 1,000 carbon copies from the files. Forty-five percent of them were for situations that could just as well . . . .)

3. *And* may properly begin a sentence, but only if you want to emphasize it.

4. *And* is not proper before *etc.;* the *et* in *et cetera* means *and.*

5. Except in formal writing, *and/or* is acceptable to mean either or both of two mentioned possibilities.

**Ap** The appearance of a written message (as of a person) should be pleasant but unobtrusive and should suggest that the writer is competent, accurate, neat, and alert. Check Chapter 2.

**Apos**trophes (usually considered with punctuation, although they belong with spelling) should appear in:

1. Possessives (except *its* and the personal pronouns): before *s* in singulars *(man's)*; after the *s* in plurals if the *s* or *z* sound is there to make the word plural *(ladies'* but *women's)*.

2. Contractions: to mark the omission of a letter *(isn't, doesn't, it's*— meaning "it is," quite different from the possessive *its)*.

3. Plurals of symbols: figures (illegible *8's*), letters of the alphabet (one *o* and two *m's*), and words written about as words (too many *and's* and *but's*), though some authorities now restrict this use to avoiding confusion.

**App**ropriateness to the situation is an important test of good English. Is your statement too slangy, colloquial, or formal for the occasion? See **Ad**apt and the discussion of levels of usage in Chapter 3.

**Assign**  Follow the facts and directions in the assignment. Although you should fill in with necessary details of your own invention, you are not to go contrary to the facts or the spirit of the assigned case; and you are to make only reasonable assumptions. See p. 503.

**BB**  Browbeating the reader is redundant and insulting.

Clark plans to use two approaches to attack the fast-food market. These approaches are: (1) . . . and (2) . . . . (Put the colon after *market* and omit *These approaches are.*) See also **P10**.

**Cap**italization is pretty well standardized (except that newspapers set their own practices and hence are not guides for other writing).

1. Capitalize the names of specific things, including the titles of people, but not general words. For instance, you capitalize the name of any specific college, university, or department; but you write:

   A university education may well cost $12,000, regardless of the department in which one studies.

   L. W. Wilson, president of the University of . . . . When President Wilson came . . . .

   You capitalize any specific course, room, lake, river, building, etc., but not the general words. So you might write:

   I am taking Economics 215.

   I am majoring in engineering.

   Now I must go to a history class in the Liberal Arts Building, after stopping to see a professor in Room 115.

   Next summer I may fish mostly in Portage Lake and some in the Ausable River, although I prefer river to lake fishing.

   Of course, you capitalize *English, French, German*—all the languages, because they derive from the names of countries.

2. In titles of books and articles capitalize the first word and (though library materials don't) all others except articles *(a, an, the)*, prepositions (like *of, to, in, on, for*), and conjunctions (like *and, but, or, nor, although*).

3. Capitalize the seasons (spring, summer) only when you personify them (rare except in poetry).

4. Capitalize sections of the country (the South, the East Coast) but not directions (east, west).

5. Capitalize people's titles *(Mr., Mrs., Ms., Miss, Dr., Colonel, Professor, Judge, Governor, President)* and terms of family relations *(Uncle Jim)* when used before names but only to show unusual respect when used in place of or after names.

6. Capitalize the first word after a colon only if it starts a complete sentence. (In an itemized listing, you may capitalize the first words of items even though they are incomplete sentences.)

**Card**inal numbers *(one, two, three; 6, 7, 9)* are preferable to ordinals *(first, second, third; 1st, 2d, 3d, 4th, or 2nd, 3rd)* in dates except in very formal invitations and legal documents, or when you separate the day from the month. Since the simple ordinal forms may be either adjectives or adverbs, they need no *-ly* endings, ever; so don't say "secondly."

On October 7 . . . ; sometime in November—probably about the 7th.

**Case** in modern English is a problem only with personal pronouns. One form serves for all cases of nouns except the possessive, and the only problem there is remembering correct use of the apostrophe. For pronouns:

1. Use the nominative case *(I, we, he, she, they, who)* for the subject of a verb (other than an infinitive) and for the complement of a linking verb (any form of *to be* except the infinitive with a subject).

2. Use the objective case *(me, us, him, her, them, whom)* as the object of a verb or preposition and as the subject or object of an infinitive (except *to be* without a subject). In informal speaking and writing, however, *who* is acceptable as the object of a preposition (especially if it is in the usual subject position) unless it immediately follows the preposition:

   *Who* was the letter addressed to?

3. Use the possessive case to show possession and to serve as the subject of a gerund (a verb form ending in *ing* and used as a noun):

   His accusing me of dishonesty . . . .

   My thinking that a . . . .

4. Watch case particularly after *than* and *as* and in compounds with a name and a personal pronoun:

> He is better informed on the subject than I (*am informed* implied).
>
> I am a more cautious man than he (*is* understood).
>
> Virginia and she went . . . (subject).
>
> I am to pick up Virginia and her . . . (object of verb).
>
> He told the story to Virginia and her (object of preposition).
>
> Remember that *myself* is not used in place of *me*.

**Chop**py, jerky, short sentences are slow and awkward. Usually the trouble is (1) incoherence (the sentences don't follow each other naturally—see **Coh**); (2) poor control of emphasis (all the ideas in independent clauses, although of different importance—see **Sub**); or (3) lack of variety (all the sentences of the same pattern, usually all beginning with the subject or nearly the same length—see **Var**). Try combining several of the sentences, subordinating the less important ideas and stressing the important ones in the independent clauses.

**Cl** Immediate clearness is a fundamental of good writing. Make sure your reader can get your meaning quickly and easily.

**Coh**erence means clearly showing your reader *the relationships between ideas.* It comes best from a logical sequence (proper organization) with major emphasis on the important ideas, with less on the related but less important ones, and with any necessary conjunctions to indicate what relationships exist. Incoherence comes from mixing unrelated ideas together in the same sentence or paragraph, but particularly from *(a)* using a causative word when the named cause is not the whole cause of the named effect and *(b)* linking unrelated ideas or ideas of different importance by *and*.

1. Plan ahead—get your ideas in logical sequence *before* you write. You can group seemingly unrelated ideas with a topic sentence such as "Three factors deserve special consideration."
2. Give your ideas proper emphasis (see **Emp** and **Sub**). Important ideas should be in independent clauses or separate sentences. Two closely related and equally important ideas can be together in a compound sentence. Put a less important idea in a dependent clause attached to an independent clause, making a complex sentence.
3. Carefully choose transitional words or phrases if you need them to smooth the natural sequence of ideas (see **Tr**). Consider the following as examples:

And . . . moreover, besides, in addition, also, furthermore.

But . . . however, nevertheless, yet, still, although, while.

Either-or . . . neither-nor, else, whether.

Therefore . . . consequently, hence, as a result, accordingly, so, ergo, thus. (Check for *true* cause-effect relation.)

Because . . . since, as, for, the reason is.

Then . . . after that, afterward, later, subsequently.

Meanwhile . . . during, simultaneously, concurrently, while.

Before . . . preceding, previously, prior to.

If . . . provided, assuming, in case, unless.

4. In papers longer than a page or two—and even more so in similar oral presentations—you probably will need even more than the three preceding means of showing the relationships of ideas and thus keeping the reader on the track. (See Topic and Summary Sentences and Headings and Subheads in the Index.)

**Conc**iseness (which is not necessarily brevity) depends on leaving out the irrelevant, leaving unsaid what you can adequately imply (see **Imp**), and cutting out deadwood. See Chapter 3 for explanation and illustration of techniques.

**Conn**otations—the overtones or related meanings of words—are often as important as the denotations, or dictionary meanings. Be sure that the words you use are appropriate in connotations as well as in denotations. Consider, for example, the connotations in the following: *cheap, inexpensive, economical; secondhand, used, previously owned; complaint department, customer service department; basement store, thrift store, budget floor.*

**Cop**ying from the assignment or from other people produces writing that doesn't sound like you. Put your ideas in your own words.

**Cpr** Comparisons require special attention to these points:

1. Things compared must be comparable. Usually the trouble is omission of necessary phrases like *that of, that on, other,* or *else.*

    The markup on Schick shavers is higher than *that on* Remingtons. (You can't omit *that on* or you'll be comparing the height of a Remington—measured in inches—with the markup on Schicks—a percentage.)

    Frank Mosteller sells more Fuller brushes than any *other* salesperson. (Without *other,* the statement is illogical if Frank is a salesperson; he can't sell more than he himself sells.)

2. Incomplete comparisons mean nothing; complete them.

   You get more miles per dollar with XXX. (More than with what?)

   This material has a higher percentage of wool. (Higher than what?)

3. Be sure to use the correct form of comparison words. Comparisons involving two things usually call for adding *-er* (the comparative) to the simple form *(cold, slow)*. Those involving more than two usually require the *-est* (or superlative) form *(coldest, slowest, fastest)*.

   *For words of three syllables or more—and for many with two and some with only one—the better form is more* plus the simple form (for the comparative) or *most* plus the simple form (for the superlative): *more frequently, most hopeful.* Some words can go either way: *oftener* or *more often; oftenest* or *most often.*

4. Watch these idioms: Complete the *as much as* phrase and use *to* after *compare* when pointing out similarities only, *with* when pointing out any differences:

   Price increases may be worth as much *as,* if not more than, the dividends on a common stock purchase.

   Comparison of X *to* Y shows that they involve the same principles.

   Comparison of sales letters with application letters shows that they have minor differences.

5. Some words *(unique, empty, final,* for example) are logical absolutes and hence cannot take comparative or superlative forms.

**CS** Comma splice—a serious error. Except when they are in series or are short and parallel, two or more independent clauses require separation by a period, a comma and a coordinating conjunction, or a semicolon (which may or may not require a following transition like *that is* or one of the conjunctive adverbs). See **SOS**2 and **P2.**

**CSP** Select a central selling point (in a sales or application letter) and give it the major emphasis by position and full development. Scattering your shots over too many points leaves the major ones weak. See **Emp** and **Dev.**

**Diction** Use a more suitable word. The big test, of course, is whether the word, including its connotations, conveys your thought accurately. Consider whether your words are easy for your reader to understand; whether they give a sharp, vivid picture by being natural and fresh instead of pompous, jargonistic, or trite; whether they give a specific, concrete meaning instead of a fuzzy or dull concept because they are general or abstract; and whether they are appropriately informal, formal, standard, technical, or nontechnical—according to the topic and reader. See Chapter 3.

Watch especially the following often-confused pairs: *accept, except; adapt, adopt; affect, effect; all ready, already; all together, altogether; allude, elude; almost, most; among, between; amount, number; appraise, apprise; beside, besides; capital, capitol; complement, compliment; compose, comprise; copy, replica; disinterested, uninterested; farther, further; fewer, less; flaunt, flout; formally, formerly; imply, infer; in regard to, with regards to; it's, its; loose, lose; marital, martial; may be, maybe; moral, morale; oral, verbal; parameter, perimeter; personal, personnel; pinch hitter, substitute; pore over, pour over; principal, principle; reign, rein; respectfully, respectively; stationary, stationery; some time, sometime; your, you're;* and *to, too, two.*

**Date** Date all messages in the standard form *(November 2, 1988)* unless you have good reason to do otherwise. Your most likely good reasons could be: (1) You are in the armed services, where the form *2 November 1988* is standard; or (2) you're writing a formal notice, where you use words with no figures; or (3) you're writing an informal note and may well use the form *11/2/88;* or (4) you're writing to someone overseas (2 November 1988). Modern business writing usually does not abbreviate months and does not use the ordinal forms. See **Card.**

**DC** Dramatized copy would be more effective here. See pp. 63, 151.

**Dead**wood phrases add nothing to the meaning but take writing and reading time. See **Conc** and the list of frequent deadwood expressions in Chapter 3.

**Dev**elop your point more thoroughly with more explanation, definition, specific details, classifications, comparisons, or examples to make it clearer, more interesting, more convincing, or more emphatic. See **Spec.**

**Direct**ness saves words, speeds up reading, and makes your ideas clearer. Don't waste words by beginning too far back in the background of the subject, by stating what the reader already knows, or by expressing what you will clearly imply if you begin with the key thought. Write direct, active-voice sentences beginning with the important word as the subject. The expletives "It is . . ." and "There are . . ." are indirect, passive, and wordy (see **Exp**).

**Dng** Dangling modifier. See **Mod** 1.

**Doc**umentation, or telling your sources, is necessary when you use the ideas of others—to avoid plagiarism and to convince your reader by showing that you have the backing of cited authorities for what you say. See end of Chapter 14.

**Emph**asis, divided among your ideas according to their relative importance, is basic to good communication.

1.  When you state important ideas, give them deserved emphasis by the methods explained in Chapter 3.

2.  When you have negative, unimportant, already known, or other ideas that don't deserve emphasis, avoid overemphasizing them. (See Chapter 3).

    Spring is just around the corner. You'll be needing . . . . (With spring just around the corner, you'll . . . .)

    On October 3 you asked me to write a report on . . . . I have finished it and am . . . . (Here is the report requested in your letter of October 3 . . . .)

    I have your letter of April 20 in which you ask for quotations on X. I am glad to give you our prices. Our present prices on X are . . . . (Just omit the first two sentences. They're implied in the third.)

3.  Transitional words like *and, but,* and *however* usually do not deserve the emphasis they would get at the beginning of a sentence; and prepositions usually do not deserve end-of-sentence emphasis. Indeed, this point of emphasis is the only legitimate reason for objection to such words in these positions.

**Encl**osures. See pp. 64, 153, 154(6).

**Etc.**  An abbreviation of Latin *et cetera,* meaning *and so forth,* is appropriate only when the reader can easily fill out the incomplete list (as in "Please take even-numbered seats 2, 4, 6, etc."). Otherwise, it can mean only "Reader, you guess what else I mean to include." Because *etc.* is an abbreviation, it takes a period. In no case should you write "and etc." *(et* means *and)* or "etc. . . . ." (the middle three dots mean the same as etc. here).

**Exag**geration creates distrust, especially in intercultural communication.

**Expl**etives *(it is, there are)* always slow up the reader's getting to significant information. They also nearly always make your writing unnecessarily wordy, weak, and passive. They often improperly dodge writer responsibility for statements. (See vividness in Chapter 3.)

Expletives usually result from a *misguided* attempt to write an impersonal style. If you write them in first drafts, revising to remove them will make better sentences at least 9 times out of 10. In general, then, you should avoid them, although sometimes they may help to soften a command or avoid presumptuousness in a recommendation, or ease reader acceptance of bad news.

It was thought that you would prefer . . . . (I thought you would . . . .)

There are four important factors involved. These are: . . . . (The four important factors are . . . .)

It will be necessary to have your . . . . ("You must send . . ." might be too commanding.)

**FI** The Fog Index is too high here. See Chapter 3 and make your writing easier to read.

**Fig**ures are better than words (except at the beginning of a sentence) for serial, telephone, page, chapter, chart, catalog, and street numbers; for money, dimensions, and (except in formal announcements) dates and time; for all quantities when several are close together (but not adjoining) in a sentence or paragraph; and for other isolated quantities requiring more than two words. (As an acceptable replacement for the two-word rule, your teacher may authorize usual newspaper practice: Use figures if the quantity is above nine.)

1. If a quantity comes at the first of a sentence, write it in words or recast the sentence.

2. When a sentence involves two different series of quantities, use figures for one and words for the other to avoid confusion; if more than two, use a table.

   On the qualifying exam, ten percent of the applicants scored 90–100; thirty percent, 80–89, . . . .

   Please make six 2″ × 3″ and three 5″ × 7″ black-and-white prints.

3. The old longhand practice of stating quantities twice—in figures followed parenthetically by words—is unnecessary and undesirable in type or print, although it still sometimes appears in legal documents, and always in checks, for double certainty and security.

4. Except in dates, street numbers, and serial numbers, use a comma between groups of three digits, counting from the right.

5. Except in tables involving some cents, periods and zeros after money quantities are wasted typing and reading.

6. Two-word quantities between 20 and 100 require the hyphen *(twenty-six)*.

7. Cardinal numbers *(1, 2, 3, 4,* etc.) are preferable to ordinals *(1st, 2d, 3d, 4th)* in dates except when the day is separate from the month. See **Card** and **Date.**

8. Since ordinals are either adjectives or adverbs, an *-ly* ending is never necessary or desirable (not *secondly* or *thirdly*).

Flattery, especially if obvious, is more likely to hurt than help. See Chapter 4.

**Frag**ments (phrases or subordinate clauses posing as sentences) are serious errors (because they show ignorance of sentence structure) except when perfectly clear and intentional. Attach them to the independent clauses to which they belong (see **P3**) or change their wording to make them the complete, independent sentences they pretend to be.

> The latter being the better way. (This is a phrase fragment that should be attached by comma to the preceding sentence. Or you could simply change *being* to *is*).
>
> One job in revising any paper is checking for and correcting any fragments. Which is easy to do. (The second "sentence" is a dependent clause and hence a fragment unless attached—by a comma—to the preceding.)

**Gobb**ledygook is big-wordy, roundabout, long-winded, or stuffed-shirt language. Avoid it like poison.

**Gra**phic devices of various kinds can often supplement words to make the information clearer, easier, or more interesting. Use them where they will help, but only if they will. See Chapter 14 and the checklist in Chapter 16.

**Gw** Goodwill, a basic requirement of a business letter, is lacking or poorly handled here. See Chapter 4.

**HS** Heads and subheads could improve coherence and transitions. See Chapters 13, 14, 15.

**Id**iom violated. Follow the natural, customary (idiomatic) way of expressing your idea. Usually an error in idiom is use of the wrong preposition. Consider *possibility of, possible to, necessity of, need for,* and *ability to.* See **Prep**.

**Imp**ly rather than express the idea, to save words or avoid overemphasis. See **Emp** and **Conc**.

**Ital**ic print, indicated by underscoring in typewritten and handwritten copy, can emphasize occasional words, mark the title of a book or journal, or mark a word, letter, or figure used as an illustration or typographical unit (instead of for its meaning). It is also the way to indicate an unanglicized foreign-language expression used in English context.

> Italics are *not* the *preferable* way to mark titles of *parts,* such as the title of an article in a journal or a chapter in a book. Quotation marks are preferable for that purpose.

Chapter 3, "Using an Effective Style," stresses clear, natural style and general linguistic *savoir faire.*

Many people misspell *convenience* and *questionnaire.* Use of fewer *I*'s and more *you*'s would improve many letters.

**Item** Itemize complex series and lists (like this) to (1) emphasize the points, (2) avoid complex punctuation, (3) force yourself to state your points more precisely and concisely, and (4) grab your reader's attention. This point is particularly important in oral communication.

**Jar**gon is fuzzy or inappropriate writing attributable to pompousness, circumlocution, deadwood, abstractness, big words, technical terms (written to nontechnical readers), or hackneyed expressions. It is the opposite of simple, natural, clear writing. Avoid it.

**Jux**tapose (put side by side) facts and ideas that the reader needs to consider together. For instance, wholesale and retail prices need to appear together (with the difference and percentage of markup figured) if they are to mean as much as they should to the retailer being asked to stock the product.

**K** Awkwardness in expression calls attention to itself, and it may confuse the reader. Reconstruct your sentence or change word order for a more natural flow.

A so-called split infinitive (putting a modifier between *to* and a verb) is usually undesirable only because it is usually awkward.

**K/S** Known to the reader. Omit or **Sub**ordinate.

**lc** Lowercase needed here, instead of capital. See **Cap.**

**Log**ic Avoid statements which will not stand the test of logic or for which the logic is not readily clear. Perhaps you need to supply a missing step in the logic. Maybe you need to state your idea more precisely. Or maybe you need to complete a comparison to make it logical. (If the last, see **Cpr** for fuller explanation.)

**Mod**ifiers Make sure that each modifier relates clearly to the thing it is supposed to modify. As a general rule, the two should be as close together as natural sentence construction will allow.

1.  Participles (usually phrases including a verb form ending in *-ing* or *-ed,* and usually at the beginning of a sentence) require careful attention lest you relate them to the wrong word (or nothing at all) and produce "dangling modifiers" (**Dng**).

Smelling of liquor, I arrested the driver. (The officer did not intend to report drinking on duty—but the words do.)

After soaking in sulfuric acid overnight, I set the specimen up to dry. (The scientist didn't really soak, either.)

Infinitives can dangle the same way:

To enjoy the longest, most dependable service, the motor must be tuned up about every 500 hours of operation. (The motor cannot enjoy dependable service.)

In order to assist you in collecting for damages, it will be necessary to fill out a company blank. (The two infinitives dangle because they do not relate to any proper doers of the actions indicated.)

But absolute phrases (a noun plus a participle) and participles, gerunds, and infinitives naming an accepted truth rather than the action of any particular person or thing do not need to relate to any subject:

The sun having set, the fish began to bite.

All things considered, Steve is the better man.

Counting all costs, the little X is not an inexpensive car.

To judge from results, that was an effective method.

2.  Misplaced modifiers, like danglers, can also make you look silly.

The girl riding the horse in the blue sweater is my sister.

There is a meeting at 3 this afternoon about morality in the president's office.

Watch especially where you put such limiting qualifiers as *only, almost,* and *nearly.* Consider the varied meanings from placing *only* at different spots in "I can approve payment of a $30 adjustment" or in "He mourned for his brother."

**Mon**otonous  See **Var.**

**Mood**  The usual indicative (for statements of fact) and imperative (commanding) moods give little trouble. But be careful with the subjunctive (for verbs after commands and wishes) and the conditional (for uncertainties or conditions contrary to fact), especially in formal writing. Consider: "Let it be said . . . ," "I wish he were . . . ," and "If I were in your place . . . ." See **SW.**

**Natural** writing avoids triteness, awkwardness, and pomposity. Clichés, trite and hackneyed expressions, and jargon suggest that you are not thinking about your subject and your reader; awkwardness suggests carelessness; and big words and pomposity suggest that you are trying to make an impression. Think through what you want to say and put it simply, smoothly, and naturally. Although you cannot write exactly as you talk, try to write with the same freedom, ease, simplicity, and smoothness. See Chapter 3.

**Negative** in letter and memo writing means anything unpleasant to your reader. Avoid the negative when you can and subordinate it when you can't avoid it. Insofar as possible, stress the positive by telling what you have done, can do, will do, or want done instead of their negative opposites. See Chapter 5; and for methods of surbordinating, Chapter 3, **Emp,** and **Sub.**

**Objectivity** Use of emotional words suggests a prejudiced rather than an objective view and therefore causes the reader to lose faith in the writer—especially a report writer. See pp. 427 and 440.

**Obvious** statements—when unnecessary as bases for other statements—waste words and may insult the reader's intelligence. When you need to establish an obvious fact as the basis for something else, put it in a dependent clause or imply it. (See **Emp** and **Sub.**)

> New York is America's biggest city. Therefore . . . . (Since New York is America's biggest city, . . . .)

**Punctuation** that follows the conventions of written English is a *helpful device for both reader and writer in communicating clearly, quickly, and easily.* Here are the conventions most commonly violated. For convenience and clarity in explanation, we divide punctuation into two categories—end-of-sentence marks (with parts **Pa, b,** and **c**) and internal punctuation (with parts **P1–P13**). Since **Pa, b,** and **c** are all sentence-end marks, they all interact with quotation marks and parentheses as explained for quotation marks in **P9.**

**Pa** Use a period at the end of a sentence unless it is a question, is questionable (see **Pb**), or is an exclamation (see **Pc**). Less than full-sentence expressions used as outline items may end with periods or remain open-ended.

**Pb** Use a question mark at the end of a question and (in parentheses) after a spelling or statement about which you can't be sure.

> Though I've heard of Mrs. Muennink's (?) varied interests and accomplishments, I've never met the lady. (The question mark means only that I'm not sure of the spelling.)
>
> When Colby first moved to Miami in January 1981 (?), I thought . . . .

**Pc** Use exclamation marks (sparingly) after sentences or (in parentheses) after lesser expressions that you want to give dramatic emphasis.

He said he wanted (!) to be the first to . . . .

The general's succinct reply was "Nuts!"

**P1** Use a comma between two independent clauses connected by *and, but, or,* or *nor* if no other commas are in the sentence; but be sure you are connecting two clauses rather than a compound subject, verb, or object.

> You may buy the regular Whiz mixer at $78.75, but I think you would find the Super Whiz much more satisfactory (two clauses).

> We make two grades of Whiz mixers and sell both at prices lower than those of our competitors' products (compound verb; one subject).

Be sure, too, that you don't use obtrusive commas before the first or after the last item in a series or between a subject and its verb, a verb and its object, or a noun and its adjective. Also, you do not usually need a comma after a transitional word *(and, but, however, therefore),* but using one emphasizes the word.

**P2** The semicolon is a pivotal mark; avoid using it between expressions unless they are of equal grammatical structure (usually two independent clauses or two items in a complex series). Use a semicolon between two independent clauses unless connected by *and, but, or,* or *nor;* and even then, use a semicolon if the sentence already has a comma in it (as in this one). Typical weaker connectives requiring the semicolon between two independent clauses are *therefore, so, moreover, hence, still, accordingly, nevertheless, furthermore, consequently,* and *however.* When these words are simple connectors not between two independent clauses, however (as right here), set them off by a pair of commas unless they fit so smoothly into the sentence that they require no marks.

> New developments in office machines have made maintenance workers relearn their jobs; the new manuals are twice as thick as those of only a few years ago (no connective).

> The preceding sentence could be two, of course; but because the ideas are closely related, it is better as one. (Commas elsewhere in this sentence require a semicolon before even a strong conjunction.)

> Good business writing requires proper punctuation; therefore you must know how to use the semicolon (weak connective).

> The proper style for letters is simpler and less involved than for most other writing, however, and therefore does not require very complex punctuation procedures. (*However,* is a simple transition, *not* used between two clauses here and *not* close-knit into the phrasing the way *therefore* is; so it needs commas, while *therefore* goes unmarked. Note, too, that the weak connective *so* requires the semicolon because it connects two clauses.)

**P3** Use a comma after all first-of-sentence dependent clauses, long phrases, or other phrases containing any form of a verb. But when these forms or appositives or transitional words appear elsewhere in a sentence, use commas only with nonrestrictive (nonessential) ones. Nonrestrictive statements add descriptive detail about an already identified word and are not necessary to the logic or grammatical completeness of the sentence; restrictive ones define, limit, or identify and are necessary to convey the intended meaning or complete the sentence. If, on reading aloud, you naturally pause and inflect your voice, the statement is nonrestrictive and requires the comma(s).

> Because the dependent clause comes at the beginning, we have to use a comma in this sentence.
>
> We do not need a comma in a complex sentence if the dependent part comes at the end or in the middle and restricts the meaning the way this one does.
>
> Having illustrated the two points about dependent clauses at the beginning and restrictive clauses elsewhere in the sentence, we now use this sentence to illustrate the use of a comma after a long phrase at the first of a sentence. (Because it includes a verb form, it would require a comma even if it were short, like "Having illustrated the point, we now leave the topic.")
>
> The three points already illustrated, which are certainly important, are no more important than the point about using commas to set off nonrestrictive clauses anywhere, which this sentence illustrates. (In fact, it illustrates twice: you could omit both the *which* clauses; they are nonrestrictive because they merely give added information unnecessary to either the meaning or the grammar of the basic sentence.)

Sometimes you need a comma to prevent misreading—especially after a gerund, participle, or infinitive:

> In the office, files were scattered all over the floor.
>
> By shooting, the man attracted the attention of the rescue party.
>
> Thinking that, he was unwilling to listen to reason.
>
> Seeing the foreman's unwillingness to help, the men gave up.

**P4** Use *pairs* of commas, parentheses, or dashes as needed to mark off parenthetical expressions within sentences. The "as needed" in the preceding sentence is a reminder that some parentheticals need no surrounding punctuation. Like dependent clauses, some appositives are restrictive or so closely related that they require no punctuation, while others are nonrestrictive or so loosely related that they do.

> Our starting point that good punctuation is a matter of following the conventions has not had enough attention.
>
> Our second point—the importance of writing letters so smoothly and naturally that they require little internal punctuation—would preclude most punctuation problems.

1. Commas are normal for short, unemphatic, and otherwise unpunctuated direct addresses like "Yes, Mr. Thomas, you may . . . ," tucked-in transitions like *however* and *on the other hand,* and brief appositives.

2. As the length increases in a side comment or an appositive (a restatement like this one, following immediately to explain a term), the call for stronger marks like parentheses becomes more likely. Commas within a parenthetical (as in the preceding) or a desire to de-emphasize it also make parentheses necessary around it.

3. If you want to emphasize a parenthetical expression—or if it contains complicated punctuation or is long—a pair of dashes such as we're using here will be your best punctuation to fence it in. Also see **P13.**

4. People in business often use ellipses in the place of dashes to emphasize parenthetical expressions . . . or if they contain complicated punctuation or are long . . . as we do here. Since this use of ellipses has not yet become a convention, we cannot recommend it; but to use ellipses in this manner is no longer absolutely wrong. (See **P13.**)

**P5** Use commas to separate coordinate adjectives. As two tests for coordinacy, see if you can put *and* between the adjectives or invert their order without producing awkwardness. If so, they are coordinate and require a comma.

Proper punctuation can help greatly in writing a clear, easy-to-read style.

Fairly heavy white paper is best for letterheads.

**P6** A comma is the usual punctuation *between* (but not before or after) items in a series (preferably including one before the *and* with the last item, because it is sometimes necessary for clearness and is always correct). But if any item except the last has a comma *within* it, use semicolons at all points *between* items. (Suggestion: If only one of a series requires an internal comma, consider putting it last and using commas between the items.)

Make your writing clear, quick, and easy to read.

Use commas between independent clauses connected by *and, but, or,* or *nor;* semicolons between independent clauses with other connectives or no connecting words; commas for dependent clauses and verbal or long phrases at the beginnings of sentences, for nonrestrictive ones elsewhere, and for simple series; and semicolons for complex series like the one in this sentence.

**P7** Dashes (like commas and parentheses—as explained in **P4**) are also acceptable (in pairs) around parenthetical expressions that interrupt the main part of the sentence.

If the parenthetical part contains internal parentheses, dashes must surround it; if it contains commas, then dashes *or* parentheses must surround it. (Of course, only a pair of parentheses can surround a sentence giving explanations, relatively unimportant additional detail, or side information, as this sentence does. In that case the period comes inside the closing parentheses, although it comes outside otherwise.)

Except as explained in the preceding paragraph, the choice depends on the desired emphasis and on the other punctuation.

1.  Two dashes (called "bridge dashes") emphasize most:

> Your main weaknesses in writing—misspelling, faulty punctuation, and incoherence—deserve attention before you write letters.

2.  A single dash—made by two hyphens without spacing before, between, or after—may mark an abrupt change in the trend of a sentence or precede an added statement summarizing, contrasting, or explaining the first part. In this second function, it is the "pickup dash."

> Errors in spelling, punctuation, or coherence—all of these mar an otherwise good letter.

> A letter writer must avoid the common errors in writing—misspelling, bad punctuation, and incoherence. (Of course, a colon could replace the dash here; but ordinarily it should not unless the preceding statement is a formal introduction, usually indicated by the word *following,* or unless it is an introduction to an itemized list.)

**P8** Hyphenate two or more words (unless the first ends in *-ly*) used to make a compound adjective modifying a following noun.

> Fast-selling product, wrinkle-resistant material, long-wearing soles, never-to-be-forgotten experience, high-level executive.

Note that you do not hyphenate when the adjectives follow the noun.

> The material is highly wrinkle resistant and long wearing.

Certainly it does not apply when the adjectives modify the noun separately. See **P5.**

> These slacks are made of a hard, durable material.

The compound-adjective principle does apply, however, to double compounds made with one element in common, where the "suspension hyphen" follows the first: three- and five-pound cans.

The hyphen also marks the break in a word at the end of a line. See **Syl.**

Other less-frequent uses of the hyphen include (1) spelling of fractions as modifiers (*three-fourths* majority) and two-word quantities between 20 and 100, and (2) prefixing words or syllables to names (*post-Hitler* Germany).

**P9** Quotation marks are primarily for short, exact quotations (not paraphrasings) of other people's words and for titles of *parts* of publications, such as magazine and newspaper stories or book chapters. (Italicize the titles of whole journals and books—underlined in typed copy. See **Ital.**) If a quotation is more than two or three lines long, you should indent it from each side, single-space it, and omit quotation marks.

When closing quotation marks and other marks seem to come at the same place, the standard *American* practice is as follows: Place commas or periods *inside* the closing quotes; place semicolons or colons *outside;* and place question or exclamation marks inside or outside depending on whether they belong to the quotation or to your sentence encompassing it.

**P10** The colon is either an anticipating or a separating mark. As an anticipator, it appears after introductory lead-ins to explanations or quotations, especially if the lead-in includes such formalizing terms as the word *following* or if the explanation is lengthy or itemized.

> The X Company's ink was even redder: its third-quarter loss of . . . .
>
> Three main benefits deserve your attention: . . . . (Enumeration follows. Notice that you do not need—indeed should not use—a browbeating, word-wasting expression like "these benefits are" before or after the colon! See **BB.**)
>
> On the use of the colon, Perrin says: . . . . (Long quotation follows.)

Because the colon is also a separating mark, however—used to separate hours from minutes and volume numbers from pages, for example—it should not serve as an anticipating mark when the lead-in phrasing fits well as an integral part of a short, informal statement.

> The three main advantages are (colon would be obtrusive here) speed, economy, and convenience.
>
> Perrin reports that (no colon; not even a comma) *"Will* has practically replaced *shall* in . . . ."

Almost invariably words like *namely, that is, for example,* and *as follows* are wasted (and browbeating) when used with a colon. The introductory phrasing and the colon adequately anticipate without these words.

> We have several reasons for changing: namely the . . . . (Omit *namely.*)
>
> We had several reasons for changing. These reasons are: . . . . (This is worse. Omit *These reasons are;* put the colon after *changing.*)

Although practice varies, usually you should capitalize the first word after a colon only if it begins a complete sentence; but if itemizations follow, you may capitalize even though each item depends on the introductory statement for completeness.

The same idea applies to the end punctuation of items following a colon. If the items make complete sentences, put a period after each; but if all are to be considered one sentence, use comma or semicolon at the end of each (except the last, of course) as in other series—or you may use no end punctuation if the items listed are fairly brief.

**P11** Underlining in typed or handwritten copy specifies italic type when printed. Its main uses are to mark titles of books and journals, to emphasize, and to indicate unanglicized words. In copy not to be printed, underlining should go with any heading not written in solid capitals. Otherwise the heading, which is really a title for the copy over which it stands, does not stand out sufficiently. (A printer would make it stand out by using big or boldface type.)

Typed underlining is preferably continuous, rather than broken by individual words, because it is easier both to type and to read that way.

**P12** Besides its well-known use at the end of a question (**Pb**), the question mark (in parentheses) immediately following a statement or spelling indicates that the writer is uncertain and unable to determine. Obviously, it should not be an excuse for laziness; but if you have only heard a difficult name, for example, and have to write to that person, you'd better use the mark than unconcernedly misspell the name.

A question mark should not appear after indirect questions and is unnecessary after commands softened by question form, but some writers feel that it further softens commands.

We need to know what your decision is. (This is an indirect question.)

Will you please ask the secretary in your office to change my mailing address. (This is a softened command, with or without the question mark.)

**P13** Ellipsis (three *spaced* periods) means that you have left out something. You *must* use this mark when giving an incomplete quotation. Note that if an omission comes at the end of a sentence, you need to add the appropriate end-of-sentence punctuation—a fourth dot for the period, or a question mark or an exclamation point. Ellipses are also coming into wide use, especially in business, as an additional way to mark parenthetical expressions; but this practice has not yet achieved total acceptance (see **P7**).

"We the people of the United States . . . do ordain and establish this Constitution . . . ."

**P14** Brackets [ ] are useful for two purposes:

1.  To make a comment inside a quotation (as on p. 65).
2.  To enclose a parenthetical expression that has parentheses or a pair of dashes inside it (as on p. 485).

**Par**agraphs in letters and reports are the same as in other writing—unified and coherent developments of topics—except that they tend to be more compressed and shorter for easier readability. (The symbol ¶ may replace **Par** to indicate an impropriety in paragraphing.)

1. Keep your paragraphs reasonably short. Long ones are discouragingly hard to read. Especially the first and last paragraphs of letters and memos should be short (rarely more than three or four lines). Elsewhere, if a paragraph runs to more than about eight lines, you should consider breaking it up for easier readability. Certainly you should ignore any idea that a paragraph has to be more than one sentence.

2. But develop your paragraphs adequately to clarify and support your points—by explanation, detail, facts and figures, or illustrations and examples.

3. Make each paragraph unified and coherent by taking out elements irrelevant to the topic, by organizing carefully, and by showing the interrelationship of the ideas. Consider beginning with a topic sentence and/or ending with a summary. See **Unit** and **Coh** for further tips.

4. **(Coh)** Show the relation of the paragraph to the preceding (by following logical sequence, carrying over key ideas, and/or using transitional words) and to the purpose of the whole paper or section (by pointing out the significance and/or using transitional words or sentences).

   Paragraph unity also includes . . . . (*Also* means that some of the explanation has preceded.)

   Carrying over key words and using transitional words are both means of providing unity between paragraphs as well as within them. (As *well as* means we've discussed unity *in* paragraphs and now will discuss it *between* them.)

5. **Par** with **No** before it means "No new paragraph needed here because you are still on the same topic and within reasonable paragraph length."

**Par**allelism means using the same kind of grammatical structure for ideas that you use coordinately, as in pairs, series (including lists), comparisons, and outlines. These structures state or imply relationships usually indicated by *and, but,* or *or* and hence should relate only full sentences to full sentences, nouns to nouns, verbs to verbs, active voice to active voice, plural to plural—indeed *any* grammatical form only to the same grammatical form in the related part. Watch for parallelism with *not only . . . but also, as well as, larger, less expensive,* and the like. (See Item 5 under "Organizing the Findings" in Chapter 14 for parallelism in outlines.)

   One of the duties of the flight attendant is to offer customers magazines, pillows, and hang their coats (two plural nouns and a verb improperly connected by the coordinating conjunction *and*).

   The No-Skid knee guard is long wearing, washable, and stays in position (two adjectives improperly connected by *and* to a verb).

   John Coleman is 39, married, and a native (two adjectives and a noun).

> If we fair each side of the arc, we produce a more practical airfoil section and an increase in performance is attained. (Active voice related to passive. Rewrite the last part as "increase performance.")
>
> The next step is baking or catalyzation. (Use "baking or catalyzing.")
>
> Swimming is better exercise than to walk (a gerund compared with an infinitive).

Parallelism in pairs, series, and comparisons is largely a question of logic; you can add together and compare only like things. See **Log.**

**Pas**sive voice (in which the subject receives rather than does the action indicated by the verb) is usually wordy, awkward, and weak. Most of your sentences should therefore use the active voice. It makes important words (usually persons or products in letters) the subjects and objects of your verbs, as they should be.

Writers often use passive constructions in a misguided effort to avoid *I* and *we* as the subject. If you feel that you must avoid them to prevent monotony of sentence pattern, Chapter 3 explains better ways. If you feel that you must avoid them to increase objectivity, you are working under a false impression; you can be just as biased without them. But you can avoid the first person and the passive at the same time, as explained in the first illustration below.

Still, you may find appropriate use for passives to convey unwelcome information, to meet a thesis director's or company executive's unsound requirement that you write impersonally, to avoid a direct accusation, to put emphasis on something other than the doer of the action, or to weaken an otherwise rankling command or recommendation.

> Your Long-Flight skis were shipped this morning by our mailing department. (Can be made active and impersonal, as "Two Long-Flight skis are on their way; they left the mailing department this morning.")
>
> The subject has been considered from the following viewpoints: . . . . (The requirement of impersonal style may justify the passive here.)
>
> The mower apparently has not been oiled adequately (avoids accusing the user).
>
> Careful attention should be given to . . . (weakens a possibly rankling command).
>
> It is recommended that . . . . (Though this weakens and avoids egotism in a recommendation, surely you can find a better way. This deserves criticism for both a **Pas**sive and an **Exp**letive.)

**PD** Psychological description (interpreting facts and physical features of a product in terms of reader benefits) is the real heart of selling. Unless your reader readily makes the interpretation, pure physical description is ineffective in selling. So when you name a physical feature of a product you're selling, show the reader what it means in terms of benefits—as explained in Chapters 6 and 8.

> The Bostonian Sporty shoe has Neolite soles and triple-stitched welt construction. (Better with **PD:** The Neolite soles and triple-stitched welt construction cause the Bostonian Sporty to last long and keep your feet dry.)

**Per**sonalized messages written for and adapted to specific readers are more effective than mass broadcasts. What seems to be for everybody has less interest to anybody. Even form letters should give the feeling that the message is directed to each reader. Expressions such as "Those of you who . . ." and "If you are one who . . ." give just the opposite impression. (See Chapter 5.)

**Plan** your message more appropriately for the circumstances as a good-news, bad-news, or persuasive one. (See Chapter 5.)

**Pom**pous  Try to express the thought simply, not to impress the reader.

**Pr**  Follow more generally acceptable business practice.

**PR**  Personal references (names of people or pronouns referring to them) not only help to keep the reader in the picture and produce you-attitude (**YA**); they help to avoid the passive (**Pas**), to make your writing specific and concrete instead of general and abstract (**Spec**), and to make your writing easier and more interesting to read. Naming or referring to persons—Flesch suggests at least 6 percent of your words—is an important element in readability.

**Prep**ositions indicate relationships within a sentence.

1.  Be sure to use the right one for your construction. Some words require certain prepositions; others vary prepositions for different meanings. See **Id.**

    Ability *to;* agree *to, with,* or *in;* compare *to* (for similarities only) or *with* (for likenesses and differences); different *from* (not different *than*).

2.  When you use two words that require different prepositions, use both:

    Because of your interest *in* and aptitude *for* . . . .

3.  Don't use many of the .45-caliber group prepositions *(according to, in regard to, by means of, in connection with, on the part of)* for squirrel-size ideas or your prepositions will "bulk too large," as Perrin says.

**PV**  Insofar as possible, keep the same point of view in a sentence, a paragraph, or a whole letter. Make only logically necessary shifts, and let your reader know by providing the necessary transitional words. Watch carefully for shifts in time, location, and those whose eyes you seem to be looking through. For effective you-attitude, look through the reader's eyes whenever possible. See **YA.**

**R** Bring your reader into the picture early—and don't forget later. The reader is the most important person involved with your message. See **Per, PR, PV,** and **YA.**

**Red**undancy includes not only useless repetition but wasting words saying things that are obvious or clearly implied. Avoid it.

**Ref** The references of your pronouns must be immediately certain and clear to your reader—not ambiguous, too far away, or merely implied. Except for the few indefinite pronouns *(one, everybody, anybody,* and *it* referring to the weather), a pronoun confuses or distracts a reader unless it refers clearly to a preceding noun and agrees with it in number and gender. *Each, every, any,* and their combinations *anybody* and *everybody* are singulars requiring singular verbs and pronouns; but see **Agr** for further explanation of agreement.

1.  Often the trouble with a pronoun reference is that the antecedent is just too far away. Ordinarily a pronoun tends to "grab onto" the closest preceding noun as its antecedent. So construct (or reconstruct) your sentences with that tendency in mind.

2.  Guard particularly against *this, that, which, it,* and *they* making vague reference to ideas of whole preceding clauses instead of clear, one-word antecedents.

    Dayton adopted the plan in 1914 and has kept it ever since, which is a good example of the success of the council-manager form of government. (What does *which* refer to?)

    After reading a book about television engineering, the young man wanted to be one of them. (One of what? The antecedent is only implied.)

3.  Don't use the same pronoun with different meanings in the same sentence:

    The directions say that it is up to the owner to change the filter whenever it needs it.

**Rep**etition of words or ideas seems wordy and monotonous unless it serves a justified purpose. Though restatement of important ideas deserving emphasis is often desirable, even then the restatement usually should be in somewhat different words to avoid monotony.

**Res**ale material—reassuring a customer that a choice of goods and/or firm was a good one—not only shows your service attitude **(SA)**; it helps keep incomplete orders and delayed shipments on the books, rebuilds reader confidence in adjustment situations, and serves as a basic idea in collections. Look it up in the Index and read about it in connection with the particular type of message involved.

**SA** Service attitude—showing a genuine desire to give the kinds and quality of goods and services wanted, favorable prices, and various conveniences, plus unselfish reassurance of appreciation for business—can go a long way toward overcoming a reader's feeling that you are indifferent. Your basic techniques are to interweave into your messages some sales promotion material (**SPM**) and resale talk (**Res**). See Chapter 4.

**SC** Show more success consciousness (self-confidence, Chapter 5).

**Shifting** of tense (time), voice (active-passive), mood (indicative, imperative, subjunctive), or person (first, second, third) should come only when the logic of the situation dictates it; otherwise it leads to incoherence and loses or confuses readers. See **PV.**

**Simplify.** Needlessly big words or involved sentences are hard to read.

**Sincerity** is essential if you are to be believed. Don't pretend or overstate your case. See Chapter 4.

**Slow** movement is desirable only in a disappointing message, where you must reason calmly with the reader to justify the unpleasant point you are preparing to present; otherwise it is objectionable.

1.  Don't use too many words before getting to an important point. Starting too far back in the background, giving too many details, or saying things that you should imply are the most frequent faults.
2.  Don't use too many short, choppy sentences and thus slow up a message that should move fast.

**SOS** Errors in sentence organization and structure are sometimes serious enough to justify the distress signal.

1.  Don't present a phrase or dependent clause as a sentence. Usually correction requires only attaching the dependent element to the preceding or following sentence (on which it depends). See **Frag.**

    In answer to your request concerning what the company is like, what has been accomplished, and the future prospects. Here is the information I have been able to acquire. (Replace the period with a comma.)

2.  Don't use a comma—or no punctuation at all—between two independent clauses unless a strong conjunction *(and, but, or,* or *nor)* is there. The error is not basically one of punctuation (as discussed in

**P1** and **P2**) but the more serious failure to recognize what a sentence is. You need a period if the two statements are not so closely related that they ought to be in the same sentence, or a semicolon if they are.

> The credit business is big business some people estimate that it is as much as 86 percent of American business (period needed before *some*).

> Running two sentences together without punctuation is about the worst error a writer can make, however it is little worse than using a comma where a semicolon is required, as in this sentence. See **P2.**

3. Don't put words together in unnatural, confusing relationships that the reader has to ponder to get the intended meaning. (See **K** and **Mod.**)

> Just because you want to sell I don't want right now to buy. (The fact that you want to sell doesn't mean that I want to buy.)

4. Don't put ideas together with connectives that falsely represent their relationship. See **Coh** and **Unit.**

Spelling errors rarely confuse or mislead, but they nearly always have an equally unfavorable effect—they cause bad spellers to lose face and their readers' faith. So here are the most important tips on spelling and a list of words frequently misspelled in business writing. If you have spelling problems, study both—carefully.

1. *Ie* or *ei:* When pronounced like *ee*, write *ie* except after *c*, as in *brief, believe, piece, wield; receive, deceive, perceive.* The exceptions are *either, neither, leisure, seize,* and *weird.* When pronounced otherwise, write *ei* (as in *freight, height, forfeit*) except in *die, lie, pie, tie, vie,* and *science.*

2. Double a final single consonant preceded by a single vowel *(a, e, i, o, u)* in an accented syllable when you add a suffix *(-ing, -ed, er)* beginning with a vowel *(plan, planning; shop, shopping).* Note that if the word already ends in two consonants, or one preceded by two vowels, you do not double the last consonant *(holding, helping; daubing, seeded).* Note, too, that you usually do not double the consonant unless in an accented syllable *(refer, referred, references).* Two new exceptions, *benefitted* and *travelled,* can now go either way.

3. Drop a final unpronounced *e* preceded by a consonant when you add a suffix beginning with a vowel *(hope, hoping; owe, owing);* but retain the *e* after *c* or *g* unless the suffix begins with one of the front vowels, *i* or *e* *(noticeable, changeable, changing, reduced).*

4.  Change final *y* to *i* and add *es* for the plural if a consonant precedes the *y (ally, allies; tally, tallies);* otherwise, just add *s (valley, valleys).*

5.  Add *'s* for the possessive of all singulars and of plurals that do not end in *s (man's, men's, lady's);* add only apostrophe for *s*-ending plurals *(ladies', Davises', students').*

6.  Hyphenate double-word quantities between 20 and 100 *(twenty-one, thirty-two, forty-four, ninety-eight)* and fractions used as modifiers *(nine-tenths* depleted) but not fractions used as nouns (increased by *one fourth ).*

7.  Most words ending with the sound of *seed* are like *concede, precede,* and *recede;* but three require *ee (exceed, proceed,* and *succeed)* and one takes an *s* instead of a *c (supersede).*

8.  Get somebody to pronounce for you while you try to spell the following frequently misspelled words. Then study those you miss (along with others from whatever source that give you trouble).

| | | |
|---|---|---|
| a lot | explanation | prejudiced |
| accessible | gauge | principal |
| accidentally | government | principle |
| accommodate | grammar | privilege |
| achievement | height | procedure |
| acquaintance | hindrance | quantity |
| acquire | incidentally | questionnaire |
| affect (to influence) | interest | receive |
| among | it's (its) | referring |
| argument | laboratory | renowned |
| attorneys | lose (loose) | separate |
| basically | maintenance | stationary |
| believe | moral (morale) | stationery |
| calendar | mortgage | surprise |
| conscientious | noticeable | temperament |
| consensus | occasionally | than (then) |
| convenience | occurrence | their (there) |
| definitely | offered | too (to, two) |
| disastrous | omitted | undoubtedly |
| effect (result) | paid | whether (weather) |
| efficiency | parallel | writing (written) |
| embarrass | passed (past) | |
| environment | perform | |
| equipped | permissible | |
| existence | personal | |
| | personnel | |
| | precede | |

Specific wording, like a sharp photograph, helps the reader get a clear idea; general words give only a hazy view.

1. If you are inclined to use the general word for a class of things, consider the advantages of giving the specific kind in that class (machine—mower; office equipment—files, desks, chairs, and typewriters; employees—salesclerks, janitors, secretaries, and others).

2. Another kind of specificness is giving supporting details, illustrations, examples, and full explanations for general statements made. If you use generalities to gain conciseness in topic and summarizing statements, be sure to provide necessary supporting explanations or further details; otherwise, your unsupported statements may not be accepted, even if understood. See **Dev.**

3. Still another important kind of specificness is giving the evidences of abstract qualities you may use. If you are inclined to say that something is a bargain, an outstanding offer, of the highest quality, revolutionary, best, ideal, or economical, give the concrete evidences for these qualities instead of the abstract words.

In an application letter, if you want to convey the idea that you are intelligent, industrious, honest, dependable, and sociable, give the evidence and let the reader draw the conclusions. You will sound too cocky if you apply these words to yourself, and your reader will not believe them anyway unless you give the supporting concrete facts.

**SPM** Sales promotion material (when appropriate and unselfish) not only shows a service attitude (see **SA**) and produces some additional sales; it helps to take the sting out of early collection letters and provides a pleasant ending for essentially bad-news letters, provided that the situation is not too seriously negative. See Chapter 4.

**Style** See Chapter 3 and (especially for reports) Chapter 15.

**Sub**ordinate Don't overstress negative ideas, facts the reader knows, or insignificant points. If you must say them, put them in the middle of the paragraph or letter, devote little space to them, and/or put them in dependent clauses or phrases. Since dependent clauses are particularly useful in subordinating, here are some of the main beginning words that make clauses dependent: *after, although, as, because, before, if, since, though, till, unless, until, when, where, while.*

**SW** Shall-will; should-would. General usage differs so much from formal usage of *shall* and *will* that formal practice now sounds old-fashioned and stiff in most letters and reports. In general usage (which is appropriate for business writing), *will* has almost completely replaced *shall*. (Formal usage calls for *shall* with the first person and *will* with other persons to indicate the simple future, and for the reverse to indicate firm promise or determination.)

More important for business writers is the distinction between the simple futures and their conditional forms, *should* and *would*. Using the simple future sometimes seems presumptuous.

> I will appreciate your giving me your answer by November 20 so that . . . .
> (*Would,* in place of *will,* would remove the presumption that the reader will answer, by using the conditional mood and saying, in effect, *"If* you will answer . . . I will appreciate it.")

**SX** Sexist language or viewpoint. Phrase your message for equal treatment of females and males. See p. 77 for common errors and means of avoiding or correcting them.

**Syl** Divide words at the ends of lines only at syllable breaks, and then only if each part has at least two letters and is pronounceable. If in doubt about where to divide a word, check your dictionary.

**Tab**ulate or itemize when you have lots of figures to present or a series of distinct points to make. Itemization will make you think more sharply and state your ideas more precisely and concisely. Thus you produce clearer, quicker reading and more emphasis. Furthermore, **Item**ization grabs readers' or hearers' attention.

**Tele**graphic style (omitting subjects, connective words, and articles, as in telegrams and newspaper headlines) is not acceptable practice in letters, memos, and reports—except in headings or subheads.

**Ten**se Watch the tense (time indicated by your verbs) for appropriateness in the individual verb and logic in the sequence of verbs.

1. Normally you use the present, past, or future according to the time of the action you are reporting.
2. The tense of the key verb in an independent clause governs a sentence. So the tenses of other verbs or verbals should indicate time *relative to* the time of the main verb:

   > I will do it as soon as I am able (a future and relative present).
   > I had hoped that I would be able to go (a past perfect and relative future).

3. A special use of the present tenses deserves careful attention, however, for some situations: You use the present (called the "universal present") for statements that were true in the past, are true now, and will be true later. We say the sun *sets* in the west (universal present)

even though it may have set hours earlier. Any statement you might make about what a book *says* fits the conditions. If you now read a book written even in 1620, it still *says* . . . . Similarly in reporting on your research findings (which presumably are still true), you use the universal present tense. To do otherwise would imply doubt about the present validity of your results.

The law of supply and demand *means* . . . .

The 1986 edition *says* . . . .

In all the groups surveyed, more than 80 percent of the people prefer (not preferred) . . . .

4. Do not shift tenses unless the logic of the situation requires that you do so.

5. Be sure to spell the appropriate verb form correctly. Remember that English has two classes of verbs. The Old English weak verbs became our regular verbs, whose principal parts go like *plow, plowed, plowed.* Old English strong verbs became our irregular ones, which change internally *(think, thought, thought; throw, threw, thrown; lead, led, led;* and *meet, met, met).*

**TM** Typing mechanics. If you are an untrained typist, these tips may help:

1. Standard within-line spacings are *(a)* five for paragraph indention; *(b)* two after a colon or end-of-sentence punctuation (including an enclosing end parenthesis); *(c)* one after all other punctuation except as explained below; *(d)* none after an opening parenthesis or before or after a hyphen or dash.

2. Abbreviations pose a spacing problem: some (like our governmental alphabet soup—HEW, IRS, SEC, CAB, for example) are solid; others (even with the same meaning) go various ways. Learn the main ones; look up the others in your dictionary.

3. Dashes (not at all the same as hyphens—see **P7** and **P8**) are preferably two hyphens with no spacing.

4. For quotations of more than four lines, space above and below, indent from each side, single-space, and use no quotation marks.

5. Though the form of headings and subheads in reports and other long papers is a **TM** problem, treatment of the topic seems most logically placed in Chapter 15.

**T-t-t** A tea-table turn is an abrupt shift from the pleasant to the unpleasant. Typically, the statement is sweet for a few sentences. Then the next begins, "However, . . . ." The situation is quite like that of several friends already at a tea-party table when they see X arriving a little late. One of those at the table makes a very favorable remark about X and adds "but . . ."—and everybody has the sinking feeling, "Poor X!"

**Tone** Watch out for a tone of distrust, indifference, undue humility, flattery, condescension, preachiness, bragging, anger, accusation, sarcasm, curtness, effusiveness, or exaggeration. See Chapter 4.

Since salutations and complimentary closes are the first and last indications of your feelings about the formality of your relationship to your letter reader, be sure they represent those feelings accurately. See Chapter 2.

**Tra**nsitions between sentences in a paragraph, between paragraphs, and between sections in longer presentations must show their relationships. Your best method is to use a thread of logic (based on careful organization) that will hold your thoughts together like beads on a string. When the logical thread does not make the relationship clear, however, you need to do so by repeating a key word or idea from the preceding or by using a connecting word, phrase, sentence, or heading that shows the relationship. See **Coh** and **Unit.**

**Tri**te expressions (a form of **Jar**gon) are usually overused and hence worn-out figures of speech that dull your writing. The remedy is to state your idea simply in natural, normal English or to use an original figure of speech.

**Unity** (of sentences, paragraphs, or whole pieces of writing) requires that you show how each statement fits in or belongs (is not irrelevant). Applied to a sentence or paragraph, **Unit** means that the statement seems irrelevant or that the several ideas are not closely enough related to be in one sentence or paragraph. Applied to a whole letter or report, it means that the content seems so varied as to lack a central theme and that you should put it in two or more separate papers. Often, however, the writer sees relationships that justify putting things together as they are, and the fault is in not showing the reader the relationships—an error of coherence (see **Coh**).

> Please put your answers in ink and have your signature witnessed by two people. One of our envelopes is enclosed for your convenience. (The envelope is not a convenience in doing what is requested in the first sentence. The two unrelated ideas should not be in the same paragraph. Or adding "in returning your answers" would help.)

**U**sage refers to the appropriateness of the language to the situation. A passage or expression marked with the symbol may be too formal and stiff, literary, flashy, or highbrow; or too slangy, familiar, crude, or lowbrow. The normal, natural English of educated people conducting their everyday affairs is neither formal nor illiterate but informal and natural. That's what you should use for most letters, memos, and reports.

Be on guard against the following illiterate forms (mostly the result of bad pronunciation): "He is prejudice" *(prejudiced),* "He is bias" *(biased),* "usta" or "use to" *(used to),* "had of" *(had),* "would of" *(would have),* "most all" *(almost all),* "a savings of" *(a saving of),* "She lead the meeting" *(led).*

**Var**iety (of diction and of sentence pattern, type, and length) is necessary to avoid monotony, which puts readers to sleep. Achieving variety should be a part of the revision process, however, and should not distract your thoughts from saying what you want to say in writing a first draft.

In your revision, see that you haven't begun too many successive sentences the same way (especially not with *I* or *we*). If you have repeated yourself, cut out the repetition unless you need it for emphasis.

The usual English sentence pattern is subject-verb-complement; in revision, vary the pattern to avoid a dull sameness.

Good style also requires variety in sentence type. Some of your sentences should be simple (one independent clause); some should be compound (two independent clauses stating two closely related ideas of nearly equal importance); and some should be complex (at least one independent clause and one or more dependent, all expressing related ideas but of unequal importance). Especially avoid too many successive simple sentences for ideas not deserving equal emphasis or too many compound sentences connected by *and.* (See **Sub.**)

Although most of your sentences should be relatively short (averaging 17–20 words for easy readability), you will produce a monotonous choppiness if all your sentences are in that range. See **Sim** and **Chop,** and revise accordingly.

**Wordy** See Chapter 3.

**YA** You-attitude. The you-attitude is certainly one of the three most important points about letter writing. People do things for their own benefit, not yours. If you want to persuade them to act, you have to show them the advantages to themselves. See Chapter 5.

To show readers what is in the situation for them, you have to visualize their ways of life and show how your proposal fits in. See **Ad**apt.

**✗**   Obvious error. Proofread carefully and correct such errors.

**∼**   Invert the order or sequence of words or ideas.

**⌣**   Close up the unnecessary space.

**¶**   New paragraph needed. See **Par.**

**#**   Additional space needed here.

**ꝺ**   or **ꝼ** Delete (take out); unnecessary.

**←↑↓→**   Move in the direction pointed.

# Index

*This book has been set Videocomp, in 10½ and 9½ point Times Roman, leaded 1½ points. Part numbers are 28 point Times Roman and part titles are 30 point Times Roman. Chapter numbers are 38 point Times Roman and chapter titles are 28 point Times Roman. The size of the type page is 34½ by 45 picas.*